A History

of

Bangor Isycoed

I hope you find something new on every page

Vivien Lavis-Jones

Vivien Lavis-Jones

A History of Bangor Isycoed
first published in Wales in 2013
on behalf of the author
by
BRIDGE BOOKS
61 Park Avenue
WREXHAM
LL12 7AW

A CIP entry for this book is available from the British Library

Cover illustrations
Front cover: Bangor, Moses Griffiths, 1781 [NLW]
Back cover: St Dunawd's Church, Bangor [C. Green]
Centre left: Pickhill Hall [Dave Walker]
Centre right: Plâs Fron [Cath Owen]
View of Bangor Bridge from the Denbighshire side, *c*.1910

ISBN 978-1-84494-093-6

Printed and bound by
Gutenberg Press Ltd
Malta

Contents

Preface and Acknowledgements   5

Introduction   9

1.   Prehistoric Times   11
2.   Bangor Monastery – Deduction and Assumption   17
3.   Bangor Parish in 1689   32
4.   Bangor Village in 1949   39
5.   The Parish Church   43
6.   Vestry Meetings   91
7.   Dissenters   100
8.   River Dee and Bridge   107
9.   The Turnpike Roads   133
10. Transport   146
11. Law and Order   163
12. Education   190
13. Village Hall   238
14. Post Office   256
15. Public Houses   267
16. The Racecourse   280
17. Wartime   299
18. Utilities   330
19. Clubs, Societies and Events   343
20. Employment   360
21. Skeletons and the Supernatural   366
22. Old Houses   368
23. Eyton Township   394

Appendices
1.   Rectors   403
2.   Churchwardens   408

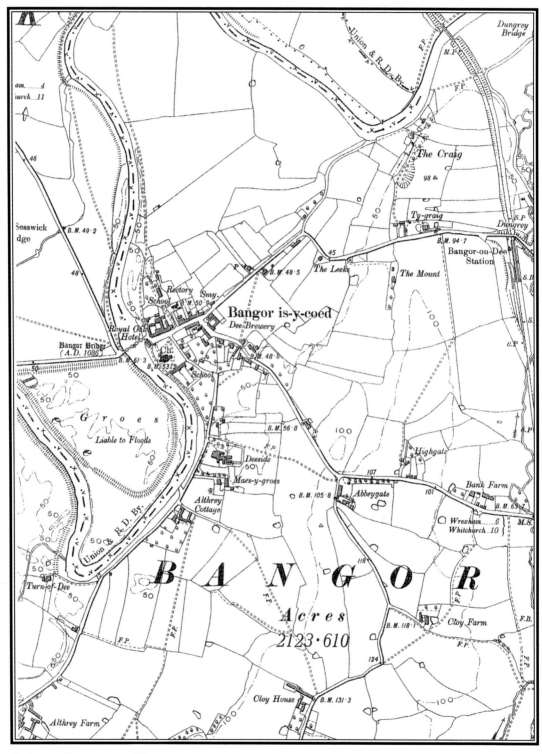

Ordnance Survey map of Bangor Isycoed, 1912.

Preface and Acknowledgements

Over the years Bangor Isycoed has lost many of its old documents and manuscripts some of which were last seen in the 1950s when canon David Thomas of Holywell wrote his booklet on Bangor entitled *Bangor Monachorum – Historical Notes on the Ancient Monastery Church and Parish*. The old vestry book(s) and the churchwardens and/or parish account books prior to 1810 and many other papers to which he had access have unfortunately disappeared. According to the historian A.N. Palmer (1847–1915), the Bangor account books predated the church registers by eighteen years, the first record covering the year 1657 during the latter years of Oliver Cromwell's protectorate. Perhaps they were the victims of a spring clean, like that of a recent incumbent whose first task on accepting the post was to clear out the 'junk' from the church. It was only by a fortuitous tip-off that the author arrived to prevent the few remaining papers from being thrown into the skip. It is thanks to a former rector, the Revd Lesley Daniel (Canon Thomas' son-in-law), that many of the remaining records were sent to the Flintshire Record Office in Hawarden for safe-keeping which has ensured their preservation and made them available for all to study.

I am not sure that grateful is the correct word to use when acknowledging the suggestion of Bob Sylvester of the Clwyd-Powys Archaeological Trust (CPAT) that someone should write a definitive book on the history of the village. My offer to cover education snowballed when no-one else came forward to help with other topics. I have always had a love of history and I have enjoyed the research, but less so the writing!

It has now been published as I am aware of *anno domini* and mindful of Peter Roberts, to whom people had entrusted their precious photographs, who died leaving no information as to their whereabouts. I have therefore decided to call a halt before history repeats itself. I would very much have liked to look at older documents but many are written in Latin, and, whilst it would be easy to brush up my knowledge of that language, the abbreviated Latin in which many of them are written is another thing entirely. It would take a while to master the art and time is not on my side. I would also have liked to carry out more research on the houses of Pickhill, Pickhill Old Hall, Emral, Broughton, Bryn-y-Pys, Plâs Fron and Gwernhaylod and many others that were at one time in the parish of Bangor, but this would have meant a further delay. I must also point out that the townships of Pickhill, Sesswick, and Royton have only had a cursory mention. Perhaps a second edition or an addendum should follow!

In the main, I have not adopted a chronological sequence of events but have researched different subjects so that each chapter stands alone. In so doing I have amassed a plethora of names of the people who lived in the parish, some of them for only a short while, others for generations – not all of whom can be mentioned. I plan to sort out my files into some logical and legible order and deposit them in the Flintshire Record Office at Hawarden for anyone to peruse if they are perhaps doing a school project or researching their family history.

In writing this book I am conscious of the many people I have contacted with a query to whom I am very grateful for their patience and time. In particular, the late Ron Evanson who shared his love of the past with me, George 'Dode' Humphreys who had to leave the village to escape the pestering and Ernie Young who regaled me with a fund of amusing stories of people and past events. My gratitude is also extended to those who have allowed me to study their house deeds or loaned me photographs, and to those of the 'old village' who patiently explained the intricacies and maze of family relationships – particularly important as three-quarters of the village are newcomers in the last forty years, or 'come-overs' as they say in the Isle of Man!

I am greatly indebted to the late Derrick Pratt for permission to include his articles on the monastery and Edward Lhywd's description of Bangor Parish in 1699, both taken from the Bangor-on-Dee Local History Society publications. I make no pretence of being an historian and am grateful to him for filling gaps in my knowledge. Last but definitely not least, I thank the dedicated staff of the Flintshire and Cheshire Record Offices and the Wrexham Local Studies Library for their help and encouragement, without whom I could not possibly have managed.

On the technical side, I must thank those people who have sorted out my computer problems, in particular Jez Jones of 'Jones, the Computer' in Wrexham for sorting out my hard-drive and who has been my life line, I give my heartfelt thanks.

Since the coming of the railway, the parish of Bangor Isycoed has often been referred to as Bangor-on-Dee in general usage. I have used the old name throughout the text.

Finally I freely admit that any mistakes are mine and I would welcome any corrections or amendments in case a reprint is ever contemplated.

I hope you all enjoy reading this book as much as I have enjoyed its research.

Vivien Lavis-Jones
2013

Aerial photograph of Bangor Isycoed shortly after the Second World War, showing the scale of the village when its population was less than three hundred.

Aerial photograph of Bangor Isycoed c.1990

Introduction

Bangor Isycoed is in Maelor Saesneg (English Maelor) which is delineated on the eastern side by the Redbrook, a stream that runs into the Wych before joining the Emral brook then finally draining into the river Dee at Worthenbury. On the south-western side, the boundary is formed by the Shell brook that drains into the Dee near Erbistock. These brooks and the river Dee also mark the boundary between England and Wales.

The parish lies partly in what was once the detached part of the county of Flintshire, and partly in Denbighshire. Flintshire itself owes its creation to Edward I who, after his conquest of Wales, proclaimed the Statute of Wales in 1284 and created the new counties of Anglesey, Caernarfon, Cardigan, Carmarthen, Flint and Merioneth out of the conquered territories, decreeing that 'there shall be a Sheriff of Flint under whom shall be the Cantref of Englefeud [Englefield], the land of Maelor Sexenyth and the land of Hope …' It was soon after 1284 that the present church was built.

Flintshire's division into three parts is a result of the Norman incursions into Wales. The Norman barons endeavoured to take over the border areas piecemeal and set up marcher lordships. One family acquired the lordship of Mold; another family seized the district around Wrexham known as the lordship of Bromfield and Yale and the king retained control of Hope and Maelor Saesneg. This situation lasted until Henry VIII suppressed the marcher lordships by the Act of Union of 1536 and the lordships of Bromfield and Yale, Mold and St Asaph were given to the new county of Denbigh. In 1541, a further Act transferred Mold and St Asaph, together with the small townships of Marford and Hoseley, to Flintshire.

Part of the parish of Bangor Isycoed – the townships of Bangor, Overton and Worthenbury – lay in the hundred of Maelor Saesneg and later became part of Flintshire, separated by the river Dee from those of Eyton, Royton, Pickhill and Sesswick which were in the hundred of Bromfield and Yale in Denbighshire. The term 'hundred' was used to denote an area of land that consisted of a hundred hides – a hide being the area of land that a team of oxen could plough in a year, usually about 100 to 130 acres depending on the terrain. The term dates from about the eleventh century and was used in the Domesday Book of 1086 to denote a unit of taxation. There is no mention of Bangor in the Domesday Book, although Worthenbury (Hurdinburie), Eyton and Sesswick are included: Eyton possessing one hide of land and Sesswick half a hide.

Just over three hundred years ago in 1689, Worthenbury was taken away from Bangor to form a separate parish, then Overton was separated off in 1867, leaving just the village of Bangor Isycoed in Flintshire. With the re-organisation of county boundaries in 1974, the whole of Maelor became absorbed into the new county of Clwyd. When the county borough of Wrexham was created in 1996, the whole of the Maelor district was absorbed into that ever-spreading conurbation.

The village of Bangor Isycoed is situated five miles from Wrexham and ten miles from

Whitchurch on the east bank of the river Dee. The name means 'a wattle enclosure (bangor) below the wood (is y coed)' and implies that there was a considerable wooded area nearby although woodland clearance in the area had probably already taken place by the early medieval period. The first recorded mention of the name 'Isycoed' is in the late seventeenth century, but it had certainly been in local use before that and it was probably used to differentiate between other places using the name Bangor.

1. Prehistoric Times

Bangor lies in the flood plain, and within a meander of the river Dee. Thousands of years ago, the river covered the valley, gradually receding leaving the telltale marks of terracing, the lower courses of which can be seen at Porthwgan. The river is now a fraction of the size that it once was and has changed its course in Bangor over time, as it has at Overton, and John Leland noted in about 1540 – 'the Dee since changing the bottom'. It would have flowed further to the western side of the flood plain, just below the bank at Royton and Plâs Fron where the Foss stream now runs It is also now much shallower since the Surveyor of the Highways stopped extracting gravel from the river for the repair of local roads. There are now extensive gravel banks in the area around the bridge that are gradually building up and narrowing the river channel and this comes from the underlying gravel bed that extends below the clay layer running under Bangor.

There is evidence that Bangor and its outlying area has been occupied since prehistoric times. A Bronze Age (2500–800 BC) axe head was found in 1937/8 during the excavation for the foundations of the Cadbury creamery at Pickhill. Two young Bangor boys, Johnny Spoor and Clem Robinson, who were watching the digging, noticed the small metal object about four feet below the surface of the ground which they called attention to. The factory manager, Mr E.W. Westwood, sent it to the Cadbury head office in Bournville where it required very little cleaning to reveal it was a fine specimen of an early bronze worker's art – an axe head, beautifully proportioned and fashioned, and in a condition so perfect that it seemed impossible to believe that it could have lain hidden for more than a year or two at the most. The British Museum stated that it was a pre-historic axe head or, to give its correct designation, a bronze socketed axe or 'celt' dating from about 2000 B.C. Using apparatus for metallurgical analysis, ICI was asked to study the composition of the axe and to make an estimate of its value as a tool. A good modern bronze contains 80% copper, and up to 20% tin with traces of other elements added, notably phosphorus. The celt contained 80% copper, 15% tin and small quantities of other metals and 0.2% phosphorus. The impurities revealed that the copper could have come from the impure copper ore such as found in Wales but may also have come from abroad. The hardness of the axe head was only about one-seventh that

Bronze axe head found near Bangor.
[*Courtesy of* Bournville Works Magazine]

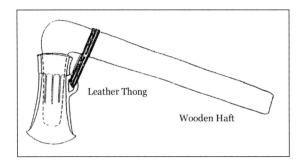

Sketch, taken from a British Museum exhibit, shows the method of 'hafting' the celt. [Courtesy of Bournville Works Magazine]

Leather Thong

Wooden Haft

of mild steel – so that as a cutting tool it would be far inferior to the cheapest modern hatchet. The British Museum was said to have recorded the find but when the author phoned them for further information, no record could be found.

There was continuous occupation of the district during the Iron Age (800 BC to 43 AD) as was discovered when archaeologist Chris Musson took aerial photographs of the Bangor area in 1979 revealing the outline of Iron Age/Romano-British farmsteads on the ridge above Royton Farm. Crop marks have shown up as possible flattened banks and filled-in ditches of farmstead boundaries.

The Romans controlled southern Britain from 43 to 450 AD. In a talk on the remains of Roman roads in north-east Wales, given by John Dutton of Caergwrle to the Bangor History Society in 1987, mention was made of having found evidence of a track from Holt to Newbridge near Chirk. The line of the track passed near Isycoed Church and Pickhill Bridge. It then ran along the ridge passing Plâs Fron and crossing the Two-mile Straight at Watery Lane Cottage, along what is now a footpath but used to be a narrow road. The line of the track then crossed the Eyton Hall to Ddôl Eyton lane and into the woods. Mr Dutton has also found traces of another road or track in the area leading from Althrey Lodge to Cloy Farm which was 28 feet wide and disappeared into the old railway line. He has since commented that he believed that this track came off the Shrewsbury to Whitchurch road two miles north of Prees and ran as far as Ffrith near Brymbo. He pointed out however that there was no evidence that the tracks at Bangor were of Roman origin and could have been mediaeval track-ways. Derrick Pratt commented:

> John Dutton has found Roman roads everywhere! This one is well off any expected alignment. Using this criteria would put some 200 townships in Cheshire/Shropshire/ Wrexham into 'potential Roman' category. The nearest 'known' Roman road is the Whitchurch–Malpas–Farndon route, but personally I would expect traces along the A525 Whitchurch–Wrexham road, but nothing has materialised to date.

The only evidence that we have for a possible Roman settlement at Bangor is a single *tessera*, a small square block of mosaic that was found in the graveyard. John Leland *c*.1539 recorded that 'squared stones' were ploughed up implying that this must be from the monastery but we know that this could not be, as those buildings would have been wooden, of wattle and daub construction. The stone could have been from any age. However could the squared stone perhaps refer to *tesserae* and not to building stone? A second-century Roman coin has been found near Cloy Farm and Leland also stated that 'Romayne monys is found there' but he did not see the coins. Before we can ascribe the title 'Roman' to Bangor much more evidence of occupation would have to be discovered. At present, all we can conjecture is that a couple of Romans were walking past with holes in their pockets!

The Dark Ages was the label given to the period immediately after the Romans departed from Britain until the advent of written records. A tradition of a monastery existing in Bangor Isycoed in the sixth century has been passed down, with embellishments, since this time. The early authority for its existence is Bede, a monk at Jarrow monastery, who wrote his *History of the English Church* in 731 AD (he died in 735) in which the monastery is mentioned. Since that time, all chroniclers, including William of Malmesbury (*c*.1095–*c*.1143), Geoffrey of Monmouth (*c*.1100–54), John Leland (*c*.1503–52) and others, have elaborated on this work and put their own 'spin' to it. Bede does not tell us the exact date of the founding of the monastery but it is generally accepted that St Deiniol (who died in 584) founded the monastery of Bangor in Gwynedd and later the monastery at Bangor Isycoed. He appointed his father, St Dunawd, also known as Dinooth, a former soldier, who had retired to lead a more contemplative life, to be its first abbot. Others assert that Deiniol founded the monastery in Bangor Isycoed first and, after appointing his father as abbot, left to found the one at Bangor, Gwynedd.

Forget the modern notion of a monastery as a large building built of stone. The Celtic monks, who were not celibate like the Church of Rome, lived with their families in dwellings made from a form of wickerwork which were spread over the flat, river plain. The monks were self-supporting and some of them would have toiled in the fields, tilling the soil or tending to the animals whilst others would have been employed in making copies of the scriptures or in teaching. There would have been one hut, larger that the rest, that would have served as a church. According to Bede, the monks were '… divided into seven groups, each with its own abbot and each of not less than three hundred strong'. That would have made a total of 2,100 monks – dare we say that Bede was guilty of exaggeration? Many of the monks would have come from an educated class of society and some were probably of noble birth. Some, like Dunawd, had also seen military service and possibly been injured, and had come to lead a contemplative monastic existence late in life. Some may have been recruited as children and been brought up to know no other life – as was Bede himself. By the fifth century, monasteries certainly existed in both Wales and Ireland.

The exact site of the monastery is a matter of speculation with various theories put forward over the years. According to Leland, the site of the monastery was on the Bangor village side of the river in Maelor Saesneg, on the flat part of the valley. Some believe that the present church could have been built on the site of the monastery whilst others assert that the most likely place was at Althrey. We will never know the truth as the only evidence likely to survive from so many years ago would be the presence of post-holes from the wooden buildings and this evidence would almost certainly have been destroyed by years of constant flooding and/or cultivation.

In 597, Pope Gregory I sent a delegation of monks to England, headed by Augustine, to meet representatives of the English and Celtic church and Dunawd was one of those present at a conference said to have taken place at a spot known as St Augustine's Oak at Glastonbury. Attempts to reconcile religious differences between the Celtic Church and the Church of Rome foundered on the belief that Augustine taught doctrines that to them were new and which they believed were unscriptural. The chief differences between the two churches were said to be:

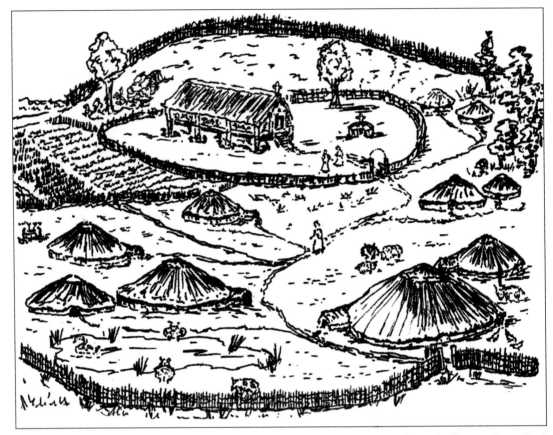

Artist's impression of a monastic settlement showing the church on stilts to keep the library above flood level. [Trish Lay]

- The shape of the tonsure. The Celtic clergy shaved the forehead, the church of Rome the crown of the head
- The observance of Easter. The Celtic church observed Easter as a fixed day whereas the church of Rome had a moveable one
- The signing of the Cross at baptism
- The celibacy of the clergy

After Augustine was consecrated Archbishop of Canterbury in 599AD, a second meeting took place in 603AD attended, according to Bede, by '... seven British bishops and many very learned men are said to have attended, who mainly came from their most famous monastery which the English called Bancornaburg, then ruled by Abbot Dinooth [Dunawd].' The story goes that the representatives of the Celtic church did not wish Augustine to be their archbishop and be in authority over them. They sought advice of an old hermit who resided not far from Bangor. His advice was to attend the next conference but to arrive late. If Augustine wished to discuss matters in a friendly manner, he would rise from his seat to meet them. However, if he wished to assert his authority and was annoyed at their unpunctuality, he would remain seated. When the delegation arrived Augustine did not rise to greet them and in consequence they would not agree to change any of their customs and conform to the Roman practices.

When the Celtic delegates refused to conform, Augustine was said to have retorted that '... since they would not have peace with their brothers, they should have war with their enemies; and since they were unwilling to preach to the Angles (the pagans) the way of life, they should suffer death at their hands as the ministers of Divine vengeance.' Augustine was, perhaps, by his words foretelling the fate of the monks at the hands of the king of Northumbria some ten years later.

Local tradition has it that this second meeting took place in Bangor, in a field at Maes-y-Groes (the Field of the Cross), near an old oak tree. There is an ancient oak tree at Maes-y-Groes known as the Monk's Oak that legend says was the very tree under which the meeting took place. However, the present oak tree, although undeniably ancient, is certainly not 1400 years old.

The monastery flourished and was renowned for its library until c.613/16 AD (date uncertain) when Aethelfrith, the pagan and ambitious king of Northumbria, wishing to expand his empire, cast his avaricious eyes on the Mercian kingdom. He met the Mercian army, whose ranks were swelled with allies from Gwynedd and Powys, at what has become known as the battle of Chester. A large contingent of monks, many from Bangor Isycoed, went to support the Welsh side in the battle against the Northumbrians, not to fight but to pray for divine intervention in the struggle for victory. When Aethelfrith saw the monks he asked who they were and why they were gathered there. When he was told, according to Bede, he was said to have replied 'If they are praying to their God against us, then even if they do not bear arms they are fighting against us' and ordered them to be slaughtered.

There is a place at Herons Bridge between Chester and Eccleston where many skeletons have been found and it is thought that this was possibly the site of the battle. Only a very limited part of the site was excavated in the 1930s and 1950s. A further excavation in 2004 uncovered further skeletons, two of which were sent for radiocarbon dating which revealed that the bones dated from around the beginning of the seventh century, and the analysis of the teeth revealed that the remains were of men who had grown up in the north-eastern part of the country, from the Peak District northwards and who were therefore probably part of the Northumbrian army. The burial site of the fallen of the Mercian army and of the monks has not so far been found. According to Bede, 1200 monks were killed and only fifty escaped. As he was writing over 100 years after the massacre, he was relying on tales told to him by others, no doubt exaggerated, as he is said never to have left the monastery at Jarrow. His writings are, however, the only record of an event that proved so traumatic for the monks of Bangor. Geoffrey of Monmouth, writing in the twelfth century, said that after the battle Aethelfrith marched to Bangor where he sacked the monastery and laid waste the land. Bede does not mention this. Did Geoffrey have another source for his information? Aethelfrith was himself defeated and killed in a later battle. The monastery may possibly have survived the massacre for a few years but, by the twelfth century, William of Malmesbury was writing that it was in ruins. The site was probably deserted soon after the battle of Chester when the surviving monks may have departed for other monastic communities in Wales or Ireland.

In 1991, aerial photography showed up mysterious circular crop marks within a meander loop of the Dee towards Pickhill, which may be associated or be perhaps contemporary, with the

Aerial photograph showing ridge and furrow in the fields between Cloy Lane (centre left to centre top) and the Overton road (just out of shot at the bottom right). [Clwyd-Powys Archaeological Trust]

monastery. There is abundant evidence of medieval farming methods in the fields around Bangor with prominent ridge and furrow field markings – the result of continual ploughing in one direction. After the abandonment of the monastery, the parish settled into a long period as a self-sufficient rural community of agricultural holdings, several big houses, along with the supporting trades such as blacksmiths, saddlers, cobblers, tailors and grocers and the population fluctuated very little until the twentieth century.

2. Bangor Monastery –
Deductions and Assumptions

by Derrick Pratt

Considering how much has been written about it, surprisingly little is known about the early Welsh Church in Bangor. Bearing in mind the period when the monastery flourished and the relatively short time-span of its working life, concrete evidence relating to Bangor is minimal. Local historians have arrived at the point where they can only retread already well-worn paths in their investigation of tired facts of doubtful authenticity.

However, prompted by an article by Professor L.A. Butler of York University[1] (perhaps better known in the Wrexham area as the excavator of Valle Crucis Abbey in 1970), the late Derrick Pratt, well-known local historian, was persuaded to re-assess the history of Bangor Isycoed in the Dark Ages. In 1988 he gave a lecture to Bangor Local History Society in which he broke new ground when he significantly re-interpreted existing 'evidence', asking listeners to turn from the traditionally romantic views of a Celtic seminary and church on the banks of the Dee and to consider in its stead a 'monastic city' that may have played a pivotal role in the development of the Welsh town. He looked at Bangor not so much from the view of a Celtic monastery of some renown, but rather as a hitherto unsuspected specimen of a nascent, native quasi-urban institution, forerunner of the Welsh medieval town, the 'monastic city' of Professor Butler's hypothesis. With his permission the following is a reprint of an article that the late Derrick Pratt wrote in 1992 in the third and last magazine of the Bangor History Society.

The extent to which records survive in comfortable quantities generally governs the competence of historians in handling such material and, more often that not, dictates the chronological limits of a particular study. If the historian is equipped to look further that the generalisation of Gerald of Wales that the Welsh 'do not live in towns, villages or castles, but lead a solitary existence, deep in the woods,'[2] he might consider the claims as pre-urban nuclei of the Welsh *maerdrefi* at Marford and Hoseley, Wrexham, Chirk, Llangollen, Overton, Llanrhaeadr-ym-Mochnant and Llanarmon Dyffryn Ceiriog.

Pursuing Professor Butler's theses, can the local historian now push back the geneses of 'urbanism' in the northeast March to the seventh century, in fact to a monastic city at Bangor Isycoed? Before initiating the discussion, it may be convenient to cite the

St Deiniol, presumed founder of Bangor monastery, as portrayed in the east window, north nave, of St Tyrnog's Church, Llandyrnog.

relative extracts from the only two works to which credence can seriously be given – the one by Bede, monk of Jarrow, because he was the authority (albeit slightly biased) writing closest to the actual existence of the monastery, and the other, by John Leland, because he gives the researcher important topographical detail of 470 years ago, especially in relation to changes in the course of the river Dee.

Recalling the events of 603AD, when Celtic 'bishops' for a second time met Augustine in an ill-fated attempt to reconcile religious matters in dispute, Bede writes: '… and seven British bishops and many very learned men are said to have attended, and mainly came from their most famous monastery the English called Bancornaburg, then ruled by Abbot Dinooth'. The latter is, of course, St Dunawd, present-day patron saint of Bangor parish church. However the dedication to St Dunawd may be comparatively recent, the older invocation possibly being that of St Deiniol. Edward Llwyd, writing in 1699 says: 'Their feast is on Daniel's [Deiniol's] Tyde.'[3] That Dunawd actually founded Bangor monastery is unlikely. That is more often attributed to his son Deiniol (died 572 or 584), Celtic bishop in Gwynedd and founder of Bangor (Gwynedd) with Bangor Isycoed as a daughter house. Dunawd could not have been abbot at Bangor for long as much of his life had been spent in arms earning himself the distinction of one of 'the three Battle Pillars of Prydyn' up in Scotland before retiring to end his days in his son's monastery in the profession of religion. He was dead by 607AD.

In referring to the battle of Chester (about 616AD) when Aethelfrith of Northumbria took on and defeated the men of Powys and Mercia, reinforced by a contingent of superannuated monks from Bangor, Bede's narrative runs:

> Most of these priests came from the monastery at Bangor where there are said to have been so many monks that although it was divided into seven sections, each under its own abbot, none of these sections contained less than three hundred monks, all of whom supported themselves by manual work … About twelve hundred monks perished in this battle and only fifty escaped by flight.[4]

Bede completed his *History* in 731, a century after the demise of Bangor monastery and almost 1400 years nearer the actual events than present-day commentators and some 411 years earlier than that other 'chronicler' of Bangor, William de Malmesbury, whose descriptions of the extent and magnificence of Bangor's ruined monastic buildings are couched in terms of twelfth century monasticism and are gross inventions. Dark Age religious communities were just not like the rigidly ordered and standardized Benedictine houses of Europe in the central medieval period.

Bede's demographic statements, however, must be treated with some scepticism – a concentration of 2,100 monks in any one Celtic mother church would be unique in Wales. But the Triads go one better and specify 2,400 monks at Bangor.[5] Neither figure is credible and are so divergent from the pattern of Celtic missionary work elsewhere e.g. under Deiniol's kinsmen and contemporaries – Saints Cadfan, Seiriol and Cybi – in Gwynedd as to be a complete anachronism. Such numbers of people and densities are not to be encountered in Wrexham Maelor until the latter half of the eighteenth century when the Industrial Revolution was well under way. Not even present-day Bangor Isycoed, in its role as a rapidly expanding dormitory village to Wrexham, can match these alleged Dark Age population statistics. Unfortunately, the only other indications as to the size of Dark Age monastic communities come from later Saints' *Lives* or *Vitae* (for Gwynllyw, Gwenfryl [Winefride] and Paul of Leon) and the numbers are very small – 7, 11, 12.[6] Figures for Bangor probably and most sensibly have to be trimmed to something approaching these proportions.

Such a move would have to be reconciled with Bede's implied picture of a considerable settlement spread over the flood plain of the Dee. In that it was 'self-supporting by manual labour' one may justifiably consider the settlement as being a focus for crafts and to some extent local trade. In the absence of towns (other than Romano-British Chester) Bangor monastery may be seen as beginning to display some basic 'urban' proportions.

If it is difficult to conceive of a monastery 'divided into seven sections, each under its own abbot' within a single restricted area, it may be that Bede's words actually hide a looser monastic federation i.e. outlying lands, churches, communities dependent on the mother church. A 'sphere of influence' may be discerned in the shape of adjacent dedications and associations. Marchwiel and Worthenbury churches, both dedicated to St Deiniol, must be regarded as ancillary to Bangor, or even as properties of that house – this in preference to the more nebulous, incidental relationships that might be construed from the emergence of a later cult. 'Ffynnon Daniel [Deiniol]' in the provostry of Pickhill and Sesswick, 'Ffynnon y Saint' or 'Saints Well' in Royton Township give further definition to former monastic property. Again, the '6 Crosses' noted by Edward Llwyd may serve to pinpoint the varying 'zones of sanctity' about Bangor monastery.

'Tyddyn Daniel' in Bedwell township (now Marchwiel parish), noted in 1562, may also be connected with Bangor; but equally well 'Daniel' may be just the name of a medieval smallholder rather than 'Deiniol'. It is mere coincidence that in 1626 Tyddyn Daniel was purchased and, according to the 1749 'terrier' its rental applied 'to the repair and use of the Church [Marchwiel].'[7]

Working on the principle that a federated community would be confined to areas within easy reach of the mother church – 50 or 60 miles, two or three days journey – one could conceivably stretch Bangor's influence to Hawarden (St Deiniol's church, Daniel's Ash), if not to Llanuwchllyn (?Llanddeiniol-uwch-y-Llyn) and Llanfor (?Llanddeiniol-is-y-Llyn).

To Bede, the local historian owes the earliest forms of the place-name 'Bangor'. As a simplex form 'Bangor' means 'a monastery, religious settlement, academy, college (within a wattled fence)' in the sense of a seminary of Christian teaching and learning, derived ultimately from its basic meaning of 'a strong upper plaited rod in a wattled hedge or fence for strengthening and binding the same'.

But interpreting 'Bangor' as applied to Bangor Isycoed is more complicated that appears at first sight as its earliest forms are complex, the final element 'bury' (OE burh = 'fortification, fortified place') being lost only in the fourteenth century:

Bancor		
Bancornaburg	731	Bede *Ecc. Hist.*, 100-102
Bankerbur'	1270	*Cal. Charter Rolls*, 11, 266
Bonkerbury	1278	*Cal. Anc Pet.*, 151
Baunkesbur'	1282	*Cal. Welsh Rolls*, 226
Bankerbir'	1283	ibid, 271
Bankerbur'	1283	ibid, 272
Blanckebir'	1283	ibid, 262
Bankerburw	1291	*Tax, Ecc.*
Bangor	1292	Flints. Lay Subsidy
Bangor	1309	*Cal. Anc. Pet.*, 341

In the light of the thirteenth century forms it is tempting to see *Bankebury'* as 'a fortified place on a bank' but the OE *banke* does not fit in date-wise with Bede's forms of 731. In *Bancornaburg*, now shortened to *Bangor* we probably have something like 'the stronghold of the men of Bangor'. Needless to say, one cannot envisage specially built 'fortifications' in the late medieval sense as imagined by William of Malmesbury.

Assuming that the *Bancor* of 731 is not an abbreviated form, it may be that the place-name forms listed above actually have two separate concurrent strands, the simplex Welsh 'Bangor' used by Welsh speakers, and the complex tautological form given and used by English/Mercian colonists unfamiliar with the 'enclosure' significance of Bangor and yet who, by appending *burh* or *bury* as a suffix acknowledged in their own vocabulary and current terminology the 'enclosure' element noted in site and physical aspect of the monastery spread-eagled between high banks on the flood plain of the Dee. One will recall that Bede wrote 'the monastery called in the *Lingua Anglorum* Bancornaburg', implying this was the form used by the English and that there was an alternative form used by Welshmen.

It is interesting to note that in the *Old English Version of Bede's Ecclesiastical History*

(Early English Text Society, (1890–8), III, 28) the element 'burh' glosses the Latin *oppidum* = 'town' (classical), 'castle' (medieval) and 'a fortified wood in Britain' (Cæsar). Thus another piece is added to the emerging picture of seventh century Bangor as being a 'town' or substantial settlement of some ecclesiastical importance.

About 1539, John Leland (1506–52), library keeper to Henry VIII and later 'King's Antiquary,' visited Bangor. He had read the standard 'historiographes' and monastic chronicles which account for an 'hearsay' element in his narrative, but the latter also had pertinent things to say about the local topography, in particular providing evidence to the shifting within his lifetime of the course of the middle Dee:

> This is Bangor where the great abbey was. A part of this parish, that is as much as lies beyond Dee on the north side is in Welsh Maelor, and that is as half the parish of Bangor. But the abbey stood in English Maelor on the hither and south side of Dee. And it is ploughed ground now where the abbey was by the space of a good Welsh mile, and yet they plough up bones of the monks and in remembrance [i.e. in living memory] were dug up pieces of their clothes in sepulchres. The abbey stood in a fair valley and Dee ran by it. The compass of it was as a walled town, and yet remains the name of the gate called Porthwgan by north and the name of another called Port Clays [Porth Klais] by south. Dee since changing the bottom runs now through the middle between the two gates, one being a mile and a half from the other, and in this ground be ploughed up foundations of squared stones, and Roman money is found there'.[8]

When Leland was writing, the river Dee had clearly changed course, if not recently, certainly within human memory. Earlier, in his description of Overton parish, he refers to the violent capriciousness of the river which even then had washed away half of the motte of Overton's twelfth century castle at Asney and was actively eroding the remaining stump.

There is abundant cartographic evidence above and below Bangor for the historic shifting of the Dee's course and that of its tributary, Worthenbury Brook, within its deferred confluence – abandoned and shifting meanders that no longer coincide with parish/township/county/national boundaries fixed post 1143 by reference to the Dee. This gave rise to boundary anomalies that were only eradicated with local government re-organisation in 1974.

There is also ample evidence for both lateral and vertical movement of the Dee in the shape of some remarkable river terrace development – and not just peri-glacial features either [Fig. I]. The edges of these terraces are noticed in the landscape by distinct breaks of slope e.g. Bryn Hovah Bank, Cock Bank, Eyton Bank, and by eroded and weathered bluff lines Royton – Gerwyn Fechan –Plâs Fron – Porthwgan. The lowest and youngest terrace is given approximate definition by the 50ft contour, its edges well marked *below*

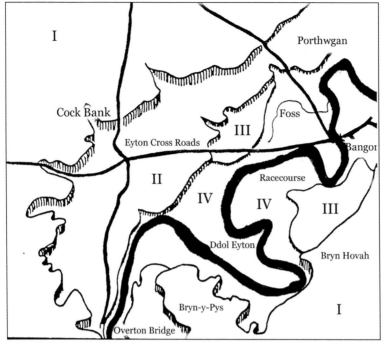

Fig. I: Vertical and lateral erosion by the Dee has created river terraces and probably removed archaeologically sensitive layers that might have held traces of Bangor monastery.
I: Original erosion surface.
II: Upper terrace.
III: Lower terrace.
IV: Flood plain

Plâs-fron, and on the other side of the river, by the abrupt change of slope that separate the track and fences of Bangor Racecourse from the enclosures and car-parks and affords punters such a natural uninterrupted overview of the running below.

At Plâs-fron the bluff line and former course of the Dee are emphasised and demarcated by the twisting upper course of the Foss, the stream that enters the Dee below Upper Sesswick Bridge (Pont Garreg). Unfortunately classical Latin *fossa* = 'ditch, trench, channel' and medieval Latin *fossus* = 'ditch dyke, moat, embankment' on the surface the name 'being so decidedly Roman (perhaps a back reference to the Fosse Way and Fosse Dyke of Lincolnshire) early antiquaries promptly sited at Bangor a Roman 'camp' and even the controversial *BOVIUM* of Itinera II of the British section of the Antonine *Itinerary*, the third century Roman road list. Such attributions ignore the fact that the 'Foss' is the Welsh *ffos* = 'ditch', no more, no less, in this case a misfit water-course devoid of any historical associations.[9]

It is possibly on the lowest terrace (III) that the monastery at Bangor was situated. The present Dee has incised itself several feet into this terrace, carving out a fresh floodplain and the wide meander belt carrying such names as Ddôl, Groes, Ddôl Eyton etc. The meanders are still actively prograding, or would be were it not for modern extensive flood prevention works. To those who seek, and have sought, in vain for traces of the monastery one can only say: 'It was here, but on an erosion surface five or six feet above present valley bottom'.

The monastery would not be the only 'monument' lost to the erosive powers of the Dee. In 1979, the aerial photography of Chris Musson revealed the remains of two Iron

Age/Romano-British farmsteads at Royton Farm [Fig. II]. Flattened banks and filled-in ditches show up as crop marks, except on the east side where farmstead boundaries have been lost to river terrace development, the denuded break of slope being marked by linear tree cover.[10] This may point to fresh terrace development taking place in Bangor post-fifth century AD.

Whatever reservations one may have regarding 'contemporary' sources, a common denominator in all narratives is the considerable Christian seminary (size debateable) laid out (exact site unknown) on the flood plain of the Dee (extent disputable), occupying a (then) secluded valley floor hemmed in by high ground, typical of the siting of early Welsh monasteries. But, in the absence of concrete physical remains, what does the local historian look for in his efforts to reconstruct and give substance to Bangor monastery?

Lacking an obvious starting point he would best emulate Professor Butler who suggests that a model of an ideal Celtic monastery may reasonably be based on a plan (Fig. III) from the *Life of St Moluaq* (530–92). Born in Ulster, Moluaq became a monk at Bangor-yn-Arfon before founding *c.*562 the island monastery of Lismore off the coast of Argyll. In that he was a younger contemporary of St Deiniol, Moluaq's protypical establishment may perhaps be of special relevance to investigations into Bangor Isycoed.

In the centre, or inner zone, is the church/monastery within its own protective bank, the most sacred in a series of concentric zones that decreased in sanctity as one moved from the centre. From the centre would radiate access roads or tracks. At cardinal points

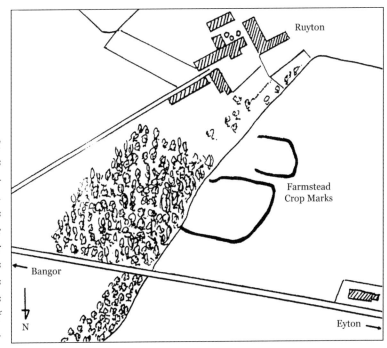

Fig. II: Not only has repeated ploughing over the centuries destroyed Iron Age/Romano-British farmsteads at Royton, but their eastern earthworks have been obliterated as the Dee has eroded river terraces, the line of which is marked by the trees. All this has important implications for recovering the site of Bangor's monastery.

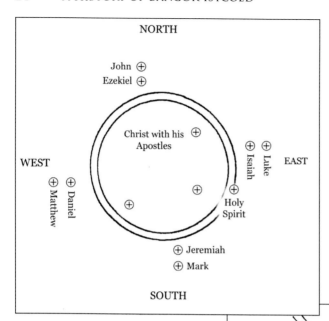

NORTH

John ⊕
Ezekiel ⊕

Christ with his ⊕
Apostles

⊕ ⊕ Luke
Isaiah

WEST   EAST

⊕ ⊕ Matthew
Daniel

⊕

⊕   ⊕
Holy
Spirit

⊕ Jeremiah
⊕ Mark

SOUTH

Fig. III: Schematic 'monastic city' based on the plan in the Life of St Moluaq *(after L.A. Butler).*

Fig. IV: An idealised development from the theortical 'monastic city' of St Moluaq – church within the oval inner zone and irregular segmental development in the outer zone according to physical constraints of the site or under only modest economic stimulii and incentives (after L.A. Butler).

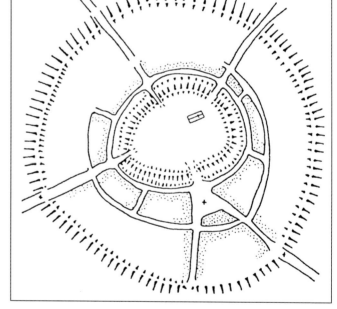

on the outskirts stood crosses but whether on the approach roads, in the open, cultivated fields or amidst dwellings, is not clear. The houses of the monks, dependants and labourers and ancillary buildings and workshops formed 'suburbs' or distinct quarters within the outer protective bank.

This model is no dry theoretic figment of a sixth-century academic's imagination. Professor Butler draws attention to the proliferation of surviving examples in Ireland e.g. Armagh, Kells, Kilkenny, where the cores of these towns still reflect the basic features of the idealised monastic city (Fig. IV). The gently rounded, easily defended hilltops preferred by founders of Irish monasteries lent themselves to the development of concentric morphological elements. That such centres abound in Ireland is attributed, *inter alia*, to the greater number of monastic/episcopal sees (over forty in 1200) compared with just four in Wales – Bangor Fawr, St David's, Llandeilo Fawr and Llandaff.[11] Also, the varied and mainly mountainous relief of Wales did not make for such unanimity of siting. The problems of identifying the 'concentric monastic city' in Wales will vary from location to location. In connection with Bangor Isycoed certain premises inevitably have to be made.

Firstly, the present consecrated site of St Dunawd's parish church is presumed to be that of the mother church. There has probably been a church here, if not since the establishment of the diocese of Lichfield in 664, certainly since the extension of that diocese westwards in the wake of Mercian conquest and territorial expansion, the limits of which are marked in the Wrexham district by Offa's (reigned 757–96) and Wat's dykes. It must be remembered that Bangor and other Maelor parishes did not become part of St Asaph diocese until 1849. The silence of the Cheshire Domesday Book (under 'Hurdingberie') does not necessarily imply the non-existence of a church at Bangor. Less than a century separates the end of Bangor monastery, implied after the slaughter and flight of most of its monks, and the imposition of some rudimentary diocesan organisation. Because of the immense sanctity of the site, the monastic church, or near contemporary, survived to become the centre of a huge parish in the Archdeaconry of Chester, also taking in Overton and Worthenbury which became parishes in their own right only in 1868 (Overton) and 1658/89 (Worthenbury). Not even Overton's later status as a castellated commotal centre under the princes of Powys Fadog and a chartered royal borough of Edward I could dent or transcend Bangor's legendary and transferred ecclesiastical prestige.

Secondly, the prime requisite in the idealised model is the circular or oval inner enclosure, a characteristic feature of Celtic *clas* churches and an assured index of the antiquity of the Christian church on site – Meifod, Pennant, Melangell, Betws Gwerful, Llansilin, etc. immediately spring to mind. At Bangor, where the broad featureless terraces of the Dee would have offered no predetermined physical constraints in the construction of the sacred enclosure, the oval or circular form would be the norm because of the ease of constructing a bank without corners or angles.

From the centre, roads or tracks radiated outwards via the four obligatory gates, in Bangor's case gates eccentrically placed rather than sited at the cardinal points as in the idealised model. Two of the gates, at Porthwgan and Cloy, are common to most literary sources. Edward Llwyd mentions a third at 'Porth Hwva' (his 'Bron Hwva', present day Bryn Hovah) and a fourth at 'Dwngre' (Dungrey). The location of these gates, even approximately, has important implications as to what actually comprised the outer bank at Bangor (Fig. V). In particular, the last three gates, which took travellers over or around the tip of the low ridge south and east of Bangor, point towards the utilisation by the monks of a convenient natural feature for a sector of a protective bank, relieving them of the difficult task, time and labour-consuming, of raising a considerable man-made 'fortification' of outer rampart and/or ditch. The disposition of the entrances thus also hints at the monastery lying closer to these three gates and at the Dee flowing some distance beyond that again, towards the north. Here marshy floodplain difficult to traverse and of access (query the existence of a causeway), and the Dee busily eroding its bluff-line below Plâs-fron and Gerwyn Fechan, focussed exit and entry traffic upon

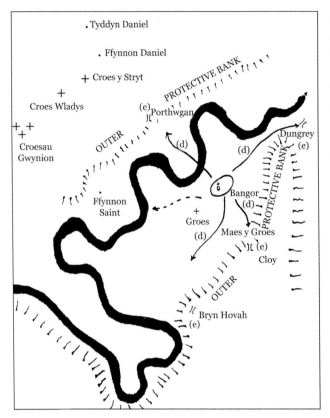

Fig. V: Provisional schematic development of the monastery at Bangor Isycoed, incorporating various aspects of the idealized 'monastic city' – (a) Inner zone (church within bank); (b) eccentric development of outer zone because of constraints imposed by the river Dee; (c) outer bank in the shape of a bluff line and ridge; (d) radiating tracks making for (e) four 'gates'. Beyond the outer bank (f) crosses and wells, visible symbols of sanctity.

one 'gate' at Porthwgan – a state of affairs that would appear to have persisted into the fourteenth century.

Significantly, in 1391, it was at Porthwgan, one of six strategically recognised entry points in the lordship, that the itinerant bailiffs of Bromfield and Yale positioned themselves on crucial market days, especially fairs and markets in Ruthin and the vale of Clwyd, to collect tolls of traders, drovers and merchants in transit as they crossed the Dee from Maelor Saesneg, Whitchurch and points beyond, and not at Bangor bridge or ford – the logical place (had they existed) as conditions pertain today. Evidence then that at the end of the fourteenth century the Dee was still flowing hard under the Plâs Fron bluff line.[12]

For a parish church with a former pastoral jurisdiction over some 22 square miles, the churchyard surrounding St Dunawd's on just three sides is a pitifully inadequate burial ground, even allowing for burials in its outlying chapelries. One would expect it to have been much larger, logically taking on the characteristic oval or circular shape hinted at earlier. Three factors may have worked to obscure this presumed earlier form. The churchyard has been truncated and squared off a) by the river Dee shifting its course to flow right under the west end and tower of the church; b) by the erection of a bridge over the new course of the river, and c) the refocusing of roads on both ends of the bridge, which involved, for example, the Overton road making its highly suspect right-angled bend to join High Street, taking off part of the churchyard in the process. Similar adjustments, with the same end result, were made to the Whitchurch and Worthenbury roads. Bangor's would not be the first oval Celtic churchyard to be so mutilated, especially in the early turnpike era – Llansilin churchyard is a case in point.

John Leland's words come to mind: '... and yet they plough up bones of the monkes, and in remembrance were digged up pecis of their clothes in sepultures', implying accidental exhumation over the former parts of the churchyard as postholes, found-ations, cess pits, etc were dug during the marking out along new alignment of Bangor's curtilages and the erection of cottages and houses thereon. This process is still on-going. In 1988, when the foundation for the extension to the village hall was dug, two skeletons were found that had been decently and properly buried which appears to support the above theory that the churchyard was at one time larger. This theory is also born out by the shortening of the nave of the church when an earlier tower was built.

Thus it is reasonable to conceive of an original church placed eccentrically within its oval enclosure. Other historical tendencies towards the idealized plan of the model are more problematical. Due allowance has to be made for limitations and peculiarities of site and position. Bangor is not a hilltop site and the Dee, wherever it flowed, was, and is, a significant constraint to expansion of settlement in one direction. Concentric 360° development would be unlikely. However, the researcher may legitimately discern some segmental development of the outer zone in favoured directions.

Bangor Isycoed's failure to emerge as an early quasi-urban institution was partly due to the limited economic resources of the area but largely to the sudden failure of the monastery and its relatively short life-span of 60–70 years, scarcely sufficient to develop fully as a focus for subsistence crafts and the little basic commerce arising from the community's struggle for self-sufficiency.

That there may have been an opportunity and some capacity for localised, low-key commercial activity can be deduced from the fact that at a later period the Dee at Bangor marked the boundary between 'the two Maelors', Maelor Cymraeg or Bromfield on the west, and Maelor Saesneg on the east, both commotes or *cymydau* first of Powys and then of Powys Fadog. The 'broom field' (Bromfield) of English colonists was by far the earliest (pre-750) place-name in use but the Malaur, Maylaur Saisneg of the Welsh expansion was current by 1200. The name 'Maelor' means not only 'land, country, plain' but also 'a market or mart' from *mael* + *lawr* = 'profit, gain + land'). As a Welsh-English dictionary of 1803 puts it, under *maelawr*: 'There are districts so called in the marches of Wales ... where trade was carried on,[13] but whether such trading activity can be projected back into the sixth century is another matter. In the later medieval period, with unassailable, if artificial, advantages of market (1279) and borough (1292) charters, Overton was to become the monopolistic commercial centre for Maelor Saesneg.

What was the nature of any development in the 'outer zone' between Bangor church and the outer protective bank? While one lacks early charters with important topo-graphical detail or is unable to refer to specific lines drawn on maps, the researcher can make some confident assumptions as to the possible character of this 'urban' growth.

Community life, whether or not the monastery was composed entirely of 'professional' monks, was the normal expression of a religious vocation in the seventh century. A monk's vocation however did not require celibacy and, as already hinted, their way of life had little in common with the popular image of the cloistered monk. Bede referred to the self-sufficiency through manual labour of the Bangor monks; this implied that landed property formed the basis for support and for income of that community. Likewise his inflated statements with regard to numbers and organisation can be interpreted as indicating a community with some degree of regulation of the day with a balance between manual labour, prayer and worship.

According to the *Vitae* or saints' *Lives* the men who founded monasteries were 'saints' by virtue of their special holiness, who determined to devote their lives to God, and encourage others to do so, in a separate and special environment – hence Deiniol founded a monastery at Bangor Fawr, but in search of greater asceticism left it shortly after with a community of monks established there and went off to found another, more spartan monastery at Bangor Isycoed, complete with disciples, companions or followers and *familae*. One cannot rule out some secular involvement and encouragement in this foundation process.

Writing about Bangor monastery, A.N. Palmer hints that it was also a royal foundation. Sources are not given, but if we accept his statement[14] that Cyngen Glodrydd [Renowned], son of Cadell Odyrnllug [Bright Hilt] and father of Brochfael Ysgithrog [Tusked], in the first instance endowed the monastery with lands, then Bangor's plantation was the result of lay *and* clerical initiative for reasons both of piety and influence, prestige and income as befitted someone deeply involved in the dynastic struggles of an emergent Powys.

As noted earlier, physical descriptions of Bangor Isycoed monastery are few, ambiguous in factual statement and therefore subjective in interpretation. Archaeology has done nothing to positively augment our knowledge. But acknowledging the 'corporate community' and 'landed endowment' elements one may reasonably imply for Bangor a) that the monastery was a separate place, marked off from the world by well defined bounds (the interpretation of the latter crucial to the concept of a 'monastic city'; b) the church or oratory of timber, sitewise possibly the most constant and enduring element within the complex; c) huts, distinctive eating and sleeping quarters, and probably a hut or house for guests; d) buildings for reading and writing. Lack of evidence does not permit one to hint at individual cells. In that Bede refers to a community supported by its own labour, the construction work at Bangor would have been performed by the monks themselves; Deiniol's companions taking their tools to cut down trees and build.

Sources do not mention different functionaries beyond seven abbots or 'section heads', but even at such an early period there must have been a hierarchy of monks responsible for managing spiritual and temporal resources and acting as deputies to Dunawd. However, it may be that the life span of the monastery was too short to permit the increased specialisation and proliferation of roles attendant upon further general growth.

While the landed basis of community support is accepted, questions of utilisation and exploitation must remain unanswered. There must have been herds, flocks, especially pigs, and barns and threshing floors. All this required labour. According to Bede we are dealing with an almost self-supporting community with necessary labour being demanded of the monks themselves. But some labour must have been supplied by others, dependants resident within the community or nearby, and possibly vocationally distinct. This implies an element of land lordship and even the existence of stewards etc to organise and oversee the workforce and its products.

Thus the monastic church at Bangor must have had adjacent to it quite a complex of more secular buildings, but where exactly in the context of present-day village layout?

As already deduced, church and churchyard, the innermost zone of Butler's 'monastic city' occupy a slightly elevated position, a matter of a metre, no more, but sufficient to make a dry island site amidst a vast lake of water during the historical annual flooding of the river Dee.

West of this enclosed 'tump' was, and is, a no-go area, being the flood plain of the Dee. Graduated posts along the roads converging on the west end of the Bangor Bridge used to bespeak possible flood hazards until removed in the last spell of road widening. East, south and north of the church, the line of the churchyard wall/embankment was partially paralleled by an encircling road from which minor streets ran away to the outer urban banks and their 'gates' (Figs. V & VI), linking the monastery with its outlying possessions. It is worth adding here that the road running roughly between the Bryn Hovah and Dungrey gates was, in the later

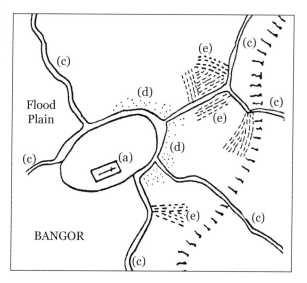

Fig. VI: Conjectural development of Bangor Isycoed after the idealised 'monastic city', showing (a) church within its circular enclosure; (b) surrounding road; (c) tracks making for 'gates' on outer ridge; (d) 'urban' development to east avoiding flood plain; (e) vanished 'open fields' of medieval origin.

medieval period, the 'royal highway' (Shrewsbury)–Overton–Bangor–Shocklach–(Chester) and figures on the British Library's Gough Map of *c*.1350, possibly the oldest road map in Britain. In Bangor it was deflected from its relatively straight line by the curve of the churchyard bank (Fig. VI). The full extent of the monastery's growth within the sixty years allotted to it by fate, will never be known, but with the evolution of even small-scale, casual 'urban' characteristics, one cannot rule out the development of a small market-place at a street intersection.

If the Dee flood-plain was avoided by the monks, the urban sprawl of both monk and lay accommodation, and the functional buildings associated with the varied 'support services' and vaguely 'commercial' enterprises, must have spread out east of the church (Fig. VI), divided into three segments by the track-ways making for the 'gates' on the outer bank – a diffusion pattern confirmed and strengthened by later source material. For the period before Bangor bent unwillingly to its new function as a dormitory village, there is ample cartographic evidence for ancient strip cultivation close to the church, particularly where the 'outer zone' rose gradually to meet its confining bank. The testimony of maps can be supplemented by medieval deeds, for example, those in the National Library of Wales Elwes MSS. In the 'open fields' of Bangor, ancient rectorial glebe was inextricably mixed with the strips of other portioners.

Leland commented on Bangor monastery: 'The cumpace of it was as of a wallid town'. But, as stated above, one does not look for defensive works in the shape of a man-made ditch and bank with timber revetment. A. N. Palmer, writing in 1889, was the first commentator to get at the true meaning behind Leland's words. A wooded ridge and river bluff-line at once gave physical definition to the 'monastic city' or quasi-urban sprawl below, as well as affording an element of natural protection and seclusion. In all likelihood these may have been augmented by the erection of a wattled fence – the 'Bangor' – which, if not exactly providing security, would certainly work to isolate the religious from the outside world. One thing is certain – the outer protective banks were never topped by the 'half-destroyed stone walls' of William of Malmesbury's vivid invention. Names on the ridge towards Whitchurch, 'Abbeygate' and the earlier 'Highgate', while apposite are modern and of doubtful antiquity.

Beyond the gates, as already noted, there were the crosses and wells (Fig. V) visible tokens or signposts marking zones of lesser sanctity, as well as perhaps marking bounds of sanctuary. They were also recognised places at which pilgrims or travellers could refresh themselves, give thanks for a safe journey almost completed, or offer prayers for a journey just beginning.

Notes on sources

1. L.A. Butler, 'The Monastic City in Wales: Myth or Reality', *Bulletin of the Board of Celtic Studies* (1979), XXVIII, 458–67.

2. *Gerald of Wales, The Journey through Wales and the Description of Wales*, (trans./ed. Lewis Thorpe, Penguin Books 1988), 251.

3. Edward Lloyd, *Parochialia &c.*, Part I, North Wales (Camb. Arch. Assoc. 1909), 134.

4. Bede, *A History of the English Church and People* (trans,/ed, L Sherley-Price, Penguin Books 1956), 100–2.

5. R. Bromwich, *Trioedd Ynys Prydein*, N⁰· 91.

6. S. Baring Gould & J. Fisher, *Lives of the British Saints*, III, 185–96, 234–41; IV, 75–86.

7. Marchwiel terriers in Denbighshire Record Office, Ruthin, 1791–1856; it would appear that the 1749 terrier (see n.9 below for source) is no longer extant.

8. Spelling is modernised, L.T. Smith (ed.), *Itinerary of John Leland &c*. (Centaur Press reprint 1965), III, 67–8.

9. A.N. Palmer, 'Notes on the Early History of Bangor Isycoed', *Y Cymrodor* (1890), X, 12–28, reprinted 1991 by Bridge Books, Wrexham, and bound along with Palmer's histories of Holt, Isycoed and Marchwiel.

10. *Archaeology in Clwyd*, 8, 6. Fig. II is based on aerial photograph CPAT 79-19-30.

11. For background to early Welsh Church see W. Davies, *Wales in the Early Middle Ages*, 141–68, especially maps, figs. 49 & 53.

12. British Library Add. MSS. 10,013, f.19v. The other 'toll-gate' in Marford bailiwick was at Pant Olwen on the boundary between Gresford and Marford townships. This, too, has similar important implications for the interpretation of landscape, especially for the course of the river Alyn and the extent of the 'Pass of Pulford' where now lies Rossett, Lavister and Darland.

13. *Geiriadur Prifysgol Cymru*, 2305–6 under mael 1, Maelor; cf. T. Morgan, *Handbook of the Origin of Place Names in Wales &c*. (1887), 118.

14. A.N. Palmer, op.cit., 15n.2. For dynastic pedigrees see D.P. Kirby, 'Greta dynastic History in the Pre-Viking Period', *Bulletin of the Board of Celtic Studies* (1976), XXVII, 81–114 esp. pp. 101–11.

3. Bangor Parish in 1699

by Derrick Pratt

Little is known about Bangor Isycoed in any detail since Bede produced his *History of the English Church and People* in 731 with his mention of the monastery until the Renaissance period when printing was invented and books such as the Bible became within reach of the ordinary man. True there are deeds/inventories, wills and letters, but these usually refer to people of substance. The occupants of the bigger houses – Althrey, Dungrey, Pickhill and the rectory – may be known, but in general not the names of the average cottager or where they lived until the 1840 tithe map or the first surviving census record of 1851. Until the twentieth century most of the smaller houses were not numbered or given names. When they were sold or described, the position of the property was fixed in relation to the owners of the property or land on their boundaries.

The period 1650–1750 was one in which many regional studies were attempted by pioneer 'antiquarian' geographers, topographers and naturalists. Not all these works were published. Much of the groundwork or research was done by the circulation, as appropriate, of questionnaires or 'Queries', printed sheets with sets of questions covering such topics as 'air (weather), water (drainage), earth and stones (geology/relief), plants, animals (ecology), arts (sociology) and antiquities (history /archaeology)'. One such was Edward Lhwyd's *Parochial Queries in Order to a Geographical Dictionary and Natural History etc. of Wales.* Some 4,000 copies appeared in 1696 as a necessary preliminary to his proposed grand opus *A British Dictionary, Historical and Geographical … and a Natural History of Wales.* Born in Loppington, Edward Lhwyd (Lhuyd), botanist, geologist, antiquary and philologist, was the illegitimate son of Edward Lloyd of Llanforda, Oswestry, and was a pupil (and later a master) at Oswestry Grammar School. When the Ashmolean Museum, Oxford, opened in 1683, Lhwyd was engaged as an assistant keeper and became keeper in 1691.

Three copies of his *Queries* were sent to each parish which were supplemented by four years (1697–1701) of fieldwork accompanied by trained helpers (unpaid 'under-keepers' at the Ashmolean) during which he visited every county in Wales. Unfortunately, with Lhwyd's premature death in 1709, his grand scheme came to naught. Both Jesus College and the university refused to buy his MSS as a corpus and they were sold and scattered and many were lost to posterity – those in possession of Sir Watkin Williams Wynn at Wynnstay, in a great fire at the London shop of his bookbinder. Fortunately, two of the notebooks containing replies to Lhwyd's Queries are now in the National Library of Wales and were published in three parts (1909–11 as *Parochialia being a Summary of Answers to Parochial Queries etc …* by the Cambrian Archaeological Association.

Included are the returns of twenty-four Flintshire (including Bangor and Hanmer) and thirty-

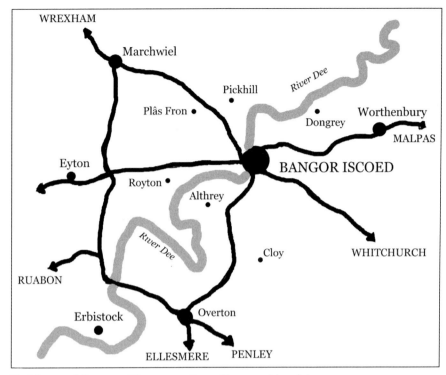

Sketchmap of Bangor with surrounding villages and hamlets.

one Denbighshire parishes (including Marchwiel) that were described by or for Lhwyd. Since this work is not easily available, local historians of Bangor might welcome the reproduction in handier form relating to their parish since it constitutes the earliest known information about Bangor parish.

[Page 45]   *BANGOR MONACHORUM*
vulgò Bangor is-y-Koed distant from Wrexham 3 miles, from Elsmere 5 or 6 small miles, from Whitchurch 8. Within the Hundr. of Maelor *seisneg*, surrounded with the Parishes of Erbistok, *Rhiwabon*, *Marchwial*, Holt, Worthenbury, Hanmer, and Overton Madok. The length from a rivulet beyond crab-tree-green betw. it & Rhiwabon on the B. of Rhiwabon and Erbistok to the white oven a house on the bord: of Worthenbury four small miles. The Breadth from a little beyond pont Pikilh (Pickilh's Bridge) on the borders of Holt to *Nant-y-Lhadron* or thereabouts on Erbistock 2 miles & a half. The number of houses in the village of Bangor is twenty-six. Overton-Madok is a parochial chap: to this and so was Worthenbury, but the Parlt have made that a distinct parish. Their feast is on Daniel's Tyde. A good rectory Mr Rees Jones the Incumbent.
E Codice Gen. Dni Rowlands de Lh: *San-nan penes* D Wyn de Mele. Upon a stone in the said Chance'ry of Bangor Church is written: *Hic jacet D'd [David] ap Madock ap Ennion* in old Saxon characters round about an Escutcheon, charged with a Lion Rampt. respecting the sinister side of the shield. And upon another Gravestone on the S. side of the Altar Chancel in Bangor Ch: is the Is. [Inscription] following: *Hic jacet Angharat*

filia Ierwerth, and she was the wife of Madock ap Gruff: dhŷ fol: 50 of this Booke.
Ibid. *Maer achæ goræ yn grych trwy gilidh iw gweled yn Vynych.*
Wrth adrodh a hir edrych.
Mae'r gwael yn deyryd ir gwych.

[Page 46] The Villages.
1. Alrhe 8 scattering houses.
2. Dyngse 5 or 6 houses.
3. Pickilh scatters much.

The Townships.
1. Bangor (in Fl: Shire)
2. Eaton.
3. Reyton
4. Seswyke.
5. Pickilh all four in D: Shire.

Of this Abby see *Primate Usher de primordio eccl'es*. Br. The field where the Abby stood
is call'd *Aniwlch* [sic]

The Better Houses.
   1. Arlhe Hall Tho: Whitley Esq.
   2. Dongrey (Brit. Dwngre) Roger Davies Gent.
   3. The rectory – all these in Bangor.
   4. Eaton Hall. Kenr Eaton Esqr.
   5. Ibid. Booth Basnet Gent.
   6. Ibid. Mr Will. Edwards.
   7. Reiton Hall, Sr Gruff Jeffrey's Heir.
   8. *Gerwyn Vawr*, Mr Edward Wyn.
   9. Bedwal. Mr John Edwards.
10. Pickilh Hall. A child, the Heir of the Late Thos. Ravenscroft Esqr.
11. Ibid. Mr. John Puleston.

Other Houses.
1. *Porth Wgan.*
2. *Bron Hwva.*   q. an *Porth Hwva*?
3. *y Klai, Porth y Klai* now. *rhai a dhwedant vod y pedwerydh porth yn Dwngre.*

Enwae Krwys: 6 Crosses.
1. *Kroes y* Street.
2. *Maes y groes.*

3. *Kroes Wladys*.

  Tîr y Prenniae a small coppice bel: to Mr Whitley.

  Twmparth yr Eirth the name of a small patch.

  Talwrn enw Fordh Lydan.

[Page 47] The Rivers.

1. Dee separating Overton and Erbistock and running thrô this parish close by the church is become the mear of Holt and Worthenbury.
2. Milbrook out of Overton thrô Bangor and into Dee 3 quarters of a mile below the Church.
3. Klywedog out of Wrexham Parish (which it divides from Marchwial) and so divides this parish from Holt and runs to Dee a mile and a half below the Ch.
4. Nant y Lhadron from ward Rhiwabon and so dividing this parish from Erbistock falls into Dee two miles above this Church a little below Overton bridge.

The Bridges.

1. *Pont garreg* over a stream coming out of *Fynnon y Saint. Fyn ...*
2. The greatest bridge is Bangor bridge a little below the Ch. on the River Dee 5 Arches.
3. Pikilh bridge on Klywedog a mile above its Fall.
4. *Pont y Pedair Onnen* on Milbrook a small h. a mile above its fall.
5. *Pont garreg*. ar ... a mile on the way to Wrexham.
6. *Pont ar Vilbrook ŷn Arch ar Fordh yr Egl Wen*.
7. *Pont newydh yn Dwngre ergid karreg odhiar i haber ar yr ŷ avon.*

  Lhyn y Vynwent (yn Dowrdwy).

Y Fynnonnydh : Springs.

1. *F Dheniol*
2. *F. y Saint.*

  Digon o Varl glâs. glô a loskant, a pheth Koed.

  Mas erw vechan a Phwlh yndhi a elwir Groft y Beydy.

   Q. *An corruptè pro Groft y meydwy; o herwydh dyna lhe*

   bydhe rhiw hên wr gynt yn gwedhio beynydh etc.

Lhwyd begins with straightforward notes on the extent and dimensions of the parish including a reference to Worthenbury's recent (1689) alienation from Bangor as a parish in its own right. It would be interesting to recover 'the white oven' landmark on the Bangor – Worthenbury boundary. Was it a kiln, brew-house or common bakehouse? Crab Mill in the Green Lane and what was Howeswood farm, Hollybush are possible contenders.

    This the earliest (so far) recorded use of the name 'Bangor Isycoed'. The qualification *vulgo* = 'commonly, generally' (the contracted sense of *linguo vulgarico* or *vulgari* = 'in the vernacular or vulgar tongue'), implies its use locally in every-day speech. The more formal *Bangor Monachorum* = 'Bangor of the monks' pre-dates Lhwyd's usage by some 22 years (NLW Coleman Deed DD 1268, indenture of 12 June 1677 – 'Bangor otherwise Bangor Monachorum') and seems to have been the preferred form in more formal legal documents.

The Revd Rees (Rice) Jones, noted as incumbent (1690–1730) was connected with the Lloyd family of Gwernheylod, Overton, patrons of the living 1680–1830. Although he was rector when Richard Trubshaw (architect for the rebuilding of Worthenbury church 1736–9) was let loose on Bangor church in his restoration of 1726–7 (the tower is to his design), it would be unfair to blame him for the loss of the two medieval gravestones mentioned by Lhwyd.

Note the size of Bangor village itself in the 1690s – only twenty-six houses compared with its outlying hamlets of Althrey and Dongrey otherwise Dyngse, Dongrey, Dwngre. These latter forms of the place-name we owe solely to Lhwyd. 1699 is a late provenance, but almost certainly indicates a British hill name referring to the ridge that separates Bangor from Worthenbury and the valley of the Millbrook. The first element is E Brit. *dûno*, OW *din* = 'a hill, fort', possibly influenced by OE *dûn* ('hill'), modified by Welsh speakers into *dŵn*. The second element is OW *creic*, W *craig* = 'rock, cliff'. There is no outcrop of the underlying Bunter Pebble beds in the entire parish, so *dun creic* = 'hill cliff' or 'fort cliff', referring to a prominent physical feature but with a probable lateral allusion to the 'monastic enclosure' that lay immediately west of the ridge. The loss of the final 'c' in *creic* offers no problem in an area subject to a constant succession of Welsh and English/Mercian influences. Significantly the second element also survives in the 'Graig Lane' and 'The Graig', right on or at the tip of, the ridge.

Under 'Better houses' (*Y Tai Kyvrîvol*) we note Althrey Hall no longer in the hands of the Ellis family. Roger Davies of Dongrey (d.1709) was of Hanmer family stock but took the surname Davies in deference to the overwhelmingly Welsh character of Bangor parish. Ruyton was an outlying estate of the Jeffreys's family of Acton Hall, Wrexham. Sir Griffith Jeffreys was the nephew of the notorious 'Bloody ' Lord Jeffreys of Wem, Lord Chancellor 1685–9. He inherited the Ruyton estate from his father in 1670 and Acton Hall from his grandfather in 1691. The heir as mentioned was Robert Jeffreys (d.1714); he had come into the property only in 1695.

The Wynnes of Gerwyn Fawr were an important family of minor Welsh gentry or yeomen, verging on the *uchelwyr* class and tracing their descent back to Tudur Trefor. Edward Wynne died in 1712. Of even more ancient Welsh stock, Kenrick Eyton (d. 1709), lived at Eyton Isaf, and was the son of Sir Kendrick Eyton (d.1681), a judge on the north Wales circuit. Four further generations were also known as Kenrick. The Eyton name died out in the 1850s with Kenrick Edward Eyton II, who lived in reduced circumstances at Fedw Goed, having been forced to sell up because of money problems in 1825.

The Basnett family had moved into Eyton Uchaf (not the present farm at Eyton crossroads) after Roger Eyton sold up in the 1590s. Booth Basnett died in 1746, aged 85. He tried to change the name of his house to Plâs Basnett, but reckoned without the conservative Welsh population. Where exactly William Edwards lived in Eyton township is not known save that, according to the church rating list, it was the second biggest house in Eyton.

The Ravencrofts, with three generations all Thomas, moved from Bretton, Hawarden, in the 1630s and lived at what is now Pickhill Old Hall. Thomas Ravencroft had died in 1699, leaving a son, also Thomas, twelve years old. The Puleston house 1609–1801 was Pickhill Hall. This particular branch of the family originated from Emral via Bradenheath. John Puleston died in 1722 and was buried in Farndon. John Edwards of Bedwell Hall (between Cross Lanes and Five Fords) was buried at Bangor 17 June 1710.

Under *Enwau Croesau* or 'Names of Crosses' Lhwyd names only three of six, *Kroes Wladys* was a boundary cross on the border of the Elizabethan manor (medieval provostry) of Pickhill, which included Pickhill and Sesswick townships, possibly to be sought along the border with Isycoed parish rather than with Marchwiel. The latter has *Kroes y Stryt*, present day 'Cross Lanes', which place-name obviously has deeper significance than just 'a junction of roads'. The other three names included by Lhwyd under this head have no known association with sites of medieval crosses. Yet some historical significance they must have, otherwise why should Lhwyd seize upon them, widely disparate as they are? *Tîr y Prenniae* (Terreprenne of 1677 and the meaningless 'Tre-a peni' of modern OS maps) means 'land with trees or wood'. What a pity the name is currently rubbished as 'Three-a-Penny'! Why should *Talwrn* in Pickhill be singled out as *Ffordd Llydan* i.e. 'the broad, wide highway'?

In any parish Lhwyd's listings of bridges may be used to gain some idea of the contemporary importance of various cross-country roads and tracks. *Pont garreg* (1.5) = 'stone bridge', both on the Wrexham road i.e. one (Upper) Sesswick Bridge and the other immediately below Porthwgan. They cannot be located in the context of today's road pattern, for the 'straight mile' approaches to the west end of Bangor bridge date only from 1819 when the B5426 was built as a 'coal road' linking Bangor with the mining districts of Ruabon and Rhos.

Pont y Pedair Onnen (4) = 'bridge of the four ash trees' and was where the Millbrook stream crossed the Worthenbury road at Bangor station, due allowance being made for diversions to accommodate railway works in the 1890s. 'The bridge on Millbrook of one arch on the road to Whitchurch [Eglwys Wen],'[6] is clearly that on the A525 below Bank Farm just before the demolished railway bridge. 'The new bridge in Dongrey a stone's throw from the mouth of the same stream (Millbrook)'[7] carries the drive/lane into Dungrey Hall.

Shorn of any historical connotation is the bare reference to *Llyn y fynwent* = 'cemetery pool' (W *mynwent* = 'graveyard, tomb'). This deep spot in the River Dee is still known as the 'Church Pool'. Like Edward Lhwyd, we leave this brief look at the Bangor of 1699 with its inhabitants 'digging turves, and burning coal and some wood'.

4. Bangor Village in 1949

A similar questionnaire to the 'Parochial Queries' sent by Edward Lhwyd in 1699 was sent by the Council for the Preservation of Rural England in 1949 to all parish councils, entitled *A National Survey of Villages*, requesting information on the village and immediate surrounding area. Under the first section 'Identification' a question 'Is there a guide book or printed local history of the village? Bangor's reply was, 'Yes, but not yet published'. No one remembers a guidebook or history being produced other than canon Thomas's booklet about the church that was printed thirteen years later, which must be the one referred to.

Question	*Answer*
POPULATION	
a. Number of children under 13 years	79
b. Number of children between 13 and 16 years	13
c. Number of persons between 16 and 65 years (approx)	200
d. Number of persons over 65 years (approx)	25
e. Total population (approx.)	310–15
f. Is the population tending to rise or fall?	Rise.
3. DWELLING HOUSES.	
a. Number of houses in good habitable order	80 out of 90 in the village
b. Number of houses condemned and subject to demolition order	Should estimate 6 pre-war 1938.
c. Number of families waiting for homes	6–8
d. Number of houses erected or reconditioned since 1939	1 by private building in 1949, none since 1914–19 war. 1 converted by private enterprise from a farm building.
e. What kind of building material has been used in the past for walls and roofs?	Brick and tile.
f. Have the new houses been constructed with these local materials?	Six are proposed to be built in 1950 allocation by Overton RDC being the first since present eight council houses erected over 25 years ago.

4. SERVICES.

Are there any of the following? Give numbers if more than one. Where not situated in the village, state the distance to the nearest.

a. Resident local doctor and/or local surgeries	2 local surgeries.
b. Dentist	No
c. Ante-natal and welfare centre	No.
d. Resident district nurse/midwife	No.
e. Registrar of births and deaths	No.
f. Veterinary surgeon	No.
g. Solicitor	No
h. Police house/office	Yes.
i. Post office	Yes.
j. Branch library	No.
k. Public telephone kiosk	Yes.
l. Public clock	None but on Church Tower.
m. Parish council office	No.
n. Bank	No.
o. Local produce or cattle market	No.
p. Street lighting (state whether electric or gas)	No.
q. Piped water supply (if not, well or rain water and if	No. Well water shortage insufficient in late summer 1949.
r. Fire hydrant (give any other fire service)	No.
s. Main sewerage system (if not, whether cesspool or earth closet)	No, cesspools and earth closets.
t. Public onveniences	No.
u. Refuse collection	Dust bins emptied every Friday.
v. Litter bins	Yes 1 in church yard.
w.Electricity (if a main supply passes through the village state whether houses are connected or not If not, how near is the supply?)	No. Nearest supply 6 miles away.
x. Gas	No.
y. Public seats	No.
z. Burial ground or cemetery	No.

5. TRADES

a. What retail shops are there? Give any others. If a Co-operative store serves the village, state which trades are so covered	3 Grocers and a Co-op van visits clients every week.

b. Provisions	Three above.
c. Greengroceries	No.
d. Meat	1 butcher.
e. Fish	No.
f. Bread and confectionary	No.
g. Hardware	No.
h. Clothing and footwear	No.
i. Boot and shoe repairs	No.
j. Fuel (coal, etc and oil)	Two suppliers.
k. Tobacco and sweets	3 grocers and 1 sweet and tobacco (4).
l. Wireless	No.
m. Dispensing chemist	No.
n. Newspapers or stationery	No.
o. Hairdressing	No.
p. Is the village served by a travelling general tradesman?	Yes.

6. TRANSPORT SERVICES

a. Is there a regular bus service? (State whether daily or weekly)	Yes. Daily.
b. Are there taxi or car hire services or motor coach facilities?	Two Taxi proprietors. No coaches in village.
c. Is there a railway service?	Yes. Bangor Isycoed 1 mile out.
d. Are workmen's and cheap day tickets available?	Yes.
e. Is there a local carrier?	No, but by GWR deliveries.
f. What improvements in bus or train services are needed?	Daily evening buses.

8. HOTELS AND INNS.

If there is an hotel, inn, guest house, hostel, etc., state in respect of each:

a. Number of each kind	2 Hotels, Royal Oak and Buck, 1 Hostel.
b. Sleeping accommodation available	12–15 in all 3 above.
c. Services supplied (e.g.) luncheons and dinners, licensed, electricity, games room etc., luncheons etc.	2 Hotels and Hostel bar, Twiss' Assembly Rooms for whist drives and dancing. Wooden village institute for whist drives, billiards and other games.
d. Whether there are garaging facilities available	At hotels.
e. Whether recognised by the RAC or AA?	Yes.
f. Is the accommodation sufficient to meet holiday demands?	Yes.

g. Would the village welcome expansion as a tourist or holiday centre?

Cannot say how any expansion can be made.

To the question on recreation they stated that there was no children's playground although the youth club rented a ground for football. There was no tennis court or bowling green and the only sporting facility offered to visitors was fishing, both salmon and coarse, on licence. There was no village or church hall. Footpath and bridle paths were not signposted and were overgrown and little used. The parish council had not undertaken any repairs on them for years but, in contrast, the road surface in the village was in good condition.

When asked about buildings of historic or architectural interest the only one they could bring to mind was the parish church. To the question 'Are there any buildings (including country mansions), structures or earthworks of historical, architectural or geological interest?' They replied, 'There was an ancient monastery but nothing remains of it. Date 600 to 800 AD. River Bridge at Bangor Isycoed dates back to 1086'! Asked whether there were any parochial or privately owned documents of historical value not properly recorded and protected, they say 'none known of.' We might not have lost so much of historical interest from the church parish chest if they had thought a bit harder!

On the question of what improvements did the council consider most needed, they replied: 'Street lighting, a village hall and public conveniences are badly needed'. They proposed to press for them through local councils and the Welsh Board of Health. They do not seem to put much store by a proper sewerage system or a piped water supply – even though they go on to state 'the village lags fifty years behind modern requirements.'

5. The Parish Church

The country was divided up into parishes in about the seventh century and all those parishes that supported a resident priest were allowed to appoint their own minister. It is not known when Bangor became a parish but it supported a rector as early as 1300 as the names of all the incumbents since then are known. At that time the parish comprised, in addition to Bangor, the townships of Pickhill, Sesswick, Royton (Ryton), Eyton, Worthenbury and Overton.

The church is dedicated to St Dunawd, a former abbot of the monastery, who died before 607AD. The date of the first church to be built in Bangor is unknown. It may have been built on the site of the earlier monastery and would have been of simple wattle and daub construction. This would have been replaced with a timber structure at a later date. The earliest part of the present church is the chancel with its red sandstone, dating to around 1300 when there was a period of church building and rebuilding in many parts of the principality after the conquest of Wales by King Edward I in 1282.

Bangor church was transferred from the Diocese of Lichfield to that of Chester in 1541 and to St Asaph in 1849. Worthenbury was part of Bangor until 1658 when, during the last days of the Commonwealth, it was made into a separate parish. However, after the restoration of the monarchy in 1660, the Revd Henry Bridgeman, restored as Bangor's rector, refused to recognize the separation and it was not until 1689 that an Act of Parliament was passed separating Worthenbury from Bangor. The then rector, the Revd John Lloyd, petitioned Parliament not to approve the separation. This petition used to be preserved among the parish records and a debt is owed to Canon David Thomas for recording its contents.

To the Honourable the House of Commons in this present Parliament Assembled.

The Petition of John Lloyd, Clerk, rector of Bangor in the diocese of Chester Humbly sheweth,

That Worthenbury in the Parish of Bangor aforesaid hath been time out of mind and beyond the memory of Man to the contrary a Chappel of Ease properly belonging to the rectory of Bangor: And that the rector of Bangor for the time being hath constantly provided a curate to officiate at the said Chappel of Ease until the Year 1683, about which time the late rector of Bangor dying, there have since been Endeavours used to separate the said Chappel of Ease from the Mother Church of Bangor, and to that end a Clerk hath been actually presented to Worthenbury aforesaid as if the same hath been a separate and entire rectory independent of Bangor.

Forasmuch therefore as your Petitioner is advised, and conceives that the Rights of the Church of Bangor aforesaid, and of your Petitioner the present Incumbent will be invaded if any such separation be made, and your Petitioner being informed that a Bill is brought into this Honourable House for that purpose, He humbly desires that he may be heard by his Councel before any such Bill do pass this Honourable House.

But his plea was to no avail and Worthenbury was lost to Bangor forever. Overton, for centuries also part of Bangor parish, was not separated from the mother church until 1867 and was constituted a rectory in 1868.

The tower

From the outside, the dominating feature of the church is the tower that has three storeys, of brick and stone, with pilaster strips, i.e. rectangular stone columns projecting from each corner. The bell openings are round-headed and the tower is topped by urn-like finials, each with a weather vane. It was built in 1725/6 by Richard Trubshaw (1689–1745), who was the mason/architect responsible for the remodelling of the façade of nearby Emral Hall, where he also added two wings in 1724 and the stable block in 1734. He also built Worthenbury church between 1736 and 1739. Born in Haywood, Staffordshire into a well-known family of masons based in Colwich, Trubshaw designed or renovated many of Staffordshire churches and no doubt employed members of his family in the work. He is buried in Colwich.

The church towers of both Bangor and Worthenbury are somewhat similar, but the ten years between their building enabled Trubshaw to refine his style and, in the case of Worthenbury, to design the body of the church to match. It has been said that Bangor's tower is out of keeping with the rest of the church and should have been made larger. Worthenbury church is a truly distinctive place of worship and is one of the finest examples of Georgian architecture in Wales and deserving of its Grade I listing. Bangor's church has been given Grade II* listing.

Trubshaw's tower was not a new feature having replaced an older tower of unknown date and design. We know that the new tower was built on the same site because in 1718, when the churchwardens applied for permission for a gallery to be erected over the west end of the nave, the description of the depth of the gallery was recorded as 'being 9 feet from the belfry wall'. This was about seven years before the present tower was built. At some time in the distant past, one bay of the nave had been demolished to accommodate the building of a much earlier tower. It is speculative to think that perhaps the oldest tower had been erected too near the river and the

foundations were undermined when the river changed its course and it was built further back necessitating the demolition of part of the nave for its accommodation.

The clock

Bangor had a church clock on the tower as early as 1725 as the churchwardens, when answering the interrogation at the archdeacon's visitation, mention this fact, but due to the loss of the early parish accounts books we have no knowledge of when or from whom it was bought. Chirk had bought a church clock in 1712 from an Ellesmere clockmaker, Edmond Bullock, who perhaps also supplied Bangor's clock.

Assuming that clocks needed replacing about every 100 years, then the parishioners of Bangor may have bought theirs

Worthenbury Church tower.

Bangor Church tower with the old diamond-shaped clock. Photograph taken on 3 August 1896, before clock was replaced and before the construction of the lych gate and the demolition of the five cottages by the bridge.

at the beginning of the 1700s and transferred it to the new tower as, about a hundred years later, the clock was giving cause for concern. In April 1811, a clockmaker was asked to come and inspect it, for which he charged the church £3 17s 6d. He also arranged for a Harry Tomkins to clean and repair part of the clock at a cost of 15s and made a new clock dial and took the old one down for £2 10s 10d. A Mr Gittings then charged 9s for a new hand for the clock, and Josh Hinton painted the clock dial and put it up – a further £5 12s 6d. This made a total outlay of £13 4s 10d – a not inconsiderable sum in 1811. The clock dial may have been of wood, as were many at that time, which explains why there is a recurring item in the accounts for painting the dial.

The clock was obviously not completely brand new

Remains of the fifth arch that was demolished to accommodate an earlier tower.

as certain parts of the old one were reused but the movement would have been. The clock was set in a diamond shaped surround and can be seen in the sketch by Moses Griffith in 1782 and in early photographs. By 1826, the clock needed further unspecified repairs and the clock dial was repainted. In 1834 a new dial was bought at a cost of £12 10s 6d. Thereafter, apart from regular maintenance such as new weights bought in 1854 and other minor work, there was no major expense for the clock.

Harry Tomkins continued to annually clean and service the clock until 1839 when the duties were taken on by Thomas Tomkins until 1844. The likelihood is that, as Harry Tomkins serviced the clock from its installation until 1839, that his employers supplied the clock and recommended him. I have not found anyone of his name living and working as a watchmaker in Wrexham, Ellesmere, Whitchurch, Hanmer or Oswestry. However there is a Thomas Tomkins in the 1841 census for Overton, sharing a house with his elder brother and described as a 'watch m[aker]'. There was a Henry Tomkins of Lightwood Green who was buried in Overton in 1843, who could be the Harry Tomkins, father of Thomas, who perhaps retired in 1839, aged 68, when his son who may have completed his apprenticeship in the same trade took over his work for a few years.

After 1844, John Jones carried out the work for some years and was succeeded by Thomas Clay, a watchmaker who lived in Bangor and serviced the clock until 1862. In that year he was convicted of stealing £20 in bank notes and three gold sovereigns from a chest, the property of Edward Maddocks, maltster, the father-in-law of Mrs Maddocks licensee of the Red Lion Inn (now Plassey House). Edward Maddocks slept in rooms over the malt kiln behind the inn. Whilst he was with an excise officer inspecting the kiln he heard footsteps overhead and found Thomas Clay with the empty chest. He informed PC Lockwood who later searched the culprit's rooms and found the missing money. Thomas Clay was given six months imprisonment with hard labour and lost his employment at the church.

When more specialised repair work was needed a watch and clock maker was sent for from Wrexham. The names mentioned in the accounts were Joseph Welch, Samuel Caldecott, Mr Leadbeater and Mr Wilks.

On 27 February 1904, the *Wrexham Advertiser* reported that:

> … the clock in the [Bangor] church tower is over 90 years old and is completely worn out and past repairing. A firm of clockmakers has given a quote of £55 for one striking the hours; for one striking the hours and 'ting tang' quarters, £85; or, for one striking the hours and Cambridge chime quarters, £115. The work could be completed in about 2 months.

The rector was in favour of Cambridge chimes and, on a proposal by William Johnson, and seconded by Thomas Williams, it was agreed to purchase one such clock from J.B. Joyce of Whitchurch. This firm which was established in 1690 continues to make clocks today and has an international reputation. Unfortunately their records were destroyed in a disastrous fire on the premises a few years ago but, as they did not start to specialise in tower clocks until 1830, they could not have made either of Bangor's earlier clocks.

To cover the cost of the purchase, a subscription was started and the Duke of Westminster, Oliver Ormrod and Henry Walker set an example to the parishioners by each giving £10. Seven people gave £5: Sir Roger Palmer, Archibald Peel, the Revd and Mrs Elrington Bisset, Captain and

List of subscribers for the new church clock, 1904.

Mrs Fenwick, General and Mrs Savage Mostyn, Hugh Peel, Miss Panton and 'Anonymous'. One hundred and seventeen people gave sums ranging from £3 down to Mrs Jane Young's 2d and the donations included one guinea from Bents Brewery whose public house, the Royal Oak, looked directly onto the church tower. The sale of the old clock made five shillings. The cost of the new clock was £125 including the casing. Henry Bostock, a local carpenter, charged 16s 6d for the woodwork in the tower and Messrs Jarman & Co charged £1 5s 11d for the printing of letters requesting donations. Thanks to Jane Young's 2d the amount collected in donations exactly matched the total expenses of £127 2s 5d.

On Wednesday, 3 August 1904, the Venerable Archdeacon Wynne Jones, taking the place of the bishop of St Asaph (who had been detained in the House of Lords), dedicated the clock and the rector of Bangor, the Revd Elrington Bisset, assisted him at the ceremony. Also present were the Revd A.G.M. Jennings of Isycoed; canon Griffith Jones, Marchwiel; the Revd C.R. Pembridge, rector-elect of Worthenbury; Elliot Simpson, curate of Overton; and G.E. Browne, curate of Bangor.

On 20 August 1904 the following appeared in the newspaper:

… a good number of people have visited Bangor to hear the chimes and their opinions are not unanimous. None can deny that they are melodious, but it is unreasonable to expect that they should be as powerful as the beautiful chimes of Wrexham especially when the amount for them is taken into account.

In 1906, it was reported that much amusement was caused when, one Sunday night in December, the clock began to strike the hours before it chimed, and then it could be heard chiming and striking at the same time. If only they had spent a little more money ...? However, this same clock (apart from being repaired in 1974 and repaired and overhauled in 2007) is still keeping good time today.

The bells

The original number of church bells nor when they were acquired is not known, but according to the churchwardens at the bishop's visitation of 1725, the belfry contained three bells. When the tower was rebuilt, the opportunity was taken to have the bells recast and to purchase an additional one. Trevor Davies, a barber of Bangor, said in his evidence to the church court in 1728 that one reason for the deficiency in the money for the building of the tower was the 'recasting & making the addition to the bells'. Four bells bear the date 1727 and were cast by Abraham Rudhall (1680–1735) – the same date and maker as the set of ten bells in St Giles' Church, Wrexham. His father, also Abraham (1657–1736), was the first of a noted family of Gloucester bell-founders, and was called 'the greatest bell-founder of this age'. The bells were hung by Samuel West, aged 21, a joiner, who had come from Shrewsbury in the August especially to undertake the work, and had remained in the Bangor area where he had since found employment.

At some point, two more bells were purchased, there is mention in the parish accounts book of taking another bell to the foundry to be recast. This fifth bell, cast by John Rudhall (1760–1835) the great grandson of the founder, bears the date 1811 and cost £40 17s 8½d and was made up as follows:

1810	
Charles Fleet (parish clerk) for taking Bell to Shrewsbury	£ 1 4s 6d
Carriage of bell to Gloucester	£ 2 10s 0d
Charles Fleet for going with the Bell & Turnpikes	12s 0d
Mr Rudhall for exchange of the Bell	£17 1s 2½d
Mr Pointon Wrexham & Mrs Frances for drink when taking the Bell down	£ 2 8s 0d
Taking the Tone of Bell & Pitchfork	£ 1 0s 0d
1811	
Carriage of the new Bell from Shrewsbury	£ 1 14s 0d
John Montford for hanging the Bell & repairing the Bell frame	14s 0d
The remainder for the New Bell	£13 14s 0d
	£40 17s 8½d

The sixth bell, by Mears & Stainsborough, is a tenor bell which bears the date 1865 and cost £43. This time, the parish clerk, William Thomas, took the bell to the station, either in Wrexham,

Ellesmere or Whitchurch – Bangor station was not constructed until thirty years later.

The churchwardens' accounts show that the bells were rung to celebrate various national events or special local occasions:

1689 Paid to the Clerk for ringing, being the Coronation Day of King William   2s 0d
1692 Paid for ringing the success of the Fleet   9d
1839 Ringing for her Majesty (announcement of Q. Victoria's engagement)   15s 0d
1862 Tolling bell on the death of Prince Consort   3s 0d
1865 Sept 25th to bill for Ringing at Rejoicing at Winstay [rebuilt after fire]   10s 0d

There were many items in the accounts for the regular purchase of new bell ropes, as they did not last long. In recent times, Joe Roberts of Abbot's Way, being an ex-navy man, used to splice the ropes together when they broke to save some money.

Hanging in the belfry is a board on which the quaint 'Rules for Ringers' is painted, thought to date from the time of the tower's construction.

In January 1892, it was reported that the bell-ringers had gone on strike. Apparently a generous benefactor had either died or had left the district and, when the usual honorarium had not been received on New Year's Day, the ringers had decided to strike. When the residents did not hear the usual sound of bells on the following Sunday, the parish clerk was hastily called and a single bell was heard to mournfully toll the worshipers to prayer. A meeting was held at the rectory the following week and the upshot was that Mr Archibald Peel gave a generous sum and the strike was at an end!

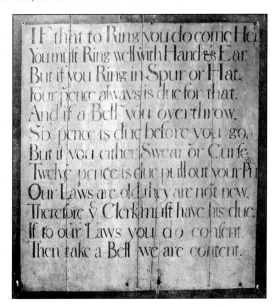

Rules for the bell-ringers.

Whenever anyone in the parish was on his deathbed it was the custom for a single bell, known as the 'passing bell', to be tolled day or night when the critical moment of death arrived to encourage the pious to pray for the soul that was about to start its journey. The death knell varied from parish to parish, but usually three strokes were repeated three times for the death of a man, two strokes repeated three times for a woman and three single stokes for a child. The difficulty arose when an apparently dying person made a miraculous recovery or when a sick person who might have recovered died sooner than expected on hearing his own death knell! At a vestry meeting in 1921 there was an objection to the ringing of the passing bell and it was decided to discontinue this practice.

Inside the church by the belfry wall is a seat with an inscribed brass plate in memory of Philip Henry Humphreys (1899–1979) who was the verger and also a bell-ringer for forty-five years and was the father of George 'Dode' Humphreys. On the pillar by the belfry wall are two marble plaques, one commemorating George Dunbabin (1844–1909) for forty-three years a bell-ringer and the other for James Poynton (1870–1917) a bell-ringer for twenty years. Another veteran bell ringer was Thomas Antley of Overton Road, who in 1934, at eighty-four years of age, was specially selected by the bell-ringers to assist in ringing a peal of bells at the parish church on Jubilee Day. He had rung a peal of bells at the same church on the occasion of Queen Victoria's Golden Jubilee, King Edward VII's Coronation and King George V's Coronation. According to a framed notice on the wall of the ground floor of the tower, the bell-ringers in 1937 were Mr Geo Humphreys, Mr Geo Humphreys Junr, Mr G. Jarvis, Mr W. Young Junr, Mr J. Spoor, Mr A. Spoor, and Mr J. Poynton.

At the time of writing, the bell-ringers are David White, Peter Furber, Alan and Rosemary Furber, Margaret Bishop, Hugh John and, until he left the district early in 2011, George 'Dode' Humphreys, aged ninety. The tower captain is Alan Furber. They rang the bells to celebrate the Queen's Diamond Jubilee in June 2012 and again on the opening day of the 2012 London Olympics in July, joining in the rejoicing with every other church. On 17 July the same year a team of bell-ringers from Liverpool were going around the country ringing the bells in each church and they visited Bangor and rang a full peal, changing one bell on every other pull. It lasted two hours and forty-six minutes and everyone remarked on the wonderful sound they made.

In the belfry is a brass plaque bearing the following inscription: 'To the glory of God as a Thank Offering for victory in World War II, 1939–1945, the bells in this tower were rehung, being defrayed by public subscription. December 1946.' Apparently the bells require recasting again.

There is in the church a set of hand-bells that were used at one time for practice and also for demonstrations that were given at various functions. In December 1897, a concert was held in the girls' school to raise funds for the purchase of lamps for the churchyard gates and the entertainment included a performance by the 'Bangor Hand Bell Ringers.' In February 1918, the hand-bell ringers under Mr Dunbabin gave a performance as part of a concert in aid of St Dunstan's House for the blind. At Christmas-time, the ringers used to visit the farms and cottages with their handbells and invite donations. In 1934, the money collected paid for the purchase of eight new hand-bells and the repair of the existing ones. Those who constituted the team in that year were: S. Dunbabin, A. Spoor, J. Spoor, G. Humphreys, T. Mercer, W. Young, J. Poynton with two boys – Joe Spoor, & Jack Fowles. In 1989, the hand-bells were restored, but two were found to be missing and it was hoped to raise funds to purchase replacements and to establish a team of ringers once again. Bill Cartwright of Hanmer who had offered to provide the training, had been a bell ringer and chorister for over seventy years in Hanmer church when he died in 2003 age 89. Nothing further has been heard about this scheme.

The nave

The pillars are one of the oldest parts of the nave being medieval in origin and dating from the same period as the chancel. A mason's mark, a reversed Z, can be seen on at least one of the pillars in the south colonnade. The original length of the nave is unknown, all that we do know, as previously mentioned, is that part of the west end of the church had to be demolished to accommodate an earlier tower as the remains of a fifth arch can be seen at the end of the north colonnade. The present length of the nave is 61 feet 6 inches with a north and south colonnade of four arches with the average width of each arch being 13 feet 9 inches. With the addition of the demolished fifth arch, assuming it was the same average measurement, the original length of the nave would have been at least 75 feet (22.86 metres).

The church has seen much repair, renovation, alterations and additions over the years, the earliest of which are unrecorded. The first repair that we know about took place in 1600 when the churchwardens reported to the bishop's visitation that 'the church was in decaye but money [is] collected for the repairing thereof.' Unfortunately no details are given as to the exact state of decay, what was repaired or the total cost.

The first recorded work was when it became fashionable to fit galleries for extra seating. In 1718, John Puleston of Pickhill, one of the churchwardens, applied for a faculty, or permission, to build a gallery at his own expense at the west end of the nave for his use and that of others. He planned to recover part of the cost by selling or renting seats to anyone who wanted them for their families and/or servants. It was to be twenty feet in length, i.e. the width of the nave between the pillars, and nine feet in depth from the belfry wall, jutting out from that wall to the point of the arch of the colonnade. The gallery was constructed in 1720 but the names of the architect and builder or its design are unknown. When the new church at Worthenbury was erected in 1736 it also incorporated, and still possesses, a gallery that was used to house the choir and harmonium. However, there is no evidence that the choir or the orchestra ever used the gallery at Bangor.

One of the rectors, the Revd Rice (Rees) Jones (1691–1736) complained many times that the interior of the church was dark and that he had difficulty in reading prayers and sermons. The church was only used in the daytime (except at Christmas), candles being too expensive, and apart from the big chancel windows, the windows in the aisles were very small and narrow. Eventually, when the long wall of the north aisle was found to be in a 'decayed state', the decision was taken to demolish it and rebuild, incorporating larger Georgian windows with dormer-style gables depicted in Moses Griffiths's drawing of 1782. This work took place at the same time as the gallery was constructed in 1720.

In 1723, when plans were under discussion to rebuild the tower, the decision was taken to ask Richard Trubshaw to rebuild the south aisle at the same time. It was only 7 feet 6 inches wide and it was decided to widen it by pulling down the long south wall and rebuilding it 3 feet 6 inches further out, with new and bigger windows to match those of the north aisle. The total cost of this work, together with the rebuilding of the tower, was estimated at £2,427. Worthenbury's bill for building an entire church was only £1,364 four years later.

This large bill may have been the result of taking the opportunity to rectify much of the damage done to the church during the Civil War and Commonwealth period (1642–60) when churches had to obey an edict sent by Cromwell's Parliament to every parish forcing them to conform to Puritan beliefs and remove 'all monuments of idolatry' such as statues, ornaments, stained-glass windows and ostentatious furnishings from the church. One of the directives was that chancel screens were to be removed and the floor was to be made the same level as the nave and the various stalls in it removed. In fact the minister during the interregnum, Robert Fogg, made the following note in the one of the registers:

1660. The Chancel hath been formerly levelled, according to the ordinance of Parliament of 1643, the stalls removed, and that it had been made even with the body of the church and seats assigned to it.

Drawing of the church by Moses Griffiths in 1782 showing the north aisle with its Georgian-style windows and gabled roof. Note the brick porch so loathed by Simon Yorke. [National Library of Wales]

Many churches had had their stained-glass windows smashed and a great deal of other damage was done in places by soldiers that were billeted, with their horses, in churches. Some of this damage must have occurred in Bangor and may have resulted in the large repair bill. £2,427 was a huge sum for a small rural parish to spend on renovating the church. How this money was raised was recorded in the parish register of Clocaenog church under the entry for 30 June 1723 when they had received a 'brief' or begging letter asking for contributions towards the £2,427 'and upwards' required for the building of Bangor church. The Clocaenog congregation collected 2s 5½d in response but the entry gave no further explanation as to why Bangor needed the money and the very next entry denotes a brief received from Holt Church, that raised the sum of 2s 3d towards their expenses of £1,939. In 1730, Worthenbury church sent a brief to raise the £1,364 to rebuild their church but only received 5d! Bangor did very well in comparison! Not that it was all profit; they had to pay the printing costs – Montford church in Shropshire is recorded as having sent out 9,804 briefs for the rebuilding of its church in 1738 and they had to pay the costs of the men who undertook to go from parish to parish to collect the money. It has been estimated that if only half the sum raised by a brief was profit, it was a good result.

Not surprisingly, the brief did not bring in as much money as had been hoped and, with the money raised and donations from local benefactors, there was still a shortfall of £260 of which £110 was owed to the workmen. The £110 was covered by the then churchwardens, Richard Jones of Pickhill, Edward Tunnah of Cloy and Edward Wynn of Royton, taking out a bond and making a lay, or tithe, assessment on the parish of £50 for the next three years which was over four times more than the usual annual tithe of £12.

Second gallery
So successful had been the first gallery in the west end of the nave that Thomas Lloyd the Younger of Halghton pressed for another gallery to be erected over the newly-widened south aisle and in

South side of church showing the Georgian windows in the enlarged south aisle matching those of the tower. Drawing by John George Wood, FSA, from The Principal Rivers of Wales *1813.*

1727 he applied for a faculty saying that he would bear a reasonable proportion of the cost. His father had had the idea of a gallery in mind when the aisle was widened some three years before and had asked Richard Trubshaw to make provision for a door in the east end of the aisle to enable access to be gained from outside. This he duly did, but just incorporated the doorframe and 'hooks' or hinges on which a subsequent door could be hung. The gallery which Trubshaw designed, was to be twelve yards long and extend to the middle of the pillars and sloped up from front to back. It was estimated to be about seven and a half feet above the floor of the nave. Fortunately, the diocesan court has preserved a copy of Trubshaw's plan so that we know how it would have looked.

It is known from his answers to questions put to him at the visitation that he had not been responsible for the design or for the build of the west-end gallery but it would be sensible to assume that he planned the second one to match, or at least to be in keeping with, the design of the first. The plan also shows the appearance of the Georgian style windows of Trubshaw's newly-built south wall of the aisle that matched those in the tower. These can clearly be seen in the drawing of the church and bridge, published in 1813 in a book *The Principal Rivers of Wales* by John George Wood, FSA, which shows the south view of the church with its uniform appearance.

There was considerable opposition to another gallery and the Revd Rice Jones, was asked to read out a notice from the bishop after divine service on 23 July 1727 informing the congregation that an inquiry was to take place at the diocesan court to consider the arguments from both sides. Those people who sat on the south side of the church and had, for over two-and-a-half years, enjoyed and appreciated the extra light coming from the enlarged windows in the newly-extended south aisle were not unnaturally opposed to the idea. The churchwardens, Edward Tunnah of Cloy, Edward Wynn of Royton and Richard Jones of Pickhill, led the opposition, supported by

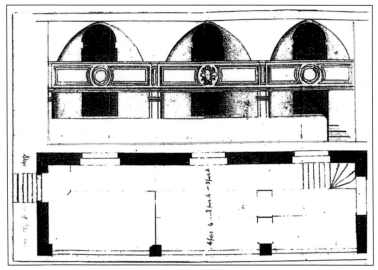

Trubshaw's plan of proposed second gallery.
[CRO EDC5/1728/2]

such people as Roger Davies of Dongrey; Thomas Evison; James Taylor; Kendrick Eyton; John Puleston and Booth Basnett. Evidence was also given by Trevor Davies, a barber of Bangor; Thomas Cope, schoolmaster and vestry clerk; and Robert Puleston of Sesswick, tailor, who all opposed the plan, arguing that:

• the building of a gallery over the south aisle would be oppressive and would have the effect of making the church dark once again as the gallery would bisect the new windows leaving two thirds of the window below the gallery and one third above.

• it would interfere with the sound and the occupants of the furthest seats would not be able to hear the minister even though the pulpit was, in those days, on the south side of the nave, opposite its present position.

• the gallery would be on a slope, the front of which was said to come down to within 5 feet 11 inches of the heads of the occupants of certain seats when standing below, in particular those of Roger Davies of Dongrey (a tall man) and Lord Plymouth, as their seats were raised above the others and required steps to enter.

The supporters of the scheme, such as the engineer William Roberts of Hanmer; John Jenning curate of Overton; carpenter Thomas Thomas of Gresford; and Edward Tunnah of Cloy, yeoman; servant to William Lloyd's uncle at Halghton Hall, then to his widow and after that to the promoter James Lloyd, said to the Court that in their opinion the gallery would not obstruct the light and would greatly enhance the appearance and be an ornament to the church. They gave as the most important reason in favour of the erection of a second gallery the income that would be generated from selling the extra seats so provided which would pay off the previous debt. It was however pointed out that not all the seats in the west gallery had been taken. There was room for seats or pews for another thirty people to bring in extra income, plus space in the widened south aisle for more accommodation.

One of the reasons given by Mr Lloyd for the erection of a second gallery was that he and his family had no seat of their own in the church and had to use those of other families when they attended divine service. However, those against the scheme argued that as Thomas Lloyd lived at Halghton Hall in Hanmer parish and styled himself 'of Halghton' – as opposed to his father who lived at Gwernhaylod near Overton in Bangor parish – that his parish church was that of Hanmer and therefore it did not entitle him to his own seat at Bangor and he could have bought or rented a seat in the first gallery. After various people had given their opinion to the inquiry, the bishop must have refused the application as the gallery was never built. Doubtless the parishioners breathed a sign of relief at not being saddled with more unnecessary expense and debt.

After such a spate of building and rebuilding the parishioners had a respite as the only known building work that was undertaken thereafter was the addition of a brick porch to the entrance of the church that may have taken place as early as 1770. This design so upset Philip Yorke (1743–1804) of Erddig's sense of what was aesthetically pleasing that he composed a verse pouring scorn on the design that he felt was so out of keeping with the fabric of the church.

> A New Brick Porch Having been added to the Old stone
> church at Bangor Monachorum
>
> What a barb'ous trick?
> With a red nose of brick,
> To patch the stone face,
> Of this reverend place,

Drawing of the church showing the new windows in the north aisle wth the battlemented roof installed in 1832 along with the small vestry on the east end. Note: the hated porch has been removed. [Courtesy of Lambeth Palace]

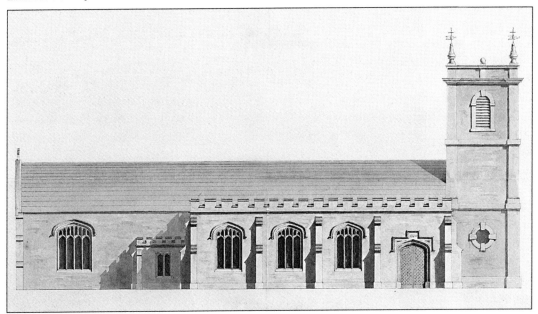

Committing of waste in the regions of taste:
Most surely the Clark,
Was much in the dark,
That he did not prevent
Such an evil intent,
And to avoid the disgrace
That attended the case,
Some Bricklay'r was Warden,
(A choice flow'r in that garden,)
Had he been but a Mason,
'Twould have had a stone case on.

O ye men, of renown,
Who inhabit this town,
Where, where, were you dosing,
When the porch was composing?
For neither were ye, slumb'ring seen
Gently snoring on the Green;
Nor on Gwernhayled's favor'd top,
Nor upon the neighb'ring cop,
When this excrescence, filthy, vile
Was stuck upon your ancient pile;
This barbarous compound of mortar, and brick;
Oh! rise River Dee then, and wash it off quick.

The next phase of alterations took place in 1832 when the north aisle was extended westward to provide seating for the poor. At the same time, the dormer gables in the roof of the north aisle, depicted in Moses Griffiths' sketch of 1782, were replaced with a battlemented roof and the new windows installed in 1723 were replaced with the present much wider ones. A small vestry was added to the east end of the same aisle with access to the chancel by a door inserted in place of an ogee window. The architect was Thomas Jones of Chester and his plans show another door leading to the vestry from the aisle but this was never implemented. At the same as the aisle was widened and extended, plans were drawn up for the gallery to be continued northwards over the church entrance and the west end of the extended aisle. It is not known whether this scheme was ever carried out. Towards this work the Church Building Society gave £160, the Marquis of Westminster, Sir Foster Cunliffe and Mr F.R. Price each gave £50, and the Earl of Plymouth £25. The donations are recorded on a board at the rear of the north aisle although this is now fading rapidly.

Victorian renovation

In earlier times, the interior walls of the chancel and nave would have been plastered and painted and often decorated with paintings depicting scenes from the scriptures. These walls were painted over at the Reformation and again in the Commonwealth period. In the parish accounts, mention is made of payment for colouring and whitewashing the interior of the church, the last time in 1866 when Mr Evans was paid £10 14s 1½d for 'colouring the church'. In the Victorian era the High

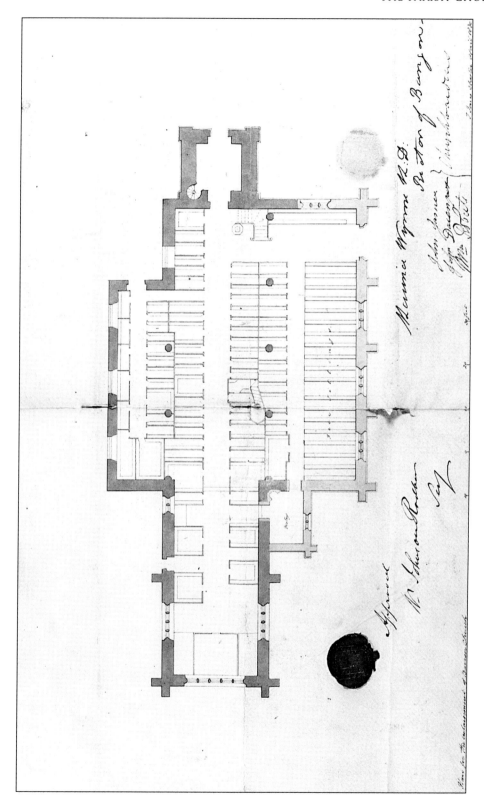

1830 plan of the interior of the church. Note the stairs to the gallery to the right of the tower doorway; the font under the gallery; the pulpit with stairway in the middle of the north side of the nave; the nave and chancel 'cut up like a modern cattle market into closed pens or pews'; Trubshaw's windows in the south aisle – now at odds with the new windows in the north aisle – and no porch. [By permission of Lambeth Palace Library]

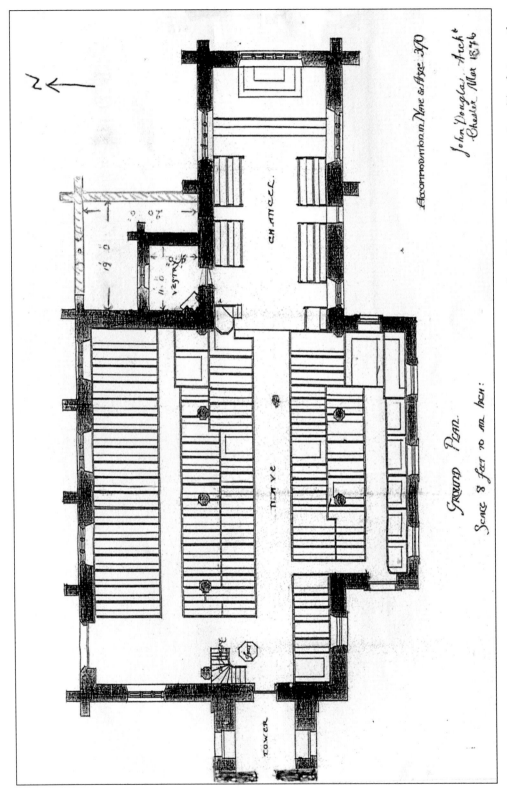

John Douglas's plan, dated March 1876, showing the suggested enlargement of the vestry. Note the pulpit moved to its present position between the chancel and the nave, box pews replaced in the chancel and still no porch.

Church movement held sway and dictated how the interior of churches should be arranged, advocating stripping off all the plaster to reveal bare stone walls and roofs, galleries demolished and less ornate pulpits installed as well as the removal of box pews. Bangor was no exception to this trend.

The architect John Douglas (1830–1911) was responsible for the next major phase of the building work. Born in Sandiway, Cheshire, in 1830, the son of John Douglas of Northampton and Mary Swindley (the daughter of the blacksmith of Aldford), he was articled to the Lancaster architect E.G. Paley in the late 1840s, remaining with him as his chief assistant. He had established his own office in Abbey Square, Chester by the time he married a local girl, Elizabeth Edmunds of Poplar Cottage, Bangor Isycoed, in 1860. They had their first two children christened at Bangor, John in 1862 (when their address was Turn o'Dee) and Colin Edmunds two years later when their address was given as being 'of Chester'.

Douglas's first major commission had been the rebuilding of the entire south side of Lord Delamere's seat of Vale Royal and the building of the first church of St John the Evangelist at Over in 1860. This early patronage established his reputation and he never looked back. His clients included the Duke of Westminster, Lord Leverhulme and the Gladstone family. In 1899, he designed the St Deiniol's Library in Hawarden as part of the National Memorial to W.E. Gladstone. In 1874/5, he designed the entrance lodge, gates and railings at Bryn-y-Pys for Sir Edmund Peel; Llanerch Panna, Penley for the Hon. George T. Kenyon and the Gelli, Tallarn Green for the Hon. Georgina and Henrietta Kenyon.

In 1868, Douglas under took major restorative work to the chancel. The plaster ceiling was removed to reveal the timber roof richly banded with early tracery. Early pulpits were usually sited at the junction of the nave and the chancel but in the eighteenth century the fashion was for them to be moved to the middle of the north side of the nave. Bangor followed this trend as is shown in the drawing made in 1830. The pulpit would appear to be one of the 'three-decker' type, with seven or eight steps leading to the upper storey. The parish clerk sat in the lowest tier, leading the congregation in responses to the prayers read by the rector who was seated in the second pulpit above him. The rector would then ascend to the 'top deck' to deliver his sermon. Douglas now moved the pulpit back to its original position at the west end of the chancel and it was replaced with a much simpler one in oak on a stone base. This was installed and dedicated by Mrs E.M.M. Parry Jones in loving memory of her husband Richard Parry Jones. A public subscription was started to defray the cost of all the building work which amounted to £400.

In 1877, Douglas was asked to make alterations to the south aisle. He removed Trubshaw's windows and replaced them with windows that were similar to those in the north aisle and

The new pulpit installed in 1868.

South side of church showing Douglas's new windows of 1868 which replaced those installed by Trubshaw.

extended the aisle to form the baptistry. The gallery at the west end was taken down and the entire roof of the nave and south aisle stripped of its plaster to reveal the old timbers so as to match that of the chancel. It was at this time that the old box pews were also removed from the nave and aisles and replaced with oak bench pews. With all the alterations and rebuilding going on the rector, the Revd George H. McGill, took the opportunity to have a stone porch built at his own expense, with a half-timbered gable in memory of his wife. All this work was recorded on a brass plaque on the west wall:

The Parish of Bangor Monachorum dedicated to St Dinooth was restored A.D. 1877.

The Duke of Westminster, K.G., Patron.

George H. McGill, M.A., rector.

Harold Lees (Pickhill Hall), Churchwardens

Thomas Brassey (Althrey Hall)

Francis Lloyd (Plassey).

To pay for this work another public subscription was started to which the Duke of Westminster gave a large donation. The present gates were put on the porch in 1996 after a spate of vandalism and misuse.

In 1909, the *Wrexham Advertiser* reported that a relic of the old Bangor parish church gallery had been unearthed.

The church underwent a process of restoration some 32 years ago and the old minstrel gallery was then removed. A portion of the timber in the form of two carved oak beams, found their way to Chester. A short time ago a gentleman wrote to the rector of Bangor informing him of the beams and the rector (the Rev. Elrington Bissett) lost no time in acquiring the relics and they are now placed near the door of the ancient edifice from whence they were removed.

The beams were part of the original chancel screen that was pulled down in accordance with the direction of Parliament in 1643 and had then been reused in the building of the gallery in 1723. The larger of the two is moulded with carving on one side and the other has indented ornamentation and they date from around 1300.

Twentieth-century restoration
In 1913, more major work was envisaged and a special meeting was held to agree to petition the chancellor of the diocese for a faculty for the following:

1. To take down the existing vestry and build a new vestry and organ chamber, at the same time to take down the organ, clean and re-erect it. To move the organ screen and place it round the organ in its new position. All the said alterations to be carried out according to the plans of Messrs Douglas, Minshull & Minshull of Chester.
2. To remove the wooden ceiling over the North Aisle and expose the timber roof so as to correspond with the remainder of the church.
3. To strip the plaster off the walls of the Chancel and North Aisle and expose the red sandstone walls.
4. To place a new floor in the Belfry for the Ringers and repair doors and windows, and provide a case for the clock weights.
5. To place additional oak work behind the choir stalls and Reading Desk.
6. To erect a Chancel Screen in memory of the late rector the Rev. George H. McGill, the cost of £100 to be born by his daughters, Miss McGill and Mrs Thorpe.
7. To place in church a font cover carved by Miss Wyberg, the cost to be borne by herself and her sister, Mrs Dronsfield.
8. To erect a new altar rail, the expense to be borne by Col Dunn of Althrey.

A brass recording this work was set into the west wall of the church:

> The Parish Church of Bangor Monachorum was
> restored by public subscription 1913 AD.
> The Duke of Westminster, K.C.V.O., Patron.
> R.J.B. Patterson Morgan, M.A.
> W.J. Mackenzie, Secretary, rector.
> Oliver Ormrod, Chairman of Committee.
> Francis Lloyd, Treasurer.

The oak litany table is decorated with a carved angel facing eastwards on either side. It was given by Samuel Leonard Hamley in memory of his wife, Elizabeth Dorothy Hamley and is undated.

At the rear of the nave are the benefaction boards or memorials of charity which list the names of people who had bequeathed money or property/land to the church for the benefit of the poor

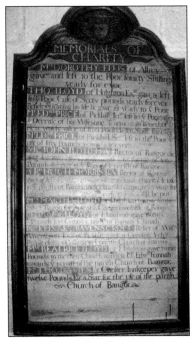

One of the two Benefaction Boards at the rear of the nave.

of the parish. One board is headed by Mrs Dorothy Ellis of Althrey who 'gave and left to the Poor fourty Shillings yearly for ever' and the other commemorates the gift of £500 by Dame Dorothy Jeffreys to found a charity school in Bangor.

The Vestry

It is not known whether the original thirteenth-century church had a vestry or where its position would have been, as no records exist but it is possible that the little door in the south side of the chancel originally led into a vestry. The first-known position of the vestry was on the north side of the chancel, accessed by a small door, and measured 11 feet by 9 feet. It was built in 1832 at the same time as the north aisle was widened and extended. By 1876, the idea of enlarging the vestry had been discussed as Douglas had drawn a provisional extension for a vestry (measuring nineteen feet by twenty feet) on the plan in pencil, but it was not until 1913 that the decision was made to act on this idea. The north aisle was extended alongside the chancel to house the vestry, together with the organ chamber from the south aisle. An arch was inserted in the north wall of the chancel for ease of access by the clergy and to accommodate the organ.

In the early twenty-first century to bring the church facilities up to date, a grant was obtained for the installation of a toilet that could be used by handicapped people and, at the same time, to construct a room with a sink and cupboards for use as a kitchen for the making of refreshments, and also for the use of the flower arrangers. Two plans were put forward for the site; the first one

using the base of the tower for the kitchen with the toilet at the west end of the south aisle, the other plan entailed the conversion of part of the existing vestry into two rooms, one for the kitchen and the other for the toilet and cupboards. After much discussion, the latter scheme was chosen and a grant was obtained for this work. This meant the construction of yet another new vestry, this time at the east end of the north aisle. At the same time, the first two or three rows of pews were removed from the front of the nave to allow performances by visiting choirs, etc. The walls of the new vestry were lined with the carved wood from the rows of pews removed.

The new vestry with the walls made from the pews removed from the north aisle.

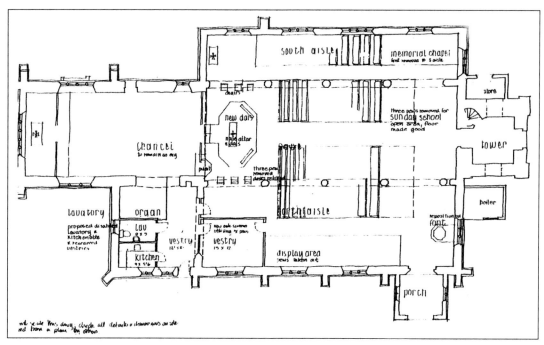

Provisional drawing of the church for the fitting of a disabled toilet and kitchenette necessitating the construction of a new vestry. Note the font was not moved from its position in the south aisle.
[Courtesy of Graham Holland Associates]

There is a note in the Revd McGill's handwriting 'Drawing of Head over door to Belfry Ward of Bangor Church' but the drawing itself has been lost. It is thought that this refers to the corbel of a human face that is now fixed to the back of the chancel wall in what is now a cupboard off the toilet. When the wooden reredos behind the altar was removed in 1913 and placed over the door to the tower, the projecting corbel that was in the way was removed and placed in its present position when the vestry was moved from the south aisle.

The Lady Chapel

In 1933, the rector, the Revd F.R. Baldock, proposed a scheme for a side chapel at the east end of the south aisle from where the old vestry and the organ had been removed. He and his wife wished to erect it in memory of his father-in-law, Frederick William Woodhouse, and his own parents, Alfred and Rebekah Ross Baldock. He submitted a design for a side altar with its appointments in the south aisle that received the approval of the church council. When the daughter chapel at Cross Lanes

Corbel of a head removed from the rear of the nave.
[David Walker]

The Lady Chapel.

was closed in 1987, the furnishings (such as the reredos and altar table) were brought to Bangor and used in the Lady Chapel which some people now refer to as the Cross Lanes Chapel.

When the chancel was restored in 1868, a wall painting was discovered which is thought to date from the seventeenth century. It was thought to represent St Dunawd, the patron saint of the church, in cope and mitre with a crosier, turned inwards, in his left hand and a book in his right hand. This was removed and transferred to the wall of the south aisle but, by 1908, had disappeared. A copy had been made however and this, restored and framed, was presented to the church in 1908 by the Revd Elrington Bisset and hung above the altar in the Lady Chapel. This has also disappeared and a hanging from the Cross Lanes Chapel is positioned above the altar.

On the south wall in the Lady Chapel in a glass case is the parish banner that used to be paraded around the village on St Dunawd's day (22 September) and on other special occasions. On the banner, the saint is depicted carrying his crosier in his right hand and a model of a church in his left hand. In the background behind the figure is a church building of similar design to the model carried by the saint. Above the saint are the words 'St Dinooth Bangor Isycoed' and at the bottom of the banner is a Latin quotation *Certa bonum aeternam certamen vitam fidei*

The Parish banner.

apprehende which translates as: 'Fight the good fight of faith, lay hold on eternal life'.

The Baptistry

At the west end of the south aisle is the baptistery that was created by extending the aisle in 1877. The floor of the baptistery was laid with black and white tiles, symbolising sin and purity. The font is of octagonal design and dates from the Tudor period. It had at some time been whitewashed and coloured and when the church was restored the paint was removed and it was set up in the new baptistery. The eight panels depict alternate instruments of the passion – hammer, nails, etc – with evangelistic emblems, with one shield of *fleur de lys*, which, with the rose, assign it to the middle of the fifteenth century. At the rear of the church is an older, eleventh-century octagonal font and a stone basin. According to a report in a Wrexham newspaper, the latter was said to have been used during the Commonwealth period, and was restored to the church by Mr John Davies, retired schoolmaster of Tŷ Graig.

In 1916, Mrs Dronsfield of Sandiway Lodge presented the church with a font cover personally carved by her sister, Miss Evelyn Wyberg of Overton Old Hall who had carved the pew ends in Overton Church. It is of intricately carved English oak and was designed by O.I. Allen of the Liverpool School of Art. The cover rises from an octagonal base to a spire in the gothic style, 2.7 metres (9 feet) high. In the niches above the font base are figures of our Lord as the Good Shepherd, of St Dunawd (being a reproduction of the mural painting discovered in 1868), St Deiniol and St George and the dragon. The new baptistery was dedicated in 1916 by canon Binney of Chester at a service taken by the Revd Paterson Morgan.

Hanging in the baptistery are three British Legion banners, two of which were dedicated in 1988 in memory of Eddie Robinson who was the standard bearer for Bangor for many years and for Wales for five years. In 1971, he was the first National Standard Bearer to come from Wales. His sister, Hazel Robinson, assumed the same position for the women's section. The standards are those of the old east Denbighshire area and the Bangor Isycoed branch that sadly folded in 2009 after the death, firstly of Harry Clegg and then of Ron Evanson.

The early Tudor font.

The Chancel

The chancel is the oldest part of the church being of sandstone and dates from *c*.1300. The large much restored east window is

The eleventh-century octagonal font.

The ogee window.

contemporary with the building of the church as is the small square-headed two-light ogee window in the south wall of the chancel. This matched a similar small window on the north side that was lost when the arch for the new vestry and organ chamber was built in 1913. Although this small window is an original feature of the church, the stained glass, depicting life and death, is modern and was given in memory of Emily, wife of Oliver Ormrod of Pickhill Hall, who died on 26 April 1903.

When the church was undergoing restoration in 1868, the east window was filled with new stained glass by public subscription in memory of the Revd G.A.E. Marsh, M.A., who was rector for thirty-two years. The glass is by Gibbs, and the subjects of the five lights comprise the Crucifixion in the centre, with scenes on either side from the Good Samaritan and from the story of the British bishops and St Augustine. The Good Samaritan is said to be a portrait of Revd Marsh. In the tracery above are works of mercy, the Adoration of the Shepherds and the Magi, surrounded by the Virgin and Child, and at the head of all the Good Shepherd in glory. A dedication reads: 'To the glory of God and in memory of the Revd G.A.E. Marsh for XXXII years rector of Bangor. Erected by public subscription 1868.'

As already mentioned, during the Commonwealth period every parish church had to conform to puritan beliefs and the floor of the chancel was lowered to that of the nave. The chancel was raised back above the nave, probably during the renovations of 1726/7. The original chancel screen that separated the nave from the chancel had also been removed and it was not until 1915 that a new, much simpler one in oak, surmounted by a cross, was erected by their children in memory of the Revd George Henry McGill (rector 1867–96) and his wife, Frances.

In 1603, every church received a directive 'that the Ten Commandments be set up on the east end of every Church and Chapel, where the people may best see and read the same'. This was painted on either side of the east window, the remains of which were revealed when renovations took place either in 1868 or

Restoring the east window of the chancel in 2013.

in 1913 and some fragments of lettering are still visible. This had been white-washed over at some stage – probably during the Commonwealth – as in 1725 the church-wardens reported to the bishop's visitation that 'the Ten Commandments are not anywhere written either in church or chancel'. In 1775, Peter Lloyd donated a reredos of mahogany panelling with gilt mouldings, depicting the

Remains of the lettering behind the altar.

Ten Commandments, the Lord's Prayer and the Creed that was hung behind the altar. This reredos, which obscured the lower part of the east window was removed in a later restoration and is now to be found at the rear of the nave, over the door to the tower. These boards badly need restoring, as it is almost impossible to read the words.

While the restoration was taking place, the opportunity was taken to remove the plaster from the ceiling in the sanctuary revealing the beautiful panelled roof, richly banded with early tracery. The restoration is recorded in a brass tablet on the sill of the east window on the north side which reads: '*Hoc sacrarium restoratum est. rectore G.H. McGill. A.D. 1868.*'

The sanctuary was again restored in 1911 and, along with an altar, re-table and credence table and two chairs, formed a memorial and is recorded on an oak panel:

> To the glory of God and in loving memory of George Capel Ralph Curzon Fenwick of
> Plâs Fron, late Captain Royal Welch Fusiliers, for nine years rector's Warden of Bangor.
> This sacrarium was restored by his widow, Mary Adela Fenwick, A.D. 1911.

The rector's stall, with its carved oak canopy, was presented in 1913 in memory of John Ellis of Althrey Cottage and Frances, his wife. In 1914, W.J. Mckenzie, rector's warden, gave a reading desk in memory of Robert and Sarah Parker of the Parkey, Cross Lanes. The panelling above the seats on the north and south sides is a memorial to Fanny Lloyd, wife of Francis Lloyd of Eyton House, erected by her husband and children in 1913. The door in the panelling on the south side was installed in memory of the rector, the Revd Leslie Daniel (1954–84) and covers an outside door that leads through an old archway to the churchyard. Mrs Oliver Ormrod presented the altar cross in 1901 in gratitude for the restoration to health of her son.

Oliver and Emily Ormrod gave the brass eagle lectern in memory of their three sons, Lionel James, 2nd Lieutenant, 12th Royal Lancers, who suffered sunstroke in India in 1913 and died from its effects on 3 May 1915, aged 32 years; Oliver Hugh Ormrod and Lawrence Moreland Ormrod who died in the service of their country during the Great War.

Church vault

In earlier times, burial within the church was quite common, at least for the members of prominent families and occasionally for incumbents, with stone slabs with the names of those buried inserted

The door in the panelling in the chancel.

The brass eagle lectern.

into the floor. A few were buried under the chancel and the person's name would be recorded on a brass or stone tablet above or nearby. As was the case of Thomas Puleston of Pickhill who, in his will of March 1668 stipulated that ' I give my body to be interred in my burying place within the Chancel of the Parish Church of Bangor.'

Some doubt has been cast as to the existence of a vault under the chancel of Bangor church. In about 2004, the author spoke to Mrs Vera (Sue) Roberts (née Spoor) who was widely regarded as possessing a marvellous memory and who was deemed to be the fount of all knowledge for all things relating to Bangor. She said that her brother, carpenter Johnny Spoor, who died in 1985, had gone into the vault from an entrance under the east window some years previously to do some work and reported seeing several lead-covered coffins that were the fashion in the Jacobean period. He also reported that there was not much headroom and he could not stand upright. The entrance was subsequently sealed.

The following is by courtesy of canon David Thomas's publication *Bangor Monachorum* that appears to be notes for counsel regarding a dispute that arose respecting a grave-space in the chancel reserved for the coffin of the Revd John Lloyd in August 1687:

Owen Barton, Esq., John Barton, Gent. and John Roberts alias Edwards are indicted that they the 23rd day of August Ano. 3 Jacobi [1687] at Bangor in the County of Flint, in the Chancell of the Parish Church of Bangor with force and riotously did meet and at a certain burying place or grave for the buryall of John Lloyd late Rector of the said Parish Church there made did throw in or fill up ag[ains]t the peace.
Thomas Lloyd
Test[emony].
Edward Mostyn.
As to the title in case Capt. Barton sh[oul]d insist any thing thereon or pretend to it –
To prove yt[that] the place was the Rector's and that he always was at the charge of the repair thereof.
Hugh Lewis, the Def[enden]t's Witness
Roger Edwards

To aske Hugh Lewis, Capt. Barton's Witness, if his Mother did not paye 10s to the Rector of Bangor for Licence to bury in the Chancell.
Ask all the Capt.'s Witnesses whether they knew or heard of any moneys paid for Licence to bury in the Chancell or leave asked to the Rector or did they ever know of any person buried

under the Communion Table yt[that] was a parishioner without leave unlesse the Rector or Rector's Wife.

Another Indictment ag[ains]t the same parties for riot and assaulting of Roger Edwards in the same place as above said the day and year above specified.

Test[imony]. Roger Edwards

As to Roger Edwards being assaulted.

Mr Thomas Lloyd

Mr Thomas Barnes

To prove the manner of the riot yt[that] the parties indicted and have forced open the church door with Clubbs and got into the grave and assaulted Roger Edwards who was working there and hindered him to work and cast up the earth.

Mr Thos. Lloyd

Mr Mostyn

Roger Edwards

That Mr Davies in whose right the Def[enden]ts made the disturbance did not offer to make any disturbance though he was present in Church when the Riot was committed.

The same Witnesses.

At the Great Sessions for Flintshire, held in Mold on 9 April 1688, William Lloyd of Halghton, the patron of the church, and Captain Barton of Knolton Hall, were concerned in a trial, 'the one for ryot, and the other for assault in Bangor Church, and found guilty of both'.

Parishioner George Humphries said there is supposed to be a passage going under the river from the vault and that there is a sandstone wall opposite the tower on the other side of the river that he thinks may be part of that passage. Any passage would have to go a long way down to get under the river and there would be a very real danger of flooding, especially when the river was in spate. The lack of headroom under the chancel also rules out a passage. The stories of tunnels or passages that are said to exist; one from the church to Althrey Hall, and one from the church to Porthwgan are just that – stories.

Church seating

In the early churches it was not the custom to provide seats for the congregation, everybody stood, perhaps to ensure that no one fell asleep during the service. The only exception would be a few, originally stone, benches for the elderly or infirm that would have been placed against the walls – this led to the expression 'the weakest go to the wall'. Gradually, from the fourteenth century onwards more and more people provided themselves with, firstly, wooden forms or benches and then with more and more elaborate seats, culminating in the box pews of the seventeenth century.

We do not know when pews were first fitted in Bangor church but we do know that seats had been allocated to various families as early as 1631 when William Furnival, a schoolmaster, summoned William Sharott to attend the church court for taking his title to a pew in Bangor church as the result of alterations to the seats. The item included references to the ownership and to the existence of forms. It was possibly after this altercation that, in 1635, a floor plan of the nave was drawn up entitled 'The Church of Bangor Uniformed and seats settled in the year 1635. John Jeffreys, Esq., Thomas Ellis, Gent, Church Wardens.' This apparently showed the allocation of seats, or seat spaces, to the various families. Some fifty seats were marked with the names of the owners. However, no trace of this document can now be found, either in the church or in the Flintshire Record Office, which is a great shame as so few seventeenth-century seating plans have survived. Canon David Thomas of Holywell mentions this plan in his 1962 booklet.

> Ninety per cent of the floor is allocated to different families so that little room is left for the unprivileged at the west end of the nave and along the walls. Fifty seats are marked bearing the names of the holders. In this plan the pulpit is shown near the centre of the north side of the church and the rector's desk on the north side of the chancel. A door is shown at the west end on the north side where the existing door is, and a corresponding door on the south side. Along the entire length of the north and south walls of the nave benches are shown with the following note: 'A long bench the sitting places of severall persons.

According to A.N. Palmer the lost churchwarden's book contained an account of the levelling of the chancel floor on 28 August 1643, according to the order of Parliament, and there is reference 'to the seats in the chancel of Kenrick Eyton, Esq., and of Andrew Ellise Esq'. The Ellises (of Althrey) probably had a seat on the south side of the chancel and the Eytons on the north. It would also appear that the east end of one of the aisles had been screened off as a chapel, and it is this chapel, then occupied as a seat by the Ravenscrofts of Pickhill, which was sometimes referred to as 'Mr Ravenscroft's chancel.'

A person wishing to alter or erect a seat in the church was supposed to apply for a faculty. In May 1750, the churchwardens presented

> Nathaniel Morris of Eyton Gentleman, for building or raising a Seat or pew in the Middle Isle of the Church of Bangor aforesaid without any lawful authority by him for that purpose first had or obtained. The same being raised so high that several of the parishioners are thereby prevented from seeing the Minister in the reading Desk.

Morris admitted that he had raised the seat one foot higher without authority, but denied that it was raised so high as to block the view of the parishioners, but added that he had since lowered the seat back to four feet.

The majority of the pews were fitted before the Civil War when the interiors of churches became increasingly filled with seats. We do know that many of them were box pews erected by prominent local persons for the use of their own families. These seats were highly prized and jealously guarded and woe betide anyone who sat in the wrong pew. The seats were often mentioned in wills, as in that of a yeoman, William Davies of Cloy who, in 1730 bequeathed two seats on the north side of the church – 'one adjoining to Mr Roger Davies and the other adjoining to Mr Edward Wynn' – to his executors, Roger Powell and John Smith. Also, Caroline Edwards in her will which was proved in 1843, mentions 'the pew in Bangor church which has my name on it left me by my late husband' and the schoolmaster, John Jones, who left his pew in the church to his wife, Sarah, in 1847.

The arrangement of the pews gave an indication of the social standing of the family with the wealthy or important families seated at the front, the middle classes in the centre and the ordinary families at the back or in the side aisles. The poorer classes however were not without their champions in support of the right of everyone to a seat in church. One of these was Hugh Jones of Pickhill who in October 1790 wrote:

> You are desired by Mr Wynn, Mr Randles, my self, and several other Friends, to favour us with your company at Bangor tomorrow by one of the Clock, where a vestry is to be held to prevent a 2nd attempt of Mr Morris's ingrossing the south side of the church to him self, and thereby excluding near 50 families from having any sitting place in the Church amongst which 3 are tenants to your Mr viz. John Edwards, John Ellis & Richard Thomas – and the s[ai]d Mr Morris has at the highest rents his Estate in this Parish was ever sett att but 53 pounds a year and he has two good seats one of each side the middle Isle. T'is highly necessary that you should be there which I hope you will (and in time).

When the Revd Maurice Wynne became rector in 1798 he took up the baton on behalf of the poorer members of his congregation and pressed for additional seats to be put in the church. A scheme was finally undertaken in 1832 whereby the north aisle of the church was extended westward for the entire length of the nave and then fitted with seats. It occurred to the rector that some document should exist that gave a brief description of each seat, thereby guarding against any future disputes that might arise respecting any of them and he had the following note inserted at the front of the baptism register.

> It having been long a matter of regret to them who felt an interest in the spiritual welfare of the poorer classes by this the Parish of Bangor that no provision existed for their accommodation in the church, they at last resolved that application be made to the different proprietors of land within the parish for subscriptions to enable them by the enlargement of the church to remedy this deficiency. In this labour of love, the applicants were eminently successful for, in a very short period, a sufficient sum was raised to enable them to commence building. By means of this addition *two hundred free and unappropriated sittings* are provided.

He went so far as to detail who was to have each seat.

> The top seat in the new part of the church, which is raised above the others, is appropriated for the use of the *churchwardens*, their old seat by the belfry door being inconveniently situated is, in consequence, a *free* seat. The two seats next to the churchwardens are free being *intended for old people*. The third seat from the churchwarden's seat belongs to Mr Smith, of Althrey, who had it in exchange for a seat in the gallery, at the sum of £5. The next seat is free. The fifth seat from the churchwarden's belongs to Mr Edwards of the Oak, who had it (in addition to the sum of ten pounds) for two seats that did belong to him in the gallery. The next seat is free. Seat no 7 belongs to John Jones, who gave the sum of twenty pounds for it. Seat 8 is free. The next seat no 9, belongs to Sir R Puleston, Bart, who gave twenty pounds for it. The *three* next seats are free. Seat no 12 belongs to Ld Mostyn, who gave twenty pounds for it. All the remaining seats are free and all the seats in the gallery are free, except a small seat belonging to Mr Cooper, of Halghton Mill.

In 1877, when further work was carried out, all the old box pews were removed and replaced with the open pews of oak with carved ends, an innovation that did not meet with everyone's approval. No doubt the little four-year-old girl about whom the *Wrexham Advertiser*'s reporter wrote in 1904 would have welcomed the change.

> ... when taken to a local church in which the pews were very ancient, when the second lesson was in progress she became refractory, and had to be taken outside by her father. On being admonished she exclaimed 'I likes the piano' (meaning the harmonium) 'but I doesn't like sitting in a cupboard!'

This church may have been somewhere like Worthenbury which still retains its old box pews, or Marchwiel where the pews were not replaced until the 1920s.

By the end of the twentieth century, with dwindling numbers attending the services, two or three rows of pews were removed from the front of the nave and a raised semi-circular platform or dais was built level with the chancel. This enabled the church to have a dual function as a venue for concerts, art exhibitions and the like. Some pews were also removed from the rear of the nave to provide room for the Sunday school, for socialising, and for the serving of refreshments. The wood from the pews was used in the construction of the new vestry walls and this mitigated to some extent those parishioners who cried 'vandalism'. At the same time, the pews from the north aisle were taken out to form a display area for a popular exhibition of photographs, finds and text illustrating the history of Bangor. A model of a monk was introduced that at the press of a button, tells the story of Bangor in either English or Welsh. The Revd R.H. Owen's son, the Revd Russell Owen, informed the author that the monk was incorrectly attired: a celtic monk of the period would have worn a white not a brown robe and would have had his forehead shaved.

Church music

The earliest mention of a choir that has survived is in the parish accounts of 1776: 'paid Thos Edwards, the Singing Master, his salary £3 3s 0d.' In earlier times, it was the custom for the choir and congregation to be accompanied by a small orchestra of players on a clarinet, bassoon, bass viol or violin and flute. In many churches, the players were accommodated in the gallery, as in

Worthenbury church, but it is not known whether this was the case in Bangor. There are several entries in the churchwardens' accounts for repairs to the instruments and to the music. By 1814, the instruments were past repair and the churchwardens paid for new instruments to be bought. They also agreed that 'a proficient person should be found to instruct them in their use', no doubt tiring of the discordant sound emanating from the musicians! The last time an entry is made concerning the instruments is in 1836 when there is an item for 'repairing the flute 2s.'

There is no mention in the accounts of the purchase of an organ

The model of the monk.

The exhibition of Bangor's history in the north aisle.

but one must have been bought in about 1839 as the first mention of it is in 1840 for paying 'the organ grinder £3 0s 0d' for his annual salary. That organist was John Jones and he played during services for many years. The last time he is mentioned as the organist is in 1868 when he was paid £4. A boy was paid for 'blowing' the organ at 2s 6d per annum. In 1892, that boy was William Poynton who received £1. When Captain Paul Griffith Panton, R.N., J.P., of Plâs Fron died in 1872, aged seventy-eight, his family erected a screen round the organ chamber in his memory.

When the Revd McGill was inducted as rector in 1867 his eldest daughter took over as the organist and played for twenty-five years. Her younger sister, Mary, became choir mistress until 1896 when their father died and they left the district. The original site for the organ was in the east end of the south aisle. This was not the ideal location for it and organists over the years had complained that they could not control the choir from that position. When further work on the church was contemplated in 1913, the decision was taken to have an organ chamber built alongside the proposed new vestry. For some reason, although the new chamber was constructed, the organ itself was not moved. In 1919, the organist again complained that he was unsighted as the organ was too far removed from the choir. He believed that a new organ would cost £800 and the old one, repaired and enlarged, and moved to its new position would cost £500. It was agreed to find out the cost of putting the organ into a thoroughly workable condition and also to obtain an estimate for moving it to the new organ chamber. This was done and the organ was at last placed in its new home, surrounded by the screen that was removed and placed round the chamber. The organ was overhauled, repaired and cleaned in 1948 and again in 2008.

Because Bangor is a Crown parish many parishioners believed that the choir had the privilege of wearing red cassocks. In 1986, the rector, the Revd Philip Owen, wrote to the Lord

Chamberlain's office to enquire whether this colour was reserved for the College of Chaplains and others in the Ecclesiastcal Household. The reply came back that the Queen had personally decreed that no church could have that privilege, whatever their royal connections. The advice from the bishop of Bath and Wells, Clerk of the Closet, was to replace them gradually as they wore out so as not to incur any unnecessary expense and perhaps to obtain ones in a deeper shade of red, called Windsor Red. The question is now academic as the church no longer has a choir, it having ceased to function in the first decade of the twenty-first century.

Lighting

Until the nineteenth century services were held in the daytime so there was no need to light the church; the only exception being the early service on Christmas Day that was held before dawn, and called *Plygain* in Welsh, a word derived from the Latin meaning cock crowing. On this occasion, candles were used and one of the earliest entries in the now lost churchwardens' accounts was for 1689: 'John Richards, Churchwarden, Pd for Candles for the Plugen and ringing: 1s 9d.' When it became customary to say Evensong after dark, the parish clerk would light them as part of his duties.

Thomas Davies, the son of John Davies who may have been a member of the Dongrey Hall family, (who had been baptized in Bangor on 19 September 1692), served an apprenticeship as a mariner and made his home in Chester where he was made a freeman of the city on 3 November 1711. In 1727, realising that he was in declining health, he made his will and left £150 each to his children, John, Thomas and Elizabeth, and left the remainder of his estate to his wife, Margaret. In addition he left 'the sum of Twelve pounds for buying a Brass Branch (chandelier) for the use of

The Revd and Mrs Elrington Bisset and the Revd Geoffrey E. Brown, curate with the Church Choir in 1908.

the parish Church of Bangor in the County of Flint', and £5 to his niece Elizabeth Davies of Overton. He made his wife and his 'good friend' Samuel Mathews, merchant, joint executors of his will. He was only about 35 when he died but had obviously done very well to be able to leave a total of £450 to his young children. In 1863, there is an entry in the accounts: 'paid the parish clerk, Williams Thomas for cleaning the chandelier'.

There is a note concerning a hanging corona written by the Revd McGill and dated 17 April 1895.

> I hereby certify that the old corona for candles, which was removed from the parish church of Bangor at the time of its restoration in 1877, was given to Mr Douglas, the architect, in exchange for a new brass tablet giving the date etc of the alterations. This (the tablet) is now in the church.

This note was enclosed in a draft of a letter to Messrs Douglas & Forshaw dated two days later that read:

> We find there is an old Corona that has been lying in a spare room a number of years. It has the following inscription round the Centre Ball: 'The Gift of Mr Thos Davies of Chester to the Parish Church of Bangor, 1727'. We have carefully looked this over & find it is in very bad condition, in fact almost past repair, it is too thin in parts to polish properly & it would cost probably £6 or 7 to make it at all decent. We send a couple of the pieces which show the general condition of it.

There is a letter from John Douglas to the Revd Elrington Bissett, dated 13 September 1897, part of which refers to the chandelier.

> I send you also to Keep the assurance of my ownership of the Corona. Unfortunately for me after giving it to Lord Kenyon & sending for it to Singers they said it was badly worn & to pieces in part. I could not draw back & paid the £6 for its complete repair.

So Douglas must have given, or loaned, it to Hanmer church.

Twenty years later, in 1917, a Mr Williams was attending a funeral in Hanmer with Ernest Foster, the licensee of the Royal Oak, when they were surprised to see the chandelier hanging in the church and proposed that Hanmer be asked to return it. This was agreed. Nothing more is mentioned about it until 1952 when the vestry minutes state:

> The Parish of Hanmer had offered to return the Candelabra loaned to them some years ago. It bears the inscription 'Mr Thomas (Davies) of Chester, 1727, presented to Bangor Parish Church.'

John Douglas' drawing of the chandelier.

It was agreed to accept its return and to hang it in the chancel. By 1959, it had still not been returned and the rector reported that it was reputed to be worth several hundred pounds but was in need of repair. It was agreed that it should be collected from Hanmer and be repaired. There is no further reference to it in the minutes and it is likely that it was in such a bad state that it was thrown away or sold. In 2010, when the author wanted to photograph it for this book, it was nowhere to be found and no one knew anything about it. However we do know what it looked like as John Douglas in 1889 had the forethought to make a drawing of it on which is written: 'May 6 [18]95 J. Douglas paid Messrs Singers & Sons of Frome £6 for repair etc and sending it to Hanmer Ch.'

The use of candles for lighting the church ceased when paraffin lamps were installed during the nineteenth century. In 1896, it was decided to light the church using acetylene gas, which was doubtless a great improvement on the old-fashioned smelly paraffin lamps. The pipes were laid, the house for the generator built and the use of gas continued for the next fifty years. In 1948, due to the failing condition of the gas lighting system it became necessary to consider another form of lighting and it was decided to wire the church for electricity even though Manweb had said that it would be another two years before the village was connected to mains electricity. A decision was made to purchase an electric generator and build a shed for its housing. In 1949, Lt-Col Fenwick Palmer made a gift of the entire cost of the wiring for electric lighting in memory of his mother, Mrs Fenwick of Plâs Fron, and the work was completed and an oak tablet was placed on the north side of the sanctuary with the following inscription:

To the glory of God and in loving memory of Mary Adela Fenwick who died
10th December, 1941, daughter of Archibald Peel of Gerwyn Hall and widow of
Captain George Fenwick of Plâs Fron, the lighting within this church was installed
by her son, Roderick George Fenwick Palmer and stepdaughter Violet Eva Owen. A.D. 1949.

An oak cupboard to cover the switches was supplied by George Lockhart Wood of Maes-y-Nant (now the Cross Lanes Hotel). In 1952, when the village was at last supplied with mains electricity, the generator was sold. The following year electric lights were installed at the lych gate and at the north-east gate.

Heating

It was probably not until the eighteenth century that any attempt was made to provide a form of heating in churches. Mention is made of the payment for coals for the stove at Bangor at the beginning of the nineteenth century. In 1835, a new (or possibly second-hand) stove was bought at a cost of £25, probably at suggestion of the new rector the Revd George Marsh for the heating of the vestry, as there is a later item for 'coals for the vestry'. Ann Powell was paid £2 17s 0d for cleaning the church and lighting the stoves for the year. In 1840, the stove was giving trouble and had to be repaired and in 1843 John Clay the blacksmith presented his bill for further repairs. In 1844, there is another repair bill from George Gittins for £5 0s 0d. Over the years, new piping for the stove occurs frequently and it would seem that the stove's performance was never entirely satisfactory.

By 1861, it was finally decided to find a way of heating the whole church and a new hot-water system was suggested. Tenders were sought and one submitted by Richard Beach & Company of

Birmingham was accepted for the sum of £97 8s 6d. Subscribers were found to partly cover the cost, with the rector starting the fundraising off with £20. Fifty-eight others contributed towards the purchase in amounts which varied from two shillings to five pounds, and the sum of £85 11s 6d was raised. The balance was paid by the rector which was in addition to his initial contribution. The system was set up and completed in January 1862. At a vestry meeting on 1 April 1864 it was resolved:

> … that in acknowledgement of the great exertion & very active services of Mr Thomas Evison, one of the churchwardens, in superintending & inspecting the setting up of the apparatus, and in collecting the subscriptions for the same, he is entitled to our warmest thanks; which we take this opportunity of tendering to him. At the same time we feel that we cannot overlook the obligations we are under to our worthy & beloved rector who has in his usual open handed & generous manner contributed so largely & handsomely towards the cost of the apparatus, & and we therefore beg of him to accept our heartfelt thanks.

This system continued in use for nearly one hundred years, albeit with a new boiler installed in about 1930. But, after many complaints that it was inadequate, it was decided to install additional electric heaters in 1958. The cost of electric heating proved too expensive however and it was decided to price oil-fired heating and, as the coke boiler was in a bad state of repair, a Mr West from the Wrexham Technical College was asked to inspect it to see if it could be converted to oil. In 1961, he reported that, as the boiler was over thirty years old, it was not suitable for conversion and, as the oil-fired apparatus was electrically operated, the boiler house was unsuitable due to potential flooding. He added that the old gas powerhouse could be used and estimated that the maximum cost of installing a new boiler, flue and storage tank would be about £700. It was agreed to ask Potterton's to send an engineer to make an inspection and give an estimate. In 1962, an estimate was received for £607 8s 6d for installing oil-fired heating and Rogers & Jackson of Wrexham was asked to undertake the work. Mains water would need to be connected to the church and an estimate for its supply was sought from the Wrexham & East Denbighshire Water Company. In the meantime, the church council expressed their grateful thanks to Tom Parry, a local builder, for his time he and his men had expended keeping the old heating system going through the very severe winter. The old radiators were repaired to stop leakages and were reused and a new boiler house was built. Mr Parry made no charge for the work, making it his gift to the church. Another new boiler was installed in 1981 with consequent improvement in the heating.

The Parish Chest

Parish chests are known to have existed in medieval times and used for the storage of written records, church plate, alms for the poor and other valuable items. During the reign of King John (1199–1216), Pope Innocent II issued an order that every church should provide 'a hollow trunk, fastened with three keys, the latter to be kept severally by the bishop, the priest, and a religious layman'. In 1538, when Thomas Cromwell ordered that every parson or vicar should keep registers for recording christenings, marriages and burials in his parish, he stipulated that they should provide a 'sure coffer' with two locks for the safekeeping of all. Again in 1552, the poor law directed that every parish should provide a strong chest having three keys for holding the alms of the poor.

The second page of the list of subscribers to the purchase of the hot-water system.

There is no doubt that most parish churches used one chest for all purposes.

The earliest known chests were of the 'dug out' type, constructed out of a single, substantial log of wood, having its inside hollowed out and its sides roughly squared with an axe. Bangor has one such chest at the rear of the nave that is carved out of a single log of wood, measuring 3 feet 8 inches by 1 foot 8 inches (110 x 50 centimetres), with iron bands and with one end narrowing slightly to a point. The inside dimensions measure 2 feet 8 inches by 1 foot 4 inches (80 x 40 centimetres). There are three locks, one for the rector and one each for two of the churchwardens. As chests go this is a small one – the one in Overton church which is of similar construction and age is seven feet long and would require three people to lift up the lid. But even this one pales into insignificance when compared to some of the chests in other churches. It would be lovely to think that Bangor's chest dates from the time of the building of the present church c.1300. However, there are examples of this type of chest being made later, so it is probably safer to describe it just as late medieval or even early Tudor.

Church plate

The church plate comprises:

A chalice with its paten bearing the inscription: 'The gift of Andrew Edwards, Citizen and Goldsmith of London, dedicated to the service of God and the Church for ever in the Parish of Bangor Monachorum. Aug. 25, 1639'. Andrew Edwards, the son of John Edwards, yeoman, of Pickhill was apprenticed in 1617 to William Leawes, cutler and goldsmith of London, for eight years. The gift of the chalice may have been made to mark the opening of his own shop in St Ann's Lane (now Gresham Street) behind Goldsmiths' Hall, London. He made his will in 1677 and left his house(s) and lands in Bedwell to his nephew, Robert Edwards who also became a goldsmith in London.

Bangor's late medieval parish chest.

Another paten, assay mark 1689.

A flagon, assay mark 1720, and inscribed 'Given by Mrs Martha Lloyd, Halghton.'

A silver wafer box.

Two silver-mounted glass cruets (containers for wine and water for the Eucharist), inscribed, 'In memory of Ernest Lewis, Manor Farm, this box and cruets were given by his wife and children, 1953'. One of these cruets came from the Cross Lanes Church when it closed.

Stained-glass windows

The east window and the little window in the south wall of the chancel have already been mentioned. There is one stained-glass window in the south aisle that was erected by Edward Randle of Bryn Avon in memory of his deceased relatives in 1877. It depicts the birth of Christ, the crucifixion, the resurrection and the ascent into heaven.

The first window in the north aisle close to the porch was erected by public subscription in 1936 in memory of a rector, the Revd Elrington Bisset (1896–1909). It depicts St Paul in the middle with St Joseph in the left-hand panel and St Lucius on the right. Incorporated into the bottom of the window is a small gothic-shaped pane of glass measuring eight inches by seven inches. It depicts a faded calvary scene with the three crosses underneath gothic arches. It is said to have come from the study window of the old rectory when it was demolished in 1868.

The second window was installed in memory of Frank Stuart Lloyd who died in the Great War in 1917, the fifth son of Frank and Fanny Lloyd of Eyton House and the Plassey. It depicts St Asaph, St Dunawd and St Deiniol.

The third window, now partly obscured by the new vestry, is dedicated to the memory of Brigadier-General Robert Henry William Dunn, R.W.F., of Althrey, who died in 1917 and his wife, Catherine Constance Selina Dunn, who died in 1935.

Parish registers

Many records of christenings, marriages and, to a limited extent, burials were kept by the monasteries prior to their dissolution, and in a haphazard way by the churches until Henry VIII directed in 1538 that 'every clergyman shall, for every church, keep a book wherein he shall register weekly every marriage, christening, and death' and that they were to provide a 'sure coffer' for their safekeeping. The entries were to be made every Sunday in the presence of one of the churchwardens. The parish of Gwaenysgor, near Prestatyn, is the only parish in the diocese that possesses a register dating from the year of institution. Most others did not keep a register until their attention was drawn to the necessity by further orders issued during Queen Elizabeth I's reign. Prior to this, most churches (and we have to assume this included Bangor) wrote up the events on loose sheets of paper that were lost. Although the bishop's transcripts (BTs) – contemporary copies of the register entries made by the rector or curate and sent to the bishop each year – begin in 1614, for whatever reason Bangor's registers do not begin until 1675 when the first entries were:

Baptism:
> 1675 January: William the sonne of Robert Davies, The Claye, was baptized the sixteenth day.

Marriage:
> 1675 April: Matrimony was solemnized between Ralph Edwards and Mary Drury the first day.

Burial:
> 1675 January: William Jeffreyes, servant to Judge Eaton, was buried the twentieth day.

On 9 April 1735 there is an interesting entry in the baptism register for a Karen Happuch, the daughter of Francis and Elizabeth Clark of Bangor. The name is a corruption of Kerentrappuch, one of a list of names in the Genevan (or Breeches) Bible from which readers were exhorted to choose names for their children. This Bible had a decidedly Puritan leaning and was replaced by the King James' Bible in 1611. For those who want to know what became of the child saddled with that name, I can tell you that she had an illegitimate son in 1766 and the churchwardens presented her to the church court 'for a base born son begotten by Samuel James, the son of Robert James of Bangor as appears by her confession on oath'. This child was baptized James on the 21 Sep 1766. There is an entry in the burial register for a James Clark on 3 November 1766, no age is given, but it may well have been Karen's son. In 1769, when Karen was recorded as being aged twenty 'and upwards' (she was actually thirty-four), she married David Jones, aged forty 'and upwards', a widower of Kinnerley, Salop by licence. They lived in Kinnerley and had three children, two girls and a boy. David, a labourer, was buried in October 1796 and Karen in May 1802 when she would have been aged sixty-five. Interestingly she is called Haranapach in the Kinnerley registers.

Tombstones and coffin lids
Over the centuries Bangor has been very careless with the medieval tombstones and/or coffin lids that were once in the church or have been periodically found in the churchyard. Some of these have disappeared over the last hundred years or so. Edward Lhwyd's own reference to missing stones was drawn from a document or source in the 'every-day book' of Revd Henry Rowlands, the Anglesey antiquarian and correspondent of Lhwyd's, in the possession of David Wynn of Melai, Llanfairtalhaiarn, Denbighshire. The two tombstones mentioned by Lhwyd as lying in the

chancel had vanished by 1699 and may have been destroyed before 1660. They were:

a) A stone with *HIC JACET D[AVI]D AP MADOC AP ENION* in 'old Saxon capitals'.
b) On the south side of the altar a gravestone with the inscription *HIC JACET ANGHARAD FILIA IERWERTH*. She was the wife of Madog ap Gruffyd Ddu.

The five coffin lids illustrated by Pennant in his *A Tour in Wales* (1784) are:

1. Stone with head above a shield carrying a lion rampant and in a border, in Lombardic capitals, *HIC : IACET : WILLIAM : LE FRENS* sword lying diagonally behind with pommel in the top dexter corner.

2. Stone with head and shoulders in coffin above shield carrying lion rampant and in Lombardic border, *HIC : IACET : ITHEL : KADWGON*.

3. 'An ancient cross' more correctly an expanded arm cross within a circle, with below, a griffin passant and lion passant, interpreted by Pennant as 'the early embracing of Christianity by the nations of our island'. The griffin (or griffon), half eagle, half lion, was anciently a symbol of divine power or a guardian of the divine.

4. A conventional chequered heraldic shield, sword behind set bend-wise, and remaining space filled with curving stems branching out into tri-lobed leaves.

5. The one survivor: this shield and sword lid went missing but was found in 1924 in the grounds of Maes-y-Nant (the Cross Lanes Hotel) and is now in the National Museum of Wales, Cardiff.

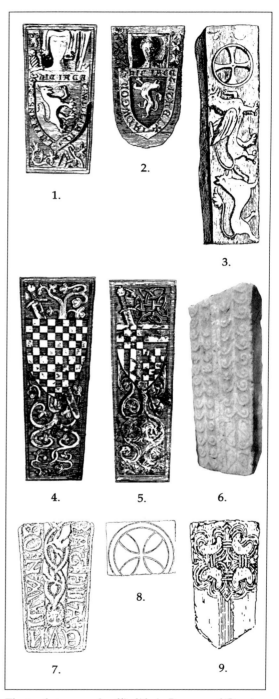

The tombstones and coffin lids in Bangor and Overton churches.

Overton Church, a former perpetual Curacy of Bangor, has been equally badly served but still to be seen in Overton are:

6. A badly mutilated fragment(s) of early 14th century four-circle ribbed cross slab.

7. The weathered lower half of a c.1300 slab to the memory of Angharad verch Einion, with a central; pattern of twisted stems and leaves emerging from lion's mouth at the bottom. A border of Lombardic capitals reads: '... RAT : FILIA : EUNIAWN : OR...'. ('Here lies Angharad daughter of Einion. Pray for her').

8. Fragment of expanded arm cross, formed in circle, inserted upside down into base of westernmost pier of south arcade.

At the present time all that survives in Bangor church is

9. The lower half of a fourteenth-century lid with a design of a simple fretted central rib with a series of curved volutes in pairs, with sufficient variation in design, style and workmanship to suggest that more than one mason worked on the stone.

Bangor Cross

The stone cross that would once have stood in or near the churchyard was removed during the Civil War or Commonwealth period on the direction of Parliament when all 'monuments of idolatry' were ordered to be destroyed. In 1849, the remains of an old cross was found by the river which the Revd Sir T.H.G. Puleston, rector of Worthenbury, described in his history of that parish.

There is at Marchwiel part of an old cross found on the farther bank of the large meadow to the north west of Bangor and about two furlongs above the church. A higher flood than usual had made a breach and exposed it. It consists of a large square pedestal with the dexter limb broken off; the shaft is about nine feet high. There were also found a quantity of black oak beams. This field is still called Maes y Groes – field of the cross. These relics were found in 1849. A section of this, the part of it where the crossbeam intersects the shaft, measuring two feet six inches by twenty inches – now rests at the foot of the lectern in Marchwiel church. Near it there is a brass plate inscribed: 'The remains of a cross found in a bulwark of the river about two furlongs from the Church of Bangor Monachorum 1849.

The place where the cross was found was called Maes-y-Groes prior to the finding of the fragment of the village cross, as local folklore says it was the field where the monks met with St Augustine. It was a pure but happy coincidence that it was found there. This fragment of the cross was returned to Bangor in 1988 and placed, with the brass plate, beneath the pulpit along with an ancient quern – the lower part of an ancient hand-mill – that was found while digging a grave in the south-east section of the graveyard.

The Churchyard

At one time, many beautiful trees surrounded the church but over the years these have succumbed to storm and tempest and now there are just four on the north side and four on the east. All the trees on the riverbank that used to frame the footpath alongside the river have gone. The last remnants had to be uprooted when the bulwark was strengthened in 2001 after the scare of the previous year when the inhabitants of the village were evacuated because the river in flood threatened their safety.

The main entrance to the churchyard is through a lych gate that was erected in 1897 which was the gift of Mrs Webster. The structure had originally been the cover over a public pump that she had sunk in memory of her husband and had the following inscription, now partially worn, carved on a stone set into the wall:

To the glory of God and in loving memory of
Robert Charles Webster, J.P., of Abbeygate, Bangor Isycoed,
who died Nov 27 1883.
Erected by his wife.

When the water in the well, and in most of those in Bangor, was condemned as unfit to drink in 1897 she had the structure removed to the entrance to the churchyard. On a beam on the side facing the road she had inscribed 'There remainith a rest to the Peace of GOD. Heb: IV: 9' and on the church side 'Let us labour therefore to enter unto that rest. Heb: IV: XI.' On one of the gates is a plaque with the simple words 'Jeanie Bruce Mackellar 1872–1947.'

By tradition, the oldest graves in a churchyard are on the south side of the church, not for any religious reason, but because it is said the north side was used for the interment of un-baptized infants, excommunicated persons and suicides. Hence it used to be regarded as the 'wrong' side. Unfortunately, the inscriptions on the ancient gravestones in Bangor have long since been worn away and the oldest one that can be identified is on the north side of the church and records a Richard Hughes who died aged twenty-nine in 1702 . There is however no corresponding entry for his burial in the parish register, nor is there a baptism record for him in 1772/3/4 so nothing more is known about him.

The churchyard was surveyed in 2005 and Dorothy Powell of Tallarn Green and David Walker of Willow Court have spent many hours transcribing the monumental inscriptions and the results have been preserved both onto a CD and in printed form. Unfortunately it has since been found that, due to a misunderstanding, a complete record of everyone buried in a grave was not made and in many cases only the first person listed on the stone was recorded. Consequently, the record should be read in conjunction with that prepared by Mrs Sunter Harrison during the 1960s which is held in the Flintshire Record Office.

It is interesting to note that when the sexton was excavating a grave in the oldest part of the graveyard in 1924 a penny dated 1707 was found in an excellent state of preservation. A piece of Roman mosaic, a *tessera*, had also been found in the churchyard some years ago which is the only evidence of Roman occupation in Bangor. An ancient quern (millstone) was unearthed when the sexton was digging a grave in 1913 which now rests inside the church beneath the pulpit.

Prior to 1864, there was a row of nine old cottages set into the east side of the churchyard on the Overton Road from Church Avenue to 'Rosecroft', forming part of the church boundary. They jutted out into the road making it difficult, if not impossible, for wagons and coaches to pass each other. The cottages were an eyesore and spoilt the view of the church and complaints were often made at vestry meetings about children playing in the churchyard. The villagers had pressed for the removal of the buildings for some time, but they were owned by various people and included two that belonged to the ratepayers which were used to house the poor of the parish. In 1863, there was a groundswell of opinion that the time had come for their removal and donations were invited to cover the cost of buying the properties and their demolition. It was quickly realised that it would take some time to raise enough money to even partially achieve the desired objective. Three people discussed the problem and the result of their deliberations was inserted in the parish accounts' book:

> In the year 1863 the Parish of Bangor received very handsome Donations which were generously presented to the parish in order to free the churchyard from a rank of Nine small cottages that formed its eastern boundary, and which had, by right of communication with the churchyard, been long pointed out as 'a grievous nuisance.'

The Marquis of Westminster purchased five of the cottages and gave them to the parish to be pulled down. Edmund Peel of Bryn-y-Pys, the owner of two of the cottages, valued at £100, also gave two of the cottages to the parish. The Revd George A.E. Marsh, the rector of the parish, purchased the two remaining buildings from the ratepayers of the township of Bangor for £53, and also gave them to the parish. The vacant site was then enclosed in the churchyard at a cost of £200. The sale of materials salvaged from the cottages raised £27 6s 6d, making the total gift worth £380 6s 6d. Thomas Bennett was paid £55 to build a new stone wall on the east side and to restore the wall on the north side of the churchyard. He was paid a further £10 12s 4d for filling up the site of the old cottages, resetting the iron railings, erecting a new wicket gate, repairing the old one, installing a new handrail and the painting of all.

At a vestry meeting on 12 April 1864, the balance sheet for the successful undertaking was read out and it was resolved,

> That the Inhabitants and Ratepayers of the Parish of Bangor take this opportunity, at the annual Easter Vestry, to acknowledge our deep obligations to the Nobleman & Gentlemen above named, for their magnificent Donations, & the liberal & generous spirit they have evinced in contributing so freely towards establishing an evident & undoubted improvement in the Churchyard of our Parish: and we beg most respectfully to tender to them our best thanks.

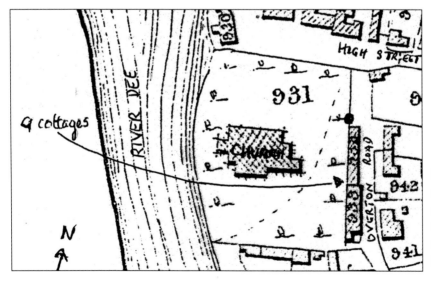

Map showing the site of the nine cottages and lock-up built into the churchyard wall and jutting out into Overton road.

The Revd Marsh and nine members present at the vestry meeting signed this tribute.

The old lock-up where drunks and ne'er-do-wells were put prior to being taken before the magistrates was another eyesore that offended the sensibilities of the villagers. This was set into the wall on the east side of the churchyard near where the demolished cottages had stood, opposite the boundary between Turnpike House in High Street and Rosecroft in Overton Road. By 1884, it was widely felt that the lock-up had served its purpose and it was finally removed. The stones and the ground were purchased from the County Council by the Revd J.H.G. Puleston, rector of Worthenbury, for £5 and presented to the rector and churchwardens of Bangor for burial purposes. Six pounds was collected in the church on 7 June 1884 towards these expenses, leaving a deficit of £1 7s 0d. On Wednesday, 6 May 1885, the land was consecrated by the bishop of St Asaph as an additional burying ground for the parishioners of Bangor and the wall made good using the stone from the lock-up, hence it being a slightly lighter colour to the rest of the wall.

The terrier and glebe land

A terrier was an inventory of the land and its boundaries belonging to the church that over the years had been donated or bequeathed for the use of the minister to either farm himself or rent out. Bangor's terrier had been lost many years ago as the churchwardens recorded at the 1725 archdeacon's visitation. The first mention of the extent of the church land is recorded by the churchwardens in a visitation of 1742

> The Terrier belonging to the Parsonage to the best of our knowledge is an House, Stable, Guarden, Orchard, Barn, Half an Acre, more or less, in a field called Stanyards bounded on the North by Mr Davies' Ground, on the south by Sarah Carter's land, on the west by the high Road (Overton Road), on the East by Mr Jones's land of the Cloy, with One quarter of an Acre, more or less, joining to the Orchard.

The field is shown on the 1840 tithe map in Overton road as N⁰· 985, being owned by Mrs Elizabeth Pooland. It is called Stanierth and is made up of several quillets, one of which belonged to the church and one to the Endowed School, and is part of the land where Abbey Gardens is now situated.

There is a mention of a tithe barn that needed restoration in 1741 as the churchwardens stated in their presentment 'the Tythe Barn promised to be repaired'. There is no further reference to it until 1846 when the Marquess of Westminster, Robert Grosvenor, had a survey made of his land in Flintshire that included 'a new croft and Tythe Barn adjoining the rectory'. The barn was located in the field between the rectory and the river marked N⁰· 913 on the tithe map, and was where the rector would have stored his tithes – one tenth of his parishioners income, whether in money, corn or hay, livestock, etc which went to the support of the rector who in return maintained the chancel of the church and saw to the provision of church worship. By the time of the first edition of the Ordnance Survey Map in 1870 the barn appears to have been pulled down. The Marquis of Westminster had bought this land in 1832 from the then rector, the Revd Maurice Wynne, who in turn had purchased it from the Earl of Plymouth in about 1815. Plymouth had inherited the land from his grandfather who had acquired it as part of a dowry on his marriage to the sister and heiress of Roger Whitley, lord of the manor of Peel in Mouldsworth near Chester, and owner of Althrey Hall. Roger Whitley's grandfather, Roger Whitley 'of London', had purchased the Peel

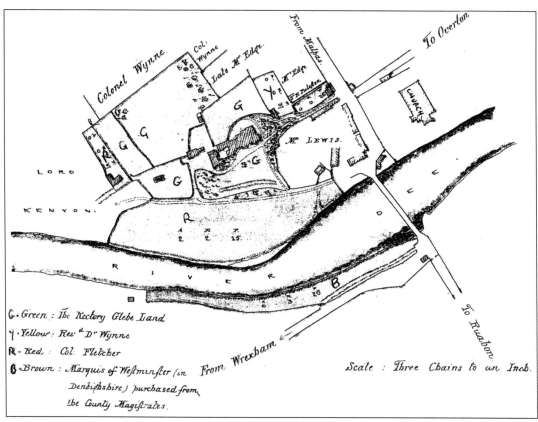

Map from a plan in an indenture dated 1832, showing the old rectory and glebe land.
[Eaton Estate Box 5 Bundle 3/5]

estate, with other lands, from Sir Richard Langley of St Martin-in-the-Fields, and his wife, Dame Cecil the only daughter and heir of Andrew and Frances Ellis of Althrey in 1677.

The Rectory

The earliest known mention of a rectory is in 1611 when the churchwardens stated at a visitation that 'the parsonage house is in decay.' Apart from that brief reference, nothing is known about its style or even its position. We automatically think that a rectory has always stood on the site behind the rectory Lodge, but we do not know for certain. That it was a large and rambling place can be inferred by the entry in the Hearth Tax Returns of 1666/7 when it was taxed for nine hearths, one of which was in a bakehouse (compared with the ten hearths that were taxed on Althrey Hall). As can be seen from old plans and maps, the old rectory was a large building, surrounded by more than three acres of glebe land. The date of construction is unknown, but it may have been built, or extended, in 1770/1 as that date appeared on a rainwater hopper on the gable end of one of the outhouses, since incorporated into the main house. If we do not know the date when the earlier rectory was built, we do at least know what it looked like as a former rector, the Revd Marsh (who died in 1867) and his wife had their photograph taken in front of the house just before it was due to be demolished.

In 1868, at the same time that the church was undergoing restoration, the decision was taken to build a new rectory. A public subscription was started and the Revd McGill, who had been inducted the previous year, mortgaged the glebe lands belonging to the church to the governors of the Queen Anne's Bounty, a fund that augmented the income of the poorer clergy. The principal was then made available for the use of churches at interest (in this case 4%) for the speedy and efficient building, rebuilding and repairing of houses for the clergy. In this way £1,000 was raised by mortgage which was to be paid off from fundraising events such as concerts, bazaars and fetes.

The new rectory, although smaller than its predecessor, was still large with a black and white gable above the front door with the Latin inscription: *Utinam Veris Hanc Amicis Impleam* (Would that I could fill this house with true friends) and it became the home of the rectors for the next 116 years. Inside there were a set of twelve heraldic crests of the rectors from the Revd John Lloyd (1662) to the Revd Paterson Morgan (1920). The last one was added in 1950 and was painted by Mrs Rome of Abbeygate. Lesley Ann Murray (née Daniel), daughter of the Revd L.M. Daniel (1954–85), although born in Bangor and resident until her marriage, does not remember any such crests being in the rectory. It is probable that the crests were removed whilst the rectory was being restored in 1964 and their whereabouts were forgotten. It is a pity that they had vanished just fourteen years after the last one was added.

In 1954, the Revd Leslie Daniel and his wife, Ann, came to Bangor from Llangollen where he had been curate for six years. On his appointment he was told by the bishop of St Asaph that the rectory was big and very damp and had been condemned, and that they should make it their first priority to find a new home. In 1962, on being given a valuation of £2,500 for the old house, the Church authorities took the decision to sell the rectory and to build a new, smaller house with the money. The parishioners however had other ideas and there was great objection to this plan and the authorities changed their minds and decided to renovate the existing rectory instead.

In 1964, after many money-raising events by the parishioners, the go-ahead was given for the renovations to begin. The alterations included the removal of the third storey at the rear of the building and the demolition of the old kitchen and back premises to make the rectory a more

The Revd and Mrs A.E. Marsh and their staff outside the old rectory prior to demolition, c.1867.

The new rectory, built in 1868.

manageable size. It was impossible for the family to live there whilst these alterations were in progress and they took up the offer by the vicar's warden, Colonel Fenwick Palmer, of a flat for the duration in Cefn Park, Wrexham. In the spring of 1965 the work was completed and the rector and his family returned to a smaller, more compact home.

The Revd Daniel's son, David, who had been born in Llangollen, entered the Church but eventually became a teacher in a private school. The rector's daughter, Lesley Ann, was born in Bangor. The Revd Daniel died in 1984 and, after Mrs Daniel eventually vacated the rectory in 1986 to live in Dudleston Heath, the building was sold and the church authorities purchased a modern house in Ludlow Road for the next incumbent, the Revd Philip Owen. The old rectory was partly modernised by the new owners, Brian and Veronica Dodd, and in 2002 it was sold to Chris and Elizabeth Jackson. Chris worked in Liverpool for the grandson of the Revd Okell, a former rector of Bangor (1920–5). They put in train a scheme of modernization and extension that has seen the old rectory turned into a comfortable family home. It has recently acquired new owners.

In the north-west corner of the rectory grounds are the remains of an old cockpit, marked by a dip in the land surrounded by banks, and there was also a cockpit at the back of the timber-framed Buck Farm in Halghton, formerly the Buck Inn. Throwing stones at cockerels was said to be a traditional sport of apprentices on Shrove Tuesday in some areas and many people were attracted by the violence and the prospect of making money by gambling on the winner. The birds were specially trained and matches were arranged between rival owners and considerable money changed hands when substantial bets were taken. Cock fighting was abolished in 1849. The last mention of cock fighting in the Bangor area was in August 1882 when Ambrose Sutton of Althrey Hall and nine others were charged with unlawfully ill-treating and abusing cocks. Sutton was also charged with keeping a place for the purpose of cock fighting. It appeared that on 28 June about forty people had gone to Althrey Hall where they were ushered through a door onto a lawn surrounded on all sides by a high wall. The door was locked and cock fighting then took place. All the defendants were found guilty and fined £2 each.

Also located in the grounds of the old rectory is a pillar sundial that used to be in the garden of the schoolmaster's house. In 1905, when the house ceased to be used by the schoolmaster and was rented out, it was removed by the rector, the Revd Elrington Bisset, to the rectory grounds for safekeeping. It is said to be an old sundial of a type that is mentioned in *The Book of Sundials* by Margaret Gatty, of which there is another example at Madeley Hall, Shropshire. That one is a cube of stone on each side of which is a hollowed-out circle, to receive the

This rather blurred photograph, taken at a church fete, shows the 'new' smaller rectory after 1964.

rays of the sun and by a gnomon, or pointer, record the hour. Around each of the circles are smaller hollows, round, triangular, and diamond-shaped, which equally serve to indicate the hour at one time of day or another. The one in the old rectory grounds has a square stone with similar hollows on each side set on a pillar base. A sundial was a common feature of churchyards before churches possessed clocks and it may be that its original site was in Bangor churchyard. There is another, more modern sundial in the churchyard, but the brass plate with the gnomon is missing from the top.

Church events

Over the years garden parties, fetes, harvest homes and other events have been held to raise money for the upkeep of the church, many of them in the rectory grounds, and opened by a local person of note, such as Mrs Ormrod of Pickhill Hall, Mrs Rosselli of Bryn-y-Pys or Philip Yorke, last squire of Erddig. The grounds were extensive and the rector would often call upon two or three parishioners to help get them in trim for the event, particularly when the rector had only recently been inducted and had not had time to do any gardening. There would be several days of scything, mowing, sawing and trimming before the big day.

The annual garden fete was the highlight of the village year. In 1942, it was held on 8 August and was organised by an enthusiastic band of helpers with the rector, the Revd R.H. Owen as chairman, H. Bellis as secretary and Pitcairn Campbell as treasurer. The event, which was opened by Mrs Gossage of Gerwyn Hall, had amongst its outdoor attractions, sports for the children, a tennis tournament, sideshows, games and competitions. A whist drive was held in the rectory with Mr F. Cheetham as master of ceremonies and there was dancing on the lawn in the evening to music provided by T. Williams and Lesley Griffiths for which Neville Cheetham acted as master of ceremonies. The stalls and stall holders were:

Produce: Mrs Cheetham, Mrs Richards;
Jumble: Mrs Barlow, Mrs Peters, Mrs Morris;
Sunday School: Mrs Westwood, Miss Berry; White Elephant, Mrs Rome, Miss Margaret Jones;
Refreshments: Mrs Owen, Mrs Norton, Mrs Higginson, Mrs Jones.

The old sundial now in the grounds of the old rectory.

Side shows:

Hoopla: Mrs Wood, Mrs Campbell, Miss Misa

Darts & Roulette: Mr Wood, Mr Sells, Major Misa

Hidden Treasure: Master John Wood, Master Geoffrey Clark

Donkeys Tail: the Misses Denton; Skittles, Mr Duggan

Weigh Machine: Mr Antley

Coin in bucket: Mr H. Bellis.

Sports: Messrs T. Jarvis and F Robinson. The winners of the tennis tournament were Mr Jack Richards and Miss Vera Keddie (evacuee).

According to Sheila McGuighan, who lived in Marchwiel as a child, the church fete was considered to be the highlight of the year and was eagerly anticipated. Even though there was little spare money for fripperies, the girls always had a new dress, either made or bought specially for the annual event and, as they began the walk to Bangor, their excitement would mount as they looked forward to the delights ahead.

The advowson of Bangor

The advowson of Bangor – the gift of the living or the right of making the appointment or of recommending a member of the clergy to a vacant benefice – goes back to very early times. Canon D.R. Thomas wrote in 1908:

> King Edward [I] had granted it to Prince Gruffydd until, through the murder of the eldest son of Madoc ap Gruffydd by John, Earl Warren, it passed by grant of Edward I to that earl. It is probable that it remained in the gift of the Warrens until the death of Earl John in 1347. Henry IV then granted the right of patronage to the Stanley family, later Earls of Derby, who held it until about 1680 when it was sold to the Lloyds of Gwernhaelod, in whom it remained until about 1830 when Philip Lloyd Fletcher sold it to the 2nd Marquess of Westminster.

BANGOR-ON-DEE PARISH CHURCH

A

VINO BEANO

AT

THE PLASSEY, EYTON

BY KIND PERMISSION OF MR & MRS. A.J. BROOKS

TUES 13 MAY, '80

8·00 PM TO 12·30 AM

LICENCED BAR APPLIED FOR - TICKET INCLUDES FREE WINE AND BUFFET UNTIL 9·00 P.M.

DANCING TO THE "M3" DISCO.

➤ TICKETS £2.50 EA.

Members of the Grosvenor family appointed the rectors until 1910 when the Duke of Westminster appointed the Revd Paterson Morgan as rector. In 1914 the Welsh Church Act was passed under which it was agreed that lay patrons would give up the right of patronage to the crown and that they were entitled to compensation for their loss. Since that time the monarch has the gift of the living and through his/her advisors appoints the rector to the church hence the term 'Crown Parish'. It has no connection whatsoever with the colour of the cassocks of the choir.

6. Vestry Meetings

When the manorial courts began to lose their authority in the sixteenth century, the church vestry meetings took over the running of secular affairs. The church in turn handed over the management of affairs to the parish councils when they were constituted in the late nineteenth century. In the early days in Bangor, before the church was heated, it was the custom to adjourn the vestry meetings to one of the local public houses. In 1811 meetings are recorded as being held in the Star Inn in 1811 (called the Lower Star in 1816), the Star and the Buck in 1814 and the Star, the Lion and the Oak in 1824. The last mention of holding vestry meetings in one of the hostelries was about the time that the new stove was purchased for the church vestry, most probably at the instigation of the new rector, the Revd Marsh.

At the Easter meeting of the vestry the parish officials: the churchwardens, the overseers of the poor, the parish constable and highways surveyor (sometimes called the 'waywarden' or 'overseer of the bye-ways') were appointed – all unpaid. The last two have been discussed in other chapters. Notice of vestry meetings were posted on the church porch such as the one called on 20 April 1856 that read:

> That there will be a Vestry meeting of Inhabitants and ratepayers of this Parish on Friday the 25th day of April at the hour of 3 o'clock in the afternoon for the purpose of granting a rate for the necessary repairing of the bye-roads and also to arrange about the making new or repairing of the pound and also to appoint places where to get the garbols [gravel] for the repairing of the bye-roads – and also to appoint an assistant overseer to serve the office for the Township of Bangor for the ensuing year ending in the 25th day of March 1857 and any other parish business.
> As witness our hand
> | | |
> |---|---|
> | James Lewis | Overseer of Bye-ways |
> | Isaac Pickering | Overseers of the poor |
> | Joseph Fowles | |
> | Chas. Griffiths | Vestry Clerk |

At this meeting it was moved by John Smith and seconded by George Cambell and carried '*nem com* (without dissent) that a rate of 2d in the pound be allowed for the repairs of the bye-ways in the township of Bangor. It was also moved by Mr Smith and seconded by Robert Bithell and carried *nem con* that James Lewis, the overseer of the highways, should apply to the magistrates to ascertain at whose expense the village pound was to be repaired and then to call a vestry meeting on the subject. Also moved by Mr Cambell and seconded by Mr Smith and carried *nem con* that the gravel for the repair of the bye-ways be obtained as normal from out of the river close to Bangor bridge.

Churchwardens

Of the four parish officials appointed annually, the post of churchwarden was the most important. The position is an ancient one, dating back to medieval times and carried some prestige and social standing in the parish. Usually two wardens were appointed, but in large parishes there could be many more. In Bangor parish, four churchwardens were appointed: two for Flintshire, representing the townships of Bangor and Worthenbury, and two for Pickhill and Sesswick and Eyton and Royton, the Denbighshire portions of the parish. After the restoration of the monarchy, Flintshire's representation was reduced to one warden when Worthenbury was made into a separate parish. The rector appointed his own choice, known as the vicar's warden, and the vestry meeting chose the two people's wardens, one to represent the townships of Pickhill & Sesswick and another for that of Eyton and Royton.

Churchwardens were responsible for the upkeep of the church, for checking for defects and dilapidations of its fabric, its furnishings and fittings as well as maintenance and repair, and also saw to the upkeep of the churchyard. They saw to the conduct of church services, kept accounts of all expenditure and were responsible for investing the money left by people in their wills towards the care and maintenance of the poor or for the upkeep of the church, such as occurred in 1443 when John de Puleston of Emral left five shillings for the repair of Bangor church.

A great deal of information regarding the running of the parish can be gleaned by perusing the accounts that they kept and a few of the more interesting items will serve as examples:

1691 A coat for Edward the idiot.		2.00
1692 Paid for stopping the Pigeons out of the Church.		1. 00
1776 By 61 doz sparrows	10.2	
10 hedgehogs	1.8	11. 10
1776 Paid for 2 padlocks and 18 Brass Hatpins (for the choir?).		3. 2
1811 John Howe for Whitewashing the Church etc.		3. 1. 6
1812 Charles Fleets Bill for washing the Surplices & Cleaning the windows and sand for the Church		3. 3. 10
1812 John Williams for Land marks and Lettering them for to divide the Poor Land at the Graig and Mr Puleston's Land.		
April 29th 1813 by Mr Poole and Mr Crane		4. 6
1820 To journey to Chester on acct of Parish Apprentice		7. 6

Churchwardens set the general rate for the parish which was used for the upkeep of the church. In 1842, the amount assessed for Bangor was £33 3s 11½d. The following is a list of the people who owed money, were too poor to pay the rate, only paid part of the rate or where a property was vacant:

Voids and uncollected		
Sarah Brown	Poor	3½
Ralphs	Void	3
Edge	Void	1½
Martha Edwards	Poor	1½

Thomas Maddox	Void	4
Miss Jones	Void	4½
Mary Roberts	Poor	3
Elizth Lloyd	Poor	4½
John Edwards Poor		2½
Sarah Dawson Poor		3
John Munford Poor		1½
Thomas Paddock	Void	1½
Mary Roberts	Poor	5
Jemima Ralph		4
Davies Millbrook.		7s 3½d

The churchwardens were the eyes and ears of the bishop and had to attend his or the archdeacon's visitations and inform him of the condition of the church. An example of the churchwardens' responsibilities is given by an entry relating to the visitation of Bangor by the bishop of Chester in 1592:

Against the Churchwardens, Thomas Mason, gent, John Rogers, Edward Eaton, gent., & Robt ap Evans – there churchyard wanteth reparation, there bible shomewhat ruinous – the two tomes of Homelies [an official collections of sermons], Mr Juells Replie & apologie wantinge – the communion table cloth but indifferent, they wante a silver cupp, noe names taken of absent[ees] from church, the last churchwardens accompt verie sclender. On wh[ich] day appeared John ap Rogers one of the churchwardens, and the Judge enjoined him to provide before Xmas a faire cummunion cuppe of silver, a communion table cloath, and a new Byble of the largest volume, and before the s(ai)d daie to repair the Churchyard, to provide the queens injunctions & to certify the Courte daie after Xmas etc.

Churchwardens Oaths.
[CRO EDV/3/57]

Advertisement.

THE Parson, Vicar, or Curate of every Parish, and the Churchwardens, are to meet together, and read over these Articles, to deliberate seriously about them, and to prepare proper Answers to them. And when they have duly considered them, the Churchwardens are to write their Answer or Presentm. (with the Names of all Offenders) unto every particular Article, distinctly and truly, according to their Consciences : And the same so written, they are to bring to the Visitation, and to deliver up under their Hands, and upon their Oaths, directed to the Lord Bishop of CHESTER, his Vicar General, or other Judge competent.

The New Churchwardens OATH.

YOU do swear, That you will well and truly execute the Office of Churchwarden for the Year ensuing, in the Parish where you are chosen ; and that you will present all such Persons and Things, as are presentable by the Laws of this Realm, according to the best of your Skill and Knowledge.

So help you God.

The Old Churchwardens OATH.

YOU do swear, That you will true Presentment make of all such Persons and Things, as are presentable by the Laws of this Realm, according to the best of your Skill and Knowledge.

So help you God.

The curate was also reprimanded for giving Holy Communion to people who could not say the Lord's Prayer by heart or did not know the Ten Commandments.

At each visitation, the churchwardens had a printed series of detailed questions in a Book of Articles that they were expected to answer. In 1725, in answer to the question whether the church was in good repair, the churchwardens, Booth Basnett, Edward Tunna and James Royds, stated that the church 'was out of repair but is sett to be repaired'. They reported that:

> We have a Parchment Register Book carefully kept by the Minister but not as the Canons direct.
> Our reading Desk and Pulpit are pretty good, Placed conveniently enough to the Congregation but inconvenient to the Minister by reason of the distance from each other.
> We have three bells and they and the bell ropes are in good order.
> We have a church clock.

They advised on such things as the state of the rectory, whether the rector was resident in the parish, whether he neglected his duties or refused to visit the sick and the dying. They listed any dissenters who were living in the parish and if they had a meeting house. They also reported on swearing and drinking and in Bangor in 1725 admitted 'that Swearing and Drinking are too much Practised in our Parish we are sensible of, but know not whether there be any Person so notorious as to be presentable.'

In 1733, the churchwardens, Will Edwards, Edward Tunna and John Thomas, replying to the question of whether the rector, the Revd Rice Jones, instructed the youth of the parish said, 'Our rector used formerly to Catechize the youth of the Parish during the time of Lent till he was disabled by some disastrous accident, he intends to do it the remainder of the Sumer,' and 'The rector used to mention the King & Royal Family in the Prayers before Sermon, but since he had been forced to preach from the reading desk has omitted it'. Presumably he found it difficult to climb the steps to the pulpit since his accident. Answering a question about the parish clerk they replied that 'The person that officiates as Clerk has been a long time but the rector can't so far approve of him as to admit him to be licensed.'

Churchwardens also looked after the social and moral welfare of parishioners and could, and did, report cases of sexual misconduct, non-attendance at church and other transgressions, the perpetrators of which were summoned to appear before the Church court held twice a year in each deanery. The most common offence was bastardy, as in 1718 when Elizabeth Kendrick of Pickhill was presented 'for bearing a bastard child by late miller of Pickhill Mill who is since gone out of the country'. By 1721 he must have thought that he was safe from a forced marriage and returned home only to find that the church, or her father, had not forgotten, as the wedding of Hugh Jones of Pickhill Mill and Elizabeth Kendrick of Bangor is recorded that year. Or we could be charitable and assume that after three years he found that he really did love her, enough to marry her – a case of absence making the heart growing fonder? Later, in the nineteenth century, when the power of the Church courts declined, cases of bastardy were dealt with by the Petty or Quarter Sessions.

Cases of fornication or adultery were also common. In 1699, Robert Shone of Bangor was presented for 'living incontinently with a woman under pretence of marriage but they produce noe certificate of their marriage.' In cases of sexual impropriety, the woman might have to appear in a white shift and confess her sins before the congregation. Men on the other hand seem to escape with a fine! If all else failed and they did not appear at the court or pay the fine, there was always the threat of excommunication but this seems to have been rarely carried out; the threat seemingly enough to bring the guilty party into line and pay the penance or fine.

Individuals could also complain to the court and seek redress for wrongs such as in 1632 when Richard and Jane Edwards summoned Robert Evans, clerk, for libel for saying they were living together unmarried, and in 1696 Alice Gough summoned Anna Olton for calling her a bagle (the handle of a shepherd's crook) implying that she was crooked – whether morally or physically is left to our interpretation.

Overseers of the poor

Each parish was responsible for the maintenance of the elderly, infirm and poor members of the community. Overseers of the poor were created under legislation of 1572 which was updated in 1601, and were appointed each year by the vestry but, unlike the churchwardens, were required to be a 'substantial householder'. The legislation stated that each local community should be responsible for its own poor by fixing a poor rate based on property. Two overseers were usually elected in Bangor who, like the churchwardens, were unpaid. Assistant overseers were also appointed but they were paid as it was their task to go from door to door collecting the money that was then disbursed amongst those in need. This poor rate was in addition to the general parish rate for the upkeep of the church. Apart from some accounts that were entered with the parish accounts for 1841–5, these records have not survived.

In 1781, Peter Lloyd left Graig Cottage in Graig Lane, 'now in the holding of Elizabeth Edwards, widow,' to the Revd Frederick Lloyd in his will. The churchwardens were to be the trustees, and were to rent out the property and use the money to buy bread for the poor of the parish every Sabbath day. He also bequeathed the sum of £200, 'secured to me by Bond From Thomas Puleston late of Emral Esq, deceased,' and stipulated that it should be invested on good security and to use the interest for the same purpose.

1842 Charity Account for Bread. Mr R. Barker [overseer]

Recd from Mr Lee for Turnpike Trust	£1 5s 0d
Recd one years Interest from the Rev. Lloyd Wynne's Bond	£10 0s 0d
Recd four years Interest from the Leather Sellers Company London	£ 4 0s 0d
Recd of Thomas Edwards one years Rent to the 25th of March 1842 for cottage at Graig	
Less stamps 6 at 4d	£11 19s 2d
	£ 27 4s 2d

After paying Caroline Edwards and Joseph Fowles for their bills, and Thomas Jones for baking, the bread was distributed to the poor each Sunday.

At the vestry meeting held on 27 December 1813 it was agreed that the rental of the tenement and land situated near Sutton Green and occupied by Samuel Dod, farmer, which belonged to the poor of the parish of Bangor, should be extended to him for a further term of ten years at a yearly

The Overseer of the Poor,
account for 1739.
[FRO D/LK/61]

rental of £16 10s 0d, exclusive of all leys and tax assessments. They also stipulated how he was to farm the land: he was to be allowed to take three crops off the land in the first half of the term and then to sow with clover and grass seed and to graze the lands thereafter. He was to be allowed five pounds off his first year's rent to put a new floor over the end of the dwelling house. By 1832, it was occupied by Thomas Garner or his under tenants and it was agreed to let the property and land to John Davies a farmer of Sutton Green at a rental of £14, but with the stipulation that the land was for grazing only.

In 1814, it was agreed to extract rock at the Graig belonging to the parish and sell it for the best price that could be got for the benefit of the poor. As well as cottages in Holt and Sutton Green, cottages in Bangor had been purchased with some of the money left by benefactors; two of the nine cottages built into the churchyard wall in Overton road belonged to the parish.

In 1842, the trustees of the poor received the following income from the investments:

Charity Account. Mr R. Barker

Recd of Jas Davies ½ years rent for Cottage at Holt	£3 13s 6d
Recd of Jas Davies ½ years rent for Cottage at Holt	
due 25th March less for repairs etc	£ 3 7s 6d
Recd share of Sutton Green Rent.	
Less for repairs and stamps etc	£ 3 3s 2d
	£10 4s 2d

This sum was distributed amongst the poor inhabitants of the township of Bangor in the form of coal, clothing or rent. In 1915, the Bangor charity account showed a balance of £166 8s 2d and the trustees stated that the amount to be given in Easter money and bread had to be reduced that year, as extensive repairs to the charity property had to be faced. Finally, in 1921, the properties belonging to the charity at Sutton and Holt were sold for £725, and in 1954 Graig Cottage was sold and the money invested.

There were other accounts held at various times by the vestry such as the Clothing Club Fund, Sunday School and Eyton Mission Accounts, Churchyard Fund, Bangor Sunday School Account, Fred Davies Charity Outfit, Eyton Mission Fund, Cassock Fund, Bangor Choir Excursion Fund, Eyton Sunday School Excursion Fund and Bangor School Excursion Fund.

Briefs

As already mentioned, a brief was an official 'begging letter' or royal mandate authorizing a collection for some deserving cause. The deserving cause would be announced by the minister and a collection would be made during or at the end of the service and handed over to the official collector with the brief endorsed with the amount of money raised and a copy was also entered in the churchwardens accounts. Briefs were frequent in the seventeenth century, but none have been issued since 1854.

Bangor did not turn a deaf ear to requests for money as the following entries illustrate from the lost parish accounts recorded by canon Thomas:

1664, Dec 20th. Collected for one Mr Lowrie, an Irish gentleman, being blind, 7s 6d.

1666. The Great Fire of London. Received the 8th day of November, 1666, of Mr Robert Lloyd, churchwarden of the parish of Bangor, in Flintshire, by the hand of Ralph Mansell, the sum of seven pounds, which was collected in the said Parish on the Fast Day, being the 10th day of October, 1666, towards the relief of those persons who have been great sufferers by the last sad fire within the city of London. I. Gay, by order of the Lord Mayor, Sam Kendall.

1675, July 25th. Collected in the Parish Church of Bangor Monachorum the summe of four shillings and ninepence towards the relief of Watton, in the County of Norfolk, by Thomas Puleston and John ap Edwards, Wardens.

1680. Received from the Minister and Churchwardens of Bangor their collection towards the redemption of captives in Turkish Slavery at Algiers the sum of £1.3.0¼.

1681. December 12th. Received from the Minister and Churchwardens of Bangor their collection towards the repair of St Albans, the sum of £1 2s 4d.

1682, July 24th. Received from the Minister and Churchwardens of Bangor the money collected towards the relief of the distressed French Protestants the sum of £1 15s 10½d.

There is preserved in Chester Record Office a brief sent by the bishop of Chester on behalf of Neston parish church in 1695 to all parish churches in the archdeaconry of Chester, requesting contributions towards the rebuilding of their rectory following a fire. Bangor collected a total of £2 3s 0d and the list of the names of the donors has been preserved:

Mr Eyton	10s
Mr Beale	5s
Mr Kenrick	5s
Mr Beck Eyton	2s
Mr Edwards	1s
Mr Basnett	1s
Tho Clark	6d
Mr Davies [churchwarden]	1s
Robert Williams	6d
Tho Tonna	6d
John Richards	6d
Mr Baker	1s
Franck Clark [churchwarden]	6d
Ellis Jones	6d
Richard Jones	6d
Charles Hassall	6d
Mr Puleston	2s
Mr Perkins	6d
James Humphreys [churchwarden]	6d
Mr Rice Jones (rector)	10s
	£2 3s 0d

Parish clerk

The parish clerk was a paid official of the Church and had to be licensed by the bishop. His duties were many and varied and included some or all of the following: opening up the church at dawn, ringing the bell, lighting the candles, acting as a witness at weddings, leading the singing and responses to prayers. He often supplemented his income by cleaning church windows, washing surplices, brushing the church floor, attending visitations, etc. The names of the parish clerks are unknown before 1718.

*c.*1718–28	John Hughes, wife Elizabeth [1722 baptism], died June 1728.
1728 – *c.*1735	John Lloyd, acting as clerk but unlicensed.
*c.*1735–71	Edward Pritchard [1735 baptism], died April, 1773, aged 82.
1771–76	William Pritchard, found strangled July 1776, aged 30.
1776–1802	John Lloyd [marriage register, 1792], wife Ester Jones, died 1802, aged 52.
1802–20	Charles Fleet [parish accounts], wife Bridget, died November 1820, aged 60.
1820–3	William Jones [parish accounts].
1836–47	John Jones [parish accounts], schoolmaster, died February 1847, aged 46.
1847–58	Charles Griffiths, tailor, born Bangor [1851 census], died May 1858, aged 67.

1858–96	William Thomas, born Bangor [census], wife Martha. Resigned 1896 [vestry minutes]. Died 1900 aged 69.
1896–1909	Richard Johnson, aged 60, Whitchurch road [1901 census] died 1909, aged 68.
1909–1919	–?–
1919	Parish clerk resigned [vestry minutes].

In many parishes the office of parish clerk had become redundant by about 1907.

The vestry clerk

The vestry clerk was a literate person from the community who recorded the business transacted and the decisions made by the vestry meetings for which he received a small payment. Again the early holders of the office are unknown.

1727 Thomas Cope, schoolmaster
1841 Edward Hanmer
1843 Thomas Speed (paid £3 3s), schoolmaster
1850 Mr Maddocks
1856 Charles Griffiths, also the parish clerk
1862 Arthur Hanmer
1867 Combined with post of parish clerk

The verger, sexton and beadle

Vergers often combined general duties in the church with the position of sexton in digging the graves, until recent times. Grave digging is now contracted out to private firms. The beadle was a minor parish official responsible for keeping order and dealing with petty offenders.

1830 William Williams as verger
1841 William Williams for looking after the church
1853 William Williams as beadle
1863 William Williams as verger
1873 George Puleston was paid 10s [50p]
1875 Edward Roberts
–?– Daniel Bartlem
c.1920 Philip Humphreys
c.1940 Philip Henry Humphreys
2000 Leslie Done

7. Dissenters

Each year the rector or churchwardens had to make a return of all known recusants or dissenters from the established Church, either Roman Catholics (Papists) or Non-conformists to the Church court. In the 1605–6 Correction Book for Bangor, preserved among the diocesan records in Chester Record Office, there is a list of recusants of the parish of Bangor with no distinction made as to faith.

Correction Book for 1605–6

Recusants in Pickhill:

Roger Griffiths and Harriet his wife
Meredith ap Roger his son
William James, Taylor, and Margaret his wife
Agnes, daughter of Maddock, widow
John ap Hugh ap Maddock, Taylor, and Matilda his wife
Janet of the New House
Katherine Owain
ly…gard daughter of Roger

Recusants in Bangor:

John Howell, gent, and Katherine his wife
Eleanor wife of Lewes ap Edward
Katherine, daughter of Edward, widow
Margaret wife of John ap Edward, Glover
John ap Ellis labourer
Elizabeth wife of John, widow
Edward ap John ap Howell, labourer, and Matilda his wife

Recusants in Sesswick:

Edwina, daughter of Roger Ellis
wife of John ap John, labourer
Widow Lowri

In 1608 the recusants for Bangor were:

Roger Griffiths and Janet his wife
William James and Margaret his wife

Janet daughter of John & Elizabeth
Ermine wife of John ap John

1669: Robert ap David; Richard Basnett and David Eaton [Eyton], gent, were presented 'for frequenting puritan meetings or conventicles and absenting themselves from the Common Prayer & Services of the church'. At the same court, Peter Griffiths; Janet Ellis; Margaret Ellis; Elleanor Draycott and Eliza Lloyd were all presented as Papist recusants.

1670: Peter Griffiths and Frances his wife; Janet Ellis; Margaret Ellis and Ellenora Draycott were reported for not coming to church. Richard Basnett of Eaton, gent; Eliza Lloyd; Robert ap David and George Draycott for standing excommunicated.

1671: Peter Griffiths and his wife Frances; Margaret Ellis; Ellenor Draycutt; George Draycutt; Bridgett Bathoe and Michael Bathoe were listed as Old Recusants. Robert ap David; Roger Urian and his wife Janet were said to be New Recusants.

1672: Ellenor Draycott (by now a widow) and her son, George; Peter Griffiths and his wife; Roger Benion and his wife and Margaret Ellis (widow) were all described as Papists or Quakers.

1674: Roger Urian and his wife Janet were said to be Quakers.

By 1700 the names of dissenters had ceased to be recorded. Many kept up the pretence of being Anglicans by attending church every so often, but several refused to pay their church dues. Thomas Whitley of Althrey Hall refused to '… pay the church lay for the township of Eaton for the year 1681, 3s 2d, as also for the Township of Bangor in the same year'. The names of those who refused to pay the church lays were presented for a few years more up to *c*.1718. The only known Catholic chapel in Bangor parish was one in Althrey Hall that was hidden in the roof.

Protestant Dissenters
The first mention of the site of a meeting house in Bangor for Protestant dissenters is when a

> … piece of Building Situate On the West side of the Church Street in the Town of Bangor in the County of Flint and Diocese of Chester commonly called or known by the name of the malt kiln now in the holding or occupation of Thomas Shone was registered in accordance with an Act of Parliament made in the first year of the reign of King William & Queen Mary.

It was registered in the Public Episcopal Registry in Chester in July 1801 and was signed by seven members of the Dissenters: Thomas Shone; Simon Hope; John Shone; William Woodhall; Charles Harris; William Nixon and John Lowe. Quite where this property was is not clear. There has never been a Church Street in Bangor, only Church Avenue along the side of the Endowed School, but this road has no house on the west side only the river, all the buildings are on the south side. If it was that part of High Street by the church that was meant, then the only property on the west side was the terrace of five cottages by the bridge where the War Memorial now stands and it may well have been one of these that was described. The cottages were small, but presumably the congregation was initially few in number.

A return of the places of worship of Non-conformists was made to the Quarter Sessions at Easter 1829 when a Wesleyan chapel was recorded in Bangor parish, but exactly where it was situated is not stated. In October 1833, the Quarter Sessions Minute Book records that it was 'ordered that the entry made by John Edwards, William Newns and Isaac Pickering all of Bangor, of a new Meeting Room for religious worship situate at Bangor be duly registered'. The congregation had probably outgrown the little cottage and had moved to larger premises. It is thought that this meeting room was the large room over Isaac Pickering's post office that could seat more than seventy people.

Between 1833 and 1839 a chapel was built and in July 1839 the following registration was recorded:

[a] … certain building situate in the parish of Bangor in the County of Flint in the possession or occupation of Isaac Pickering and others intended to be used as a chapel for religious worship by Protestants Dissenting from the Church of England.

The names attached are William Minshall, James Lewis, Edward Moses, Edward Davies, and Isaac Pickering. The chapel must have been built just prior to the 1839 registration and was later described on an O.S. map as an Independent Chapel.

These applications for registration are the first mention of Isaac Pickering in Bangor. He was baptized on 4 January 1801 in Llanarmon-yn-Iâl church, the seventh of ten children of miner Francis Pickering and Sarah (née Bryan), when the family was living in Eryrys. Isaac is listed on the 1840 tithe map apportionments as the owner of the chapel, a little cottage and the post office/Orme Lodge. The little cottage has since been pulled down. The occupants were himself, John Kilham and others. In the 1851 census, he is described as a draper and grocer and ten years later was also the sub-postmaster.

The chapel probably served as a place of worship for Dissenters regardless to which sect they belonged but, for some unknown reason, by 1867 it was no longer being used for worship. At some stage the chapel was converted into a residential property and in 2013 is about to undergo yet another conversion into a branch surgery for the Overton Medical Practice.

After 1867, the Non-conformists were holding services in a room above a shop belonging to William Davies. This had been fitted with benches, a reading desk and lamps and could seat between 80 and 100 people. Services with no denominational allegiance were held here every Sunday. When a group of Calvanistic Methodists came to live in the neighbourhood and joined the congregation, they encouraged the members to think about building their own church. Among these new members were William Dicken of Porthwgan and Robert Evans of Halghton Mill. William Davies offered them a plot of land for £50 where a building had stood attached to Winifred cottage (the present doctors' surgery) in Whitchurch Road near the corner of High Street. This may have been the property where the congregation had actually been meeting. The services of an architect (T.M. Lockwood of Chester) were engaged and plans were drawn up and approved.

The new church was to be built in the gothic style, utilising red bricks with stone facings and a porch with iron palisades on the front. The interior of the church was to be thirty-three feet long by twenty-four feet wide and was designed to accommodate 140 people. It was to be lit by two pendant lights suspended from the ceiling and heated by a hot water system. Attached to the back of the church was a schoolroom (measuring twenty feet by eighteen feet) with an entrance from the church and by a side door. The total cost of the building was between £500 and £600. The

The Independent Chapel in the High Street circa 1930, lately a private residence, now about to be converted into a doctors' surgery.

foundation stone was laid on 9 August 1869 by John Roberts of Bryn Gwenallt, Abergele, using a silver trowel presented by Robert Evans. The stone bore the following inscription:

> This stone was laid by John Roberts, Bryn Gwenallt,
> August 9th 1869.J Lockwood, architect; Benjamin Owen, builder.

After the ceremony, the company sat down to a tea in two large tents erected in the field opposite owned by Mr Bithel of the Star Inn and in the evening they were entertained to a concert featuring singers from the Presbyterian Chapel, Rhostyllen.

The new church opened in 1871 with services on Friday, 15 April and Sunday, 17 April. After the service on the Friday everyone again sat down to a tea in two tents erected in the field opposite. The tea was served by Mrs R. Evans, Halghton Mill; Mrs William Dickin, Porthwgan; Mrs Bithel, Star Hotel; Mrs Lewis, Bangor; Mrs Morris, Worthenbury; Miss Edwards, Cross Lanes; Miss Billington, Bangor, Mrs Lee, Halghton Hall; Mrs Suckley, Cloy; Miss Edwards, Mount House; Miss Maddocks, Gwynn; Miss Shaw, Twll; Mrs Wright, Cross Lanes; Mrs Barnett, Lion and Mrs Fowles, Bangor. The Presbytery for Lancashire and Cheshire recommended that £50 be given each year towards the engagement of a pastor for the church, but in the meantime Dr Edwards of Bala sent the Revd Thomas Davies to care for the fledgling congregation until such a time as they appointed a minister of their own. Mr Dickin of Porthwgan was appointed secretary of the church, a position which he held for thirty-seven years before finally resigning in 1905.

The first anniversary service of the Presbyterian Chapel was held on 18 May 1872 when the Revd William Howell, president and theological tutor of Treveen College, preached three sermons.

The attendance was not so numerous in the morning and afternoon, but in the evening the chapel was well filled and the collection totalled £5 16s 2d. On the following Monday evening a tea was again held in a tent, set up in Mr Bithell's field near the chapel.

In September 1875, a bazaar and tea party were held with the object of clearing some of the debt of just over £300 still remaining on the Presbyterian chapel. It was opened at 2 p.m. in a tent while preparations for the tea were being carried out in another tent. Four stalls containing articles of drapery, millinery, etc which had been very tastefully arranged, were presided over respectively by Mrs Cambell, Mrs Jones, Mrs Dickin, Mrs Evans and their friends. The bazaar raised over £125 and this, with contributions of friends and promises of £90, had the happy result of reducing the debt to under £100.

In October 1875 an interesting meeting was held at the Presbyterian chapel in connection with the departure of the Revd Richard Jones (their late pastor) from the neighbourhood. He had accepted the charge of the church at Llanymynech, near Oswestry. The Bangor congregation was then without a resident minister until 1882 when Revd Robert Phennah was introduced as the new pastor. In May 1887, Salem and Eyton congregations were joined with Bowling Bank and Bangor under his ministry.

In January 1886, one of the teachers of the Presbyterian chapel Sunday school, Margaret Dickin, second daughter of W. Dickin of Porthwgan, was leaving the neighbourhood to attend the 'North Wales College' at Bangor, Caernarfonshire, and was presented with a set of books by her class. Mr Evans of Dee House made the presentation on behalf of the children. In 1888, she passed the first division of the matriculation examination of the London University and distinguished herself in Latin and gained a scholarship.

There was always a flourishing Sunday school and in 1925 Mr and Mrs Wilfred Jones of Orchard Farm gave the officers, teachers and scholars of the Presbyterian chapel an excellent tea. After tea a pleasant hour was spent in games and each of the children was given a bag of sweets by Master

The Presbyterian Church in Whitchurch Road.

Interior of Presbyterian Church. [David Walker]

William Jones and Miss Florence May Jones, two children who were to remain stalwart life-long supporters of the church.

Frequent entertainments were held such as one in 1934 in the Assembly Rooms when the Congo Follies Concert Party from Whitchurch was invited to entertain in aid of the Presbyterian church. The concert party was said to be very popular and this was the fourth consecutive year that they had appeared. They always attracted a large and appreciative audience.

In August 1939, a fete took place on the Groes Field in aid of both the Bangor and Bethel Presbyterian churches. A comic football match held between Bangor ladies and Abenbury ladies resulted in a win for the latter team by one goal to nil. George Parry of Cacca Dutton was the referee. The sports events were in the hands of Tom Jarvis, the well-known local athlete, the handicapper was Leslie Griffiths of the post office, who also acted as the starter and Albert Fowles and George Jones of Abenbury were the judges.

In recent years, the congregations of the Anglican and Presbyterian churches have occasionally held combined services, showing the spirit of friendly cooperation that now exists between them. As recently as Christmas 2012, a combined carol service was held in the chapel with the tightly-packed congregation of well over 100 singing their hearts out in a glorious uplifting sound of thanksgiving for the birth of the holy child. Rhos or Brymbo Male Voice choirs could not have sung better!

The ministers known to have served the Presbyterian church were:

1870–5   Revd Richard Jones
1879–81   Revd W. Williams
1882–7   Revd Robert Phennah
1887–94   Revd R. Morgan Rees
1904–06   Revd W. Morgan Williams
1908–16   Revd Philip O. Williams

1917– ?   Revd David Manuel
1924–25 Revd J. Harris
1927–34 Revd E.V. Pierce
1934–40 Revd W.E. Davies
1941–?   Revd E.D. Notman
1959–?   Revd C.H. Nicholas
1977–78 Revd J. Couch
1979–82 Revd R.H. Kendrick
1989–96 Revd Geoffrey Barrington
1998–2006 Revd Richard Evans
2007–10 Revs Stewart and Paula Miles

8. The River Dee and Bridge

The bridge, a Grade One scheduled monument, is medieval in origin and is said to have replaced an earlier stone one, the remains of which some people say could at one time be seen a few yards slightly down stream. There are five, unequal elliptical arches and three full height splayed cutwaters on each side with refuges at the top for pedestrians to avoid the, not inconsiderable, traffic. The arches are principally of red sandstone with a parapet and cutwaters of mainly yellow sandstone. The parapet is of large dressed slabs.

The date of its erection is unknown, only that of the first recorded restoration in 1658, which was part of an inscription on a stone inserted into the southern side of the bridge in the fourth course of the second pier from the Bangor side. The lettering became eroded with time and can no longer be seen. According to Thomas Pennant (1726–1798), in his *Tours in Wales*, a 'learned schoolmaster' (not named) had recorded and deciphered the letters and numbers before they became too worn.

MVND 5607	DENB. CC	CONCIT
REPARAT AN CHRIST 1658 SVMP E COMIT	LIB	MA
HEGYR 1036	FLINT. C.	

Which translates as:

> Repaired in the year of the World 5607, in the year of Christ 1658 and the year of the Hegira 1036, at the expense of the county of Denbigh £200 and of Flint £100. M.A.

It is thought that 'M.A.' was the mason who did the work. Denbighshire appears to have borne the major part of the expense – £200 as against Flintshire's £100, but most probably the final 'C' had already become eroded as the cost was afterwards always shared equally between the two counties. The 'learned schoolmaster' would most probably have been one of the curate/schoolmasters with a working knowledge of Latin. For an explanation, I quote from the *Archaeologia Cambrensis* Volume XIII (1895):

> First of all of the three dates given by Pennant, the first (the year of the world) is, I think, copied inaccurately – 5607 instead of 5662, a mistake easily made. It is quite clear that the three dates indicate the same year, calculated from different standpoints viz:
> 1. The year of the World
> 2. The year of Christ
> 3. The year of the Hegira, or that year from which the Mohammodans reckon.

Bangor Bridge.

According to Usher's calculation, AD1658 would correspond to AM5662, and Usher's reckoning was, after the middle of the seventeenth century, equally accepted, and is indeed still accepted by many. But 5607 will agree with no mundane reckoning known to me. On the other hand the year of the Hegira 1036, and the year of Christ 1658 absolutely correspond.

There had been a bridge across the river in earlier times, as there is mention in an Overton deed of 1292 of 'the King's highway leading to the bridge at Bangor'. The bridge must have fallen into disrepair, or had been washed away by floods, as by 1388 a ferryboat had replaced it. In that year, there is an account of the repairs carried out to the boat, details of which included:

> And in expenses paid to Ieuan Sayr, carpenter, and helper, for the repair and renewal of the lord's boat at Bangor, for 12 days for which he received 4½d and the other 3d a day, 7s 6d. And in carrying planks from the castle [Holt] and timber from Eyton Park for the said boat, 16d. And for two gross of nails bought for the said work, 4s. And for one pig of iron for a chain to be made for the said boat, together with the smith's work, 18d. And for 30lb of pitch bought for the said boat, 5s. And for 10lbs of grease bought, 10d.

In 1391, the boat was farmed out at two marks. When the stone bridge that replaced the

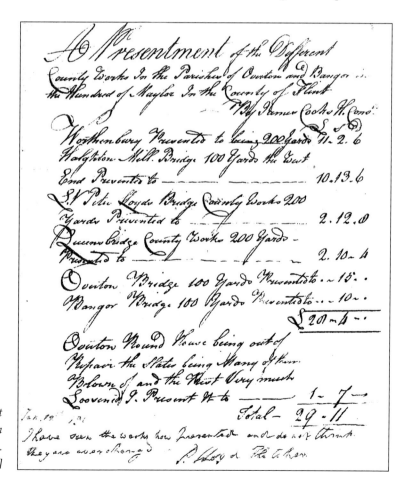

The constables' presentment of the various bridges in need of repair in 1791.
[FRO QS/SR/160/3)]

ferryboat was built is unknown but Derek Pratt states it was after Owen Glyndŵr's rebellion c.1401 when, despite decrees to the contrary, a steady stream of 'wet back' cattle from Broxton are said to have regularly swum across the Dee at Bangor en-route to Ruthin market. The inference is that if the bridge had been built there would have been no need for the cattle to swim the river. However, a bridge had been built by 1464 as Jankyn ap Madoc left '10s to the fabric of the bridge at Bangor' in his will.

It has been said that the present bridge dates from the sixteenth century although no-one knows for sure. When John Leland toured the area sometime in the 1540s, he praised the stone bridge at Llangollen but did not mention the one at Bangor. This has led people to assume that it had not been built. But it is just as likely that it did not warrant a mention when compared to the Llangollen Bridge (not the present one) that was more impressive, being much longer and most probably wider, beside which Bangor's paled into insignificance. We know that there was a bridge in 1556 as Rue Lloyd alias Rice ap Gruff ap Edward Lloyd of Erbistock in his will gave 'Unto the reperacion of Bangor Bridge xl.s.' What we do not know is to which bridge the will refers. Again Roger Puleston of Emral in his will of 1587 said '… if at any time hereafter the bridge of Bangor be builded new out of the ground I do hereby give and bequeath twenty pounds towards the making of the said Bridge'. From these sources we know that there was an existing bridge that was constantly in need of repair but whether it was the present stone bridge will continue to exercise minds for many years to come.

Perhaps the building of a new bridge had been deferred and the authorities just kept on patching up the old. The £20 given in the will – a significant sum being a fifth of Flintshire's total contribution nearly a century later – may have proved to be the spur. If the present one was built just after the Puleston will was written then it could just be described as sixteenth century, although it should not have needed major restoration seventy years later. It has been said that Inigo Jones (1573–1652) built the bridge as he may have designed the present one at Llangollen in similar style, but no bridge that he built would have needed major restoration just six years after his death. It is far more likely that he oversaw the restoration of the bridge and then copied the design when he built the one at Llangollen.

The bridge has been repaired many times over the years, being damaged either by floodwater or by carts, wagons, coaches, and since 1900, motor vehicles of all kinds. There is frequent mention in the Flintshire Quarter Sessions Records of it being presented by the High Constables of 'Mayler' as being in need of repair. Usually the nature of the repair is not specified, however in the Quarter Sessions rolls for 1761 the following is written:

> Estimate for the repair of Bangor Bridge by Edward Pritchard, mason, there being about 50 yards of stone work destroyed by the flood. Viewed by Robert Williams, Richard Parry Price & Robert Davies Esqs & the Rev. Mr Frederick Lloyd of Bangor, £11.10.0. Repairs to the battlements of the bridge £1.11.0.

Again in June 1793, when it was necessary to repair the Flintshire end of the bridge, details are given:

> The Battlements to be taken down and a new stone Battlement to be erected in the same manner as the Denbighshire end is done: fourteen Inches at the Bottom and Seven Inches at the top and

not to be shorter lengths than four Feet and Cramped with Iron Cramps eight Inches long properly leaded into the stone with Strong Post, an Iron Rail at the Angle next to the house, and the Stone Work of the Piers to be properly repaired.

The estimate for the work was eighty-two pounds.

Many stories have been told about two vehicles meeting in the middle of the bridge with neither driver prepared to give way and reverse. As early as the Michaelmas 1764 Quarter Sessions one such incident was reported at which estimates were given 'to repair Bangor Bridge thrown down by two carts meeting on the bridge'. In 1906 it was reported in a Wrexham paper that:

> ... a local farmer and his wife were travelling home from market with their pony and trap and had gone about one third of the way across the bridge when a car came rushing up from the opposite direction. Its greater speed meant that the car arrived at the centre of the bridge first. The result was that neither of the two could proceed, and as neither would back off the bridge, all traffic was held up for quite some time. Eventually the farmer, probably because he could not afford the time to argue the matter, gave way, although he most certainly had the sympathy of the large crowd of onlookers who had assembled to witness the fun.

Traffic lights were finally erected about 1953 and a restriction was placed on the width of vehicles trying to squeeze over the bridge. With a maximum width of 2.7metres (9 feet), the bridge is now restricted to smaller vehicles and is one-way only, although late night revellers have been known to take a chance in driving home from the pubs in the wrong direction.

In 1909, a lot of work was done to the bridge. On the Flintshire side, the bridge was stripped down to the arches, the County Council having decided to adopt the French patent reinforcement process, known as Hunebique's patent, the work being entrusted to the Yorkshire Hunebique Contracting Co Ltd, Leeds. This process consisted of laying a double lattice or caging of steel rods about six or seven inches apart over the arches and then filling in the whole of the interstices with fine concrete. The inventor claimed that bridges treated in this way were capable of bearing loads many tons in weight and would therefore multiply the strength of the bridge many times. In addition to this, half a dozen tie rods were inserted through the bridge to strengthen the parapet. On the Denbighshire side the authorities relied on a much more simple, and cheaper, method. They merely took off the old roadway down to the upper masonry after which they made a foundation for the new road by making a concrete of the gravel off the old bridge, to which was added a certain quantity of cement and pouring it into all the holes and crevices. It will be a matter of time as to which method will prove to be the most durable.

In 1967, a report was commissioned into the condition of the bridge. This reported that the bridge:

> ... is still remarkably well preserved. Investigations have shown that the bridge is founded on good supporting material and is well built. The findings of a underwater survey team of local skin divers located and recorded the spandrel ties which were installed 50-60 years ago having been prepared for the Flintshire half of the bridge by the local village blacksmith and for the Denbighshire half by a Wrexham firm believed to be Cuthbert [sic - Cudworth] & Johnson. The arched piers and abutments and the main arch rings are strong and fully capable of supporting

live loads of up to full 'Construction and Use ' limit and no weight restriction is considered necessary. The County Surveyor of Denbigh arranged for an underwater survey by Messrs T.R. Parry and J. Beckitt of a local team of skin divers to report which was borne out when the river level dropped unexpectedly to enable a visual survey to be undertaken.

They reported that the spandrel walls, connecting ties and parapet walls were weak. It was agreed to fix a 10-ton weight limit that would allow cars, buses and industrial vehicles of normal size to pass.

If you think that it was the invention of the motorcar that brought forth requests for a new bridge across the river, then you would be wrong; calls for a second bridge over the Dee were being made two hundred years ago! In February 1810, the Clerk of the Peace to the Quarter Session was ordered to write to Colonel Puleston to know whether he would consent to the disposal of his cottages at the east end of the bridge for the purposes of erecting a new bridge. Nothing came of that request. In 1826 an attempt to widen the bridge was made when Mr Turner, the county surveyor, was asked to prepare a plan and estimate for the improvement of Bangor Bridge by adding a footpath and railing on each side. Twelve months later the magistrates met at the Buck Inn in Bangor to consider his proposed plan.

The magistrates agreed to put an advertisement in the two Chester and the two Shrewsbury newspapers asking for tenders for widening and repairing the bridge, according to the plans and specifications, in iron as well as stone. On receiving the tenders they then asked for a meeting of the county surveyors for Flintshire and Denbighshire with Mr Hartley, engineer of Liverpool, to assist them in determining the best method of widening the bridge. A month after this meeting Flintshire Quarter Sessions received a letter from their counterparts in Denbighshire saying that they were of the opinion that it would be

> … most expedient to build a New Iron Bridge over the Dee at Bangor according to the plan produced by their County Surveyor as soon as the incumbrances on their County Rates, which

The Old Bridge Cottages.

are considerable, are paid off, but were willing to unite with this county in making such temporary repairs as may be necessary.

Mr Hartley's report on the state of Bangor Bridge having been read, the magistrates present were unanimously of the opinion, with the magistrates now assembled of the county of Denbigh, that it would be inexpedient to widen and repair the present bridge but that it would be more desirable to build an entirely new one. They therefore recommended to the next Court of Quarter Sessions for the County of Flintshire that the sum of £500 be annually laid out to meet an equal sum from the County of Denbighshire towards the erection of a new bridge. It is not known whether this recommendation was ever put into practice. The Flintshire magistrates were not happy at the contemplation of a long and inconvenient suspension of the co-operation of their Denbigh colleagues in the erection of a new bridge. They would have been in despair if they had known that it would take over 150 years before the two counties finally agreed on a plan!

As wider and heavier loads and vehicles tried to negotiate the narrow approach to the bridge on the Flintshire side, damage to the structure was inevitable. The approach was still restricted by the five cottages that protruded on one side of the road – where the War Memorial now stands - and was not helped by the outbuildings of the Royal Oak on the other. Flintshire County Council had agreed to pay one-third of the cost of purchase and demolition of the cottages, amounting to £210, if Bangor could find the remaining two-thirds. A petition was started in 1913 led by Hugh Peel of Bryn-y-Pys who, along with R. Fenwick Palmer and Frank Lloyd, wrote the following letter to all their friends, acquaintances and many of the local firms who regularly used the road, requesting donations.

We feel sure you will be interested to know that the block of five old cottages, which have for so many years obstructed the view of Bangor Bridge, have been purchased for £300, and the cost of conveyance.

In these days of motor traffic, it is an absolute necessity to get a clear view of the Bridge, which, owing to its narrowness and bad approach, is exceedingly dangerous to all traffic, and we consider the price reasonable for the advantage that will be gained.

The Flintshire County Council have unanimously decided to pay one-third of the cost, the remaining two-thirds (which, with the expense of demolishing the cottages and protecting the site, will be about £225), we have every confidence, will be willingly met by voluntary contributions.

Knowing the use you make of the Bridge, and the interest you have in the removal of such a dangerous obstacle, we venture to ask you for a contribution.

To overcome any difficulty the present tenants may have in finding other dwellings, a scheme is under consideration for the erection of eight or ten new cottages, with gardens, adjacent to the village, which will be ready for occupation before the old ones are demolished.

Your co-operation in the movement, and subscriptions, will be welcomed by the undersigned, who have made themselves responsible for the purchase.

Philip Yorke of Erddig replied to the letter on 29 December 1913:

The scheme in which you are interesting your self ought to be well supported, & I would suggest that Sir Watkin might like to subscribe, & also certain others whose names are not yet here to be found, notably Mrs Summers of Emral & Col. Dubb [Dunn], all of whom are motorists as I believe, & all having very frequently to make use of the Bangor-Is-coed bridge.

I have much pleasure in sending my cheque for £5.0.0, & hope the amount required may soon be raised....

LIST OF SUBSCRIBERS

Mrs Fenwick	5. 0. 0.
Wrexham Motor Co.	1. 0. 0.
R. Fenwick Palmer	5. 0. 0.
O. Ormrod, Esq.	10. 0. 0.
The Duke of Westminster	10. 0. 0.
Charles Jones, Esq.	1. 1. 0.
Frank Sowler, Esq.	2. 2. 0.
P. Ormrod, Esq.	5. 0. 0.
T. Arthur Acton, Esq.	5. 0. 0.
The Hon Mrs Tighe	1. 1. 0.
Capt. D. M. King	2. 2. 0.
A. P. Campbell, Esq.	2. 2. 0.
P. H. Ashworth, Esq.	5. 0. 0.
Mrs Rayner	2. 2. 0.
W. J. MacKenzie, Esq.	1. 0. 0.
Bent's Brewery Co.	5. 0. 0.
P. Yorke, Esq.	5. 0. 0.
Mrs Summers	5. 0. 0.
The Lord Kenyon	10. 0. 0.
Captain Lloyd	1. 0. 0.
Mrs Dixon	5. 0. 0.
H. W. Ethelston, Esq.	5. 0. 0.
Mr W. Chesters	10. 0.
Col. Dunn	2. 0. 0.
Hugh Peel, Esq.	10. 0. 0.
G. Dutton & Son	1. 1. 0.
Mrs Pilkington	1. 0. 0.
Mr John Mort	2. 0. 0.
J. Howard, Esq	10. 0. 0.
A. Summers, Esq	5. 0. 0.
Mr A. Sutton	2. 0. 0.
Sir W. Hanmer, Bart.	10. 0. 0.
Sir W. W. Wynn, Bart.	5. 0. 0.
Frank Lloyd, Esq.	10. 0. 0.
Bangor Race Committee	10. 0. 0.
General Mostyn	2. 0. 0.

H. Dyke Dennis, Esq.	3. 3. 0.
Dr S. Edwards Jones	2. 2. 0.
Rev. R. Paterson Morgan	10. 0. 0.
W. Dromfield, Esq.	5. 0. 0.
	————
	£ 184. 6. 0.

To make up the deficit, Hugh Peel loaned an additional £60 and by 1915 the old cottages had been demolished, the land made good and the inhabitants re-housed.

By now the demand for a new bridge was gathering momentum as the impact of motorised vehicles was beginning to be felt – quite literally as the lorries, charabancs and tractors bounced off the stone parapet when they failed to negotiate either of the entrances! Both Denbighshire and Flintshire authorities prepared their own plans for a new crossing but neither side could agree and the intervention of two world wars did not help. The design of the proposed bridge advocated by Denbighshire was for a new channel to be cut in the river which would eliminate the Turn o'Dee loop and redirect the river to emerge nearly opposite the old bridge. The majority of village people thought that when the river was in flood it could cause pressure to bear on the bank opposite the village at what was always regarded as its weakest points opposite the High Street and Church Avenue. If the bulwarks failed to hold, a column of water would surge straight down the High Street with devastating results. The design favoured by Flintshire County Council was for the Wrexham–Whitchurch road to continue parallel to the river for a hundred yards before swinging left to ascend to meet the other end of the same road at the junction of Cloy Lane. Finally, commonsense prevailed and the Flintshire plan was chosen in 1972.

It was a pity that the new stretch of road was not continued past the bends at Raggs Hill, as was originally planned, but Flintshire decided that to carry on pressing for total acceptance of their plans would further delay the

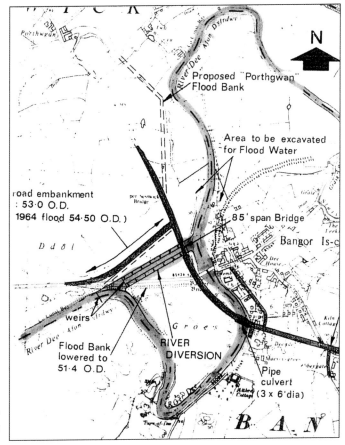

Denbighshire County Council Scheme
for the diversion of the river. [FRO]

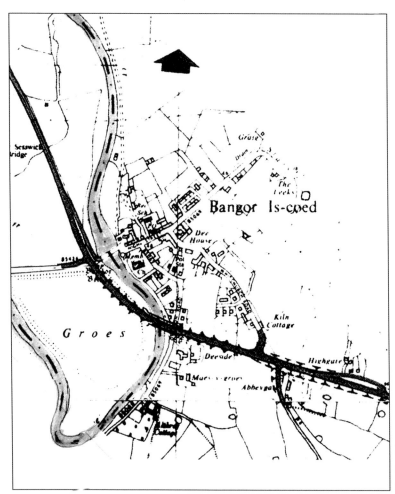

*Flintshire County Council's
successful proposal.*
[FRO FC/13/25]

work. Also for reasons of economy the opportunity was not taken to raise the level of the main road when it was widened and straightened for the approach to the new bridge. This would have prevented the flooding of the roads that regularly occurs at least once every winter during periods of heavy rain causing the river level to rise and to back up the drainage ditches. The A525 is a major artery from Wrexham, the Wrexham Trading Estate and the A483 Wrexham–Chirk bypass and it is disappointing that, in the twenty-first century, the roads are closed for several days at a time and traffic diverted. This is inconvenient for the villagers and lorry drivers who have to make a detour, for the ageing residents' loss of public transport and for the transport firms themselves who have to absorb the financial implications.

According to the 1905 Ordnance Survey map there was a ferry from the Graig to Pickhill and one further down stream at the Wern, Worthenbury but it was not a manned public ferry as the boats belonged to the Pickhill or Lower Hall estates and were for their use and their retainers and tenants and each had a boat house on their land.

There are several places where it is, or was, possible to ford the river. The first was below Asney at Eyton at a place called Dulsford or Dutford marked on the 1912 O.S. map. In April 1901,

Building the new bridge.

the enterprising landlord of the Boat Inn, Erbistock with an eye to business paddled his canoe from Erbistock to the ford at Eyton where, for a few pence, he had a most successful time ferrying passengers across the river to Bangor races. It is said that this ford became impassable when the weir at Erbistock was raised. The other place was at the Graig where it used to be possible to walk across the gravel bed to Pickhill Hall. When the railway bridge was built, the family used to walk along the track to church, which saved them having to sit with wet feet during the sermon! In 1903, they had a bridge built where the ferry used to be that is still there although in a dilapidated condition and is not now safe to use.

Pickhill bridge in its heyday when it was passable by pony and trap.

Coracles

The ancient British boat, the coracle, was used for centuries for salmon fishing on the Dee and probably dates back to prehistoric times. In 1188 Gerald of Wales (Giraldus Cambrensis) wrote in *The Description of Wales* how '… for fishing and crossing rivers [the Welsh] make coracles out of withies. These are not oblong but rounded…' (Thorpe 1978, 252). According to Derrick Pratt, the earliest references to coracles on the Dee between Overton and Bangor dates from 1430–50 when '… a certain John Eyton of Eyton on occasion made gifts of a coracle to deserving fishermen …'.

The coracle was a flat-bottomed boat with rounded ends with a seat across the middle. It was made of willow and would originally have been covered in hides but this was changed to canvas, which made a lighter boat, coated with up to twelve coats of pitch or tar. They differed from boats made at Llangollen, being lighter – 35lbs, to Llangollen's 55lbs. Bangor coracles were designed to hold just one person unlike boats on other Welsh rivers many of which were designed for two people. They were manoeuvred using either a short paddle or a long pole. Fishermen would sling a net between two boats and then drift down-stream with the flow of water to catch the salmon. They would then land and carry the net, paddles and coracle back up stream to repeat the process. Many of the inhabitants of Bangor have for centuries made a living out of the river and were described as fisherman or coracle fishermen in census returns.

By the mid nineteenth century, coracle fishing was said to be denuding the river of salmon and when the Fishery Board was formed, coracle fishermen were required to have a special licence. Eventually they were discouraged from fishing altogether and permits became difficult to obtain or were not renewed. The fishermen were compensated with the youngest getting the most money. In 1920, the Dee Fishery Board paid the last six men on the lower reaches of the river £1,000. In October 1922, it was claimed in a newspaper '… that since Net fishing has been prohibited on the Dee the river had been overrun by pike.'

Prominent among the coracle owning families in the village were the Poyntons, the Johnsons and the Stants, all of whom were mainly dependent on fishing for a living. Two brothers James and Charlie Johnson supplemented their income by making baskets and they used to cut the willow that grew by the river and weave baskets to sell when the fishing was poor. This business slowly grew until the First World War when James' son, also James, volunteered for the army and was badly wounded. He was sent to Beckitts Park, Leeds where he had an operation to graft a small bone from his leg into his arm – the first operation of its kind. During his time in hospital, he learned of a firm of basket makers in Leeds and, after he was discharged, took up the

Cyril Johnson making baskets.

offer of a two-year apprenticeship with the firm. He returned
to Bangor and, with his son
Cyril, was responsible for the
development of the Johnson
business. After the First World
War, James planted his own
willow bed rather than being
dependant on the natural
source. Charlie Johnson (died
in September 1922) was the
spokesman for other coracle
men appearing before the Dee
Conservancy Board, Chester
and at the Fisheries Commission in London. He was a fine
swimmer and saved many
lives in the deepest parts of
the Dee for which he was
awarded a certificate of the
Royal Humane Society. He was
also active in parochial affairs.

Bangor fishermen with their coracles. The figure on the left is believed to be W. Stant and on the right, Charlie Johnson – one of the last coracle fishermen to hold a licence.

One of the last coracles in Bangor belonged to W. Stant who had built a specially constructed shed in his garden in which to store it. As a result of negotiations by James Hornell, a leading expert on coracles, it was purchased for £5 in 1935 by the Welsh Folk Museum at St Fagans Castle near Cardiff where it can still be seen. They also purchased several fishing nets, along with examples of coracles from Llangollen and Ironbridge.

Prior to the twentieth century, regattas and coracle races would be held each year when the fishermen would compete over a length of river for prizes. When sports days were organised, the programme usually included a coracle race such as one held in May 1871 when first place went to Philip Cartwright for a prize of ten shillings [50p]; second place to Richard Griffiths 2/6d [12.5p]; third place, Moses Young and fourth was John Lewis. When celebrations took place in the village to mark special occasions, a coracle race was often included in the day's events. One such occasion was Queen Victoria's Jubilee celebrations of 1897 when a coracle race was very keenly fought and was won by C. Johnson with J. Johnson as runner up. Bangor's coracle men also took part in the Chester Regattas such as one held in August 1878 in which seven men from Holt and seven from Bangor competed over a straight course of 440 yards. The first prize of £3 was won by G. Dunbabin of Bangor, second prize of £1 by T. Chadwick of Holt, third prize of 10 shillings [50p] by G. Challoner of Holt. C. Johnson of Bangor came fourth. The *Chester Observer* reported that 'As usual the race was productive of much amusement.'

Early in 1910, some people were reminiscing about old times when the subject of the old coracle races, which used to be such an interesting and popular sport in Bangor were mentioned. When

Hugh Peel of Bryn-y-Pys offered to donate the prizes, it was decided to revive them. Mr Peel agreed to act as starter and Mr G. Goswell offered to be the secretary and the date was fixed for April. Any coracle fishermen living in the vicinity of Bangor were eligible to take part. The event created quite a stir in the district and among those present to witness the competition were: Lord Kenyon, Mr and Mrs Hugh Peel, Mr Peel junior, Miss Peel, Colonel and Mrs Dunn, Miss Dunn, Mr K. Dunn, Mr W.Y. Hargeaves, (Llanycefn), Mr A.J.P. Child, (agent for Bryn-y-Pys estate), Mr and Mrs Corbet, Mr Talbot, Mr L. Townshend, Mr and Mrs Fenwick, Mr and Mrs G. Goswell, Mr & Miss Fenwick, Mr Mort, Mr Payne, Mr Pennington, Mrs and Miss Williams and the Misses Bennett.

The following excerpt from the *Wrexham Advertiser* takes up the story:

> … in the first event there were nine competitors but the race from the commencement was confined to three men; J Johnson, H Rogers and C Johnson. At the Turn O'Dee the first two named competitors kept together until Turn o'Dee when J Johnson pulled ahead owing mainly to his opponent getting amongst the bushes. The second race provided plenty of excitement for the spectators. There were eight competitors: B Payne, R Hargreaves, C Hargreaves, S Dunbabin, W Poynton, Chris Thomas, John Lewis, and R G Fenwick. In the race Dunbabin made the pace and getting well away at the start he soon passed all those to whom he had to concede a start and won easily. W Poynton (scratch) started well and looked like passing all the others but he soon came to grief through overbalancing himself whereby his frail craft capsized and he plunged into the river. He swam out but his coracle continued downstream for some considerable distance before being recovered. John Lewis, the other scratch man, waited to render assistance if necessary, then set of after leaders with strong regular strokes and at Turn o'Dee was challenging Payne and Fenwick for second place, there being no hope of catching the leader. Owing to the currents he had shipped a lot of water and was compelled to pull into the left bank to empty his coracle. He resumed the race and overtook the other two, younger, men 100 yards from the finish to gain a very well deserved second place. Payne finished in third place and Fenwick was in fourth. At the conclusion of the races Lord Kenyon presented the prizes to the successful competitors.

In recent times, raft racing has taken over from coracle racing on the river. In 1976 when the Bangor Carnival was revived, the villagers organised a river spectacular as part of the celebrations. Items included a walk on water competition between pub teams attempting to cross the river on a line of pallets stretching across the river, and a tug-of-war competition across the water. Another of the events was a raft race with the launch site at Turn o' Dee and the finishing line at Bangor bridge. For several weeks beforehand, the sound of hammering and welding could be heard as competitors designed their own version of rafts – petrol drums and tyres were in short supply in the area for weeks prior to the race. When the event was repeated another year, Val Green, who was looking for a fellow 'nutter', persuaded the author to crew a raft constructed by her husband, Chris. The idea was for Chris to tow the raft with the girls onboard upstream to the starting point. However, when Val and Viv, dressed as Bunny Girls, arrived at the riverbank it was just in time to see the raft disappearing in the distance – he had forgotten he was supposed to tow the crew as well! By the time the girls had run all the way to the starting point the race had already begun. To the rhythm of Val repeating 'Just wait until I get the b**** home, I'll **** him', they powered their way down stream overtaking several competitors on the way, but the leaders had too great a start and they just could not catch them. If only the course had been a few yards longer – 'we was robbed'!

Illegal fishing

It was very tempting to fish outside the permitted times or in private pools and many men made quite a profitable sideline out of illegal fishing and there were many cases of poaching brought before the magistrates. Such as the case of Richard Griffiths, blacksmith, who in September 1874, was summoned for illegally fishing for salmon half-a-mile below Bangor bridge contrary to the byelaws of the River Dee Conservators. He pleaded guilty and was fined 6s 6d and costs and he had his expensive fishing net confiscated. At the same Petty Sessions, John Hunt and William Griffiths, fishermen of Bangor, were luckier when they were charged with netting salmon in the Dee, near Pickhill Hall, during the weekly close time at 8.15 p.m. Mr Pritchard, solicitor of Chester, appeared to prosecute on behalf of the River Dee Board of Conservators, and called PC James Taafe stationed in Cross Lanes, to prove the case. The officer stated that he saw the two defendants coming down the river in coracles, having a salmon net stretched across the stream. On seeing the constable they took the net up, and put it into Hunt's coracle, and went on down the river. Both denied they were fishing for salmon and said they were fishing for eels. The magistrates, after retiring to discuss the facts, gave the defendants the benefit of the doubt and dismissed the case.

The next month, the magistrates must have decided to increase the penalties for illegal fishing when Charles Johnson and William Williams, both fishermen of Bangor, appeared before them and pleaded guilty to four charges of using an illegal fine mesh net and for taking seventeen salmon. They were fined £4 and 10s costs, or fourteen days imprisonment. At the same court, Thomas Roberts and William Pointon, fishermen, of Bangor, were also charged with fishing at Graig Pool, near Pickhill, and for refusing to permit the water bailiff, Williams, to search their boat. They too were fined £4 and £1 costs or fourteen days imprisonment for each offence.

However in June 1908, James Johnson of Bangor was luckier when Mr Goswell summoned him for alleged illegal fishing. Mr Goswell said he was going to fish in the private pool of Mr Hugh Peel at Turn O' Dee when he saw the defendant in his coracle dragging a net. James Johnson said he was mistaken and that it needed two men in two coracles to drag a salmon net. He was laying lines to catch eels for which he had permission, as they were very destructive of salmon. The magistrates said that they had a very strong suspicion that he had been illegally fishing but that there was not enough evidence to convict.

The *Wrexham Advertiser* of 8 February 1856 published a poem *The Battle of the Deee, Fought at Overton, Feb. 2, in the year of Grace 1856,* by an unknown author, on a case of illegal fishing that had been brought before the magistrates at Overton just six days before. Its style is very similar to a lengthy one that was written twenty-two years later in praise of steeplechasing and may well have been penned by the same person who knew the gentry of the locality intimately. It is worth reprinting.

> But what's to do at Overton on the banks of the sylvan Dee,
> Where gather all the chiefs to-day of rustic chivalry?

Sure some impending clash of arms hath stirred the sluggish town,
Where crowd the excited peasantry and squires of high renown?
There's Cambria's foremost commoner rides over from Wynnstay,
And from the first to last stood by a witness of the fray;
There's brave old Panton from the Fron, who never seems to tire,
There's Dymock from old Penley hall, the parish priest and squire.
There's dapper Pentrebychan, and Warter of Bangor Bank,
And Puleston erst of Emral, but now of (leave that blank,
I don't know where he lives just yet) and Cotton from Marchwiel,
And the paragon of country squires the courteous Edmund Peel,
(You would'nt sneeze if he grows a-tired of Bryn-y-pys,
And give't you at a peppercorn rent on a comfortable lease).
There's Colonel Jones of Knolton with his bright and ruddy face,
And silvery headed Eyton, last of an illustrious race;
And the stalwart Drake of Malpas spurred and booted to the thigh,
And the doughty Marsh of Bangor who had sworn to do or die.
And there were venerable parsons who had come the fight to view,
The Douglas priest of Overton, and Smith of Bangor too;
And there were learned men of law, and one or two of rhyme,
And among them an old friend of mine-but I'll let him go this time.
And scribblers of the 'fourth estate,' who'll tell you all about it,
And verify this tale of mine should any of you doubt it;
There was Wyatt with his 'case'– crammed head like a digest made to walk,
And Lewis with his six inch tongue – the Gods, how he did talk!
And Ayrton with his sombre face, and one with a moustache,
Call'd Horsfall, whom today some came to save and some to smash.
Now ho! the lists are ready, and the magnates all are come,
Let every hat be taken off, and every voice be dumb.
Now bring the miscreants forth to hear the information read –
What say you plundering rogues to that? guilty or not guilty you plead?
Say did you on the day herein the laws of Britain break,
And with a net from out the Dee the aforesaid salmon take,
And throw it in anon quite dead, when it lay on its side,
Then poke it with your oar to make it down the current glide?
'Not guilty' – very well; and now the wordy strife begins,
And happy men their dole who bring thereout unbroken shins.
The unshaven and unwashed have called for vengeance deep and loud,
And round their doughty champion Marsh with eager faces crowd.
Within a sack two monster fish before the court are brought,
'Tis said that they had died because by Horsfall they'd been caught,
They bore his number and his mark upon a piece of tin –
Were numbered 35 and 6 upon a 'dorsal fin.'
And now the temper of the crowd like ocean rose and fell,
And for a moment who would win twas rather hard to tell.
On one side charged the great unwashed FOR AND AGAINST the laws,

On the other, well digested sense, and the battle seemed to pause,
When Panton to the rescue came, and in a moment more
The great unpaid gave their decree and the stern fight was o'er.
Ho! ye fishermen of Bangor where are now your lusty threats?
Ho! go and burn your coracles, and hang in your own nets;
That is if during 'Fence Days' your instincts you cannot school,
For you shall not poach the river nor abolish Horsfall pool.
But first discharge your lawyer's bill, and let the day you've lost,
Teach your children when they go to law not to count without their cost.

Fish were not the only things that were caught in the river. In 1871, William Thomas junior, and Samuel Stant were netting for salmon in the Dee, when to their great surprise they caught a fine otter, measuring three feet eight inches long, and weighing about 18lbs which they had great difficulty in landing. Two years later, Benjamin Poynton and Moses Young were out fishing by the Graig ford and they closed the net upon what they believed to be a very fine fish but imagine the surprise of Ben Poynton, on pulling it into his coracle, to find the 'fish' had seized him by the heel of his boot! It was an otter weighing 15 pounds and measuring 3 feet 10 inches long. In 1926, six otters were seen sporting near Bangor Bridge. With the heartening news that otters are once more returning to many British rivers perhaps it will not be too long before we see the return of these engaging creatures on the Bangor stretch of the river Dee.

On 22 September 1923, a rate was levied for the first time by the Dee Drainage Board upon the occupiers of land drained by brooks empting into the river Dee. This rate in some cases amounted to only 4d, but in others as much as £10, £12, and £19. There was much resentment and the rate was only paid after extreme measures were threatened. In the September there was an election at Bangor for five seats on the Board and amongst the candidates were Messrs Remer Sutton of Althrey Hall; Charles Jackson of Isycoed Farm; Eddie Tomlinson of Holt; Leonard Houlbrooke of Lane End Farm, Shocklach; Mark Darlington of Caldecott, Farndon; and Mr Shaw who lived Farndon way. The results of the election are not known.

The houseboats

In 1902, three houseboats belonging to Messrs Galt, Lee and Page, all of Liverpool, were stationed at Bangor. In April a party of over twenty Liverpool ladies and gentlemen paid a visit to inspect the boats and were intending to stay on board. However, the boats were quite unable to provide the necessary accommodation for such a large number of people so Mr and Mrs Cain Ratcliffe of the Buck Hotel offered to put them up and the party remained for four days.

A local man was paid to keep an eye on the boats and to prepare them for use each year. He would ensure that they were put in the water in the spring and taken out in the autumn. In 1905, John Dodd from Bangor was engaged along with a number of others, in getting one of the houseboats onto the river, when one of the rollers under the boat caught his foot then along his leg to his thigh imprisoning him under the heavy boat. He was quickly released and conveyed home. He was very lucky to only sustain badly bruised muscles and no broken bones.

The next mention of the houseboats was in a newspaper report of 8 September 1923 which reported that the Bangor Harvest Home and Flower Show was held in the rectory grounds. By

Bangor boathouses.

this time the houseboats had probably been replaced by boathouses as the report said that the sports had been held in Mr Tom Williams' field, 'who also threw open the houseboats for the use of the committee'. By October 1934, people were actually living in the boathouses as in that year Thomas Basil Woodcock was buried in Bangor churchyard and his address in the burial register was 'the House Boats, Bangor'.

The biggest boathouse was called *Maisie* where in 1934, Thomas Basil Woodcock committed suicide by hanging himself from a beam. According to Ernie Young, who was about fourteen at the time, PC Price asked him to come to the boathouses to give him a hand with something. When they opened the door, Ernie had a shock to see the body and he had to support it while the officer cut the rope. Ernie was only gingerly touching it and when the rope was severed the unexpected weight of the corpse caused it to fall backwards on top of him and both fell to the floor. This was an experience he has never forgotten. The next occupant of *Maisie* was William Fisher and both the 1936 and 1947 electoral registers give his address as 'The Boathouse'.

In 1949 it was reported in a local newspaper that there had been a fire in this chalet and

> Mrs Elwyn Morris of Kiln Cottages, tenant of the boat houses and other women, ran across the fields with buckets to fetch water from the river to put out the fire before the fire brigade arrived. But the fire had got a hold and the fire brigade was unable to prevent the boathouse occupied by Mr Lawrence from being destroyed.

The boathouses were situated on the Royal Oak side of the river in the second field. It has not been possible to discover who actually owned them, nor when the houseboats on the river became the boathouses on the river bank. The fire was the last occasion that there is mention of them in the newspapers, but it is known that one of the remaining two was seen floating downstream during one of the floods.

Ownership of the riverbank

The question of ownership of the riverbank between the bridge and Turn o'Dee was an ongoing dispute between the Parish Council, the County Council and the Quarter Sessions in the early part of the twentieth century which began when the Parish Council requested the County Council to crop the trees on the bulwarks on their land on the south side of the bridge. They claimed that the bulwarks abutting Bangor bridge were county property and should any damage be caused by the trees falling on the church or the grave stones, then the county was liable. The Parish Council added that in the County Council's *Year Book* of 1889 listed the land as County property. They also asked whether the County owned the land on the lower side of the bridge, abutting the yard of the Royal Oak. The County Council replied that they did not lay any claim to the land known as the bulwarks nor the land near the Royal Oak and repudiated all liability for damages that might be caused by fallen trees or branches. The County was then asked 'to define on a plan the slang of land at Bangor, which they claimed to own in past Year Books'.

In order to find out the historical facts about this contentious issue, the Quarter Sessions minutes were searched and a mention was found in July 1825 'that Edward Hanmer, the tenant of the land at Bangor near the Dee belonging to the County, have notice to quit, and that the same be advertised for sale by public auction'. In January 1826 it was ordered that 'the sale of the county land on the side of the Dee near Bangor be confirmed to the purchaser Joseph Edwards on his paying the sum of One hundred and eighty-two pounds the purchase money to the Treasurer'. That would appear to settle the matter.

Whether the land in the aforementioned paragraph was the same as the land quoted in 1840 in *A List of County Buildings & Property* is difficult now to say. It reads: 'A slang of land running north to south situate above the Bridge at Bangor and lying between the River Dee and a line of trees with mound on the west side of the churchyard,' and in October 1842 it was ordered: That William Jones let the slip of land between the churchyard at Bangor and the water works (the breech in the riverbank at Maes-y-Groes) to any person who will pay the most for it.' From these last two items it appears that the County did indeed own the land. Unfortunately, the oldest surviving *Year Book* only dates from the 1890s and contains no reference to this 'slang of land'. The dispute rumbled on until a joint meeting of the representatives of the various councils was arranged to meet and hammer out the issue, but the result of the meeting was not stated. Nothing further is heard about the matter, but it is presumed that the County must have won the argument!

Wrexham County Borough Council now owns the riverbank on the A525 side of the river, between the two bridges, having acquired it from Royton farm to construct the bypass. They let it on a 25-year lease to the Community Council for £100 and they in turn in turn sublease it to the Dee Angling Club, also for £100. In 2011, the Community Council laid out part of it as a riverside walk to create an attractive recreation area between the river and the A525. Funding was secured through the Rural Development Plan, the Countryside Council for Wales (CCW) and Bangor Community Council. The project involved creating a circular footpath, wide enough for wheelchair users, and a surfaced picnic area cum viewpoint with seven oak benches and tables. A full-size model of a coracle was made and displayed at the side of the walk as a talking point and two interpretation boards were erected, designed by local artists, one to show the local wildlife and the other to show the history of the area. This coracle has since been stolen and discussions are currently taking place about whether to commission a replacement.

The riverside walk.

Fatal accidents

Where there is water, there will always be accidents with fatal results. In the church registers, there are occasional mentions of death by drowning and when a coroner was called out to investigate a death, he would submit a report, which does not survive, with a claim for his fee and expenses which would be noted in the Quarter Sessions records. The victim is usually named such as in the inquest account of Michaelmas 1822 by the coroner, Peter Parry, on John Fenna (Phennah) who was 'casually drowned by sinking of a certain boat at Bangor', or the inquest report of Midsummer 1827 on John Davenport who was drowned in the Dee at Bangor. When the police force was formed the retrieval of bodies became a frequent unpleasant aspect of their role.

When a local boy was drowned in the 1930s, the villagers started a fund for the purchase of a boat, which was kept in one of the rectory outbuildings. This was mainly used to rescue people marooned by the regular flooding by the Dee, or to take food and milk to them in their homes. The problem was that if anyone got into difficulties in the river then it would take about ten minutes before the boat could be launched.

In 1956 after a young boy, John Glyn Mytton, was drowned in the Dee, the villagers determined that there should be no more lives lost in the river. The Bangor Public Safety Committee was formed with Councillor Tom Parry as chairman and William Jones as treasurer and, along with such people as Peter Roberts, Val Green and her husband Chris, they organised events to raise money to buy a boat. They rattled collecting tins at Bangor Racecourse to persuade race-goers to part with their money in the worthy cause and eventually raised £200, enough money to buy a shallow-draught boat with an outboard motor for £65 and to pay for the erection by craftsmen from the Cadbury creamery of a boathouse in which to keep it. Life jackets were donated by a Liverpool firm who also gave lifebelts to be erected on posts at strategic points on the riverbank.

In 1958, a service was held to bless the boat by the rector, the Revd Daniel, and attended by the archdeacon of Wrexham, the Venerable P. Jones-Perrott. Mrs Marda Ormrod of Pickhill Hall named the boat and after the ceremony, tea was served on the rectory lawn. Twelve men initially volunteered to undergo training to make up the three-man crews needed to man the boat with the aim of eventually training every able-bodied man in the village to handle the boat. The following year, when the river was once again in flood, the boat was used to rescue some sheep from a watery grave. The scheme, which was financed by voluntary donations had thirty trained divers on call at any one time. Neighbouring police authorities were quick to realise the value of the service to aid in searches and following the initial publicity in the press, the Cheshire Constabulary requested their help on a couple of occasions. The crew members often gave demonstrations and advice on lifesaving and one year were invited to go to Flint to give a talk and a demonstration launch and rescue. Afterwards each member of the crew was presented with a box of pencils bearing the following inscription:

Bangor lifeboat, L–R: Peter Roberts, Revd L. Daniel, Cllr Tom Parry, –?–, Marnie Thelwell, Val Green, PC John Davies, Richard Owen, Chris Green.

> Presented to the crew of the Bangor-on-Dee rescue boat on behalf of Flint rescue boat committee by the chairman, her worship the Mayor of Flint, Counc. Mrs C.E.M. Edwards, JP, in appreciation of services rendered at the Flint rescue boat demonstration Saturday, 9th March, 1957.

The scheme was a very laudable one, but suffered from one major flaw: a suitable launch site. The riverbank by the boathouse ended in a gravel bank and the boat had to be carried down the bank and over the gravel to reach the water. By the time the alarm had been raised, crewmen contacted and the boat taken out of the shed and launched, up to half an hour could have elapsed and the victim could be a long way down stream, particularly if the water level was high with a strong current. The boat was never used to rescue anybody and gradually deteriorated and the lifebelts were often thrown into the river by revellers after a night out in one of the hostelries.

In 1980, when a meeting of village organisations met to discuss the future of the boat and the boathouse and of the public safety committee, it was decided to disband the committee and to ask the Community Council to assume responsibility for river safety. It was proposed to sell the boat and associated equipment and the money raised, together with existing funds, was used for the purchase and installation of new life-saving equipment.

The riverbank and the maintenance of the boathouse became the responsibility of the Community Council and when the roof of the boathouse needed repair some twenty years or so ago, discussions with the Bass Charrington led to the brewery agreeing to maintain the area and the boathouse, if the tenants of the Royal Oak were allowed to use the building for such things as the sale of ice cream in the summer months. They have since kept the riverbank mowed, erected seats and generally maintained a tidy area. A wood carver provided a tourist attraction for two to three years demonstrating his craft outside the boathouse. The seats have since been replaced with tables and benches. The brewery sold the Royal Oak in 2012 and it is hoped that the new owners will honour the arrangement made for the upkeep of the boathouse and riverbank.

Flooding of the Dee

For centuries, Bangor has had to endure the problem of water overflowing from the river in times of heavy rain. Certain places along the riverbank were often breeched, particularly opposite Maes y Groes and orders for the mending of the 'water works' are frequently mentioned in the Quarter Sessions records. The bulwarks were built of the clay that underlies Bangor to protect the village from the water. It kept minor floods at bay but when the water reached a certain level, the water would overflow the bank down at the Graig.

The onset of the water was usually signalled by the milkman on his early morning round who, on seeing the water creeping up Graig Lane, would spread the word that the flood was coming. This would usually give the occupants an hour or two to move their valuables and retreat upstairs. There was never any panic, it was just regarded as a cross they had to bear. In bad winters the water often came in over the ground floor windowsills – the Old Smithy Cottage and some houses in Abbot's Way spring to mind – and the second group of houses in Abbot's Way were built slightly higher than the first ones for that very reason. On the Royal Oak side of the bridge there is a chain hanging from the first pier, which the older residents say was a good indication of the height of the river – when it was covered by the water, they knew that a flood was imminent. Many of the older residents take great delight in recounting tales and showing photographs of past floods to newcomers to the village and it was often a topic of conversation at dinner parties!

An indication of the speed with which the floodwater advanced is illustrated by the following anecdote told by Brian Hamlington of Overton from his first days as a plumber. Having not long completed his apprenticeship with Jim Woolley, he was working with Jim's son Ian maintaining all the council's serers in the hundred of Maelor when they were told that flooding was imminent. They made a series of regular checks on the holding tank in the field between Abbot's Way and Field Oaks which was 30–40 feet deep and worked on a ball-valve system so that when the

sewerage reached a certain level in the tank, it pumped it all up to the Graig tanks. The first check (at about six o'clock in the morning) revealed no problems and no sign of flooding. The next time they went, about two hours later, they had to put on wellington boots to reach the tanks. By ten o'clock they had to don waders to undertake the inspection. At noon they were knocking on Clem Robinson's

1947 flood in the High Street.
[Mike Stratton]

1947 flood at Bangor.

door asking to borrow his canoe – that was how quickly the water could rise!

In times of flood, coracles were used to transport food to beleaguered residents who had moved upstairs to escape the water. Baskets would be lowered from the upstairs windows to receive loaves of bread, milk, etc. They were also used to take the sick or infirm to a safe refuge, or to rescue animals from a watery grave. The meadows between Bangor and Overton bridge would be completely covered and only the tops of the hedges could be seen. Rabbits, driven from their burrows by the water, had to take refuge in the hedge tops and men in coracles were seen rescuing them. In March 1868 a newspaper reported that one man was said to have collected four pairs of rabbits, three brace of partridge, and three salmon. A welcome addition to the cooking pot!

One of the worst floods seen in Bangor in living memory occurred during the winter of 1947. It is still referred to by the 'old hands' as the benchmark for high water. The floodwater was said to have reached 'Abbey View' and 'The Cottage', the two cottages in Whitchurch Road where the 30 m.p.h. signs used to be. Following this, in 1951 Flintshire County Council and the Dee and Clwyd River Board presented a Bill to Parliament to enable them to carry out works at Bala to regulate the flow of the Dee to ameliorate the flooding and increase the flow of water in dry weather and to improve agricultural & fisheries extraction from the river.

The last time that the village was under water was in 1963/4 resulting in further work at Bala,

1947 flood in High street with the coracles.

Whitchurch Road with Mount View and Hillview on the right.

High Street looking towards the Buck Hotel and War Memorial.

since when it has not been flooded, although the A525, the Two-mile Straight and fields around are regularly inundated in winter. However, during the winter of 1999/2000, even the older members of the village were getting worried when the police knocked on doors advising everyone to vacate their houses and move to high ground as there was a danger that the bulwarks would not hold. This was the year that places nationwide that had never flooded before were suddenly underwater. In December 2002 major work was commenced by the Environment Agency Wales to raise and strengthen the embankments downstream of the old bridge as far as the Graig. This was followed in 2003 by work on the area between the two bridges, consisting of steel sheet piling, rock revetment and geotextile membranes being placed along the embankment to stabilise and strengthen the defences.

Eleven volunteer flood wardens have been trained and appointed, each one being responsible for a specific area in case of future evacuation and they have developed the Bangor-on-Dee Flood Warning, Communication and Action Plan which includes useful information and advice on what action will be taken by the various author-ities in the event of flooding. Hopefully the danger of flooding is now well and truly in the past.

George Stratton at Plassey House 1947. Note the high flood mark.

High water in winter of 2000/01 when people were advised to vacate their houses until the water subsided.

9. The Turnpike Roads

In the sixteenth century, the roads that had been partly maintained by the monasteries and partly by the manors were falling into disrepair after the dissolution of the monasteries by Henry VIII, and they became the sole responsibility of the manors. It has been estimated that a man on horseback could only comfortably average about twenty-five miles in a day and by the sixteenth century, it became obvious that the state had to interfere and parliament passed the Highways Act of 1555. This stipulated that each parish was responsible for the upkeep of the roads within their boundaries and that all able-bodied males had to do compulsory, unpaid, highway labour for four days each year, later increased to six days. All the materials, tools etc were to be provided by the parish. They had to appoint a man, the surveyor of the highways, to take charge of the work, under the supervision of the local magistrates. This surveyor, or waywarden as he was sometimes called, was appointed by the manor court and later by the church vestry annually, and like the parish constable, also appointed by the court, the position was unpaid. It was the surveyor's responsibility to report on the condition of the roads, bridges and pavements and to see that repairs were carried out on the stretch of highway lying within the parish. He often had no training for the job of bridge and road construction or of keeping the books and accounts. Those people with road frontage in villages or hamlets were responsible for keeping the highway clear of rubbish and mending broken causeway in front of their property, cleaning out their ditches and trimming their hedges or they would be presented to the manorial court and fined.

With the increase in road traffic, parishes and townships struggled to cope. By 1700 with the wide use of wheeled vehicles, coaches, carriages, and carts carrying heavy loads, many of the main roads were in a ruinous state and the maintenance of them was beyond the means of local parishes. Often people left money in their wills for the repair of the highway such as John Lewis of the Cloy in 1664 who left 'Five shillings towards the repair of the highway betwixt Bangor and my dwelling house'. To solve this problem, turnpike trusts were set up and the main highways were maintained by making a charge to supplement the local rates for the stretch of road within their jurisdiction. This money then paid for the officers of the trust such as the clerk, treasurer and surveyor but still using local unpaid labour.

By the mid seventeenth century, most of the major roads had been 'turnpiked' by various private Acts of Parliament and trustees had been appointed. The trusts' capital was raised from local landowners and people of note who would receive interest on the money loaned as a bond. Turnpike roads developed somewhat piecemeal nationwide with each turnpike trust only responsible for the main roads within its boundaries. Consequently some highways where the volume of traffic was greater, the increased income from the tolls was such that they were kept in better repair than others. In the meantime the local minor roads were still the responsibility of the parish.

The first mention of the Marchwiel & Whitchurch Turnpike Trust was in an Act of Parliament of 1767 that authorised repairs to the highway from Marchwiel to Whitchurch, Bangor to Malpas and Redbrook to Penley '... the roads being ruinous and in several places very narrow and incommodious, and cannot be properly amended, widened and repaired by the Law now in being.' The Act, which normally lasted for twenty-one years, was renewed in 1798, 1810 and in 1830.

The trustees had the power to appoint surveyors, repair roads, fix toll charges, set up toll bars, and erect toll keepers' cottages. The trustees, or turnpike commissioners, were drawn mainly from the local gentry or landowners with property or land in the three counties of Cheshire, Flintshire and Shropshire and included at various times; Edward Lloyd of Pengwern, Philip Lloyd Fletcher, several members of the Hanmer family, Sir Rowland Hill, John Jones of Llwyn Onn, members of the Kenyon family, John Leche of Carden, members of the Puleston family of Emral, Sir Watkin Williams Wynn, Simon Yorke and Philip Yorke.

In the preamble to the 1767 Act it stated that it was 'An Act for repairing and widening the Road from Marchwiel in the County of Denbighshire, through Bangor, Worthenbury and Hanmer, in the County of Flint, to a house in the Possession of Thomas Jenks, in Dodington, in the Parish of Whitchurch, in the County of Salop; and from Bangor aforesaid to Malpas, in the County of Chester; and from Redbrook to Hampton, in the said County of Salop'.

In 1767, 101 trustees were appointed, with a minimum of five or more required to make a quorum, and the Act stipulated that they should meet

> ... at the house of Thomas Edwards, known by the sign of the 'The Three Spread Eagles' [the old name for the Wynnstay Arms], in the Town of Wrexham, on that day fortnight next after the passing of the Act, and shall proceed to the execution of this Act, and shall then, from time to time afterwards, adjourn themselves, to meet at such Place or Places near the said Roads ...

Meetings took place at various public houses along the route; the Buck Inn (Bangor), the Emral Arms (Worthenbury), and the Hanmer Arms (Hanmer) being the ones most used but the [Red] Lion Inn (Marchwiel), the Buck Inn (Willington), the White Lion (Whitchurch), were occasionally frequented. The Bowling Green (Overton) and the Plough (Worthenbury), were each recorded as having been used once.

All meetings were held on a Saturday and a Special General Meeting was held in February each year at which the treasurer's and clerk's accounts were approved. Meetings frequently had to be adjourned because of insufficient numbers of trustees attending. The early records of the Trust have not survived and the first minute book dates from 1804 when the clerk was Joseph Stokes, the schoolmaster of the Endowed School in Bangor. He died in August 1808 and his successor in that office was Thomas Jones of Messrs Kenyon & Parry.

The charges were fixed by the Act and were displayed on each tollhouse, gate or toll bar and varied depending on what type of vehicle or number of animals passed through. For example in 1767 the tolls were:

> For every Horse, or other beast, drawing any Coach, Chariot, Landau, Berlin, Chaise, Hearse, or Chair' i.e. vehicles designed for conveyance of passengers 'the sum of Three Pence.

For working vehicles:

> For any horse, or other beast, drawing any Wagon, Wain, Cart, Tumbrel or Sledge, the sum of Two Pence.

For a horse or other beast not drawing any wheeled vehicle the charge was 1d. Cattle were charged 10d per score and other animals at 5d per score or *pro rata* for a greater or lesser number. Local traffic was exempt from paying a toll: worshippers going to church on a Sunday; people attending a funeral; ministers; farmers with cattle going to or from water or pasture, or with ploughs and other farming implements; soldiers on the march; mail coaches; carts of gravel or stone required for the repair of the roads, etc.

When the Act was renewed in 1810 and 1830, the charges were increased. No person was required to pay a toll more that once in twenty-four hours at any gate within the trust boundaries and payment at one gate allowed for free passage through all the other gates, but only within the area covered by the

EVADING TURNPIKE TOLLS.

WHEREAS by an Act of Parliament (3d. Geo. 4th. Chapt. 126.) it is enacted that if any Person shall with any Horse, Cattle, Beast, or Carriage, go off or pass from any Turnpike Road through or over any Land or Ground near or adjoining thereto, (not being a Public Highway, and such Person not being the owner or occupier or servant or one of the family of the owner or occupier of such Land or Ground,) with intent to evade the payment of the Tolls granted by an Act of Parliament; or if any owner or occupier of any such Land or Ground shall knowingly or wilfully permit or suffer any Person (except as aforesaid,) with any Horse, Cattle, Beast, or Carriage whatsoever, to go or pass through or over such Land or Ground, with intent to evade any such Tolls, or if any Person shall do any other act whatever in order or with intent to evade the payment of all or any of the Tolls, and whereby the same shall be evaded, every such Person shall for every such offence, forfeit and pay any sum not exceeding

FIVE POUNDS.

And whereas several Persons have of late, unlawfully evaded payment of the Tolls on the Turnpike Roads leading from Redbrook to Welshampton, from Marchwiel to Whitchurch, and from Bangor to Malpas:

NOTICE IS HEREBY GIVEN,

That all Persons who shall be found so offending in future, will be proceeded against according to law.

BROOKES AND LEE,
Clerks to the Trustees of the above Roads.

Evading Turnpike Tolls. [Hatchers Solicitors, SRO 1416 box 26]

trust. One of the last cases of prosecution for evading payment of the toll was in November 1875 when Thomas Gregory of Pandy Farm, Worthenbury was summoned at Bangor Petty Sessions for evading payment at the tollgate at Bangor. The defendant produced a ticket he had received at Pandy that cleared the gate at Bangor. Case dismissed.

It soon became the practice to rent out the tolls and, after placing an advert in the local papers, and displaying a notice on the turnpike gates and bars, an auction would be held, often at the Buck at Bangor. The 'Taker of Tolls' appointed by the trust was the person who made the highest bid at the auction for the right to collect the toll at all the gates and to appoint his own gate keepers. He was required to pay one month's rent in advance with payment of the remainder in monthly instalments, and to give the names of two people, approved by the trustees, to act as his surety. It is known, for example, that the tolls arising from the turnpike gates at Bangor were assigned to Edward Lloyd of Pengwern for £100 in 1769 and by 1807 Humphrey Edge of Bangor, innkeeper, paid £510 for the privilege. In 1824 David Platt of the parish of Hope, yeoman, made the successful bid of £817, and again in the following year but now described as 'of Bangor'. His sureties were Kitching Midgeley of Manchester, fustian manufacturer, and Publius Platt of Garside in the parish of Bradford in Yorkshire, toll collector. Four years later, David Platt, now of Hough Green Gate, Cheshire was once again the successful bidder and his sureties were Joseph Platt, of Cotton Hill, Salop and James Platt of Llandegla, toll collector. In 1832 the highest bidder was Joseph Platt, 'the present gate keeper' who proposed his father, David Platt and his brother, James Platt as his sureties. Nothing like keeping it in the family! If there was no bidder for the tolls, the treasurer, or the trustees, had to take the tolls and appoint toll keepers. In 1846 Edward Leah was the successful bidder at £843. After 1843 the auction raised a smaller sum each year as the coming of the railways affected the income from the tolls.

The gatekeepers appointed had to be of good character and above all, trustworthy, as the temptation to divert the tolls for their own use was great thus reducing the income of the taker of the tolls. It was also possible for the gatekeeper to let friends pass through without payment, and this undoubtedly went on. In June 1833, a letter was received from one of the gatekeepers that some such irregularity was occurring. The treasurer had to take charge of the gate and receive the tolls, whilst this was being investigated. The treasurer reported 'that the debt owing by Platt the keeper is £146 17s and that the said keeper was in gaol for other debt' and agreed to make inquiries into what means Platt had of discharging the debt. In 1861 James Platt, and his wife Elizabeth, were removed as keeper of the Bangor gate and from any employment with the trust. They were ordered to give up possession of the gate and house. John Wright and his wife, Hannah, were appointed as keepers in their place. In 1865 Mary Larkins, the keeper at Redbrook was removed and discharged and Thomas Davies and his wife were moved from Pandy gate and took over the Redbrook gate. Thomas Humphreys and his wife, Mary, then took over the Pandy gate.

For the repair of the roads, the Marchwiel and Whitchurch turnpike trust extracted gravel from various sites; one of which was a field in Overton Road, opposite Turn o'Dee, and known as the 'Gravel Hole Field'. The Dame Dorothy Jeffreys Trust owned this field, and the rental income was used to help fund a charity set up for the teaching of poor children within Bangor parish. The extraction of gravel frequently caused damage to the surface of the field and to the fences and gates and a sum for repair was allowed for in the annual financial report of the turnpike trust. Gravel was not the best stone to use for filling in holes as it was too small in diameter and it was only after John Loudon McAdam (1756–1836), a road engineer and surveyor for a turnpike trust in Bristol, published reports and books on road making that it was superseded. His reputation became nationwide as he and his sons and grandsons became surveyor and trustees of many other turnpike trusts. According to the *Dictionary of National Biography*, he had observed that when holes were filled with large stones, that carriages passing over them would crack and scatter them but that when stones of a certain minimum size were used the holes stayed filled longer! He laid down recommendations for road construction; a careful preparation of a well-drained subsoil with a slight fall from the centre of one inch to the yard covered by stones just large enough to put in your mouth, about six ounces, were used to a depth of ten inches, compressed by workmen, and consolidated by traffic.

The turnpike trust had taken notice of the recommendations and, in 1871, the trust ordered stone from as far afield as Penmaenmawr 'at a cost not exceeding £25,' to be laid on the Whitchurch–Marchwiel road. It was not until after the coming of the motor car, with its accompanying clouds of dust, that tar began to be applied to main road surfaces giving rise to the terms 'tarmacadam' and 'tarmac', and still longer before all the minor roads were covered. Some of the older people can well remember the condition of the minor local roads, describing them as being dusty in summer and muddy in winter.

The state of the roads was an ongoing problem not least because of the recurring floods and, as early as 1809, at a meeting held at the Buck in Bangor, an order was made that 'the present Gatekeeper be allowed £5 on account of holes in the turnpike road caused by the floods in the course of his year'. His income from tolls had been reduced owing to the state of the road being 'dangerous many Teams were prevented [from] passing the Gate.'

In 1831, the trust ordered that posts be put up between Porthwgan and Bangor, and between Bangor and Worthenbury showing the depth of the water in times of floods. In 1851 a surgeon from Manchester, John Owen, (1815–1902), visited the Bangor area to research his family and he wrote in his diary,

> Pursuing the road to Bangor [from Marchwiel] … the road sloped down into a valley and coming to a post by the roadside with figures marked upon it and the words 'when the water reaches this post the road is dangerous', gave indications that the vale was subject to inundations.

Unfortunately, no one had thought to take a photograph of one of these posts. The post near Porthwgan, or its replacement, was still there until about the time of the building of the new Bangor bridge in 1980 when the A525 was straightened and widened. No one can remember a post on the Worthenbury road but it would have been in the dip just before the junction with the Dungrey road and probably vanished at the time of the building of the railway bridge. There was a third one towards the Bangor end of the two-mile straight and this one vanished at the time of the strengthening of the flood defences in 2001/2. It is a little piece of history that has gone forever.

In 1872, the floods had been so extensive and the rain so heavy that the cost of repairing the roads, bridges, and culverts and other property injured by the floods of that year amounted to over £250 and it was agreed that the trust request an order from the Justices of the Peace for the payment of this expense out of the rates. The Pandy Bridge at Halghton had been completely destroyed and the surveyor brought in for the purpose, Mr Fairclough of St Asaph, the Flintshire county surveyor,

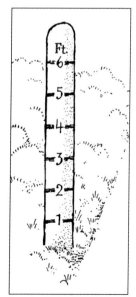

Artist's impression of one of the posts indicating the depth of flood water.
[Les Newland]

estimated that the cost of rebuilding that alone would be £150. The old bridge was only six feet wide and six feet high and the stream was twenty feet wide. He proposed that it be rebuilt with bricks to a width of twelve feet and a height of eight feet, the road over the arch raised two feet, and the parapet walls to be built with bricks with a stone coping. In September 1872, Sir John Hanmer of Bettisfield, summed up the feeling of the users of the road when he sent a letter to the clerk to the trust:

> We should be very glad in these parts of a little intelligence, as to when you propose to replace the Pandy Bridge. The short days and the long nights are approaching and the present mode of crossing that chasm is dangerous to man and beast, life and limb, goods and chattels.

The trust spent a significant part of their income on improving the roads, in particular in lowering the height of many of the hills along the route. In 1823 mention is made of building a culvert at the bottom of Porthwgan hill and that the hill 'be lifted and reduced' and a gutter paved along the side. Likewise in 1824, the surveyor was ordered to make an estimate of the cost of building a culvert under Dungrey bridge and raising the road above the same and improving the hills on either side. In 1825, the trust agreed to a request from the Overton Turnpike Trust to contribute £200 towards the cost of completing alterations to the hills at Kingsmills, Wrexham, as the Overton trust funds 'shall be deficient for the repair of that road.'

In 1835, Wrexham civil engineer W. Merritt was asked to produce a plan and report on the best method of improving the road at Bangor Bank; the first hill on the Bangor to Whitchurch road. The trust paid the owner of the adjoining land, Daniel Rowland Barker of Carden, £50 6s for part of two fields, amounting to two roods and thirty-five perches, taken to widen the road. The contract for the work was awarded to Robert Jones of Whitchurch for £180. In February 1836, the trust paid the surveyor of Worthenbury Parish £20 'in satisfaction of the injuries done to the roads in that parish by reason of the turnpike road at Bangor Bank having been stopped in consequence of the works there and no temporary road having been made'. The line of the old road can be seen where it passed immediately in front of Highgate Cottages, emerging by Bank Farm. This explains why today the cottage on the left hand side of the A525 road going towards Wrexham towers above the highway at Porthwgan, and the road to Worthenbury at Tŷ Graig is below the council houses.

In 1845, the inhabitants of Worthenbury and Halghton wrote to the local magistrates complaining that the state of the hills on either side of the bridge at Halghton were once again causing problems, 'that within the last few years more accidents had occurred and two people had been killed in consequence of the strength of the hills'. The Flintshire Court of Quarter Sessions made an offer of £100 towards the cost but the trust decided that this sum was not sufficient to justify the expense of the work. However they must have had a second look at the problem for they employed Merritt, to survey the hills and report on the 'best mode and cheapest way of lowering them'. He stated that nearly the whole of the road would need to be altered or improved for 100 yards on each side of the bridge. The trust was already encumbered with a debt of £3,990, but agreed to authorise the treasurer to defray the expense of lowering the slopes and improving the road upon the condition that half the sum was to be paid out of the county rates.

Left: Early milestone on the A539 Overton–Ruabon road.

Right: Milestone erected in 1767 on Wrexham–Whitchurch road.

Left: Milestone erected in 1820 on the B5426 near the Plassey.

Right: Metal milestone erected in 1898 on the Bangor–Malpas road.

By 1766, all turnpike trusts were required to erect milestones along the roads covered by the trusts, one mile apart. This allowed travellers to know how far they had travelled and also allowed stagecoaches to accurately price their 'stages'. These were made at first of stone with the distance, inscribed in statute miles, given to the nearest town or large village. One of these early stones can be still be seen on the Overton to Ruabon road (A539), 150 yards back on the left-hand side of the road from the junction with the A528 Marchwiel to Overton Road at Rosehill bearing the legend 'Ruabon 2, Wrexham 5, Overton 5.' There is also one stone remaining on the right-hand side of the A525 Bangor to Whitchurch Road, just past the turning for the A539 to Hanmer, opposite the London Apprentice Farm and a convenient lay-by. Carts and coaches trying to pass each other on the narrow roads often caused damage to the milestones and by 1822 it had become such a problem that an Act of Parliament was passed in that year to curb the outbreak of broken or battered milestones that littered the highways.

The later milestones were made of iron and in 1846, the trust ordered that iron mileposts be purchased and placed on the road between Bangor and Malpas. Some trusts reused the old stone posts and just attached cast iron plates to the front of them. One of these could be seen on the left-hand side of the Plassey side of the roundabout on the Marchwiel–Overton (A528) and the Bangor–Johnstown road (B5426). Unfortunately it was knocked down in 2010 by a lorry reversing when work was being carried out on the approach roads on either side of the roundabout. It was lying in three pieces at the side of the road in the hedgerow on top of the hubcap from the offending vehicle. The highways department of Wrexham County Borough Council were informed

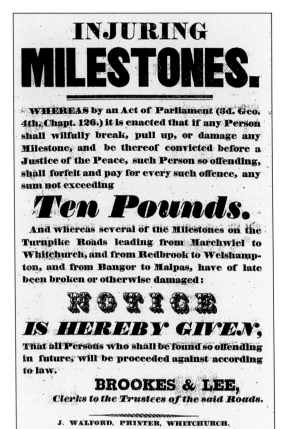

Injuring milestones.
[Hatchers Solicitors, SRO 1416 box 26]

and explicit directions given to its exact position. A verbal promise that they would look into the matter was made. Six months later they had still not collected the milestone and they were contacted once again. By March 2011 the stone had gone. The highways department was rung once again in August to ask how they were getting on with repairing the stone and the response was 'What milestone?' Nobody knew anything about it! It is a shame that a 200-year-old piece of history has been lost forever.

It is possible to trace the course of a turnpike road if a series of such posts are found. Many of them have not survived road widening but Cheshire County Council were particularly good in carefully erecting modern replacements in their original position in 1898 when the county councils came into being. One of these can be seen going from Bangor to Malpas just before Cuddington and again a mile further on just before the turning signposted Chorlton, both on the right-hand side of the road. Unlike Cheshire, Denbighshire and Flintshire County Councils just remove the posts when road widening takes place and do not replace them. It is a lovely quirky piece of history, but for how long before some philistine council uproots them when more road widening takes place?

The term turnpike is derived from the toll bar that was supposed to resemble a pike. The turnpike consisted of either a gate across the road, or a bar that was 'turned' or lifted to allow passage. Most gates or bars had a toll cottage or house, usually built projecting onto the road, to accommodate the toll-keeper and his family, but some just had a shelter for the keeper like the one at Fenns Bar that, in 1876, was described as 'no more that a thatched cabin'. At first there were only two turnpike gates, one at the junction of the Whitchurch and Ellesmere roads at Redbrook, and one at Bangor. The Bangor gate spanned the High Street to the rectory Lodge, with a second gate across the Overton Road. A toll-keeper's cottage, on the corner of Overton Road and High Street, served both gates. The cottage and tollgates are clearly marked on the 1840 Tithe Map of Bangor and on the 1870 Ordnance Survey map. The exact design of the toll-cottage is speculation as no drawings or pictures are known to exist but it would have been built when the turnpike trust was set up in about 1767.

When the tollhouse was valued on the termination of the trust in 1876, it was described as 'a poor house with no ground but what it stands on'. This cottage is commemorated in the aptly named, but modern, Turnpike House erected on the site about 1973. Another tollhouse was erected at Hollybush in 1822, and the gate spanned the Penley road with another across the Wor-thenbury road and was described as 'an old house with only one bedroom and no garden'. In 1850, a toll bar with house was built at Pandy, Halghton, on the Whitchurch road, 100 yards on the Bangor side of the bridge over the Pandy Brook. In 1876 the building was said to be 'a good commodious house with every accom-modation'. This last tollhouse was on the Bangor–Whit-church road on the right-hand side, standing right on the edge of the road, opposite Halghton Farm, just past the turning to Halghton Hall, and was only demolished in the 1990s.

Toll cottage erected in 1850 on the A525 Bangor–Whitchurch road at Pandy, Halghton. It was demolished in the 1990s. [FRO Sunter Harrison D/DM/1201]

Tollgates also had their uses in the catching of criminals – or runaway brides. Policemen, or outraged fathers, could enquire of the toll-keeper whether their quarry had passed through the gate. By this means if they had a fast horse they could go from gate to gate following the path taken. This is illustrated in a report in the *Wrexham Advertiser* of March 1872 when, by this means, the Bangor constable, PC William Mathews, succeeded in catching a thief who had stolen a horse and cart, by tracing him to Audlem where he was arrested as he was feeding the horse in the yard of the Combermere Arms. Sadly, it often proved very tiring for the policeman's horse if his quarry had a head start as is shown by an article in July of the same year when PC Edge of Overton was granted a £30 gratuity and a payment of £30 was given to a W. Roberts of Whitchurch as compensation 'for a horse that died from being over ridden in pursuit of an escaped prisoner'.

In addition to the tollgates in Flintshire there was also a tollgate and cottage over the Bangor bridge in Denbighshire at the end of the 'two-mile straight' linking the Whitchurch–Wrexham Road with the Bangor–Eyton Road. Many people think that this was a Roman road but it was constructed about 1820 to transport coal from the coalmines of Hafod and Ruabon. In October 1813 the following was inserted in the Quarter Sessions Minute Book.

> Whereas some of the committee for the building of Overton Bridge being desirous that a Tollgate should be erected at the end thereof and likewise at the end of Bangor Bridge and the subject having been referred to the court and the court having taken the same into consideration are of the opinion that it would not be expedient to erect any gate at either end of the said bridges.

This decision was reversed in as far as Bangor Bridge was concerned as a tollgate was built at the end of the straight, near the bridge and all traffic approaching Bangor from the 'coal' road turning left to Marchwiel would have to pay a toll.

This toll house was set in a triangle of land on the corner of the 'two-mile straight' and is called

Engraving by Henri Gastineau c.1830, showing the toll cottage that was located just over the bridge on the junction of the Two-mile Straight.

the 'New' Gate House on an 1831 plan of land bought by the Marquis of Westminster to distinguish it from the other Bangor tollgate. It would have been built around the time the 'coal' road was constructed and was therefore of a later date than the one over the bridge in Bangor. It has been depicted in the 1830 book *Wales Illustrated* which contains engravings of a series of views drawn by Henri Gastineau which shows the tollhouse as a single-storey building. This gatehouse was erected by a separate trust, the Bangor & Overton Turnpike Trust, which collected the tolls and was responsible for its upkeep.

In 1851, the New Gatehouse was home to John Edwards (aged 51) and his wife Mary (aged 46), both born in Marchwiel, with four of their children. In the 1871 census, the tollgate keeper was Thomas Bowker (aged 34), an agricultural labourer who had been born in Wem. With him were his wife, Jane (aged 40) born in Threapwood, and their son Thomas (aged 13) born in Bangor. In 1868 they had another son, Edwin, christened in Bangor church. In more recent times, the triangle of land on which the New Gatehouse stood was cultivated as a garden by Herbert Williams who had a butcher shop in the High Street that is now part of the Stableyard.

Unfortunately, the 1841 Census for Bangor has not survived but the 1851 census shows that the gatekeeper at the tollgate in the High Street was Joseph Hughes (aged 40). Living with him was his sister Jane and both were born in Malpas and were unmarried. On census night, they had two visitors staying with them: Thomas Pritchard (the Bangor school master) and a scholar, Thomas Ridgway (aged eight). Pritchard had been newly-appointed as the schoolmaster and was waiting for the widow of the previous master to vacate the schoolhouse. In the 1861 census, John Wright was the toll collector and was living with his wife, Hannah. Both were born in Audlem, Cheshire. Staying with them was their grandson, Joseph (aged ten), born in Market Drayton. The tollgate was still operating in 1871 as the census reveals that the keeper of the gate was then Thomas Davies and his wife Ellen, both born in Bronington. Living with them was their twenty-one year old son, John, who was a groom, born in Hanmer. By the time of the 1881 census, the turnpike trust had been dissolved and the tollgate and cottage removed.

Apart from the early years, the income of the trust was always inadequate to meet its expenditure. At a meeting in August 1810, the trustees stated that 'the tolls should not only equal the annual expenditure but that there should be a surplus of one hundred pounds per annum to diminish the debt.' It is doubtful, even at the very beginning of the trust, if this was ever achieved. At various times, to raise additional income, the commissioners erected new tollgates or bars at other places. A tollgate was placed on the Redbrook–Welshampton road at Bradenheath in 1813, only for it to be removed two years later as it 'not being so profitable as some expected and no gatehouse having been erected'. They tried again in 1843 only to have it removed one month later.

As well as the gentry, merchants and landowners loaning money to the trust, ordinary folk were encouraged to invest their savings in a bond knowing that the repayment was guaranteed on the tolls. The overseers of the poor of Hanmer, of Bangor and of Worthenbury had invested their charity money in the turnpike trust fund and the interest received went towards the relief of the parish poor. In 1845 the Revd William Cotton produced a mortgage on the tolls dated 13 June 1769 and claimed the payment of arrears of interest thereon since 1815 from the turnpike trust. As no interest had been paid since that time his claim was rejected. In 1856, Mrs Mary Roberts was luckier when she required payment of £100 due to her on mortgage of the tolls and she was offered £50 on account.

In 1857, the trust wrote to the Home Office for advice as to the best way of repaying the bonded debt of the trust and received the following reply.

Two courses appear open to the trustees to enable them to provide for the repayment of the bonded debt namely; either to receive aid from the parishes toward repairing the road, or to obtain the consent of the creditors to reduce the rate of interest. Sir George Grey thinks that if some arrangement as suggested can be made, the creditors may not resort to the extreme course of seizing the Tolls.

A letter from the local magistrate to the constable of Bangor probably dates from this time with its order '… to remove Edward Allman who has taken possession of the Bangor gate house, & put in the appointed gate keeper Jane Elliot'. In 1858, the Revd G.A. Marsh, rector of Bangor, applied for repayment of £500 due to the Bangor Club only to be told that the commissioners had no funds for the repayment of the money. In 1867 he was offered, and took, £100 in part payment.

The advent of the railway sounded the death knell for the turnpike trusts. As everyone flocked to use the trains, the roads gradually deteriorated once more as the income from the tolls declined, particularly when the transportation of heavy goods was transferred to rail. Like many others, the Marchwiel and Whitchurch trust struggled to pay its debts and by 1870 the list of creditors included Worthenbury Club (£400), Bangor Club (£400) and Bangor Poor (£25). In 1871, the clerk sent a circular to the mortgagees informing them that notice had been received from the Home Secretary of the intention to discontinue the local Act of the Trust and asking them whether they were prepared to forgo all the instalments on their debts.

In 1872, a petition was sent to the Select Committee of the House of Commons from the Bangor Old Men's Club signed by Revd G.H. McGill, rector and treasurer; Edward Massey, chairman; four stewards and the secretary, which stated that

> ... the members of the Club are Agricultural Labourers, in number about sixty, all old men, the youngest nearly sixty years of age, and that it would be ... very unfair to deprive them of the hard won earnings of their youth, at a time when the infirmities of old age are pressing so heavily upon them.

It went on to beg that the turnpike trust should be allowed to continue collecting the tolls until the creditors had been repaid. The rector and churchwardens added an additional plea on the bottom of the letter on behalf of the charity funds of the Bangor poor who had advanced £25. A copy of the same petition was sent from the Worthenbury Friendly Society, signed by the Revd T.H.G. Puleston (treasurer), Richard Griffiths and John Humphreys (stewards).

The trust was allowed to continue for another three years but was of no benefit to the Bangor creditors as the balance of the debt remained the same. In 1876, the Bangor Friendly Society was offered £50 in full payment of the debt of £400 and the Bangor Poor were offered £9 7s 6d of the debt of £25. The balance of £230 in the turnpike trust's funds was offered to Worthenbury Club to repay their debt of £400. Worthenbury Friendly Society and Hanmer Poor were paid out in full, the cost being borne by the rest of the creditors. Why Worthenbury Club were paid so much and Bangor Club was repaid only one-eighth of the balance outstanding was not recorded.

In 1876, the tollhouses were valued by J.H. Lees of Redbrook and advertised for sale. The Redbrook tollhouse was described as:

> Toll Gate house belongs to Trust, no garden: Is a good house, and if standing might be worth, with its outhouse and pigstye £45 or £50. Gate & Posts are worth £3 but it is a great question whether anyone will give it for them.

Because he owned the land around the gatehouse, Earl Brownlow purchased this for £35 to add to his holding.

A tollhouse was sold to Ellen Williams, wife of Dr George Harvey Williams of Wrexham as it was 'surrounded by lands belonging to the said Ellen Williams'. Although called the Hollybush

Sale of Bangor toll cottage.
[Hatchers Solicitors, SRO 1416 box 26]

gatehouse, this must have been a clerical error and would have been the one at Pandy as included with the house was 'the yard, gardens and ground, together with the wooden shed, bars, gate, and posts' and valued at £90 to £100' and we know that the Holly bush tollhouse is described by Lees as having no garden. Martha Hanmer wrote to the trust that she wished to buy the Bangor tollhouse, but the surveyor, Thomas Billington, reported that 'The Road Authority is unanimous in recommending that a portion of the site of the tollhouse should be thrown into the road so as to make the turn to Overton a curve instead of angular as at present.'

On 6 December 1876, the turnpike trust advertised the auction at the Buck Inn of the Bangor toll house by auctioneers Cooper & Son of Whitchurch. The auction was to be in two lots – the bricks and other materials of the Bangor Toll house and the tollgates and posts. The materials from the house had to be removed at the purchaser's expense within one month of the sale and the posts and gates were to be removed within one week of the sale.

When the Marchwiel to Whitchurch Turnpike Trust was dissolved in 1875 the Highways Board, accountable to the magistrates at the Quarter Sessions, took over the responsibility for repair and maintenance. The upkeep of the roads was still dependant on local, but now paid, labour as is illustrated by the County Surveyor's report to the Flintshire Quarter Sessions in 1883 that

> … he could find scarcely any improvement in the state of the road in the Hanmer and Overton end of the county. At the other end of the county where the roads were repaired – under the new system of highway boards – the roads were steadily and surely improving. Here he could not go in any direction without finding men employed on the roads, whilst at Hanmer end, he could go from Bangor to Redbrook, 9 miles, and thence via Hanmer to Overton, 7 miles without seeing one roadman. Under the new system advantage was taken of the right seasons for preparations, under the old, the men were kept on the farms as long as their services were required, the roads being allowed to take there chances. At the same time he felt reluctant to cut those defaulting parties and townships from the benefits of county and Government grants.

But he could not declare that the roads had been satisfactorily maintained. No explanation was given as to why one part of the county's roads was maintained by the old system and the other part by the new system.

In 1888, county councils were created which took over the responsibility for the main highways with a more uniform plan of maintenance and many of the tollhouses were demolished for road widening. An Act of 1894 completed the transfer of the remaining 'parochial' roads to the new district councils and brought to an end an era forever associated by romantics with the coaches, post chaises, runaway brides and highwaymen.

10. Transport

After the Romans left Britain many roads deteriorated into cart tracks that were rutted and dusty in summer and muddy in winter, skirting around fields and meandering between settlements. Each hamlet or village had to be more or less self-sufficient with its own baker, blacksmith, saddler, shoemaker, etc. as it could take too long for goods or services to be brought from the nearest town. When more sophisticated modes of travel such as coaches became common in the London area it was obvious that the other roads had to be improved and, as we have seen, the solution of creating toll roads worked for some time and the quality of the principal roads generally improved.

By the beginning of the seventeenth century, coaches and carriages had appeared but the first coaches were a most uncomfortable means of transport with no springs or tyres to cushion the passengers from the rutted tracks. By 1700, when the 'S' spring was invented, their use by the gentry and the richer members of society increased. Public stagecoaches were seen on most principal highways by the mid 1700s. These ran a regular service in stages between hostelries approximate every ten miles apart where the horses could be changed for fresh ones and the passengers could obtain refreshment or could get accommodation for the night. The affluent rode inside the coach, the less well-off rode in a seat at the rear or on top with the luggage! The poorer people still had to rely on farm carts or shank's pony.

A stagecoach inn was one that had many rooms for hire for weary travellers and with a large yard at the rear with, either space for the coach to pull in and turn around without backing, or with a rear exit. The inns in Bangor were not coaching inns as they did not possess many rooms for hire nor did they have a large yard. They did provide stabling for horses and the Buck Inn had a range of stables that were burnt down in 1937, along the wall that separates it from the rectory lodge. Towards the end of the nineteenth century a regular service was started by a stagecoach that ran daily between Shrewsbury, Ellesmere, Overton, Bangor, Wrexham and Chester. In 1905 it was reported that:

> Ye Old Town Coach continues to pass through the district daily and appears to be well patronised, and also to attract as much attention as ever. What a pity no-one can see their way to cater in that way for the less affluent residents and visitors, say, the Great Western Railway Company with their motor omnibuses, or any other regular service of cars to & from Wrexham.

By August 1908 the service only ran during the summer months and, as motor buses became more reliable and less prone to breaking down, it ceased to operate in 1913 as it just could not compete with the modern forms of transport.

'Ye Olde Town Stagecoach,' photographed c.1910 outside the Red Lion Inn, Marchwiel, with the licensee, Cain Ratcliffe (formerly of the Buck Inn, Bangor).
[Courtesy of Glyn Jones]

Bicycles

Since the advent of the turnpikes with the improved roads the bicycle now came into its own. The earlier ones of the 1860s with their solid tyres were known as 'bone shakers'. In July 1871, it was reported that the Eyton Amateur Bicycle Contest took place which was a race along the Ruabon to Bangor turnpike road for a prize of two guineas. It started at 8 o'clock over 2,500 yards which a Mr Lloyd won by ten yards, completing the course in 6½ minutes despite falling when he hit a stone. The main race was between Williamson, Lloyd and Edwards over a half mile. After a false start Lloyd again won, this time by fifty yards. Edwards was second by three yards. Upwards of eighty spectators watched the race.

The penny-farthing which succeeded the earlier 'boneshaker' in the 1880s never really caught on with its large, four or five-foot front wheel and small one-foot rear wheel, the rider being perched above the solid front wheel and, although there were brakes, a rough road or small stone could cause a very nasty accident. The Yorke family had a penny-farthing bicycle on which Philip Yorke, the last squire learned to ride and often gave demonstrations at fetes and carnivals.

The advent of the 'safety' bicycle in the 1890s with its pneumatic tyres and slightly smaller rear wheel caused a sensation. They were much easier to ride although the first of the new bicycles had no freewheel and coasting downhill presented difficulties when the wheels flew round. Riders often rested their feet on a special metal bar fitted on each

Philip Yorke, last Squire of Erddig, on a penny-farthing bicycle. [FRO D/E/3097]

side of the front wheel fork, although practice was needed to resume the spinning pedals afterwards. Bryn Hovah hill was the cause of many an accident with its sharp bends at the top and bottom.

It is hard now to realise how revolutionary it was for the ordinary person to possess his own wheels. The bicycle was a cheap form of transport that could be enjoyed by everyone and meant they no longer had to walk or wait for a carriage or cart to come along. They were suddenly released, free to enjoy their off-duty time, Sundays mostly, exploring the surrounding countryside. The police forces in Flintshire were slow to catch on to the benefits of providing bicycles for their men, although individual officers who could afford one were soon to be seen in and around the Maelor area on their bicycles. It made the patrolling of the rural district very much easier. As late as May 1895, at the Flintshire Joint Police Committee the question of reckless and dangerous riding of bicycles in Rhyl was brought up and, amid great laughter, someone suggested that the policemen should be equipped with bicycles to catch the offenders.

All over the country, cycle clubs were formed and men in plus-fours and woman, often in divided skirts or bloomers, were seen everywhere. One such club, the Wrexham Bicycling Club, later called the Wrexham Cycling Club was formed in 1877. Their itinerary would be published in the *Wrexham Advertiser* and members would gather in Wrexham and travel to different places, a run to Hanmer or Ellesmere via Bangor-on-Dee being particularly popular. Many other clubs such as the Chester Cyclists also liked the Bangor route. The *Cheshire Observer* of 20 May 1899 made the following comment:

> An early and enjoyable afternoon can be found in a circular route to Bangor Isycoed leaving Chester by the Wrexham Road and travelling via Rossett and Wrexham, the cyclists will find the

A cycle club in the Royal Oak yard about to continue their outing.

road to Bangor smooth and inviting. The interesting little hamlet on the Dee is looking its best in its early summer garb, and the river, viewed from the old bridge is always interesting. The return journey for the sake of variety is made through Worthenbury, Shocklach and Farndon. The whole distance from Chester Cross is about 30 miles. I am agreeably surprised the other day to find the section of road from Bangor to Shocklach wonderfully improved compared with its condition a few years ago and the roadside near Worthenbury was quite brilliant with a wealth of cowslips.

Cyclists' services were held in Bangor church and one Sunday afternoon in July 1901 the officials of the Wrexham Cycling Club carried out the arrangements with some 120 cyclists from different parts of the district attending. A procession was formed, marshalled by Ernest Foster of the Royal Oak, led by the Ruabon Volunteer Band, which marched through the village to the church. The curate, the Revd Ellis Rowlands, and the rector, the Revd Elrington Bissett, took the service.

Motor Cars

The first cars with an internal-combustion engine were introduced in this country in the 1880s but their use was restricted by the edict that they had to be preceded by a person carrying a red flag and their speed was limited to four m.p.h. (two m.p.h. in towns). This was repealed in 1896. The first mention of a motorcar in the Maelor area was in October 1899 when Mr Price, the Unionist candidate in the General Election, was telling some of his friends at Overton that he had travelled from London to Holyhead in twelve hours in his motorcar. What a revelation that must have been as not so long before it would have taken about five days to cover the same journey by stagecoach. The first person known to own a motorcar in the Maelor was Hugh Peel of Bryn-y-Pys who, according to a newspaper, had been seen travelling the district in his motorcar, in November 1900. A doctor in the Overton district was also spotted doing his rounds in his car in 1901.

The passing of the 1903 Motor Car Act made the registration of cars compulsory. The first person to register in the Maelor was Hugh Edmund Ethelston Peel of Bryn-y-Pys, Overton. In fact he registered two cars in November 1903 – DM 2, a 24-hp De Diebrich car with a grey tonneau body, weighing about 24 cwt and DM 3, a smaller 8-hp De Dion car with again a grey tonneau body, weighing about 12 cwt. Presumably the small one was for his personal use and the bigger car was to transport his family. In August of the following year he bought a third car, DM 71, a 16-hp, 18 cwt, 5-seater, Pritchetts & Gred in dark blue with light blue lines that on his insurance policy was said to have cost £750 new. In 1907, he also bought a 40-hp, Siddeley petrol car, in dark blue with

Hugh Edmund Ethelston Peel in one of his early motor cars.
[FRO D/BP/33]

white lines, weighing 32½ cwt that he gave up or sold in January 1911.

Not to be outdone, Lord Kenyon of Gredington Park registered his first car in August 1904, registration DM 74, a lead coloured 2-seater, 16-hp, FIAT that he kept until 1912. In 1905, he purchased a second car, DM 103, this time a 10-hp Vulcan 2-seater with a yellow body picked out in blue. He cancelled the registration of this car in 1907 and transferred the number to his third car, another FIAT, a 60-hp with a phaeton body in yellow with a hood and glass screen, which he sold in 1915. At the same time as he bought the FIAT he also bought a second Vulcan, this time a 14-hp car with a side entrance, tulip tonneau, yellow and blue underbody and blue lines. This last car was sold in 1913. Both these two gentlemen owned three cars at any one time. In comparison, Sir Wyndham Hanmer of Bettisfield Park was a bit slow off the mark as he delayed registering his first car, an 18-20 hp Wolseley until 1907 by which time the other two were purchasing their fourth vehicles.

Hugh Peel often employed men from Overton to act as chauffeur, men like Victor Lee who was driving car registration DM2 in 1907 when it was reported that the 'car skidded on tram lines going over Grosvenor Bridge, Chester, [the] front struck an electric light post and the back struck a tramcar going in the opposite direction'. Two years later, Edward John Hopley was driving the same car when a 'pony being lead behind a trap & as the car was overtaking, the pony took fright'. There was yet another accident involving the car in 1910 when it was being driven by a chauffeur, which resulted in the death of a horse and damage to a governess cart on a road leading from Marchwiel to Crabtree Green. The car was insured for £300.

The first person to register a motorcar in Bangor was the rector, the Revd Elrington Bissett, who bought a 6-hp, green, two-seater vehicle, registration number DM 213, in December 1907. Unfortunately the make of the car has not been recorded. He sold it in 1911. The rector was soon followed in the car ownership stakes in 1908 by Mrs Pitcairn Campbell of Deeside who bought a 6-hp Rover, followed in 1909 by Douglas Maitland King of Abbeygate Cottage who registered a 14-hp Darracg. The next rector, the Revd Paterson Morgan was reported as saying that, although a car was very useful to get around his parish, he had found there was not the same atmosphere when he stopped to talk to people as when he went around on foot, cycled or on horseback; as people were more anxious to get out of his way. However he did concede that it was much easier to keep in touch with Wrexham and St Asaph.

In 1903, the first of many complaints was made about the excessive speed taken by motors when passing through Bangor village with its sharp bends. Many early accidents involving horses and horse-drawn vehicles were caused by the noise and speed of the cars or motorbikes when they met, particularly on narrow lanes, when the horse would rear up depositing its rider on the ground and often overturning the trap before galloping off dragging what remained of the vehicle behind. In October 1908, W.S. Huxley of the Bangor Motor & Bicycle Works was riding his motorcycle down a hill near the Cloy when he met with a herd of cattle. The brakes of the machine failed to act and, to avoid hitting the cows; he flung himself off the machine and sprained both his arms in addition to other injuries. He was not put off motorbikes as he registered a 6-hp Antoine motorcycle with a black and brass tank for his business the following year.

In March 1905, there was great excitement in the village when a motor omnibus passed through Bangor and Overton, the property of the Great Western Railway Company. It came from Wrexham to Bangor giving a free ride to all who cared to avail themselves of the opportunity. On arriving in Bangor, a stop was made at the Red Lion Inn where it was boarded by quite a few for the journey to Overton, Wrexham and back. It was said to be a trial run to see if there would be enough interest to make it profitable, but it is not thought ever to have operated from Bangor although it did from Wrexham to Holt collecting would be passengers for Wrexham railway station. In the same year nothing more was heard about a motor-bus service from Wrexham to Ellesmere after the unfortunate experience at Bangor Races when they had to employ horses to heave it off the field after it had became stuck in the mud.

If you think that speed traps were a modern invention then think again. In 1906, it was reported that the Cheshire police had adopted a new method of timing the speed of motorcars. The method hitherto had been to station constables at $\frac{1}{8}$ or ¼ of a mile apart and within sight of each other. Under the new system, the police took up positions at milestones armed with stopwatches and printed cards. On the card they set down the number of the car and the exact time it passed them and the direction in which it was travelling. Afterwards a sergeant, mounted on a bicycle, went from one to the other and compared cards. If the time, therefore the speed, had been exceeded then a summons was issued.

The first cars in production were not very reliable and breakdowns were frequent. In July 1907 the *Wrexham Advertiser* reported that,

… a motor car which was on its way to Bangor, Caernarvon, on the Saturday for the use of the king [Edward VII] on his visit to Wales, broke down, strange to say at Bangor, Flintshire where it had to be put up at the Red Lion Hotel for repair. It was found that a cog attached to the axle was broken and the chauffeur had to telegraph to London for a new axle and also for a mechanic to execute the necessary repair. They arrived on Saturday and the work was completed the same day. The car continued on its way to Bangor where it arrived in time for the king on the following day.

Again in April 1906 that,

… a motorcar, said to be 12 horsepower, had a breakdown outside the village. Mechanics from Birmingham were brought to execute the necessary repairs. It restarted its journey to Wrexham only to break down again. It was reduced to a one horsepower vehicle when it was towed back to Bangor by a horse belonging to a local tradesman.

The East Denbighshire bye-election in August 1908 caused a great stir in the district with motorcars being much in evidence. Hugh Peel of Bryn-y-Pys sent no fewer than three cars to convey voters to the polls. One eighty year old man was brought from Eyton to Marchwiel in a car belonging to the Duke of Westminster. On being asked afterwards how he had liked the ride, he expressed himself as highly pleased with the sensation and he had decided that he would go up to heaven in it!

Many minor roads were still unsuitable for heavy traffic and during the bad winter of 1912–13, after snow had fallen, followed by hard frost, there were reported to be six or seven motor lorries stranded on the Worthenbury bank for several days unable to move. In 1912, the Wrexham

Omnibus Company began running a service from Wrexham to Overton, and in 1913, from Wrexham to Whitchurch (via Bangor and Overton) every Friday. In January 1919, the company started a regular service three times a week on Mondays, Thursdays and Saturdays. There were seven buses a day with the first bus leaving Wrexham at 8.15 a.m. and arriving at the White Horse Hotel, Overton at 8.50 a.m.. This then became the first bus of the day to go into town, departing Overton at 9 a.m., Bangor church at 9.13 a.m. and arriving in High Street, Wrexham at 9.40 a.m. The last bus from Wrexham left at 9.15p.m. and the return journey from Overton departed at 10 p.m. The single fare from Overton to Wrexham was one shilling (5p) and from Bangor 9d. The fare to Overton from Bangor was 5d. This service was of little use to those villagers who worked in Wrexham as it only operated three days a week and did not arrive in Wrexham until after 9.40 a.m.

In April 1916, the Rural District Council resolved that a letter be sent to the Chancellor of the Exchequer requesting that a tax be placed on motor omnibus vehicles owing to the serious damage done to the roads – so perhaps Bangor is to blame for putting the idea of a road tax into the

Wrexham and District Transport Co., Ltd.
'Bus Offices—6, Lord Street, Wrexham.   Telephone 182 Wrexham.

MOTOR OMNIBUS SERVICES

WREXHAM BANGOR & OVERTON.
MONDAYS, THURSDAYS & SATURDAYS.
JANUARY 11th, 1919.

		a m	a m	a m	p m	p m	p m	p m
Wrexham (High Street)	dep.	8 15	10 10	12 30	3 0	5 30	7 45	9 15
Marchwiel (Red Lion Hotel)	...	8 27	10 23	12 43	3 13	5 43	7 58	9 28
Cross Lanes ...	...	8 32	10 29	12 49	3 19	5 49	8 4	9 34
Bangor Church	...	8 38	10 35	12 55	3 25	5 55	8 10	9 40
Overton (White Horse Hotel)	arr.	8 50	10 49	1 19	3 39	6 9	8 24	9 54

		a m	a m	p m	p m	p m	p m	p m
Overton (White Horse Hotel)	dep.	9 0	11 20	1 50	4 20	6 50	8 30	10 0
Bangor Church	...	9 13	11 33	2 3	4 33	7 3	8 43	10 13
Cross Lanes ...	...	9 20	11 40	2 10	4 40	7 10	8 50	10 20
Marchwiel (Red Lion Hotel)	...	9 26	11 46	2 16	4 46	7 16	8 56	10 26
Wrexham (High Street)	arr.	9 40	12 0	2 30	5 0	7 30	9 10	10 40

SINGLE FARES.

	OVERTON.	BANGOR CHURCH.	CROSS LANES.	MARCHWIEL Red Lion Hotel.
Wrexham (High Street) ...	1/-	9d.	7d.	5d.
Marchwiel (Red Lion Hotel) ...	11d.	5d.	4d.	
Cross Lanes ...	9d.	4d.		
Bangor Church ...	5d.			
Overton (White Horse Hotel) ...				

The Wrexham and District Transport Company, Ltd., give notice that they do not undertake that the Motor 'Buses shall start or arrive at the Time specified in the Time Table, nor will they be accountable for any loss, inconvenience or injury arising from delay or detention from any cause.
    The Company reserve the right to alter the Times and the Fares without any previous notice. All Fares are collected in the 'Buses, and Passengers are requested to see that they obtain a new Ticket, punched in the section to which they are entitled to travel.
    All Children occupying seats must be paid for at the full scheduled rates, and Parcels occupying seating or gangway space will be charged for.
    All enquiries should be addressed to the MANAGER at the Local 'Bus Office, 6, LORD STREET, WREXHAM—TELEPHONE 32 WREXHAM—and complaints to the Local Office.

                                                          A. A. HAWKINS, General Manager

Timetable for the service to Bangor and Overton from Wrexham, 1919.

Chancellor's head, a levy that motorists have been complaining of ever since!

In 1922, the county surveyor conducted a seven day census of traffic using the Bangor bridge between the hours of 6 a.m. to 10 p.m. This was repeated in 1925 and 1928 and showed a steady increase in the volume of traffic.

	1922	1925	1928
Bangor Bridge	4,821	5,092	6,317

It is not known whether a count was only of motorised transport or whether it included horse-drawn vehicles. An increase of 271 between the first two surveys had shot up to 1,225 three years later. In 1923 and 1929 censuses were also undertaken of traffic using the Overton to Bangor road at Bryn Hovah but the results of these have not been recorded.

By 1919, the number of motorised vehicles had increased and drivers required a more convenient means of obtaining petrol other than driving into the nearest town and the first applications for permission to store petrol were made to the RDC in 1919. In December, Mr Higgins, the licensee of the Buck Hotel, was the first to be given permission, followed in August 1921 by Billy Griffiths of the post office. In 1924, when he renewed his licence Billy also submitted a plan for a 'Bowker' Outfit petrol pump for the storage of petrol. This old pump, with its shell-shaped sign on top advertising 'Shell' petrol was to be found outside the shop until the last quarter of the twentieth century and several people remember using the pump to fill up their tank. It was probably removed when Ken Rees was the postmaster (1968–74) and had certainly gone by 1981 when the Sunderlands took over the post office. J.T. Twiss applied for a licence in 1922 and his old pump is still to be seen in the High Street outside Hendy although, unlike the post office, the petrol was for his personal use and was not for resale.

In 1930, a licence was granted to George Thomas Griffiths to store 1500 gallons of petrol at Hollybush which was probably when the garage was erected there. It was demolished about twenty-five years ago. In 1931, an application was made by A.E. Peters of Birkenhead for the erection of a garage adjacent to Walnut House in Whitchurch Road and in 1935 William Austin Peters was granted permission to install a petrol storage and filling tank there. This garage has now also ceased to operate and the pumps have been removed.

Philip Humphries, George's father, started a taxi service in the 1920s for the people of Bangor before there was a regular daily bus service. He had two cars, one of which was a Ruston Hornby with a silver bonnet. For 6d return the taxi would take them to the Wynnstay Arms Hotel in Wrexham and park in the Wynnstay yard under

The old petrol pump still outside Hendy in the High Street.

Philip Humphries and his wife with their coal lorry.

the watchful eye of Billy Pickup, the yardman, ready for the return journey. He later gave up the taxi business and started a coal delivery service. The first person in Bangor to advertise cars for hire was H. Berry in *Bennett's Directory* of 1922 where he is listed as a motorcar proprietor of Laurel Cottage, Worthenbury Road and advertised 'an up-to-date car for hire for any time or distance with own driver. The only closed car in the village'.

A regular daily bus service was started in the 1930s by Williams & Hudson of Marchwiel who charged 9d return from Bangor to Wrexham. The driver stopped at every passenger's house and would help to carry in their shopping. When children came along, the mothers could not get their prams onto the bus and had to use the train.

Fire fighting

Many places such as Whitchurch or Wrexham would have had a system in place for the fighting of fires within the town. Because of the close proximity of houses everyone needed to be vigilant in case of fire as many properties were built of timber with thatched roofs. Early fire engines would have been pulled by hand or drawn by horses to the site of the conflagration. Because of the distance of the towns from any fire that might occur on a large estate such as Wynnstay or Bryn-y-Pys they found it advisable to have their own fire engines drawn by horses which would often reach a fire before the town engine arrived.

The Wynnstay estate had its own engine which attended a fire at 'Deeside' at the beginning of February 1904. It was reported in the *Wrexham Advertiser*:

> A fire broke out at 'Deeside', the home of the Hon Alexander Parker, brother to the Duke of Westminster's agent. The fire was discovered at about 8.30 a.m. in a bedroom at the front of the house and the flames spread rapidly. With the aid of willing helpers much of the valuable furniture was saved. The Wrexham Fire Brigade arrived in response to a telegram and the flames were soon brought under control. The Wynnstay Brigade (Sir Watkin William Wynn's) also turned out. All the principal rooms were practically gutted but the fire was prevented from spreading to the servant's quarters at the rear of the house and the outbuildings were unaffected. The outbreak was thought to have started from a large old-fashioned grate in this ancient house. The damage is estimated at £2000 and the house and furniture were insured.

Major Hugh Peel of Bryn-y-Pys, Overton had also bought a horse-drawn fire engine for his estate. It was a Shand Mason of London patent steam-engine and the first fire that it attended was in a stack of hay belonging to Thomas Williams, butcher, of Turn O'Dee, Bangor in July 1909. A report of the fire was given in the *Wrexham Advertiser*:

> An alarm had at once been given and Mr A.J.P. Child, agent to Mr Peel who happened to be in the village at the time at once wired for the Bryn-y-pys steam fire engine. The engine was soon

on the spot and with the plentiful supply of water from the river the fire was completely extinguished within an hour. Fortunately the wind, which was blowing very strongly at the time, was from the opposite direction and did not fan the flames. Mr Stokes, foreman on the Bryn-y-pys estate, had charge of the fire engine, and this being the first time the brigade had been called to a fire since Mr Peel had purchased the machine all remarked on the smart and expeditious manner in which they arrived and fought the blaze. Everyone felt that the machine was a great acquisition to the district and that the owner deserved the warmest thanks.

The Bryn-y-Pys fire engine on display as part of the Fire Historical Collection of the Fire Service College in Moreton-in-Marsh. [Michael Kernan, archivist]

The Bryn-y-Pys fire engine was last known to have turned out to a fire in 1937. The shafts were later replaced by an attachment for attaching it to a tractor and when it was no longer used for fighting fires it was used for an annual journey to the Bangor racecourse to fill the water jump. In 1947, it was called out to Bangor to pump out the cellar of the Royal Oak Inn after the river Dee had flooded the village. In 1950, Major Peel died and when the estate was sold, builder Tom Parry of Bangor bought the engine for £24 in memory of the great sportsman and planned to show it at carnivals and fetes. In its boiler there was still a bundle of creosoted sticks, while in a box below its body was coal ready to heat its furnace when the alarm was given. He towed it back to Bangor behind his car and gave a ride on the engine driver's seat to Miss Chris Spoor, a 72 year old Bangor shopkeeper who had always wanted to ride on a fire engine. On entering Bangor she donned the fire helmet and villagers were brought to their doors by the ringing of the fire bell. For some years Tom Parry's daughter allowed her two boys to play on it but, when Tom died it was stored in Wrexham Fire Station. It was their intention to renovate the engine and put it on display, but lack of money put paid to that scheme. It was finally sold to the Fire Service College in Moreton-in-Marsh, Gloucestershire where it has been renovated and is now part of their Fire Historical Collection and is displayed in the foyer of the building where it is much admired.

The Wrexham and Ellesmere Railway

The Cambrian Railway Company was formed in July 1864 by the combination of four lines including the Oswestry, Ellesmere and Whitchurch line. There had been a previous plan to run a railway between Wrexham and Whitchurch as a continuation of the Wrexham, Mold & Connah's Quay line some twenty years earlier, but it had been abandoned. The original route of the railway was to have been from Wrexham to Bangor Isycoed and thence to Penley, omitting Ellesmere altogether, linking up with the Whitchurch–Oswestry line at Bettisfield. Not unnaturally Ellesmere objected to this proposal and the plans were revised. Two engineers, Henry Robertson and Benjamin Piercy, were the prime movers in the railway scheme, but both died in 1888 before work was started, causing further delays. George Owen, a Cambrian Railways engineer was then appointed the engineer-in-chief and David Charles Jones became the resident engineer to oversee the work. The contractors were Davies Brothers of Wrexham and the value of the contact was £93,000.

After various delays, mainly caused by disagreements as to the exact route to take, work eventually began in June 1891 with the pegging out of the line, commencing at the Ellesmere end. An amusing incident that caused a great deal of talk in the immediate locality involved a certain freeholder and his wife who lived on a four-acre property on the outskirts of Lightwood Green. The line had to pass through the middle of their land and they were determined that the engineer should not put his pegs in the ground. When the time came for the engineer and his men to pass through, the freeholder and his wife stood at the gate of the entrance into the yard, bidding them defiance. The officer tried to persuade them by fair means, but without avail. As the work was bound to continue, four of the men were ordered to open the gate by force which resulted in a tug-of-war which the railwaymen won. This was said to be the only unpleasantness that had been experienced along the route.

By mid 1892 the whole of the line had been pegged out from the Cambrian system at Ellesmere to the outskirts of Wrexham, a distance of 12¾ miles, and the first sod was cut in a field off Caia Road, Wrexham by the Hon. Mrs G.T. Kenyon, the wife of the chairman of the Ellesmere & Wrexham Railway Company, in the presence of Frederick Soames, mayor of Wrexham. In January 1893, a number of boys employed on the new railway went on strike when their employers reduced their pay from 3½d to 3d an hour. So determined were they that in the end the company was obliged to look for non-union workers. By now the work was progressing very satisfactorily and at Bedwell the building of the bridge across the road had commenced, and in order to get the sand for the services, the navvies had commenced cutting the road from Marchwiel to the station.

In June 1895 a dreadful accident occurred when a youth named Alfred Young of Bangor, who was engaged on the new railway at Lightwood Green was run over by a lorry containing rails. It tore away the fleshy part of his leg and exposed the bone. George Beckingham, the ganger, did all he could to stem the fall of blood until Dr Richmond arrived and the sufferer was then conveyed to Wrexham Infirmary.

The railway bridge that spanned the River Dee near the Graig at Bangor.

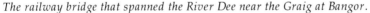

The line between Bangor and Pickhill required the spanning of the river Dee by a bridge, the building of which was one of the most talked about and controversial features of the railway for most residents. Many feared that the pillars would restrict the flow of water and cause the river to back up and cause worse flooding to the village. The bridge had a clear span of 195 feet and was one of the longest single spans in the country with two bow-shaped lattice girders resting thirty feet above the river on pillars that were built of pink stone obtained from a quarry on the south side of the railway at Abenbury owned by the contractors. This stone was known for its good weathering qualities. Pearson & Knowles of Warrington supplied the ironwork for the bridge, one end of which was fixed whilst the other was left free to allow for expansion. The Dee bridge carried a speed restriction of 25 mph and all stations were limited to 10 mph. Latterly there was a limit of 40 mph all along the 12¾-mile track.

The railway was single track for its entire length, with passing loops provided at Marchwiel, Bangor and Overton. But, in anticipation of increasing traffic in the future, all the viaducts: at Gwenfro, Abenbury and one over the Liverpool-Fyrnwy pipeline, as well as the over-bridges, were designed with sufficient room for a double track to be laid if required. The gradient on the south side of the river up Bangor Bank was 1 in 85.

Davies Brothers had purchased land at Abenbury in 1892 containing about ten acres of clay over forty feet deep and works were erected especially for the manufacture of the blue and red bricks required for the stations and some of the bridges on the line. Bangor's station was built on land purchased from the Trustees of James Mellor of Liverpool and was about ¾ mile from the village and was more convenient than Overton's Station, which was a 1¼ miles trek. The station was timber framed and clad, similar in design to all the stations on the line, and it had two long platforms with a passing loop. William Astons & Co of Wrexham were entrusted with the furnishing of all the stations. The Bangor signal box contained twenty-four levers and was in telephone communication with Overton and Marchwiel stations.

The station building was on the 'Up' platform and comprised a booking office, general waiting

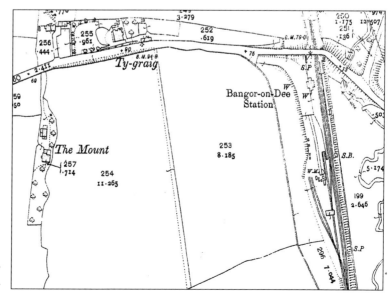

OS map of Bangor Station, 1912.

Bangor Station. [FRO Sunter Harrison D/DM/1201]

room, ladies waiting room and WC, with a gents WC in a little annex. The 'Down', or north-bound, platform on the left had a gothic-style tiny platform shelter with signal box tacked on to the south end. Bangor's station could be accessed via steps from the top of the road bridge as well as by the long station approach, at least on the 'Up' side. The station had ample horse and carriage docks. There was a goods yard with a small goods shed and coal wharves and cattle pens as the transport of livestock was an important part of railway business, at least in the early days.

At the end of May 1895, a special train journeyed to Ellesmere to make an official inspection of the line. On board were the directors of the Cambrian Railways: J.F. Buckley (chairman); A.C. Humphreys Owen, MP; J.W. Maclure, MP; Bailey Hawkins; H.P. Slattery; the Hon H.C. Herbert; Edward Davies; Alfred Aslett (general manager); George Owen (engineer); Mr Aston (locomotive and carriage superintendent); A.H. Aslett (engineer Wrexham & Ellesmere Railway), Howel Davies (Davies Brothers, contractors) and their guests. They found that the work was in a very forward state with the stations nearing completion. All the signal boxes were in process of being erected and the signalling equipment would be installed when the contractors had completed their work.

It was hoped to open the line to passengers by July 1895 but for one reason or another the Board of Trade inspection was postponed, but as everything was in place, a special Church of England excursion train was allowed to travel the line to Ellesmere on 2 July. It was arranged between the vicar of Wrexham and the contractors, and about ninety people were conveyed in a train of four coaches, including Charles Murless, the mayor of Wrexham. After a service in Ellesmere's Oteley Chapel, followed by the Wrexham bell-ringers ringing a quarter of Grandsire Triples, all were entertained to a tea at the Bridgewater Hotel. After several speeches by the mayor, Hwyel Davies of Davies Brothers and others, the party departed well satisfied with their day.

On 2 November the line opened without any formal ceremony as the earlier excursion trip had come to be regarded by many as the official opening of the railway. The first train consisted of five coaches and a guard's van. The third-class coaches were of the corridor type and were superior to the first-class coach in having the benefit of a lavatory. The train, with twenty-eight passengers on board, left Wrexham's Central Station amid a salvo of fog signals. At Ellesmere, a large number of people had gathered to watch the arrival and departure of the first train. Nearly forty passengers boarded the train for the first return trip. It reached Overton in eight minutes where it picked up a number of people and steamed into Wrexham in half an hour to be greeted by a crowd of well-wishers and another salute of fog-signals. More than 400 paying passengers boarded the train during the day from Wrexham, many of whom were reported to be carrying fishing rods. Although there was no official opening, specially invited representatives from other railway companies travelled in a coach during the morning for the journey to Ellesmere including William Pollitt, the general manager of the Manchester, Sheffield & Lincolnshire Railway Company; Mr Meldrum, the general manager of the Cheshire lines, and Thomas Cartwright, the general manager of the Wrexham Mold & Connah's Quay Railway, along with officials of the Wrexham & Ellesmere Railway and the contractors. At Ellesmere, they were joined by other friends and officials and all travelled back to Wrexham and the party then settled down to a lunch served aboard the train in the Central Station.

Push-pull engines were employed on the line and the original service operated five or six trains a day in each direction. By 1954, the line operated four passenger trains, usually with just one carriage, and two freight trains a day in each direction. The original fares, fixed by the Wrexham & Ellesmere Railway Act of 1885, were:

Passengers:

1st class	2d per mile
2nd class	½d per mile
3rd class	1d per mile

Animals:

Horses – beast or draught	2d per mile
Cattle	1½d per mile
Calf, pig small animal	½d per mile

Goods:

Coals, coke, etc.	1d per ton per mile
Pig iron, etc.	1½d per ton per mile
Sugar, grain, hides, potatoes	2d per ton per mile
Lace, furs, silks, china, glass	3d per ton per mile

OPENING OF THE WREXHAM AND ELLESMERE LINE.

THIS LINE WAS OPENED ON

SATURDAY, NOVEMBER 2ND,

And the following Train Service is in operation :—

	a m	a m	p	m	p	m	p	m
Oswestry..............dep	8 40	11 45			4 15		6 30	
Whitchurch	8 30	10 5	1 35				6 30	

UP.

	a m	a m	p	m	p	m	p	m
ELLESMERE.........dep	9 5	12 10	2 15		4 40		7 10	
Overton-on-Dee .... ,,	9 13	12 18	2 28		4 48		7 23	
Bangor-on-Dee .... ,,	9 20	12 25	2 40		4 55		7 35	
Marchwiel .... ,,	9 26	12 31	2 53	5 1			7 48	
WREXHAM (Central) ..'arr	9 30	12 35	3 0	5 5			7 55	

DOWN.

	a m	a m	p	m	p	m	p	m
WREXHAM (Central) ....dep	8 10	9 55	1 35		3 45		8 30	
Marchwiel .... ,,	8 17	9 59	1 39		3 52		8 34	
Bangor-on-Dee .. _ .... ,,	8 28	10 5	1 45		4 1		8 40	
Overton-on-Dee .... ,,	8 36	10 12	1 52		4 11		8 47	
ELLESMERE .... arr	8 50	10 20	2 0		4 25		8 55	
Whitchurch .... arr	9 25	11 30			5 5		10 15	
Oswestry....... ..——.... ,,	9 20	10 44	2 25		4 55		9 15	

For the Through Train Service to other Companies' Lines, see the Cambrian, Manchester, Sheffield, and Lincolnshire, Cheshire Lines Committee, and Wrexham, Mold, and Connah's Quay Companies' Time Tables.

Full particulars in regard to Passenger Fares, Rates.&c., can be obtained from Mr W. H. GOUGH, Passenger Superintendent, Oswestry, and Rates and general information in respect of Goods, Mineral, and Live Stock traffic, from Mr J. SHEPHERD, Goods Superintendent, Oswestry.

BY ORDER.

Oswestry, October, 1895.

Opening timetable of the Wrexham–Ellesmere line.

Bangor station was a busy station in its early years and people from the outlying villages of Tallarn Green, Sarn, Threapwood and Malpas would walk or cycle to the station to travel to Wrexham or Ellesmere and as many as 400 passengers would travel on Saturdays and market days. They would leave their bikes in the station before boarding the train knowing that they would still be there on their return. Farmers would send their milk, chiefly to Reece's of Liverpool, and when the milk fell off in the summer months they turned to cheese making. One stationmaster, J.W. Hobbs, remembered as many as eighteen vans being loaded with cheese on a Saturday morning.

The Wrexham–Ellesmere line was a friendly little line and the communities of Marchwiel,

Bangor and Overton soon got to know the regular drivers, station staff, signalmen and the permanent-way staff who serviced the line. Many, such as Sid Barclay, E.L. Mitton, Frank Packham and Bill Williams, lived in Bangor and are still remembered by the older inhabitants. The drivers of the trains would keep a lookout for any late passengers, usually a breathless woman pushing a pram with a child or two in tow, and the driver would even reverse the train back to the station.

Incidents on the railway line were thankfully few, but when derailments occurred they could block the track causing long delays to passenger trains. A less serious incident happened in 1898 when it was reported that by some means or other the wagons and engine on the Wrexham and Ellesmere Railway parted company.

> As this happened on an incline, the engine had to go at its very best to avoid being overtaken by the trucks. There was an exciting race, and the wagons looked the winner until Bangor Bank was reached. Fortunately, no damage was done.

An accident happened at Bangor on Saturday, 8 June1901 when Mr Wilkes, a relief porter from Oswestry, fell between an engine and the platform just as the train was moving out. The train stopped and he was conveyed in the luggage compartment to Wrexham Infirmary having sustained a broken finger and two scalp wounds.

The Bangor Steeplechase which is held in April each year certainly benefited from the opening of the new railway and the organisers praised the arrangements made by the Cambrian Railways who ran fifty-three trains on the Wrexham and Ellesmere line and over 3,000 tickets were said to have been issued at Wrexham station that first year. On race days, horseboxes were tagged onto every passenger train or made up into 'specials' at Ellesmere and Wrexham Central. On such occasions, a shunter from the Oswestry sheds would be sent to Bangor to help out. Fields near the station were pressed into use for temporary grazing, both before and after races, whilst horse owners awaited their own particular horse-box to be shunted into the horse-landing at the bottom of the 'Up' platform.

However not everyone benefitted from the advent of the railway and the motorcar. Many of

Train at Bangor station.
[FRO Sunter Harrison
D/DM/1201]

Train at Pickhill Halt with the Cadbury's creamery chimney in the background.

the villagers had cause to lament the passing of horse-drawn vehicles, as those who had any kind of building could get almost any price asked for stabling accommodation on race days and those villagers who offered accommodation to jockeys and stable hands found that now they often travelled to Bangor and back in one day and no longer needed bed and board.

In 1898, the RDC had to decide at what level to fix the rateable value of the railway. Until now the Cambrian Railways had not been rated, so to make up for the arrears the overseers had assessed the company at the rate of £90 per mile. The company objected to this as they said that the line could not afford to pay the 3½% it was paying its shareholders and this had to be guaranteed by other companies. Three months later the company gave in and decided not to contest the issue.

The question of the blocking of a public footpath by the railway was raised by Mrs Meredith Jones of Abbeygate and when approaches to the company did not produce the required result, she and other inhabitants engaged a Mr Kendrick a Wrexham solicitor, to act on their behalf. She claimed that a right-of-way existed from a point on the Whitchurch road close to her house, which ran along the right-hand side of Mr Done's field and came out by the station. The end of this footpath had been obliterated by the cutting of the railway track and required a bridge over a culvert. Mr Done was asked to place stiles along the path indicated on a plan and the railway company was asked to allow the footpath to proceed along the railway embankment nearest to Bangor instead of crossing the track and proceeding along the far side as had previously been the route. The company agreed to do the work if the parish council undertook to be responsible for its maintenance.

The trains soon acquired a reputation for unpunctuality as was sarcastically reported in a Wrexham newspaper:

> The Bangor Church Clock has to weather something besides storms. It was only 20 minutes late the other night. What an excellent clock it would make for the Cambrian Railway Co; it would suit their purpose to a T, and give them a semblance of punctuality.

The Cambrian Railways merged with the Great Western Railway (known as GWR or God's Wonderful Railway) in 1922. To help reduce the costs of running these rural lines the posts of stationmaster at Bangor, Marchwiel and Overton were cut in the early 1930s. In Bangor's case, it is thought that this may have coincided with the retirement of E.L. Mitton, thought to have been a class five stationmaster. All the stations then became effectively halts and the two signalmen stationed at each place were given the responsibility of maintaining the service.

When Cadbury's bought Twll Farm at Pickhill where they built a creamery which opened in 1937, the railway opened Pickhill Halt with a private siding to the factory in 1938 and as many as five wagon loads of chocolate at a time were said to have been carried. When war broke out in 1939 the factory was requisitioned by the War Office to make bars of 'ration' chocolate, containing no milk, as well as receiving and distributing milk to the north-west region.

During the Second World War the railway was closed to passenger travel from 8 June 1940 until 6 May 1946. It reopened again soon afterwards, but by this time everyone had become used to using the now reliable and regular daily bus service and sending goods by road and the increased traffic anticipated when the line was laid never materialised. It was always very much a rural line and, except in its very early days and on race day, never carried many passengers. Gradually the number of carriages was reduced until latterly there was just one. The railway fell victim to Dr Beeching's axe on 8 September 1962. The tracks were taken up soon afterwards and the line is now just a memory.

Stationmasters:

1895 – April 1898 William Lewis, born Aberdyfi, promoted to chief clerk in the goods manager's office, 1898.

1898–December 1899. Mr Williams who later moved to Carno, near Caersws, Powys.

1899–1906. Evan Griffth Jones (aged 26 he was boarding at Tŷ Graig in 1901), single, born in Llanwddyn, Merioneth. Awarded fifth prize out of one hundred entrants for the best-kept Cambrian Railways station in 1905. He resigned April 1906 to work in Wrexham as a clerk and had returned to live at Orchard House with his wife, Jessie, by 1918.

1906–11. Unknown.

1911. Ellis Davies appears as the stationmaster in the 1911 census, aged 25. He was single, born Ellesmere, the son of John Davies, farm labourer, and Martha. He boarded at Dongrey Farm with William Edward Owen.

August 1911–May 1913. John William Hobbs. Married to Winifred, he had daughter, Mary Dorothy Jane, who was baptised in Bangor church. The *Wrexham Advertiser* reported that he had been 'lately appointed to Bangor Station, brother of the famous Surrey cricketer [he was not], has moved to Fenns Bank station.' He retired as Ellesmere stationmaster in 1946.

1913–33? Ebenezer Lewis Mitten, (grandfather of the builder Gordon Mytton). He lived at Orchard House in April 1921. He died in May 1953, aged 85.

At dates unknown, Billy Williams, Joe Evison or Frank Packham may have combined the duties of signalman with that of stationmaster.

11. Law and Order

Prior to the development of the police force, maintaining law and order was the responsibility of the manor courts presided over by the lord of the manor or his steward. A manor could vary in size according to the lord's land holdings and could cover two or more parishes. Each year the court would appoint a man to be the unpaid constable from amongst the residents of the manor whose duties were many and varied and included: maintaining law and order; apprehending miscreants; maintaining the stocks; administering punishment; inspecting alehouses, apprehending rogues and vagabonds and the removal of itinerants and paupers not resident in the parish who were a drain on the parish resources. Consequently, it was not a popular post and frequently the person appointed would pay someone else to act on his behalf. Later, in many areas, the constable, as well as overseers of the poor and surveyors of the highways became parish officials, appointed by the church vestry, and under the supervision of the churchwardens and local magistrates.

An Act of 1405 made it compulsory for every village and town to provide stocks for the public display of people caught for such things as blaspheming, drunkenness or for breaking the Sabbath. In Bangor, mention is made in a bond of 17 April 1654, between John Davis Ellis of Dungrey, John ap Williams of Bangor, yeoman, and Humphrey Ellis of Althrey, gentleman, ' ... to make a good pair of stocks and whipping post, and also find locks, keys and other iron work.' The site of the Bangor stocks is said to have been in Overton Road, opposite the churchyard and near the junction with High Street. This was the most obvious place where people passed by and could witness the sight of minor villains and transgressors being humiliated. The use of stocks had generally ceased by the first half of the nineteenth century.

There was a gibbet at Lightwood Green near Overton. This was a post from which the corpse of an executed criminal was hung to deter other wrongdoers. The criminal would have been executed elsewhere and the body would probably have been that of a local person or of a person gibbeted at the scene of his crime. In 1898, when the land around the

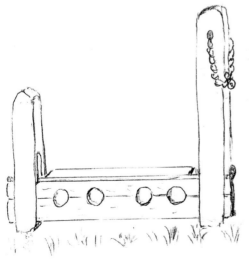

Typical stocks with whipping post.

163

Ruabon Round House, located alongside the road below Ruabon Parish Church, is thought to be very similar to the one at Bangor.

gibbet pole was being ploughed, several of the gibbet chains were unearthed.

In earlier times most places possessed a ducking stool but there is no record of one at Bangor, although they were common in the area. It is likely that one would have been in use in earlier times given the convenient proximity of the river.

In the nineteenth century Bangor, like many places, had a stone lock-up that was used as temporary accommodation to sober up drunks, or for holding prisoners before they taken before the magistrates. It was set into the wall of the churchyard, jutting out into Overton Road between the little side gate on the corner of the churchyard and opposite the site of the village stocks. This site can be identified by an eight-foot length of wall which is constructed of slightly lighter stone to that of the churchyard wall, opposite the boundary of Turnpike House and Rosecroft. The lock-up, which was marked on an early edition of the Ordnance Survey map, was described as a dome-shaped, round structure (hence it being sometimes referred to as the 'round house') built of sandstone and consisted of a single room about six or seven feet in diameter with a circular opening in the roof to let in light and, according to the Revd Puleston, JP, was 'built in the castellated style'. It sounds very similar in size and design to the one that can still be seen in Ruabon just below the church, although that one has small windows with bars, which may have been a later modification. There was also a round house in Overton as, at the Epiphany Quarter Sessions of 1791, a presentment was made by James Cooke, the high constable for Overton, that it needed repair as 'the slates being Many of them Blown of and the Rest Very much Loosened'. The repair to the Overton Round House was estimated at £1 7s 0d. Local magistrate Philip Lloyd Fletcher thought 'the estimate fair and not overcharged'. The court would authorise the local JP to arrange to pay for, and report on, the work. It was again presented as being in need of repair in 1816. The need for a new lockup was being requested as early as 1783 but it was not until 1823 that it was finally replaced by a bigger 'house of correction'. Another round house stood in Caergwrle, opposite the Castle Inn. It appears in an 1830s print by Henri Gastineau and was said to have a stone slab about a foot off the ground on which the prisoners could rest. It was demolished in 1887. Mold also had a round house that was mentioned in the Quarter Sessions records for Easter, 1814 and Hawarden had a single cell 'square' house, that can still be seen at the junction of Cross Trees Road and High Street.

The date of erection of these round houses has not so far been identified, but the Bangor lock-up probably dated from the same period as the one at Overton. It was certainly well before the formation of the police force. In 1851, John Owen, a surgeon from Manchester who came to Bangor researching his family, recorded in his diary a conversation which he had with a local resident:

The site of the Bangor Round House marked by the slightly lighter stone in the church wall.

On a vacant space of ground east of the churchyard and close to its wall [was] a dungeon building for the safe custody of prisoners previous to being taken before the magistrates at Overton. The man said 'he could not see why there should be any occasion for a building of that sort now that the village was so much quieter than formerly when every public house was of a night thronged with carriers, and one public house did as much business as all the stock do at present.

The lockup was heartily disliked by the villagers who for years had pressed for its removal.

At the Quarter Sessions in January 1851 it was ordered '… that the plans & estimate for work to be done on the lockup house at Bangor should be approved and the work commenced subject to the approval of magistrates of that division.' In July it was agreed that the sum of £58 18s was to be paid to Samuel Davies for building the Bangor lockup house. Thomas Roberts, a saddler who lived in Overton Road by the churchyard was appointed its keeper at an annual salary of 10s in 1852. This lockup was not a complete replacement for the old one and more of a renovation. In October 1855 it was ordered that the lockup house at Bangor be ventilated as suggested by the county surveyor. Twenty years later in a report to the Quarter Sessions of September 1875 on the state of the division, the chief constable reported 'that a strong room attached to the PC's station at Bangor is much required in lieu of the old round house of bygone age which is still in use there & certainly too damp.' At a meeting of the Flintshire Quarter Sessions in January 1884 the Revd H.G. Puleston, JP, called the attention of the court to the lockup at Bangor which he likened to a castor or pepper pot and called for its removal as it was very damp and dilapidated. He said it was an excrescence built half in the churchyard and half in the road. The chief constable, Peter Browne, when asked whether the lockup was a proper place to put a criminal, replied that 'it was all right for a criminal but not for a drunken man.' The deputy chief constable, James Bolton of Hanmer, said that it was a disgrace to civilization and that

… he had seen as many as seven people in it at one time during the (Bangor) races and if the court

Overton Court House built in 1886. [FRO D/BP/904].

had seen the state of the prisoners owing to the insufficient accommodation in a room only six or seven feet in diameter they would not allow it to be used again. It belonged to a past age.

After much pressure, the old lock-up in Overton Road was finally removed and the site was purchased from the County Council by the Revd Puleston, rector of Worthenbury, and presented to the rector and churchwardens of Bangor to be used for burial purposes.

Unlike England, which introduced the office of Justice of the Peace in 1361, Wales did not appoint them until the Act of Union in 1536. Up until the seventeenth century, justices of the peace, or magistrates as they are more commonly called, were appointed according to their position in society and normally came from the land-owners for this was one of the qualifications for appointment. They varied in quality from the conscientious that saw it as a duty to uphold the peace, to the downright lazy who saw the position as purely a boost to their social standing. In most areas, magistrates convened in rooms in public houses and those of the Maelor were no exception, meeting in the Bowling Green Inn in Overton (which was the tall building partly occupied, until recently, by the curtain and fabric shop, Inspirations, and now by a café) on the corner of Church Road and Station Road, or the first floor of the Buck Hotel in Bangor. Occasionally, the Hanmer Arms in Hanmer was pressed into service and there is an instance of the Buck Inn (now the Buck Farm) in

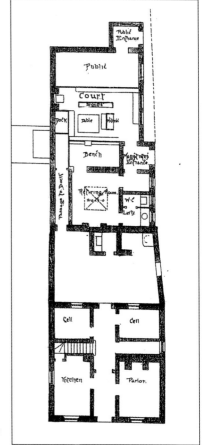

The interior plan of the Overton Court House. [FRO D/BP/904]

Willington being used. In the Maelor Division, the magistrates met on the first Saturday of every month and dealt with petty offences and the proceedings became known, as the Petty Sessions. One of the sessions held each year, known as the brewster session, had as the first item on the agenda the granting, renewal, or withdrawal of public-house licences.

By the nineteenth century, magistrates had become increasingly more professional and in many places special courtrooms or shire halls had been built. All the court proceedings were transferred to Overton in 1886, when a new courthouse was built attached to the police station on the other corner of Church Road and Station Road. Two or more magistrates presided over all matters with the more serious cases being referred to the Quarter Sessions which were usually held in Mold or Flint every three months. The Assize courts dealt with capital and other serious offences and were presided over by judges who travelled around their circuit; Bangor Isycoed being in the North Wales circuit. The Assize Court and the Court of Quarter Sessions were amalgamated in 1971 to become the Crown Courts.

Quarter Sessions

The records of the Court of Quarter Sessions for Flintshire only survive from 1720, but these are well preserved and are held at the Flintshire Record Office in Hawarden and consist of the quarter sessions rolls and the minute books. The minute books were the formal record of each session kept by the clerk of the peace, whereas the rolls consist of the letters, papers, bills and accounts for repair work done to roads and bridges, etc. that were dealt with at each sitting. After the end of each session these were rolled up into a bundle and stored.

Flintshire was divided into five divisions: Mold, Maelor, Prestatyn, Rhuddlan, and Coleshill, and a high constable was appointed to each division who was responsible for, amongst other things, the reporting of those roads and bridges that were in need of repair, obtaining estimates and presenting them in court. This was the case in 1759, when the high constable presented a report that the banks of the river Dee at Bangor 'being 400 yards in length and much broken and fallen in. Should be repaired for a sum of £52 18s and a further £20 18s 8d to repair the bridge'. In 1761, the estimate was given for the repair of Bangor bridge by Edward Pritchard, mason,

> ... there being about 50 yards of stonework destroyed by the flood. Viewed by Robert Williams, Richard Parry Price and Robert Davies Esqs & the Revd Mr Frederick Lloyd of Bangor. £11 10 0. Repairs to the battlements of the bridge £1 11 0.

In 1791, James Cooke, high constable, presented Worthenbury bridge, Halghton Mill bridge, Sir Peter Lloyd bridge, Queensbridge, Overton bridge and Bangor bridge as being in need of repair.

The high constables also had to present to the Quarter Sessions each year a list of the freeholders in the Maelor who were aged over sixteen and under seventy and eligible for jury service. The jury list for 1791 included Thomas Davenport of Halghton, George Davenport of Halghton, Humphrey Edge of Bangor, Joseph Stokes of Bangor and Edward Roberts of Maes-y-Groes. Woe betide any one of the jurors or the high constables who failed to attend the court when summoned without good reason. In 1772, the court ordered that John Thomas, one of the high constables for the hundred of Maelor, be fined forty shillings for non-attendance.

The court frequently dealt with cases establishing legal settlement. Each township or parish was responsible for relieving and maintaining the poor people of their parish who had gained a legal settlement by right of birth. The Poor Law Act of 1662 had set out ways in which a poor person could claim to be legally settled; a new place of settlement could be gained if a person had worked in the parish for more than a year or through an apprenticeship. On marriage, a woman took on the place of settlement of her husband. Children obtained settlement in the place where they were born, so that the parish constable was always anxious to escort any vagrants likely to give birth over the parish boundary and so become a burden on the next parish's rates. The churchwardens would apply to the petty sessions for an order to remove the person or persons concerned to his official place of settlement. Appeals from parishes to the Quarter Sessions against the order could be expensive if, as was often case, each side engaged attorneys. This was the case of Charles Capper who, in 1779, had been removed by the constable on the order of the churchwardens and overseers of the poor of Worthenbury, from Worthenbury to Bangor, which was adjudged to be his last legal place of abode. Bangor appealed against the order and after argument by the attorneys for both sides, the order was quashed and Worthenbury had to pay the costs of both the appeal and the maintenance of the pauper whilst in Bangor prior to his being shunted back over the parish border to Worthenbury.

Bastardy cases were sometimes heard in the Quarter Sessions if the reputed father did not acknowledge parenthood and/or appealed against the decision of the Court of Petty Sessions or had defaulted on payment. An example of the latter is the case of Ottywell Ralph, a fisherman of Bangor who, in September 1779, was brought by the churchwardens and the overseer of the poor of Worthenbury before the Quarter Sessions having defaulted on his payments for 'the relief of a male bastard child begotten on the body of Anne Bradshaw, single woman and whose child was now chargeable to the parish of Worthenbury'. He was committed to Flint gaol without bail until such time as he could find sufficient surety.

Many of the convicted cases were fined, but whipping was occasionally ordered for more serious or repeated cases of larceny or felony. On 15 of January 1785 the jury found Edward Cash guilty of petty larceny and ordered 'that he be stripped naked from the waist upwards and then whipped by the Master of the House of Correction at Hanmer between the hours of Ten and Two through the Market Place of Overton and afterwards to be discharged'. Nor were females exempted from this form of punishment as there is an example of Anne Rhodes who was ordered to be conveyed from the gaol at Flint to Holywell and that 'she be there whipped between the hours of eleven and one o'clock from the Cross to the entrance of the road at the Upper End of the same Town leading towards Brynford and back again, she being first stripped naked from the waist upwards.' Public whipping ceased after 1851 and private whipping was substituted instead.

Transportation to the colonies was another recourse of the magistrates in certain cases. In 1774 in a case of the Crown against Thomas Williams, the jury having found him guilty of a felony, fined him and ordered that 'he is to be transported to some of his Majesty's Plantations in America for the term of seven years'. The last time that a prisoner was sentenced to transportation by the Quarter Sessions was in 1852. In 1779, William Anwyl having been convicted of petty larceny, offered himself as a volunteer in his Majesty's service, most probably to escape being whipped! The clerk of the peace was ordered to write to Sir William Innis, commanding officer of the forces at

Chester, to request that Anwyl be taken into His Majesty's service and engage him for five years.

Flintshire police

Denbighshire had a police force soon after the Constabulary Act of 1839 was passed, but the Flintshire county magistrates felt the system of parish constables was working very efficiently and cheaply as unpaid parish constables were appointed each year. It was not until the passing of the County and Borough Police Act of 1856, which made the formation of a police force compulsory that Flintshire followed in its neighbour's footsteps. In January 1857, a Peter Browne of Plâs yn Cwm, St Asaph, was appointed as the first chief constable of Flintshire. A Welsh speaker, born in Abergele in 1813, he was the son of Thomas Browne a former army surgeon who had served at Waterloo and who afterwards practised in the St Asaph area before moving to the family estate of Brynllithrig in Rhuallt parish. Peter Browne was brother to the Revd M.T. Browne, rector of Bodfari and uncle to the Revd G.O. Browne who became the rector of Gobowen. After he was appointed, Peter Browne married in 1858 Frances Cockson, a girl some twenty years his junior, in Lambeth, London. When first appointed he made his headquarters in the Holywell division but then he moved his base to Rhyl and lived in Rhuddlan. As chief constable, he was responsible to the magistrates and made a report to the Flintshire assizes each quarter on the state of the police force, the type and number of crimes reported and the number of persons apprehended, discharged or committed for trial. He also reported on the various lock-ups and police stations that required attention, and the number, if any, of the vacancies in the force. The magistrates set the rates of pay and in the first year of Peter Browne's appointment they were:

> Chief Constable: not less than £250 and not more than £500 a year
> Superintendent: not less than £75 and not more than £150 a year
> Inspectors: not less than £65 and not more than £120 a year
> Sergeants: not less than 19s and not more than 25s a week

The strength of the force was initially to have been thirty but this figure was reduced to twenty-five which included the chief constable, two superintendents and three sergeants. However it was not long before it was increased to the original figure.

   The Flintshire Constabulary was divided into three divisions: Mold (which included Hawarden, Buckley, Caergwrle Penyffordd, Broughton and Saltney); Holywell (which included St Asaph, Flint and Rhyl) and Overton (which comprised the whole of the Maelor). Superintendents were put in charge of the Mold and the Holywell divisions and the Maelor was in the charge of an inspector. In the early years of the force there was a higher than average number of resignations amongst the men when they found the hours were too long or the job did not come up to their expectations, or they learnt that the pay was higher in another county. There were many dismissals for misconduct, such as for drunkenness or taking bribes, but things tended to settle down after the first few years as the chief constable honed his skills at picking trustworthy men. He said he preferred his men to be married as 'they were much more content and reliable after than before the event.'

   In December 1857, the position of inspector for the Overton division was advertised:

Flintshire Constabulary. Wanted: An Inspector of Police for the above named force. Salary 25/- a week, £50 per annum (for keep of horse), and uniform police clothing. Only men experienced in police duties need apply. Application in candidates writing, stating age, height, etc and enclosing copies of testimonials to be forwarded to the Chief Constable, Holywell.

The person appointed, with overall responsibility for the Maelor area, was James Dale Bolton, a Yorkshireman born in Askwith, who was serving as a sergeant with the Liverpool Constabulary where he was well thought of. He was appointed in December 1857 and initially lived in Overton until repairs to the 'Bridewell' in Hanmer were completed. In the 1861 census he was shown as being aged thirty-three, living with his wife, Mary (aged thirty-four). Living with them was a nephew, Thomas David Kitching, age six, born in Bradford. There do not appear to have been any children of the marriage. The nephew lived with them for a number of years before becoming the Hanmer post-master and, in 1907, relieving officer for the Ellesmere Board of Guardians. He was the father of Hubert Vaux Kitching, a well-respected surveyor and estate agent of Wrexham.

The county supplied each division with a cart, a harness, a saddle and a bridle, but the superintendents and inspectors had to find their own horses. When he was first appointed, Inspector Bolton may not have had much riding experience nor much money as he was a little reluctant to purchase a horse. There is a letter from the chief constable asking whether he had taken any measures to provide himself with a horse, and if not, why not? It took a second letter from his chief saying, 'Provide yourself with a

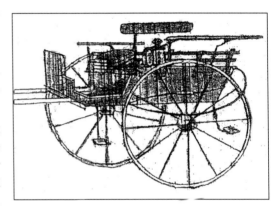

A spring cart was supplied to each division.

horse without delay' to galvanise him into action. Presumably, up until then, he had been hiring someone to transport him around at a charge to the police. However he must have complied with the order as there is an extant letter from the chief constable ordering a saddle and bridle from a Mr Henderson of Chester, priced at £3 13s, for his use. Soon after, he was to be found driving about the Maelor District supporting his officers in his phaeton. According to a report in the *Wrexham Advertiser* of June 1858, when

> … driving from Overton to Bangor at a rapid pace he was thrown out of the vehicle by Bryn Hovah, lacerating his head and hands. After righting the vehicle he set off again at a gallop and in Bangor came into contact with a cow, the property of Mr Edwards of the Star Inn. An altercation ensued.

After the appointment of the first chief constable in 1857, the other ranks were soon appointed to the force and were graded first, second or third class depending on their experience and aptitude. First-class officers wore a double stripe on their sleeve and second-class men, a single stripe. A first-class officer with a merit badge wore the badge above the stripes, an acting sergeant a single chevron with the merit badge over and sergeants wore three chevrons. Not only did the magistrates fix the salary scale for the county's constabulary but at first they also chose the uniform with each county adopting its own variation. They must have made a rather motley collection of men when a neighbouring police force requested help. There is a letter from the chief constable's office in December, 1857 ordering uniforms that included a blue, single-breasted dress coat (frock coat) with a stand up collar, trousers in an Oxford Mixture, a great coat, a cape and strap, a pair of boots, a stock and clasp (worn around the neck), a button stick and brush, a belt and plate, an armlet, a hat (similar to a top hat), and two pairs of gloves. The frock coat had the Flintshire Constabulary badge in white metal with the Prince of Wales feathers on the collar. Officers were also issued with a lantern, a pair of handcuffs, a truncheon, a Red Book, a daily book and an instruction book. It was not long after the formation of the force that the chief constable questioned the suitability of top hats for police officers and by 1869 had ordered helmets as well as top hats. It was not until December 1879 that the chief constable ordered tunics instead of the frock coats.

How the constables patrolled their beat is not specified, but they could not afford the luxury of a horse on their pay so they would have had to obtain a lift or walk – quite some distance in the case of the three Maelor men stationed in Hanmer, Overton and Bangor, although later on they would have used their own bicycle as the Flintshire force did not provide such items until very much later and then only one per station. The officers were expected to regularly meet with their counterparts in the Cheshire, Denbighshire or Shropshire forces at conference points on their beat on the county borders, such as Sarn bridge, Bangor bridge or Redbrook where they would liaise and exchange information. They had to keep a record of where they patrolled each day so that if the inspector needed to speak with them he could call at the police station and consult their daily record book – and woe betide if they were not where they said they were going to be, without a very good explanation.

Police officers were restricted as to where they could go when off duty and they had to seek their superior officer's permission before leaving the premises in case they were needed in an emergency. They had to apply to the chief constable for permission to marry and an investigation would be made as to the suitability of the women as was the case in August 1858 when a Flintshire constable, Peter Roberts, applied to marry Mary Lewis 'late servant at the Belvoir Hotel, Rhyl, & now living with Mrs M. Lloyd in 10, Church Street, Rhyl'. Superintendent Casey was asked to inquire into her character and connections.

In January 1858, Thomas McLaren, a former member of the Liverpool Constabulary, applied to join the Flintshire police. He was a former colleague of Inspector Bolton. After the chief constable received a good report of his previous conduct he was appointed as a first-class constable and posted to the Overton division under the direction of the inspector and put in charge of the Overton House of Correction. He appears in the 1861 census, aged thirty-six, with his wife Jessie (Janet, aged forty) and six-year-old daughter Marjory, all born in Scotland. He also had a son, John, who had been born in Liverpool and a second son, James, born in Overton. By 1871, McLaren was an inspector in charge of the station in Rhyl. There was a third son, Donald, who was also born in Overton. All three boys followed their father into the police force. In 1901, Donald McLaren was living in Tŷ Broughton with his wife and six children. He had been stationed in the Mold division before being transferred to the Hanmer area. His wife died in 1907 aged only thirty-seven and he died suddenly in 1910, aged forty-nine, leaving nine children.

In January, 1858, third class police constable (N°· 10) Francis Loughrin, an Irishman and a former member of the Manchester Constabulary who had joined the Flintshire force in November 1857, was appointed as Bangor's officer. The previous month he had been dismissed from the Flintshire police service after a misconduct report for drunkenness whilst serving in Mold but had been reinstated the next day after appearing suitably penitent and making promises to amend his behaviour. He was transferred from Mold to the Overton division and told to report to Inspector Bolton. He was then to go to Bangor where he was to be stationed and told to report to the local magistrate, Joseph Warter, who lived at The Cottage (now called Abbeygate Cottage) in Cloy Lane.

Inspector Bolton was not impressed by PC Loughrin and on 23 January received a letter from the chief constable's office asking him to explain more fully why he had written in his report of his 'entire want of confidence' in the constable. Two days later the chief constable received his report of drunkenness against Loughrin. When the incident occurred Inspector Bolton had been in Worthenbury on police affairs and he was asked to make the fullest inquiries and under no circumstances to overlook the most trifling act of misconduct. In February, there was a further report of drunkenness and on 10 March PC Loughrin was fined and reprimanded. He finally blotted his copybook in May when, in the course of escorting a prisoner to Flint Gaol, he allowed him to get drunk and, being drunk himself, to escape. This time the chief constable's patience was at an end and Loughrin was immediately dismissed from the force. Francis Loughrin is next heard of in the 1861 census living in Gun Street, Manchester, with his wife, Ann, and seven children, and working as a licensed victualler!

In May 1858, PC 28 William Lockwood became the next village constable in Bangor. Born in Keighley, Yorkshire, he had joined the Flintshire force on the same day as Thomas McLaren, both having been colleagues in the Liverpool Constabulary. He too was appointed a first-class constable and was initially sent to the Rhyl division under Superintendent Casey before being transferred to the Overton division on the dismissal of Francis Loughrin in May. Lockwood was a widower with a young daughter, Mary (born in 1854), his wife Judith (née Sharp) having died in June 1855. He must have been told by the chief constable to regularize his private life and he and Rebecca Stevenson with whom he had formed a relationship, were married in Wrexham Register Office on 26 October 1858. In the 1861 census William Lockwood (aged thirty-two) was living with his wife, Rebecca (aged twenty-five) and two daughters, Mary (aged seven) and Ruth (aged two), in Overton Road, Bangor. His wife had been born in Douglas in the Isle of Man and contributed to the family income by making hats.

It was PC Lockwood's responsibility to summon wrongdoers to appear before the magistrates at the monthly petty sessions. The first mention of him by name in the *Wrexham Advertiser* was in 1860 in a report of the proceedings of the Overton Petty Sessions when he presented Robert Darlington, Thomas Martin, John Edwards, George Butler and Thomas Henson before the magistrates (J. Warter of Bangor, C.R. Cotton and the Revd J. Puleston of Emral) for being drunk and disorderly. All were fined five shillings (25p) plus costs. According to newspaper reports, PC Lockwood was kept very busy in Bangor and the surrounding area apprehending drunks, breaking up fights, prosecuting people for riding without reins, catching robbers – and removing bodies from the river.

We know from the Bangor church register that there was a police officer named George Dutton stationed in Cross Lanes as he and his wife Mary had a son, George Edmund, christened in Bangor Church on 11 of August 1861 by the Revd Marsh. They had a further four children christened at the church, the last one in 1871. The police station was in one of the cottages at the Cross Lanes junction, on the corner of Kiln Lane and the Wrexham road. There was also a police officer based in Pickhill who, in 1863, was Henry Green. He and his wife, Harriet, had a daughter, Sarah Jane, christened in the church. These officers were both members of the Denbighshire force.

In 1863, Inspector Bolton was promoted to superintendent and, when PC McLaren was promoted to sergeant-in-charge in Flint in 1864, William Lockwood took his place in Overton and the Bangor position was given to PC 30, John Crackell Armer, who gave evidence in a case of accidental drowning in 1865. He must have joined another force just prior to 1861 as he is to be found in the census of that year, unmarried, living in 15 Kilshaw Street, Preston (aged twenty-seven), born in Dent, Yorkshire and giving his occupation as a police officer. In June 1862, he married Agnes Robertson in West Derby, Liverpool. There do not appear to be any children of the marriage. There is only the one mention of him in and around Bangor so must have been there only a short time as, by 1867, he had been moved to the Mold division. In the 1871 census, he is living in the Sealand area with Agnes but giving his place of birth as Burton, Westmoreland (not far from Dent, but just over the county border). By 1881, according to the *Wrexham Directory* of that year, he was the police constable in Caergwrle. He was made acting sergeant about 1881 and remained in Caergwrle until he applied for retirement in 1891 when he was granted a full pension having served for thirty-three years: twenty-one years in the Flintshire force, three years and nine months with Liverpool and two years and two months with the Lancashire force. He died two years later, age sixty.

In November 1866, PC 27 Henry Simpson, another Yorkshireman, was stationed in Bangor and was the arresting officer when he summoned the licensee of the Royal Oak Inn, Benjamin Bithell, to appear at the petty sessions for allowing drunkenness on his premises on 10 January 1867. In February 1868, Simpson wrote to Inspector Bolton at Hanmer to report

> I have examined the lock at the Bangor lockup. I went inside & locked myself in and found that I could pick the lock by pushing my finger between the staple and the wall so there is nothing to depend on but the padlock and that is a very common one of the smallest size. It is the only padlock I have for both lockup and pinfold and not fit for either being a kind of padlock that any person might have a key to fit.

Two new locks were required to be fixed before the races on 5 March.

In February 1868, Simpson was fined ten shillings for being seen in a public house whilst on duty and in June he issued a summons against John Jones, Thomas Green and Henry Humphreys for throwing stones at houses including that of the local magistrate, Mr Warter, and frightening the maids. Jones was fined one pound plus costs; Green and Humphreys were each fined ten shillings plus costs. Jones was also bound over in the sum of ten pounds to keep the peace for six months for threatening a police officer. Following the Overton Petty Sessions, the inspector wrote to the chief constable:

PC Simpson gave evidence very badly, in fact he is thoroughly frightened. The defending [?] advocate was very severe upon him for showing animosity against Jones for threatening to report him [Simpson] for being drunk in Marchwiel on the 1st May.

On 10 August, PC Simpson was called to a disturbance at the Bangor tollgate where a man named John Owen was drunk and abusing the toll keeper, John Wright. An altercation took place and Owen struck the officer who, after a struggle, assisted by John and James Hunt, locked up the prisoner. He was taken before the magistrates and fined with costs and repairs to the constable's coat, which had been split from waist to collar in the melée.

Despite his initial success in the post, PC Simpson failed to give satisfaction, presumably he had been reported once too often for drinking, and the chief constable wrote to him in 1868:

> If your conduct at the Overton Flower Show had been officially and formally reported, as it should have been, your instant dismissal must have followed. As it is far from my wish to blast men's future prospects, I will withdraw the notice and allow you to send in your resignation.

PC Simpson left Bangor and the police force and appears in the 1871 census living in Toxteth Park, Liverpool, age 42, with his wife and three children. His occupation is now given as a railway porter. By the time of the 1881 census he had died.

While awaiting the appointment of the next constable to Bangor, a problem arose regarding the police station as Inspector Bolton wrote to the chief constable on 3 October 1868:

> ... there are two cottages empty at Bangor. It appears that Wm Thomas, the owner of the cottage usually occupied by the constable has promised it to someone else. What his object is I do not know. He professes not to know that Simpson was leaving, or whether there was going to be another constable at Bangor in the future. This of course is nonsense. Mr Warter [the local magistrate] thinks it is more for annoyance than anything else. He is a very old man! The only recommendation his cottage had was its proximity to the lockup.

They managed to get another cottage in Overton Road, owned by Mr Cheetham, which was described in another letter to the chief constable on 8 November:

> Re the cottage at Bangor. I have seen Mr Cheetham and pointed out to him that the pump has not been repaired, nor garden railings at the back and also found coal yard wants repairing, door to outlet of pigsty is missing. House and privy require cleaning, all of which he promises shall be done forthwith. Now that the kitchen grate has been repaired I don't see much to find fault with. There is an oven!! and a slide on each side of the grate so that the fire can be either contracted or enlarged at pleasure.

In the meantime, the incoming officer, PC (25) James Wood, was lodging with the schoolmaster, Thomas Pritchard. He soon integrated himself into the village life and supported village events as, in 1869, he is believed to be the James Wood of Bangor who entered Worthenbury's annual flower show. He exhibited a model of a cottage, with a garden in front that was commended by the judges. In November 1869, he summoned Ambrose Sutton of Althrey for allowing a pig to stray onto the road. Owing to the prevalence of foot and mouth disease, the police had received strict orders to summon people for allowing animals to stray and thus allowing the disease to spread. PC Wood is last heard of in January 1870 when he summoned Charles Lea for being drunk on a part of the thoroughfare in Bangor. In February 1870, he was transferred to the Mold division and by census day 1871 (aged twenty-eight) was living in Gwespyr with his wife Martha. He was another police officer who was not Welsh, giving his place of birth as Colne in Lancashire, although his wife had been born in Tremeirchion. The chief constable dismissed him from the service for gross violation and neglect of duty in 1872 and nothing further is known about him.

On 19 May 1869 there was a disturbance at Leeswood Green Colliery when the miners took action against John Young, the underground manager, with whom they had a grievance. For some time he was said to favour his relatives and friends when allocating duties involving overtime which made a considerable difference to their pay. A crowd of 200–300 people had forced the hated manager out of his house towards Hope station, intending to send him to Chester, but two policemen managed to rescue him from the crowd. The men had removed everything from his house and deposited the articles in the railway wharf, all the while encouraged by their women folk who were clapping and cheering. To prevent the colliers from loading his goods onto a train, the manager, being forewarned, took the precaution of clearing the wharf of empty trucks. The station manager, on asking where the goods were to be sent received the reply, 'Send them to Birkenhead that he [Young] might go over to America with them'. Two or three police constables witnessed this but, as the crowd had by this time grown to around 500, many of whom were armed with sticks, stones and other missiles, they took the view that 'discretion was the better part of valour' and stood by and watched whilst making note of the chief actors. The local magistrates issued eight warrants for the arrest of the ringleaders who were to appear at a special quarter sessions.

A week later, on the day the first of the prisoners was being brought to the court, a large number of miners and supporters thronged into Mold for the hearing and the crowd was estimated as being around 1,000, many of them armed with sticks and bludgeons, the number being swelled by men from neighbouring collieries. Anticipating trouble, the chief constable issued orders that the whole strength of the force should assemble at Mold that day and some thirty-nine or forty officers were in the town at an early hour on Wednesday. Superintendents Thomas (Mold), Adams (Rhyl) and Bolton (Hanmer), with all their inspectors, sergeants and constables in their respective divisions appeared in their new helmets, and armed with cutlasses. William Lockwood was made an acting sergeant for the occasion. Anticipating trouble, the chief constable also requested the presence of the militia from Chester to help control the crowd.

Afterwards at a meeting of the Flintshire Assizes on 26 June, the Chief Constable Browne reported on the police officers that had been injured in the colliery disturbance. Of the men known to have been based in the Maelor district, Inspector Bolton had suffered contused wounds to the spine, left shoulder blade and neck; Acting Sergeant Lockwood had contused wounds on various parts of the body, an injured left hand and right knee joint; PC William Matthews suffered a right knee joint contused wound and was still lame from the injury; PC John Armer had suffered a scalp wound and bruising. He also reported that:

Nine helmets were cut open in the affray, and about the same number of uniform dress coats were so stained and saturated with blood and damaged that they were almost worthless. The men are doing well, and have with one or two exceptions assumed pretty nearly their usual routine duty.

In March 1870, at Overton Petty Sessions an eighteen-year-old girl applied for an affiliation order against Sergeant Lockwood, claiming that he was the father of her child. She had entered into service with the family in April of the previous year and had brought a charge of rape against him two months later but the magistrates had dismissed the case. Now she sought to prove that her child, the outcome of the rape, was his. It was contended that it was a conspiracy to ruin a meritorious officer. After a long deliberation the court chairman, Mr Warter, said they had given great attention to the case and had come to the conclusion that there was insufficient evidence to satisfy the requirements of the law. However, so much interest had been manifested in the case that it was thought wise to move Sergeant Lockwood to another division and in 1871 he is listed in the census as living with his wife and younger daughter in Saltney. He was later moved to Hawarden and died in December 1880. Reporting his death to the Flintshire Quarter Sessions in January 1881, the Chief Constable described him as

A most efficient and meritorious officer had died. He had served the force for 22 years and 10 months. An allowance of £78 was given to his widow [a years salary]. Mr Gladstone said the deceased had merits so great that they were quite exceptional. There was but one opinion in Hawarden as to his merits, and he had during his stay there vastly improved the character of the place.

He was buried in Hawarden churchyard. His widow, Rebecca, and Ruth, a medical nurse, appear in the 1881 census in Gwyddelwern, Cynwyd Fawr, Merionethshire, but by 1884 Ruth had died and on William Lockwood's gravestone the inscription states that she was interred in Kirk Braddan in the Isle of Man.

No doubt William Lockwood was suspended from duty whilst the rape case was being brought against him as in April 1869 a PC James Edge had replaced him in Overton and was active in the area. On 9 April 1870, Edge was summoning George Stanley, 'a seedy looking customer' to appear at Overton Petty Sessions for passing base coins at Bangor Races.

In February 1870, PC (16) William Matthews, a native of Ireland, replaced PC James Wood as the Bangor constable. In the 1871 census, he was living in Overton Road with his wife, Mary Anne, and their five children. Before being transferred to Bangor, Matthews had been stationed in the Hanmer area, firstly in Bronington and then, when his family outgrew the small, damp police station, to Ty Broughton for five or six years, where his eldest four children were born. He was very diligent in pursuing criminals and arresting the obligatory drunks. His job could, on occasion, be dangerous as was reported in August 1872, when several men savagely attacked him near Cross Lanes. 'He received a blow to the nose, it is supposed by a brick, almost entirely demolishing that organ, and he was rendered insensible'. A large reward was offered for the apprehension of the assailants by the magistrates and members of the public also promised substantial sums.

In May 1874, PC Edge of Overton resigned from the police force due to ill health and PC

Matthews was appointed in his place. In May 1875, Edge died after a long and painful illness and it was reported that the funeral was attended

> … by tradesmen of the town, Mr Matthews, the present police officer and the officers of Bangor and Hanmer. The deceased was only 53 years of age and had been a member of the police force upwards of 15 years. He had been a teetotaller for more than 16 years and in consequence was always a little severe on those who happened to indulge too freely in intoxicating drinks.

PC Matthews was a popular and well-liked police officer and, when he was promoted to acting sergeant and moved to Overton in 1874, the inhabitants of Bangor presented him with a handsome inscribed silver watch as a token of their regard. In the evening, a public dinner was held in the Buck Inn when, under the chairmanship of the Revd McGill, a large company of well-wishers enjoyed a good meal and entertainment. He only remained in Overton for a couple of years before being promoted to full sergeant and moved to the Rhyl division where he was stationed in Holywell. He appears to have remained as sergeant for the remainder of his police career. His health was not good and he was known to suffer with stomach problems and he had several periods of sick leave. He eventually applied for early retirement when he was fifty-seven years of age in 1891. He had served thirty-two years and nine months with the Flintshire police force and four years and two months with the Irish constabulary. His pay was £85 3s per annum and he was granted a pension of two-thirds of his annual pay, amounting to £56 15s 6d.

Third-class officer PC21 Walter Pagan, much against his wishes, was moved from St Asaph to Bangor in April 1874. He promptly sent in his resignation from the force but was persuaded to withdraw it the following month. He was promoted to first-class officer in the September. He was assaulted whilst on duty and was appointed an advocate to fight his case. In February 1875, he again resigned but withdrew his letter on the strong recommendation of Superintendent Bolton. He was moved to Tŷ Broughton having exchanged beats with PC John and appears to have settled down after leaving Bangor as by 1884 he was as an acting sergeant. He retired in 1903.

In February 1875, the incoming officer was PC35 William John who hailed from south Wales. In 1871, he had been living in Holywell with his wife Rachel and son Edwin, all born in Haverfordwest. Before transferring to Bangor he had been living in Tŷ Broughton, near Hanmer for three or four years where he and his wife had two children. They had a daughter, Louisa, christened in Bangor Church in 1878. In November of that year he was awarded a one pound reward for catching a man named Davies who was an army deserter. He remained in Bangor for five years and is last mentioned at the Overton Petty Sessions in May 1880 when he successfully charged a man with cruelty to a horse. It appears that he met Thomas Hall of Threapwood with a horse and cart laden with coal and noticed that the horse looked very weak and in pain. On examining it he found that under the horse's collar were several oozing sores. In June 1880, PC John was transferred to Rhyl. He had rather a chequered career after leaving Bangor as he was demoted from second-class constable in September 1887 then, twelve months later, to third class. By 1890 he was back up first class. In December 1892 he was transferred back to Bronington where he was once again in trouble and was demoted to third class for misconduct and fined one week's pay. He was restored to first class in 1895. He retired from the police force in December 1897 and went to live in Cadney, Bettisfield where he took up an agency with Billingtons the coal merchants.

In 1880, PC22 John Williams was appointed to Bangor and he is mentioned in a case before the monthly Bangor Petty Sessions in March 1881 when he summoned Richard Hughes, alias Dick Spot, a well-known horse breaker, with being drunk and refusing to quit the Royal Oak, Bangor on 14 February when requested to do so by the landlord, Mr Hanmer. In the census a month later, John Williams (aged 27 and born in Rhyl) is recorded as living in Overton Road with his wife Eliza and their infant son John Alid. In November 1882 PC Williams charged William Williams of Threapwood at the petty sessions with being asleep in his cart on a public highway in Bangor. The defendant denied the charge protesting that he was not sleeping, but admitted that he was resting his head in his hand and nodding a little. The magistrates must have been in a good mood that day for they accepted his explanation and dismissed the charge.

In July 1883, the first funeral conducted by a Nonconformist minister took place in Bangor Isycoed churchyard and was reported in the local newspaper as being that of a child of PC Williams. This interment is not mentioned in the Bangor burial register, as the family were not members of the Church of England. Later the same year, PC Williams was transferred to Sealand in the Mold division, where he and his wife had a further three children. By the time of the 1891 census he had once again been transferred to Leeswood, still in the Mold division.

By December 1883, the police officer for Bangor was PC47 Joseph D. Hughes having exchanged places with PC John Williams. In that month he summoned the landlord of the Buck Hotel, George Douglas Hughes, with being drunk on his own premises. The police officer had visited the inn at 5.30 p.m. and found the defendant drunk and quarrelsome. At 8.00 p.m. he again visited the inn, this time accompanied by Sergeant Burton of Overton, and found the landlord very drunk but quiet. It not being his first offence he was fined ten shillings (50p) with eight shillings (40p) costs and his licence endorsed.

In 1884, when Superintendent Adams of Mold resigned as deputy chief constable due to a serious illness and 'utter failure in health' the chief constable appointed Inspector Bolton of the Maelor division as Superintendent of the Mold division and deputy chief constable whilst retaining supervision over the Maelor district. Sergeant Jonathon Burton of Overton was appointed in charge of the immediate care of the whole of the Hanmer division.

In April 1886, PC Hughes arrested Owen Shone of Holt, a water bailiff, and escorted him to the Bangor court where Alice Jones of Bangor stated that he was in arrears of a bastardy order, and had made promises to her but never carried them out. Holt was sentenced to two months imprisonment. In May of the same year, a new courthouse was opened at Overton and one of the first cases to be heard was that of Sarah Few of Bangor, the wife of James Few, the water bailiff, who was charged by PC Hughes with being drunk and disorderly. She was fined and allowed two weeks to pay.

PC Hughes summoned George Griffiths a farmer from Cloy for being drunk in charge of a horse and shandry (a rickety vehicle) when coming home from Wrexham Fair on 12 August. It appears from the evidence of the constable and a woman named Bowker that the defendant was so drunk that he ran his vehicle over a little child in a perambulator at the roadside. The child had a very narrow escape and the defendant was fined one pound with fifteen shillings (75p) costs.

In 1888, Chief Constable Peter Browne resigned 'having attained a considerable age and far from well' – he was aged seventy-three. He had been a well-respected chief constable who had demonstrated on many occasions that he had the welfare of his officers at heart. It is known that when he was not satisfied with an officer's performance he would give him the opportunity to resign the force rather than dismiss him so as to avoid a black mark on the officer's record which might prevent him from obtaining a post with another force. He took an almost fatherly interest in his men as is shown by the following letter sent in 1878 to Inspector McLaren's son, John, who sometime before had obtained a post with the Isle of Ely Constabulary and wished to apply for a better paid position with the Windsor police.

> January 26. To John McLaren. I am in receipt of yours of the 24th intimating your intention to apply for another and apparently better berth in the matter of money. I cannot see that any testimonial from me will serve you, as you well know you were not giving me satisfaction when you left. All will and must depend on the recommendation of your present Chief Constable but if you were to ask me whether you should apply for the situation or remain were you are, I should never hesitate to recommend you strongly to stick to your present ship. You are a very young man and your school, so to speak, is a good one. I think you owe Captain Foster a debt of gratitude and it would be scarcely fair under the circumstances to cause him inconvenience now that your services are becoming of some little value to him. I am glad to find that you have at least improved your handwriting and I shall be glad at all times to hear of your well doing – and if you are bent on going in for the Windsor affair I will of course give you the same testimonial that I gave to your present Chief Constable.

The choice of new chief constable was rumoured to be between Major Leadbetter (the chief constable of Denbighshire) and the deputy chief constable of Flintshire, James Dale Bolton, but it was considered advisable to advertise the vacancy. In the event, Major Leadbetter did not put his name forward and seven candidates were short-listed for the post and presented themselves at the October Quarter Sessions. They were: Major R.T. Webber (Royal Welsh Fusiliers, of Wrexham), Superintendent J.D. Bolton, Captain Reuben Norton (Durham Light Infantry), Superintendent Innes (Hertfordshire Constabulary), Captain Arrowsmith (from Kent) and Mr Edward Lingard (Cheshire Constabulary). It will be noted that there were a number of army men on the list and certainly in the early years of the police forces the top positions tended to go to men with military experience. A ballot was held amongst the magistrates present and the result was: Bolton 18, Webber 16, Morgan 9, Lingard 5, Norton 4, Arrowsmith 0, and Innes 0. A second ballot then took place between the top four candidates and the result was: Webber 22, Bolton, 20, Morgan 8 and Lingard 2. The two with least number of votes were eliminated and the remaining two entered into a third ballot with the outcome being a tie: Webber and Bolton 27 votes each. It was only by the late entry into the room of another magistrate that the stalemate was resolved in a fourth ballot: Webber, 29, Bolton, 26.

In May 1889, James McKnight, a travelling draper from Hanley in Shropshire, was charged by PC Hughes of Bangor with being drunk when in charge of a horse and trap the previous evening. The officer said that shortly before 10 o'clock the night before, he found the defendant lying on the side of the road dead drunk and that two men were trying to arouse him. He had been seen falling from his trap and under the horse's hooves and it was feared that he had hurt himself. With help of the men the officer got him into the trap and held him up whilst a young man drove the horse to Overton where the defendant was locked up and his horse and trap put up in a public house. He was fined fifteen shillings, including costs.

In March 1890, PC Joseph Hughes left Bangor for New Brighton near Mold. He had been a member of the Presbyterian Chapel in Bangor and a teacher in the Sunday school. On the Sunday evening before he left a farewell meeting was held at the chapel, when reference was made to the numerous valuable services rendered by Mr Hughes, who acknowledged the kind expressions of goodwill.

PC13 George Wright was the next resident constable. He had previously been stationed in Hawarden for a couple of years where two of his children had been born Prior to that, he and his wife were living in Mold. The police station was still in a cottage in Overton Road. He was soon off the mark charging his fair share of drunks, when he successfully summoned William Williams a hay dealer from Threapwood for drunkenness when in charge of a horse at Bangor. This was most probably the same man that PC Hughes had successfully prosecuted for drunkenness in 1882. However, PC Hughes did not always win his cases as occurred when Richard Povah, a nailer of no fixed abode, was charged with stealing a waistcoat at Worthenbury, the property of Joseph Harris of Wallington Lane. Harris gave evidence that on 13 June he was carting from Wallington Lane to Worthenbury and where he lost his waistcoat. PC Wright said that he had apprehended the prisoner at Malpas with the waistcoat in his possession. Povah said in answer to the charge: 'I found it on Worthenbury Bridge about 9 a.m. on Saturday last'. The prisoner repeated that statement and having been cautioned was discharged.

In April 1895, a case of vagrancy was heard at Overton when PC Wright charged John English of Liverpool with begging. The officer stated that because of complaints received he had patrolled the roads between Overton and Bangor, saw the prisoner begging and arrested him. The prisoner said that he was making his way to Bridgend in south Wales and, on the understanding that he was going to south Wales to find work, he was discharged.

In August 1895 John Dodd of Overton and David Adams of Bangor were charged by PC Wright with committing a breach of the peace at Bangor, and John Mort, Bryn Hovah was charged with aiding and abetting. The constable said that on 10 July he saw Dodd and Adams fighting and that there was a crowd encouraging them to fight it out. All were fined ten shillings (50p).

In April 1896, PC Wright was transferred to Flint but it was not long before his health broke down and he was permitted to retire on medical grounds aged forty-seven, having completed fifteen years and two months service. His pension was £73 per annum.

In July 1894, Deputy Chief Constable James Bolton retired, aged sixty-six years, having completed forty-six years and seven months service, of which thirty-six years seven months were with the Flintshire Constabulary and ten years with the Bradford and Liverpool forces. Chief Constable Webber expressed his thanks for the loyal support and valuable assistance which he had always afforded him and he wished him and his wife many years of health and happiness to enjoy the pension so well earned and richly deserved. A presentation of an illuminated address and a purse containing £80–100 was made to Bolton on his retirement. In reply he said

… that he had started his career in Bradford in 1847 and had transferred to Liverpool in 1854. When off duty one day he went to the aid of a fellow policeman who was being attacked by a mob. He was stuck by a heavy object and rendered insensible and came round to find himself in hospital. For his action he was promoted to sergeant. He saw the advert for Flintshire police force for a man to take charge of a district of the county with the rank of inspector and applied. In 1884 he moved to Mold as DCC. He was particularly happy to see his dear old chief [Peter Browne] present at his presentation.

James Bolton and his wife retired to live at Trowstree Farm, Willington on a pension of £106 12s 4d. In May 1897, he was made chairman of Willington Parish Council. He died on 20 April 1901, aged seventy-three. His wife died in 1909, aged eighty-three years, having moved to live in Hanmer presumably with or near her nephew, Thomas Kitching.

In April 1896, PC46 Josiah Barker of Flint became the Bangor village policeman, having exchanged beats with George Wright. He stayed for twenty months before being moved to Bronington, only to be dismissed from the service one month later.

In December 1896, PC19 Edward Parry became the next police constable for Bangor. He had been born in Edgehill, Liverpool and was appointed to the Flintshire force on 1 August 1894 as a third-class officer, stationed in Mold. He was promoted to second-class twelve months later and to first class in September 1896 when his pay rose from 23s 4d (£1.17) to 24s 6d (£1.22) a week. He was soon active in the village and, at the Overton Petty Sessions in the following February, Thomas Dodd of Wrexham was fined for working a pony in a lame state. He saw the defendant driving a hawker's cart drawn by a very old pony in a distressed condition. It was lame and perspiring heavily. The constable told him he must walk the pony back to Wrexham and he promised to do this but later on was seen driving the pony at a fast trot through Bangor. Parry wired ahead to Inspector Jones of the RSPCA who met the defendant on his way into Wrexham. The inspector said that he had spoken to Dodd about the pony before.

PC Parry was a keen sportsman and represented the Flintshire police in June 1898 in the championship race at the police sports in Liverpool, which was open to any police force in the UK. He also took part in the police sports at Shrewsbury in September, winning the one-mile cycle race. He was a very fit young man and he needed to be, as in January 1899 after a fierce storm which caused the bulwarks to burst, he discovered an elderly man, Joseph Fowles, who had been living alone, in a very bad way and on four occasions carried the doctor through the floods to attend to him. The man subsequently died and PC Parry had to swim to the station at Bangor to use the telephone to inform the coroner, who lived in Oswestry, of the death as the water was too deep for him to wade. An inquest later said he deserved great praise and he was afterwards seen going about his rounds in a coracle.

The following month, the *Wrexham Advertiser* reported that

PC Parry, who figured so prominently during the late flood, and of whose conduct the jury had so high an estimation is now paying the price for his pluck, rheumatism is claiming him for one of her victims.

At the beginning of March the same newspaper reported

… that PC Parry of Bangor will shortly [in April] leave here for Prestatyn. We have no doubt that he is of the opinion that Bangor on Dee is a misnomer, for when he has been there the village has

Graig Cottage was used as a police station for a short while until it was sold in 1905.

several times been nearly under the Dee. It is no use any constable going there unless he is an expert swimmer and can manage a coracle.

In April 1899 PC19 Edward Spencer, who had joined the force in 1896, was the next police constable in Bangor. He and his wife, Sarah, had their daughter, Selina, christened in Bangor parish church on 5 May but he lost them both a few days later and they are buried in the village churchyard. He did not remain long in Bangor and by the end of August had been transferred to Connah's Quay. He resigned from the service in May the following year after just five years in the force.

In August 1899, PC13 John Connah, a native of Buckley, was the next police officer who had been stationed at Iscoed. In the 1901 census, aged twenty-nine, he was living with his wife, Sarah in Graig Cottage, Graig Lane. Until recently, Marjorie Bayliss and her husband lived in the cottage and were told that the policeman used to lock up the prisoners in a building at the side of the house. This explains why Graig Lane was at one time called Policeman's Lane by the fishermen who came from Liverpool to fish the river. The police station was moved from Graig Lane when Graig Cottage, owned by the trustees of the Bangor Peter Lloyd Bread Charity, was sold in 1905.

In November 1899, PC Connah caught and charged John Thelwell of Willington Lane and F. Jones of Wallington Farm with being on licensed premises during prohibited hours. They said they had travelled from Wrexham and called in the Royal Oak at 3.30 p.m., falsely claiming to be travellers. They were both fined.

PC Connah had his share of drunks to deal with as a case at Overton Petty Sessions in February 1905 illustrates. He charged John Jarvis and David Cooper with being drunk and disorderly on the Whitchurch road having found them helplessly drunk and using disgraceful language. Both were fined. Also at the same court he charged the auctioneer Frank Lloyd with driving through Bangor without a light. The defendant said in his defence that the candles must have gone out. He was fined.

In February 1904, the *Wrexham Advertiser* reported that

> PC John Connah is about to leave Bangor where it may truly be said he had proved himself a most efficient officer. He is a man who is bound to do well and is a credit to the Flintshire force.

He was promoted to sergeant in charge of Mold and in 1912, only eight years after leaving Bangor, was promoted to inspector and was given charge of Overton and the Maelor division.

In 1904, PC44 Thomas William Nelson, the son of Robert Nelson, a retired police sergeant of

Mostyn, was appointed police constable for Bangor. During his stay in the village he must have always associated Bangor with sad tidings as, on 5 May, his parents came to stay with him and his family and shortly afterwards his mother was take seriously ill and died aged fifty. The following year his father left to visit his daughter in Texas. Whilst in New York on his journey home to stay with his son at Bangor he was suddenly taken ill and died. He was sixty years of age and had only recently been superannuated from the Flintshire county force. He was buried in Meliden besides his wife.

In April 1905, PC Nelson was congratulated on successfully arresting a man who had evaded the vigilance of the police for over two years and in August he summoned Thomas Matthews to appear at the Overton Petty Sessions charged with indecently assaulting Margaret Stant on her way back home along the bulwarks after buying groceries. She screamed and he ran off. PC Nelson took him to the lockup where he was charged with the offence. The magistrates sentenced him to one month in prison with hard labour.

FLINTSHIRE CONSTABULARY,
Superintendent's Office,
MOLD, 28th May, 1900.

HORSE STEALING

THE FOLLOWING IS THE DESCRIPTION OF

JAMES STEWART

Wanted at this Office, charged on warrant with Stealing a Horse (recovered) at Saltney, in this Division, on the 24th inst.

Age—18 to 20 years.
Height—5ft. 3 or 4 inches.
Complexion—Fresh.
Hair—Brown.
Build—Stout.
Native of Bury.
" J.S." tattooed on one arm.

DRESS—Light Cap, Dark Serge Jacket, Waistcoat and Trousers, strong Lace-up Boots, wears Leggings. Has the appearance of a Groom.

The above had in his possession on the 24th, an aged Cream Coloured Horse, 14 hands high, Hog Mane, Shod with Leather, Sore Back, Black Stripes on Forelegs, and a Low Trap to seat four, Varnished Body, Shafts and Wheels painted Yellow, 2 Steps on each side, Splashboard on near side damaged and repaired with 2 plates underneath, Driving Box, Dark Brown Cloth Cushions, India Rubber Mat (nearly new), Maker's Name on Cups, A. Graut, Oxford Road, Manchester, also a set of old Black Leather Silver Mounted Harness, Wheatleaf on each side of Pad, Brown Bridle, with Brass Ringed Snaffle, Black Reins (all supposed to have been stolen). The Trap and Harness are now in the possession of the Police, and the Horse was bought by a Dealer in this County.

Please cause enquiries to be made, and if above man is found, arrest, and communicate with

Supt. J. IVOR DAVIES, as above.

W. N. Bellamy and Company. Limited. Printers. High Street. Mold.

Horse Stealing. [FRO FP/3/6]

On 11 April 1908 Nelson successfully prosecuted Patrick Collins a well-known showman and proprietor of roundabouts, for driving a traction engine in the county of Flintshire without paying the fee and obtaining a licence. 'It was an oversight,' he said, 'I did not know that I was in Flintshire.'

In the July of the same year PC Nelson was walking with his wife and two little boys near Graig Lane when he was hit by a cyclist coming round the bend. He managed to get his wife and children out of the way in time but he suffered a broken nose and severe bruising. He went to the Infirmary in Wrexham where Dr Edwards Jones administered medical help. Several requests for the easing of the bend, which was surrounded by high hedges, had been made to the district council but no avail and now, yet again, a request was forcibly put to the council demanding action. Finally, in March 1910, Flintshire County Council widened the Worthenbury road close to Graig lane and cut down the high hedge which was replaced with an iron fence.

In 1909 PC31 Samuel Chesters was posted to Bangor from Connah's Quay. Another native of Buckley, he only remained in the village for just over two years before being transferred to Bronington in May 1911. It was reported that in this short space of time he had managed to win the respect and esteem of the villagers.

In 1911 PC44 William Edward Price (William Evan Price in the Bangor baptism register), born in Abergavenny, was transferred from Holywell to be the next police officer. He married a local

Deva House (centre) was the police station from 1905–37.

girl and in October 1912 they had a son, Joseph, christened in Bangor church. He proved to be a very efficient officer and made many friends. Mary was a great support, representing him at many functions, funerals and weddings. He retained a fondness for the village and, in April 1916 after he had been moved to Shotton, he and his wife returned to have a daughter, Anne, christened in Bangor church. He was promoted to sergeant and stationed at Rhyl where he died in 1924, aged 50.

The middle cottage, Deva House, at the junction of High Street, Station Road, and Whitchurch Road now became the home for several police officers and their families. It later became a fishing tackle shop run by Miss Ainsworth.

By 1915, telephones had been installed in the main police stations and it was not long before all and sundry were making use of this new facility. This soon necessitated the sending of the following letter to all officers:

> Use of police telephones. Road foremen and others should be discouraged from the phone especially trunks except in an emergency such as an accident. Any calls made should be entered in the telephone call check book and any trunk calls refunded.

By 1923, Overton police station (telephone number 11) had been connected to the national telephone system. The first phone number for Bangor police station was Overton 33 but, after the new automatic telephone exchange was established in Bangor in 1931, the number was changed to Bangor-on-Dee 22.

In 1915, PC Richard Ellis Jones came to Bangor from Pwllheli. He was the maternal grandfather of siblings Richard and Margaret Owen of Abbot's Way. He was based in Bangor for five years and left Bangor in 1920 (when his eldest daughter, Mary Winifred Jones, the mother of Margaret and Richard, was five years old) to move to Tremeirchion and she attended school in St Asaph. She had a sister, Iris, who was five years younger being born just after they left Bangor. PC Jones later retired to live in Four Crosses, Pwllheli. His daughter, Mary, trained as a nurse and answered an advert for a district nurse in the Maelor where she worked during the Second World War, lodging with Bob Crouch in Worthenbury. If she heard the bombers coming when she was cycling on her rounds she hid in a ditch. If she was called out at night for a baby case or an emergency, Bob used to drive her in his car with no lights on. Mary married Edward Donald Owen and lived at Dongrey Farm, her husband's family home. She died in 1986 aged seventy-three. Her mother-in-law, Kate Owen, was the daughter of Tobias Martindale, the headmaster of Penley Madras School (1892–1912). Before her marriage Kate was a governess to the family at Cholmondeley Castle.

PC Richard Ellis Jones 1915–30.

PC1 Thomas Joseph Parry was transferred to Bangor from Flint on 23 January 1920. He had joined the Flintshire force as a third-class officer on 1 May 1906 and was promoted to second-class twelve months later and to first-class on 12 August 1908. He had been born on 1 July 1885 in Swansea and married Mary Jones in 1915. On 5 July 1929 he was awarded a chevron for twenty-two years' service. His son, Tom, married Gladys Parker Twiss of High Street, Bangor in 1939 and he became a well-known local builder and county councillor. He recited some of his memories of life as a policeman's son to A.F.M. Jackson that were included in the second issue of the Bangor-on-Dee Local History Society magazine in 1989. He recalled that his father had to work long hours; twelve hours a day and six days a week, but he was never really of duty. He provided himself with a bicycle and had to cycle to the conference point to meet colleagues from other beats between 12 midnight and 2 am. He always walked around with a stick and was not afraid to use it to keep unruly children in order. A favourite prank of boys was to tie a button to the window of a house with cotton that would tap on the window in a breeze to the great annoyance of the people inside. Use of the stick was a great deterrent in such cases. In those days, the police would just administer a good clout for minor offences that left no hard feelings on either side. One time a boy climbed onto a barrel to tie a button to a window but lost his footing and fell into the barrel, which was nearly full of water. This time PC Parry forbore to use his stick as he felt that the boy had been punished enough. In the 1920s, when foot and mouth disease was rife in the Maelor area, he would be stationed at a farm gate to ensure that everyone stepped in a bath of disinfectant before entering or leaving the premises. He

PC Thomas Joseph Parry 1920–31.

could be on duty twenty-four hours a day for up to ten days at a time, sleeping under canvas with just a sofa and a brazier for company. He could then be moved on to another farm.

PC Parry was on duty when the Bangor Races took place and was particularly vigilant for pickpockets and other tricksters. A popular trick, called 'Crown & Anchor', was to put a canvas sheet on the ground and invite the public to gamble and throw money down. An accomplice would call out 'police coming' and the man would bundle up the sheet with the money and disappear into the crowd. The pickpockets were very professional and difficult to spot and as many as fifty empty wallets, retrieved from hedgerows, could be handed in to the police station after race-day. Some people reckoned that the bookies were in league with the thieves, tipping them off which pocket the punter put his money in after paying out his winnings.

The police were often called out to incidents connected with the river and PC Parry was involved in some of them. One particular one that his son remembered was when a man who was sleeping rough on the river bank near Worthenbury fell into the water and drowned. He must have been in the river for some considerable time before being noticed. Young Tom, who was in his early teens, went with his father to give a hand to help pull out the body. He took hold of his boot and the whole foot came away with it! Tom admitted that he could not sleep for a week after his experience. The body was taken to Worthenbury for identification by his brother who, on seeing that the dead man was wearing a good pair of boots, asked whether he could have them. The reply was ' If you would like to take them off, you can have them'.

On 14 February 1931 PC Parry resigned from the force with effect from 30 April. He died in 1938 aged only forty-five. At the annual August Flower Show and Harvest Festival held that year on the Groes field his daughter, Mary, came fourth in the swimming race and the family remained in the Bangor area.

PC3 Richard Thomas Victor Price had been stationed in Bronington for 3½ years before being transferred to Bangor in 1931. He was thirty-two years old. Ernie Young still tells the tale of the time when Billy Griffiths (from the post office) and a friend were walking in the village and saw PC Price and his wife getting on the bus to go into town. He noticed that the sash windows in the living room of the police station in Station Road were open a fraction and, without more ado, lifted the window up and climbed in. He had previously observed that they had several family paintings/photographs on the wall, and now, he proceeded to lift them down and swap them onto different walls. When the couple returned they did not notice the change for a while and then the policeman asked his wife why she had moved the pictures. Of course she denied having done so and the argument raged for quite some time, much to the amusement of Billy and his friends. In 1937, PC Price was promoted to sergeant and transferred to Rhyl. A native of Gwernysgor he was based in Halkyn when he died in 1944, aged forty-five, having been with the Flintshire force for nearly twenty-five years.

In 1937 PC47 Alf Connah, who had been stationed in Connah's Quay, was the next policeman and was the first officer to occupy the new police station, Westgate House in Overton Road. When John Mort died in March 1937 the property was acquired by the Flintshire Constabulary as a police house. Mike Stratton remembers coming home from school in Wrexham riding on the crossbar of his friend's bike. Because of the floods they had to make a detour via the Cloy and when they reached the junction of Abbeygate Hill and Whitchurch Road who should appear from behind a hedge but Alf Connah who promptly told them off in no uncertain terms for riding two on a bike. The police constable was stationed in Bangor for the duration of the war.

PC54 Reuben Edgington was transferred from Lloc near Holywell in December 1946. Born in Southport in 1912, he was brought up in Flint where his father was a baker. He married Dilys Jones a native of Mold in 1938. He was transferred to Bangor in December 1946, during one of the worst winters seen that century when the river broke through the bulwarks just opposite the police

Wartime police officers and special constables outside Bangor police station L–R: PC Alf Connah (Bangor), –?–, –?–, Albert Pierpoint, Austin Peters (Bangor), Philip Humphreys (Bangor), Albert Williams (Tallarn Green), George Johnson (Tallarn Green). The police officer in front was based in Overton and is believed to be either Sergeant Hugh Williams or Walter Smith. [Ruth Bennion]

station in Overton Road and flooded the house. Six months later, when they were finally able to move back into the police station, they could still see the tidemark where the floodwaters had reached.

Whilst he was in Bangor, PC Edgington helped to form a youth club that met in the old village institute hut that stood alongside the present village hall. This led to the formation of a football team that was later accepted into the Denbighshire Youth League. When he retired he made some notes about his police service in which he recalled being summoned to a fire that had broken out in the evening after Charlie and Ruby Duggan's (née Spoor) wedding reception in March 1948, held in a room at the back of the old smithy in Whitchurch Road. The wedding couple had fortunately already left the reception when the fire broke out. It was especially memorable for the officer as a gas cylinder exploded near to where he was standing, fortunately not causing serious injury to humans although killing a cat.

In 1949, he and his wife Dilys had a daughter, Olive Denny, christened in Bangor church. Reuben was awarded a medal from the Royal Humane Society for saving a boy from the river Dee, who had absconded from the Bryn Estyn Home in Wrexham. The old boathouses that once stood near the Old rectory on the riverbank were often the hiding place for boys absconding from the approved school. The centre of the bridge was the dividing line between the Denbighshire and Flintshire police forces and there was often debate as to who should deal with the matter when a problem arose concerning the river.

Reuben Edgington died in 1986 aged 74. Margaret, one of PC Edgington's daughters, married Jeremy Stratton of Plassey House that was, until about 1916, the Red Lion Inn. She was the receptionist at the Bangor surgery for several years. Mrs Stratton, Margaret's mother-in-law, later ran a betting shop at the Plassey House and died in 1992.

PC54 Reuben Edgington 1947–56.

Westgate House was the police station from 1946 until the early 1990s.

PC Harvey F. Northcott came to Bangor in the late summer of 1956. He and his wife, Myfanwy, had four girls, three of whom, Linda, Sandra, and Mary were born in the village. By 1967 he was an inspector in Mold.

In 1961, PC John Davies and his wife Margaret became the next inhabitants of the police house.

In 1965, PC12 Joseph D. Turner and his wife Lorna came to live in Bangor. When the Flintshire force was merged with the Denbighshire and Gwynedd forces to form the Gwynedd Constabulary in 1 October 1967, he transferred to the CID as a detective constable.

In 1968, PC124 David S.C. Cartmel, with his wife Elspeth, was the next police officer to be posted to Bangor.

In 1971/2 PC1009 Garry James Bentley was the next police officer. He had married Penelope Houlbrooke of Knolton, Overton in 1968 and they had their first child, Christopher, christened in Bangor in 1975. He was active in village life, serving on the village hall committee as treasurer. When the committee decided to hold a village bonfire party he stored the fireworks, which had to be ordered early, in a secure outhouse at the back of the police station. When the village hall lottery scheme was set up in 1973 he became its first treasurer. Gary Bentley went on an exchange visit to America in 1972 where he caused a sensation when he directed traffic in his uniform. The American police were amazed that he patrolled without a gun and wondered how he could keep law and order with only a twelve-inch club-type instrument (his truncheon) that he had admitted he had never had to use. He died of cancer in 1994 aged forty-six.

In 1978 PC862 Alan T. Farley and his wife Glynis came from Llandudno to Bangor. He was at school in Connah's Quay with the son of PC Joseph Turner, a former Bangor police officer. He too involved himself in village life and was chosen as one of three judges in the Miss Carnival Queen contest in 1979 when Sheila Done was chosen. Alan was sent to Liverpool in 1981 to help quell the Toxteth Riots and he remarked on the contrast from Bangor, where everyone greeted you as a friend, to Toxteth where he was petrol bombed. Alan was transferred to Wrexham in 1982. He is no longer a serving officer, although he worked for the police force until 2011. He now lives in Overton.

PC165 Richard C. Gostage came to Bangor in 1982 with his wife Bronwen. He went on to do undercover work and died when he lost control of his motorbike at high speed at Pentrefoelas.

PC Peter Lloyd and his wife Michelle was the next occupant of the

PC1009 Gary James Bentley 1971–9.

police station. He was the son of Hugh Lloyd (also a policeman and latterly the coroner's officer). Peter went on to CID work before emigrating to Australia.

In 1991 PC625 John McCarthy was the last officer to be based in Bangor. He and his wife Karen bought the house from the North Wales Police when it ceased to be a police station. He is still a serving officer.

In the early 1990s due to financial restrictions the village lost their resident policeman and the police station once more became a private residence, Westgate House, and Bangor came under the care of Ruabon police station.

12. Education

The first system of education in Bangor would have been private and/or dame schools. The first mention of a schoolmaster that has been found is in 1631 when William Furnival, schoolmaster, summoned William Sharott to appear at the church court in a dispute over a pew. Any schoolmaster or mistress was required to have a licence to teach from the church to ensure that the information being disseminated was in accordance with the Anglican faith. There was a school in Bangor in 1665 as the schoolmaster, Christopher Paxton, was presented by the churchwardens to the church court 'for working a private school but whether licensed we know not.' He must have obtained a licence as he was still there in 1671. By 1674, John Williams was the curate and schoolmaster and he was presented because; 'He has no licence to neither place.' In 1705 Roger Jones was mentioned as a schoolmaster but by 1709, he too had left. At Easter 1712, William Furnival, no known descendant of a previous schoolmaster, held the post but by the autumn had moved to Harthill where he was again presented to the court as being unlicensed. In 1723 Thomas Cope was a schoolmaster and also the vestry clerk. All of these men would have run small private schools for the children of families who could afford to pay for their education. In the early twentieth century, there was a private school at Tŷ Graig run by the retired schoolmaster of the Endowed School, John Davies, that Marshall Humphries' father, Gordon, attended.

A dame school was normally a school run by a woman, often a widow and usually in her own home to supplement her income. Paying pupils would receive a very basic education and in many cases, it was simply a child-minding service. The first mention of the name of a schoolmistress is that of Anne Miress recorded in the Bangor church register as having been buried on 7 September 1734.

Bangor Endowed School

The first educational establishment in Bangor as we know it today was a Endowed School founded by Dame Dorothy Jeffreys of Acton, widow of Sir Griffiths Jeffreys of Acton Hall, who died in July 1729 and left money in trust for the setting up of a school. Her husband was the nephew of 'Bloody' Judge Jeffreys, also known as the 'Hanging Judge', notorious for presiding over the trials of rebels who took part in the Monmouth Rebellion of 1685. Dame Dorothy left £500 in her will to found a school in Bangor Isycoed to teach poor children to read and write, to learn the catechism, and to apprentice poor children to learn a trade. The persons appointed as trustees were her sons-in-law, John Robinson and Philip Egerton Esq. of Oulton Park and the money was invested in land and property in Holt and Bangor.

The Dame Dorothy Jeffries Trust was formed to administer the income and it was not until 1747 when the bequest had grown with interest to £800 that it was decided, on the recommendation of the rector, the Revd William Phillips, to buy a terrace of three thatched cottages in Overton Road with land attached on which to erect a purpose-built schoolroom. The end cottage nearest the schoolroom, with a thatched barn alongside, was for the use of the schoolmaster with the income from the rent of the other two cottages as part of his salary. Sir Thomas Hanmer owned the freehold of the land the chief rent of which, in 1784, was 1s 2d a year.

The schoolroom was built of brick with a slate roof. Inside there was just one room measuring approximately 15½ feet x 34 feet (4.70 x 10.34 metres) with a large fireplace at the south gable end and four windows on the long east front facing Overton Road. It had a brick floor and the entrance door was on the extreme right of the front elevation, with a porch that may have been a slightly later addition. A stone tablet was fixed to the outside of the porch com-

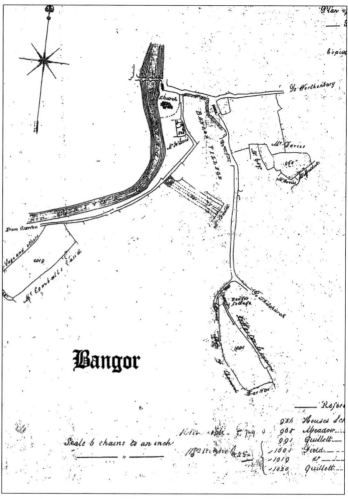

Plan of land purchased in Bangor by the Dame Dorothy Jeffreys Trust to be let for income.

memorating the endowment and inscribed 'This school was built and endowed by the Charity of Dame Dorothy Jeffreys late of Acton and by her Will bequeathed the sum of five hundred pounds

Artist's impression of the Endowed School built in 1747.

for the teaching to read and write and instructing in the catechism of the Church of England and for putting out apprentices poor children of the parish of Bangor'

The first schoolmaster appointed on 16 March 1748 was Francis Clarke of Bangor. He was a member of a long-established local farming family; members of each generation of whom were given the christian name Francis, many serving as Bangor churchwardens. As previously mentioned, all schoolmasters had to be licensed by the Church of England but for some reason, Francis Clarke had omitted to apply for a licence when he was appointed to the post. In May 1749, he was presented to the church court by the rector, the Revd William Phillips, and churchwardens Edward Jones, Randle Randles and Thomas Evison '... for presuming to teach without a license.' Little is known about him other than that at the Easter Court of Quarter Sessions on 27 February 1752, he summoned Richard Lee of Bangor, bricklayer, to answer a charge of assault and battery on his wife, Elizabeth. Richard Lee made a counter charge of assault by Francis Clarke on his wife, Mary, on 18 March. At an adjourned sitting of the court in the July, Richard Lee pleaded guilty to assault and was ordered to pay a fine of twenty shillings. In 1754, in addition to being the schoolmaster, Francis Clarke was also appointed the petty constable for the parish of Bangor (unpaid) at the annual vestry meeting and, whilst going about his duties in that post, he was violently struck by Mary Yates, wife of Joseph Yates, yeoman, without any provocation. Mary was summoned to appear at the Quarter Sessions where she was bound over to be of good behaviour and to keep the peace. He continued as the village schoolmaster until 1764 when he resigned due to infirmity. He died five years later and was buried on 9 August 1769 in Bangor churchyard, followed in the December by his wife.

Philip Egerton Esq, by now the sole surviving trustee, appointed the son, John Clarke, to succeed his father as schoolmaster on 2 November 1764. When the trustee died his successor, John Egerton Esq, confirmed the appointment of John Clarke on 2 February 1767, 'as long as he behaves well in that office'. However all was not well and on July 1768 Clarke was asked to present himself for examination at a Bangor vestry meeting. On being sent for, he refused to attend or undergo any examination. The meeting agreed to ask Mr Egerton to nominate another master or to leave it to the churchwardens to advertise and appoint a suitably qualified person. No action was taken at the time and Clarke must have been given another chance. On 17 February 1770 he may have been the John Clarke who, with a Francis Clarke, was a witness at the marriage of, Mary Clarke, by licence to Edward Edwards, the schoolmaster of Dodleston. However, John Clarke must finally have been asked to leave his post as a new master was appointed in 1774.

That man was Joseph Stokes who belonged to a family of the name in Bickley, near Malpas. He had married Hannah Lightfoot on 19 August 1770 in Malpas by licence when he was twenty-five and she was twenty. Their first child, Jemima, was christened the following year in Malpas parish church. They then moved to Whitchurch where their second child, Thomas, was christened in 1772, finally moving to Bangor on his appointment to the Endowed School in 1774. Joseph and Hannah went on to have a further eight children, Mary, Sarah, Justina, John, Joseph, twins Samuel and William and finally George; all christened at Bangor between 1774 and 1791. As the schoolmaster he received a salary of £22 10s 0d a year that was increased to £25 in 1795. He paid two guineas a year rent for his house and barn, later increased to three pounds.

Each schoolmaster kept a record of all expenses incurred on behalf of the school and presented bills for the maintenance of, and repairs to, the schoolhouse and schoolroom to the trustee's agent. In comparison with the purpose-built brick schoolroom, the schoolmaster's house and the other two cottages were old, timber-framed properties with thatched roofs that required considerable maintenance. Local people such as Ambrose Sadler, glazier, John Clay, blacksmith, William Munford, carpenter, Humphrey Edge, slater, William Bebington, thatcher and Joseph Thomas, bricklayer were just some of the names that presented accounts for repairing the properties. In 1798 John Jones, mason, was paid for 'cutting afresh and cleaning the letters on the stone tablet' over the porch. As well as the repairs to the Bangor properties the land at Holt required constant attention and bills for cleaning the Devon Brook, repairing or replacing a bridge and draining the land after flooding occurred frequently.

In 1780, Joseph Stokes was asked by Humphrey Hughes, a surveyor of Oswestry, to measure and map the area of land in Bangor at Maes-y-Groes that had been flooded. He was called as a witness when Hughes sued Thomas Witton in the King's Bench at Shrewsbury for non-payment of the cost of repairs to the breech in the riverbank at the same place. For his work in mapping out the land and his 'loss of time in attending as a witness' Joseph Stokes was paid £3 10s 6d. Ten other witnesses were called to give evidence and Hughes paid all the expenses for them and their horses at the Fox and Coach Horses Inn in Salop. Hughes paid Humphrey Edge £3 2s 6d for 'chair hire' to transport some of the old members to the trial. A second hearing took place and the schoolmaster was asked to compare the old maps and to mark up those places where the breaks in the bulwarks had occurred. This time the witnesses were put up at the Red Lion Inn in Shrewsbury and Joseph Stokes was paid another £3 3s 0d.

The schoolmaster was often called upon to adjudicate in village disputes, to witness wills and to serve on the jury at the Quarter Sessions. In 1800, a dispute arose over the boundary between a property at the back of the schoolroom owned by Mr John Knight and a strip of land at the rear of the schoolroom and he was asked to find out the truth of the matter. In July 1800, he wrote the following letter to W. Kerfoot of Nicholas Street, Chester who was acting as agent for the trustee:

> I thought it proper to acquaint [you] that Mr Knight sent Mr Turner of Whitchurch to Bangor to make what inquiry he could about the boundary betwixt Mr Knight's premises and the school premises ... I then promised Mr Turner that when I had seen you and had made some inquiries concerning the business I would write a letter to Mr Knight and of which letter I have sent you a copy.

This is the letter that he sent to John Knight:

> Since Mr Turner was at Bangor I have made some little inquiry respecting the space of ground betwixt your Stable and the school and also respecting the fence betwixt your garden and my garden and yard.
>
> Respecting the fence Mrs Dixon says that from the school to the necessary [the privy] is yours and that below is mine. This is a matter that I never heard before that she ever claimed any of it as belonging to your premises but to make good her assertion she says a Dutch Codlin grew in that part of the fence and that she always gathered the fruit of it. Now the truth is that there is no tree at all in that part of the fence neither has there ever been any for 27 years. T'is true also

there is a Dutch Codlin but it grows out of the hedge about 3 feet on your side and consequently on your premises. Now you please to take into consideration whether or not this is to be credited when the chief stress is laid on a real falsity.

Respecting the space between your stable and the school Mr Lewis of Bangor said that Mr Hugh Jones who was church warden at Bangor at the time the school was built and [had] the care and direction of the boundary of it told him that he left a space at the back side of the school (of which that is a part) in order that a ladder might be raised up to the school at any time and to stand upon school premises giving for a reason for so doing to Mr Lewis at that time he did it in case neighbours might not be quite so agreeable that such a space might be obtained without interruption as belonging to the school as a freehold property.

Mr Edwards of Dongray uncle or relation used to put muck or such, also coals, in that place sometimes but he doesn't say that the late rector of Bangor observing that the muck injuring the wall of the school obliged his uncle to take it out and ordered me to put a door on it the which I did till I set it and then I took the door away this I well remember to be true for the rector well knows that the space belongs to the school and for what purpose it was left.

If that space of land had not belonged to me Mrs Davies of Dongray (the previous owner of the cottage) would soon have ordered my door away.

Reply to letter 24 January 1801

I have looked over all my papers and find none for the purpose you mention … The purchase Deeds of the school land I have not a doubt are in Doctor Wynne's [rector] keeping among the Parish Papers. I did not think proper of saying anything to him about them till I heard from you again but from what I have overheard or know of the business the case is as follows:

£500 was left by Lady Jeffreys and it was paid for several years after her death and had accumulated with the interest to about £800 which sum was received by Mr Phillips who was rector of Bangor at that time and with the money he purchased the land and built the school and I make no doubt but that the Purchase Deeds were made in his name. I have often heard Mrs Lloyd mention of her father [Mr Phillips] bringing the money home and considering how to lay it out for the best.

Alas, we are left hanging in mid-air, as we have not been told the outcome of the dispute!

It was not long before Joseph and Hannah found the schoolmaster's cottage too small for their needs and they rented the cottage involved in the above dispute, owned by John Knight, and situated at the rear of the school. It was a bigger, half-timbered, thatched property and more suitable for their ever expanding family. They then sublet the schoolmaster's house to bring in additional income.

In 1798, the Revd Frederick Lloyd, rector of Bangor, had a seat erected in the chancel of St Dunawd's church for the schoolmaster's use at a cost of £1 5s 0d. However, he died before the bill was settled and his niece, Ann Lloyd, as his executrix paid out the money. In addition to his duties as schoolmaster, Joseph Stokes had served as the rector's churchwarden twice, in 1794 and again in 1807. He was also appointed as clerk to the Marchwiel and Whitchurch Turnpike Trust.

Joseph Stokes died on 21 August 1808, aged sixty-four. In his will, dated 15 August, he requested that he be buried 'in the Church Yard of Bangor and as near to my children who are gone before as conveniently may be done'. Unfortunately a survey of the churchyard has not revealed his grave, nor that of his children. He was survived by seven of his ten children and his widow retired to live in Wallington, Worthenbury and died in April 1824, aged seventy-five. Joseph owned a property in Whitchurch, as he mentions in his will that 'in case my loving wife Hannah Stokes should think the [rent from the] copyhold estate at Whitchurch shall not be adequate to her dower I give her the sum of Four pounds a Year'. Joseph left his youngest son, George, age seventeen, 'my large Globe and all and every my Mathematical Books and Instruments'.

His second child and eldest son, Thomas, succeeded him as schoolmaster. It is not known where he and his wife, Sarah, were living when the first five of their children were born before his appointment to Bangor. They had one child, Charles Whitehead Stokes, in Bangor in 1810 who sadly died the following year. Thomas Stokes had only been in the post for six years before he fell ill and 'being in a weak state of body,' hastily made his will on 4 May 1814. He died four days later aged only forty-one. His widow was paid a year and a half's years salary (less rent). According to the will his surviving children were Josias Wadsworth, John, Sarah, Mary and Hannah Stokes.

An application for the vacant post of schoolmaster was received from a Daniel Whatmough, the assistant head of Malpas School for five years, who had just married Sarah Sanders in Malpas the month before. The applicant was described as: 'a very discerning young man and well qualified' by Thomas Crane, a tenant farmer of Sir Richard Puleston of Emral. A Mr C. Vaughan also supported this application. However, on 26 May 1814 at a vestry meeting held at the Buck Inn, the churchwardens recommended Benjamin Harris, also known as Benjamin Harry, to the position of schoolmaster. Edward Hanmer, vestry clerk, signed the minutes. Mr Harris had made

> … a very handsome offer to Mrs Stokes, widow of the late Thomas Stokes, to teach the scholars for her till Midsomer next and give her the benefit and likewise has offered to teach her children until Christmas gratis if she should happen to stop in Bangor till that time. [He had also] offered to pay every expense for all fixtures belonging to Mrs Stokes and anything in the garden and house at a fair valuation.

It was reported that 'the school is empty in the meantime and the children doing nothing but mischief in the street'.

Benjamin Harris was born c.1763 and married Anne Ken(d)rick in Bangor church on 4 May 1795, aged about thirty-two, at which time he was described as a bachelor and a labourer. He was a local man and related to a Marchwiel family named Harry. His wife was a Marchwiel girl whose two sisters were married in Marchwiel church in 1798 and 1809 with Benjamin acting as a witness. On 14 June a vestry meeting approved his appointment at a salary of £30 with the proviso that he was to make a return each quarter of the number of scholars under tuition to the minister and churchwardens in order that the names of the negligent parents whose children failed to attend could be noted. The children were to be brought to church every Sabbath day and the churchwardens proposed that Mr Egerton be asked to establish a Sunday school out of the charity.

At the vestry meeting, it was further proposed that the trustee be asked to settle a small bill for damage to the church and church bells by the scholars and that a small bell be purchased for the use of the school instead of the scholars using the church bells and doing damage to the bell wheel and to the church. It also appeared that the pupils of the Endowed School were being accused of playing ball games against the tower wall and damaging a shutter and it was agreed that a quantity of rough stone should be placed in front of the tower to discourage such activity!

In 1815, the school pump was repaired, the well was cleaned, the brickwork pointed, and a new spout and bucket provided at a total cost of £3. Further work to the property was needed as on 15 April 1816, it was reported at a vestry meeting that an inspection of the Endowed School had been made and it had been found that all the window leads had decayed and that, as the glazier had declared them beyond repair, it was recommended they be replaced. The walls around the schoolyard and the school door were also 'very much out of repair and had been so for a long time'. In 1819, more work was required on the schoolmaster's house and schoolyard at a cost this time of over £24. Sir John Grey Egerton, by now the trustee, informed the rector that he was appointing his brother, the Revd Philip Egerton, rector of Malpas, to be his attorney and trustee of the school whilst he was abroad, with powers to admonish or discharge the present schoolmaster if necessary and appoint another.

Benjamin Harris had also spurned the schoolmaster's house and lived in the same large cottage at the rear of the school. In addition to the thirty scholars that he was contracted to instruct in reading, writing and accounts, he was also allowed to take fee-paying pupils on his own terms. He made a charge of one shilling when they first entered the school and one shilling each annually 'for firing.' He was allowed to receive as many scholars as he could 'with convenience' manage helped by his wife, Anne. She taught the younger children, both boys and girls, until they could read in her own school after which they were then removed to the endowed school. Some times there were reported to be as many as fifty children in the schoolroom at any one time. The fee-paying pupils were supplied with any stationary that was required but the free children had to provide their own. Three weeks holiday was allowed at Christmas and again at harvest time as the children were needed to help with the gleaning of the fields that interfered considerably with their instruction.

In November 1819, a theft occurred on his premises and Harris summoned Thomas Prince, described variously as 'of Chester' and 'now of Bangor, labourer', to appear at the Quarter Sessions charging him with stealing a 'Yelve' or muck fork valued at 10d. He called John Clay, blacksmith, of Bangor and William Kettle, shoemaker, to give evidence in support of his case. Unfortunately for Harris the case was dismissed. In 1820, the rector, Revd Maurice Wynne, appointed him as his churchwarden at the Easter vestry meeting.

In 1828, when the schoolmaster was aged sixty-five, he engaged, and personally paid, John Jones, aged sixteen, to act as his assistant and he continued to teach at the school until he retired in 1837. He died on 20 April 1839. In his will dated 8 March 1836, he appointed his wife, Anne, and nephew, John Kenrick, as executors and his estate was valued at £450. He does not appear to have had any children.

John Jones, Harris's assistant, succeeded him as schoolmaster at Bangor in 1837 when he was twenty-five, on a salary of £30 (with the rent of the two adjoining cottages included, but by now his own house was rent-free). He combined his duties as schoolmaster with those of parish clerk for which he was paid £15. He also received money from paying pupils. He had never received any formal training as a teacher but, with his position as schoolmaster now secure, and with an income of at least £45 a year, he could afford to wed and in September, 1839 he made a good marriage to

Mary, the daughter of Charles Edwards, a well-respected farmer of Sontley, at Marchwiel parish church. Aged twenty-three, she was employed as a governess and, like her predecessor, assisted her husband in the Endowed School and also ran her own school in a cottage where she taught the girls needlework and was said to maintain good order. This cottage (N$^{o.}$ 916 on the 1840 tithe map) was situated at the corner of the National School grounds and was given rent-free by the rector who in turn rented it from the marquess of Westminster. When a report was ordered into the state of education in Wales in 1846, John James, the assistant commissioner, visited the schools in Bangor in January 1847 and described this building as 'a ruinous old cottage, where the rain dropped from the ceiling onto the children's desk and the furniture and apparatus were very insufficient'. He found that the endowed school had sixty-eight scholars enrolled, forty-two of whom paid between three shillings and ten shillings per quarter and twenty-six were taught free in consideration of the endowment. He observed that the boy's schoolroom was

> … out of repair, and required an additional window but was of good height and dry. The furniture and apparatus were insufficient and the outbuildings (the privies) were in bad repair.' He added that on the day of his visit '… there were present 25 boys and 24 girls; 8 of these pupils were above 10 years of age (chiefly boys), and 22 had attended the school for periods varying from two to above five years. I found 15 who could read with ease … only 6 were learning arithmetic … only 17 could repeat the Catechism; 6 well. The girls were more intelligent and better conducted than the boys than the boys, who were ill-mannered, and grossly ignorant. One of them said that the Fifth Commandment was 'Thou shalt NOT honour thy father and thy mother,' etc. They receive no instruction in Scripture history from any person. The rector does not take any part in the religious instruction of the pupils, but confines his attention to the Free [National] school. He states that the ignorance of the scholars is such that it would be necessary for him to undertake the charge of their entire education. He expressed his anxiety to establish the school upon a better footing, but alleged that the schoolmaster is at present in such a state of health as would make it dangerous to remove him. He thinks it important to keep the present Endowed school distinct from the Free school, the later being already sufficient for the wants of the poorer inhabitants, whereas the endowment of the former, and the privilege of taking pay-scholars, would command an able master, who could impart more substantial instruction to the children of farmers and small tradesmen, which class would generally not frequent a school to which the poorer and lowest were admitted. The master was absent from the school during my visit. The person who acted as his deputy was very inefficient. Though an Englishman, he could with difficulty understand the meaning of the word arithmetic.

Just nine days after the inspector's visit, John Jones died on 6 February 1847, aged forty-six. In his will he left everything, including his pew in the church, to his wife, Mary, and named her and his father-in-law as his executors. His estate amounted to under £800, a large amount of money at that time. The witnesses to the will were David Jones, junior, of Worthenbury, schoolmaster, and John Edwards of Bangor, innkeeper. There were no known children of the marriage. The trust paid his widow half-a-year's salary. On his death certificate the cause of his death is stated as unknown.

His successor was appointed on 19 February 1847. As this was within two weeks of the death of John Jones he was, most probably, the assistant master, name unknown mentioned in the above report, as yet unpublished, with its scathing reference. With the death of John Jones, the shortcomings of his deputy to be the schoolmaster became more obvious and it did not take long before the trustees were informed of his unsuitability and appointed George Thomas Rice of Croydon in his place. Rice had just graduated from Battersea Teachers' College. Nothing further is known about him and in October 1850, the trustees appointed another local man, Thomas Speed, as the schoolmaster.

Thomas Speed had been the church vestry clerk at Bangor since at least 1841. In 1842 he and his wife, Elizabeth, had their son, Thomas, christened in Bangor church. They went on to have a further five children, George, Fanny, John, and twins Henry and Frederick christened in Bangor, at each of which he was described as a schoolmaster in the church register. He may have taught at somewhere like Worthenbury or Overton before he was appointed to Bangor, or had run a private school. Unfortunately, no sooner had he been appointed master in 1850 than he succumbed to typhoid fever on 24 December 1850 and was buried in Bangor aged 40. He left a widow aged thirty-nine and seven children including one-month old twins. Elizabeth Speed, who had also been a schoolmistress, was paid the salary owing for the quarter up to Christmas 1850 and eventually went to live next door to (or possibly in an apartment at the rear of) the Buck Inn. Until she vacated the schoolhouse the next appointed schoolmaster lodged with the tollgate keeper, Joseph Hughes, in the tollhouse on the corner of High Street and Overton Road. As he was unmarried, Mrs Speed continued to help with the education of the girls. She died in September 1880, aged seventy-one.

The new schoolmaster of the Endowed School, Thomas Pritchard was aged forty and was born in Overton according to the 1851 census, but in Harthill by the 1861 census. Apparently he had been a butler in the employ of Archbishop Wrangton, the father in law of Chancellor Henry Raikes' son, who had died some time before he had resolved to take up scholastic work. Thomas Pritchard began his teaching career by assisting his friend, John Edwards, who had been for many years the master of the Blue Coat School in Chester. He was afterwards recommended by the Revd P. Harrison to be master of Painters Green School, Iscoed, near Whitchurch, to which office he was appointed by Joseph Lee of Redbrook. When that school closed, Mr Lee then recommended him to the Revd Marsh of Bangor as suitable for the post of master of the endowed school in 1851. His salary was £30 per annum and he was also given an annual allowance of £2 for coals.

The question how many scholars could be taught in the Endowed School was raised at a vestry meeting in 1854 as it had become the custom to limit the number of free scholars according to the following formulae: thirty of the poorest children in the following proportions: ten from the township of Bangor, ten from the Township of Pickhill and Sesswick and ten from the Townships of Eyton and Royton. The children were to be recommended by the churchwardens of each respective division. A search was made for a copy of Dame Dorothy Jeffreys will (made in 1728, the year before she died) to see whether the number of pupils was stipulated therein – it was not.

At the same vestry meeting it was decided to ask John Palin of Christleton to undertake a valuation of the property and land belonging to the Endowed School. In his report Palin said the value of the property and land in Bangor was put at £35 8s 0d and that in Holt at £22 13s 0d, which included the value of trees growing on the land. In his report on the property, he stated that

> … the school is much improved with taking down the ceiling and exposing the roof, the timbers of which are oak. The roof had been re-slated and the schoolroom is now, with the exception of the windows that needed re-leading, in very good repair.

The schoolmaster told him that during the summer the school, although much improved since the ceiling was taken down, was

… still rather close and some contrivance to ventilate it would be an improvement. The Small Cottage used by the schoolmaster has been improved and made the most of and is very neat as is the garden which was formerly a yard and has been picked up and levelled by the schoolmaster with the assistance of a labourer for which he paid £3 0s 0d. The [middle] Cottage and garden occupied by Christiana Baker, timber framed fitted up with Bricks and thatched in good repair except the windows which want new leading. Rent £3 0s 0d, which is enough. Cottage and garden occupied by Samuel Taylor similar to the above under the same roof, in similar repair and rent the same. There is a channel in the front of the cottages irregularly paved. Mr Pritchard said he would take it up and re-pave it.

In December 1854, John Edge, a builder of Overton, drew up an estimate for the erection of a new school privy to be constructed in brick with a floor of Buckley tiles, roofed in Llangollen slates, with the addition of a urinal and a new seat in the old privy, all with proper drains to a new cesspit, six feet deep by three feet in diameter and a new drain from the cesspit to the bottom of the garden to take the overflow. At the same time, the commemoration stone was to be removed from above the entrance door to the school and placed in the centre of the wall to provide room for a new six-feet square porch to be built which was to be fitted with a seat on either side and with three rows of coat pegs above. The door was to be of red deal and the whole slated in Llangollen slates. The estimate for the work amounted to £27 17s 0d. The work was carried out over two years along with a new iron entrance gate (with oak posts) to the schoolyard, paving the yard, fitting boards to the inside of the schoolroom windows, a new desk and form and whitewashing the schoolroom interior and was completed by 1857. The final cost was £35 7s 5d. The school-master certified the account and John Edge was finally paid in May 1857.

Up until 1859, the Dame Dorothy Jeffreys charity had been run with a cash surplus each

Final bill for work completed in 1854.
[FRO D/BC/2837]

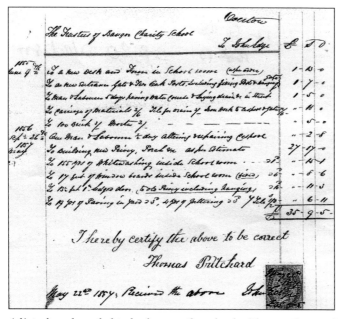

A list of work needed to be done on the school with an estimate of cost. [FRO]

year, overseen by the rector and churchwardens and responsible to Mr Egerton, or his successors, through his solicitors/estate agent, the forerunners of Birch Cullimore & Co of Chester. However, disaster struck about 6 o'clock in the evening in late January, 1859, when the schoolmaster's cottage and the two adjoining cottages burnt down. According to one report in the *Wrexham Advertizer* the cause of the fire is unknown but it was said to have started in the school-master's cottage. There was little chance of extinguishing the flames once the cottages were alight as they were timber framed and with thatched roofs. The barn alongside, although also thatched, was saved from the fire, as it was not attached to the other properties.

Mr Pritchard managed to get most of his furniture and other things out of his house but the occupant of the middle cottage, Mr Ridgway, a joiner, lost nearly everything he possessed in furniture, clothes and tools. A child who had been in bed in the middle cottage was rescued and no fatalities or injuries were reported. Samuel Taylor in the end cottage lost £17–£18 but by careful riddling of the ashes, was able to recover most of it in gold and silver that was very little the worse for having been in the fire. The loss by the different parties amounted to £45, exclusive of the value of the buildings, and a collection was soon under way with the rector, Revd Marsh, generously starting it off with £5. Pritchard was paid £5 as a gratuity and in June a further £5 'in consequence of his loss by fire'. The Revd Marsh gave the village constable, PC William Lockwood, 2s 6d (12.5p) for his exertions in getting everybody out of the burning buildings, which the chief constable gave permission for him to keep.

Plans and estimates for the rebuilding work were sought and a sketch was received from J. St Aubyn of 35 St John Street, Chester in April 1859 for

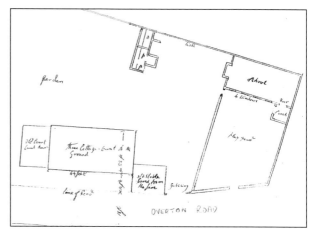

Site of the burnt cottages in 1859.
[FROD/BC/2854]

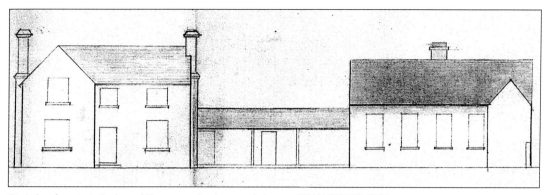

St Aubyn's rejected plan of the new schoolmaster's house. [FRO D/BC/2854)]

> ... a new master's house with the following accommodation: living room 12 x 12, bedroom 12 x 12, pantry & scullery all to be upon the ground floor.

This was obviously not to the trust's liking as in February 1859 an estimate with plan was received from William Whalley of Kingswood Cottage, Mollington, near Chester, stating

> I have taken into account the bricks from the cottages burnt down and everything useful for the new work to be taken by the contractors. I will engage to do the work in a substantial and workmanlike manner for the sum of £200 & 10 pounds. P.S. The fencing not included in the estimate.

In a memorandum dated 15 February 1859, Mr Whalley wrote to a Mr Humberston (who was acting on behalf of the trustees) that the rector thought

> ... it would be best not to build more than one good house for the Master of the School and perhaps five pounds more salary can be allowed him as that same he got in rent for the two

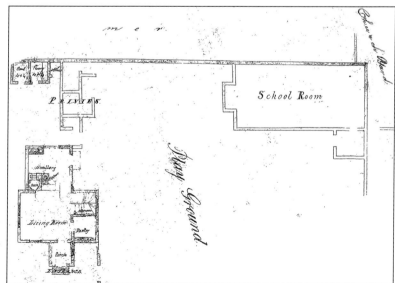

William Whalley's successful plan for the new school-master's house.
[FRO D/BP/1057]

cottages burnt down. Mr Marsh also wishes to ask whether the cottages were insured or not. Also he would like the old stable that is saved from the fire to be taken down and wishes the play yard to be enlarged… I beg to add that I think with Mr Marsh that it will be much the best to take down the old thatched stable and make the play yard more than twice the present size. I have made a plan for your inspection which I think will be convenient and look well.

There was no mention of insurance in the accounts for the charity before the fire, but there was an item for Sun Fire Insurance of 13s 6d thereafter, a classic case of the horse and the stable door.

The Dame Dorothy Jeffreys trust could not afford to rebuild the schoolhouse on the income from investments and the decision was taken to borrow the money. A loan was raised from Helps & Co (through Birch Cullimore & Douglas) of £252 9s 4d, being the total cost of rebuilding at an interest rate of 4%. In March 1860, John Edge of Overton put in the successful tender for £153 3s 5½d that was countersigned by Henry Bollin of 43 Watergate Row, Chester as 'very fair and reasonable' and rebuilding was soon underway. By July 1861, the new schoolhouse was ready for occupation by Thomas Pritchard.

Under the terms of Lady Dorothy Jeffreys's will, part of the charity's remit was the recommending of poor children such as orphans, illegitimate children and children of unemployed parents, to be bound as apprentices. It was an easy method of dealing with local poverty on the assumption that training in a skill would set a child up for life and would reduce the chances of the child being a charge on the parish in later years. It was also seen as a way of controlling adolescents and ensuring a steady supply of labour.

The child was usually bound for seven years, or until he was twenty-one, to be taught a trade and would have to reside with his apprentice master who provided him with his board and lodging. Although no distinction was made in the will between boys or girls, in practise, only boys appear to have been chosen. Being a rural community, many boys were apprenticed to farming in the parish or neighbouring parishes, but the officials were not confined to their search for masters within the parish of Bangor. Some were sent to apprentice masters in the nearby towns and were indentured to the most useful trades such as, shoemakers, tailors and blacksmiths. The children were chosen from each of the townships in rotation and two of the parish officials, usually the overseer of the poor and a churchwarden for the township in which the boy or girl lived, would sign the indenture papers, two copies being made at a cost of seven shillings. The charity paid a premium to the apprentice master, initially of £5, to cover the boys living expenses. On average, three apprentices were placed every two years until the income from the charity reduced which resulted in not so many boys being sent. Until 1859, many of the names of children recommended for apprenticeship, usually by the schoolmaster, are recorded with, in most cases the name of the boy, the apprentice master to whom he was sent and the trade. After 1859, because of the need to repay the loan for the rebuilding of the schoolmaster's house, the apprenticing of boys ceased, as the trust could not afford the premium, by now eight pounds. Only two boys thereafter were apprenticed; one out of school funds as a special case, and the other by the kindness of the Revd Marsh, who provided the necessary funds out of his own pocket.

On 24 July 1860 the school received a very favourable report when the Revd L.R. Henshaw examined the pupils in the presence of the Revd Marsh, rector of Bangor, and Mrs Panton of Plâs-fron and others. The examination comprised arithmetic, grammar, geography and English history.

The report in the *Wrexham Advertiser* of 28 July stated: 'From the very state the school is in great credit is due to Mr Pritchard who is untiring in his exertions to promote the welfare of his scholars.' Afterwards, the children marched a mile to Plâs-fron where Mrs Panton provided refreshments.

Whether the boys and the girls were educated in separate schoolrooms is not known but by 1865 the girls and boys had been separated, all the infants were being taught by Miss H.A. Jeffries, the older girls taught by Mrs Elizabeth Speed in the National School and the boys sharing the Endowed School building in Overton Road. On 29 June 1867, there was another visit by the Schools Inquiry Commission which reported that the parents of the pupils in the Endowed School were chiefly agricultural labourers and that the number of male pupils was forty-six.

Thomas Pritchard held the post of schoolmaster until he was sixty-one in 1872. According to a report in the *Wrexham Leader*, the Revd McGill said that the schoolmaster used to conduct the school in a 'quite a burlesque manner.' It sounds as if lessons could have been great fun! Thomas Pritchard had been appointed on the understanding that he would receive a pension at the end of his service and he retired to live in Weaver Street, and later in Trinity Street, both in Chester, on a pension of £20 a year paid for out of the charity funds. The payment of his pension depleted the Endowed School's income and it was suggested that it be stopped, but they were told that he was legally entitled to it. He died in June 1890 having been retired eighteen years.

The next schoolmaster, John Pritchard (no known relation to the previous master), was appointed at Christmas 1872. He had begun his teaching career at the National School in Oswestry as he is recorded in the 1851 census as a twenty-two year old living with his widowed grandfather, also John, a gardener, and his uncle, David. He then became the master of the National School in Dudleston Heath, Ellesmere, where he taught for several years. He was married and he and his wife, Emma, formerly a governess, had three sons and a daughter.

In August 1876, it was reported in a Wrexham newspaper that:

Tuesday being the birthday of Capt Mostyn Owen of Althrey Woodhouse, Bangor, the children of the boys' and girls' schools, also the Sunday school children from the chapel, altogether numbering 130 were regaled with tea and plum cake etc on the lawn in front of the hall. After doing ample justice to the good things provided for them they enjoyed themselves in running races and other sports for prizes viz; books, pocket handkerchiefs etc.

Although the work of the schoolmaster was initially satisfactory – a report not long after he was appointed remarked that the school was 'beginning to look up' – by October 1876 the rector had asked the trustees to send Mr Pritchard a letter putting him on three months notice to give up Bangor school. The reason is unrecorded but it was undoubtedly because of his health, which had latterly caused him to miss a lot of the teaching curriculum. Whatever the reason, notice was duly given and they advertised for a replacement.

As the new master could not take up the post immediately, Pritchard was allowed to stay until 25 March 1877. However, when the time came to vacate the premises he held fast and on 29 March the Revd McGill wrote to the trustees that Pritchard

… declines to give up the keys of the school and house though the new master is working the school and has been since Monday last. I do think that a sharp letter from you would be the best way.

This had the desired effect and Pritchard left, dying of Bright's disease and pneumonia just four months later, aged only forty-nine. Four years later, his widow and daughter (Emma, a dressmaker) were living near the Red Lion Inn in Whitchurch Road. All their children stayed in or near Bangor and Mrs Pritchard was the oldest inhabitant in Bangor when she died in May 1914, aged 91. She is buried in Bangor churchyard.

It is interesting to note that the salary of the master had changed very little in nearly 100 years since 1795 when Joseph Stokes was receiving £25 a year and 1809 when Benjamin Harris was paid £30. Both of these masters had also had the rent of the other two cottages in the terrace in addition to their salary. Now the new schoolmaster, Thomas Whitehead, took up his position at a salary of £28. The trust was unable to offer more as the payment of £20 a year in pension as well as the interest on the loan was crippling.

The new schoolmaster, Thomas Whitehead, was aged forty-five and had been born in Hutton, Lancashire, the son of Robert Whitehead who was a schoolmaster in Turton, Lancashire. He began his career as an apprenticed pupil teacher, aged fifteen, to James Rutter a schoolmaster at Trinity Street School in Bolton in 1851. He had taken over from David Jones as the schoolmaster of Worthenbury sometime prior to 1872 and was a keen gardener as in August 1875, he had entered several of the classes in Worthenbury Horticultural Show and he was placed second in the peas, second in the large potatoes, second in the kidney potatoes and second in the lettuce sections. Once appointed to the Endowed School he wasted no time in marrying Sarah Clark, the mistress of Bangor Girls School the same year. The following year, he was congratulated by H.M. Inspector of schools on the improvement in the school in the twelve months since his appointment. The inspector added: '… This school has undergone a reformation since Mr Whitehead has been in charge of it. I shall be disappointed if it does not become a very good school'. He said that the geography was about 'fair' and the grammar 'weak,' but the order kept by the schoolmaster and the 'tone' of the school was excellent. The amount of the government grant received as a result of the inspection was nearly double the amount given in 1877.

In 1880, education was made compulsory for all children up to the age of ten (raised to eleven in 1893 and to twelve in 1899, except for those employed in agriculture). Schools had been required to keep admission registers for some years, but none of these have survived for the Bangor schools. Logbooks had been introduced in the 1840s but only exist for Bangor between 1886 and 1948, and then only for the National School. The school board paid the fees for poor children from 1876 until 1891 when all fees were abolished and education became free for all.

In May 1880, the report from Morgan Owen, H.M. Inspector, was very satisfactory:

In the boys' school: 'the infants were good in spelling and form, fair in reading and tables, their writing only moderate. I regret the geography was lacking in intelligence and grasp. The grammar of the second and fourth Standards was good of the third weak of the fifth and sixth fair. The work of the first, second and fourth standards and the style of the paper work were good, and rest of the work was approaching very fair. Order and tone were excellent. The school accounts are excellently kept (by the rector). The managers are giving evidence of interest in the school by providing it with a wooden floor and other improvements.

Thomas Whitehead stayed in Bangor for three years and then, no doubt spurred on by the knowledge that they were expecting their first child and needing an improved income, he sought another post. Not long after the publication of the above report, he left to become the schoolmaster of the National School in Winteringham, Lincolnshire.

In 1880, John Davies became the last schoolmaster of the Endowed School. Prior to coming to Bangor he had held a teaching post in Flint. He was aged twenty-nine and had been born in Brymbo. His wife Bessie (aged thirty), born in Wharton, near Winsford, Cheshire, was a schoolmistress. They had a son, Albert (born in Wharton) and a daughter, Mabel Emma, christened on 7 January 1883 in Bangor. The schoolmaster had been a choirboy at Beverley Minster and possessed a trained voice. Like her father, Mabel was musically gifted and won a scholarship to the Royal Academy of Music. She sang with the Carl Rosa Opera Company and went to South Africa with the George Edwards Opera Company where she married a Lionel Abrahams and was known to have one daughter who was said to have inherited the family musical talent.

John Davies had the unenviable task of teaching the boys of the Endowed School and the older boys of the National School together in the one-roomed Endowed School building – all ages from seven to ten together in one room in a building that must have been very cold in winter, with the ink often frozen in the inkwells, and with only a single fireplace at one end and its roof open to the rafters with no modern thermal insulation. At least by now the brick floor had been replaced with wood, which would have been warmer under foot. At this time, the infants' school was also sharing the Endowed School premises.

In February 1881, the school was examined in religious knowledge by the Revd E. Owen, diocesan inspector of schools, who reported:

This school possesses a very fair knowledge of the Holy Scriptures. The repetition in the various classes is good, and so also is the writing from memory'. The following boys received honour certificates: Group 1, William Gregory, William Boote, and Alfred Bennett; Group 2, James Mullock, William Young, and James Poynton; Group 3, Charles Hughes, Reuben Johnson, and Charles Davies; Group 4, Herbert Hughes, Edward Fearnall, Joseph Mullock, Henry Poynton, and Frank Young.

In December 1883, John Davies was charged with assaulting Enoch Brookfield of Eyton, whilst in school on the 5 November. As the schoolmaster was ill and unable to attend his wife appeared on his behalf. The complainant stated that the master struck him three times across his back with a cane and also hit him with his hand. Mrs Davies read a statement giving evidence of the bad conduct of the complainant whilst in school. A note from Dr Gopat, and evidence given by PC Hughes who had seen the boy soon after the alleged assault, showed that the assault was of the most trivial nature and was consistent with simple chastisement. The case was dismissed.

By July 1884, the report of the H.M. Inspectors, T.M. Owen and his assistant E. Morris, showed an improvement all round.

The geography of the first standard was good: of the second weak in map but good otherwise: of the third standard good in part and weak in part, with fair map knowledge: of the fourth, fifth and sixth standard pretty good, and the map knowledge good. The Grammar of the second and fifth standards was pretty good, of the rest fair. The poetry of the first, second and third standards was good: of the fourth, fifth and sixth standards very good. The work of the third standard was good in reading, pretty good in spelling, fair in arithmetic: that of the other standards were good. The singing, tone, order and registration were good. The school accounts are excellently kept by the rector.

The inspectors went on to comment that an extra classroom was needed along with new desks and maps and that the infant boys' school should be sent to the girls' school. The infants were transferred to the National School once again but the trust could not afford to extend the school and new desks were out of the question. The condition of the schoolhouse and school was deteriorating as the trust was in debt and only absolutely essential repairs were undertaken.

By 1893, the school inspectors had pointed out that work was needed to improve the ventilation at the school and several other things required attention. The rector wrote to the trustee's agent that the work, estimated at £8 10s, could be done at the same time as work on the girls' school. The trustees did not feel inclined to fund the money needed and suggested that it should come from the parish. As the school managers already had to find £259 for work on the girl's school and £100 for Eyton School, the rector wrote back:

> When I came to Bangor in 1868 Sir Philip Egerton asked me to take charge of the instruction in the Boys school at considerable cost of time and money but I did not undertake the care of the buildings. We cannot ask the farmers to help as they are in a very depressed condition. Several are giving up their farms through the bad times.

So once again nothing was done.

The accounts for the Endowed School for 1894.

BANGOR BOYS' ENDOWED SCHOOL,

FOR THE YEAR, 1894,

RECEIPTS.	£	s.	d.	EXPENSES.	£	s.	d.
Sir P. Egerton—Endowment	35	0	0	Master's Salary	77	1	0
O. Ormrod, Esq	2	2	0	Poor and Highway Rates	0	13	3
Rev. G. H. McGill	1	1	0	Books, Stationery, Drawing, &c,	7	7	8
Hon. Mrs. Tyrwhitt	1	0	0	Cleaning	2	2	6
Mrs. Randles	1	0	0	Furniture, Fuel, and Lights	8	10	8
Capt. & Mrs. Fenwick	1	0	0	Repairs, &c.	1	0	2
Capt. & Mrs. Pocklington	1	0	0	Balance due 1893.	0	5	11
Government Grant	31	7	0				
Fee Grant, 12 Months.	19	5	0				
Government Drawing Grant	2	17	0				
Balance due to Treasurer Nov. 1st, 1894	1	9	7				
	£97	1	7		£97	1	7

As the rector was in failing health, John Davies had taken over keeping the accounts for which he was paid £5 in addition to the £30 he received from the trust as master of the endowed school and by now his salary had been made up to £77 1s, as he was now also master of the boys of the National School. In July 1897, the school managers, who were now responsible for the running of both schools, agreed that he needed an assistant and they interviewed a Miss Isobel Winifred Morris for the post. Her references proving satisfactory they decided to employ her at £20 per annum with the addition of a railway season ticket.

In 1898, as the inspectors had condemned the condition of the boys' school on several occasions, a decision was taken to amalgamate the schools under one roof. This would entail the enlargement the girls and infant school by the building of a new infants classroom thus releasing the big classroom for the older children. To facilitate the scheme, the Duke of Westminster had offered to hand over the ownership of the girls' school buildings to the National Society for use as a Church of England school. This required plans to be submitted and approved and the sanctioning of the closure of the boys' school and the diversion of its endowment.

By February 1899, the Education Dept and H.M. Inspectors had approved the plans for the extension of the girls' school by twenty-one feet to accommodate a classroom for infants with sliding doors to separate it from the other room. It was proposed that Mr Davies should retire and that Mrs Davies be appointed mistress over the whole school with the necessary assistance, and that the income arising from the charity would be applied towards the salary of the mistress.

When the plans were shown to a public meeting of the ratepayers of the parish called to approve the scheme, despite the rector pointing out that there would be a saving of nearly £50 per annum on the working expenses, they voted not to adopt them. The main reasons given by those against the scheme were: opposition to the idea of a mixed school and either the making of a public subscription to defray the expenses or an addition to the rates. However by the time a further public meeting was called, especially when the school managers let it be known that they would resign unless a satisfactory outcome was forthcoming, the opposition had faded away and the scheme was approved with the cost of the work to be raised by public subscription.

It was decided to retain the schoolhouse for the schoolmaster and to charge a rent for its use. There was talk of selling the schoolroom but the trust finally decided instead to rent out it out to increase the income of the trust. Birch Cullimore & Douglas prepared a statement of the charity:

On the 31st December 1860 the rental of land and property was £53 per annum and there was a balance of £53 3s 7d in hand. After the cost of rebuilding the schoolmaster's house in 1861 when Messrs Phelps & Co advanced the whole of the cost of £252 9s 4d at 4% interest. £159,94 had been repaid, leaving a balance of £93 outstanding. Since the payment of £20 a year pension to Thomas Pritchard the Charity became overdrawn and now the balance due from the Charity amounted to £263 2s 7d.

By August 1900, the Charity Commission had given its consent to the closure of the boys' school and the diversion of the endowment, not towards the teacher's salary as the National School had wished, but to applying the whole of the income to the purpose of liquidating the debt. In February 1901, the building work was at last underway. Unfortunately the duke died before he had formally handed over the property to the National School and things were delayed once again whilst the school board waited to see if the new duke would ratify his intentions.

In July 1902, a formal application was made to the Charity Commission to close the Endowed School (sole trustee Sir Philip Henry Egerton) and to transfer the children to the Westminster/National School, although the children had actually been transferred a few months previously. The position of John Davies as headmaster was causing concern to the rector who wrote enquiring what was his position as he was 'a servant of the Charity' and was in limbo and had not received a formal letter ending his employment. John Davies decided to pre-empt the situation by sending in his resignation. He wrote that some time previously he had felt that his health was failing due to 'varicose'. A physician had examined him and had certified that he was unable to carry on in this, or any similar, post. He was subsequently informed that he could claim 'disablement allowance' but that he had to cease being a teacher at once and was, at the age of fifty-one, resigning as master from 31 July 1902 after twenty-two years' service. He asked the trustee and the Charity Commission for a little compensation as an acknowledgement of that service as, even in good health, he would find it difficult to obtain another situation, as the age limit for teachers was forty. The commissioners felt considerable hesitation in allowing any gratuity to be paid in view of the financial position of the charity, but they wrote to say they would not oppose if Sir Philip Egerton agreed to a sum not exceeding half a year's salary.

A letter was sent from the Charity Commission informing Birch Cullimore that they were prepared to sanction the closing of the Endowed School and that they were further prepared to authorise Sir Philip Grey Egerton to offer the school, schoolhouse and garden for sale. In their view, a sale of the other land in which the trust had its money invested would not be advantageous to the charity. The trust, however, decided not to sell, but to rent out the buildings.

In January 1903, Mrs Bessie Davies wrote to the agent:

> … that the schoolhouse is now so damp and dirty and is in such a bad state of repair that it is not fit to live in. The offices (the privies) outside are in ruins and the boundary walls are crumbling. It needs urgent attention. Houses in the village are extremely scarce.

Exactly one month later, John Davies informed the trust that a brick wall about fifteen yards long by two feet high, dividing the whole premises and the neighbouring property had fallen into the garden. Six days, later Richard Bostock wrote that

> … the high winds of last night have blown the chimney tops in pieces in Mr Davies's school house & damaged the slates & the roof must be attended to at once. Estimate £31.16.0 by Joseph Edwards for work needed to be done.

By the June, the roof and the chimney had been attended to but the wall had still not been rebuilt. In October, the schoolmaster complained of the state of repair of the ends of the house as rain was coming in and he felt that they should have the last six months rent-free.

The trust considered a proposal to sell the schoolhouse and paid for an estimate of the likely selling price. Despite the condition of the house, John Davies had put in an offer but as this was below that figure, he now offered the full estimate of £200. In the end the trust decided not to proceed with a sale but to continue letting the building. Davies had a lucky escape as, not long

Overton Road looking south with the schoolmaster's house on the right.

after he gave up the tenancy, high winds once again blew off the slates.

At the beginning of 1904, Mr and Mrs Davies gave notice that they were giving up possession of the schoolhouse for which they were paying rent of £6 per annum and the trust advertised for a new tenant. It received several replies, including one from H.B. Twiss, manager of the British and Continental Stores of Henblas Street, Wrexham and one from Samuel Lee, a shoeing smith of 252 Manchester Road, Castelton, Lancashire. The trustees agreed to rent the house and garden to Griffith Jones, tailor, at a rent of £8 a year. At the beginning of June, John Davies relinquished the tenancy.

Soon after taking up the tenancy Griffith Jones wrote to the trust:

… I find that the ancient Sun Dial on stand that stood in the front of the House has been taken away this week. I am given to understand that it has been there a long time. We have people in Bangor that lived in the House about 40 years ago and they tell me it was there then. I would like to have it back if you will kindly see to it.

The sundial had been removed by the rector and installed in the rectory garden and had not been returned. Jones and his family lived at the schoolhouse for some years and the trust continued to rent it out before finally selling it to Gordon Mytton in the 1960s . The schoolroom was rented out as a warehouse for storage until the debt was finally paid off in 1913, much to everyone's relief. The trust then considered a scheme to equip it to give the boys a course of handicraft and the girls a course of lessons in housecraft. In May 1917, the old schoolroom was reopened as a handicraft centre fitted out with worktops for the practice of carpentry that could be fitted over the cookery range and appliances for laundry work for the girls. The schoolroom was latterly also used as a dining room until one was built in the National School grounds. It was finally sold to the trustees of the Village Institute in 1963.

The Dame Dorothy Jeffreys Trust is still in existence. Apart from a nominated representative of the Egerton family, the trustees are members of the Eyton, Sesswick, Bangor and Overton community councils, the rectors of Overton and Bangor and a county councillor. It meets four times a year and continues to devote the income to providing pupils with such things as prizes for school work and, until recently, blazers, hats, school ties, etc, when they passed the eleven-plus to go to senior schools.

Bangor Apprentices

A parish would often place the children of families who were in receipt of poor relief into apprenticeships so as they would no longer be a charge on the local community. The schoolmaster or rector would recommend the children and it was customary for an apprentice to serve for seven years or, occasionally, until they were twenty-one years old. The master who agreed to take the child and instruct him in his trade would receive a sum of money to cover food, lodging and clothing.

> 1775 May 13. Received of the Rev. Frederick Lloyd the sum of five pounds towards the putting out of John Griffiths an apprentice for the township of Eyton. Received by me Robert Tamberlaine, Overseer of the Poor.
> Paid Samuel Turner towards putting out Samuel Edwards a poor apprentice for the Township of Pickhill. £5 to Samuel Weston, taylor. Signed Saml James, churchwarden & Ed Pritchard, Overseer of the Poor. Witness: William Leicester.
> 1776. Paid John Ellis towards putting out ... Edwards as poor apprentice £5 0s 0d for the township of Eyton
> 1777 Mar 31. Pd Edward Lloyd towards putting out Richard Jones an apprentice £4 0s 0d for the township of Sesswick.
> 1778 June 6. Pd John Davies for putting out J. Owen for the township of Pickhill, £5 10s.
> 1778 Aug 22. Pd John Wynne for putting out Edward Cook for the township of Eyton, £5 10s.
> 1778 Dec 12. Pd Mr Hughes & Thomas Hopley for putting out Charles Ralph for the township of Bangor, £5 10s.
> 1778 Dec 12. Pd Mr Hughes & Thomas Hopley for putting out Thomas Woollam for the township of Bangor, £3 3s.
> 1779 Nov 26. Pd Thomas Davenport, Overseer of the Poor for Eyton for putting out ...
> 1780 Ap 24. Pd John Rowlands, Overseer for Bangor, for John Jones to Daniel Edwards of St Mary's, Chester Parish, brick maker, £5 10s.
> 1780 Ap 26. Pd Richard Hughes, Overseer for Pickhill, for Edward Edmunds to Fred ... David Edwards for the township of Eyton. £5 10s Tesseman of Wrexham. £5 10s.
> 1780 May 3. Pd Richard Hughes, Overseer for Pickhill, Samuel Ollerhead to Jonas Evans of Gresford, shoemaker, £5 10s.
> 1781 Jan 15. Willm Roberts. Apprentice: John Ellis for Sesswick, £5 10s
> 1781 Feb 27. John Hoskings (signed Hotchkins), churchwarden, Overseer for Bangor, for Richard Prince to John Edgely of Halghton. £5 10s, for 7 years.
> 1781 Feb 27. ditto for John Clay to John Fruen of Willington, for 7 years.
> 1781 Feb 27. Geo Taylor for Richard Cathard to Thomas Blethin of Malpas blacksmith for 7 years. Witness J Stokes, for 7 years.

1782 Jan 10. John Hoskins for John Roberts to Thomas Jones of the Royal Oak in Wrexham, butcher for 7 years.

1782 May 7. John Hoskins for Owen Cathard to Thomas Roberts of Dodington, Salop, brick-maker, for 7 years

1784 Sep 27. Pd James Small for Bangor for James Hughes to John Williams of Penley, shoemaker, £5 10s for 5 years.

1785 Mar 30. John Evison for William Francis of Eyton to Thomas Richards of Wrexham, £5 0s 0d for 7 years.

John Evison for John Jones of Eyton to Wm Hughes of Eyton, taylor, £5 10s.

1786 July 14 Pd for Wm Hughes to Humphery Hughes of Wrexham, taylor, for 7 years.

1788 Jan 23 Pd for John Kenric to John Jones of Ruabon, wheelwright for Eyton township. £5 0s 0d.

1788 Mar 17 for the township of Eyton for James Davies to Samuel Ollerhead of Holt, taylor for 4 years £5 0s 0d.

Ap 14. William Cathard to Stephen Rodenhurst of Wrexham, builder for 7 years £5 10s.

Aug 4. Pd for the township of Bangor for William Fleet to Simon Jones of Ruabon, weaver for 7 years, £5 0s 0d.

1789 Jan 1. Edward Jones to James Pritchard for 7 years.

July 13. George Smith to Joseph Meredith for 4 years.

Aug 20. For Ryton, Daniel Davenport to Rich Jones of Wrexham, staymaker; for 3 years

1791 Feb 21. Pd Tristram Davenport & Thos Pearson for Roberts Edmunds for the township of Pickhill, £5 10s.

Ap 25. For the township of Eyton, William Cross to Thomas Bickley, taylor, £5 10s.

1792 Jan 8. For the township of Eyton, Edward Francis to Humphrey Hughes, taylor of Wrexham for 7 years.

Ap 21. Thomas Hopley to John Meredith of Hanmer, for 7 years.

May 14. For the township of Bangor, Joseph Evans.

Oct 27. For the township of Pickhill, Alexander Murdock to Edward Roberts of Wrexham, for 7 years.

Nov 6. For the township of Sesswick, Edward Hughes to John Hughes of Wrexham, taylor, for 7 years.

Dec 4th. Paid Elizabeth Pugh with Mary Ann Jones, an apprentice to a mantua maker in Wrexham for 1 year £5.

Paid Richard Edwards with Benjamin Holland, an apprentice to a Staymaker in Wrexham for 6 years £7.

Paid William Davies with Thomas Hughes for an apprentice to a Cordwainer in Wrexham for 4 years £7.

1793 Feb 16. For the township of Pickhill, David Rowland Jones to Edward Roberts of Wrexham shoemaker, £5 10s.

Ap 15. For the township of Eyton, John Reeves to Edward Parsonage of Wrexham, hairdresser, for 7 years.

1794 Feb 12. Wm Hughes to … £5 10s.

1795 Mar 7. William Stretch to William Powell of Wem, Salop for carpenter. £6 0s 0d.

Oct 11. Robert Hopley to Thos Jones, shoemaker, for 7 years.

Moses Edwards to Thos Edwards, Blacksmith for 7 years £6. 0s 0d.

1796 Ap 18. For the township of Bangor, Frances Edwards to William Hawkins of Ellesmere, carpenter.

1798 Nov 3. For the township of Ryton, Samuel Barnes to William Jones at Wrexham Abbot, shoemaker for 5 years, £6 0s 0d.

1799 Nov 4. For the township of Bangor, Thomas Matthews to Humphrey Hughes of Wrexham, taylor for 7 years, £6 0s 0d.

For the township of Sesswick, Thomas Jones to Edward Rogers of Wrexham, taylor, for 7 years, £6 0s 0d.

1802 Apr 19. For the township of Bangor, Charles Lloyd to Smith & Kendall of Liverpool, grocers, for 7 years, £6 0s 0d.

May 7. For the township of Eyton, Thomas Hughes to Edward Pritchard of Esclusham, shoemaker, for 5 years, £6 0s 0d.

Oct 18. For the township of Bangor, Robert Jones to John Jones of Worthenbury, shoemaker for 7 years.

1803 Feb 10. Robert Davies to Thomas Smith of Sesswick, joiner, for 5 years, £6 0s 0d.

1804 Jun 30. Edmund Kaye to Edward Davies of Wrexham, carpenter & joiner, £6 0s 0d.

Nov 1. John Edwards to John Jones of Bersham, taylor.

1819. Owen Taylor of Pickhill, an infant under the age of 21 to Richard Davies, cordwainer, of the parish of Wrexham for 7 years. Edward James of Pickhill, farmer, & Edward Edwards, farmer overseers of the poor for the parish of Pickhill.

1820 Aug 5. John Manley of the township of Bangor, an infant under the age of 21 apprenticed to Richard Edwards of the parish of Overton, wheelwright, for 7 years.

Signed: John Newnes of the parish of Bangor, farmer, overseer, & William Roden of Eyton, farmer, churchwarden, of the poor for the parish of Bangor.

1821 Feb. John Hanmer of the parish of Bangor, son of Jane Hanmer of Bangor, widow, to Thomas Davies of Wrexham, barber, for 7 years. Signed: Thos Wynn, Jno Smith, churchwardens, Edward Hanmer, overseer.

William Thomas of Gresford, blacksmith agreed to take David Thomas of Bangor for 7 years. Signed: M Wynn, Benjamin Harris, churchwarden, Edward overseer, Hanmer,

1844 Jun 1. Thomas Rogers of Sesswick to Thomas Griffiths, tailor of Overton, churchwarden.

Tho Griffiths had not received any money for the boy and had returned the boy.

Write to him. No indenture received offer 4 months.

Thomas Morris of the township of Bangor to John Darlington of Bersham, tailor for 7 years. Signed: Maurice Wynne, minister, Edward Davies, churchwarden, Sam Barker, Overseer.

Thomas Morris not bounded to John Darlington but to Thomas Davies.

1854. Edwards Ellis to Thomas Roberts of Pickhill, blacksmith, £8 0s 0d.

H. Thomas to W. Smith, machine maker, £8 0s 0d.

1856. Thomas Davies to …

1858. Jas Mumford to …

1859. D. Jones to Nathaniel Davies, £8 0s 0d.

Bangor National School

The Society for the Promotion of Christian Knowledge (SPCK), which had been founded in 1698, set up the National Society for the Education of the Poor in the Principles of the Established Church in 1811, whose aim was to set up a church school in each parish in England and Wales. In 1833, the society was supported by a government grant and as a consequence, from 1839 the schools had to be inspected. In 1832, the Marquess of Westminster bought a plot of land adjacent to the rectory from a former rector of Bangor, the Revd Maurice Wynne and at some time, possibly as early as 1840, had a schoolroom erected there at his own expense. The school was run under the auspices of the National Society for the 'children of the poorer classes' and was free, hence the alternative names of the Free or Westminster School.

A schoolmaster was appointed who ran the school with the help of an assistant pupil teacher and/or child monitors. The marquess was the patron and the school was maintained by a grant and subscriptions from local benefactors, with the patron heading the list with a large donation. Unlike the Endowed School little is known about the early days of the Free School. Logbooks had been introduced in the 1840s but only survive for this school from 1886 and the school managers minutes that exist only from 1897 – for a short time. From 1870, the school was required to keep admission registers but none of these survive. Apart from official inquiries and inspections much of the information has been obtained from newspapers.

In 1846, an inquiry was ordered into the standard of education and the provision of school premises in England and Wales and in January 1847, Henry Vaughan Jones sent his assistant, John James, to visit Bangor and to make a report. This report makes interesting reading and, if the report on the Endowed School was damning, that of the National School was much more encouraging. Unfortunately, the name of the first schoolmaster has not been recorded but from the inquiry we know that he was thirty-six years of age, married with a wife of the same age, was formerly engaged in farming and had been a teacher for six years. He had received no formal training other than six months in Pulford School in 1840. He was paid a salary of £40 per annum and he was also the vestry clerk for which he received £3. He was provided with a rent-free house and garden and his wife taught needlework to the girls every afternoon for two hours. John James reported that he 'does not speak good English: but he is careful, maintains good order, and his manner towards the scholars is good. His acquirements are limited'.

The front elevation of the early National School, date unknown. [FRO D/BP/1051]

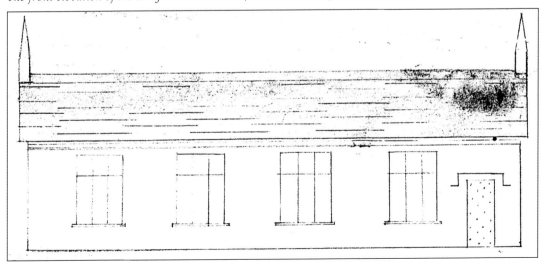

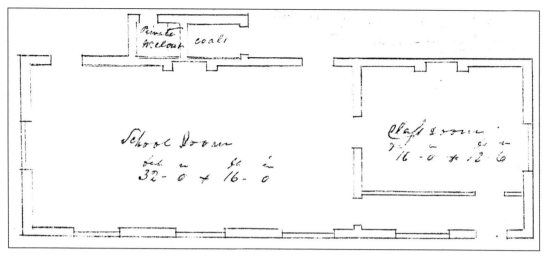

Ground floor plan of the early National School, date unknown.[FRO D/BP/1051]

According to the report the school had fifty-one scholars on its books: twenty-four boys and twenty-seven girls, of whom twenty-six had attended school from three to five years and twenty-nine of the pupils were over ten years of age. The subjects taught were reading, writing, arithmetic, the scriptures and the Church catechism. When the school was examined there were twenty-nine scholars present of whom fourteen could read with some ease; two out of twenty-five copies were well written. John James found that

> ... out of 18 children learning arithmetic, two could work sums in Proportion; the rest had not advanced beyond the simple rules. Every child present could repeat parts of the Church Catechism, nearly two-thirds perfectly; 19 answered Scripture questions, 14 of them with remarkable religious intelligence. Indeed, these were the best-informed children that I have met with, as regards religious knowledge. This appears to be owing to the care taken by the minister, who takes charge of the religious instruction of the scholars. Their attainments in other subjects did not match their scriptural knowledge. Boys and girls who could answer any question from Scripture were unable to work a plain sum in one of the first four rules of arithmetic.

An infant school for boys and girls had been opened on 20 May 1846 which shared the same building as the National School. The number of infants on the books was seventy-seven; with eight older pupils employed as monitors which was, by now, the accepted way to train pupil teachers who could be as young as thirteen. A mistress was employed to teach the infants at a salary of £15 per annum, with her dinner provided at the rectory daily. At the time of the report, she was nineteen years of age, had been a dressmaker and her only experience as a teacher had been a residence of one month at Threapwood Infant School in 1846. Her name is not given, but she may have been Judith Gregory, born in Worthenbury to John Gregory, a carpenter. At the time of the 1851 census she was aged twenty-three and was an infant school teacher lodging with James Munford and his family at Althrey Lodge.

The subjects taught were 'Reading, Scripture, Catechism, tablets etc'. On the day of the visit, there were twenty-two boys and twenty-two girls present of whom twenty-four were above five years of age. The inspector found that four children could read an easy verse in the New Testament; the rest were 'learning to read letters and monosyllables, or ignorant of the alphabet. There were 20 who could repeat 'The First Step in the Catechism;' and 4 could answer a few Scripture questions'. The school provided 'a kind of couch or bed in the room for the use of the smaller children. Seven children attend this school from a distance of more than a mile and a half'. John James adds 'It appeared that sufficient precaution had not been taken to drain the ground upon which the school stands'.

At some time after 1847, the children were separated, with the boys of the National School being taught with the boys of the Endowed School and the girls and infants sharing the National schoolroom. Whether this was at the recommendation of the inquiry is not known. This may have been because they did not want the expense of employing a man as he would be paid a higher salary than a women. There is no further mention of any subsequent masters of the National School, only mistresses, except for an article about the history of Bangor held in the Flintshire Record Office to which someone has added 'Written by Mr Acton, former Bangor headmaster'. There is no further reference to him and nothing is known about him.

The size of the annual grant was dependant on a favourable report by the school inspectors, and the Revised Code, published in 1862, introduced payment by results and the teacher's pay depended in part, on the children's performance in the examinations.

Judith Gregory left to be married in December 1860 to John Neale, a twenty-four year old schoolteacher from Ottery St Mary in Devon. Judith's age is not given in the Worthenbury marriage register but she would have been thirty-two. The next teacher of the National School whose name is known was a Miss H.A. Jeffreys who, with Thomas Pritchard, master of the Endowed School, organised a party for all the school children at Christmas 1864. She probably left Bangor in 1865 as Miss Elizabeth Coffinson aged eighteen, was employed as mistress of the girls' school later that year. She was still there in 1871 and, according to the census, had been born in Manchester and was lodging with Elizabeth Speed the widow of the late Endowed School master, Thomas Speed.

In January 1869, the children from all the schools in the parish, some 185 in number, were entertained with tea and plum cake kindly provided by Mr A. and Lady Georgiana Peel in the schoolroom. Afterwards fifty-two prizes, given by the rector, the Revd MᶜGill, were distributed to the most regular attenders of the day and Sunday schools. Such prizes often comprised such things as hard wearing frocks for the most deserving girls and peaked cloth caps for the boys.

In March 1869, another examination of the girls school took place and the following report was presented to the school managers.

This school has made a good beginning. The girls are intelligent and well taught in elementary subjects. The reading throughout the school is good and on the whole the examination has been satisfactory. Seventy pupils were present … there was not a single failure in reading, and in other subjects the girls acquitted themselves in a manner highly creditable to their teachers. The boy's school, being endowed, is not under Government inspection.

In 1870, the Education Act made attending school compulsory for all children and was no longer free. School Boards were elected to manage the schools and all were now subject to government inspection. This encouraged local patrons to improve the facilities provided in accordance with recommendations in the inspector's report. The School Board was made up of the *ex officio* (not known to attend) patron, the rector, and others who had to be members of the Church of England and who were drawn from amongst the list of subscribers.

In May 1872, Elizabeth Coffinson left to be married and was presented with inscribed tea and coffee pots, milk jug & sugar basin in electroplate. It was under her ministration that the school had received the excellent report and the managers would certainly have been sorry to see her go. The next schoolmistress to be appointed was Miss Sarah Clark, who had been born in London in about 1845, the daughter of William Clark a ship merchant. The following year the inspector's report on the girls' school was very favourable. 'Miss Clark has begun with energy, and the school already shows a decided improvement, both in attendance and discipline'. That year the combined grant for all the schools – boys, girls and Eyton, exceeded £70.

In 1877, Sarah Clark married Thomas Whitehead, the master of the Endowed School, not long after his appointment to that position. They had obviously been 'keeping company' for some time. The following year the school again had a good report:

> I was pleased to be able to complement the managers upon the improved appearance of the surroundings of the school, and upon the enlargement of the playground. The singing was 'particularly good.' I should advise that the boys and girls be taught singing together. The specimen work in sewing and knitting was 'praiseworthy.' The work in my presence was 'very good' throughout the school and in other respects the school has passed a pretty good examination. The work done is creditable to Mrs Whitehead.

In April 1879, the inspectors gave the school another good report:

> … the infants know the tables capitally, the rest of their work will need more attention. The grammar of the 111 standard was very fair, and 11, 1V, and V standards fair. The specimen needlework was, as usual, good. The work done in my presence was fair. Some of the spelling was weak. In other respects the standard work was pretty good. The tone, order and singing were all good. The school accounts are excellently kept by the rector. A pupil teacher was advisable. The government grant is £44.13.

There was another good report the following year from Morgan Owen, H.M. Inspector.

> The infants in the first class were good in reading, spelling and form; pretty good in arithmetic and tables. The reading throughout the school was of a good character and the singing of the whole school was decidedly good. The accounts were kept in the most proper and methodical order. Mrs Whitehead should have the help of a pupil teacher – managing with just monitors.

The combined grants of the schools exceeded the largest that had ever been achieved in previous years amounting to £115, based on population.

Sarah must have been pressing the managers for the assistance of an assistant or pupil teacher since the 1879 inspection report without success and when she found she was expecting their first child she supported her husband in looking for another, better paid, post – no doubt armed with a copy of the excellent inspector's report. In 1880, soon after the report was published, she and her husband departed for pastures new.

Obviously the school managers were trying to keep cost down by paying senior pupils to act as monitors, who since 1870 had to be fourteen years of age, instead of employing an assistant teacher with more experience, to help the mistress. Fundraising events were frequently held to boost the school funds such as a concert in January 1878, which was reported in a newspaper.

A musical entertainment was given in the girls schoolroom at Bangor Isycoed, the proceeds being devoted in aid of the Bangor and Eyton National Schools. There was a very full attendance, the schoolroom being crowded long before the concert commenced, and several were unable to gain entrance. The programme, which contained a very excellent selection of readings and songs, was admirably gone through, and gave great general satisfaction.

Members of the wealthier local families often provided treats for the children of all the schools such as in August 1876 when, according to the *Wrexham Advertiser*:

Tuesday being the birthday of Capt Mostyn Owen of Althrey Woodhouse, Bangor, the children of the boys' and girls' schools, also the Sunday school children from the chapel, altogether numbering 130 were regaled with tea and plum cake etc on the lawn in front of the hall. After doing ample justice to the good things provided for them they enjoyed themselves in running races and other sports for prizes viz; books, pocket handkerchiefs etc.

In 1891, the National School was given the gift of a grand piano by Mr and Lady Georgiana Peel of the Gerwyn and in 1895 Captain Tyrwitt, RN, of Althrey Hall, who was in the Mediterranean with his squadron, forwarded two cases of oranges for distribution amongst the children.

In 1880, with the departure of the head teachers of both the Endowed and National Schools, the trust and the school board advertised for a master and mistress to run the two schools, no doubt saying that preference would be given to a married couple. Mrs Bessie Davies was the successful applicant, her husband being given the post of master of the Endowed School. She had the charge of the girls, but still with only the help of senior pupils as school monitors.

In addition to annual visits from Her Majesty's inspectors, the Church inspectors also visited the school and reported in February 1881:

The school passed a satisfactory examination in Catechism, Old and New Testament history. The repetition and writing from memory were good. The following received honour certificates: Group 1, Annie Pritchard, Group 2, Janet Mullock, Alice Blake, Lizzie Thomas, and Florence Johnson, Group 3, Mary Roberts, Mary Edwards, and Louisa Johnson, Group 4, Mary J Green. The Infants school prizes were given to: Deborah Williams, Gertrude Johnson, Thomas Mullock, and Sarah J Powell.

In September 1881, Mrs Peel of Bryn-y-Pys distributed the sewing and knitting prizes gained by the girls attending the school. After the rector had expressed the hope that the good instruction given them would be of benefit to them in the future, the prizes for sewing were given to Elizabeth Thomas, Mary Roberts, Judith Davenport, Annie Cheetham, Margaret Lewis; and for knitting to Mary Ann Jones, Janet Young, Phyllis Mullock, Alice Taylor, Sarah J Davies, Sarah Powell and Sarah Goswell.

In 1883, Mrs Davies started the first of the two log books that have survived. That year she reported that the average number of children attending was sixty-nine out of eighty enrolled in the school. Boys shared the infant class with the girls until they were seven years old when they were sent to the boys' school. The rector, Revd McGill, took a couple of classes each week and the curate Revd McGonigle took an average of one a week in scripture and arithmetic. The Misses McGill checked the needlework and tested the pupils. The pupil teacher was Louisa Johnson, a local girl born in Bangor who had just been appointed, aged fourteen, and she took charge of the infants. Senior pupils were appointed at 1s a week to act as monitors. In 1889, two girls, twelve-year-old Jenny Hughes and Fanny Griffiths agreed to share the job on alternate weeks.

In 1890, Louisa Johnson was examined in all subjects and Mrs Davies decided that she needed more attention before sitting the scholarship exam. In the 1891 census she was now nineteen and staying with Richard Holland, a tailor, and his wife Alice. In July 1891, she was given the greater part of the week off to study for her forthcoming scholarship, which she gained and, proudly bearing her certificate, she left for an assistant's post in another school. Jenny Hughes, still under fourteen, was put in charge of Standard I and, until a permanent teacher was obtained, Emily Davies, aged thirteen, was made a monitor at 1s a week to take the infants class.

In 1891, when Mrs Davies had to attend her mother's funeral and Emily Davies was away all week, rather than closing the school, John Davies brought the boys over and taught the combined school assisted by the rector's two daughters. This happened on several occasions. Sometimes she had to resort to borrowing an assistant from Eyton School to help out.

By January 1892, Emily Davies had left and Jenny Hughes was off sick, so Mrs Davies had no choice but to close the school. The inspector's report that year said that 'she was about to resign her position as she needs more help'. He adds that the schoolroom required whitewashing and a stove. The following year he recommended that a large porch be built, that new windows were needed and new toilets, which could be built at the back of the school, were required.

As Bangor did not possess a village hall, the National schoolroom was used for most social events and meetings held in the village. Mrs Davies was irked by the need to close the school so that the classroom could be prepared for these functions, as it disrupted the smooth running of the school and she began keeping a record in the log book. Entries such as: October 1893 '... schoolroom required by rector for a clerical meeting at 2.30 p.m.. School closed'. One wonders why did he not use either the church or the rectory? 30 November: 'School ends on Thursday this week as schoolroom is required on Friday preparing for a dance in the evening'. 15 December: 'No school on Friday afternoon as the choir were giving an entertainment in the evening'. She really was incensed when she wrote in March 1897: '... classroom has been scrubbed before school and soaking wet for the children to sit in. Done by a person who had been given permission for a dance to be held in the evening. This quite upset the school as all pictures had been taken down and some things thrown disorderly in the porch.' The pupils probably did not mind being given the time off.

All these days or half days were in addition to the school being closed for events taking place in the village such as, a half-day holiday to mark the wedding of a local person such as Miss F. Fearnall in May 1896 and five months later for her sister's wedding; when it was Race Day; when one of the Friendly Societies was holding a sports day or when Bostock's Menagerie visited the village. It made it difficult for Mrs Davies to maintain the teaching curriculum, particularly when an epidemic of one of the childhood diseases such as scarlet fever or measles swept the school, necessitating the closure for several weeks. Schooling was also disrupted when the weather affected attendance and heavy snowfalls or flooding kept the children at home.

By the end of 1893, Jenny Hughes had left and a new pupil teacher, Miss Helen Stott was appointed and given charge of Standard I and the infants class. Lydia Bostock, a monitor, was put in charge of the second-class infants but failed to keep them in order. Mrs Davies tried the new teacher with Standard II but found that she had little control over them and had refused to use the blackboard. A week later, she again urged Miss Stott to use blackboard with her class but still did not do so. At the end of March, Mrs Davies had to ask one of the older girls to take the infants in singing as 'Lydia Bostock is incapable and neither does Miss Stott sing'. In April, when Mrs Davies was taken ill, her husband had again to bring the boys over to join the girls' school as 'the girls' staff was incapable of managing the school on their own.

The following item appeared in a Wrexham newspaper:

An incident has occurred in connection with the Bangor Girls School that has caused a great deal of feeling. The staff consisted of the head mistress, Mrs Davies, who has conducted the school with great interest for upwards of 15 years, and a female teacher. Everything was going on remarkable well until the other day, when the younger teacher asked for an increase in salary, which the rector refused, the consequence being the teacher 'struck'. A young, inexperienced teacher was then appointed, but Mrs Davies at such a critical period, the Government examination being near, refused to stake her reputation as a teacher, and she too 'struck'. The school difficulty was amicably settled.

In May, on the day of Morgan Owen's inspection, Helen Stott left. When his report was published he again laid great stress on the need for proper help to be given to the mistress and that new desks and benches were needed for the infant school. In June, Lydia Bostock, a paid monitor, took the whole day off to help her mother with the washing, leaving the schoolmistress without any help whatsoever for the whole day. Finally, in October, Lydia Bostock left and, as Mrs Davies wrote in the log book, 'without giving notice of her intentions, she had no delight in her work and the infants were much neglected by her'. In her absence, the girls from the first class taught the infants and Standard I class.

In 1895, Mrs Davies had to request help from Eyton School and a pupil teacher named Mary Evans came to help with Standard I, II and infants' classes for one month. Later in the same year she borrowed Mary Williams of Royton, a pupil teacher as a temporary help. The inspector reported again that the mistress needed the help of an assistant teacher or two pupil teachers. In September, Jenny Hughes returned to school as an Article 68 pupil teacher and took charge of the infants. This year the inspector's report stated that

… the old offices [toilets] had not been pulled down as recommended in my last report and the surface drainage requires attention. Infants: 'On my visit the infants were not taught in the classroom as it is not big enough and would be overcrowded. The first class infants were taught by an article 68 teacher in the main room, the rest were looked after by one of the older girls.

He was clearly not impressed. A month later, the walls and floor had been cleaned, the old offices removed and the bad spouting and drainage attended to.

Two years later, he again said that 'the infants are still being taught part in the main room and part in the classroom, which should be enlarged. The gallery should be furnished with suitable desks and backrests'. This is the first time that the presence of a gallery in the school has been mentioned. It was probably put in when the school was built or not long after. In 1898 the inspector's report said that 'the managers had improved the playground by drainage and had covered it with gravel. The classroom will I hope be made more attractive and the present antiquated gallery removed'.

Discussions were now underway to combine the schools under one roof, initially by building an extension on the boys' school. Plans were drawn up to that effect but an alternate suggestion was made that extending the girls' school would be the better option. The rector wrote to the education department with reference to the buildings at the boys' school mentioned in the HMI's report, requesting that work on these buildings be postponed as the managers were now investigating the possibility of enlarging the girls' school to make it a mixed school.

At the manager's meeting in February 1899, the dilapidated condition of the boys' school, which had been condemned several times by HMIs, was discussed. There were only ninety children on the books of the two schools and, as there was already sufficient accommodation for that number in the present girls' school, it was decided that a mixed school should be formed. In order to meet the requirements of the education department it was agreed that a new classroom for the infants should be built and all the necessary alterations be made to the school buildings and playgrounds. Plans to this effect were submitted by the architects and were accepted subject to the approval of the education department and the inspectors.

In December 1899, a public meeting was called, chaired by the Revd Elrington Bissett, to discuss the recommendations of the school inspector who advocated extending the girls and infants school to take in the boys under one roof by building a twenty-one feet extension to form another classroom. They had two courses open to them, one was the repair of the boys school, which was in a dilapidated state, and the enlargement of the classroom and other improvements which, 'in his opinion would be like putting new cloth onto old garments'. It would be throwing away money that could be devoted to the second scheme – extending the present girls school to accommodate the three departments under one roof. Such a scheme had been sanctioned by the education department and, if adopted, would mean a saving of £60 a year.

The rector said that he foresaw one difficulty with respect to the proposed alterations, and that was with respect to the ownership of the girls' school and the land on which it was built. In 1900, the Duke of Westminster with his well-known generosity had offered to transfer the ownership of the building and land to the National Society for the benefit of the parish. In addition, he had offered to give a strip of land to provide a better access and driveway to the premises from the High Street. Up until then, the children had been walking up the rectory drive in order to reach the school. There were three schools in the parish and owing to the increasing requirements of the education department it was a difficult matter to keep them all going. If they fell in with the second scheme, there would not only be a saving of about £60 a year but also the only extra staff that would be required would be an assistant mistress and a pupil teacher. The rector estimated the amount of money required for the extension would be about £250 to £260.

The rector was asked whether it was intended to do away with a schoolmaster and whether it was advisable to conduct the schools on a 'mixed' system. He replied that you had only to look at the Eyton mixed school to see that it was an excellent school. The money from the endowed school would, it was hoped, be transferred to the new school for the employ-ment of a headmaster or mistress. Mr Sutton remarked that he was an old school manager, a large ratepayer and his family had lived in the parish for 400 years and he proposed that things remained as they were. His remarks carried weight with the meeting, the propos-ition was seconded and put to the vote and the motion was carried.

This was a setback and at a meeting of the school managers in June 1900 chaired by rector, with the Hon. Alex Parker and Mr Ormrod present, the special report from the education department with reference to the condition of the boys' school and the infant classroom was again reconsidered. The managers decided that unless the ratepayers in the parish agreed to adopt the amalgamation scheme and made a offer to subscribe a sum of money towards defraying the expenses of the building, that the managers would be unable to carry on the work on the schools and must resign their position. It was decided that another public meeting would be called. In the meantime, the duke had died before he could formally hand over the ownership of the school and land and there was a delay whilst the managers waited to see if his successor agreed to carry out his intentions. A second public meeting was held on 2 July 1900, by which time the opposition to the amalgamation of the schools had faded away and, subject to a satisfactory outcome over the ownership, the meeting voted to proceed with the second scheme and to fund it from a voluntary subscription. Tenders for the work were invited and finally that of Messrs Parker of Chester was accepted and work commenced in July 1901. By the September, the school had been enlarged and the playground divided. It was decided to double the insurance of the school to £1,000 and to cover the schoolyard with cinders.

The question arose about the representation of the Bangor Parish Council on the committee, as Dr Edwards Jones was anxious that they should be represented. After some discussion the following motion was proposed by Mr Ormrod and seconded by Mr Fearnall – that the parish council should have one direct representative on the committee, elected by themselves (that representative being a member of the Church of England and a subscriber of not less than 20s to the school). This was carried unanimously.

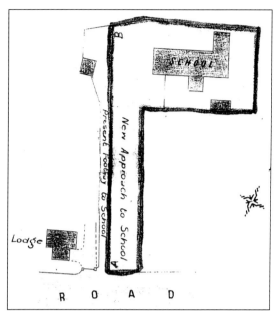

The Duke of Westminster gave the land on which the school was built and the strip of land in front to improve access to the school in 1901. Note the exten-sion at the rear built to accommodate the boys from the Endowed School.

The educational system in England and Wales was completely reorganised in 1902 when responsibility for all levels of education was given to local education authorities (LEAs). The question of the four foundation managers for Eyton and Bangor schools under the new Education Act was discussed and the following were elected to serve for both schools: Revd Mordaunt Elrington Bisset (rector); the Hon Alex R. Parker, Deeside, Bangor; Oliver Ormrod Esq. of Pickhill Hall, Denbighshire and Mr Thomas Fearnall, of Royton, Denbighshire.

In June 1901, the work commenced on the building of the new classroom and on 8 October the school reopened after thirteen weeks with the painters still on the premises as the work had been more extensive than had been anticipated. Ten days later, John Davies brought the boys over to join the girls and the Endowed School was closed. After the initial novelty of being a mixed school had worn off, the children soon settled down under the tutelage of two senior teachers. In February, Mrs Davies wrote in the log book: 'Teacher (Jenny Hughes) late no books out. Bell should be rung 10 minutes before 9.0 a.m. and all books out in readiness for lessons'. Again a few months later she reported: 'Jenny Hughes again late. No bell rung, front not unlocked and no preparation for day's work'. In the August, John Davies resigned due to ill health and the managers decided to offer the post of head mistress of the combined schools to Mrs Bessie Davies at a salary of £85 per annum and advertised for a second mistress, an Act 50 teacher, at a salary of £45–50 and a Mrs Williams was appointed. By September, Mrs Davies was recording: 'Boys much improved in discipline and obedience,' and in October, 'Boys are becoming much more orderly and attentive'.

In October 1902, Jenny Hughes resigned her position and in January Miss Matilda Sperring was appointed in her place as an Act 68 teacher in charge of the infants at a salary of £35. Two older pupils, Annie Shone and Ethel Williams, were paid as monitors, but were warned about absenting themselves on several occasions and A. Cassell was made a temporary monitor. In May, the inspector's report was received: 'the enlargement of the Girls School and the conversion into a mixed school is a great success. Discipline is satisfactory. A urinal and lavatory are needed'.

In September 1903, Miss Sperring resigned and was replaced by Miss Helena Bostock. Mrs Williams also resigned in December and Miss Isobel Winifred Morris was appointed in her place and commenced her duties on 1 February 1904. In March, it was reported in the log book: 'Four boys rebellious whilst being taught by assistant: William Jones, Leonard Jones, William Poynton and Alf Holland.' In October, we learn that 'William Taylor and George Humphreys both big boys were marked absent coming in at 10.0 a.m. after registers had closed. Both are idle boys.'

By now, the school was known as a Voluntary Provided (V.P.) school. In 1906, the system of using senior pupils as monitors was abolished. The staff now settled into a routine after a period of constant change until March when Helena Bostock left and Mrs Davies had to ask her daughter, Mabel, and Miss Mary Jones to take temporary charge until Miss E. Martin came as the new infant teacher. In December, Mrs Bessie Davies retired as headmistress. Her time as head had been a constant battle to have more staff to help her and having to use pupils to help with the infants.

On 26 January 1907, John and Bessie Davies were given a present subscribed by past and present pupils of the schools as a mark of the esteem in which they were held. They remained in Bangor, initially at Orchard House, and later at Tŷ Graig where John ran a small private school for several years. He was always very active in village affairs, being clerk of the parish council and an assistant overseer of the poor for twenty-seven years. He had at various times been secretary of many local societies as well as a member of the church choir, occasionally playing the organ and serving for twelve years as churchwarden. In 1927, he and his wife retired to Birkdale, Southport to be near their son where they died in 1929 and 1937 respectively.

On 10 December 1906, George James Moss, a twenty-five year old bachelor, was appointed headmaster of Bangor Schools. He had come from Flint, but he was a local man said to be a native of Coedpoeth. He took over the log book begun by Mrs Davies but his entries were sparse and not as informative or as interesting as previously.

In 1908, when Miss Martin was off sick, initially with flu and later with rheumatism, Miss Eva Williams and later Miss Alice Davies were appointed temporary supply teachers in her place. Miss Martin finally resigned in November of that year and Miss Margaret (Maggie) Lloyd Jones came as a temporary uncertificated teacher in December and stayed on as an assistant, sitting her teachers certificate examination in March 1912. She was appointed headmistress of Erbistock School a year later. She was the sister of John Arthur Lloyd Jones who was killed in the First World War and is commemorated on the War Memorial. John Davies, although retired, stood in for the headmaster for a fortnight when he was ill with flu in March 1909.

After an inspector's report in November 1907 which stated that the schoolyard needed improving, people rallied around and organised a concert that took place to a crowded audience to raise the necessary funds and in November 1910 the scholars gave another concert to a crowded schoolroom at which the mayor and mayoress of Wrexham, Dr and Mrs Edwards Jones, were present.

In 1912, George Moss married Isobel Winifred Morris in Caernarfon. She had joined the staff of the school in 1904 and their son, Stanley, was born in January 1916. In December 1913, the annual prize distribution took place when Mrs Fenwick of Plâs Fron unveiled an honours board, the gift of the local authority, and also gave out the prizes. The school had been extremely successful during the year winning half of the scholarships offered in the district. This honours board is now propped against a wall in the church tower, abandoned and forgotten. There are twenty-nine names inscribed on it. The names are:

1907	Herbert Welborn	1916	John William Bloxham
1909	Thomas E. Prichard		Albert Bloxham
1911	Violet May Edwards	1919	Gladys Hopley
1912	Gertrude Lloyd Jones		Hilda Pady
	Ethel Louisa Bennett	1920	May Jones
	William J. Jones		William Griffiths
1913	Joseph Hughes (*Daily Sketch* Comp)	1921	George Dunbabin
	Eva Goswell	1922	Denis Daly
	Joseph Hughes	1923	Bartlem Henry Griffiths
1914	Louisa Welborn	1926	Thomas Flanders Preston
	Florence Pritchard		Margaret Dunbabin
1915	Gladys Williams		William Edward Barlow
	John Raymond Blake	1928	John C. Woolley
	Ethel Parry		Thomas A. Dodd.
	Herbert Hughes		

No new names have been added since 1928.

The HMI's report of 1914 stated:

Since the last report the adaptability of the school for teaching purposes has been greatly improved by the erection in the main room of a sliding partition. The small classroom, which is found very convenient for the instruction of a few older scholars, is encumbered by large cupboards, which might advantageously be moved to another part of the premises'. He goes on to criticise the antiquated desks still in use and advocating their replacement. He finishes by remarking that 'the tone and discipline of the school is highly satisfactory however one class has had five different teachers since last August but under its present capable teacher is rapidly gaining lost ground.

For some time, the managers had contemplated equipping the old Endowed School to give the boys a course in handicraft and the girls a practical course of lessons in house-craft. When the old schoolroom had been equipped with a cookery range, appliances for laundry work and benches for woodwork, the opening ceremony was performed by Mrs Peel of Bryn-y-Pys in May 1917. The centre was under the charge of Mr Moss but the teaching and the staffing were the responsibility of the Flintshire Education Authority. The cookery classes were in the charge of a Miss Holdsworth. The children of the village school were admitted on attaining the age of eleven years and it was planned that the centre would be open to scholars from Overton and Worthenbury.

In December 1922, the annual prizes were distributed by Mrs Edwards Jones, the doctor's wife, who congratulated the winners, but urged everyone to try their very best and to remember that those who do not win prizes often went on to be very successful in life. The following prizes were awarded:

Dame Dorothy Jeffreys Prize for Religious Knowledge: Olwen Pritchard.
Managers' Prizes for Religious Knowledge: Frank Young, Leslie Humphreys, Bartlem Griffiths, Elizabeth Madeley.

Most Womanly Girl (given by the rector): Dorothy Lamb.
Most Manly Boy (given by Mr Oliver Ormrod): Bartlem Griffiths.
Needlework Prize (given by Mrs Fenwick): 1. Doris Madeley, 2. Dorothy Lamb,
    3. Barbara Brazendale.
Needlework Prize (awarded by Mrs Pitcairn Campbell): Vera Lewis.
Gardening Prize (awarded by Mr A Pitcairn Campbell): 1. Harry Griffiths & William Spoor, 2. Frank Young & Frank Hewitt, 3. Arthur Done & Tom Green.
Arithmetic Prize (awarded by Mr J. Mort): Dorothy Lamb, Louie Williams, Joseph Armstrong, Vera Parry.

Bangor V.P. School Honour's Board erected in 1913.

Bangor school pupils in 1914.

General Knowledge Prize (awarded by Mrs Mackenzie): Stds V& VI: Bartlem Griffiths, Olwen
     Pritchard, Madeleine Daly. Special: Harry Griffiths'. Std IV: Walter Young.
Prizes awarded by Mrs Oliver Evans for proficiency in Sunday school work: Olwen Pritchard
     and Lena Mullock.
Certificates were awarded to a large number of scholars for proficiency in religious knowledge
     and also for certificates in attendance awarded by the local education authority.

In January 1923, the HMI reported:

On the whole the school is being maintained in a thoroughly creditable state of efficiency and that
some of the work tested in the senior class merited the summary mark 'Excellent'. The oral
answering in general knowledge, history geography and arithmetic was thoroughly satisfactory.

Bangor pupils c.1950.

Class of 1923/4. Back Row L–R: –?–; –?– Prandle; –?–; Jim Johnson; 'Rusty' Spoor; Bill Davies; –?–; –?–; Connie Matthews; Daisy Jarvis (Dodd); Ursula Butler(?); Sue (Vera) Spoor; Louie Lewis. Front Row L–R: Jessie Fowles (Poynton); –?–; –?–; Linda Lewis; George (Dode) Humphreys; Mary Crawford; –?– Roberts; Annie Johnson; Gladys Roberts (Dedicot); Trix Clarke (France); Ursula Butler (?); Doris Oliver; Lettie –?–; Dolly Thomas.

In January 1924, Gwendoline Green of Johnstown began her duties as a certificated mistress. She had been educated at Grove Park Girls' School and trained at St Mary's College, Bangor, under canon John Fairchild. At the school prize giving that year the following prizes were distributed by General Peel:

Dame Dorothy Jeffreys Prize for Religious Knowledge: F Bartlem Griffiths, Frank Young.

Most Manly Boy (rector): George Evans.

Most Womanly Girl (Mr Ormrod): Nancy Dodd, Elsie Bevan.

General Knowledge (Mrs Mackenzie): William Jones, Edith Mitton, and William Prandle.

Needlework (Mrs Pitcairn Campbell): Mary Hughes.

Gardening (Mr Pitcairn Campbell): Jack Prandle, Frank Young, Joseph Fowles and
    William Spoor.

Arithmetic (Mr J Mort): Louie Williams, Margaret Griffiths, Margaret Dunbabin and
    Jack Fowles.

Regular Attendance (L.E.A.): Harry Young and Mary Poynton.

Empire Day 1924 was celebrated at the Bangor Schools with the scholars singing a selection of national airs. Mrs Fenwick Palmer presented the prize for needlework to Doris Madeley and Mrs Okell gave a prize to May Spoor. An exhibition of country dancing was given by the senior girls, trained by Miss Green, accompanied by Miss Twiss who also played for dancing.

At the annual prize-giving in January 1927, Mrs Gossage of Gerwyn Hall made the presentation.

For unbroken attendance: Harry Young; for two years unbroken attendance Ivy Prandle; 96%
    attendance James Poynton, William E. Barlow, Thomas F Preston, Mary Poynton, John Spoor,

In 1925 children were allowed to watch the Bangor Races traffic: 3rd from left, Jessie Fowles; 4th from left Hilda Morris' sister, Elsie; boy in front in light jumper, Charlie Spoor; boy behind Charlie, Harry Young; boy in front row eating, George Dode Humphreys; girl to left of George, Elsie Mytton; boy to right of George, Joseph 'Rusty Spoor; girl peeping over head of little girl in front row, Maggie Roberts (Mrs Jack Roberts's daughter); two boys to right of little girl in front, cousins Geoff Dodd (left) and Tom Dodd (right).

John C Woolley, Margaret Roberts, Edwin Bevan, Connie Matthews, Mary Thomas, Jessie Fowles, Vera Spoor; 98% attendance Elsie Bevan, Mary Hughes, Lily Griffiths, Thomas Prandle, Annie Johnson, Henry Preston and Joseph Spoor.

Dame Dorothy Jeffreys Prize for Religious Knowledge: Tom Preston, Elsie Bevan and Emma Woolley.

Managers' Prize: Walter Young, Margaret Dunbabin, Eddie Barlow.

Needlework (Mrs Fenwick of Plâs Fron, Mrs Baldock, wife of the rector and Mrs Phoenix): Class A – Mary Hughes, Elsie Bevan; Class B – Emma Woolley; Class C – Muriel Jones.

General Knowledge (Mrs Mackenzie): Class A – William Turner; Class B – Elsie Jarvis. Class C – Stanley Moss. Juniors: John Woolley and Muriel Jones.

Arithmetic Prize (Mr J. Mort): Seniors – Tom Presto, Elsie Jarvis, Tom Dodd. Juniors – John Woolley, Leslie Betteley.

Gardening (Mr A. D. Pitcairn Campbell): 1. William Prandle, Walter Young; 2. James Poynton, Tom Parry; 3. James Betteley.

Headmaster's prize for conduct: James Poynton.

Mrs Gossage gave each of the successful scholarship candidates – Thomas Flanders Preston, Margaret Dunbabin and William E. Barlow – a copy of *Chambers Twentieth Century Dictionary*.

Prize-winning scholars of 1927 proudly wearing their medals. Back row L–R: Stanley Moss (schoolmaster's son); –?–; –?–; John Woolley. Seated L–R: Elsie Jarvis; Myra Woolley; –?– Roberts (Mrs Jack Roberts' eldest daughter). Bottom Row L–R: Geoff Dodd; John Spoor; –?–.

After the prizes were distributed, the managers provided the children with a tea in Twiss's Assembly Room, and Professor Humo entertained them with his doll, Joe King, and clever conjuring tricks. Each child was presented with a gift and a bag of sweets.

In the September, the diocesan inspector reported that the children were keen to do work and gave proof of having been thoroughly well taught. The Dame Dorothy Jeffreys' prize for Religious Knowledge went to Harry Young and the Managers' Prize for Religious Knowledge was won by John Spoor and Geoffrey Dodd.

In 1928, Mr Moss, the headmaster, moved his family to live in Wrexham and thereafter caught the bus to Bangor each day, but often walked home. He was said to have later suffered from 'St Vitus' Dance.

Captain Holford Harrison of Maes-y-Nant (now the Cross Lanes Hotel) presented the annual prizes in January 1931.

The local education authority's prize for unbroken attendance for three years was won by Hilda

Bangor pupils dressed as soldiers c.1930. L–R: –?–; Sarah Roberts (daughter of Mrs Jack Roberts); May Jones; Hilda Roberts; Michael Daly; Lesley Griffiths in front with Kathleen –?–; Gerald Dodd above Kathleen; third from right Nesta Hopley; second from right Geoff Arrowsmith.

Roberts; one year unbroken attendance: Leonard Prandle, Dode Roberts, May Shone, Olive Humphries. Over 98%: Edna Berry, Len Dunbabin, Sarah Roberts, Joyce Berry, George Bartlem Humphries, Geoffrey Arrowsmith, Reginald Shone, and Thomas Roberts. Over 95%: Elsie Woolley, Dorothy Prandle, Violet Spoor, Nesta Hopley.

Dame Dorothy Jeffreys Prize for Religious Knowledge: Joseph Spoor.

Managers' prize: Hettie Large, Vera Spoor, Thomas Prandle, Lena Fowles.

Honours certificates: Daisy Jarvis, Doris Roberts. Gold: Hilda Fowles, Elsie Woolley. Violet: Cyril Spoor, Reggie Williams, James Johnson. Red: Reggie Shone, Richard Prandle, Eunice Bennett, Sarah Roberts, May Shone, George Humphreys, Alfred Fowles and Allan Spoor. Blue: Denis Arrowsmith, Joyce Berry, Rose Woodfine, Hilda Roberts. Black: Ronnie Blackford, Ronnie Stevenson, Leslie Griffiths, Sybil Jarvis. Infants: Thomas Roberts, Newton Dunbabin, Mabel Bellis, May Jones, Hilda Pugh, Doreen Roberts, John Robinson.

Needlework: Senior (Mrs Fenwick): Elsie Mitton, Mary Thomas. Junior (Mrs Bostock & Mrs Phoenix): Elizabeth Pugh, Elsie Fowles.

Gardening (Mr A. D. Pitcairn Campbell): 1. Edwin Bevan and Joseph Spoor, 2. Daisy Jarvis and Elsie Mitton, 3. Eric Green and Leonard Prandle.

Arithmetic (Captain Harrison): Class I – Elsie Woolley, Tom Prandle; Class II – Joyce Berry, Zena Dunbabin; Class III – Denis Arrowsmith, Ronnie Blackford.

Diligence and good behaviour (Mrs Gossage): Class I – Edna Berry, Edwin Bevan; Class II – Eric Green, Eric Shone; Class III – Michael Daly, Hilda Pugh.

Royal Sanitary Institute (Health Week essays): Elsie Woolley (prize), Sheila Copnall (certificate).

Due to an influenza outbreak, the 1933 prize giving was postponed until July 1934. Stuart Peters had made the maximum number of attendances whilst Leslie Jones had won a scholarship to Grove Park School and Cyril Peters had also done well, gaining free admission to the same school. Presenting the prizes, Major Hugh Peel said that a number of scholars had gone on to great success in their careers and he quoted Herbert Welbourn who having gained a scholarship in 1907 was now the headmaster of a Manchester school. Others had been admitted to universities and colleges and now held responsible positions. The outstanding example he quoted was that of Joseph Hughes of Graig Lane who won a scholarship from Bangor and later went to Oxford where he gained a first in Chemistry and was employed as an analytical chemist at Brunner Mond & Company in Stockton-on-Tees.

In 1936, to celebrate the headmaster's thirty years at Bangor school, the pupils were given a day's holiday. Mr J.T. Phillips, a former pupil and superintendent of the Municipal Gardens at Slough, sent a message of congratulations. He had been successful in getting into royal service after the war, in which he had served in the Royal Flying Corps. He became royal florist at Buckingham Palace. He was later gardener to HRH Princess Victoria and after her death he took up his appointment at Slough.

In December 1937 annual prize giving Mrs Gossage presented the prizes to the following children:

Dame Dorothy Jeffreys Prize for Religious Knowledge: May Jones, Kathleen Barlow, John Campbell Pritchard.

Managers Prize: Arthur O. Prandle.

Honours certificates: Beryl Prandle, Gladys Prandle, Kathleen Barlow, May Jones.

Gold: John Campbell Pritchard, Dennis Prandle, J. Thomas Roberts, Eddie Robinson,
    Doreen Robinson; Violet: Susie Roberts, Ruby Spoor, Joan Robinson; Red: Fred Beckett,
    Reggie Norton, John Robinson, Greta Williams, Hazel Robinson, Joseph Roberts;
    Black: Vera Williams, Noel Taylor, Fred Robinson, Charles Vickers, John Astbury;
    Blue: David Davies, Harold Roberts; Green: Joan Prandle, Betty Phillips, Ivy Phillips, Kathleen
    Davies, William Roberts, Ernest Young, Geoffrey Clark, Geoffrey Edwards.

Three years perfect attendance: Greta Williams, John Campbell Pritchard.

Two years' perfect attendance: Harold Norton, Beryl M. Prandle, Dennis Prandle, Susan Roberts;
    98% attendance: Maureen Duggan, Doreen Roberts, Charles Duggan, Kathleen Barlow, Vera
    Williams, John Astbury; 95% and over: Gladys Prandle,
    Joseph Roberts, Gwyneth Williams, Mona Humphreys, Muriel Clarke, Joyce Carr,
    Olive Betteley.

For diligence and progress: Senior prize – John Campbell Pritchard, Beryl Prandle, Hazel
    Robinson; Infants prize – Ivy Phillips.

Needlework prize (Mrs Fenwick): May Jones, Hilda Pugh;

Prize awarded by Mrs Baldock: Doreen Roberts

Prize given by Mrs Phoenix: Joan Astbury.

Prizes awarded by Deeside Animal Welfare: Doreen Robinson, Amy Woolley.

Essay on the Coronation (Captain Hoadley Smith): Kathleen Barlow, May Jones,
    John Cambell Pritchard.

Handwriting (*The Daily Herald*): Kathleen Barlow, Arthur O. Prandle.

Mrs Phoenix resigned from her post as assistant teacher in 1938 and was presented with a clock for her fourteen years service. Miss Gwendoline Mary Williams was appointed in her place. Mrs Phoenix was thought to have been persuaded to return for the duration of the Second World War and is remembered by Ernie Young and Noel Taylor because she rode a motorcycle, dressed in a helmet, goggles and a long leather coat.

In October 1944, Mr Moss retired and was presented with a cheque by senior pupil, Noel Taylor, representing the contributions of the school, staff and scholars. Miss Pitcairn Campbell presented a cheque on behalf of the managers and others, including old scholars. Noel remembered that Mr Moss was a strict disciplinarian and was very quick to give a back-hander to any child that erred and often caned their backsides. George Moss was another who was persuaded to return for the duration of the war and finally retired in 1946. He died in 1954, aged seventy-three.

In January 1947, the local education authority advertised for a temporary headmaster and Mr Hibbert was appointed for a short time until the new head took up his appointment. He had been demobbed and was in his forties. Ernie Young and Noel Taylor remember that they were taught to touch their caps in respect whenever one of the 'toffs' went past. One day, when Mrs Owen of Plâs Fron was in Bangor, some school-boys did not touch their caps to her when she passed by. She promptly went into the school where Mr Hibbert was taking a class and demanded that the boys be taught their manners and the respect that was due to her. You can imagine her amazement when the master turned the tables on her by telling her off for the discourtesy of interrupting his class with such a minor thing.

Later the same year Eric C. Woodward became the new headmaster, a post he was to hold for the next thirty-three years. He was born in Llanarmon and trained at Chester College before taking up his post at Bangor. When he joined the staff there were eighty-nine children aged between three and fourteen, compared with 160 when he came to retire. He often recalled how in his early days the school had no running water, no electric light and had two buckets of drinking water delivered each day. School meals were provided at 1s 8d (8p) and woodwork and cookery classes were taken in the old Endowed School. Gardening was then a popular subject and the school worked on a quillet (allotment) located where Abbey Gardens was later built.

Mr Woodward was a youth leader for eight years, running a youth club boasting of fifty members from Bangor and surrounding villages. During the 1950s he was secretary of the Maelor National Savings Committee and, at one time, president of the Flintshire County Branch of the National Union of Teachers. He was a founder of the County Federation of PTAs. He continually pressed for new school premises with more room and better toilet facilities. The school was still occupying the building erected about 140 years ago with its earth closets. He was very keen on football and ensured that the school's football teams practised until they won their respective leagues.

The cast of a school production of a nursery rhyme/nativity play in 1946/7. Front row L–R: Josie Spoor; Arthur Betteley; –?–; Jean Dodd; Kathleen Roberts (as a dog); Albert Green; Frank –?– ; Ann Twiss. Second row L–R: Melvyn Roberts (as a cat); Jim Poynton; Godfrey Wynn; Raymond Poynton; Graham Wynn; Doreen Wraight (as Bo Peep); Jeremy Stratton (with cap); –?–; Doug Roberts; –?– (with hood); Victor Beckett; Joyce Williams; Edna –?– (sister to Frank); Everard Sheldon; John Taylor; Peter Phillips (shepherd); Mary Shone. Back row L–R: Cyril Johnson; Victor Green (Wise Man); Jim Davies (shepherd); Jean Roberts (Joseph); Rosie Roberts (Mary); Gwen Barber (above unknown with hood); Vera Wraight (second Wise Man); Jackie Wynn (in white, below Wise Man); John Richards (shepherd).

Mr Woodward's class, c.1952. Front row L–R: Pam Morris; Jean Forsey; Gaynor Sheldon; Margaret Owen; Hilda Francis; Maria Williams. Middle row: Walter Ellis; Beryl Grifiths; Jennifer Forsey; Jean Dimelow; Rosemary Blake; Ann Jones; Richard Francis; Stuart Lloyd. Back row: Phil Duckett; Malcolm Davies/ Brian Huxley (?); Lawrence Wynn; Peter Roberts; Brian Clark; Geoff Done; Arfon Mytton.

Mrs Capper's class, c.1955/6. Front row L–R: Pauline Bayliss; Gail Brereton; Kathleen Griffiths; Sandra Northcott; Christina Fowles; Christine Dooley; Janet Davies; Peggy Bayliss. Middle row: Ann Franklin; Jonathan Franklin; Sheila Underwood; Ann Blake; Edwin Phillips; Richard Owen. Back row: Reggie Williams; David Spoor; David Fowles; Dennis Jones; David Daniel; Barry Barlow.

Mrs Evans's Infants class c.1967. Front row L–R: –?– Thelwell; –?–; –?–; Paul Johnson. Second row: Angela Thelwell; –?–; Karen Roberts; –?–; Yvonne –?–. Third row: –?–; Sue Young (?); Carol Poynton; Julie Johnson; Susan Thelwell; –?– Griffiths; Ann Evanson; –?–. Back row: –?–; Tony Leach; –?–; Michael Davies; –?–; –?–.

St Dunawd's Primary School

With the increase in the numbers of young children in the village, the school urgently needed new premises. A site was eventually earmarked in the middle of the Dee Farm estate at the end of Sandown Road and after talking about it for a long time, the first turf was cut in June 1976 and building was completed by December 1977, at a total cost of £103,435. The school was designed to accommodate 154 pupils of nursery, infant and junior age ranges.

The building consisted of: entrance foyer, headteacher's room, main hall, three junior class areas with general teaching/wet area, two infant class areas with general teaching/wet area and a nursery/reception unit. A fully-equipped kitchen was located adjacent to the main hall, designed to serve 150 meals each day. The external play facilities comprised a playing field, playground, infant play area and a nursery play-garden. The school was to be open plan with cushioned floors and some areas were even carpeted. This was greatly appreciated by the staff as it made for much quieter movement of pupils around the school.

The school was traditionally constructed with a concrete tiled roof on timber trusses with concrete block walls: the external walls were rendered Tyrolean finish. Internal walls were generally fair-faced block work, with floors covered in a variety of finishes. The architect was G.G. Tomlinson and the builder was H. Roberts of Coedpoeth.

Mrs Tennant's class c.1954.
Front row: Glyn Mytton; –?–; –?–;
–?–; –?–. Second row: all unknown.
Third row: Richard Owen; –?–; –?–;
–?–; –?–; Edwin Fowles; –?–; Clive
Edgington. Back row: all unknown.

Mrs Capper's class c.1955.
Back row L–R: Gordon Mytton, June
Roberts, Joan Davies, Joan Richards,
Audrey Roberts. Middle row L–R: Ken
Griffiths, Sylvia Clark (?), Valerie
Dodd, June Owens. Front Row: Beryl
Griffiths, Malcolm Davies, Margaret
Spoor, –?–, Sidney Underwood.

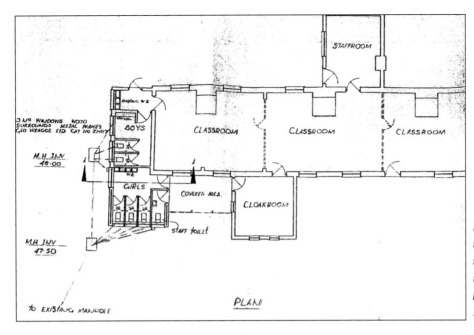

Plan for installation of modern toilets in the 1960s. [FRO FC/A/2/68)]

In the playground.

Below right: Phil Duckett at the top of a Heath Robinson climbing frame.

Mr Woodward's class.

On 20 February 1978, 123 children moved into the new school and the school routine in the new premises was already established by the time it was officially opened by Princess Alexandra on Friday, 28 April. Pupil Samantha Wright of Ludlow Road was chosen to present the princess with a bouquet at the opening of the Kellogg's factory on the Wrexham Industrial Estate in the morning, and Donna Griffiths presented a posy of flowers at the school in the afternoon.

The nursery was not utilised straight away, presumably because of financial restrictions, but with thirty-six local children in the qualifying age group waiting to attend it was not too long before the money was found to engage the necessary staff and the nursery department opened in November 1978 with a part-time teacher and assistant. With an active Parent Teacher Association already formed, plans were soon afoot to equip the nursery and furnish the central courtyard with plants and shrubs and, subject to certain limitations, for the keeping of pets. The children enjoyed the space to work off surplus energy with gym lessons on the apparatus in the hall and running freely in the playing fields.

Mrs Evans, the deputy head, decided to retire after thirty-one years service and Mrs Noreen Turner was appointed in her place. After two years sorting out the teething troubles in the new school, Mr Woodward retired in 1980 after thirty-three years as headmaster. Before leaving he presented the new village sports field with a seat that would serve as a memory of his many happy years spent in Bangor. Mrs Turner composed the following poem bidding him farewell:

> Long ago, a new head came to our village by the Dee
> And through the years we got to know how kind this man could be.
> His name was Mr Woodward and football was his game,
> Teams at Overton and Penley would shiver at his name!
> We know he taught some of our dads and taught some of our mothers
> And when you stop to think of it, there were many, many others.
> Soon the school was far too full and getting very old,

We will build you a nice new one said the men who came from Mold.
They showed to Mr Woodward lots of exciting plans
Showing bases, halls and areas where we could wash our hands.
To open up this school so grand a royal princess came,
She walked around and saw our work and gave us a new name.
Ysgol St Dunawd is what we're called; we think it very good,
But one thing makes Mr Woodward mad, that dreadful thing called MUD!
If our headmaster thinks of us as he's working in his garden,
For all the naughty things we did we'd like to beg his pardon.
We never will forget him in the years that are to come,
He gives us lots of things to do and made our schooldays fun.
And so it's time to say goodbye and say it without tears,
For we wish you joy and happiness through all the coming years.

Malcolm Powell,
headmaster 1980–2.

Mr Malcolm Powell, the head of Isycoed Primary School was appointed as the next head teacher. He was born in south Wales but later moved to Oswestry, read Philosophy and Psychology at the University of Wales, Cardiff, and completed teacher training at Exeter. He taught at Warley near Birmingham, then in Ellesmere before accepting the post of deputy head at Overton. About three years later he became head teacher at Isycoed where he remained for four years before accepting the post at Bangor in 1980. He stayed only a couple of years before he was appointed to the post of head of St Mary's Church Primary School, Ruabon.

The next headmaster was John E. Braybrook. He had come to teaching after an interesting career in the RAF. After serving a technical apprenticeship at RAF Halton he did several tours of duty, one of which was with a bomb-disposal squad based in such places as

The new school in Sandown Road.

Singapore. He was in Germany when the Berlin Wall was being constructed and, by sheer coincidence, was visiting his daughter who was stationed in Germany when the wall came down. His final tour of duty was with the Red Arrows. After he retired from the RAF in 1970, he started a second career as a teacher. After college and final teaching practice in Bryn Coch School in Mold he was appointed to a school in Kinnerton and after twelve months was made deputy head. In 1981, he took a year's sabbatical to do a post-graduate diploma in primary maths education and was then appointed head of Bangor school in 1982. He retired in 2004.

Mrs Julia Whitby had been appointed an assistant teacher in Bangor in April 1990 before becoming head in 2004. She left in March 2012 and a temporary head, Stephen Jones, was appointed until the new head, Miss Sara Tate, formerly deputy head at Tan-y-Fron, arrived to assume her duties.

Staff c.2000.
Back row L–R: Jean Allen, nursery
teacher; Rebecca Hughes, infant teacher;
Lesley Nightingale, secretary.
Front row L–R: Julia Whitby, deputy
head; Jill Milligan; John Braybrook,
headmaster; Sue Cauldwell, (now head of
Eyton School). [John Braybrook]

13. Village Hall

The Village Hut

In earlier times the church was not only a place of worship but also the only building of any size for social use. It served as a centre for parish meetings and village life. In many respects the Endowed School took over this former use of the church and the schoolroom was used occasionally as a parish room. When the National School was erected it took over this role. After the two schools merged in 1902, the Endowed School building, built in 1747, was declared to be surplus to requirements and was badly in need of repair and maintenance. A suggestion was made in 1900 by the then rector, the Revd Elrington Bissett, that the schoolroom could be used as a parish room, but nothing came of this idea and the Dame Dorothy Jeffreys Trust decided to rent it out at £10 per annum to Griffiths Jones, a tailor, for a number of years. Many of the older people still remember going to the house to be measured for garments.

In 1919, the national Village Club Association was been formed to try to repair the damage to village life that the Great War had wrought. It included representatives from the Women's Institute, the Soldiers' Club Association, and the Village Clubs Association and its aim was to encourage people to return to, and participate in, village life and to have a place to meet. Arrangements were

Overton Road with the Great War army hut just protruding behind the wall in the background. Westgate House on the right.

238

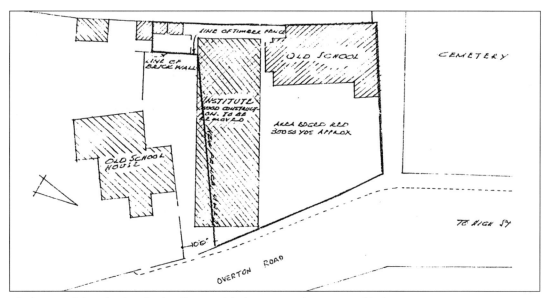

The layout of the school and schoolhouse with the ex-army hut squeezed in between.

made to supply lecturers to address village audiences on subjects of general interest. Plans and estimates for building clubs and halls were available and it was suggested that club premises could be constructed of steel and concrete and be built in three stages, commencing with the main hall, to which wings could be added at a later date as funds became available. The price quoted for the hall only, size forty feet by twenty-five feet, was about £450. Wealthy communities could afford this sum, but it was out of the question for Bangor and they looked around for other alternatives. With the increase in the number of pupils using the village school and the consequent lack of space, the old Endowed School had once again been used for educational purposes for woodwork classes for the boys and cookery classes for the girls and so was no longer available for use as a village institute.

When the army began disposing of old army huts now surplus to requirements in the post war period (they were initially promoted as being suitable for low-cost housing for workers) a proposal was made that a hut be acquired for use as a village institute. This suggestion was followed through and on 21 March 1921 a hut, sixty-five feet long, was purchased and installed in the space between the schoolhouse and the schoolroom. The Dorothy Jeffreys Trust added the hut onto its insurance policy but, because of an increased risk of fire, they felt that the insurance on the school should be at least doubled to £400 with the institute being asked to bear the difference in the premium.

As soon as the hut was erected, the first management committee was appointed with the rector Revd F. Okell as chairman and Captain Holford Harrison as treasurer and Mr H. Williams as secretary. At the annual general meeting of 1923 E. Young, F. Cheetham, and Evan G. Jones of Orchard House (an early stationmaster) were appointed to fill vacancies on the management committee. The rector presided over the meeting and it was agreed to reduce the membership fee. At the 1925 AGM, the previous officials were re-elected and the committee was strengthened by the election of Mr H.H. Davenport of Halghton Mills.

A stove in the middle of the floor provided the heating for the hut and the old earth privies belonging to the school were still used until a chemical toilet was installed inside the building. The hut was divided across the width into two rooms by a partition and used for such things as whist drives, youth club, keep-fit classes, Cubs and Scouts and, for a short period during the Second World War, as a cinema. A billiard table was purchased, but such was the popularity of the game that twelve months later a second one was acquired which meant that single matches as well as pairs could now be played. This meant that the partition in the hut had to be removed to allow room to use the second table and a band of volunteers soon made light work of the alterations thereby enabling the Institute to take part in competitions against other local villages.

Once the two billiard tables had been installed it soon became apparent that there was little room for functions of any size and the hut became more of a male meeting room, although women were tolerated for such things as whist drives. Travers Twiss solved the problem by acquiring a second army hut and installing it at the end of his garden at Hendy in the High Street and this became known as the Assembly Rooms and was were village dances, keep-fit classes, revues and any sizeable function, even wedding receptions, were held for many years.

In 1927, Mr W.H. Davies had been appointed honorary secretary of the entertainment committee and it was proposed to hold a carnival followed by a fancy dress ball in the summer in aid of the Institute. Classes were commenced at the Institute under the auspices of the Flintshire Agricultural Education Committee in 1928. In June 1929, the rector, the Revd Baldock, presided at the AGM when the secretary, Archie Morris, reported that the cup, given by Mr Stevenson for the best billiards player amongst the members, had been won by Mr J.E. Morris. Mr Holford Harrison's vase had been won by Mr H. Dodd. The treasurer, Captain Holford Harrison, produced a financial report that showed a slight balance. All the officers were re-elected. In 1937, at a meeting held in the school on 7 October, Hugh Arrowsmith tendered his resignation as secretary, a position he had held for some years and William Griffiths (Post Office) was appointed in his place.

When the Second World War broke out in 1939 the Local Defence Volunteers, later known as the Home Guard, at first used the old school room as their headquarters and drill hall. They later used the Institute and when on duty became expert billiard players which Joe Roberts said was responsible for ruining both the tables and the hut floor! Bangor's hut fell into a bad state of repair during this period, as there was no money to spend on maintaining the fabric of the building, every spare penny having been donated towards the war effort.

After hostilities ended, a new institute committee was formed in November 1948, the officers were: Lt-Colonel S.V. Misa (chairman); Miss Joyce Berry (secretary) and Mr Edward Duggan (treasurer) – the father of Charlie Duggan who married Ruby Spoor. One of the first things they did was to obtain estimates for stripping and re-felting the roof, repairing the floor and the guttering, installing new lighting and heating and purchasing a new, three-quarter-size billiard table, the cost amounting in total to £188. To cover this expenditure the committee applied to the Flintshire Welsh Church Fund for a grant, but were not successful. However, they did manage to obtain a grant from another source and the hut continued as a centre for village social life for the next twelve years and any event was always well supported. The hut was also used as the village library and Joseph Spoor, who was a carpenter, repaired an old cupboard to house the collection of library books. This was in the days before television became such an attraction – or distraction!

The Village Hall

By 1960, the floor of the hut had been declared unsafe and other major work was urgently needed and the committee decided the time had come to demolish the hut and build a new village hall. In the intervening years, the population of the village had grown as the Abbot's Way council estate had been built and the first of the many private residences – bungalows in Abbeygate Walk – were in the planning stage. It was proposed initially to build on the site of the army hut but this was declared unsuitable, as there would be no space for a car park.

Some eight years earlier to celebrate the coronation of Queen Elizabeth, the parish council had been negotiating to buy the site of the old toll cottage on the corner of Overton Road and High Street, owned by Bents Brewery (now occupied by Turnpike House and Fernhill), for a bus shelter and had been offered the site at a cost of £50 plus legal fees and expenses. After much discussion, the council had not proceeded with the idea and it was now suggested that this site would be an ideal place for a village hall and the committee wrote to enquire whether the brewery was prepared to renew their original offer. The reply came back that, as the offer had been made some years before and land values had in the interim changed very much, it was no longer the company's policy to dispose of any land. As a result of this, the possibility of using the old Endowed School as a village hall was reconsidered. The old schoolroom had last been used as a dining room for school meals (with the food being cooked elsewhere). Many people still remember the crocodile of school children walking to the school for dinner each day. A dining room had then been built on the National School site and the old building was available to be put to another use. The schoolroom had no kitchen of its own, no toilets and the only form of heating was from an open fire at one end of the hall that had been supplemented at some time by a stove at the other. As with many old buildings that had had no money spent on them for several years, the schoolroom had deteriorated badly and needed a considerable sum of money spent on it if it was to be adapted for use as a village hall.

The residents of Bangor held a meeting on 16 January 1962 to ascertain how much support there was for the idea of purchasing the property. Under the enthusiastic leadership of Colonel Misa, backed by William Jones, it was unanimously agreed to go ahead with the scheme and an approach was made to the Dame Dorothy Jeffreys Trust to see if they were prepared to lease or, preferably, sell the schoolroom. In March 1962, the trustees of the charity, Sir Philip Reginald le Belward Grey Egerton, the

Two rather blurred photographs showing (above) the old Endowed School in the late 1950s [Sunter Harrison] when it was bought for use as a hall and (right) the same building in 1966 after conversion into the Village Hall. [FRO D/DM/1201]

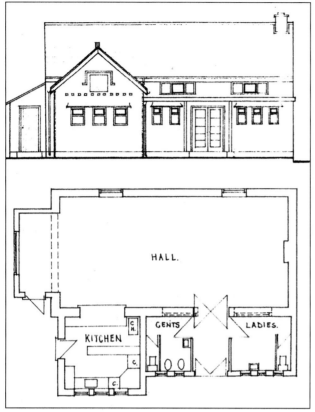

Front elevation and plan of the old schoolroom for its conversion into the village hall in 1966.

Revd Leslie Mills Daniel (rector of Bangor) and Colonel Fenwick Palmer of Cefn Park, with the agreement of the Ministry of Education, agreed to sell to the trustees of the parish Institute,

All that piece of land in the Parish of Bangor in the County of Flint comprising 300 square yards or thereabouts together with the old School Building and Institute erected thereon situate on the South East side of the road leading from Overton to Bangor.

The property was to be sold for £200, subject to the following conditions:

That the purchaser agreed to erect and forever thereafter maintain a good and sufficient fence at least 4 feet in height between the schoolroom and the schoolhouse; that the purchaser shall agree to contribute to the cost of relaying or renewing any service pipes or cables enjoyed by both properties; that the purchaser shall remove the First World War hut standing partly on the property being sold and partly on the land retained by the charity (the schoolhouse) within 6 months and shall level the site.

On 4 March 1963, the charity trustees conveyed the property to the trustees of the Bangor Institute: the Revd L. Daniel, Harold Clarke of Althrey Farm, Mr W. Jones of the Orchards Farm and Colonel S.V. Misa of Althrey Woodhouse. The opportunity also arose of purchasing the property located to the rear of the schoolroom, which has once been owned by the wife of the Revd Paterson-Morgan, known as the Church House, for £250. This could be used as a car park for the hall. Negotiations were soon underway with the estate agent and chartered surveyor, Hubert Vaux Kitching of Horsemans Green, Whitchurch (the son of Thomas Kitching of Hanmer and great nephew of a deputy chief constable for Flintshire, James Dale Bolton). The property was conveyed to the trustees on 22 September 1962.

With a debt of £450, the residents of Bangor set to with a will to hold special events in order to raise enough money to renovate and adapt the building to its new role. The great day arrived when the former army hut, having served its purpose as one of the centres of village life for over forty years, was demolished and the land made good. The old schoolroom porch was taken down, the dormer windows were removed and a ceiling inserted. The roof was re-slated with a gift from a generous benefactor, thought to be Mrs Ormrod, and a kitchen, toilets and foyer were built on the front facing the road. The old heating system was removed and gas central heating installed. Finally, the old stone tablet commemorating Dame Dorothy Jeffreys' bequest was once again fixed on the outside. All this did not happen overnight and it took three years from the date of purchase before the converted building was ready for use and the old schoolroom reopened in January 1966 as the Village Institute.

New officers were appointed, still under the chairmanship of Colonel Misa: Mr D. Adams of Pania, Whitchurch Road (secretary); Colonel F.C. Macvie, licensee of the Buck Hotel (treasurer), with a committee made up of: Mr & Mrs T. Clarke, Laurels Cottage (later of 29, Abbot's Way); Mrs T. Green, Overton Road; Mr J.E. Harries, Abbeygate Walk; Mr G. Oliver, Abbeygate Walk; Mr & Mrs E. Robinson, River View, Graig Lane; Mrs M. Rowling, Wayside, Whitchurch Road; Mrs Richardson, The Mount, Station Road; Mr Simmons, Overton Road and Mrs V. Williams of Coed Aben Farm. This new committee inherited an outstanding debt of £200 owed to Tom Parry, timber merchant and local builder (and the son of a former Bangor policeman, PC Thomas Joseph Parry). The committee made repaying the debt its first priority and a fair and regular whist drives and bingo sessions were organised to raise money. Two years after the hall had opened, the debt had been repaid. In March 1967, Colonel Macvie proposed that a manager should be appointed to take over the care of the building and Mr J.E. Harries initially agreed to act as caretaker. However, it was not long before he gave up the job and Colonel Misa asked Mrs Joan Furber to act as caretaker, a post that she was to hold for thirty-two years before retiring in 1998. As well as cleaning the hall, she also took the bookings, opened and closed the hall and put out the tables and chairs for each group.

In 1968, Tom Parry applied to purchase a strip of land (approximately fifteen feet by sixty feet) at the end of the car park from Overton Road for a vehicular access to his cottages in Church Avenue for which he was offering £69. At the same time, MANWEB were seeking permission to erect a transformer station on part of the land. The deeds of the village hall where examined to ascertain where the exact boundary line lay and the chairman stated that there was a 7½-foot path parallel to the church railings and the village hall land and that the part in front was set back six feet from the road as the path was to be widened by the council in the near future. The committee decided that it should keep all its land and not sell any to Mr Parry and declined his offer. Mr Parry then built a boundary wall between his property and the hall.

In 1970, Colonel Misa did not stand for re-election as chairman as he felt it was time to make way for a younger man and Mr J.E. Harries was elected in his place. It was agreed to paint the outside of the hall (at a total cost of £20) and to concrete the area in front of the building and the side (cost £124 12s 6d) the actual work to be done by volunteers.

The first extension
The population of Bangor was growing fast as the housing estates of the Laurels, Abbeygate Walk and the Nurseries had been built, and by 1970 the houses on what was known as the Dee Farm Estate were under construction. A new, younger, population, many with children, injected fresh life into the village. The village hall was well used and it was not long before it was bursting at the seams when community events were organised and was plainly too small for the burgeoning

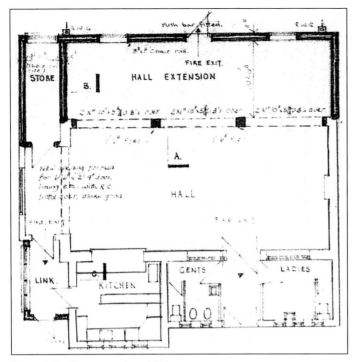

Plan of the first extension, 1972.

population. In 1970, a request was sent to the Church in Wales for a possible grant but it had been refused as the Institute was not a registered charity.

In 1971, a letter was received from the Flintshire Welsh Church Fund stating that it may have money to spend on improving facilities, but rather than just improve facilities the committee was now planning an extension to the hall, initially planning to increase the width by between five and six feet, with a storeroom at one end. The Director of Education offered to provide a grant of 75% of the projected cost of £3,700 with the balance of £925 to be found by the committee. It was soon realised that the sum required would be considerably in excess of the £925 quoted when additional work was carried out and in 1972 the committee decided to approach the Maelor Rural District Council to see whether the balance could be borrowed from them and repaid from a rate to be levied which the committee would undertake to repay.

In December 1972, the parish council held a public meeting to discuss the plans for the proposed new extension and to suggest means whereby the loan could be repaid. Permission was given by the council for a loan up to a limit of £2,000. A new committee was voted in at the meeting and consisted of: chairman, Mr B. Hutchings of Sandown Road; secretary, Mr P. Bryan of Sandown Road; treasurer, Mr G.J. Bentley of the Police Station, Overton Road and nine committee members viz Mr P. Hughes of Hillview, Whitchurch Road; Mr G. Griffiths of Raggs Hill; Mr J. Firth of Worcester Road; Mr A.M. Powick of The Nurseries, Overton Road; Mr T. Osborne of Bryn Hovah; Mr E. Robinson of River View, Graig Lane; Mr H.K. Rees of the Post Office; Mrs D.M. Nunnerley of Dongray Hall and Mrs A. Adams of the Stores. Tom Osborne was appointed as a

Members of the Village Hall Committee at the opening of the first extension in 1972. L–R: Andy Powick, Gary Bentley, M. Jones, Peter Bryan, P. Hughes, B. Hutchings, Mrs J. Ackerley and Mrs Ann Adams.

trustee in place of Harold Clarke who had left the district.

Quotations for the extension were received from E.N. Rogers, G. Mytton and B. & P. Construction Consultancy and the latter (for £2,907) was accepted. The total sum, together with resurfacing the car park and ducting came to £3,700. It was now planned to build a ten foot, single-storey, flat-roofed extension on the back of the hall, running the whole length of the existing building

The smart appearance of the Village Hall after all the hard work.

and supported by two pillars with a storage room at one end. At the same time the opportunity was taken to have a covered way built between the side door of the hall and the door to the kitchen to avoid the necessity of going outside to enter the kitchen – something that the ladies in particular had been requesting for some time. The plans were submitted to the local fire-officer for his comment and his report. The cost of his recommendation for exit signs, emergency lighting and the re-hanging of the kitchen door to open outwards was agreed to be included in the building programme. He also recommended that attendance in the hall be limited to 130 people at any one time. Building work went ahead and on 19 May 1973 its successful completion was celebrated by a dance attended by the Director of Education, Mr T. Glyn Davies with his wife. Colonel Misa entertained Mr and Mrs Davies and the chairman, Mr Hutchings, and his wife, at the Royal Oak prior to the official opening.

The original constitution of the hall forbade its use for religious or commercial purposes but this was not felt to be in accordance with current thinking and a revised constitution was drawn up stating:

1) The objects of the Institute shall be the provision of facilities for the social, intellectual and physical welfare of the inhabitants of the parish of Bangor Isycoed and of such other persons as the institute may from time to time admit.

2) The ownership of the freehold and leasehold property, cash, investments and chattels used for the purposes of the Institute shall be invested in Trustees … of whom there shall be not less than three and not more than five.

In view of the extra work involved following the increase in size of the hall the caretakers fee was changed to £1 flat rate plus 40p per hiring. The hiring rates were also raised to reflect the new facilities.

Village lottery

To help raise the money to pay off the loan, a village lottery scheme was set up in 1973 whereby each person in the lottery paid 10p a week – £5.20 a year. Half the income was to be paid out in

Volunteers painting the hall in 1977.
L–R: Lawrence Stevenson, Ernie Young,
Ron Evanson, Peter Hannah (on ladder)
and Val Stevenson.

prize money with four prizes of £5 and one of £10 drawn each month, and several large prizes once a year. To run this scheme a lottery treasurer was appointed with eight lottery collectors who divided the village up between them to collect the money weekly, monthly or yearly according to the wishes of the members. It was envisaged that this scheme could pay off the loan in less than twelve months, after which time it could be used to fund the purchase of equipment and provide a much-needed regular income for the maintenance of the hall. The first lottery secretary/treasurer appointed was Garry Bentley and the promoter was the village hall secretary, Peter Bryan.

The lottery fund proved to be a great success with an average membership of 333. The proceeds paid for the purchase of twenty chairs and ten tables (24 ins x 24 ins) for £162.32 from Matthews of Liverpool, a loan of £25 to the Youth Club, the purchase of a £70 mowing machine for the children's playground, and the repayment of the £1017.49 loan plus interest for the extension. One of the first uses to which the lottery income was put was to treat the roof timbers of the old part of the hall where dry rot and woodworm had been suspected and confirmed by Rentokil. The cost of treatment was £115 with a twenty-year guarantee. The committee agreed to accept the estimate and the work proceeded without delay.

On a proposal by Peter Bryan, it was agreed to re-name the hall Bangor-on-Dee Village Institute and Social Club. A social sub-committee of four was formed consisting of Mr Bryan, Mr Powick, Mrs Adams and Mrs Ackerley who were to report back at monthly meetings with ideas for activities to be run for fundraising events. The first suggested programme of events was for a country and western evening in July, a tramps' supper in September, a halloween dance in October, a bonfire and firework display in November and a Christmas dance in December. In addition, it was proposed to hold a series of monthly junior disco's for under sixteens and prize whist drives in June and December.

In the past, the vacant school house had been used to store playgroup equipment but, as it was now no longer available for this purpose, they were using the new storeroom in the hall. Difficulties had arisen when the committee wanted to use the storeroom as a bar for social functions. Mr Powick, by now the chairman, offered the use of his garage as a temporary store whilst investigation was made into the possibility of acquiring a wooden shed (10 ft x 8 ft) to be erected in the car park for the playgroup. The secretary was asked to write to the chief executive officer and county clerk at the Shire Hall in Mold expressing the committee's interest in the school house and to ask that they be given first refusal should it become available for purchase.

The hall committee held the first fireworks display and bonfire in the village in 1974 on Mr Bebbington's field at a cost of £110 plus VAT for the fireworks, the expense being covered by running a prize bingo and draw. Gary Bentley offered to store the fireworks in a secure outhouse at the back of the police station in Overton Road. All male members of the committee were asked to help prepare the site and the ladies and/or wives to serve refreshments under a shelter provided by Gordon Mytton. The following year there was a small overall loss of £2.86. In 1976, because of the committee's involvement with other projects, a decision was taken not to run a prize bingo and draw but instead to defray the cost of the event by making a charge for admission to the field for adults of 20p. Not surprisingly the event produced a deficit of £55.88, despite a donation of £26.66 from the Youth Club. In 1977, the loss on the bonfire, bingo and draw was down to single figures again but because of the difficulty of finding a suitable site and the increased cost of the fireworks, the committee decided not to repeat the event.

The officers for 1975 were: Andy Powick (chairman); G.M. Thompson (secretary) and John Welbourn (treasurer). One of the trustees – Eddie Robinson – had died during the year and John Welbourn was appointed in his place.

Sports field

After the Second World War, when all agricultural land was needed for crop growing, the village lost the Groes field across the river opposite the church, which had been used as a bowling green, sports field and for other village events. Although a small play area near Abbot's Way had been provided for young children, and Mr Bebbington had kindly allowed the school to use his field, the situation regarding general recreational facilities in the village was poor and there was a need for a designated sports area. The Cubs chairman, Dave White, suggested in 1974 that a village hall sub-committee should be formed to discuss the purchase of land within walking distance of the village centre. It was felt that this was a more worthwhile project than the possible purchase of the old school house. They asked for the plan to be discussed at a Community Council meeting as the provision of recreational facilities was primarily their concern. A map of the village was inspected and various suitable fields were examined.

It was decided, with the support of the Dame Dorothy Jeffreys Trust and the Community Council, to approach Wrexham Maelor Borough Council for outline planning permission and the change of use of two fields in Station Road/Graig Lane from agriculture to sports and social, and to terminate the agreement of the existing tenant, Gordon Humphries, a local farmer. The land was a little over four acres in area and was owned by the trust. The project had the support of the district councillor, Mr Reid, and the county councillor, Colonel Misa.

The Dame Dorothy Jeffreys Trust offered a renewable lease for a period of twenty-one years at a rent of £50 per annum for the first seven years, thereafter at the market agricultural rate. As a condition of the lease they stipulated that:

A twelve-feet-wide hardcore right of access be made to provide access for the tenant of the third field.
The water supply be extended from the existing point to the third field.
The entrance to the playing field site to be from the mid-point of the Graig Lane site.
The committee to be liable for the payment of compensation to Mr Humphries for his loss of tenancy.
That land drainage would be undertaken in due course.

Geoffrey Morris & Ashton the solicitors for the hall's trustees, were instructed to apply for a change of use of the field from agricultural to sports and recreational use. Mr Gordon Humphries who rented the land was to be approached for his co-operation in giving up the tenancy of the two fields. Grants towards the cost of the project were to be sought from the District Council based on their statutory responsibility, the Community Council, the Dame Dorothy Jeffreys Trust, the National Playing Fields Association, the County Council and the committee's own resources. A meeting with the Leisure and Recreation Officer and the Parks Superintendent of the District Council had been encouraging and they recommended that a formal application be made as soon as possible in the form of a comprehensive statement explaining the recent population explosion in Bangor, the present lack of recreational facilities, coupled with the successful 'self-help' progress already made. In addition, they would require a balance sheet and financial implications, together with the time scale for the development. A timetable of proposed developments with approximate costing was drawn up:

Year 1:	Works to comply with lease	approx £1000
Year 2:	Drainage and regrading	approx £7000
Year 3:	Possible car park and/or tennis courts	approx £17,000
Later	Sports-changing facilities/club house/community centre	

By 1977, the change of use had been granted, a survey of the field undertaken and plans drawn up for the drainage work and the provision of access. It was now felt that it was time to separate the sports field project from the village hall committee as it was taking up a great deal of time and discussion at meetings when the primary task of the committee was the maintenance and running of the building. A public meeting was held on 10 May 1977, at which thirty-five members of the public attended, and it was agreed to formally set up the Sports Field Management Committee with its own trustees and bank account. The hall committee did not just cast it adrift and agreed to credit the sports field account with £1,000 from the Lottery account and to donate 50% of the Lottery income each year to the project until such a time as it could stand on its own feet. The saga of the sports field is continued in the chapter on clubs and societies.

In the meantime, new metal posts with chain linkage (donated by Mrs Gwen Robinson of River View) had been erected to the front of the hall, the central heating improved and a notice board erected on the front wall. The British Legion had donated thirty pre-formed chairs to the hall and, in addition, new tables and more folding, wooden chairs had been purchased.

All hirers were asked what facilities or improvements they would like to see in the hall. Reorganisation of the kitchen and the plumbing of hot water to both the ladies' and the gents' toilets were high on the list. The waste-pipe leading from the kitchen sink to the drain that had caused waste water to overflow across the car park was still giving trouble and it was proposed to extend the pipe into the drain by the addition of a rubber tube. Over the years the problem of the drainage was never entirely resolved, despite various solutions being tried but, in 2013, the grid was encircled with bricks and it is hoped that this has finally solve the problem.

At the AGM held in December 1975, Andy Powick indicated that he did not wish to serve as chairman for a third term but agreed to be acting chairman until a successor was forthcoming – but effectively ended up serving a third year when no replacement was found. Peter Hannah was appointed minutes secretary and Gordon Thompson became the correspondence secretary. John Welbourn was the treasurer.

On 1 May 1976, following increase in the payments made to the caretaker, the hiring fees were raised:

Occasional Hiring:	£2.25 per hour + 75p for use of kitchen. Minimum charge £9 per evening.
Contract Hiring:	£1 per hour, including free use of kitchen if required. £1.50p per hour each hour past 11p.m..
Commercial Hiring:	(If accepted) £2.25 per hour, £1 for use of kitchen. Minimum charge £12. Cancellation: 25% of total hiring charge to be levied.

Village carnival

At the next meeting of the village hall committee in January 1976, Dave White, on behalf of the Cubs, proposed that the village should revive the carnival as a joint venture with other village groups at which a Carnival queen, chosen at a special function, could preside. He suggested that, as most of the village organisations were users of the hall, that the event be organised by the Village Hall Committee. This suggestion was enthusiastically received and a carnival sub committee was formed with Dave White acting as the co-ordinator between the two committees.

In the first year, Peter Bryan was the total event manager, with Andy Powick in charge of the procession, the route and the stewards. Kate Warner organised the fancy dress competition; Gordon Thompson co-ordinated the stall, the stands and the field layout; John Griffiths overseeing the car parking and the gates; Peter Hannah was the treasurer and Dave White was responsible for the publicity, the catering and the provision of toilets. The tug-of-war organiser was Frank Morris. The carnival was held at Bangor Racecourse with the tug-of-war competition at Turn o'Dee. A carnival queen, Karen Roberts, had been chosen and paraded through the village on a decorated float drawn by a tractor. Trailers and lorries loaned by people such as Les Done and Peter Furber were gaily decorated for the different village groups. The carnival was a great success and it was agreed to repeat it the following year. The money that was made was donated to the Sports Field Project. Further information on the carnivals can be found in the chapter dealing with clubs and societies.

In 1977, the committee rule of twelve members appointed at an AGM was changed and it was agreed that it be six elected members and six other members, one from each of the organisations on contract hire. New officers of the Village Hall Committee were appointed and as Andy Powick had only reluctantly agreed to serve a third term the previous year, Peter Bryan was voted in as the new chairman with Andy acting as secretary. As John Welbourn wished to stand down as treasurer, Vivien Lavis-Jones was persuaded to take on the duties by fellow pharmacist, Peter Bryan. Peter Hannah was appointed lottery treasurer. The committee was made up as follows:

Nominated Representatives:
Young Wives	Mrs K. White
Play Group	Mrs E. Nicholls
WI	Mrs R. Rome

Church   Mr B. Evers

Elected Representatives:

                                Mr P. Bryan
                                Mr J. Griffiths
                                Mr P. Hannah
                                Miss V. Lavis-Jones
                                Mr A. Powick
                                Mrs V. Stevenson

Second extension

Having successfully launched the carnival and sports field schemes, the committee soon began to discuss the idea of again enlarging the hall, as almost as soon as the first extension was complete, the Dee Farm estate, Friar's Court and Friar's Mews, had been built. The demands for the use of the hall for evening functions were such that the Village Hall Committee and the Young Wives Group had to find other venues, and the problem was solved by the committee being offered the use of the old people's bungalow in Abbot's Way for their monthly meetings and the Young Wives Group being accommodated at the school.

A development subcommittee was formed to investigate how best to meet the social amenity requirements of the village in the years ahead. It was felt that the purchase of the sports field with the building of a social club facility of larger dimensions than the hall should solve the problem but this was a long-term project. At first, just a storeroom was added to the rear of the hall to take the tables, chairs and big enough to provide all the storage facilities for the various groups was mooted. However it was soon decided to build a second 10–11 feet flat-roofed extension the complete length of the hall, with a room on the end as before, for the storage of the tables and chairs that took up much needed space.

The committee was informed of the Manpower Services Commission which was a scheme whereby young people would be engaged on the project supervised by an experienced builder with the cost of erection met by the training scheme and only the cost of an architect's fees, materials and tools to be met by the committee. It was decided to apply for the scheme and plans were drawn up and estimates sought for the extension and agreed at £9,268. The money was to come from a 50% Welsh Office Grant, 25% from the Community Council and 25% from the village hall funds. Notice had been received that, as the hall was no longer designated as a listed building, there should be no problem with the planning application.

Once plans had been accepted and planning permission granted, work commenced on the foundations at the beginning of 1986. When a 6ft deep trench had been dug at the rear of the hall the lads working on the site had a nasty shock when one day the side of the trench collapsed revealing part of a skeleton. On further investigation the remains of at least two skeletons were found and the coroner was informed. The bones were declared to be ancient, at least 200 years old, and were re-interred in the churchyard. After the hold-up whilst the find was investigated, the building work continued apace and it was not long before the extension was finished.

The original estimate for the building work when added to the cost of items such as a new central heating system, meant the final figure totalled £11,522.47. During the course of the work, it was found that the first flat roof had not been insulated and there was not enough fall allowed so that water collected on the roof and this had to be corrected. To save money, the floor in the new extension was covered in a lino tile instead of the wood boards in the rest of the hall.

As soon as the hall was finished, the committee were somewhat taken aback when the playgroup requested permission to use both storage rooms as they were outgrowing their original allotted space. However, several other village groups also required space to keep their equipment, the Cub Scouts in particular, wanted a separate room for one-to-one instruction of members. The problem was solved by allocating the slightly larger new room to the Playgroup with the suggestion that they could fit in more things if they put up shelves. The toddlers were asked to share the Playgroup's room if the latter were allowed to keep their chairs and tables in the hall. The other room was given to the Cubs as they were one of the original hirers of the hall and had been inconvenienced the longest! As the Youth Club had not met during the year, their needs were not considered but the committee was told that if they did regroup they would be need a second table tennis table. It was decided that the problem would be faced if and when it arose. In the meantime, the Cubs had the sole use of the room, and wooden wall cupboards would be built in the hall for some of the groups when funds permitted. The hall would still have to keep all the tables and chairs on display.

To celebrate the successful addition to the hall, an opening dance was arranged and 142 tickets sold which made a profit of £169. After the event, it was agreed that 120 should be the maximum number allowed when seated at tables as complaints had been received that the room was too crowded. In 1988, a second toilet was fitted in the ladies' cloakroom and hand driers were purchased for both cloakrooms, the new cupboards were constructed and another gas oven and a separate gas hob were installed in the kitchen. A new water heater was bought for the kitchen and the interior of the hall was painted. In 1989, Roy Jones moved to work in Bristol and his post as lottery treasurer was taken over by Vera Walker.

In March 1990, William Jones, formerly of Orchards Farm and latterly of Highgate Cottage, died. He had been a trustee of the village hall since 1963, a past chairman when no willing person could be found, a parish councillor for more than twenty years, an elder in the Presbyterian church and a good supporter and an encouraging voice and helping hand whenever anything needed doing. The committee bought a bench and had a small brass plaque fixed with the words 'Donated by the Village Hall Management Committee in memory of William Jones, 1990.' The Community Council paid for its installation at the corner where the Whitchurch Road joins the bypass and his sister, May, often interrupted her walk home to sit on it for a few moments of quiet reflection. The British Legion offered to mow around the seat for the next year until the Wrexham Maelor Borough Council could put it on their work schedule. There now being two vacancies, the remaining trustees appointed George Humphries and Ron Evanson. Later, when Tom Osbourne died, Allan Hayes of the Buck Hotel was chosen and the updated information was forwarded to the solicitors.

In 1994, fifty gold upholstered chairs and some tables were purchased for £500 from the Buck Hotel which was being refurbished. The aim was to gradually replace the wooden folding chairs and the pre-formed plastic chairs. Unfortunately, the new chairs were not popular with the older ladies groups as they were heavy to move around and took up too much storage room.

By 1995, the caretakers wages had been increased to £10 per week (plus £1 per booking). After

Presentation in 1998 to retiring care-taker, Joan Furber, by the chairman, Ken Manchester.

thirty-two years of sterling work as caretaker, Joan Furber retired in 1998 and the committee held a small reception to which the various villages groups were invited to send representatives and contribute to a gift in gratitude for her service. The chairman, Ken Manchester, presented her with a bouquet, a crystal bowl and a cheque. A new caretaker was appointed, but only after the wages had been raised to £15 per hour plus £1 per booking.

In 1999, the joint in-between the pitched roof and the first extension was found to be leaking and the committee was told that the flat roof would need replacing during the next twelve months as it was 'bubbling'. A roof fund was set up and donations invited, with the British Legion giving £65 and the Friendship Club £100 to start it off. The committee organised an Easter draw and a total of £1,100.50 was realised thanks to the efforts put in by all the user groups who made a special effort to sell the tickets outside the village. Quotations were received from B. Simon (£1,509.30 for a ten-year guarantee and £2078.75 for a twenty-year guarantee). The hall's finances were currently running at £200 expenditure over income and the hiring charges, last fixed in 1996, were increased to: contract hire – £3.50; private hire – £7 and £8 per hour: commercial and local government hire – £12.50.

Efforts were made to try to find the source of a grant to pay for the new roof from the National Lottery, the Maelor Borough Council and the director of environmental bodies from Shanks & McEwan Waste Solutions (who deal with the granting of monies from Customs and Excise Landfill Tax). The last named was oversubscribed in the financial year but were sympathetic to the request and suggested applying again the next year. In August 2000, a grant of £4,500 was obtained from the Millennium Small Grants for Wales along with £150 from the Community Chest for roof repair, floor repair, plasterwork and painting. The Simons roof estimate now stood at £2,120 with a twenty-year guarantee and a quotation from Universal Builders for the interior decoration of £1,105 (plus VAT) and £1,365 (plus VAT) for the lighting. These quotes were accepted and as soon as two or three days of dry weather occurred then the roofing work would begin. It was bad luck that the roof needed repairing just when there was almost continual rain for months and the river was at its highest for many years. The roof was finally re-felted in January 2001 and the interior work commenced the following month. In the meantime, all user groups became adept at leaping over the row of buckets and bowls placed to catch the leaks!

In about 2004/5 grants became available to fit handicapped toilets in public buildings and it was decided to take advantage of the scheme and at the same time update the two existing cloakrooms with new wash basins, toilets, tiling and flooring. The result improved the entrance but focussed attention on the main hall, which was marred by the clutter of tables, chairs and the overflow from the playgroup. It was decided that a storage room was badly needed. The kitchen too was not a good advert for the twenty-first century as it had not been touched since the hall was converted in 1966. Plans were provisionally drawn up for the building of a small storage room on the back of the hall which would tie in with a kitchen upgrade. The scheme was abandoned on being told that it would only receive planning permission if the extension had a pitched roof. In addition, the two existing flat roofs would probably also have to be converted to a pitched roof. Grants were unlikely to be awarded, as increased hiring of the hall could not be demonstrated. However, in 2006 funding was obtained from the Association of Voluntary Organisations in Wrexham (AVOW) to the tune of £2,500 which was used for the purchase of twenty new, blue upholstered, folding metal chairs and twenty tables and trolleys on which to keep them. The aim was to gradually replace the gold upholstered metal chairs.

In 2007, the playgroup, having installed a metal shed in which to keep the outside play equipment, received a grant from the Dame Dorothy Jeffreys Trust of £244 for the erection of wrought-iron gates from Paul Belmont across a section of the car park to provide a secure play area for the children that could be folded back at other times. The hall committee agreed to pay the balance of £200. Resurfacing of the car park at the back of the hall was now added to the list of things that needed doing but, in the meantime, woodworm had been found in the floor and the bottom of the door jamb leading from the hall to the kitchen lobby and, after three different quotes had been obtained, that of Timberwise for £686 (plus VAT) was chosen.

In 2007, the treasurer announced her intention to retire from the post which she had held for thirty years having found an able, and willing, replacement in Roy Jones – now back in Bangor from Bristol. Unfortunately, this prompted the chairman and secretary, Ken Manchester and his wife Denise, to put into action their previous threat and announce their resignations from the committee. Roy set about recruiting new officers from among his friends in the village and came up with Andy Powick, a chairman from forty years earlier who was prepared to act in the same office again; John Firth, an able vice chairman, and Jan Gresty as secretary. Viv, having agreed to remain on the committee, offered to continue taking the bookings for the hall and to report any repair and maintenance problems to the monthly meetings. For this she was given the grand title of Hall Manager.

With the new team at its head, the committee was revitalised and the reason soon became obvious why the officers were chosen – apart from being willing, they were all of a like mind and wanted to see the pillars removed that for forty years had blighted the inside of the hall. This now became their prime objective. In 2008, after problems had been encountered with the heating, it was discovered that there was no insulation in the loft over the oldest part of the hall and kitchen and Andy Powick and John Firth remedied the omission by laying insulation felt. A few months later, with the support of a Wrexham Borough Council grant of £2,500 the single-glazed wooden and metal-framed windows throughout the building were replaced with double-glazed units from Northern Glass.

The committee planned the renovations in three phases and, succumbing to female pressure, decided that the fitting of a new kitchen was a higher priority than the removal of the pillars and that work was designated as phase one. Although there had been plans to alter the kitchen at the time of the building of the second extension, these had been dropped in favour of enlarging the hall and, apart from tiling the walls, new work surfaces and a new boiler, nothing major had been done to the old kitchen. Three members of the committee paid a visit to Bettisfield village hall to see their revamped kitchen for which they had funding from Northern Marches Cymru. Whilst it was realised that it was not possible to enlarge the kitchen, it was possible to re-design the interior layout to incorporate a new condensing combination boiler, a fridge, a range cooker and granite worktops, as well as plenty of cupboard space.

Three contractors were invited to quote for the work and Robertson & Jones was chosen. Within a short time a grant of £18,948 (85%) was obtained from Northern Marches Cymru and £3,000 of the remaining £3,213 (15%) was granted from AVOW. Additional expenditure was incurred with the purchase of a five-litre, hot water drinks dispenser that would reduce the condensation from kettles and for the fitting of cupboards in the kitchen passage for the use of the cleaner and housekeeper, and for the storage of brushes mops, buckets, etc. The ladies also felt that instead of the oddments of crockery and cutlery that had infiltrated the kitchen over the years, it was time for the hall to have its own. To their surprise, the committee approved everything they suggested. Once grants had been obtained and the kitchen constructed, two of the committee paid a visit to a china warehouse in Stoke-on-Trent where, reigning in their inclination to buy prettily patterned ware, they opted for tough, plain, white crockery at half the price – £500 – that could easily be replaced. The hirers all voted the new kitchen a great success. The total cost being £25,046. An open day was arranged to which the mayor of Wrexham was invited. The different village groups were offered the chance to put on a display of their activities and this, along with the history of the village hall and schoolhouse found during research, created great interest.

Now that the ladies had been satisfied the boys were free to plan phase two, their greatest achievement, the removal of the pillars, the extension of the heating system, the laying of laminated flooring throughout, the improvement to the disabled access and the fitting of a sliding partition. The total cost of this work, including redecoration, was estimated at £40,150. A structural survey was undertaken, planning permission applied for, quotations received and grants sourced. Approval for grant funding from the Landfill Communities Fund by Waste Recycling Environment Ltd (WREN) was successful and £35,000 was obtained. Dee Valley Builders of Llangollen began work at the beginning of August 2009 and completed by the beginning of September, the work being timed to take advantage of the holiday period so as to create the minimal disruption to hirers. The work cost the village hall £4,000 of its own funds.

At the time of the second extension, a partition was installed that could be drawn across the room just behind the pillars to enable the room to be used for two functions. This, which had been sourced from a redundant school, ran on a track and was never very successful as it was heavy to move and was often found pulled off its runners. An added problem was that it was not entirely sound proof and once, when two meetings were taking place at the same time, one group remarked on the hilarity issuing from the other. In 2008, when the suggestion was made that a moveable partition should be installed, there was a less than enthusiastic reception from those people who had long memories. However, on being assured that it would be a motorised, lightweight and soundproof screen with an integral door, the scheme was given the go ahead and was included as part of phase two.

Under phase three, with a grant from AVOW of £7,500, it was planned to make a small corner stage, provide sound, lighting and projection equipment, and install a hearing loop. Eight new cupboards up to the ceiling were fitted for the use of hirers, with two long cupboards overhead. An open day was arranged and early in 2010 the mayor of Wrexham, Councillor Arwel Gwynn Jones accompanied by his mayoress Mrs Mair Jones, was invited to formally re-open the building.

Above left: Phase Three completed in 2010. View looking towards the kitchen with the hall now pillar-free.

Above right: The new kitchen installed in 2009.

Right: View of the hall in 2013 with some of the art group.

Also attending were County Borough Councillor Rodney Skelland, the chairman of the Community Council Malcolm Jones, and over 120 residents.

The Bangor Cub Scouts had amalgamated with the Overton pack in 2009 and no longer met in the hall and the opportunity was taken to move all the wooden and gold metal chairs into their storage room before anyone else could stake a claim. Another twenty blue chairs, without the trolley, were bought which, with a bit of ingenuity, were also fitted into the same room.

Later in 2010, with the aid of a Wrexham Maelor Borough Council grant of £1,500 and a grant from AVOW, the car park was finally resurfaced with tarmac and marked out with parking spaces. The work cost £6,700, which used up only £212 from hall funds. It was voted a great success and significantly improved the external appearance of the hall. The chairman, and particularly the treasurer, were thanked for all their work in obtaining grants for all the upgrades in the last two years, in addition to the financial and practical support provided by Gordon Mytton Developments Ltd, and other local benefactors. It was noted that, of the total spend of £88,096, only £8,400 had been a direct charge on the hall funds and had resulted in an increase of 50% in private hire income in the succeeding twelve months.

Having brought the saga of the village hall up to the present time it can be said that the committee is as enthusiastic as ever, that the hall is used every weekday and several times on some days. The committee is now concentrating on building up a financial safety net for any future remedial work needed on the roof. The old Endowed School, built with the money bequeathed 285 years ago by Lady Dorothy Jeffreys, is safe for several more years to come.

14. Post Office

During the reign of King James I (1603–25) a 'Postmaster of England' was appointed for the 'taking up, sending and conveying of all packets and letters'. By 1809, this had been styled the Royal Mail. At first, the post was carried on horseback with the horses being changed at 'posts' along the main highways. Innkeepers were paid about 2d per day to keep post-horses for the exclusive use of the Royal Mail. Robbery was a frequent occurrence, but when main roads were 'turn-piked' and coaches introduced from 1786, the carriage of mail became safer and faster. Although highway robbery was still an occasional hazard, the mail coaches carried guards armed with blunderbusses for just such eventualities.

All letters were charged by weight and by distance travelled and consequently the Royal Mail was too expensive for the ordinary man to use. Acts of Parliament in 1763 and 1794 meant that delivery to villages could be made at a charge of an extra penny from the nearest post town, either Wrexham or Oswestry. Overton was classed as a sub-post town but Bangor was not, consequently Overton had a sub-postmaster as early as 1610, although the names of the office holders are unknown. Envelopes were not generally in use in Britain before 1801 as the charge was based on the number of sheets of paper used – paper was expensive – and an envelope would have added to the weight. The charge for a single-sheet letter from Overton to London went up from 6d in 1784, to 8d in 1796 and 11d in 1812.

POST OFFICE REGULATIONS.

On and after the **10th January,** a Letter not exceeding **HALF AN OUNCE IN WEIGHT,** may be sent from any part of the United Kingdom, to any other part, for **ONE PENNY,** if paid when posted, or for **TWO PENCE** if paid when delivered.

THE SCALE OF RATES,

If paid when posted, is as follows, for all Letters, whether sent by the General or by any Local Post,

Not exceeding ½ Ounce .... **One Penny.**
Exceeding ½ Ounce, but not exceeding 1 Ounce **Twopence.**
Ditto   1 Ounce .... 2 Ounces **Fourpence.**
Ditto   2 Ounces .... 3 Ounces **Sixpence.**

and so on; an additional Two-pence for every additional Ounce. With but few exceptions, the WEIGHT is limited to Sixteen Ounces.

If not paid when posted, double the above Rates are charged on Inland Letters.

COLONIAL LETTERS.

If sent by Packet Twelve Times, if by Private Ship Eight Times, the above Rates.

FOREIGN LETTERS.

The Packet Rates which vary, will be seen at the Post Office. The Ship Rates are the same as the Ship Rates for Colonial Letters.

As regards Foreign and Colonial Letters, there is no limitation as to weight. All sent outwards, with a few exceptions, which may be learnt at the Post Office, must be paid when posted as heretofore.

Letters intended to go by Private Ship must be marked " Ship Letter."

Some arrangements of minor importance, which are omitted in this Notice, may be seen in that placarded at the Post Office.

No Articles should be transmitted by Post which are liable to *injury* by being stamped, or by being crushed in the Bags.

It is particularly requested that all Letters may be *fully* and *legibly* addressed, and posted as *early* as convenient.

January 7th, 1840.

By Authority :—J. Hartnell, London.

Post Office Regulations 1840 relating to the introduction of the 'penny post.'

256

When Sir Rowland Hill introduced the so-called 'Penny Post' in 1840, the volume of mail being distributed greatly increased and brought it within reach of the working man. For the sum of one penny '… a letter not exceeding half-an-ounce in weight, may be sent from any part of the United Kingdom, to any other part, if paid when posted, or two pence if paid when delivered.' The postal service was advertised in the town directories. *Slater's Directory* of 1850 states that 'letters from Bangor arrive (by footpost) every evening at 6.30 p.m. and are despatched thereto at 6 a.m. Delivery of letters commences in the morning at 7 a.m. in the summer and in the winter at 7.30 a.m.'

The postmasters

The first pillar-box was erected nationally in 1855, about the same time that Isaac Pickering, was appointed as Bangor's first postmaster. He had been baptized in Llanarmon-yn-Iâl on 4 January 1801, the seventh of the ten children of Francis, a miner, and Sarah (née Bryan) and living in Eryrys. In the 1840 tithe apportionment he was listed as being the owner of all the property on the north side of the High Street, from the chapel up to what is now called Orme Lodge, making three or four properties in all, one of which was attached to the chapel side of the post office, since demolished. Why and when he moved to Bangor or how he came to own four properties in the village is unrecorded. He may have been left them by a wealthy, deceased relative, but was certainly in Bangor by 1833 when he was one of the signatories applying for the registration of the protestant meeting room. In 1836 he applied for a licence to marry Sarah Gibbons (née James) the widow of Samuel Gibbons a wheelwright, who already had two daughters, Eliza (who died aged twenty-one in 1850) and another, name unknown.

Isaac and Sarah were married on 30 June 1836 in the church of St Martins-in-the-Fields, Liverpool and their marriage certificate gives his occupation as 'teacher'.' He would not have taught in Bangor schools, because he did not belong to the Church of England, but may have been a Sunday-school teacher at the chapel or at the Presbyterian church in Wrexham. The couple had two children; a daughter, Sarah, born in April 1837 whom they had baptised in the Presbyterian church, Chester Street, Wrexham, and a son, George, born in 1838, who died three weeks later. Shortly after his death, his mother died aged forty. Both were buried in Bangor churchyard in the grave of her first husband, Samuel Gibbons. Isaac never remarried.

The next mention of Pickering is in October 1849 when he successfully prosecuted Ann Edwards (alias Ann Giles, aged 40), and Charlotte Lloyd (aged 35) at the Quarter Sessions for stealing items from his shop. Both pleaded guilty to larceny and were sentenced to two months imprisonment with hard labour in Flint gaol. In the 1851 census, he is described as being 'a draper and grocer and a widower, aged 50' and living with him were his daughter Sarah (aged thirteen) and his niece, Mary Pickering (aged thirty-one) of Llanarmon, who was acting as his housekeeper. In April 1856, Isaac, along with Joseph Fowles, was an overseer of the poor when he attached his name to a notice in the church porch of a vestry meeting to fix a rate of 2d in the pound to cover the cost of repairing the bye-roads and the village pound, and for the appointment of an assistant overseer.

In May 1860, Isaac's daughter married Mark Vickers, a builder of Netherfield Road, Everton, the son of William Vickers, also a builder, in Walton Parish Church, Liverpool. In the 1861 census, Isaac Pickering was listed for the first time as a sub-postmaster and staying with him was his

Bangor post office soon after Billie Griffiths took over in 1921. His sign is over the door, but no petrol pump and no post box on the wall. Note the little cottage that was then attached to the post office.

daughter, Sarah Vickers, described as an 'architect's wife.' Sarah and her husband went on to have three children, Joseph Pickering, buried in Bangor in November 1862, aged five months, Sarah Pickering, buried in March 1864 also aged five months and Florence who was buried in May 1868, aged five weeks, before separating and eventually divorcing. No doubt the ordeal of losing three children put a great strain on the marriage.

In the 1868 *Slater's Directory* the postmaster for Bangor is given as James Pickerington, an obvious error, the handwriting having been carelessly misread by the printer. Isaac Pickering supplied the church with sundry items from his shop and presented his bills to the churchwardens for payment until his death on 17 March 1873, aged seventy-three. After her father died Sarah carried on the post office and shop and is listed as the postmistress in the 1874 *Worrall's Directory*.

In December 1877, Sarah married Charles Cheetham, a thirty-one year old bachelor farmer who was probably living on the family farm in Marchwiel. He then took over the position of sub-postmaster. The rector, the Revd McGill who conducted the service, obviously did not object to Sarah's earlier divorce, as he wrote 'the divorced wife of Mark Vickers, spinster.' Sarah Whitehead (the wife of the schoolmaster), William Thomas Cheetham (Charles's younger brother) and Mr Bickerton (the innkeeper of the Buck) were the witnesses. Sarah and Charles had just one child, Marian Pickering, in February 1879 who sadly also died aged just three hours. Sarah died in January 1890, aged fifty-two. Charles remained a widower for just twelve months before marrying Amy Cash in Birmingham in the first quarter of 1891.

In 1906, at a parish council meeting the increase in the number of visitors to the village in the summer months was discussed and with it the need for better postal facilities. With the support of Charles Cheetham, a letter was sent to the head postmaster at Wrexham requesting that in addition to the morning delivery a second delivery of post in the afternoons be undertaken. He responded by extending the time for posting and improving delivery. By 1907, Charles Cheetham, having been in failing health for some time, died aged sixty. His widow, Amy, carried on the post office and shop until 1913, when aged fifty-two, she sold the business and returned to live in her home city of Birmingham.

Bangor's next postmaster and proprietor of the grocery shop was Thomas Austin Pemberton who had been born in Market Drayton in 1889, the son of Benjamin Pemberton, a grocer and sub-postmaster and his wife, Harriet. In the 1911 census, Pemberton had been working as a farm worker and living with his wife, Ellie, and daughter, Lily, in Market Drayton. He probably stayed in Bangor for the duration of the war, but by 1918 he had moved from the village.

The next postmaster was Frederick Joseph Mayland but within three years he and his wife Charlotte Elena Mary had taken over the post office in Caergwrle. He was born in 1881 and died in March 1932 whilst staying at the Great Central Hotel in Marylebone, London. Nothing more is known about him.

William Griffiths became the postmaster with his wife, Elizabeth Mary, in 1921. One of his first actions was to apply to the District Council for a licence for the storage of petrol at the post office and he submitted a plan of a 'Bowker' Outfit for a petrol pump that was approved, provided it was at his own risk. He sold Shell petrol and the illuminated shell glass dome could be seen with the pump until relatively recently. In those days most villagers who had a yard or garden kept chickens and a few also had a pig and Griffiths (known to locals as Billy) had a warehouse at the back of the shop where he sold animal food – chicken corn, pig meal. If you were on the tall side, the general shop could be a death trap as hanging on hooks from the beams were such things as stable-brush heads, bunches of black-lead brushes and even rabbit snares. Over the entrance door was a shelf where tins of paint were stored – you could have any colour as long as it was white,

Billy Griffiths with his wife. By now he was supplementing his income with advertising posters on the shop front and by the sale of petrol. Still no post-box.

green or brown. Like many shopkeepers he had a bacon slicer and would order a side of bacon every week from a butcher in Wrexham to be sent on the train each Saturday. He would pay a couple of the local lads sixpence to go to Bangor station where they would sign for it and bring it back on the back of an old postman's push bike. On a Saturday morning there would be a gang of schoolboys outside the post office waiting for it to open, each one hoping to be chosen to 'bring home the bacon' – or the 'tiger' as Billy called it.

One day Billy received a telegram addressed to Mrs Margaret Young – an illiterate Irish widow who lived in Post Office Cottage (no relation to Ernie Young) from a Pat Maloney, an Irish jockey who used to lodge with her when the races were on. Billy went to her cottage with the telegram and informed Margaret that the jockey would not be coming to Bangor races on that occasion. She refused to accept it, saying that he always came and would be coming that time too. Billy finally got annoyed and brandished the telegram under her nose saying, 'Here's the telegram he sent to tell you.' She snatched the paper out of his hand, looked at it and said, 'That's not his handwriting!'

Billy was very gregarious and was involved in many village affairs serving at various times as treasurer of the cricket club, secretary of the bowling club and of the Institute, and was at one time a member of the parish council. In 1936, a carnival was organised in Bangor in aid of the local boys football team and on the Saturday the village was *en fête* with flags and bunting. The schoolchildren turned out in fancy dress and the local boys football club band, conducted by Billy, led the parade. His son, William Leslie Griffiths, was also very musical and passed Grade 4 in piano with the RAM & RCM (London). The following year he formed the Leslie Griffiths Band which provided music for the annual children's fancy dress party and for dancing after the church fetes.

In 1947, when the Bryn-y-Pys fire engine was engaged in pumping out the cellar of the Royal Oak, Billy lent a hand. He was the talk of the village as he proudly displayed his baldhead that he had shaved for a bet! He has been described as a rum character who was very fond of playing practical jokes. He also liked to drink and was said to keep a pint of beer behind the counter and, as the years went by, was often found in his shop somewhat inebriated. One year, the post office was flooded and his goods were seen floating down the High Street but he was too busy drinking in one of the hostelries to care. When he was in the pub people used to help themselves to any thing they wanted from the shop and leave the money on the counter. By 1949, his drinking had reached such a level that he had to retire from the post office and was finally admitted to a home in the Colwyn Bay area having been Bangor's postmaster for twenty-eight years.

In 1949, Thomas Clifford Knight took over the post office with his brother Arthur and sister Helen. They were local residents as Arthur had buried his wife, Ethel, in Bangor in 1945. One of

his first actions was to buy the little cottage that was attached to the post office, the occupants of which had recently been accommodated in the newly-built council houses. He had the house demolished to allow him room to build a garage. The family were well liked in the village and when Clifford delivered the groceries to his customers he was very obliging and took any post that had come for them as well. Arthur

Clifford Knight and his sister, Helen.

Knight also did a lot with the village youth club. After nearly twenty years they sold the post office and retired to live in Worthenbury where Helen ran that post office for a few years.

Wing Commander Henry Kenneth Rees and his wife, Mary, became the next occupants of the post office in 1968. He was the eldest brother of the late Hélaine and Marjorie Rees of Maes-y-Groes. Betty Starr, another sister, lived in Post Office Cottage where Hélaine came to live after Marjorie died. They were all brought up on a farm at Gardden Hall, Ruabon. In September 1938, Ken volunteered for the RAF aged only seventeen. Whilst undergoing training as a bomber pilot, he flew in a Wellington bomber, with a crew of six, under the Menai Bridge for a bet. He was shot down into a lake in a remote part of Norway whilst on a bombing raid and spent the rest of the war as a prisoner-of-war in *Stalag Luft III* and was involved in the famous Great Escape. He wrote a highly readable book *Lie in the Dark and Listen* based on his experiences. He carried on farming for a short while after the war but could not get used to civilian life and rejoined the RAF attaining the rank of wing commander in charge of 148 Squadron flying Vickers Valiant bombers. He retired in 1968, aged forty-eight, and bought Bangor post office where he and his wife lived for five years during which time he did a lot for the village and for the village lads who were then running riot and getting up to mischief. He organised activities for them in the village institute and dances in Twiss' assembly rooms. During his stay in Bangor, he converted the ground floor of the post office premises into one room by demolishing a couple of walls and thereby making the shop premises more spacious and inviting. The shop had previously been one of a chain of grocer's stores and had a sign 'VG Grocers' over the entrance and the villagers

Caricature of Ken Rees by Pat Rooney, an RAF colleague, in 1948. [Helaine Rees]

nicknamed him the 'Virgin Grocer'. He eventually decided that the life of a postmaster-cum-shopkeeper was not for him and moved to Anglesey where he bought a private members club – the Sandymount – in Rhosneigr where he could entertain the members with his reminiscences. There he was honoured by a surprise visit from Prince William, Duke of Cambridge in 2010/11.

In 1974, Alfred J.G. Lake became Bangor's next postmaster but did not stay long.

In 1976, Denys Longworth had become Bangor's postmaster and was succeeded by Martin Sunderland, a surveyor, and his wife Veronica, in 1981. They had lived and worked in South Africa and the Middle East and returning to this country, decided to buy Bangor post office for Veronica to run. For reasons of security, as the post office used to be immediately on the left of the entrance door, one of the first things they did was to block up the left-hand entrance and open up the right-hand door. Veronica remembers Miss Twiss, who lived in the old bungalow in Whitchurch Road, delivering the letters on her bicycle around Halghton, even on Christmas Day, and would often be invited inside for a glass of sherry before weaving her way back to Bangor. She also recalled three elderly ladies, Mrs Mytton, Miss Pryce and Miss Price, who were very particular about their bread, each specifying a specific type and would accept no other. One winter, thought to be 1981/2, the snow was thick on the ground and so bad that the local milkman, David Lewis, helped by his wife, was delivering milk on sledges. The bread had been delivered and left on the floor of the back premises. When Veronica came to make up the orders she discovered that their labrador dog had taken all the bread and buried it in the garden. In order to fulfil the orders for their pernickety customers, Martin drove through the snow to Coedpoeth to buy more from the Village Bakery. The three ladies had no idea of the trouble he took to satisfy their dietary needs at the time. The dog was happily digging up bread in the garden for a long time afterwards.

The Sunderlands had plans to divide the large upstairs room into two to make a separate flat but decided to move instead. They bought Cloy Farm and lived in rented accommodation in Bronington whilst it was renovated. They then sold this and bought a very busy post office in Tarvin which they again sold and bought another in Whitchurch. They finally retired to Worthenbury where they still live.

In about 1985, John Edwards and his wife Valerie took over the post office. He had retired from a job in industry and thought he would try his hand at being a sub-post master. He divided the premises into two separate properties once again and rented out the other half for extra income. The smaller shop meant that they could not stock the same range of items as the previous owners with the result that the turnover was down. They complained that the Sunderlands had exaggerated the income from the business only to be told that the books perfectly represented the turnover and had not been 'cooked.' Unfortunately, John's health failed requiring several hospital visits and the postmaster in Overton would often stand in for him in at Bangor. The Edwardses finally decided to retire to the Wirral.

Ann and Kenneth Stegall were the next occupants of the post office in 1987. Not long after arriving they divorced and were not at the post office long enough to make much impression on the local population and people have struggled to remember them.

In 1991, Mark Groom, formerly manager of a supermarket in Lymm, Cheshire, became the postmaster, with his wife Deborah and four boys. Both properties were offered to him but at the time he was only interested in the post office, a decision he has since come to regret as in 2011 he had to build a granny annex to accommodate his mother-in-law. A keen golfer in his younger days, his son Josh is set to follow in his footsteps or even surpass him, and has enrolled on a two-year course at the Lee Westwood Golfing Academy and has been gaining experience as part of his training stewarding at St Andrews, shadowing all the big names in the golfing world.

Village postmen and women
The mail used to come from Wrexham early in the morning and it was tipped out onto the shop floor (or later the garage floor) to be sorted for the postmen or women to deliver to the village and outlying hamlets. The district was split into two, with Bangor and Worthenbury in one round and Hollybush/ Halghton area in another. The first postman that can be identified was Isaiah Jones who was described as a 'post messenger' in the 1861 census. He was aged thirty-six, born in Overton and living with his wife, Mary (aged thirty-seven, a baker) at the back of one of the public houses. By 1881, Mary Davies, aged forty-eight, of Raggs Hill, but born in Wem, was a letter carrier and charwoman.

In 1889, Miss Elizabeth Sarah Clay, born in 1832, the daughter of the village blacksmith,

William, and his wife Harriet, began working as a post-woman. She used to cover the Hollybush and Halghton area walking up to fourteen miles a day. In 1911, aged fifty-three, she was described as a 'post office letter carrier' and living with her in what has come to be known as Clay's Cottage was her widowed mother (born in 1828 in Isycoed). After the death of her husband in 1896, Mrs Clay helped her daughter with the delivery of letters and was well known to the local inhabitants. She died in 1912. Lizzie Clay retired as postmistress in 1927 when aged seventy, having been a post-woman for thirty-eight years and it was reckoned that during her long service she had walked about 170,000 miles. She is known to have been absent from duty only once when she injured her ankle. She died in August 1932.

Elizabeth Clay standing outside her cottage in Whitchurch Road.

The other postman with Lizzie Clay and who worked the Bangor and Worthenbury round, was a Mr Baker who was a keen cyclist. According to a Wrexham newspaper in 1902 he carried off the first prize for collecting the most money for the second year running in connection with the Wrexham Cycling Carnival. In 1906, it was reported in the *Wrexham Advertiser* that a letter was posted in Overton at 6 p.m. which then went to Ellesmere, Chester and then Wrexham before finally reaching its destination in Bangor by post-cart at breakfast time the following morning. All this before the post office had mechanised transport.

In the 1911 census, John T. Roberts was recorded as being a postman in Bangor. He was single, aged twenty-six, the son of Mary Roberts with whom he lived in what is now called Frazer Cottage, opposite the post office. A native of Bangor, he served with both the Cheshire Regiment and the King's Liverpool Regiment during the Great War. His wedding was the first to take place in the Congregational chapel. His wife was always known as Mrs 'Possie' (Postman) Roberts, to distinguish her from any other Mrs Roberts living in Bangor at the time. John retired due to ill health in 1938 and died four years later aged fifty-seven. At his funeral, the mourners included postmen Eddie Roberts and W. Martin.

Eddie Roberts lived in Kiln Cottages behind the Royal Oak and did upholstery as a sideline. He had served for twenty-three years with the Royal Welch Fusiliers, fifteen years of which were as a physical-training instructor. He was a gymnastics instructor for a Wrexham gym club and held keep-fit classes at the old baths in Tuttle Street in Wrexham. He was always in charge of the procession at the village carnivals and made sure that everyone marched in step.

Mr Martin drove the post office van that delivered the post to Bangor. He used to entertain the Bangor children at their Christmas party by playing the piano and singing. He was thought to have lived in Wrexham. There was also a Jack Lewis who was thought to have been a postman.

Jane Mytton, daughter of E.L. Mytton of Orchard House, married Thomas Twiss in 1941 and was a post-woman for a time, covering the Raggs Hill, Pandy and Halghton area. Joan Duckett was a post-woman with Jane Twiss and delivered to Bangor and Worthenbury. After Jane Twiss

Left: Joan Duckett with her 'trusty steed'. Right: Her certificate of appreciation after twenty-five years of service.

retired, Marjorie Bayliss took over her round. Hilda Morris was also a postmistress for a time. When Joan had been postmistress for twenty-five years she was given a certificate from the GPO for her service. She retired in 1977 and was thrilled to receive a gift from her customers in Worthenbury who had made a collection and bought a small, round, silver box which was inscribed 'In appreciation from Worthenbury.' Inside the box was a silver model of a letter box on a post with a bicycle leaning up against it. The handlebars of the bike turn and the wheels and pedals revolved.

The telephone service

It seems strange now to think that residents of Bangor had to wait until the 1950s before they had piped water and the 1960s before they had a sewerage system and yet a hundred years ago they could talk to people miles away using the new-fangled telephone. By the start of the twentieth century the General Post Office (GPO) was introducing an embryonic telephone service. We do not know who was the first person to have their own private telephone, or when it was installed, but it was probably a tie between the local magistrate and the rector.

In 1915, the parish council asked for a telephone exchange to be built in the village but were told that the GPO could not proceed with the scheme with the country in the middle of a war. Four years later, the parish council requested that a public telephone be installed in the Bangor post office and this was done in 1920 with the number Bangor-on-Dee 1. As more and more local people

acquired phones, the GPO erected an automatic telephone exchange in Whitchurch Road which opened on 15 April 1931 complete with a UAX5 Unit Automatic Exchange System. The GPO had obtained the services of the noted architect Sir Giles Gilbert Scott to design the familiar red public phone box, known the K6 and one was installed outside the exchange. There used to be a further three red phone boxes in Bangor: one opposite Tŷ Graig by the council houses, a second at the bottom of Raggs Hill and the third at the Racecourse. These were removed when the new-style kiosks were produced in the 1980s and were not replaced.

One of the original old 'candlestick-style' telephones.

The telephone exchange was serviced by a technical officer or linesman called Geoff Dodd, who latterly lived in Cloy Lane. He, together with trainees, used to service the little automatic exchanges of Bangor, Overton and Dutton Diffeth in his designated area. One of these trainees was Terry Davies of Overton Road who fondly remembers travelling around the exchanges in the GPO van with Geoff, and often with Jess or Ted Jackson, two other linesmen. He less fondly remembers how cold these little buildings were with their lack of toilet facilities!

The old telephone exchange on Whitchurch Road.

It is almost forgotten now, but in the early days to make a long distance phone call you had to lift up the receiver and dial 'O' to speak to the operator in order to be put through to the number required. Bangor was attached to Ellesmere Manual Exchange in the early days until Wrexham's Manual Exchange took over. In 1983, the Bangor exchange was updated to a TXE2 system in a new electronic telephone exchange building and moved to Station Road. All Bangor phone numbers then had '780' added in front of their old number and now everyone can pick up the receiver and dial direct to any country and by-pass the operator.

The K6 phone box was replaced by the K8 box in 1968, still red but now made of fibreglass instead of metal, with larger glass panels. After the GPO was privatised the new company, British Telecom, re-branded everything and had a new, modern, yellow glass phone box designed for them in 1985, the KX that replaced the old red kiosk in Whitchurch Road. There was an instant

outcry and residents in many places started petitions and mounted campaigns for the re-instatement of their old red box – the one they never knew they loved so much until it was taken away. When the old exchange was sold *c*.1989, thought to be for £15,000, the new style phone box was moved to its present position in Station Road. It was not long after this that Terry Davies and his wife came to live in Overton Road and, with his GPO connections, was able to buy one of

A red telephone box.

New telephone exchange on Station Road.

the old red phone boxes (as had Geoff Dodd) which he installed in his garden. When it was spotted by the residents he thought he was in imminent danger of being lynched by a mob shouting 'Give us back our red phone box, it's ours!' until he persuaded them he had bought it in a fair sale. Incidentally, there is another old red phone box in the village, in the rear lobby of the Buck Hotel, which is actually used for its original purpose.

The GPO provided employment for several Bangor people – Ron Evanson, Geoff Dodd and Walter Young spring to mind. The last named was presented with a Civil Service Long Service Medal in 1942 and, during the Second World War, due to the shortage of manpower, continued working long after his official retirement.

15. Public Houses

From earliest times, ale was the drink of choice for most of the population who could not afford wine and, as water was boiled in the brewing process, bacteria were destroyed so making it the only safe drink that was cheaply and readily available. The alcohol content was low so it was drunk by all ages. Water was drunk only by the very poor. In 1830, the government removed the duty on beer and allowed householders, on purchasing an annual excise licence for two guineas, to brew their own beer and they were allowed to sell it to the public. These beerhouses, as they were known, flourished, particularly in towns and cities, often established in the front parlour of people's houses, and many shopkeepers such as grocers sold their own beer over the counter.

Unlike the public houses, the condition under which the beer was brewed and sold in beerhouses was not regulated until 1869 when the Wine and Beerhouse Act was passed which laid down the conditions under which the drinks were brewed and sold and the issuing of licences came under the control of the magistrates who could refuse the renewal of existing ones. Many of the beerhouses closed, or were taken over by pubs, inns or breweries, and became tied to selling a particular brewery's own beers.

Malting was a small-scale business, and was usually carried out by women on a domestic scale in malt kilns in villages and towns, until the development of common breweries in the eighteenth and nineteenth centuries. It is known that there was a malt kiln at the back of the Royal Oak, behind Bridge Cottage, at the rear of the Red Lion and at Kiln Cottage in Whitchurch Road, and probably others connected with the Star Inn and the New Inn. The village also had its own brewery in the nineteenth century at the side of the Star Inn (Dee House), now occupied by a dental surgery and a local builder's office.

In the nineteenth century, Bangor could be a noisy place to live with little restriction of pub opening hours and groups of men would spill out of the inns into the streets fighting and shouting. Many families led a very poor existence because the men and women spent all their wages on drink. At one time, there were seven public houses in the village, of which only the Royal Oak and the Buck Hotel now remain. The others were: the Star Inn, the Ship Inn, the New Inn and the Red Lion Inn, all of which premises can be identified. The exact site of the seventh, the Boar's Head, has not been discovered. That there was once another inn is confirmed by John Owen (1815–1902) in his diary where he wrote of his visit to Bangor in 1851, 'I think there are 6 public houses besides one that is discontinued.'

When the temperance movement was born in the nineteenth century, meetings were set up in every town and village of any size to combat the effects of the 'demon drink.' People were urged to 'sign the pledge' to encourage abstinence. The magistrates gradually restricted the number of public houses, particularly after the police force was formed, and first the Ship Inn, then the New Inn and the Star and finally the Red Lion were refused permission to renew their licence.

The Royal Oak

The Puleston family of Emral Hall, Worthenbury owned the Royal Oak from at least the middle of the eighteenth century. The inn was bought from the family when the estate was broken up and sold to Bent's Brewery, a family firm whose head office was in Stone, Staffordshire. The brewery also owned the land on which the Turnpike House and Fernhill now stand as well as the field at the back of the council houses fronting onto Station Road. The north Wales district manager for Bent's Brewery was an accountant, Eric Charles Lavis-Jones, the author's father, who had come from the firm's office in Liverpool in 1929 to take over from the then manager, Walter Spradbury, who was retiring. His office was at the bottom of the Wynnstay Arms Hotel yard in Wrexham and he also held the licence for that hotel. Mr Spradbury had previously acted in a similar capacity for Thomas Montgomery (whose properties were absorbed by Bent's Brewery) in May 1902. The Wrexham office was amalgamated with the Chester branch in about 1964. Bass Charington took over Bent's Brewery and in 1971, it was restyled Bass Charington (North West) Ltd with a red door as its trademark. It later amalgamated with Mitchell & Butler to become Bass, Mitchell & Butler. Latterly, the Royal Oak was owned by Punch Taverns, and has had several landlords/ladies in the past five years and was eventually advertised for sale in April 2011. In 2012 it was bought by the consortium that owns the Holt Lodge and the Alyn, Rossett.

According to a drawing by Moses Griffiths in 1781 the Royal Oak was a thatched building situated next to a slated property, with a slightly higher roofline, opposite half-timbered cottages by the bridge. We do not know what the original Royal Oak was like nor its age as, according to a date on the brace of the dormer window facing High Street, it was rebuilt in 1900. It is now a two-storey building of half-timber and painted render. The frontage to the High Street is five-bays wide and most of the windows to the ground floor are casements with multi-paned leaded lights. The old entrance to the vaults has been converted into a window, still with its round-headed canopy. Quite how much of the interior was remodelled in 1900 is difficult to say as there has been considerable revamping on at least two occasions recently, but some of the old beams are likely to have been reused. The newspaper correspondent who used to send articles about the goings-on

The Royal Oak, rebuilt in 1900. The door to the vaults is now a window.

in Bangor is strangely silent on the issue.

When the village was flooded the Royal Oak's cellars used to fill with water and the barrels of beer would be found floating. The author remembers her father saying that the office had been contacted to ask if the regular brewery wagon could bring with it certain perishable items of foodstuffs for the beleaguered residents as it was one of the few vehicles that could get through the flood.

The Royal Oak today. Its exterior has changed very little.

Landlords/licensees:

1814	Mr Joseph Edwards
1840	Daniel Done (1840 Tithe Map)
1851	John Edwards, born Worthenbury, wife Susan, born Bagthorpe, Norfolk, and three daughters (1851 census)
1858	Arthur Hanmer
1862 February	Thomas Hanmer, brother of previous licensee.
1867	Benjamin Bithell, took over the Star Inn.
1868	Joshua Hewitt – went bankrupt (*Wrexham Advertiser*).
1874–81	Thomas Hanmer, born Overton, wife Isabella, born Hanmer (census).
1881 July	John Jones
1881– Dec 1900	John Parry, born Crewe, wife, Margaret, born Chippenham, Wiltshire (census). Left to take over the Trevor Arms, Marford (*Wrexham Advertiser*)
1901–August 1902	William Bibby, 33, b Manchester, wife, Rose, born Birmingham (census). Left to take over the Black Lion, Ellesmere (*Wrexham Advertiser*).
1902 August– November 1935	John Ernest Foster. He died in November 1937, buried at Bangor. (Brother-in-law to Horace Blew, a Wrexham councillor and footballer).
1935 November– January 1940	Edward Hywel Price & Margaret Ella, formerly of the Red Lion, Christleton.

1940 January– February 1942	The licence was transferred to Margaret Ella Price when her husband was convicted of selling intoxicating liquor to non-*bone fide* travellers, on a Sunday.
1942 February	Thomas Prior Downs and Dora
1952 June	Robert Albert Savage
1958	George R. Forsey and Eleanor
1959	William H. Niven and Lily
1969	Arthur W.N. Bates
1971	Jeffrey James Jones and Wendy
1976	Anthony Wood and Irene (Elect Reg)
1978.	David Thompson and Christine (baptism & elect Reg)
1986	Michael Gary Willard and Irene (Elect Reg)
1999 ?	Alan and Beth Last
2001	Beth Last
2005	Michelle Booth
2007	Andrew Smith
2010	Temporary managers
2013	Mark Finlay

The Buck Hotel

This is an early eighteenth-century building with later additions and alterations and has a façade of rendered brick. There is a first floor room that was used as a former courtroom where the local JPs heard cases brought before them. Like the Royal Oak, it belonged to the Puleston family of Emral Hall, Worthenbury. Mention of it is made in an indenture of 1810 when it was leased to George Mellor.

> … all that messuage or dwelling house now and for a long time past used as an inn or public house and commonly known as the Buck's Head, with the yard, garden and outbuildings and appurtenances thereto belonging situated and being in Bangor, with several fields and parcels of land …

The Buck Hotel today.

The licensee was Richard Francis.

When the Emral estate was sold in 1852, the hotel was bought by George Cambell for £858 13s:

All the messuage or Public house … the Buck Inn in Bangor with outbuildings yard garden and
two crofts or parcels of land in the occupation of John Davies or his under tenants.

Cambell died in 1876 and his trustees leased the Buck to the Wrexham brewer F.W. Soames. In
1905, his trustees sold it to Messrs Bate, brewers of Wrexham who, in turn, sold it back to F.W.
Soames in 1908. By 1909, the inn was owned by Peter Walker & Co. of the Union Brewery,
Wrexham, whose head office was in Burton-on-Trent. This brewery in turn sold it to Greenall
Whitley. In 1978, Greenall Whitley sold the hotel at a public auction and it was bought by Albert
and Dorrie Cooke for about £25,000. Mrs Cooke described the pub as the 'Marie Celeste' when she
came to view for the first time: all the beds were made, the tables laid, all the drawers full of cutlery
and the collection bottle for the Frank Wingett Cancer Fund was still on the bar counter.

Landlords
c.1810–18	Richard Francis, (Emral Estate papers)
1818	Anne Francis, widow (will)
1834–c.45	John Orford (Tithe Map) and Ann, daughter of above
1852	John Davies (Emral Rental)
1854	John and Mary Maddocks (baptism)
1858	Mr Thomas Humphries, butcher & publican and Elizabeth his wife (census)
1871	Mr Richard Edward Bickerton
1881	ditto
1883	Joseph Twemlow (*Slater's Directory*)
1883	George Douglas Hughes (*Wrexham Advertiser*) was charged with selling alcohol without a licence. He had never had it transferred from the previous licensee and nor had he applied for a temporary one. The inn was closed until the next Petty Sessions.
1884–95	Thomas Barron, late of the Shropshire Inn, Eyton (*Wrexham Advertiser*), born North Meols, Cheshire, wife Eliza.
1895–1903	Cain Ratcliffe, born Upstone, Staffs, wife Ester, born Hadley, Salop (1891 census). Overseer & Bangor parish councillor, former coachman to Squire Yorke of Erddig. Moved to the Red Lion, Marchwiel, died 1910
1903 March–1906	Stephen Copnall
1906 November	Richard Thomas
1908 July–July 1920.	William and Mary Higgins from Southport
1920–2	Walter & Hilda Crosse

The old brewery on
Whitchurch Road.

1922–7	Mrs E. Foster
1927–9	Alfred William and Mary Crohill
1929–32	Harrop (d April 1932) & Elsie Mary Mallalieu
1932–3	Mrs Elsie Mary Mallalieu
1933–5	Joseph Edward Walley (Elect Registers)
1935–7	Edmund Hoadley Smith, buried 5 February 1937
1937–9	Wilfred & Elsie Howarth
1939–45	Edgar and Kathleen Lea
1945–7	Leslie C. Crabtree
1947–50	John H. and Ruby Lockett
1950–72	Colonel Frank C. and Janet Macvie
1972–6	Frank N. and Maureen Whitham
1976–8	Peter J. and Margaret Freeman
1978–89	Albert and Dorothy M. Cooke, moved from the Lion Hotel, Moulton, Cheshire
1989	Fredrick Allan and Kathleen Hayes

The Star Inn

The earliest record of this inn is an entry in the bishop's transcripts on 6 April 1673 when the baptism of John, son of John Edwards of the Star, is recorded. It is now known as Dee House, but it is not known when the present house was built. Farming and brewing traditionally often went hand in hand and the Bennett family farmed the Dee House farm and also ran a small brewery for some years. Until a means of controlling the temperature was found, the fermentation of the brew was seasonal work and took place in the autumn and winter and temporary workers would be recruited from the farm labourers. Many farmers would have a barrel delivered to the farm for their workers.

Brewing continued until 1907 when John William Bennett, the brewer, fell into a vat of boiling liquid and, although he managed to get out, subsequently died. He was only thirty-seven years of age and had two children. The secret of good brewing died with him and although another brother

The Star Inn now Dee House.

took over as brewer, it was not a success and the brewery closed. Eventually, in the late 1960s the farmland was sold for housing and was known officially as the Dee Farm Estate (but unofficially by many as the Racecourse Estate when all the roads were called after different racecourses). The old farm buildings and the brewery were later sold to Gordon Mytton for building in the 1980s and called Dee Court,

The inn was owned in 1840 by Miss Elizabeth Davies who lived at the Mount and the tenant was Samuel Chesters. By 1881, the inn had closed and it reverted to being a farmhouse and brewery.

Landlords:

1840	Samuel Chesters.
1851 census	John Davies, 35, unmarried, farmer, born Bronington
1858 April	Mr Thomas Edwards (will)
1861 February	George and Ann Bather (baptism)
1863 January	Richard Edward Bickerton, later took over the Buck Hotel
1868	James Burton (*Slater's Directory*)
1869 December	Mr Benjamin Bithell
1874	Ditto (*Worrall's Directory*)

The New Inn

This inn is now called Walnut House in Whitchurch Road. The building is thought to be eighteenth century and is said to have been mentioned in an indenture of 1788 where the names Charles Poyser, William Bradshaw, John Smith and Edward Bevan were mentioned, but whether these were the owners or their tenants is unknown. According to the tithe map, Thomas Bradshaw owned it in 1840. Little is known about this inn and by the 1880s the licence was not renewed by the magistrates, there being more than enough inns in Bangor.

The New Inn, now Walnut House with the attached Rose Cottage.

Landlords:

1716	John Pennant, (burial of son)
1840	William Bebbington and James Clark (tithe apportionments)
1851–69	James Lewis, age 33, born Llansantffraid, wife Mercy age 35, born Whitchurch, (census)

The Red Lion

This inn was located in Whitchurch Road on the site now known as Plassey House and Plassey Court. There used to be an old well at the back, known as the Monk's Well or Deiniol's Well, which tradition said was the well that the monks of Bangor Monastery used. It was said to be one of the few deep-water wells in Bangor and was filled in when the property was converted into apartments. In 1840, it was owned by Robert Bateman and included with it was the field at the back (where Plassey Gardens is now located) and the field on which Abbeygate Walk has been built. His son, John, lived at Welshampton and by 1891 his grandson, Thomas Bateman, had sold it to Mary Bennett (a widow), Alfred Bennett and John William Bennett for £995.

The old Red Lion rebuilt, divided into apartments and renamed Plassey House

Landlords:

1812	John Jones and Anne (baptism register)
?	
1840	Charles Jones (tithe apportionments).
1844	Mr and Mrs Maddocks
1851 census	Roger Parker, born Farndon, age 34, butcher and farmer of 38 acres, wife Catherine, 53, born Caldecott, sons Richard (27), born Worthenbury & Roger (24), born Bangor, both butchers, and daughter Mary (18), born Bangor. This family may just have been staying at the inn at the time of the census and were not the landlords.
?	John Maddocks, 'mysteriously disappeared' (*Wrexham Advertiser*).
1858	Mr Higgins (held the license for Mrs Maddocks)
1862	Mrs Maddocks
1868	William Bennett (*Slater's Directory*)
1881	William Bennett (41) (died 1890), wife Margaret, 5 sons & one daughter, Edith (census).
1891–8	Margaret Bennett, 49, widow; sons Alfred, 28, and John, 21, both brewers (census).
1898 June	Licence transferred to Benjamin Boffey on a testimonial being received from the police superintendent for the Delamere Division, Cheshire, died August 1899 aged 55. (*Wrexham Advertiser*).
1900	Mrs Mary Richardson Boffey, widow.
1901	Reginald Parry '... the son of Mr John Parry who left the Royal Oak to become the Licensee of the Trevor Arms, Marford who had been such a popular face in Bangor' (*Wrexham Advertiser*, April).
1910	William and Bessie Dunbabin (Baptism)
1913	William Thomas Morris and Grace (Baptism).
1916	Thomas Alfred Maddocks and Mary (Baptism)

At the annual licensing session in March 1916 the police objected to the renewal of the licence of the Red Lion on the grounds of redundancy.

The population of the parish being only 470 persons of whom 134 were adult males, 178 adult females and 180 were over the age of 16. In the village there were only 256 persons comprising; 67 adult males, 101 females and 88 over the age of 16 and, at that time there was one licence for every 85 people. The Royal Oak and the Buck were said to be 'practically hotels constantly accommodating visitors.

The Red Lion had only three bedrooms and there had been three transfers of licence in the previous four years. There was no record of complaints on the character of the house nor against the

The Ship Inn now the Stableyard.

character of the people associated with it. In February 1917, the magistrates again refused to renew the Red Lion's licence and it was referred to arbitration between the County Licensing Committee and the Board of Inland Revenue. In the meantime, the house remained open. The compensation must finally have been accepted by the owner as in 1918 it was no longer an inn and was rented by John and Elizabeth While (the parents of Ron While who died in 2012). The Stratton family afterwards occupied the house and Mrs Stratton latterly ran a betting shop on the premises. Gordon Mytton bought the property and rebuilt the old inn as apartments on the same footprint and converted the barn into cottages.

The Ship Inn

According to Mrs Sunter Harrison, the earliest date mentioned in the deeds for this property is 1670. Now known as the Stableyard, it was originally built as two houses probably in the early seventeenth century and had eighteenth- and nineteenth-century extensions either side. The roof was raised and the exterior walls partially rebuilt in brick probably during the late eighteenth or early nineteenth century. The interior has two rooms divided by a timber-framed wall with chamfered beams. In one room there is a fireplace with a heavy bresummer beam. In 1840, the owners were John Edge, Edward Hanmer and Elizabeth Bithill.

The property was sold in August 1876 when it comprised, in addition to the former inn, a large yard, garden, brew house, milk house, stabling, cow house, barn, coach house, piggeries and other out offices. Also sold with it were two cottages and a saddler's shop adjoining the inn and several quillets, and part of a croft and a garden tenanted by Richard Griffiths and Cadwaladr Williams, a saddler.

Landlords:

1840	Joseph Sandilands
1851 census	Thomas Davies, aged 49, born Llanasa, wife Jane, aged 48, born Pwllheli, son David, aged 2, born Bangor
1861 November	Jane Davies, widow
1871 September	Mrs Davies was refused renewal of her licence – appealed
1873 September	Mrs Thomas, renewal of licence finally refused by the magistrates as there were four other inns in Bangor

The Boar's Head

Confirmation that there was a seventh inn comes in the Bangor burial register for 1720, when a John Davies of 'The Boars Head' was buried on 25 February and, two years later, on 6 December 1722, when Robert Jones, son of John and Margaret Jones of 'The Boars Head' was buried. In 1739, when a survey of land and property belonging to Emral Hall was made it included the Boar's Head tenement in Bangor, occupied by John Jones. The tenement consisted of:

	Acres	Rods	Perches
One Butt in the Lower Trous a Forth [in pencil has been added 'Traws y Ffordd' – across the road]	-	-	28
One Butt in the nearer Trous a Forth	-	1	2
Croft at the Towns end	1	1	25
Three Butts & a half in the Placey	-	2	16
Two Cuttings in the Placey	-	-	33
Site of Housing, Fold & Garden	-	-	23
	2	3	7

Included with this written survey is an estate map with all the fields and properties marked with the corresponding numbers that pinpoint exactly where the properties were, but unfortunately the map only covers Worthenbury, Willington and Halghton. Bangor was presumably on a separate map that has been lost.

When John Puleston died intestate in 1756 an account of the rentals of the Emral estate was made and continued whilst his heir was under the age of twenty-one. This listed properties in Bangor and there is an entry for Mary Jones of the Boar's Head. Her rent was £5 a year and she was £14 5s 1d in arrears. Her husband must have just died as thereafter she is recorded as Mary Jones, widow, of the Boar's Head, and by the next year had paid off all the arrears. She was still there in 1775.

In 1810, Richard Puleston leased the Emral estate to George Mellor, gentleman of Chester. Mentioned in the indenture were parcels of land including: 'Lloyd's tenement lately held by Joseph Edwards together with the Boar's Head Public House containing together 3 acres 2 rods and 8 perches,' plus several quillets in various parts of Bangor. There is still no indication of where it was situated.

The Boar's Head survey 1739. [FRO D/CL/49]

Mrs Vera (Sue) Roberts (née Spoor, died 2005), was brought up in the smithy and remembered playing as a child in buildings at the rear of the premises and seeing a beam inscribed with the name 'The Boar's Head'. She assumed it was the name of an inn run on part of the smithy premises at one time. Interestingly, when the smithy was sold to Joseph Spoor in 1901 the description of the property was 'All that messuage or dwelling house, shop, warehouse, malt kiln and garden ...' which seems to give credence to this assumption. George Humphreys thought that it had been in Overton Road, on land where Greylands and Greenacres now stand. A track once ran at the side of the smithy in Whitchurch road, emerging in Overton Road in between Orchard House and Greylands. The inn could have been at either end of this track, but its exact location is lost and no mention can be found as to when it ceased to be a public house. The nearest we can get is that it was after 1810 (when it is mentioned in the indenture) and before 1840, as it is not listed as an inn in the tithe apportionment. It had ceased to operate as an inn by 1851 as John Owen records that it no longer exists in his diary.

Innkeepers and Landlords

There is in the Flintshire Quarter Sessions records for Easter, 1753, a recognizance to keep orderly ale houses, inns and victualling houses in the parishes of the Hundred of Maelor with the names of the keepers listed, and the names of two people who stood surety for them. Those for the parish of Bangor were:

Keeper	*Surety*
Trevor Davies	Thos Reece, John Ralphs
John Evans	Thos Reece, Thos Bethel
Widow Jones	Mr Probart, William Jones
John Williams	Thos Bethel, John Ralphs
Mary Roberts	Thos Bethel, John Williams
Thos Bethel	John Ralphs, John Williams

Signed by W. Hanmer and Lloyd Kenyon

This list of inns is for the whole of Bangor parish and it is a pity that they did not also record the names of the inn occupied by each innkeeper. It is difficult to find out where these landlords had their premises as some of them were most probably not in Bangor village but in one of the townships. Trevor Davies had one of the bigger inns in the village, probably the Buck or the Oak, as, according to the Puleston manuscripts, he was paying £24 a year in rent to the Emral Estate in 1756 – nearly five times more than Mary Jones was paying for the Boar's Head. In 1751, he was over £92 in arrears but gradually reduced his rent arrears and by the time of his death in 1761 was only £41 in debt. His widow Jane took over the licence, paid off the arrears, and thereafter until her death in 1767 kept up regular payments.

In 1767, Humphrey Edge became the landlord of one of the inns, most likely given the coincidence of date, the same inn that Trevor Davies had run. In August 1769, aged twenty-seven, he married Mary Griffiths of Pickhill by licence. The following August, they had a son, William, baptized in the parish church who sadly died twelve months later. A second son was also christened William in September 1772. By 1775, Humphrey Edge was paying a rent of £27 6s a year.

His first wife must have died between 1772 and 1777 as in August 1777 he married Anne Evison, a spinster of Bangor. They both claimed to be twenty-eight 'and upwards' (he was actually thirty-two and she was thirty-eight – if her age of sixty-five at death in 1803 was correct). There were no children of this second marriage christened in Bangor church. Humphrey Edge was churchwarden in 1792 and again in 1806. He died in December 1819, aged seventy-five.

16. The Racecourse

The racecourse at Althrey, three-quarters of a mile from the village on the road to Overton, has always been on land that is part of the Bryn-y-Pys estate. The races date back to 1858 when Captain Richard Myddelton-Biddulph of Chirk Castle and the Hon. Lloyd Kenyon of Gredington could not agree who had the better horse and a challenge was thrown down and accepted to decide the matter with a race. Edmund Peel offered part of his land for the venue and flat ground by the river at Althrey was chosen as the most suitable site. It was agreed to race for approximately three miles over fences and the route was roughly marked out. Various friends offered to act as starter and course officials and the excitement and anticipation grew as word spread amongst their large circle of friends, neighbours and acquaintances.

When the day arrived, a large crowd had gathered, swelled by many farmers and local tradesmen who had heard of the event, it being the main topic of conversation at every market and in every public house for miles around, and bets had been placed on the outcome. Lloyd Kenyon was to be on his horse Skip Jack and Captain Biddulph on his horse Grayling, for a wager of £50. Both weighed in at the identical weight of twelve stone and were evenly matched and everyone looked forward to an exciting race. In the event Grayling won easily when Skip Jack refused several of the fences, giving the winner a distinct advantage. The event proved so popular and attracted such a crowd that it was decided to 'make a day of it' the following year with more races, but restricting the entrants to members of the Wynnstay Hunt and people who had hunted with them.

On 25 February 1859, the first official Bangor steeplechase meeting was held. It was a beautiful day and the setting for a racecourse could not have been bettered. There was a large crowd (estimated to have been between 4,000 and 5,000) and most of the principal residents of the district were present. Although there was no official entrance fee, about £22 was given at the entrance gate. Colonel Cotton, the master of the Sir Watkin Williams Wynn foxhounds, was in overall charge, and George Cambell of Althrey Cottage was the starter.

The main race of the day was the Grand Wynnstay Steeplechase, popularly known as the Farmers Race, which was run over three miles. The first prize was a cup valued at £25, with £50 in prize money given by the gentlemen of the hunt. The race was

George Cambell of Althrey Cottage, the first starter of the races.

restricted to horses that had hunted with Sir Watkin's hounds, *bona fide* the property of farmers, innkeepers and tradesmen. The second prize was £5 and £2 10s the third prize. The entrance fee was one sovereign. The race was won by Charley, a six-year-old, owned by Mr Jones and ridden by Harry Gaff. Second was Mr Oswald's five-year-old horse Polly, ridden by Webster, and third was Mr Humphreys' horse Lottery, three years old, ridden by Fox. Twelve horses ran, amongst whom were Mr Whalley's Lucy Long, Mr Powdrell's Elastic John, Mr Hassall's Malster and Mr Platt's Welsh Harrier. All the horses stumbled at the first fence and the resulting melee set the tone for the race, with only four in contention at the finish. An objection was raised against jockey Gaff for 'shooting the post' but the result was upheld.

The second race, called the Owner's Cup, was for horses ridden by their owner with an entrance fee of £5. It was won by the Hon. R.O. Hill on Lady Bird. Second was Captain Palmer of Cefn Park on Blackmare. Third was Mr Peel on Young Ireland and Captain Cotton came in fourth on Dublin. This was said to be the best race of the day, with Dublin making all the initial running but before halfway he was overtaken by Captain Palmer who rode a cautious race and for some time looked to be the winner but his mare ran out of steam at the finish.

There was also a race for ponies under fifteen hands with a prize of £50. Only four entrants started the race and Mr Birch of Marchwiel was a runaway winner by nearly a mile. Two of the ponies could not leap the brook and galloped through, soaking their riders.

The final race was for horses that had not won a race, for a prize of £50. It was won by Mr Foulkes on Tommy Tickle, second was Mr Powdrell on Elastic John, third was Captain Cotton on Dublin, fourth was Mr Thomas on Smoker. From the start Tommy Tickle took the lead, with Elastic John in close contention and the others far behind. About half-a-mile from home Elastic John threw his rider twice thus permitting Tommy Tickle to romp home an easy winner. The Bangor Steeplechase was declared to be an unqualified success and the decision was made to hold it every year.

In 1860, the stewards were Sir Watkin Williams Wynn, Lieutenant-Colonel the Hon Wellington Cotton of Cherry Hill, the Hon Lloyd Kenyon, J.O.H. Leche of Carden and Major Owen of Althrey. Sir Watkin acted as judge, Major Francis Owen as starter and Mr Cambell as clerk of the scales. There were six races and the rules were relaxed to allow members of the Shropshire, Cheshire and North Staffordshire Hunts to enter certain races, which no doubt accounted for the increased attendance as many of their supporters came to cheer on their riders.

The first, and most important race was for the Wynnstay Cup – value £25 and £50 in prize money given by Sir Watkin Williams Wynn. Twelve horses again ran and this year it was won by Mr Platt's Jerusalem. Second was Mr Hassall's Elastic John, ridden by Butler. Elastic John must have been sold after the previous year's race meeting as occasionally happened if a horse ran well. The third horse passed the post was Mr Birch's Stella, ridden by its owner. An objection was lodged against the winner, claiming that the horse was not qualified to enter, but the stewards were satisfied that Jerusalem fulfilled all the criteria for the race and the result stood.

The second race for £5 was for gentlemen who hunted regularly with the hunt and was won by Captain Cotton's horse Sir Rufus. The third race was open to members of the Wynnstay Hunt and neighbouring hunts for a prize of £50. Race four was the Owners' Race, for horses ridden by their owners who belonged to one of the above mentioned hunts. Captain Starkie, riding his horse

Skylark, won by a head. Race Five was an open steeplechase for beaten horses for a prize of £20. The sixth and last race was for ponies under fifteen hands for a prize of £15. Mr Minor's Tea Dealer was the winner but was disqualified when it was found to measure half-an-inch higher than the rules allowed and the race was given to the Mr Birch's pony, Actress.

The earliest known race card that has survived is dated 1861 and was printed by G.C. Griffiths of the Telegraph Office, Wrexham, and cost four pence. The race cards were printed in a different colour each year in white, pink, yellow or green, clearly setting out the rules and prizes for each race. The stewards for the 1861 meeting were Lieutenant-Colonel the Hon. W.H.S. Cotton, Major Owen, the Hon. Lloyd Kenyon, Sir Watkin Williams Wynn, J. Hurleston Leche and R. Ethelston. The first race, the Wynnstay Cup, was won by Mr Birch on his horse Stella. Mr Mulliner's Doubtful, ridden by Mr Peel, took the lead but threw his rider who promptly remounted and came in a creditable third. The second race for the gentlemen of the Wynnstay Hunt (prize of £5 plus a silver cup) was won by Captain Cotton on King Edward, second was Captain Palmer's Slasher, ridden by Archibald Peel, and third place was taken by the Hon. Lloyd Kenyon on Salopian. The rules of the third race were altered slightly to include followers of Mr Meynell Ingram's Pack. The entries for the pony race (prize £15) were allowed to be entered on the morning of the race at the Buck Hotel and the favourite, Captain Cotton's Fosco, proved a popular winner. The money given at the gate that year was £34 13s 1d. Many well-known faces were seen at the racecourse, amongst whom were Viscount Ingestre, Sir Watkin and Lady Williams Wynn, Lord Alexander Paget, Lord Berkeley Paget, the Hon. Lloyd Kenyon and Miss Kenyon, Colonel and Mrs Biddulph, the Misses Biddulph, Colonel the Hon W. Cotton with his wife and daughters, the Hon. Rowland Clegg Hill, Captain Peel, Colonel Brooke and Mr A. Brooke, Captain and Mrs Cotton and R. Corbet.

By 1863, the cost of a race card had been raised to 6d and racing now began at noon and for the first time racing colours were noted on the cards. The stewards were the Hon. W.H.S. Cotton, Sir W Williams Wynn, Major Owen, the Hon. Lloyd Kenyon and Edmund Peel. In previous years, people attending the races arrived mainly in carriages of varying descriptions, but the number coming on horseback had been steadily increasing and it had become the custom for 'young bucks' to try out the course, before or in-between races. The stewards were therefore forced to introduce a new rule that anyone other than those taking part in the races would be fined £1 if they rode on the course and jumped the fences.

In 1864, the best race of the day was the amateur steeplechase for the gentlemen of the Wynnstay Hunt. It was won by a neck by Captain Cotton, riding in his own colours of blue and scarlet, on his own horse Garibaldi. Mr Jones, riding his horse Grimaldi, in his colours of blue with a rose coloured cap, was second and third home was Mr Topham's Kate Coventry, ridden by M. Blake, in white with an orange cap. Sir Watkin Williams Wynn acted as starter and Mr Leche of Carden as judge. The clerk of the course was Major Francis Owen of Althrey Hall. This year the race cards were printed by Potter & Snape, Steam Power Printers of Wrexham.

In 1865, there were seven races on the race card. The event was notable for the presentation after the fifth race of a silver cup each to the first and second whips of the Wynnstay Hunt, Mr Tocock and Mr Orbill. A handsome testimonial had been presented to Mr Walker, the huntsman, some time ago, subscribed by those gentlemen who appear in the field in the scarlet. Now the presentations were the result of a subscription got up by those gentlemen of the hunt who did not don the scarlet. The cup that was presented to the first whip contained sixteen sovereigns and Mr Crane of the Woodlands, performed the ceremony on horseback. At the close of the races, three hearty cheers were given for Sir Watkin Williams Wynn. Isaac Hodgson of Sodyllt was the judge and Major Campbell, clerk of the course.

In 1866, the clerk of the course was Captain Owen of Althrey. In that year, and in 1867, the steeplechase was run under Market Harbro' rules and the printers of the race cards were Griffiths, Machine Printer of Chester. In 1868, the starter was Isaac Hodgson and there were eight races run under the National Steeplechase Rules. For the first time a charge was made for people bringing their own horses onto the race ground: saddle horses 2s 6d (12.5p) each, harness horses 5s (25p) each.

In 1869, a twelve-year-old boy in his first season as an apprentice jockey won his first race on Maid of Trent in the pony race, and after that his career never looked back. He went on to become a champion jockey thirteen times riding 2,748 winners. That jockey was Fred Archer, who was to become a legend in the world of racing. He was born Frederick James Archer in Cheltenham in 1857 and became jockey, later a partner, to horse trainer Mathew Dawson and won the Derby at Epsom five times. In 1885, he rode 246 winners in a season. Following the death of his wife, Ellen Rose, in 1884, he became depressed and committed suicide four years later aged only twenty-nine. That wonderful pony Maid of Trent, belonging to Mrs Willins, known as Coffey because of her coiffeur, carried on winning, or was placed, for a number of years, finishing with a win in 1875. The last time a pony race was held at a Bangor meeting was thought to be in 1878.

By then the Bangor Steeplechase, run under Grand National rules, had become firmly established as an annual race day. The villagers lined the streets to see the gentry dressed in their finery drive past in their barouches, broughams, phaetons, carriages, gigs, hansom cabs, followed by the not so great in their donkey-carts, dog-cars and shandries. The tolls taken at the turnpikes boomed. The gatekeepers had a busy time and often had a welcome bonus to their wages when the driver was in a hurry to reach the racecourse to gain a good vantage point and did not stop to collect his change.

Many of the carriages were taken onto the ground, like the cars of today, and were used for seating, particularly by the ladies to save their shoes and the hems of their long dresses from becoming dirty. They had a good view over the racetrack; a comfortable seat and they could see and, more importantly, be seen. The picnic hampers would be brought out and the champagne corks would pop. Many well-known people attended and most of the local gentry held house parties and invited their friends to stay, the highlight of their visit being attendance at the races. Sir Watkin Williams Wynn of Wynnstay attended every year and was usually accompanied by a large party of friends that often included the Earl of Shrewsbury, Earl Grosvenor and Lord Richard Grosvenor. Race-day was always a big event for Bangor with every farm and large house called upon to provide stabling for the horses and places within two miles or so of the racecourse offered board and lodging for the stable lads and jockeys. The farm labourers would act as grooms adding a welcome few shillings to their farm wages. Young boys would offer to hold a horse whilst the rider went to one of the hostelries for refreshment. In the High Street, trestle tables would be erected outside the shops and refreshments were piled high in the pubs in an effort to catch the people arriving by carriage, bicycle, or later by train, or walking to the racecourse. When the railway closed in 1962, the passing pedestrians, and consequently the income, was considerably reduced.

In between races the race-goers were entertained by the many sideshows such as Punch & Judy shows, shooting galleries, trials of strength, even boxing booths added colour to the scene, as well as rows of drinking booths, refreshment tents, nut stalls and cake stalls – all designed to separate people from their money. However, as well as the legitimate temptations to spend and lose money, the races also attracted pickpockets, five-card tricksters and other conmen. A typical episode took place in 1895 when William Fox of Liverpool was charged with stealing a spade guinea, the property of Edward Fitzjohn of the Boat Inn, Erbistock. PC John arrested the prisoner and took him to the weighing room and searched him without success. Acting Sergeant Farrell of Wrexham entered the room and put his hand into the prisoner's mouth and produced the guinea.

For the first meeting in 1859, the chief constable had sent Inspector Bolton four extra men to help the three resident policemen: PC Edward Jones (Bronington), PC Loughrin (Bangor) and PC McLaren (Overton) to police the course. The following year, he sent eight men. Eight years later, in 1868, the contingent had increased to fourteen men – four of whom were in plain clothes. This number, plus the three resident constables, was a third of the entire Flintshire police force of forty-one officers tied up in this one event. He stressed that the cost of supplying the extra police presence was to be borne by the race committee. He was also now borrowing men from the Denbighshire Constabulary, the chief constable of which had complained that they had been out of pocket the previous year. The following year, the number had jumped to twenty-four officers from Flintshire plus, in addition to the assistance from Denbighshire, he also requested a detective from Shrewsbury and one from the Chester forces. When a charge was made to enter the ground, part of their duty was to patrol the riverbank for people arriving without paying on horseback across the fields, by boat or by walking or riding across the ford at Royton. According to Jeanie Chantler, general manager of the Racecourse today, only on big race days such as Ladies Day would they request a couple of police officers. Police might be in the road controlling traffic and generally keeping a watchful eye on proceedings, but once they go onto the race ground there is a charge made – and they are expensive. The racecourse now employs its own security staff but in general, apart from the odd counterfeit note, it has a good clientele which is much more law abiding.

After every race meeting, the local magistrates were kept busy dealing with cases such as theft or drunkenness. In 1889, a case was brought before them by the police and the RSPCA for maltreatment of a horse. James Duxbury, a licensed cross-country jockey was summoned for ill-treating a racing mare named Baroness, the property of Captain Baldwin, by violently spurring it during a steeplechase. Blood was seen running from her side on returning to the paddock and Inspector William Jones of the RSPCA called the attention of Sergeant McLaren of the Denbighshire police to the horse. At the subsequent hearing, the sergeant gave evidence to the bench that he had seen the mare being spurred until she passed the winning post although she had no chance of winning. Captain Baldwin called the jockey 'an ignorant rider'. The magistrates fined Duxbury 16s 6d and £2 3s 6d costs.

In 1871, the stewards included Viscount Combermere, Sir Watkin Williams Wynn, Edward Peel and S.K. Mainwaring. The clerk of the course was Captain Francis Owen, the judge was

W. Maysmor Williams and the clerk of the scales was F. Minton.

1873 was characterised by the most beautiful weather and there was a large attendance. The turf was in splendid condition owing to the previous day's rain and this encouraged a large number of ladies and gentlemen to appear on horseback. Among those present were: Lord and Lady Hill Trevor, Lord Richard Grosvenor, Viscount Combermere, Miss Cotton, Prince Saphieha, Lord Hanmer, Sir Watkin Williams Wynn and Lady Wynn, Edmund Peel and party, Archibald Peel and party, the Revd T. Puleston and party, the Revd E. Dymock and party, R. Ormesby Gore and party, C.M. Owen and party, T.H. Leche and party, Mr & Mrs W.C. West and party, H.C. Raikes, G.H. Whalley, Marshall Brooks, officers of the 14th Regiment of Dragoons and officers of the 5th Dragoon Guards.

The meeting in 1875 was not as well attended as usual, with fewer people in carriages or on horseback, and it was thought that a fair day and also a market day in Wrexham were to blame. Whatever the reason, there were also fewer horses entered in many of the races. The Marchioness of Lorne (Princess Louise), the Duke of Argyll and Earl Grosvenor all came with the Duke of Westminster's party. Also present were Major West, lord lieutenant of the county and Mrs West, Lord Hanmer, Viscount Combermere, Lord Hill Trevor, Sir Roger Palmer and the Hon. T.G. Kenyon. The Grand Wynnstay Steeplechase attracted only four entrants and, apart from 1868 when only four horses ran, this was the smallest field for fifteen years, but was a good race nonetheless. Major Bulkeley had won this race in 1868, 1873 and 1874 and was second in 1871 and third in 1872. Now, riding Mr Lloyd's horse Baron, he had to settle for third place behind Mr Baughs' horse Orange Blossom which won by six lengths. Mr Morris's horse Charlie, ridden by W. Morris, was second.

The most exciting race of the afternoon was the Bryn-y-Pys Steeplechase that also attracted only four competitors. Mr Peel on his own horse Spring Flower and Captain Baldwin on Blue Bell were unhorsed at the second fence. After jumping over two fences Major Bulkeley on Burgular had a clear lead of 100 yards but came to grief at the third fence by which time Captain Baldwin and Mr Peel had remounted and continued the race. On reaching the third fence BlueBell refused. Mr Peel managed to get his horse over safely and was soon leading the field by three meadows. Major Bulkeley and Captain Baldwin started off in pursuit once again and were slowly gaining on Mr Peel, who by this time was only cantering slowly. Alongside the river, he quickened his pace only to slow down on reaching the straight, but this was enough to win him the race by twenty lengths. It was later found that Spring Flower had burst a blood vessel and could not have gone much further.

1876 saw Sir Watkin Williams Wynn appear in public for the first time since his return home from the Mediterranean where he had passed the winter in search of better health. After the third race Lord Combermere presented him with an address congratulating him on his safe return to comparative health. The stewards were the Duke of Westminster, Viscount Combermere, Sir Watkin Williams Wynn, the Hon. R.W.S. Cotton, E. Peel and S.K. Mainwaring. The clerk of the course was Captain Francis Owen of Althrey. The judge was W.M. Williams and the clerk of the scales was Mr F. Minton. The glorious weather at the start of the meeting attracted a great crowd, but the day was spoilt by several thunderstorms in the afternoon. There was one noticeable alteration in this year's course: the water jump had been moved to immediately under the eminence

The forerunner to the modern clay pigeon trap – a glass ball trap and ball. The trap turned on a wooden base and the direction of the shot could be varied by means of hand lines attached to the cross piece.

on which the carriages were placed each year, a change that was much appreciated by the spectators. The stewards were determined to enforce the rule that stated 'Any one riding in a race in colours other those listed on the card will be fined.'

The weather was good at the start of the 1878 meeting and thousands of spectators flocked to Bangor on 12 April for the twentieth anniversary steeplechase, which Sir Watkin Williams Wynn unfortunately again missed owing to ill health. This year, the water jump was placed near the judges' box and there were nine races in all. It is thought that this was the last time that a pony race was held. Again it was won by one of Mrs Willins ponies, Hurdle. A new rule was passed that shooting at glass balls was not permitted and posters were prominently sighted on the ground advertising the ban. Glass balls, the forerunner to the modern clay pigeons, were released from a trap by hand. Most probably someone had been blinded or injured by flying glass, hence the ban – Health and Safety would have had a field day!

1881 was a very successful meeting for Captain Myddelton of Chirk. In the second race he rode Colonel Lloyd's horse Planet to win by a head and in the third race he won on his own horse New Year from Mr Francis's horse Vivien, ridden by Mr Hayhurst. Captain Myddelton also won the sixth race, again on New Year. In those early days, a horse could take part in two or three events in an afternoon and, if there was a dead heat as happened in the fifth race in 1885, between Capt Hayhurst on his own horse Nightingale and Mr Peel on his horse Goatfell, then they had a runoff to decide the winner. Captain Hayhurst declined to race again, and Peel was declared the winner.

In 1883, the meeting was abandoned owing to the death of Miss Nesta Williams Wynn, Sir Watkin Williams Wynn's youngest daughter. In 1884, the presence of Sir Watkin Williams Wynn was missed having been ordered by his doctor to Brighton to recoup his health. In his absence, Lord Combermere officiated as starter. The judge at this meeting was Edmund Peel and the clerk of the scales was S.R. Pickering. Also present were: Lord Rocksavage and party, P. Lane of Plâs Power, Captain Best of Llangollen, R. Howard of Broughton, Mr Fletcher and party of Pant-yr-Ochain, Mr Peel of Bryn-y-Pys and party, S.K. Mainwaring of Otley, Mr Piercy of Marchwiel and party, Captain Godfrey of Bryn Estyn and party, Mr and Mrs the Hon. Tighe of Ash Grove, Mr J.F. Edisbury, Mr Archibald and Lady Georgiana Peel of Gerwyn and party, and Mr Palmer. The stewards for the meeting were the Duke of Westminster, Lord Kenyon, Sir Watkin Williams Wynn, Lord Cholmondeley, the Hon G. Ormsby Gore, Lord Hill, Mr E. Peel, Mr R . Middelton-Biddulph and Captain Ethelston. The starter was Sir Watkin Williams Wynn, the clerk of the course was Mr F.E. Cotton and the handicapper was R.K. Mainwaring.

In 1887, a person who identified himself only as RKMB wrote a poem in praise of steeple-chasing and in it are thinly disguised references to well known members of the racing fraternity.

It was obviously written by someone who knew the racing personalities very well and who mixed in the same social circle. It is printed in full at the end of this chapter. In 1889, a jockey, Fred Hassall rode five winners in one meeting – a record that still stands today. The winning horses were: Miss Palmer, Bagman, Candytuft, Curiosity, and Sweet Ethel.

For the fortieth anniversary in 1898, the prize for the Great Bangor Handicap Race was £300, of which £250 was for the winner, £35 for second and £15 for third and the race attracted thirteen runners. It was won by a six-year-old horse, Mum, owned and trained by D. Mann and ridden by E. Matthews. Reid Walker's aged horse Surplice was second, followed home by Major Orr-Ewings' horse Ford of Fyne, ridden by Withington. In addition to the Great Bangor Handicap Race, the other races were: the Grand Wynnstay Steeplechase for £74, the Bryn-y-Pys Steeplechase, the Flintshire

Bangor Wynnstay Hunt Steeplechase poster, 1893.

Steeplechase, the Wynnstay Hunt Cup, prize £100, the Selling Steeplechase for £50 and the Combermere Plate for £50.

Many of the horses that won at Bangor went on to compete in the Grand National at Aintree such as Gamecock, which won in 1887 and Cloister, ridden by Ernest Piggott, the grandfather of champion jockey Lester Piggott, that, in 1893, became the first horse to win at Liverpool under 12st 7lbs. Piggott won again in 1895 on The Wild Man from Borneo, having previously won at Bangor two years earlier. In more recent years Amberleigh House, owned by John Halewood from Manley and trained locally at Cholmondley, won at Bangor in 2003 and went on to win the National

Ernest Piggott, Lester Piggott's grandfather.

the following year to give trainer Ginger McCain his fourth Grand National winner. In 2004, Comply or Die won the novice chase at Bangor and then went on to win the National in 2008.

Ernest Piggott, who rode Poethlyn and The Wild Man from Borneo, also rode Jerry M to victory in the Grand National. He was a well-known jockey and was born in Nantwich. According to an article in the *Chester Guardian* in April 1919, he gained his first experience of racing on a donkey that was famed throughout Cheshire for the number of races that it won. Donkey races were a feature of the programme at sports meetings and Piggott had trained it to start by rattling stones in a tin can. The story is still told in Nantwich of the day that the jockey, tiring of rattling stones, decided to use a whip. When the flag fell the donkey refused to answer to the whip and they were left at the starting post!

A horse that had a connection with Bangor, although it was not known to have won a race there, was Tipperary Tim, owned by H.S. Kenyon and trained by Joe Dodd, the great grandfather of Brian Gresty of Bangor. It was trained at Marley Green, near Marbury, Cheshire and won the Grand National in 1928. Prior to the race the horse was brought to the smithy at Bangor to be shod by the Spoor family who had made themselves quite a reputation for fitting horseshoes made of aluminium that, being lighter in weight, were said to enable the horse to run faster. His usual jockey, George Richard Owen (always known as Bruds), was thought to be too young to ride in the National – about eighteen years old, and a solicitor from Chester, W. (Billy) P. Dutton, who was himself an amateur

Tipperary Tim, owned by H.S. Kenyon. [Brian Gresty]

Poethlyn, owned by Hugh E.E. Peel and his wife.

rider, was given the ride. Forty-two horses started the race and at the canal turn on the first circuit there was a massive pile-up and only seven horses were left. By the start of the second circuit this number had been reduce to only five. With two jumps to go there were just three horses left – the favourite, Billy Barton, Great Span and Tipperary Tim. At the penultimate fence Great Span's saddle slipped leaving just two horses to finish the race. At the last fence the favourite Billy Barton fell but was remounted to finish second, leaving Tipperary Tim the clear winner at 100–1. During its career the racehorse was renowned as an excellent jumper and never fell. The silver Trainer's Cup was donated by the family and can now be seen on display at Aintree racecourse.

The following year, 1929, George 'Bruds' Owen was the jockey when his mount Fenwick Court, owned by his father George R.E. Owen of Dodleston Hall, won the Bryn-y-Pys Steeplechase at Bangor. Bruds went on to become a professional jockey and later a trainer, and three well known jockeys rode for him, Dick Francis, Tim Brookshaw and Stan Mellor. Dick Francis was later to become a best-selling writer of 'whodunnits' – all based on horse racing. He rode his first winner at Bangor in 1946 on Wrenbury Tiger and later achieved a hat trick by riding three winners in an afternoon at a meeting. He won the Welsh Grand National at Chepstow with Fighting Line and competed several times in the Grand National at Aintree. Although he never won the National, he came second on Roimond behind Russian Hero ridden by Stan Mellor at the 1949 meeting. The trainer of both, George Owen, gave Dick Francis the choice of horse to ride, but he chose the wrong mount.

Dick Francis with Frank Perks and owner Charlie Read of Tŷ Graig. [Felix Francis]

Dick Francis was quoted as saying that Bangor was his favourite course because of its flatness and the absence of sharp bends. His brother, the well-known trainer Doug Francis, lived about this time at Deeside Cottage, Overton Road, which was later pulled down to make way for the new bridge. Doug, when asked why he had chosen to live in Bangor, said that it was an ideal place with plenty of open ground and hardly any ice or snow. The inhabitants of the village can vouch for the weather as many

Dick Francis (left) with his brother, Doug, at Aintree. [Colin Turner]

times it can be snowing heavily in Wrexham just five miles away, but only a light smattering in Bangor.

Tim Brookshaw also rode at Bangor and is remembered locally principally because his brother Tony and wife, Della, bought the Plassey Farm two miles from Bangor and have built it up into a thriving business comprising: a nine-hole golf course, garden centre, caravan park, restaurant, café, blacksmith's shop, hairdressers as well as converting all the farm buildings into various boutiques.

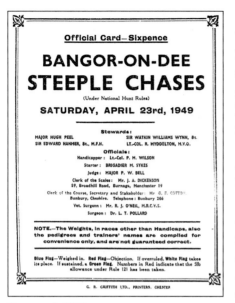

Race card, 1949.

A local horse, owned and trained by the late Lieutenant-Colonel Fenwick Palmer of Cefn Park, was Eternal which could often be seen training on the roads in the Cefn Park area in the 1960s. It won fourteen races in twelve seasons, including the Emblem Chase in Manchester in 1960, the Lancashire Chase in Manchester in 1960 and 1961 and the Grand Sefton in Liverpool in 1962. But perhaps the horse most associated with this area was Poethlyn (1910–40), owned by Hugh Peel of Bryn-y-Pys. It had been born on the estate but thinking that it lacked potential as a racehorse, was sold at an auction in Wrexham for £8. The buyer used it to draw a milk float in the Wrexham area where it was spotted by a local trainer who persuaded Hugh Peel to buy it back. After placing it with a new trainer it won several races and was entered in the 1918 Grand National which had been relocated to Gatwick because of the cancellation of the Aintree meeting owing to the First World War. Here it was ridden by Ernest Piggott and won by four lengths. It went on to win the 1919 Grand National at Aintree, by eight lengths and looked set to repeat the performance the following year but was unfortunately brought down by the eventual winner at the first fence. Every betting man in the district had money riding on that race and there were a few sore heads the following day after they had drowned their sorrows in one of the local hostelries. Its most successful season was 1918–9 when it went unbeaten through ten races, including the Prince of Wales Chase at Sandown and the Lancashire Chase, twice. It was eventually retired to Bryn-y-Pys where it could be seen living happily with its great companion Truthful, a greyhound that was a winner of the Waterloo Cup. Both are buried on the estate.

Prior to the race meeting on 20 April 1923, the members of the Wynnstay Hunt entertained about 1,000 farmers and their wives to luncheon. Major Hugh Peel proposed the health of Sir Watkin and on behalf of the company thanked him for maintaining the traditions of the hunt and for providing them with a splendid pack of hounds. In 1924, racing had to be cancelled because of an outbreak of foot and mouth disease. Although the meeting was not held, some one rang the bell at the racecourse on the day originally fixed at two o'clock, the starting time of the opening steeplechase.

1929 was notable for the first time a charge of 2s (20p) was made for admission to the course. The race-goers grumbled at being asked to pay and that year there was a slight reduction in attendance. In 1934, the water jump was replaced with a plain fence and was once again moved to just in front of the paddock. In 1940, members of the armed forces were admitted free and this was the last race to be held until after the Second World War. In 1946, racing resumed with a record attendance of 11,000.

The following year, when two meetings were held in the spring, a hurdle course was built which attracted more entries and a better class of horse. In 1953, a company was formed and was

Morning exercise, with Fred Robinson of River View on the leading horse and Helaine Rees of Maes-y-Groes on the third horse, watched by trainer Doug Francis and a reporter from the Sporting Chronicle. *[Richard Francis]*

named Bangor Steeplechases Ltd. In 1954, stabling was built on land adjoining the racecourse with accommodation for horses and their attendants who had to stay overnight that can now accommodate eighty-five. Entries are now received from all over the country and from Ireland. During the late 1950s the racecourse was used as the backdrop for filming part of the popular *Adventures of Sherlock Holmes* television series starring Jeremy Brett.

Two two-day events were tried for the first time in 1962, on 6/7 April and 27/28 April. The attendance at both was sufficiently encouraging to persuade the stewards to repeat the experiment in 1963 which, despite the closure of the railway, showed no evidence of dwindling crowds. On 3 April 1965 a record attendance of 15,502 passed through the gates. A two-day event took place on the 23/24 April. Four of the events on the second day were televised for the first time and people had been forecasting a smaller attendance in consequence. However, this forecast proved to be unfounded. On 15 March 1968, the meeting was transferred to Haydock Park, because of foot and mouth in the district. The ban had been lifted on the movement of livestock in infected areas but not in time to save the meeting at Bangor.

In 1970, the Autumn meeting had to be cancelled partly due to cattle grazing the track and the Jockey Club having declared that the course was unfit for racing unless the course was fully enclosed by railings. The following year, Bangor Steeplechases Ltd negotiated a long lease on the land with the owners, the Peel Settled Estates, which ensured that the course would only be used for racing in the future. In 1972, the racecourse was closed for almost twelve months whilst the required improvements were made including draining, levelling and enclosing the track. In 1999, another problem arose when a local farmer grew a crop of maize in the centre of the course that became so tall that it obscured the far side of the track from the spectators' view.

In the early days, Major Francis Owen of Althrey was clerk of the course, followed by Frank E. Cotton in 1883. Cotton rode many winners at Bangor and took part in the Grand National of 1886.

He was appointed manager of the course until 1921 when his son, Major Gilbert E. Cotton, took over. Gilbert Cotton won the National Hunt Chase at Cheltenham, on Rejected in 1912 and also rode in the Grand National the following year on the same horse but unfortunately fell. He brought home a number of winners at Bangor. Nearly fifty years later he saw his grandson Sir William Piggott-Brown win the National Hunt Chase at Cheltenham on Superfine. He remained in charge of the course until 1970 when he retired after nearly fifty years as inspector of National Hunt courses. He was unfortunately killed in a car crash the following year near his home at Priestland, Tarporley. He was ninety-one and his funeral took place in Bunbury church. He is commemorated by the Gilbert Cotton Memorial Hunter's Steeplechase.

Bangor Races became Bangor Steeplechases then, in 1953, Bangor Steeplechases Ltd was registered as a company limited by guarantee without share capital. The original number of members was seven, each being liable for £1 in the event of winding up. The management was vested in a committee, the first members of which were: Major Gilbert F.R. Cotton of Priestland, Bunbury, director of Manchester Racecourse Co. Ltd.; Lieutenant-Colonel Godfrey E. Fitzhugh, Plâs Power, Wrexham, director of Alliance Assurance Co., Wrexham Local Board; the Rt Hon. Lord Kenyon, director of Watkin's Nurseries Ltd.; Sir Griffth W.E. Hanmer, Bart., M.F.H, (chairman); Lieutenant-Colonel Ririd Myddelton, M.V.O.; Colonel Roderick G. Fenwick Palmer; Lieutenant-Colonel Sir Owen Wynn, Bart, G.F.H.; director Alliance Assurance Co., Wrexham Local Board. Secretary: Major Gilbert F.E. Cotton. Solicitors: Walker Smith & Way, Chester. Registered Office: Priestland, Bunbury, Tarporley.

In 1988, when the first brick building was being planned, the board, headed by the chairman Major Malise Nicolson, decided to finance the project by issuing 120 £500 shares and people such as Lord Hanmer, Sir John Barlow, Bobbie McAlpine and Peter Rosselli were invited to purchase.

Mention has been made of the idyllic setting of the racecourse on the banks of the river Dee but not to its downside – the problem of flooding. In 2000, several months of continual rain caused the cancellation of six meetings when the Dee flooded the course taking away a complete steeplechase fence and several sets of plastic wings. This, combined with a foot and mouth outbreak, brought about financial difficulties. In 2002, the Chester Race Company bought the shareholding in the race company paying £21,664 per share – an excellent return for those people with foresight. The racecourse is now jointly owned by Chester Racecourse and is part of the same company, each one complementing the other with flat racing at Chester and 'over the sticks' at Bangor.

Major Malise Nicholson (chairman) and Peter Occleston (secretary) ran the steeplechases for a few years until Major Michael Webster was appointed manager in 1996. The present manager, Jeanie Chantler, was employed as a stable girl in the 1970s by Tony Brassey of Nomansheath who had a permit to train his own horses and she used to bring them to the racecourse. In 1977, she was offered work at the course on race-days. This became two days a week, later increased to three days, until she was employed full time. She took over from Major Webster as general manager in 2004.

In 1993, the racing world mourned the death of Colonel Seymour Valentine Misa. He was the son of Major and Mrs V.P. Misa of Heron's Court, Epsom and had married Elizabeth Joan Stevenson, daughter of Mr and Mrs H. Geoffrey Stevenson of Worthenbury Manor in 1934 whilst stationed with the 22nd Cheshire Regiment at Chester Castle. In 1936, they came to live at Althrey

Woodhouse. Living next to the racecourse he was closely associated with its activities, acting as stable manager for fifty years and also steward of the meeting. Horses gave him continued enjoyment and he was a founder member of the British Horse Society and a life member of the British Show Jumping Association. Always active in local affairs he was chairman of the Bangor Village Institute and served on both the Flintshire and Clwyd County Councils.

Because of the high water table of the Dee, racing after heavy rain can be difficult as the racecourse is often waterlogged, especially during the winter months, and very occasionally racing has to be cancelled. Usually the ground staff manage, by some adjustment of the fences, to achieve the near impossible. As soon as race day is over, the staff walk the

Frank Lloyd being presented with the Gilbert Cotton Hunter Chase Trophy on 12 February 1993, by the wife of Major Nicolson.

course checking for any damage to the surface. No two meetings are run on exactly the same track and after every meeting the white rails are moved to a slightly different place to spread the wear and damage to the surface and to give it a chance to recover. The staff spike the ground to aid drainage and also fertilise and spread a seed, sand and soil mix onto worn areas. As well as regular mowing, they also water the course in times of drought and are licensed to draw water from the Dee.

When Sir Watkin Williams Wynn was in charge of the course, Richard Bostock was head groundsman and he was responsible for getting the course ready until 1919 when, after fifty years, his son, Fred, took over. Tom Osbourne was head groundsman from 1932 until he retired after

forty years then Len Maylam took over. After twenty-seven years, he was followed by his son, John. Andrew Maylam is now the head groundsman and he is assisted by his brother, Brian. The last building to be erected was the bungalow for the head groundsman so there is now permanent staff on site.

In 2006, a point-to-point track with eight fences was developed on the inside of the traditional National Hunt circuit. It covers just under 1½ miles – slightly shorter than the main track, which has nine jumps. All point-to-point races are run over three miles and the horses are trained and ridden by amateurs. Since March 2006, point-to-point racing, for many years held at Eaton Hall, is now held at Bangor and attendance

Jeanie Chantler, the present general manager of the racecourse.

averages 4,000 with a high of 7,000 in the summer. The entries for the races come in five days prior to the day but are not finalised until twenty-four hours beforehand so race cards are now printed overnight by Weatherby's, British Horse Racing's central administration, and arrive at the course on the day of the meeting.

In 2009, when the 150th anniversary of the first race was held, the day chosen was 25 February, which was the actual date of the first race in 1859. Many improvements have been made to the course in the last twenty years with the timber buildings of previous years being replaced by modern brick-built structures. There is a new paddock restaurant, new parade ring, new hospitality suite and a veterinary building. They now have two restaurants and, with the addition of marquees, can cater for up to 1,000 people. All these facilities are now available for private hire for functions such as weddings, conferences and celebrations of all kinds. Bangor-on-Dee races have certainly come a long way between 1859, when only one race day was held, to 2012 when sixteen steeplechases and two point-to-point meetings took place during the year.

A poem in praise of Bangor Racecourse was sent to Jeanie Chantler in 2006:

Bangor on Dee Races, 2006

I really had to write to say,
I'm just so glad you came my way.
Your Facilities are best by far,
In fact I rate them all five star.
Bangor races are really great,
So tell your family and your mate.
In Summer, Autumn, Winter, Spring,
Bangor on Dee Races are just the thing.

At Bangor Races you get so much more,
Quality, value and that's for sure.
You will pay your cash and still be jolly,
When their bargain prices save you lolly.
The racecourse is clean, the staff real smart;
Warm and friendly from the start.
They are also courteous and kind,
Ask any question they won't mind.

So come along and have a ball,
Bangor Races are here for all,
Bet with the bookies, on the Tote too,
Bangor Races are the place for you.
Bangor on Dee Races makes your life complete,
The opposition just can't compete.
I send my best to Management and Staff
And hope this rhyme gives them a laugh.

These words are true I do not jest –
Bangor on Dee Races are just the best.

Derek Robinson, Stockton-on-Tees

In praise of Bangor Steeplechase, 1887

I hate your flat-racing, give me steeple-chasing,
and Bangor the scene of my lay,
Where the meadows so sound are the very best ground
For the sport we're enjoying today.
The crowds that are seen are far greater I ween,
Than ever were seen here before,
And the card it is longer, the entries are stronger;
The starters are better and more;
The sweepstakes attractive, the managers active,
The bright charming morns are the cause.
We'll enjoy the great treat, our luncheon we'll eat,
It tastes best of all out of doors.

They have come from Welsh Wales, with mountains and vales,
They have come from the country around.
In thousands 'The masses' enjoy with 'the classes'
The fun that is here to be found.
There is one from North Wales my muse always assails,
He is not here, thank goodness its so;
If a patriot you be, read Jennings, M.P,
And quote him where ever you go.
Wynnstay has a party, its popular Bart. he
is known as a patron of sport,
and Combermere's Lord, by Cheshire adored,
His experience as steward has brought.

There is Sal, from the mere he, looks happy and cheery
and the Squire from Bryn-y-pys Hall,
and Archie from Gerwyn, and Best from Berwyn,
with welshers I cannot recall.
Next the Kaffir I see, and Whitmore from King's Lee,
Owen John from the famed Bara Chaws;
There's Bobby from Cefn, to whom Bangor's a Heaven,
He can ride and sit still as a mouse.
Tho' Althrey is left of its tenant bereft,
The old bird and the cygnets are here,
He has found a new nest, with a mate of the best,
and has come to enjoy the good cheer.

From Mossfields comes Jack, when hounds run you may back
him to follow as straight as a whip.
Though a carriage he's brought full a Darby looks thoughtful,
lest his pedigree chicks have the pip.

From Cholmondeley comes Rock, wth of course Arthur Brock,
and his dug-up old fossils equine;
Though good is his jockey, and talented Rock,
of winners has not found a mine.
From the cottage of oak, with four quads in the yoke,
River's Bulkeley arrives on the scene;
Though his team is but scratch, it would hard to match,
the dash they display o'er the green.

From Cheshire comes Corbet, you search through the orbit,
a vulpecide greater to find;
Young Reg with his Dad, looking cheery and glad
to use language lad's not inclined.
Where's Shropshire's keen master? T'would be a disaster
if hunting were stopped as some say;
Ah! perish the thought . Here's success to the sport
Our best thanks to Lonsdale we'll pay.
From Wem comes bold Harry, I wish I could tarry
to tell of his riding of yore,
when he won o'er the course, on his very best horse,
two or three times, if not more.

And Puffles and Dandy, good naturally bandy
their jokes from the backs of their hacks,
and an M.P. or two, with sensation quite new,
from the meeting of holiday smacks.
From Marbury's Poole, who since he left school
has thickened and grown you may bet,
From Cherry Hill's Sandy, who thinks he'll be handy
with the daughter of old Etiquette.
But my muse travels fast the pace cannot last
so I can't tell you everyone here.
Enniskillen (late Cole) I'd forget on my soul
Where ever there's sport he'll be near.

But 'Borderer' keen, with Price ever Green,
Audits the accounts of the fray.
Which way the wind blew, Arundel will tell you
in the 'field' of next Saturday.
Now the Wynnstay Light Horse are clearing the course,
and the farmers are saddling their cracks,
and Holland is there with his though-bred mare,
that they back as if others were hacks.
A second over, and backers in clover,
for success still the favourite attends,

Old pals we meet, and we cordially greet
our neighbours, relations and friends.

Its luncheon time now, so away from the row,
and hubbub in Paddock and Ring.
For I hear the corks pop, and I must have a drop,
Before further glories I sing.
Oh! what fun there is there! see the elderly mere
Through her specs watching Caroline Finnick,
for the young ones will play, youth will have its day,
Its natural – where's the harm in it?
So just one more glass to the health of the lass,
each drinks to the flame he admires.
[line missing]
The bookies of odds are the criers.

The fun's fast and furious, the fair sex are curious
to know how to win the kid gloves.
The open Race-runners are voted A-oners,
the ladies have dubbed them all 'loves'.
The Clerk of the Course runs a very fine horse
his jockeys not Chalk, but of Cotton,
But he never one minute appears to be in it,
and his form must never be forgotten!
But for the fun! we must see what's to run
for the Sweepstakes a new race this year.
See! Sir Watkin is riding, a good horse bestriding,
If he cannot win he'll be near.

And horses galore in the Paddock they pour
on Greddington's jockey – like Lord.
There are five or six more, on the favourite's young Gore
may his confidence meet its reward!
What sport is this race! and a rattling good pace
the first round has settled the black.
Sir Watkin is riding, and Grosvenor biding
his time with Seymour on the crack –
The colours flash by, and I'm sorry that I
cannot tell what's first past he post,
for I'm lunching again, and in sparkling Champagne
the health of the rider I'll toast!

Here's good luck to Chasing, it's better than Racing
and sportsmen like 'Mr E. Jay',
Who run on the square and never despair,

if they own a sound nag that can stay.
So Bangor Iscoed, where the silver Dee's flowed,
for centuries past to the sea,
of sport meritorious and rivalry glorious
may your meadows the scene ever be.

R.K.M.B.

17. Wartime

We know that Wales was active in the Wars of the Roses that were fought between the rival houses of York and Lancaster, because of the Welsh ancestry of Henry Tudor, the Lancastrian claimant to the throne. Henry defeated Richard III at the battle of Bosworth Field in 1485 and ascended the throne as King Henry VII. Interestingly, the remains of the body of Richard have just been discovered during an archaeological dig beneath a car park in Leicester in the foundations of Grey Friars, a Franciscan friary, where Richard was said to have been buried after his defeat. The results of radio carbon dating and DNA tests of a known descendant, have just confirmed that the find is the body of the king. Henry Tudor had the support of such local gentry families as the Pulestons, the Myddeltons and the Eytons. A John ap Ellis of Eyton fought at Bosworth and is known to have received land along the Welsh border for his services. No doubt at times the conflict impinged on the everyday life of Bangor, but to what extent is not really known. The first event for which we have reliable evidence of its effect on the village is the Civil War of 1642–6.

The Civil War
North Wales was regarded on the whole as Royalist territory, a rich source of recruitment for the army. Many of the local gentry were prominent supporters of the king, principal amongst whom were Sir Gerard Eyton and his son Ken(d)rick Eyton and both were captured by the Parliamentary forces at Eyton House, Eyton in February, 1644. Kenrick Eyton later became a judge and was knighted in 1675. Also on the side of the king were the Broughtons of Broughton Hall, Sir Edward Broughton of Marchwiel, Sir Thomas Hanmer of Hanmer, Major Francis Manley of Manley House, Erbistock, Edward Phillips of Worthenbury, Colonel John Robinson of Gwersyllt and Lieutenant-Colonel John Royden of Isycoed. Thomas Ravenscroft of Pickhill was also a Royalist and was in command of Hawarden Castle when it was under siege in 1643. The main Parliamentarians in the area were Colonel Thomas Myddelton of Chirk Castle and his son Thomas, Captain Andrew Ellis of Althrey Hall, Sir Roger Puleston and Judge John Puleston of Emral Hall (although Sir Roger's father and grandson were both Royalist supporters). Parliamentary

Colonel Thomas Mytton 1608–56, commander-in-chief of the Parliamentary forces in north Wales. [FHS Publication, Volume 6]

headquarters were established in Wem under Colonel Thomas Mytton and at Nantwich under Sir William Brereton.

Colonel Mytton lived at Halston near Whittington in Shropshire. He was born in 1608 and married Magdalen, daughter of Sir Robert Napier of Luton in 1620 by whom he had three daughters. Magdalen was the sister-in-law of Sir Thomas Myddelton. After the war Thomas Mytton, finding that Cromwell and his party had further designs than the defence of liberty, the cause for which he was engaged, resigned his commission and retired. He died in London in 1656 and was interred in St Chad's Church, Shrewsbury.

Found among the papers of Revd Sir T.H. Gresley Puleston of Emral (died 1890), rector of Worthenbury, were orders from the Commissioners of Array regarding the raising and disposition of troops during the early period of the Civil War. The papers show the unsettled state and alarm that prevailed along the Welsh border. During 1643 and 1644 the constables of the hundred of Chirk were constantly receiving orders to raise men for the defence of the approaches. We read of 124 musketeers from the hundred of Bromfield being put under orders to guard the crossings of the river Dee and

> ... to raise a sum of money to pay the 300 firemen appointed to continue for a constant guard upon the several passages of Holt, Bangor and Overton which charge ought to be maintained since the safety of the whole country depends upon making good these passages.

In an appeal addressed to the Field Marshal General of all His Majesty's Forces, on behalf of the distressed districts, it is stated:

> Having seriously taken into consideration the distressed estate of these parts, having for no little space lain in the mouth of danger and too near the enemy garrison at Wem, a strong receipt of rebels, daily subject to their sallies and incursions we do humbly supplicate and certify your honour that, according to our knowledge strengthened with the judgement of most expert and able old soldiers, with whom in that behalf we have conferred, that the passage near the river of Keriog under Lower Chirk, is so convenient and necessary, and conduceth so much for the good of these poor parts of Wales, that without utter neglect and great danger of the country it cannot be any longer left without a sufficient guard of Soldiers.

The appeal seems to have produced some effect as on 22 February 1643 there came an 'order for the raising of a sum to pay the 400 foot soldiers of Colonel Hunke's regiment, in garrison at Wrexham, for the defence of the county' and on 20 March a further order containing several instructions, among them were the following:

> That twenty men armed with muskets be sent out of every hundred to Wrexham within eight days to be immediately drawn down to Bangor to garrison that place, and to be paid out of the general contribution of the county. The men not to be brought to Bangor before the horse and foot now quartered there be called away from thence; that £50 be raised for furnishing Captain Robinson company with muskets, and £20 for furnishing Captain Manley's men that are unarmed. That the Commissioners of the county meet as a committee at Wrexham upon each

Tuesday, and that five or more of them, in the absence of the rest, upon every such meeting to have power to 'agitate and conclude' the business of the whole county.

These orders are confirmed by an entry in William Maurice's diary, that on 15 February 1643 'Bangor in Flintshire began to be fortified for the King'. The orders were supplemented on 18 April 1644 by an order from Prince Rupert to Sir Evan Lloyd, sheriff of the county of Denbigh, for the impressing of another 134 men.

Later in 1643, the Parliamentary forces under Colonel Myddelton recruited men for an invasion of north Wales and for the recovery of Chirk Castle, by now in Royalist hands. The Royalists suffered casualties when they encountered the Parliamentarians at Wem and the skirmish came nearer home when Sir Edward Broughton and his two sons were taken prisoner at their home in Marchwiel. No doubt by this time most of the defenders of Bangor bridge had been sent as reinforcements to the Royalist side and the crossing of the Dee had been left with just a small number of men who were easily overcome, as we are told that in 1643 'Col Mytton came over the Bangor Bridge in the Civil War.'

In 1644, when Chester was under attack, we learn that 'The King's soldiers burnt Bangor upon Dee and other great houses that if fortified might annoy the garrisons of Salop and Chester.' The houses were burnt to prevent them being used for billeting enemy troops. Which house or houses in Bangor were set on fire is not revealed and nor has any written or oral history been passed down of a house being burnt. The two possibilities that spring to mind in the immediate vicinity of Bangor are Althrey Woodhouse and Plâs Fron. That there was an older house on the Woodhouse site is borne out by the old half-timbered barn in the grounds alongside the house, but whether the old house was burnt or simply replaced is not known. Plâs Fron at Porthwgan was demolished about forty years ago, but we know was built in 1657, not long after the end of the war, on the ridge with a commanding view over Bangor. This could have replaced an older property that had been burned. All this is pure conjecture as there is no known evidence to support the theory. When the old Bangor cross was found in 1849 a quantity of black (burned?) timber was also found near Maes-y-Groes. It may be that the burnt house was somewhere near there or at Deeside.

Farmers suffered greatly by the soldiers being garrisoned in or near Bangor. At first the army of both sides paid for any food or animals that they requisitioned. Many of the commanding officers had raised their own regiments and probably initially paid the men's wages themselves. As the conflict dragged on and the men were owed money they took to scavenging for food – a complete herd of cattle being driven off without payment was not unknown. When complaints were made to the commanding officer he would say that the owner would be compensated at the end of the war.

When no other accommodation could be found, churches

Sir Thomas Myddelton, major general of the Parliamentary forces in north Wales. [FHS Publication Volume 6]

were commandeered as lodgings for the troops and their horses. Some churches such as Holt still bear the scars from musket balls when the fighting spilled over into God's house. This was quite apart from the deliberate damage to stained-glass windows, statues and other 'items of idolatry.' Householders were expected, or even compelled, to provide lodging for the soldiers without much expectation of recompense. When Emral Hall was occupied by Royalist forces, Judge Puleston complained of the plundering that took place and the Parliamentarians were no saints either, as any Royalist house that they occupied would be stripped of items of value for the 'cause'. Even churches were not immune as we are told that the Parliamentary forces stripped Wrexham's parish church of its organ pipes to make much-needed ammunition.

Both John Jeffreys of Acton Hall, father of the infamous Judge Jeffreys, and Colonel John Robinson of Gwersyllt were prominent Royalists. Robinson, who defended Holt Castle in 1643, recaptured Hawarden Castle in 1644 and was in Chester during the siege by Parliamentary forces, later joined King Charles II in exile until the restoration. These two families were to become linked by marriage and established ties with Bangor when John Jeffreys' eldest grandson, Sir Griffith Jeffreys, married John Robinson's granddaughter, Dorothy. It was this Dorothy Jeffreys who founded the Endowed School in Bangor run by the Dame Dorothy Jeffreys Trust.

Thomas Whitley of Aston Hall in Hawarden, and his eldest son by his second marriage, Colonel Roger Whitley, were also ardent Royalists and had a connection with Bangor. After the restoration of the monarchy, Roger Whitley bought the manor of Peel Hall in Aston Hayes, Cheshire and married the daughter of Andrew Ellis of Althrey Hall. On the demise of the Ellis line, his wife inherited her father's estate. Roger Whitley died in c.1696 and his daughter, Elizabeth, eventual heiress to her father's estate on the death of her brother, married the second earl of Plymouth in 1705 and brought Althrey Hall estate in Bangor and Whitley estates in Cheshire and north Wales to the marriage. This explains how the earls of Plymouth came to own properties and land in and around Bangor and why the Plymouth name occurs in deeds, subscription lists and in church affairs.

After the restoration of the monarchy, wars did not really impinge on the daily life of village people. True, villagers might know someone who was fighting in a conflict, such as the father of Edward Jones of Raggs Hill who fought with the Duke of Wellington at Waterloo, or Sir John Power, who, whilst serving with the Irish contingent of the Imperial Yeomanry in the Anglo-Boer War, was killed in the Orange River Colony in South Africa. He had lived at Abbeygate in Bangor with his mother, Lady Power. However, they would usually be regular soldiers or members of the gentry for whom the army or navy was a career. Of course, the villagers were aware that a war was going on and of battles that were won, such as Trafalgar, because the victory would be announced from the pulpit and the church bells would be rung enthusiastically in celebration. Events such as the Anglo-Boer War and the relief of Mafeking on 17 May 1900, were celebrated, as reported in the *Wrexham Advertiser*, in the village,

> ... with much merrymaking until the early hours of the morning. Everyone was beside themselves with excitement. As much ammunition as could be procured was fired away during the night's festivities. The bells rang out merry peels.

First World War

The real horror of battle was not generally felt as, since the Civil War, wars had been fought overseas by the regular army or volunteers so that when war was declared on 4 August 1914 young men enrolled enthusiastically for what was regarded as a bit of a lark and a welcome break from the daily toil of agricultural labour. They were going to show those Germans a thing or two; after all it would all be over by Christmas. As the full horror of trench warfare, with its appalling conditions of mud and disease, started to filter through, and particularly when conscription was introduced in 1916, villagers realised that this war was different. The First World War was the first conflict since the Civil War that really affected everyday lives.

Soon after war was declared, farmers felt the immediate effect as horses were requisitioned to haul gun carriages and farm-workers and skilled men, such as village blacksmiths and wheelwrights, were encouraged to join up leaving a shortage of labour for food production and the maintenance of farm implements. A major part of our food such as fruit, cereal, sugar and meat was imported but the outbreak of war and the loss of ships due to enemy submarines had a great effect on food supplies and other essentials.

Each county council was asked to set up a War Relief Committee and Flintshire appointed an executive committee in August 1914. Bangor parishioners were invited to form such a committee at the invitation of the lord lieutenant of the county, Mr G.C. Gladstone, and the clerk to the Flintshire County Council. A meeting was held on 6 August at which the following were present: the rector, Revd Paterson Morgan; Mrs Fenwick; Miss Fenwick; Mrs Paterson Morgan; Revd R.C. Williams; W.J. Mackenzie; Dr S. Edwards Jones; H. Roberts, Eyton; Miss Sutton; Miss Head; Mr Pitcairn Campbell; F.W. Cheetham, and the relieving officer for the district, Mr Kitching, in addition to the members of the parish council; J. Mort; J. Davies; T. Blake; E. Owen; J. Lloyd Jones and J.E. Foster. It was agreed to form a committee made up of everyone present. The joint secretaries were to be the rector and John Davies, the ex-headmaster. The problems of fundraising and the appointing of collectors in each township in the parish and the support for the rural district council were discussed. There was a difficulty in that the parish fell into two counties and it was agreed to split any money raised into two portions.

In June 1915, a national register was drawn up and volunteers were sought for the duties of enumerator to make a list of all single men aged between eighteen and forty-one who would be encouraged to volunteer. Leaflets were distributed calling attention to the provisions of the National Registration Act of 1915 and requesting assistant overseers to distribute them when they deliver their poor rate assessments. On 30

The famous Kitchener recruiting poster of 1914.

October 1915 Overton District Council appointed Major Godsall, G. Wardle, Captain Cotton, Mr Hockenhull of Tŷ Broughton Hall and Ambrose Sutton of Althrey to the local committee of the RDC in connection with the government's recruiting scheme. After the disastrous first battle of the Somme fought between July and November 1916, which won little territory and cost a huge number of lives, enlistment became compulsory. Married men were no longer exempt, although there were exemptions such as widowers with children, ministers, men suffering from poor health and certain occupations such as farming and mining.

One of the first circulars sent out by the lord lieutenant and the Flintshire War Relief Committee (WRFC) was a request for articles of comfort for the soldiers, especially for members of the first and second battalions of the Royal Welsh Fusiliers. The second battalion was already at the front and urgently required items such as shirts, socks, handkerchiefs, cardigan jackets, balaclavas, scarves and caps as they had not been able to recover any of their kit from which they became separated during the forced marches at the beginning of the war. Other things suggested were bootlaces, tobacco, cigarettes, tobacco, chocolate, pocket-knives, boracic ointment, antiseptic powder, newspapers, magazines and pencils. Thus began the habit of sending regular comfort parcels that were greatly appreciated by the soldiers in the trenches. Even the smallest child was encouraged to knit scarves for the troops.

A War Agricultural Committee was formed in each county to encourage farmers to produce as much food as possible and to plough up pasture for cereal production. This committee arranged for the bulk purchase of fertilisers and animal feed. They also supplied such things as seed potatoes (again bought in large quantities) and had arranged with potato merchants in Scotland for a consignment of seed potatoes specially selected by Professor White of the University College of North Wales for the ensuing season and distributed to farmers, allotment holders and anybody with land to encourage them to become more self-sufficient. Even cottagers were encouraged to grow sufficient potatoes for their own needs in their gardens. Bangor parish council decided to try the new potatoes and ordered a supply, but those who planted the new variety thought that there was very little, if any, improvement to their usual crop. British Summer Time was introduced in May 1916 to make the most of the longer hours of daylight.

An inspector visited each farm and fixed a quota for the production of corn and root crops depending on the acreage available and the suitability of the land. In general the Maelor farmers managed to reach their quotas, although like everyone else they struggled when the bad weather decimated the crops. The loss of skilled labour and horses had the effect of introducing the tractor to the farming community much earlier than would otherwise have been the case. The county bought some Titan tractors and then five Fordsons that were available for hire by the farmers, as well as other farming implements such as threshing machines and ploughs. Horses were still needed and some were obtained from such places as Harpers of Liverpool but the quality was variable and some had to be returned as they had sore shoulders and were unfit for work.

In 1917, a very thorough report was made on the cultivation of land by each farm and smallholding. It noted the total number of acres under crops such as wheat, barley, rye, potatoes, peas, beans and roots crops, and the total acreage of permanent grass or meadow that could be ploughed up for 1918. The inspector even reported on the condition and sufficiency of the farm buildings, the amount of fertilizer required, the number of working horses, sheep, pigs, milk cows, other cattle and even the amount of cheese, if any, produced in 1916.

Women were encouraged to volunteer for farm work and in January 1917 the Women's Land Army was formed, small in number, and the carefully selected recruits were given free uniforms and transport. Local women had always helped with such things as milking and general dairy work as it was one way of boosting the family income that they could fit in around their own domestic responsibilities. In 1918, it was estimated that there were 130 women employed in farm work in the county. Older schoolchildren were recruited to help out and in February 1915 Maelor children aged between thirteen and fourteen were granted exemption from attending school for the duration of the war – although the schoolmasters had always had problems with absenteeism during harvest time. Even convalescent soldiers and men on leave were encouraged to help. It was said that the Maelor district could not have brought in the harvest without the soldier labour, practically every farm had one man and some had as many as three men helping.

On 5 November 1915, Bangor Parish Council received a letter from J. Bevan Evans, honorary secretary of the Flintshire War Savings Campaign, with the news that a county committee has been appointed to organise a campaign throughout the area to advocate public, personal and household economy and to encourage small investments in the War Loan. They hoped for the parish council's active and sympathetic support. Bevan Evans was in attendance at the meeting and the council said they were in sympathy with the scheme and promised to arrange a public meeting. Even school children were encouraged to bring in their pennies and, by the end of the war, the parish of Bangor had done very well, taking into account the population, and £7,000 had been raised for the various war loans and savings schemes.

A Food Economy Campaign Committee was also started in each parish to call public attention to the need to reduce waste. A Mrs Protheroe was asked to give a talk on the use of potatoes, the headmaster spoke to the children about food economy and even church ministers were asked to give a sermon on economy at their next service. Soup kitchens were set up in towns and it was agreed to give the idea a try in Bangor. Mrs Fenwick of Plâs Fron managed to secure a good person to manage a communal kitchen which proved to be a great success, the soup being sold for just a few pennies a pint. The first soup makers were Mrs Tom Williams, Mrs Antley (Greylands) and Mrs Foster (Royal Oak).

By March 1915, gifts of things like flour, cheese and potatoes had been received from the people of Canada and America and were distributed throughout the county. The rationing of sugar was introduced in December 1917, followed by meat and fats in April 1918. Weekly rations per person were 15 oz meat, 5 oz bacon, 4 oz fats and 8 oz sugar. Rationing was continued for a short while after the cessation of hostilities in November 1918 and an important notice was issued by the Overton Local Food Control Committee requesting that all persons resident in the Rural District of Overton should fill up the reference leaves in the ration books and forward them to the local Food Office in Ellesmere to enable the new books to be given to them.

In April 1918, the Flintshire War Agricultural Committee sent out a circular requesting hospitality for members of the Australian Forces who were on leave. Thomas Bourne reported that he had interviewed several farmers in the district with reference to the entertainment of overseas troops and he had obtained the names of thirty people who were prepared to offer a billet for a period of seven to ten days.

In May 1918, when the final push began to finish the war, the Flintshire Agricultural Committee was required to find 350 men from those engaged in agriculture in the county, to be called up for military service. They wrote complaining that the quota was excessive and they pointed out that 25% of the total male agricultural population was already serving in the army and that the military admit that Flintshire had recruited better than any other county in Wales. They also stated that there were not 350 men of Grade I status, under thirty-one years of age employed in agriculture. Towards the end of the war, to relieve the labour shortage, prisoners of war from camps such as Oswestry were allocated to farms to help with the harvest at a payment of 5d a day.

After the war was over, Bangor Parish Council received a circular from H.N. Gladstone at the War Office about War Trophies. Apparently there were many items of military equipment that were either surplus to requirements or had been captured from the Germans which were being offered to the district councils to purchase and through them to the parish councils. In December 1918, the RDC agreed to apply for six trench mortars to be placed at Hanmer, Overton, Bangor, Worthenbury, Bettisfield and Iscoed and that a trophy of crossed rifles be given to each school in the district. In May 1919, the lord lieutenant of the county reported that sixteen German rifles would be distributed, but Bangor must have refused to display them as it was not included on the list. The following additional trophies were also distributed: Hanmer – one German helmet, one pair of German wire cutters, one water bottle and two German rifles. These were reported as having been received at the RDC meeting of 17 September 1919. In January 1920, the lord lieutenant wrote informing the RDC that two machine guns had been allotted to the Maelor, one for Overton and one for Hanmer. In August 1921, Mr Downward of Overton asked the RDC to remove the two machine guns that were still being stored on his property; did the RDC still want them or could they be offered to other parish councils? Overton parish council decided that they still wanted them. The country seems to have been awash with guns as a letter was also sent from the officer commanding, the Royal Welsh Fusiliers Depot in Wrexham asking whether the committee wanted any German guns. What happened to those trophies? Do the various parishes still have them rusting away in some forgotten barn or were they collected for scrap metal and used to defeat the enemy during the Second World War? There is a report in the *Wrexham Advertiser* of 7 May 1927 that the gun that was placed in the grounds of Grove Park School needed attention, as it had not been maintained over the years. After a vote the governors agreed to its disposal. As some one remarked ' there are better ways of remembering the dead.'

In 1919, as well as War Trophies, there were also army huts of various sizes that were now redundant and which the War Office advertised for sale being anxious to recoup some of the enormous expenditure of the war. These were offered as ideal for use as temporary housing for local authorities, for use on farms as hen houses, hay barns or for the storage of agricultural implements and for meeting rooms. As

Sale of war surplus items by Dodman, Wrexham.

already recorded, Bangor and some other townships in the Maelor bought one for use as a village hall. Surplus army equipment such as boots, tunics and trousers were also sold off. The tough hard-wearing material made them ideal for farm work and for many years farm workers could be identified by their army uniform.

On 12 July 1919 the 'Old Scholars' of the Bangor C of E School presented the school with a Union Jack flag in memory of all the old scholars who had laid down their lives in the war. The flag was hoisted by Sergeant Humphreys, RWF, J.T. Roberts and Harold Humphreys, demobilised soldiers, saluted.

After the war life gradually returned to a semblance of normality. The owners of large estates faced the prospect of managing their land with fewer men and increasingly elderly retainers. Many of the farm labourers had either been killed or maimed in the war and there was not enough labour to work the land. A lot of the younger men were seduced by the higher wages being paid in towns and did not want to return to their old agricultural life. Mechanisation was introduced and tractors replaced the horses that had been requisitioned for the war. Many of the estates struggled or were put up for sale as the heirs had been killed. Women in particular had become used to the higher wages and relative freedom of factory life and had no longer wished to return to the drudgery of domestic service.

Second World War

Thanks to Winston Churchill's foresight, planning for a possible outbreak of war began as early as 1936 when a conference on air raid precautions was arranged at Mold and the county council was asked to send two representatives. This time the general public was under no illusions as to the hardships that would have to be faced in the coming months. From the beginning volunteering would not be an option, military service would be compulsory.

In April 1938, William Morris, the rating and valuation officer, was appointed organiser and clerk to the Rural District Council with responsibility for the organisation of Air Raid Precautions (ARP) and the formation of a Food Control Committee. In January 1939, the Home Office requested details of all the First Aid posts and Ambulance stations being planned for the Maelor district. Bangor, Bettisfield and Iscoyd were first off the mark having already made arrangements for such posts, the rest were told to hasten their preparations.

Planning for the rationing of food was one of the first priorities as no one thought this time that the war would soon be over. The weekly ration allocated for each person, which appears meagre by today's standards, was: 12oz of minced beef, 4oz bacon, 2oz cheese, 2oz butter, 2oz lard, 8oz sugar, 4oz jam, 2 pints milk, 2oz tea or coffee, one egg and 2oz sweets. No doubt some illegal poaching of salmon must have taken place to supplement the rations.

Soon after the commencement of hostilities in September 1939, the Rural District Council were told by the Welsh Board of Health that they should make provision for a stock of building materials, to the value of £10, for repairs to buildings rendered unfit as the result of aerial bombardment or other war action. The problem of where to store the materials then arose with Overton being the first choice, but Rogers & Jackson solved this by offering to provide storage facilities in Wrexham.

Additional arrangements had to be made for the very real prospect of fire. As well as cover provided by the Wrexham, Ellesmere and Whitchurch fire services, the Overton RDC put in an application for a motor trailer pump to be stationed at Overton and a light two-man fire pump at Bangor. Bangor Parish Council also wanted a motor trailer pump as it was felt that a single two-man fire pump was not sufficient protection for the whole parish. Other parish councils were not happy with the arrangements either and Overton RDC amended their application to two motor fire-engine trailer pumps, one for Hanmer and one for Overton, and six two-man manual fire pumps to be stationed at Overton, Bangor, Bronington, Hanmer, Horseman's Green and Tallarn Green. Sometime later, an additional motor trailer pump was purchased. Stirrup pumps also were available from Overton RDC and could be purchased by individuals. The cost of a pump with nozzle and twenty-five feet of hose was £1, or a pump with nozzle only, 15s 6d. Initially only four people in Bangor made an application. A supply of sand was also made available from Overton RDC to be kept in buckets outside the back door as an additional precaution to smother any flames. It was rare that these buckets were used for their original purpose and most people used them as a receptacle for cigarette butts.

Overton RDC purchased a stock of steel sheets in various sizes to provide householders with improvised shelters for protection from splinters and bomb blasts. The steel sheets were not of the same gauge as those used in Anderson Shelters (which for some reason were not available in Flintshire). These were in addition to the Morrison shelters that saved many lives and which consisted of a steel tabletop with solid steel legs which measured 6 feet x 6 feet and were designed to be self erected and form a permanent fixture as a combined table and shelter. Not everyone constructed such shelters as many people preferred to take cover under their stairs as this was reckoned to be the strongest place in a house.

The anticipated shortage of petrol was another problem that had to be addressed. The RDC decided that an emergency store of 450 gallons, representing six weeks supply, would need to be provided for ARP and National Defence purposes; half of this was to be stored in a garage in Overton and half in a garage in Hanmer. The clerk to the council was to issue one-gallon permits per horsepower for vehicles belonging to the following people:

The Morrison shelter could be converted for use as a table by unscrewing the sides

ARP wardens.
Dr Caspar, Mr R.L. Higgins, Mr W. Morris (clerk to the RDC)
The three district nurses stationed at Hanmer, Overton and Worthenbury
Dr M°Coll, Hanmer
The two ambulances
The two first-aid squad cars
The two first-aid sitting cars

Mr T.A. Whitfield of Penley for one lorry to be used for decontamination purposes

All police officers

The garages in Hanmer and Overton were to be paid 2s 6d (12.5p) a week for the reservation of one of their pumps for emergency storage use and, in addition to defray reasonable charges for supplying petrol for defence and ARP purposes.

In 1939, E.L. Mytton of Orchard House, grandfather of Gordon and Arfon, was appointed group organiser for transport for the hundred of Maelor. All vehicles employed on ARP services had to be readily recognizable by police and wardens so that they could proceed when other traffic had been stopped and bear the initial of the council and the words: 'On ARP Service' affixed to the left hand side of the windscreen.

In 1940, the Ministry of Transport proposed that all road signs should be removed starting with trunks roads and with unclassified roads to follow in due course. This was designed to cause as much confusion as possible to the enemy in the advent of Germany successfully invading Britain. Village place names outside built-up areas were also to be removed and milestones dug up and placed the other side of the fence or hedge or in a nearby place of obscurity. Milestones of considerable historic significance were to be treated with care when being removed or, preferably, covered with a heap of manure or rubbish. This could explain why so many of the ancient milestones have vanished from our roads.

Air Raid Precautions (ARP)

In March 1938, recruiting of volunteer personnel for the various ARP sections began. The rector was asked to advertise for volunteers at the church services. The four chief air-raid wardens appointed for Bangor were A. Pitcairn Campbell, H. Bellis, E. Duggan and P. Humphreys. A handbook and explanatory letter on the training necessary for air raid wardens were received in September 1938 and each warden had to be trained in the following subjects:

Anti-gas precautions

ARP organisation and important details about locality

ARP wardens householders' register and fitting respirators to the public

The principles of the air-raid warning system, and local air-raid and gas warnings

Protection against high-explosive (HE) bombs

Methods of dealing with incendiary bombs

Auxiliary Fire Service organisation

Relations with police and public

Message writing and reporting

Equipment of warden's post

Elementary first aid

Complaints were received from the Bangor wardens that of the four people appointed from the village, two were asked to go to Overton to serve there weekly in case of an air raid. This only left one to serve the needs of the whole of Bangor parish, the fourth person being required to man the telephone. Early on the chief constable had taken over all matters concerning the organisation of

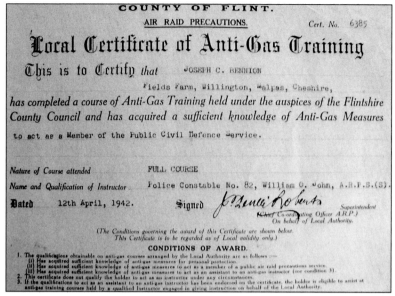

Anti-Gas Training Certificate for Joseph C. Bennion of Fields Farm, Willington (cousin of William and May Jones of Orchards Farm).
[Ruth Bennion]

the ARP and his response to the air-raid wardens complaint was:

> 16 wardens have been appointed for the Maelor district and the manning of Overton Report Centre. Can you not ask some of the parishioners to act as Civil Defence? Volunteers could qualify as wardens as there was a scarcity of wardens.

It was felt this was not a satisfactory reply. None of the wardens had volunteered to serve at the report centre in Overton. They had been told to report there under threat of suspension from the commencement. No scarcity of wardens existed except on nights when they were at the report centre. The clerk to the parish council was asked to write to the chief constable pointing out the

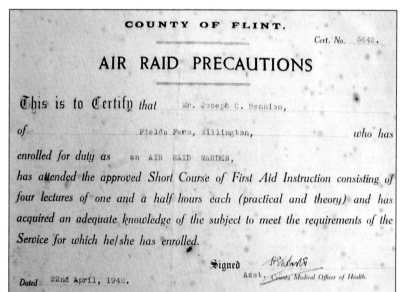

Air Raid Precautions Certificate for Joseph C. Bennion. [Ruth Bennion]

facts and pressing for the return to former arrangements as the council did not think they could ask for further volunteers as it had already furnished the original four required which the chief warden at Overton thought was too many.

A directive was issued that all warden posts should be fitted with blast- and splinter-proof protection and, if newly built, should be of concrete or steel sheeting, and provide accommodation for at least six wardens. In August 1939, the weekly rates of pay for volunteers was announced: £3 per man; £2 for women; youths aged 16–17; youths aged 17–18, £1 5s 0d. People under the age of sixteen were not considered suitable. These rates of pay were increased two years later. Higher rates were given for foremen and skilled members of rescue parties. Each warden had to be provided with a whistle and each post supplied with handbells and first aid boxes, unless there was a first aid post nearby.

In December the state of the ARP posts was causing numerous complaints:

Concrete floors were very cold and either lino or felt was requested.

An electric radiator was needed and, if no fireplace, a kettle.

A water supply (with a wash basin) and a lavatory were needed.

Two bunks were required with as many as six blankets and shelves fitted.

Blackout curtain for the windows should be fitted.

Each post required a cleaner (at 2s per week) and a tradesman's account should be set up for food and coal.

Two years after the outbreak of war these defects had been remedied in most places.

Each station had to keep a register in which all the messages received were to be logged. There is only one surviving register for the Overton station, dating from 24 September 1940 and ending 6/7th May 1942. In it are recorded all the messages received from Ruabon police station which then had to be passed on to the police stations at Bangor, Hanmer, Bronington, the Ordnance Depot at Overton and the Royal Corps of Signals at Overton. The signals were colour coded: yellow – air raid warning; purple – lights warning; red – action warning; white – cancel action. The height of activity was probably recorded during the night of 6/7 November 1940 when ten air raid messages were received. On the night of 21/22 October 1941, telephone reports were received of four HE bombs being dropped in Willington parish, all of which exploded on impact.

Bomb 1 at 21.45 hours Tuesday 21/22 October 1941.

Crater size: 6ft x 4ft.

Soil: Grassland, clay subsoil.

Size of bomb: 50 kg.

Place: 40yd from Plassey Lane, Willington, in field of Mr Butler, The Bungalow.

Casualties: Nil.

Bombs 2, 3 and 4 were all logged at the same time – 21.45 hours – at Whalebone Farm on the north side of Whalebone Lane; at Fields Farm, Plassey Lane, Willington and the last one 300 yards on north side of The Fields, Willington. No casualties were reported. All these places were about ¾ mile ESE of Bangor Police Station. The bombs fell in practically a straight line from south to north.

The following night, seven air raid messages were received and a report that an HE bomb had dropped at Bradenheath in Bettisfield parish. No casualties were reported but there was damage to roofs and high-tension cables in the district. Two HE bombs also exploded in the same parish, breaking house windows and causing damage to an electricity pole. No air raid messages were received during this period. On Friday night, 24/25 October, two bombs were reported dropped in Bettisfield parish. These turned out to be parachute mines, one at Little Hall Farm which caused damage to chimneys, and the other one 500 yards WNW of Bettisfield Park, breaking glass in the library and drawing room windows. Bangor got off very lightly in comparison.

Nothing is recorded in the book after 6/7 May 1942, and other books have not survived. The centre was supposed to be manned every night by two men, but after 1941 things quietened down and on many occasions the duty men failed to turn up. On the nights when they did, there was often nothing to report. The men manning the centre from Bangor included: Edward Duggan, Whitchurch Road; L.M. Reeves, Orchard View; William Jones, School House; Denis Prandle, Kiln Cottage; W.H. Maws, River View and Lewis Mytton, Overton Road.

In the autumn of 1939, all parents of children attending the village schools received a note from the headmaster outlining a scheme, approved by the education authority, that was to be adopted in the event of an air raid during school hours. The plan was for the pupils living in the village to run home as soon as the warning of an air raid was given. Those living some distance from the school would be allocated a home to go to that was willing to give them shelter. A list of these places was to be hung up in each classroom. By this means, every village child could leave their gas masks at home and only those children from a distance would need to bring their masks to school. Rehearsals would take place from time to time so that all pupils would be under cover within seven minutes and be aware of his or her place of shelter.

Friday afternoons at the school were spent practising putting out imaginary fires with a stirrup pump. Mike Stratton recalls that his family used to keep pigs on the land at the back of Plassey House and one day the door of the schoolroom burst open and one of their sows rushed in and lay down beside his desk – just like Mary and her little lamb. The children were delighted as anything that interrupted lessons was always very welcome. However, Mike was roundly told off for it.

There was a manned searchlight battery on Cloy Farm land and about every two days the men went to Plassey House with a wagon to draw water from their well to cool down the generator. A detachment of Royal Signals was stationed in nissan huts at Abbeygate and used the stables as their canteen, and the Royal Artillery had light anti-aircraft guns on the racecourse. The army requisitioned Emral House for the duration of the war, which, no doubt, contributed to the building's dilapidation, and American soldiers had a camp in Bryn-y-Pys and in Penley. When there was a dance or other entertainment in the Bangor Assembly Rooms (the old First World War hut at the rear of Twiss's shop) there was always a contingent of solders from one or other of the camps in the area to provide plenty of partners for the local girls.

One afternoon the Royal Engineers swept into Bangor on a training exercise and began erecting poles, wires and signals and building a bridge over the river opposite the rectory, roughly where the boathouses used to be. The bridge was of the pontoon type and another bridge was constructed over the river near Turn o'Dee to take more heavy vehicles such as tanks. Unlike the first bridge, the second had no sides. The soldiers worked though out the night and by morning the bridges were in place and the soldiers were demonstrating their skill by driving lorries across the river. They then promptly dismantled the structures and drove away again.

Evacuation

Under the government's evacuation scheme, planning for the evacuation of women and children in the event of the bombing of cities such as Liverpool was a major priority. A list of emergency centres was drawn up and officers appointed for each parish in the Maelor district, A.D. Pitcairn Campbell of Deeside being appointed for the parish of Bangor. In Overton, the village institute was the main centre used, being estimated to hold 200 people sitting or 100 people sleeping, with the Methodist chapel schoolroom taking a further 50 people sitting and 20 sleeping. These centres were also used to store the cases of emergency rations for distribution to the evacuees. Some idea of the scale of planning that was required can be gained by the initial stockpile of food cases in the centres, based upon a potential maximum of 800 evacuees: 1,008 tins of meat; 816 tins of condensed milk, 816 tins of evaporated milk, 800lbs of biscuits, 216lbs of chocolate and 800 carrier bags.

Notification of such a scheme was received with details of the initial numbers to be billeted in each parish. In the first phase Bangor parish was allocated 150 evacuees, mainly children. Each parish was to prepare a list of people who were willing to provide accommodation and a reception committee of ten or twelve people was to meet the evacuees at Overton station and conduct them to their billets. This welcoming committee also comprised six members of the Women's Committee, the Air Raid Wardens, the person making out the billeting books and representatives from the Women's Institute. Each child was to be given a carrier bag containing a 12 oz can of meat, a 14 oz tin of milk (sweetened), a 16oz tin milk (unsweetened), two packets or one pound (approx) of biscuits and ¼ lb chocolate. An adult received the same, with the addition of an extra can of meat. This was regarded as sufficient for a maintenance period of forty-eight hours to enable the receiving family to obtain additional supplies. With the bag, the Food (Defence Plans) Department included a copy of the Emergency Rations Instructions:

> The food in this bag is provided free of cost. It is an emergency ration for your consumption during the next 48 hours. After that interval, the retail food shops will, it is anticipated, have received sufficient supplies to meet the requirements of the additional population in the area where you are to be billeted. You are asked to make as few purchases as possible during the first 48 hours.

In the first panic after war was announced, even before the bombing began, the first group of evacuees, mainly children, arrived. There were not as many as originally expected and they were allocated to their hosts for the duration. It was a steep learning curve for everyone as people were horrified at the verminous state of many of the evacuees and had to clean up the children as soon as they arrived before they could be introduced into the local community. The drift back to Liverpool began almost immediately as the expected bombing did not materialise and mothers in particular realised that they were billeted in a place where there was no Woolworth, and no Marks & Spencer! That first, short-lived evacuation did help to serve the residents of the Maelor district as a practice run for the future and helped to crystallise what preparations needed to be made. For example, it was soon realized that when dealing with frightened young children in strange surroundings, most without their mothers, that bed-wetting was a distinct possibility and extra bedding was a priority. Many cottages simply did not have enough spare bedding and a plea was put out around the Maelor for 100 spare blankets to be sent to Overton police station.

In 1939, the rector of Overton wrote in the *Church Magazine*:

> Before the children arrived many were busy preparing to receive them into their homes, feeling sorry for them and hoping to make them happy. But when the mothers and children arrived all were shocked at the condition of many of them, and naturally wondered how they could be asked to take them into their homes. It was therefore a great relief when the majority of them asked to be allowed to be return to their own homes. How is it possible that they could prefer the slums of Liverpool to the lovely country? … It opens our eyes to the great work yet to be done in our great cities to improve the conditions under which so many are living.

In March 1940, the parish councils were notified that plans were being considered for the evacuation of 600 children from Wallasey to the Maelor district and they were asked to submit their arrangements and what accommodation could be offered. Each parish was to receive a quota – Bangor's was to be seventy. The Evacuation Committee was told that the accommodation originally offered by Bangor was no longer available, having been taken up by workers at the Royal Ordnance Factory in Marchwiel and still further accommodation was needed for that purpose. The Ministry was requested to cancel the allocation for the Maelor district and it was scaled down to 300. How many evacuees were eventually accommodated in Bangor is unknown. In October, Overton RDC was informed that 400 children under plan VIb were scheduled to arrive who were in addition to the 300 children under plan VIa. The parish council passed a resolution they could not accept responsibility for the further 400 children because there was no more suitable accommodation, the water supply and sanitation was generally not capable of sustaining such an increase without serious danger to health and lodgers working at the Royal Ordnance Factory and some 700 soldiers stationed nearby, were already taxing the capabilities of the district.

Mr and Mrs Stratton of Plassey House, Whitchurch Road had at least two lots of evacuees staying with them and their two sons, Michael and Jeremy: a married couple with their son who stayed about a year, and later, in about 1940/1, Thomas Keddie and his wife Eva from Liverpool and their three girls – Vera, thought to be in her late teens, Jean aged about twelve and Rhona aged about seven. They stayed for the duration of the war. Vera was a good tennis player and, partnered by Jack Richards, won the tennis tournament three years in succession at the annual church fete.

Mr and Mrs Perry at Cloy Farm (now Cloy House) also had evacuees billeted with them. The first ones came from Liverpool and had no idea of personal hygiene and the Perrys were glad when they left. They then refused to have any more but relented when they were told of a family by the name of Sharp from London who had been billeted in different houses in Dudleston and were not allowed to meet. They accommodated the wife and children for the remainder of the war while the husband lodged in Ellesmere where he had a job. The families have kept in touch ever since.

Mr and Mrs Platt at Hollybush Farm also had evacuees staying with them with whom they too remained in contact afterwards. There was thought to be another girl aged about eleven who was evacuated to Bangor and stayed at Deeside Cottage in Overton Road, but her name cannot be recalled.

The Home Guard

The Home Guard, or the local Defence Volunteers as they were originally called, used to meet at the beginning of the war in the old Endowed School room until they were given the use of the Institute. They met every week, when a rota for duty was organised with regular patrols around the village at night. Duty hours were: 8 p.m.–10 p.m., 10 p.m.–2 a.m., 2 a.m.–4 a.m., and 4 a.m.–6 a.m., with two men to a patrol, ten men slept in the hut and everyone had night duty once a week. When not on patrol or sleeping the men occupied themselves with darts, draughts and billiards in the Institute.

The Home Guard used to meet on Sundays and on Monday evenings for two hours when there would be instruction in signalling with flags by two men from Worthenbury or in the use of weapons by Army personnel or drill practice. The men were sent to such places as Acrefair for instruction in new weapons or bombs. They also travelled to Llangollen and Ellesmere for exercises with other Home Guard units. Billy Morris of Halghton Mill was the commanding officer; Pitcairn Campbell of Deeside was a captain; Edgar Lea, licensee of the Buck Hotel; was a lieutenant as was William Jones of the Orchards (Horns) Farm. Tom Osborne of Bryn Hovah was in charge of Nᵒ· 2 platoon. George William Jack Stratton of Plassey House, who worked at the Royal Ordnance Factory in Marchwiel, was also a member.

One typical exercise to test their observation skills was for a party to go to Howes Wood (which no longer exists) to hide and carry out different activities around the wood to simulate the enemy. When a patrol, usually of about eight men, arrived later the first party would then make sounds like barbed being rolled out (chicken wire drawn through a hole in a tin can) or men talking. The second party then had to report back with their interpretation of what they thought the enemy had been doing to the officer in charge. The object of the exercise was to see if the men could correctly report and interpret enemy activity.

The Home Guard used to go on manoeuvres with the army and on one occasion the army was to attack Overton and Bangor bridges, which were to be defended by the Home Guard. The local contingent was given the task of defending Bangor bridge and they heard gunfire (dummy ammunition) in the distance from the battle at Overton bridge and the news filtered through that the army had won the skirmish. They were determined that Bangor bridge was not going to fall into 'enemy' hands and, by the evening the enemy had still not been sighted and news arrived that the army was spending the night at Porthwgan in a hay bay. Someone had the bright idea of sneaking up to their camp and throwing a dummy bomb into the hay bay. Everyone was declared killed and so ended the battle of Bangor bridge!

William Jones, a lieutenant in the Home Guard.

Lt Tom Osborne who commanded
Nᵒ. 2 Platoon of the Home Guard.

On another occasion, the Home Guard and an army platoon planned an exercise and met in the Buck Inn yard. The army, playing the enemy, hid themselves in the area around Bangor and the Home Guard had the difficult task of finding them. The army were quite confident that the amateur Home Guard would not succeed but they had reckoned without the local lads' knowledge of every inch of the surrounding fields and meadows. The enemy was soon winkled out of its hiding places much to their annoyance and discomfiture. There used to be a dugout near the Wrexham side of the bridge that was manned by the Home Guard. They took great pleasure in stopping and searching all vehicles going over the river, much to the annoyance of certain well-known local 'bigwigs'.

A gang of schoolboys had built some huts in a group of trees and someone discovered them and informed the CO saying that he thought that they were being used to signal to enemy aircraft. The boys owned up to erecting the huts but Captain Pitcairn Campbell said it was not possible that school children could have built the huts as they were too well constructed. On one occasion when the Home Guard was on patrol at 3 a.m. they were notified that a parachute had been seen landing at Worthenbury and were sent to investigate. It turned out to be a parachute flare and, as they were returning they heard shouting coming from Bangor bridge and on investigation they found that 'Khaki' Campbell as he was called – an old 1914–18 soldier – had stopped and, with fixed bayonet, boarded a bus containing workers for the Royal Ordnance Factory and was demanding to see their identity cards. They were not best pleased.

When the Home Guard was on manoeuvres, Mr Griffiths of Turn O'Dee would turn out with his big, square, old Ford car that had been converted for use as an ambulance. It was normally used to transport sheep and had only the one seat for the driver. When it was used for the Home Guard, he used to hang pillows on the side, each one painted with a red cross. All very Dad's Army!

Another time some boys found parachutes in a field and the Home Guard were sent to investigate to see if there were any signs of airmen or bodies. No men or spies were found and it is thought that it was at a time when there was a threat of invasion and the enemy was dropping landmines by parachute. At least one was thought to have landed in the river and another was supposed to have killed some cattle between Worthenbury and Hollybush. However, Noel Taylor does not remember any landmines coming down so near to Bangor but does remember hearing the one that exploded at Bettisfield as he was on his way to choir practice at Althrey Lodge.

Clement Robinson was aged about fourteen and was six feet tall when he joined the Home Guard along with his palls. When he had his first pair of glasses, he became the village crack-shot and won several competitions. They use to practise on a thirty-foot range at Deeside, the home of Captain Pitcairn Campbell, using rifles with 22mm ammunition. They also had competitions at Llangollen against local teams such as Monsanto, Penley and Overton. Mike Stratton remembers that his father had a 22mm rifle and as children they used to practise in an old barn at Plassey

Officers of the 7th Denbighshire/Flintshire Battalion, Home Guard at Bettisfield Park, April 1944 just before disbanding. William Jones, top row second from left; Tom Osborne, third row, second from left.
[Sheila Graver]

House, firing at a tin can on a piece of string. He also remembers hearing about a coal merchant who was on patrol with his own gun strapped to the cross bar of his bike. When he reached the left hand bend before Bryn Hovah hill near the racecourse, he saw the enemy appear over the hedge. He promptly opened fire with both barrels and killed a donkey!

In 1944, the Home Guard was stood down and a final parade was held at Overton when 450 officers and men gave their final salute to their commanding officer Lieutenant-Colonel Sir Edward Hanmer. Mr Parry donated some geese to thank the Bangor contingent of the Home Guard for their efforts and Tom Downs of the Royal Oak cooked them for a meal which was held at the Institute. A Mr Whitchurch entertained them to an evening of jokes, singing and music.

Plane crashes
There were several planes crashes in or near Bangor, the first one involved two Spitfires which collided in mid air on a Saturday afternoon. Fred Beckett remembers being in his bedroom and hearing a loud bang that he thought was a road accident. Going to the window he heard an aircraft engine and then saw an aeroplane in a steep dive towards the ground. He noticed something flapping behind the plane that looked to be attached by a piece of string. He later learned that this was the pilot's parachute that had become entangled with the plane when the pilot baled out. The plane crashed into the rock near the sewerage works at the Graig. Ernie Young, aged about nine at the time, rushed up to Tŷ Graig and found the body of the airman and, as it was the first dead person that he had seen, it made a lasting impression. His nationality appears to be a bit of a mystery as Ernie thought that he was a New Zealander as he had the initials NZ on his jacket, whereas others said that he was an Australian. Fred was told that he was a French Canadian. The next day Fred was talking to Roy Arrowsmith and was told that the pilot's body had been found

near his house, Tŷ Graig, in Station Road. The second plane came down in Done's Wood, not far from Raggs Hill, and the pilot parachuted safely to earth.

Ron While, Roy's cousin, remembers being told about the collision:

> Roy was helping my Uncle Hughie with some gardening work and was unaware of the accident until he suddenly heard a noise around him. He had just passed through a gate with a wheelbarrow & left it open. Suddenly a wing from the spitfire crashed onto the gate & something fell out to pass in front of house, never found what it was. There was a whooshing sound & falling branches in the field at the rear & Uncle Hugh told Roy to keep away, it may be a fuel tank. Roy went to find the pilot, a Canadian officer, to ask if he was OK but the body was buried in the earth. The remainder of the plane was in the rock by the railway line & only the tail could be seen from the house.

Another crash, said to be that of a Thunderbolt, flown by an American, crashed near Gerwyn Farm killing the pilot. The next day Fred and a small gang of lads went to the site to look at the plane but were disappointed to find it had already been removed. All that was remained were some small pieces of wreckage and some belts of machine-gun bullets. The lads collected some of the bullets and took them home. Fred tried to hammer some of them to extract the bullets from their casings so that he could display the casings. He went to bed as usual that night but was wakened by his father at about one o'clock in the morning with the news that a policeman was at the door asking if Fred had taken any of the bullets. He gave the policeman the bullets, having first hidden a couple for souvenirs. The next day he went to the village to meet his friends who told him that one of them, David Davies, had been taken to hospital as one of the bullets had exploded in his hand. They had been told that the bullets were in fact cannon shells. Needless to say Fred could not return home quick enough to throw the ones he had kept into a pit in the field.

Ernie Young remembered another plane, also thought to be a Spitfire, that came down on Green Lane on a Sunday and the local boys raced each other to get to the site only to be shooed away by the pilot as the ammunition was exploding in all directions. Noel Taylor, who was on his way to church to sing in the choir, confirmed this as he heard the plane come down. Ernie also thought that another plane had crashed near Halghton Mill.

Another crash was more of a forced landing. A Westland Lysander was brought done on the racecourse. The pilot was uninjured and made a phone call to his base then remained on guard by the aeroplane until the arrival of a recovery crew some hours later. They removed a camera from the Lysander and drove off. The pilot then allowed the boys to swarm all over the aircraft. Some time later a recovery crew came and remained in the area for several days dismantling the plane and taking it away in huge lorries. They lodged at Plassey House with Mr and Mrs Stratton for the duration of their stay.

War Savings

As during the First World War, everyone in Bangor was exhorted to save as much they could with the National War Savings scheme or to give towards the war effort in various ways. Mrs Rome of Abbeygate was the local organiser. Different schemes were launched to give impetus and incentive such as a Spitfire fund, a War Weapons Week and a Warship Week. In 1941, the hundred of Maelor was given a target sum to save for Warship Week with the aim of purchasing the hull of a motor torpedo boat. This goal was easily surpassed when they raised £63,840 11s 1d, and they were told that if another £5,000 could be raised before the fund was closed then they could purchase a whole boat. The Admiralty presented Bangor with a plaque to commemorate the adoption of MTB 29 which Mrs Rome was asked to display in her office for War Savings, after which each of the shops in turn could display it for a week. It was finally put in the church porch by arrangement with the rector but has since vanished. In addition to the plaque, the Admiralty also awarded certificates to the various parish councils in appreciation of the work done and the money raised.

A Wings for Victory week was declared for June 1943 and the Maelor again broke all records by leading Flintshire in the amount saved per head of population. Group Captain R.G. Harman, a distinguished fighter pilot, presented a plaque awarded by the Air Ministry to mark this achievement. The Maelor had aimed to raise £25,000, sufficient to meet the cost of a Wellington bomber and a Spitfire fighter plane. The amount actually raised was £77,000, enough for three Wellingtons and four Spitfires. Again certificates were presented to all the parish councils.

In February 1944 a Salute the Soldier campaign was planned with targets set for each of the eleven parishes to raise £3,000 during the week 8–15 July, with the intention of raising £33,000 for the Maelor. This target was probably once again exceeded.

Also in 1944, the lord lieutenants for north Wales launched a £10,000 appeal on behalf of the Y.M.C.A., for the benefit of soldiers engaged in the various theatres of war.

In addition to these service collections, there were also various flag days organised. In 1942, one was organised in connection with the Lord Mayor's National Air Raid Distress Fund, another in aid of the Special Prisoners of War Fund in conjunction with the Duke of Gloucester's Red Cross and St John's Funds. This last one was organised throughout the parish by Mrs Roberts of the Women's Voluntary Service. In 1943, Mrs Peters agreed to undertake the organisation of two flag

---

HIS MAJESTY'S LORDS LIEUTENANT NORTH WALES

Col. Sir Robert Williams Wynn, K.C.B., D.S.O.   (Denbighshire)
The Right Hon. Lord Harlech   (Merioneth)
Rear Admiral Rowley Conwy, C.M.G.   (Flintshire)
Eric J. W. Platt, Esq.   (Caernarvonshire)
The Marquis of Anglesey   (Anglesey)

£10,000 APPEAL
TO ASSIST THE
Y.M.C.A.
TO HELP YOUR MAN
IN

FRANCE, ITALY, UNITED KINGDOM, EGYPT, PALESTINE, NORTH & WEST AFRICA, LIBYA, SYRIA, TRIPOLI, IRAQ, IRAN, SICILY, ICELAND

Contributions will be gratefully acknowledged by Col. Sir Robert Williams Wynn, K.C.B., D.S.O. (Hon. Treasurer, Y.M.C.A.), AREA OFFICE, GLANMORFA, RHYL, North Wales

MAYBE THE Y.M.C.A. IS HELPING YOUR MAN—

PLEASE SEND US AS MUCH AS
—————— YOU CAN ——————

Y.M.C.A. appeal on behalf of its services to the troops, 1944 .

days – Aid to China and Prisoners of War.

Bangor very nearly had an aerodrome on its doorstep as a plan was mooted to build one at Hollybush, partly on land farmed by George Downward and five other farms stretching from Cloy Hall to the A525. In 1943, surveyors were seen taking soil samples and roughly marking out the lines of the runways and the perimeter of the site. Nothing came of the scheme, most probably because of the objections of the farmers, supported by the National Farmers' Union who, obeying orders from the Flintshire Agricultural Committee, were intensively farming their land. If the plan had gone ahead, it would have involved the closure of the A525 to through traffic and would have caused considerable inconvenience to local people who would have had to use minor roads to skirt round the proposed site, to say nothing of the noise and the increased threat of bombing once the Germans became aware of the aerodrome.

In 1944, when the tide of war had turned and victory was in sight, Bangor set up a Welcome Home Fund for all those serving with the forces. The local children decided to put on a carnival, organised entirely by them, to start off the fund and a substantial amount was raised. The following year a gymkhana with sideshows and swings was held that was reputedly attended by over 5,000 people. This may have been a printer's error and an extra '0' had inadvertently been added. After the gymkhana, a dance was held in the Assembly Rooms in the evening. Dances were also held every fortnight to help swell the funds and by October 1945 a considerable sum of money had been raised. A notice was then placed in a Wrexham newspaper with a list of persons eligible for participation in the Welcome Home Fund and asking for anyone not included in the list to get in touch with Miss Joyce Berry of Laurel Cottage. Anyone who had been in the forces, or Auxillary Territorial Service (A.T.S.), etc. was eligible and enough money was raised to give everyone about £18 and some of the money was spent on taking the children and their parents on a victory trip to Rhyl where each child was given two shillings to spend.

After the war, the government awarded medals to those who had served in the armed forces, but refused to recognise those who had served in auxillary, but vital, services such as the Fire Service and the Merchant Navy. Ruby Spoor who served with the Women's Land Army (W.L.A.) and was sent to farms in Ruthin, Corwen and Gresford, before ending up at Done's Bank Farm in

BANGOR-ON-DEE WELCOME HOME FUND.

LIST OF PERSONS eligible for participation in the above Fund :—

Sgt. G. Evanson, Cpl. R. Woolley, Pte. H. Norton, Pte. T. J. Roberts, A/C D. Hallett, Dvr. G. B. Humphreys, C.S.M. Norris, Bdr. C. H. Norcross, L.A.C. J. Pugh, L.A.C. G. I. Hodnet, Sister E. Matthews, Cpl. A. G. Fowles, Pte. F. C. Fowles, Pte. S. A. Fowles, W/O S. Peters, Cpl. M. L. Lewis (W.A.A.F.), L.A.C.W. M. Charlesworth Sgt. J. H. Fowles, Gunner J. Poynton, A.C.1. G. Matthews, Sergt. A. Crowther, A.B. E. E. Shelton, L.A.C.W. V. Spoor, Sapper J. P. Spoor, Fus. R. Shone, L.A.C. G. Jarvis, Dvr. H. Dodd, Cpl. J. Spoor, Sgt. E. Blake, Pte. D. Prandle, Sgt. T. Prandle, Pte. A. Prandle, Gdsm. L. Prandle, Gnr. E. Done, P/O J. C. Pritchard, Sgt. J. Peters (A.T.S.), O.S. J. Roberts, A.C. C. Betteley. P/O D. Arrowsmith, Cpl. G. H. Arrowsmith, P/O T. L. Keddie, L/Cpl. T. Leach, Capt. I. W. Pitcairn Campbell, Tpr. A. E. Wynn, Lt.-Col. Misa, Pte. F. Beckett, J. Mytton, Pte. G. Leach, L.A.C.W. D. Woolley, Sergt. J. Johnson, Pte. Cecil Crew, Pte. R. Norton, Gnr. J. Weston, Hilda Pugh (W.L.A.), Ruby Spoor (W.L.A.), Mr. Simmonds, Levi Studley, Wm. Fowles, Charles Wraight, Vera Spoor, Roland Lee, Ivor Evans, Mr. E. Price.

Will anyone who is not included in the above list and who is eligible, please submit their qualifications to Miss J. Berry, Laurel Cottage, Bangor-on-Dee, before the 26th October, 1945.

The Denbigh and Flint Local Medical War Committee announce that Dr. W. H. M. Jones has resumed practice at Yale Lodge, 37, Ruabon Road, Wrexham.   c

Advert in the Wrexham Leader *for the Welcome Home Fund.*

Bangor, or Charlie Duggan, her future husband, who became a Bevan Boy and had to go down the mines in Doncaster for 4½ years, were exempted. He had not volunteered for this work but every so often a name was chosen at random as the country was desperate for coal and many of the miners had been called up. Mr Peters and Charlie's father, Edward, tried their best to persuade the British Legion to include their names on the list for an award but to no avail. The government refused to recognise the service rendered to the country by these men and women and it is only in the last few years that it has been finally agreed to recognise those who served with the W.L.A., the Fire Service, the Bevan Boys, etc and they have been awarded medals, in many cases posthumously. Ruby was so disgusted at the treatment she and her husband had received that she refused to send for her medal.

Bangor Isycoed War Memorial
On 24 October 1924, a meeting was held to consider the best way to perpetuate the memory of those men who lost their lives during the First World War and representatives were sent from each of the townships of Eyton, Pickhill, Sesswick and Royton that, together with the civil parish of Bangor, make up the parish. It was decided that the memorial should be erected just outside the churchyard, near the lych gate, on the site of the five cottages that were pulled down in 1915. A committee was set up with the rector, the Revd Baldock acting as chairman, Major Fenwick Palmer as treasurer and G.J. Moss (headmaster) secretary. Subscriptions were invited and by December the treasurer stated that £220 had either been donated or promised. A number of designs from various sculptors were exhibited and it was decided to accept that of Herbert Tyson Smith of Liverpool, an honorary instructor in craftsmanship at Liverpool University School of Architecture. His principal works included sculptured portions of Accrington, Southport, Birkenhead and the Liverpool G.P.O. war memorials. Ernest Jones, grandfather of Alan Jones of Overton, who built the Overton War Memorial, is thought to have also erected the one at Bangor.

On the War Memorial is inscribed:

In grateful remembrance of the men of this parish who gave their lives in the Great War. 'All these were honoured in their generations and were the glory of their times.' Ecclesiasticus, XLIV, VII.

The dates of the war are displayed on two stone balls and on the back of the column is written 'Ad Majorem Dei Gloriam'. The names of the fallen were inscribed on the front. After the Second World War, the dates 1939–1945, were added and the column was dismantled to enable the names of the fallen of both wars to be recorded in alphabetical order.

Invitation to the dedication of the Bangor Isycoed War Memorial.

Bangor Isycoed.

The War Memorial will be Unveiled
by
Major Hugh Peel, J.P.,
and
Dedicated by the Archbishop of Wales,
on
Sunday, May 24th, at 2·30 p.m.
1925
You are cordially invited to be present.

In order to defray the amount outstanding on the War Memorial Fund, an Offertory will be taken at the Service.

The dedication of the Bangor Isycoed War Memorial, 24 May 1925.

The dedication of the War Memorial took place on Sunday, 24 May 1925. At the last moment the archbishop of Wales was taken ill and was unable to take part in the service and the Revd R.J.B. Paterson Morgan of Sandiway Lodge, Cheshire, who had been rector of Bangor for the period of the war, took his place. After a service in the church a procession proceeded to the War Memorial led by the band of the 4th Battalion, Royal Welsh Fusiliers, under the direction of Bandmaster Delancy, followed in order by ex-servicemen under Major Fenwick Palmer, the choir, the clergy, the churchwardens, Major Peel, the relatives of the fallen, the Girl Guides, the local school children, the Oddfellows and the rest of the congregation.

After a prayer had been offered and the rector, the Revd F.J. Okell, had read out the Roll of Honour, Major Peel unveiled the memorial and saluted. He then addressed the large crowd that had assembled, saying that he regarded it a privilege to be asked to unveil the memorial. He had known most of the men whose names were inscribed on it and had the honour of serving with some of them and a number had been his friends. The memorial had been erected to their memory and he quoted the words of an old treatise, 'So long as the sun shines and the river runs'. Two hymns were then sung and the Revd D. Manuel offered a prayer which was followed by the blessing. The singing of the National Anthem and the sounding of the *Last Post* and *Reveille* by the Royal Welch Fusiliers' buglers brought the ceremony to a close. Among the clergy present on the occasion, in addition to the Revd F.J. Okell, rector of Bangor, were Revd Paterson Morgan, the Revd M. Elrington Bisset, a former rector and now Chaplain to the Guards, and the Revd D. Manuel, Presbyterian Minister.

The Bangor Isycoed War Memorial in 2013.

The rector was given a book bound in red morocco leather that had been prepared by F.E. Barlow, assisted by P.H. Howard, an employee of his at Overton, both ex-servicemen. The manuscript is illuminated and the front page is embellished with the crest of St Asaph, the Prince of Wales Feathers, the crests of Denbighshire and Flintshire and with the Welsh national flower – the daffodil – in each corner. The frontispiece bears the following dedication:

> Those whom this volume commemorates were numbered among those who at the call of King and Country left all that was dear to them, endured hardness, faced danger and finally passed out of the sight of man by the path of duty and self sacrifice, giving up their own lives that others might live in freedom.

This page bears the signatures of Hugh E.E. Peel, R. Paterson-Morgan, M. Elrington Bissett, David Manuel, Frank Okell and George J. Moss. Inside the book are listed the names of the men who had fallen in the war. It is kept inside the church in a glass-topped desk. There is also a wooden commemorative board, erected by the Revd and Mrs Paterson Morgan, which bears twenty-one names displayed which, with the exception of William Mort and Thomas Dodd, are also inscribed on the War Memorial. The exclusion of Thomas Dodd is understandable as he was did not fall in combat, but William Mort was confirmed killed in action in France according the Commonwealth War Graves Commission (CWGC) and on a card filled in by the Revd Paterson-Morgan and now held in the Flintshire Record Office. It is hoped that this will be rectified by the centenary of the commencement of the First World War in 2014.

The unique card record held by the county record office is one of a unique series of cards which was instigated by the lord lieutenant, Sir Henry Neville Gladstone, third son of the former prime minister, as a means of perpetuating those men who served in the First World War, listed parish by parish. Unfortunately there are many omissions, and only sixteen of the men from Bangor who did not come back are included. But, as the completion of the card was left to the family of the man who died, or to the soldier himself in the case of survivors, there were bound to be some cards which were never returned to the rector.

In 1995, the Community Council planted a cherry tree by the side of the War Memorial to commemorate the fiftieth anniversary of the end of the Second World War. They also placed two wooden seats there to celebrate Her Majesty's Golden Jubilee in 2002.

The men who died in the First World War were:

Edward Boffey of Cloy Hall, Bangor Isycoed. Born Wettenhall, Northwich, he was the son of Benjamin and Mary Richardson Boffey of the Red Lion Inn, Whitchurch Road, Bangor Isycoed. Private (N$^{o.}$ 23146), 6th Bn, King's Own Yorkshire Light infantry. Joined the 5th Dragoon Guards in September 1914 then transferred to the Scots Greys and the Royal Welsh Fusiliers. He went to France in July 1915 and was killed in action on 6 January (5th January according to the CWGC) 1916, aged twenty-seven. He is buried in New Irish Farm Cemetery, Belgium.

James Carr of Walnut House, Whitchurch Road, Bangor Isycoed, the son of William Alfred and Elizabeth Ann Carr. Private (N$^{o.}$ 54278), 9th Bn, Royal Welsh Fusiliers. He joined Denbighshire Yeomanry (N$^{o.}$ 1453) on 6 September 1915, before being transferred to the Royal Welsh Fusiliers. He went to France on 31 August 1916 and was believed killed in action north east of Thiepval on 28 October (29th church book) 1916. He is commemorated on the Thiepval Memorial to the Missing.

Thomas Dodd, Church Avenue, Bangor Isycoed, the son of Thomas Dodd of Church Avenue. He was married with two children. Private (N$^{o.}$ 7658), 2nd Bn, Royal Welsh Fusiliers. He joined the army on 25 February 1903 and had served in India. He was called up as a reservist in August 1914 and discharged as time expired on 23 February 1916. He was awarded the Mons Star. He was accidentally drowned in the Dee at Bangor on 4 March 1916, aged thirty-five. His name is not recorded on the War Memorial as, at the time of his death, he was not serving in the army.

Robert Henry William Dunn, of Althrey Hall, Bangor Isycoed, son of General William Dunn of Inglewood, Hungerford, Berkshire. He was a justice of the peace and deputy lieutenant for Flintshire. Born in 1857 in London and educated at Eton. Brigadier-general, he had been commissioned into the army in 1877 and joined 1st Bn, Royal Welsh Fusiliers in 1880, serving in India and in the Burma campaign. He resigned his commission in 1896 and was in the Reserve of Officers. Recommissioned, he commanded the regimental depot at Wrexham during Anglo-Boer War and was brigade major and later brigadier-general commanding the Welsh Border Brigade (Territorial Force) 1907–12. In August 1914 he formed a 'Pal's' battalion of the Royal Welsh Fusiliers and was given command of a brigade in the Welsh Army Corps. He died on 8 January 1917, aged fifty-nine, having been thrown from his horse at Kinmel Bay Camp. He married twice: firstly in 1882 to Mary Louisa (died 1884), the daughter of Colonel Stokes, and then in 1890 in Lucknow to Catherine Constance Selina, daughter of General George Erskine of Chelsea. He is buried in Wrexham Cemetery.

Frederick Hugh Fearnall, of Pickhill Old Hall, Bangor Isycoed, was born 1891 the son of Frederick and Kate Fearnall. Lance corporal (N⁰· 22601), 6th Bn, Queen's Royal West Surrey Regiment, formerly with the 7th Reserve Cavalry (N⁰· 17215). Died of pneumonia 17 February 1917 in France, aged twenty-five. Buried at Hilaire Cemetery, Frevent, France.

Roger Mansel William Fenwick, younger son of Captain George and Mrs Fenwick of Plâs Fron. Born in 1898, he was trooper (N⁰· 4596) in the 1st Life Guards. He was killed in an air raid in France on 19 May 1918, aged 20. He is buried in Étaples Military Cemetery.

Thomas Ernest Goswell, of Althrey Lodge, son of George & Hester Goswell. He was born at Bangor on Dee in 1893 and became a well-known steeplechase jockey. Private (N⁰· 32538), 14th Bn, Royal Warwickshire Regiment. He had joined the Welsh Horse in January 1915 and been promoted to sergeant before transferring to the 9th Lancers and then the East Surrey Regt, the Middlesex Regt, the 17th Lancers, and finally the Royal Warwicks. He went to France in November 1916 and fell on 26 October 1917, aged twenty-four. He is buried in Hooge Crater Cemetery, Belgium.

Henry George Gravenor, Church Avenue, Bangor Isycoed, husband of Mrs H.L. Gravenor of Porthwgan. He was born in Bodenham, Herefordshire. Private (N⁰· M272702), driver, 348th Motor Transport Company, Royal Army Service Corps. He made many attempts to join the army but was rejected on medical grounds before being accepted in December 1916. He was posted to Grove Park in London, Salisbury Plain, Birmingham, back to Salisbury Plain and then to Oxford. He died on 23 October 1918 (22 October church book) of double pneumonia at III Southern Military Hospital, Oxford, aged twenty-eight. He is buried in Bodenham Chapel yard in Herefordshire.

Joseph Haycocks, son of collier James and Mary Haycocks of Crabtree Green, Eyton. He was born in 1885. Private (N⁰· 8149),2nd Bn, Royal Welsh Fusiliers. He died of wounds on 10 June 1915 in France and is buried in Bailleul Communal Cemetery Extension (Nord).

George Humphreys, of High Street, Bangor Isycoed, the son of George and Mary Humphreys, and uncle of George 'Dode' Humphreys. Private (N⁰· 49753), Cheshire Regiment. He enlisted in the Denbighshire Yeomanry at Eccleston Camp, Chester on 14 August 1914 (N⁰· 641) and later transferred to 11th Bn, Cheshire Regiment where he was the colonel's runner. He was wounded on 26 February 1917 and hospitalised Rouen and Birkenhead. He rejoined his battalion on 27 May 1917 and was believed killed in action in France between 10 and 20 April 1918. He is commemorated Tyne Cot Memorial to the Missing, Belgium.

Harry Humphreys, of High Street, Bangor Isycoed, brother to George Humphreys above. Private (N⁰· 49752), 1st Bn, Cheshire Regt. Like his brother, he volunteered for the Denbighshire Yeomanry in October 1914 and was transferred to the Cheshire Regiment. He was posted to France on 26 August 1916, and was killed in action at Ypres on 5 October 1917 (9 October in church), aged thirty-two. He is buried in Tyne Cot Cemetery, Belgium.

Frank Stuart Lloyd, fifth son of auctioneer Francis and Fanny Lloyd of Eyton House and The Plassey, Bangor Isycoed. He was born in 1893. Temporary major, 13th Bn, Royal Welsh Fusiliers. He died of wounds on 5 September 1917 and is buried in Dozinghem British Cemetery, near Poperinge in Belgium.

John Arthur Lloyd-Jones, of The Stores, Bangor on Dee, second son of John & Elizabeth Lloyd-Jones of Glan Aber, Hope, Wrexham. He was the brother of Maggie Lloyd-Jones, an assistant teacher at Bangor before she was appointed headmistress of Erbistock School in 1913. Born in 1891, he had just gained his teacher's certificate and a diploma in music at Bangor Normal College. He enlisted in Liverpool in 1915 into the 6th Bn, King's Liverpool Regiment and was transferred to the Cheshire Regiment in January 1916. He was posted to France on 24 June 1916. He was serving as a lance corporal (Nº 33148) with 'B' Company, 1st Bn Cheshire Regiment and is believed to have been killed in action at Guillemont on 9 September 1916, during the first battle of the Somme. He is commemorated on the Thiepval Memorial to the Missing.

Thomas Matthews, of Kiln Cottages, Bangor Isycoed, son of Joseph and Eliza Matthews of Millbrook Bank, Bangor Isycoed and husband of Elizabeth Jane Matthews (died 1925). He was born in Shrewsbury in 1879 and enlisted in the Royal Welsh Fusiliers in Wrexham (Nº 6563). He was a reservist when war broke out and was recalled in August 1914 to serve with 1st Bn, Royal Welsh Fusiliers. He is believed to have been killed in action, aged thirty-five, on 30 October 1914, during the first battle of Ypres. He is commemorated on the Menin Gate Memorial to the Missing at Ypres.

William Mort, of Althrey Cottage, Bangor Isycoed, was the son of James and Mary Mort of Threapwood, Malpas and the husband of Mrs E.L. Mort (later of Sunnyside, Chorlton Lane, Malpas). He enlisted in May 1917 and served as a gunner (Nº 160900) in the 190th Siege Battery, Royal Garrison Artillery. He was killed in action in France on 20 May 1918, aged thirty-one. He is buried in Brandhoek New Military Cemetery Nº 3. His name is not recorded on the Bangor War Memorial.

Capt. Lawrence Ormrod, MC.

Lawrence Moreland Ormrod, MC, second son of Oliver and Emily Ormrod of Pickhill Hall, Bangor Isycoed and uncle of Captain John Moreland Ormrod of Sutton Green Farm and Major James Jardine Ormrod of Pickhill Hall Farm. He was born in 1889 and was a captain in 1st Bn, Royal Welsh Fusiliers. He died on 25 August 1917 in the Grosvenor Hospital, London, aged twenty-eight, of wounds received in action on 27 May 1916. He is buried in Bangor Isycoed churchyard.

Oliver Hugh Ormrod, son of Oliver and Emily Ormrod of Pickhill Hall, Bangor Isycoed. He was educated at Sandroyd and Eton after which he studied farming and land agency and was commissioned as a lieutenant into the Denbighshire Hussars. He emigrated to Vancouver, Canada. On the outbreak of war he returned to Britain and was commissioned as a lieutenant in the Royal Field Artillery in October 1914. He was promoted to captain in February 1915 and served with the British Expeditionary Force in France and Flanders from July 1915, as adjutant of the 87th Brigade, Royal Field Artillery.

In December he contracted enteric fever and was invalided home in February 1916. In May 1916 he transferred into the Royal Flying Corps where he trained to become a pilot. Promoted to captain he died in a flying accident at Gosport in Hampshire whilst testing a plane on 12 September 1916, aged thirty. He is buried in Bangor Isycoed churchyard.

John Rees, son of Stephen and Elizabeth Rees of Fedw Goed, Eyton. Lance corporal (Nº 25305) 16th (17th in church book) Bn, Royal Welsh Fusiliers. He enlisted in Ruabon and was killed in action in France on 8 November 1918, aged twenty-eight. He is buried in Dourlers Communal Cemetery Extension.

Harry Roberts, of Fraser Cottage (opposite the post office), Bangor Isycoed, son of William and Mary Roberts and brother of postman John T. Roberts. Private (N⁰˙ 44033). He enlisted in November 1917 into the South Wales Borderers (N⁰˙ 41691) and was later transferred into the 2/8th Bn, Worcestershire Regiment. He was killed in action in France on 11 November (2 November church book) 1918, four hours before the Armistice. He is buried in Valenciennes (St Roch) Communal Cemetery.

Henry (Harry) Leo Rogers, of Whitchurch Road, son of coal miner Henry Rogers and grandson of Thomas Hodnett of Station Road, Bangor. He was married to Elizabeth and had a young family. He worked in the engineering department of the Post Office Telegraph Service. Private (N⁰˙ 81022) 2nd (Garrison) Bn, King's (Liverpool) Regiment. He enlisted into the Royal Welsh Fusiliers (N⁰˙ 44052) on 6 January 1915 and was killed in action at Salonika in Bulgaria on 27 February 1917. He is buried in Salonika (Lembet Road) Military Cemetery in Thessalonika, Greece.

Ernest Shone, of Cloy Villa, Bangor Isycoed, was the son of William and Elizabeth Shone. Private 35213 in the 6th Battalion Royal Berkshires. He joined the army in June 1917 and was a private (N⁰˙ 35213) in the 6th Bn, Royal Berkshire Regiment, training at Portsmouth before going to Belgium in August 1917. He was presumed to have been killed in action on the Menin Road during the opening rounds of the third battle of Ypres. There is some confusion about the date of his death which is recorded as 10 August 1917 by the CWGC, 11 August 1917 in the Roll of Honour in Bangor church and 8 August 1917. At the time of his death he was aged nineteen. He is commemorated on the Menin Gate Memorial to the Missing, Ypres.

William (Edward) Stant of Church Avenue, Bangor Isycoed, son of Harry and Margaret Stant. He joined the Denbighshire Yeomanry at Wrexham on 1 September 1915 (N⁰˙ 1451) and was later transferred to the 10th Bn, Royal Welsh Fusiliers (N⁰˙ 56766) and served as a private in Ireland and France. He was presumed to have been killed in action on 14 June 1917, during the battle of Arras, aged nineteen. He is commemorated on the Arras Memorial to the Missing, France.

Thomas Edward Studley, the son of Edward Groom and May Elizabeth (née Studley) of Cae Dyah Farm, Bangor, was born at Overton on 27 August 1890. He enlisted in the Cheshire Yeomanry in August 1914 which later became the 10th (Shropshire and Cheshire Yeomanry) Bn, King's Shropshire Light Infantry (N⁰˙ 230744). He served as a private in Egypt and Palestine and was presumed to have been killed in action on 30 November 1917 during the advance on Jerusalem. He is commemorated on the Jerusalem Memorial to the Missing.

Thomas Edwin Williams, son of Edwin and Charlotte Williams of Overton Road, Eyton, was born in 1892 in Penley. He served as a private (N⁰˙ 202027) in the 4th Bn, Royal Welsh Fusiliers and died of accidental injuries on 20 August 1918, aged twenty-seven. He is buried in Heilly Station Cemetery, Mericourt l'Abbé, Somme.

Edgar Wilson, son of Daniel Wilson (born Sesswick), a general labourer with the GPO, and Mary J. Wilson (born Hanmer), of Whitchurch Road, Bangor Isycoed. He was the grandson of William and Elizabeth Wilson also of Whitchurch Road. Born in 1898 in Carrington, Cheshire, he served as a private (N⁰˙ 201393) in the 1/4th Bn, King's Shropshire Light Infantry and died of wounds, probably at the N⁰˙ 1 General Hospital in Étretat, France, on 14 January 1918. He is buried in Etretat Churchyard Extension Cemetery, Seine-Maritime, France.

Those who died in the Second World War were:

Lionel Francis Worsley Barker, the son of Francis Worsley and Beatrice M. Barker (née Ormrod) of Neston, Cheshire. Born in 1920, he was commissioned as a lieutenant (N°· 100215) into the 5th Bn, Royal Welch Fusiliers. He died on 9 October 1943, aged twenty-three, and is buried in Salerno War Cemetery, Italy.

Ivor Evans, son of William Owen Evans and his wife Annie, and husband of Mabel Evans of Bangor on Dee. He served as a fusilier (N°· 4201922) in the 6th Bn, Royal Welch Fusiliers. He died on 17 July 1944, aged twenty-nine. He has no known grave and is commemorated on the Bayeux Memorial to the Missing, Normandy, France.

Sgt Jack Johnson.

Jack Raymond Johnson, the son of Thomas and Alice May Johnson, New Council Houses, Eyton and grandson of Mr and Mrs Wilbraham, 13 Maesgwyn Road, Wrexham, was born in 1921. Sergeant (Wireless Operator/Air Gunner) Johnson, RAFVR (N°· 1087702), served in 35 Squadron, Royal Air Force, one of the original Pathfinder Force squadrons, flying Halifax bombers. He died on 24 May 1943, aged twenty-one, and is buried in the Reichswald Forest Cemetery, Germany.

Rowland William Lea, only son of Edgar and Kathleen Mabel Lea, licensees of the Buck Hotel, Bangor Isycoed, was born on 14 December 1922. Sergeant (Flight Engineer) Lea (N°· 577749) served in 57 Squadron RAF, flying in Lancaster bombers. When based at RAF Scampton in Lincolnshire, he was only aged twenty when his aircraft went missing whilst on a mission over St Nazaire, France on 2 April 1943. He is buried in Nantes (Pont-du-Cens) Communal Cemetery, Loire-Atlantique and also commemorated on a plaque on the Lea family grave at St Oswald's Church, Lower Peover, Cheshire.

Oliver Ogle Ormrod, DFC, eldest son of Maurice Sarsfield Ormrod and Eva Margaretta (Marda, née Irving) Ormrod of Coed-y-Glyn, Wrexham and of Pickhill Hall, Bangor Isycoed, and brother of Captain J.M. Ormrod and Major J.J. Ormrod, was born 1922 in London. He died whilst serving as a pilot officer (N°· 110128) with 185 Squadron, flying

P/O Oliver Ormrod, DFC.

a Hurricane single-seater fighter in the defence of Malta on his twentieth birthday, 22 April 1942. He is buried in Malta (Capucci) Naval Cemetery.

Roger Scott, third son of chauffeur Joseph Ernest and Sarah Jane Scott of Cock Bank, and brother to Joe Scott of Marchwiel. Sergeant (Flight Engineer) Scott (N°· 220599), RAFVR, served with 514 Squadron, flying in a Lancaster bomber on his forty-third mission, a daylight raid over Hamburg, on 21

Sgt Roger Scott.

November 1944, aged nineteen. He is buried in the Reichswald Forest War Cemetery, Germany.

Charles Edward William Wraight, the son of Charles Wraight and stepson of Elsie Wraight of 43 Salop Road, Wrexham, husband of Anne (née Johnson) and father of Vera Marian, Colin James and Doreen Gwenda. He was a painter and decorator and lived at The Leeks, Bangor Isycoed. He had been born in Kent in 1911. He joined the 49th Bn, West Riding Regiment (N°· 4191160) before being attached to the Reconnaissance Corps of the Royal Armoured Corps. Promoted to sergeant he was killed in action in Belgium on 28 August 1944, aged thirty-one. He is buried in Leopoldsburg War Cemetery, Belgium.

Sgt Charles Wraight.

18. Utilities

The unsanitary condition of Bangor and the water supply

By the nineteenth century, people had become conscious of the insanitary state of their towns and cities with the condition of London with its 'great stink' receiving great publicity in the press. In the mid 1800s the great clean-up began with the construction of London's underground sewers and the smell was finally eradicated. The attention of the sanitary engineers then turned to other towns and cities. The gradual demolition of the narrow streets and overcrowded cellars of the slums and courts in places like Liverpool and the introduction of piped water with the construction of Lake Vyrnwy in 1880 meant that an abundant supply of good clean water was available to all.

By the end of the nineteenth century, the focus of attention was on the condition of the many villages throughout the country. The idyllic 'roses round the door' country cottage often concealed living conditions that were just as bad as any town slum. In 1891, a report was published in the *Daily News* on the conditions of one such village, the cottages of which were described as 'alive with vermin' and 'literally saturated with sewage.' Whilst not daring to suggest that Bangor was as bad as this description, we can get a very good idea of the problems facing the average inhabitant from the parish council minutes.

In 1896, the council agreed to have six sources of water analysed: the wells belonging to Mrs Webster (the public well); the school; H. Williams; Sarah Poynton; B. Edwards and the river. When the result of the analyses were received, the wells were found to be polluted and the water unfit for drinking. The handles of the wells were removed to prevent access. There was considerable disagreement amongst the councillors on the quality of the water. Alfred Bennett of the Red Lion Inn said that they could not get better water than the present supply otherwise his beer would not be so good. John Parry of the Royal Oak said there was no good water in the village and that for his own supply he was reliant on the generosity of his neighbour and that if Mr Bennett had his well analysed it would probably be condemned like the others.

The result of a survey commissioned by Overton Rural District Council was presented to a meeting of representatives of Parish and Rural District Councils and the sanitary inspector ('Inspector of Nuisances' as he used to be called). The Medical Officer of Health, Dr Thursfield, reported that,

> Bangor consisted of 65 houses with a population of under 300. The water supply was obtained in nearly every case directly from the river. There were about fifteen pump wells, one of which was a public well near the churchyard that had always had a problem. The wells were not deep and

Facing: Survey of wells in Bangor in 1925–7 (part one). [FRO PC/3/14]

WREXHAM AND EAST DENBIGHSHIRE WATER COMPANY.

———oOOoo———

Proposed Water Supply to Bangor-is-y-coed.

Particulars as to property within area of Scheme.

(1925 - 1927)

Asst. No.	Address	Tenant	Owner Name	Owner Address	Descrip. of Premises	Gross Asst. £	Water Rate per Qr. On Asst. £	Sundries	Total £	Favourable to supply Yes	No.	Source of present supply	Remarks
	High Street.												
							s d		s d				
19.	Dee View Cottage.	T.W.Mercer.	Bents Brewery Co.	High St. Wrexham.	D.H.	21.	12/1	—	12/1	—	No.	River.	—
76.	2.Kiln Cttg.	Mrs.Reddy.	A.K.Jones. (Agent)	43,Regent St. Wrexham.	"	7.	4/-½	—	4/-½	Yes.	"	"	—
78.	3, "	J.Taylor.	"	"	"	7.	4/-½	—	4/-½	"	"	"	—
75.	4, "	Mrs.Clarke.	"	"	"	7.	4/-½	—	4/-½	"	"	"	—
66.	5, "	A.Prandle.	"	"	"	7.	4/-½	—	4/-½	"	No.	"	—
74.	6, "	D.Prandle.	"	"	"	7.	4/-½	—	4/-½	Yes.	"	"	—
77.	7, "	E.Roberts.	"	"	"	7.	4/-½	—	4/-½	"	"	"	—
144.	Royal Oak Hotel.	J.E.Foster.	Bents Brewery Co.	High St. Wrexham.	P.H.	68.	39/1	Bath 2/6.	41/7	—	No.	Pump & River.	—
25.	Hse & Shop.	Mrs.Beavan.	H.Williams.	P. O. Overton.	H.&.S.	26.	14/7	—	14/7	Yes.	—	"	—
32.	House.	J.Humphreys.	"	"	D.H.	11.	6/4	—	6/4	"	—	"	—
143.	Buck Hotel.	Mrs.E.Foster.	—	—	P.H.	60.	34/6	Bath 2/6. W. C.2/6.	39/6	—	No.	Pump (own)	—
73.	Rectory Lodge.	H.Arrowsmith.	Duke of Westminster.	—	D.H.	10.	5/9	—	5/9	Yes.	—	"	—
139.	The Rectory.	Rev.T.R. Baldock.	—	—	"	60.	34/6	Bath 2/6.	37/-	"	"	"	"
	Schools.	—	—	—	L. up.P.	—	—	—	(say)7/6 (minimum)	—	—	—	80 to 90 children
70.	Chapel Hse.	C.Roscoe.	W.Welch.	Yorke St. Wrexham.	D.H.	8.	4/7	—	4/7	Yes.	—	Pump – butchers).	"
58.	House.	J.Evanson.	"	"	"	7.	4/-½	—	4/-½	"	—	"	—
22.	Post Office.	W.Griffiths.	W.Griffiths.	—	H.&.S.	20.	11/6	—	11/6	"	—	" (own)	—
59.	House.	J.Jarvie.	A.K.Jones (Agent)	43.Regent St. Wrexham.	D.H.	7.	4/-½	—	4/-½	"	—	"	—
60.	"	Mrs.Young.	"	"	"	7.	4/-½	—	4/-½	"	"	"	—
54.	"	J.Roberts.	"	"	"	7.	4/-½	—	4/-½	"	"	" – butchers).	—
141.	"	F.Taylor.	"	"	"	7.	4/-½	—	4/-½	"	"	" (own)	—
12.	" & Sh.	T.T.Twist.	T.T.Twist.	—	H.&.S.	26.	14/7	—	14/7	—	No.	"	—
55.	" " "	F.Humphreys.	H.Williams.	P. O. Overton.	H & Shop.	9.	5/2.	—	5/2.	Yes.	—	"	—
	Police Stn.	—	—	—	D.H.	—	—	—	—	—	—	—	—
6.	Butcher's Shop.	G.H.Williams.	C.H.Spoor.	—	H.&.S.	29.	16/4.	Butcher 1/-	17/4	—	No.	Pump (own)	—
45.	House.	J.T.Roberts.	Warburton.	—	D.H.	8.	4/7.	—	4/7	Yes.	—	River	—
	Station Road.												
—	Smithy Cttg.	Miss Davies.	W. H. Williams.	P. O. Overton.	D.H.	8.	4/7.	—	4/7	Yes.	—	Pump	—
84.	House.	J.Davenport.	"	"	"	6.	3/5½	—	3/5½	—	No.	"	—
83.	"	Mrs.Matthews.	"	"	"	7.	4/-½	—	4/-½	"	"	"	—
5.	Rhos Cttge.	D.Barthlem.	D.Barthlem.	—	"	12.	6/11	—	6/11	"	No.	" (own)	—
27.	House – Graig Lane.	W.Young.	J.Johnson.	Leek Cttge. Bangor.	"	12.	6/11	—	6/11	Yes.	—	"	"
43.	Leek Cttge.	J.Johnson (Senr)	"	"	"	6.	3/5½	—	3/5½	"	—	"	"
42.	"	J.Johnson (Junr)	"	"	"	9.	5/2.	—	5/2	"	—	"	"
(39.	Old Smithy Cottage.	T.Hodnett.	J.Mort.	West Gate, Bangor.	"	12.	6/11	—	6/11	—	No.	"	"
35.	"	A.Davies.	"	"	"	9.	5/2	—	5/2	—	No	"	"
81.	House.	Mrs.M.Berry.	J.Johnson.	Leek Cttge, Bangor.	"	14.	8/-½	—	8/-½	"	—	"	"
82.	"	Mrs.L.Clarke.	"	"	"	13.	7/5½	—	7/5½	"	—	"	"
38.	"	A.Roberts.	"	"	"	8.	4/7	—	4/7	—	No.	"	"
40.	"	S.Crewe.	"	"	"	8.	4/7.	—	4/7	—	No.	"	"
41.	"	Mrs.H.Rogers.	"	"	"	8.	4/7	—	4/7	—	No.	"	"
8	Council Houses.	Overton R. D. C.	Overton R. D. C.	—	"	15/10/-	8/11 ea.	Bath 2/6 11/5 each.	11/5 ea. 14.	Yes.	—	—	(assumed)
24.	Graig Hse.	J.C.Moore.	A.Fearnall.	—	"	32.	18/5	Bath 2/6.	20/11	"	—	—	do
	Whitchurch Road.												
117.	Dee House.	J.Bennett.	J.Bennett.	—	"	25.	14/5	Cows 16/- Horses 2/- Refrigerator 8/-	6/-	—	No.	Pump (own)	—
						(1)							

Asst. No.	Address	Tenant	Owner Name	Owner Address	Descrip. of Premises	Gross Asst. on Asst. £	Water Rate per Qr. s.d.	Sundries	Total s.d.	Favourable to supply. Yes.	No.	Source of present supply. Rem.
Whitchurch Road (Continued)												
80	House.	F.E.Barlow	Mrs. Eaton. (Agt.The Laurels, Bangor)	J.Griffiths.	D.H.	14.	8/-½	–	8/-½	–	–	Pump	–
79	"	S.Dunbabin.	"	"	"	14.	8/-½	–	8/-½	–	–	"	–
121	The Laurels.	J.Griffiths.	"	"	"	18.	10/4	Cows 5/– Horse 1/–	16/4	Yes.	–	" (own)	–
126	House.	F.Bostock.	F.Bostock.	–	"	9	5/2	–	5/2	–	No.	" "	"
	"	"	"	"	"	9	5/2	–	5/2	–	No.	" "	–
85	The Bungalow.	T.Williams	A.D.P. Campbell.	Dee Side, Bangor.	"	10.	5/9	–	5/9	Yes.	–	" "	"
	Kiln Cottage.	Minshull.	–	–	"	12.	6/11	–	6/11	"	–	Carry from Bostocks.	
49	House.	J.Roberts.	Miss Sylvester.	Kings Mills Rd. Wes.	"	9.	5/2	–	5/2	"	–	Pump (own)	
48	"	A.F.Norton.	"	"	"	9.	5/2	–	5/2	"	–	" "	–
47	"	C.Robinson.	"	"	"	14.	8/-½	–	8/-½	"	–	" "	–
23	Red Lion.	–	J.Bennett.	Dee House, Bangor.	"	32.	18/5	–	18/5	–	No.	" "	"
90	House.	W.Purcell.	H.Shillem.	Whitchurch.	"	6.	3/5½	–	3/5½	–	–	–	–
52	"	E.Matthews.	"	" v.p	"	6.	3/5½	–	3/5½	–	–	–	–
51	"	J.Fowles.	"	"	"	7.	4/-½	–	4/-½	–	–	–	–
17	Walnut House.	E.A.Peters	Mrs. "	"	H & Gar D.H.	26.	14/7	–	14/7	Yes.	–	Pump (own)	–
18	"	J.Fowles.	"	"	L.up.S.	7/10/-	4/4	–	4/4	–	No.	" "	
10	Smithy.	H.Spoor.	H.Spoor.	–	H.&.S.	15.	4/4	–	4/4	Yes.	–	" "	
9	House & Shop.	"	"	"	D.H.	15.	8/-½	–	8/-½	"	–	" "	
21	"	Mrs.Jones.	"	"	"	6	3/5½	–	3/5½	–	No.	" "	
30	Mrs.House.	Mrs.K.Boffey	F.Bostock.	–	"	8	4/7	–	4/7	–	No.	" "	
26	House.	Dr.E.Jones	T.Williams.	–	"	15.	8/7	–	8/7	–	–	" "	
Overton Road.												
56	House.	A.Thomas.	P.Simpson.	–	"	7.	4/-½	–	4/-½	–	No.	River.	
57	"	S.Wright.	Wm. Jones.	–	"	7/10/-	4/4	–	4/4	Yes.	–	"	
46	Greyland Hse.	J.Antley.	J.Antley.	–	"	16.	9/2½	–	9/2½	–	No.	"	
16	Orchard Hse.	R.L.Mitten	J.Mort.	West Gate Bangor.	"	20.	11/6.	–	11/6.	–	No.	Pump (own)	
91	West Gate.	J.Mort.	"	"	"	30.	17/3	Bath 2/6.	19/9	–	No.	" "	
88	Orchard Villa.	E.Jones.	"	"	"	14.	8/-½	–	8/-½	–	No.	" "	
89	"	J.Reeves.	"	"	"	14.	8/-½	–	8/-½	–	No.	" "	
72	Bungalow.	Holmes.	A.D.P. Campbell	Dee Side, Bangor.	"	9.	5/2	–	5/2	–	No.	" "	
142	Dee Side.	A.D.P.Campbell	"	"	"	90.	51/9	Bath 2/6.	54/3	–	–	" "	
65	School House.	G.Jones.	–	–	"	10.	5/9	–	5/9	Yes.	–	Pump	–
93	Institute	–	–	–	L.up.P.	5	–	–	–	–	–	"	–
–	Schools	–	–	–	"	5	–	(say 5/–)	–	–	–	–	–
44	Church Avenue.	J.Manuel.	Jones.	–	D.H.	14.	8/-½	–	8/-½	Yes.	–	River water	–
36	"	J.Shone.	"	–	"	5.	3/3;	–	3/3;	"	–	"	"
37	"	Mrs.M.Young	"	–	"	6.	3/5½	–	3/5½	"	–	"	"
62	"	H.Stant.	"	–	"	7.	4/0½	–	4/-½	"	–	"	"
63	"	E.Dodd.	"	–	"	7.	4/-½	–	4/-½	"	–	"	"
64	"	Mrs.H.Shone.	"	–	"	7.	4/-½	–	4/-½	"	–	"	"

Survey of wells in Bangor in 1925–7 (part two). [FRO PC/3/14]

the level rose and fell with the river and drew water from the same source. He had taken samples from four of the wells, one of which was the public one, the other three to dwelling houses and he found them to be so contaminated as to make them unsafe for potable use and the other wells would be similarly polluted. He thought that the sanitary authorities should make available to the parish a general piped water supply for the village.

Two months later, a report from Mr Maxwell Smith of Wrexham recommended that the best way to get a good supply of water was to extend the Wrexham Waterworks Company's main drain from Marchwiel to Bangor, a distance of 2½ miles. The Bangor ratepayers objected to this on the grounds of cost as there were only 162 ratepayers, the rateable value was £3,788 and the scheme proposed would necessitate a higher annual rate. They also said that the village was healthy and the death rate low. The scheme was put to a meeting of the parish ratepayers and was defeated by a large majority, despite the district councillor for Bangor, Ambrose Sutton of Althrey Hall, and others, trying their best to get the villagers to agree to the plan.

In June 1910, a letter was received from the Wrexham Water Company regarding the proposed extension of their water main to the village at an estimated cost of £821 to be borne by the company on receipt of a guaranteed water rate for the whole village of not less than £82 per annum. The guarantee was to run for twenty years from the date the water was laid on. Members thought that only the owners of properties should be the guarantors and have to pay since it was their properties that were being improved and not the tenants and it was again outvoted. In 1915, the question of extending the water main to Bangor was deferred until after the war.

After the conflict ended, the question of the water supply was again raised and in 1925, the Wrexham Water Company was again asked to give an estimate to supply Bangor with water. By now, the cost of an extension of the mains from Marchwiel had escalated to between £2,000 and £3,000 on account of the need to cross the river and the RDC was asked to write to the Liverpool Water Company to see whether a supply could be made available by connecting to their pipeline at Halghton which ran from Lake Vyrnwy.

The breweries were asked if they would agree to contribute towards such a scheme. Greenhall Whitley offered £250 and a guarantee of £10 per annum for ten years and Bent's Brewery made a similar offer, but only if the Wrexham Water Company scheme was chosen. It was then decided to get an estimate for the cost of piping water for the village only, for a distance of ¼ mile from the centre of the village on the Overton, Whitchurch and Worthenbury roads. This naturally upset the owners of Althrey, Highgate, Raggs Hill, Cloy Lane and the surrounding properties who, although outside this limit, would still have to pay the increased water rate for no benefit.

A survey of all the houses in the village with their source of drinking water was again commissioned by the Overton Rural District Council in about 1925 that gives the name of the owner, the tenant, the water rate assessed, whether the occupant was in favour of a piped supply and the source of his present supply. Predictably those people who had their own well were not in favour of spending money on obtaining a piped supply. These included T.T. Twiss (The Stores), G.H. Williams (butcher), E.L. Mitton (Orchard House), J. Bennett (Dee House) and the Buck Hotel. Those people who had their own well but were in favour of a piped supply included J. Griffiths (The Laurels), H. Spoor (The Smithy), W.A. Peters (Walnut House), W. Griffiths (Post Office) and J. Johnson, senior and junior (Leek Cottages).

Perhaps more surprising was the number of the inhabitants whose sole source of water was the river and who were apparently quite happy to continue using that supply. In 1928, the RDC asked the owners of land whether they were willing to pay for a water main to be laid to their houses and whether the RDC could extend the distance to have a water main laid to the new council houses opposite Tŷ Graig. The distance now suggested was from the Highgate to Whitchurch Road and from the Althrey Farm on the Overton road.

The question of the water supply rumbled on with various plans put forward. In 1933 the RDC were asked to consider a scheme to bring water from Raggs Hill, which was said to have a plentiful supply. The surveyor, Mr Higgins, on behalf of RDC, said it would cost £1,050 and that a 4d rate would cover it and the council agreed to ask whether there was a possibility of a grant from the county council. In 1934, the parish council agreed to accept the Liverpool Water Company's scheme and to make a rate of 8d in the £1 and to canvas the farmers around Whitchurch Road, Hollybush and Green Lane to see if they were in favour of the scheme as they were convinced that the

Liverpool company would provide a more economical supply. In September, the RDC said they were prepared to adopt a water supply scheme, but only if they could get a grant that would cover 40% of the cost.

In 1935, an offer was considered of a supply of water from Major Peel by tapping into his private link to the Liverpool water main at Plâs-yn-Coed Gate, at a cost of £1,200. This was accepted by the parish council, but later the same year, two more schemes were considered costing £1,968 and £1,441. All the schemes were rejected on the grounds of excessive cost and limited service. An alternative was then put forward whereby the parish would provide its own supply by pumping water into a storage reservoir after proof of ample supplies had been given. Again, this was rejected.

In October 1937, the parish council met to discuss the Medical Officer of Health's report on the matter and the following resolution was passed:

> This council having thoroughly discussed the same concluded that their objections on the matter were now exhausted as the report simply confirmed the complaint made by the Council some few years ago.

The matter was then shelved and was not taken up again until after the Second World War.

In 1944, the RDC proposed to lay a four-inch water main alongside the highway from the Liverpool Corporation aqueduct at Bowen's Hall to the boundary of Bangor parish at Hollybush, passing through the parishes of Halghton, Willington, Hanmer and Worthenbury. The parish council was unanimously in favour of the plan, but the scheme does not appear to have materialised. But now, farmers such as H. Machin of Cloy Hall, L. Huxley of Elm Farm, Hollybush and Mrs J. Huxley of the Woodlands, Hollybush were pressing for an urgent supply of water. Selwyn Lowndes, the secretary of the Wrexham & East Denbighshire Water Company, wrote to say that it was then a good time to consider the scheme as a whole rather than just a supply the three properties as there was a possibility of a capital grant being obtainable under the Rural Water Supply Act 1944. His company proposed a new scheme, costing £3,349, and gave details of a payment plan which would provide a domestic supply only; special provision would have to be made for fire-fighting, etc. In accordance with this, pipes would only be laid to the village itself and objections were again raised that the provision of a grant could not be assumed.

The following year, when the cost of a four-inch mains extension from the parish boundary to Hollybush, Cottage Gorse on the Bangor to Wrexham road, and to Bryn Hovah on the Bangor to Overton road was quoted, the estimated cost was £5,279, making the total cost of the augmented scheme now £8,440. This was the fifth scheme submitted by the Wrexham Water Company, all of which were unacceptable on account of excessive cost and insufficient facility to service the whole parish and that it would bring serious financial anomalies and burdens on the ratepayers.

By 1948, most people had had enough and a letter was sent to the Minister of Health, with copies to the Welsh Board of Health, Flintshire County Council and the local MP, by John Dutton (of Abbeygate Cottage) and J. Norris (chairman and clerk of Bangor Parish Council) forcibly expressing their frustration over the whole question:

The condition under which the inhabitants have to provide water for drinking, cooking, ablutions and general use with the disposal of the liquid element after usage can be favourably compared with village life in any prehistoric age when no Ministry of Health existed. It is an insult to civilization that in the year 1948 Bangor-is-y-coed householders have to draw their water in open buckets from a common well and the river Dee and, at the same time, pay the levy charged for the privilege of water and public health service enjoyed by others. In the current rating 6.81 pence for water and sewerage, or just over 5% of the full rate, is the charge made for the privilege of carrying water in buckets, and living in stinks rising from lack of sewerage.

The village school had a pump over a well that has been put out of use, because the medical officer condemned its supply for drinking purposes. No wonder, it is within 18ft of the school's three ashen privies, and urine. Their present drinking supply has to be conveyed by modern methods, viz: in a churn, along with the village milk supply, from another well.

Letter from Bent's Brewery regarding contaminated well at the Royal Oak. 1947. [FRO RD/C/1/128]

Before the removal of the older children to a central school, they could regularly be seen carrying buckets of water from a pump 150 yards distance for drinking purposes.

There are 35 houses in the densest part of the village without a supply of any kind and those nearest the river use this for all purposes.

The parish council views this disgraceful state of affairs and the apparent unconcern of the higher authorities to their oft repeated applications for better living conditions of its electorate with the utmost concern and demands an immediate inquiry by an inspector of the Welsh Board of Health.

Further to their complaints they repeat their application for a public electricity supply to be brought to the village realising that this is a essential part of a future sewerage scheme for the village following immediately a water supply is given.

After another stalemate, the parish council must have conceded defeat and the Wrexham Water Company's offer was put to a public meeting and finally accepted. The charge to the consumer could either be based on the rateable value of the property or by meter. In August 1950, the county council approved the final scheme and work began almost immediately and by October 1951 the

THE PUBLIC HEALTH ACT, 1936
AND THE
LOCAL GOVERNMENT ACT, 1933

Parish of Bangor-is-y-coed

WHEREAS the Council of the Rural District of Overton propose to carry out works for the purpose of affording supplies of water in the parish of Bangor-is-y-coed, which parish is within the limits of supply of the Wrexham and East Denbighshire Water Company and the Council have made application under Section 116(2) of the Public Health Act, 1936, for the consent of the said Company to the affording of such supplies ;

AND WHEREAS the said Company have withheld such consent and the question as to whether or not consent has been unreasonably withheld has been referred to the Minister of Health ;

NOTICE IS HEREBY GIVEN that a public local Inquiry into the matter will be held and B. C. Wood, Esq., B.Sc., A.M.I.C.E., the Inspector appointed, will attend for the purpose of holding the Inquiry at The Assembly Rooms, Bangor-is-y-Coed, on Thursday, the 22nd day of September, 1949, at 10-30 o'clock in the Forenoon, and will then and there be prepared to receive the evidence of any persons interested in the matter of the said Inquiry.

GEOFFREY CRAWSHAY,

Chairman.

Welsh Board of Health,
5th September, 1949.

Notice of a public inquiry 1949. [FRO RD/C/1/129]

water main had reached to within 300 yards of Turn o' Dee cottages in Overton Road. By January 1952, the work was finished. The official scale of charges were:

a) Metered supplies: 2s per 1,000 gallons with a minimum charge of £2 p.a., plus meter rent of £1 p.a.
2) Fixed charge: private dwelling house 3s, based on the rateable value of a house with a minimum charge of £1 10s.
3) Cattle trough: £5 for the first and £2 15s for each additional one. The fixed charge for troughs would be waived when the field was ploughed and a written notice was given.
4) Churches and chapels: £1 p.a.
5) Garages, gardens and schools: £2 p.a.

By 1957, substantial parts of eight out of ten parishes in the Maelor were now served with a piped water supply. Overton had 212 habitable buildings of which 68 had no piped water supply and the rest were supplied from Bryn-y-Pys who had their own private arrangements with the Liverpool Water Company. In 1960, the RDC agreed to the acquisition of the Bryn-y-Pys water main in order to increase the supply to premises not at present served in Overton and to cover Knolton. Their water supply was assured when in the same year Liverpool began the undertaking to flood the Tryweryn valley by making a dam for an additional water supply.

So, after over fifty years of planning and counter planning, Bangor had finally moved into the modern age with a source of clean potable water available at the turn of a tap. This must have come as a great relief to the schoolchildren whose job it had been to fetch buckets of water from the river to fill the boiler for the weekly wash or for baths before they went to school in the morning.

Sewerage
In 1897, J.M.W. Smith of Wrexham wrote a report to the RDC on the problem of sewerage.

Bangor village contains mostly small tenements and these appear to be fully occupied and with the few houses of a larger class would number about sixty-five, the drainage area within the village proper being about 15 acres, throughout which no adequate means of drainage exist. As a consequence slops and other foul water accumulates in the channels and on the sides of the roadways, in many cases close upon the dwellings. This, together with the ill smelling stagnant sewage in the main ditch or conduit situated near to, and running parallel with, the Worthenbury Road, combine to form what can only be described as a most unwholesome nuisance highly dangerous to health.

There was no public system of sewerage. A number of houses had their own cesspits but many discharged their liquid waste to open channels lined with brick, which were unfitted to act as efficient sewers. This led to a stagnation of sewerage, particularly in Worthenbury Road where some of the channels and drains were inadequate and the smell was very offensive. Many were originally road drains.

He went on to recommend: 'that a precise and detailed house-to-house survey should be undertaken, as if the village had a severe epidemic they would not be able to cope' and suggested a proper outfall drain about 450 yards long be laid along the narrow field which contained the foul drain. It was proposed that two water-tight tanks should be constructed for these drains to be flushed which might be made to work automatically by having a flusher fixed in each. A gradient of 1 in 200 was possible along that part opposite Worthenbury Road and the flat part of the village would be 1 in 250 or 270 – which would, if properly laid, would make the drains self-cleaning. Also the sewerage could be removed by gravitation to a disposal tank situated on land below Graig meadows where it would be allowed to settle before being filtered and thence run over some land, which would complete its purification. When the river overflowed its banks in times of flood the system would be rendered useless, but would return to normal working when the water level subsided.

Mr Smith estimated that the cost of such a scheme would be in the order of £450 which would be inclusive of the laying of pipes, the provision of settling tanks and a filter, and inspection chambers and flushing tanks. To this figure would be added the cost of any necessary land purchase and the payment of way-leaves. Predictably, the Bangor ratepayers objected to the scheme and to any other that was suggested on the grounds of cost. Over the years the RDC and Bangor Parish Council made many attempts to do something about the drainage problem but, when each solution was put to a public meeting, an overwhelming majority voted against it because of the potential increase in the rates. Their main objection was that they, along with the rest of the inhabitants of Maelor, were already paying a rate for a non-existent water and sewerage system and did not think that they should have pay for a scheme which would result in an even higher rate. Similarly, residents of other Maelor parishes that had piped water did not think that they should pay a higher rate because of Bangor. The result was a stalemate.

In 1900, a scheme was devised for a drain-flushing system, with a chamber located near the old bridge and a pipe and hand-operated pump. Water was to be pumped on a daily basis from the river into the chamber which could then be released, via the flush valve, to provide a surge of water which would clear the main drain along High Street, but did not make much impression on the foul ditch in the Worthenbury road. The system was initially operated each day, but soon dwindled to twice a week. There is a plaque commemorating this innovation at the side of the Bangor War Memorial.

Nothing further appears to have been done and in 1938 the surveyor stated that the total length of open sewer alongside the Worthenbury road was approximately 212 yards and the estimated

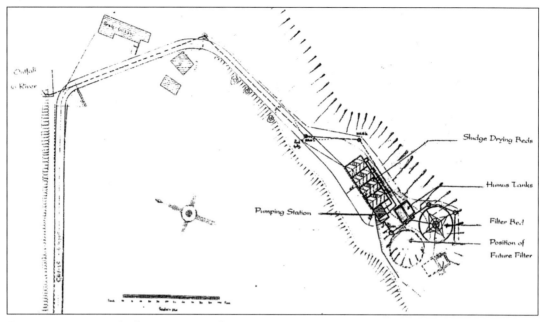

Bangor Sewerage Works. [FRO RD/C1/142]

cost of piping this and providing manholes was £105. The parish council agreed to the sewage scheme, but the clerk was asked to find out whether a grant was available from the Ministry of Health. Again nothing appears to have been done, or if it was it was not very effective, and the scheme was probably abandoned because of the war.

In October 1949, the chairman of Bangor Parish Council sent a letter to the RDC asking why no action had been taken on their letter of 24 December 1948 complaining of:

> The stench [which] arises from the foul water drain so badly that the residents have to resort to placing damp sacks over the grids when the stench becomes unbearable. The pump at the river Dee, placed there for the purpose of flushing the drains, is the responsibility of the RDC to maintain.

Finally, in 1955 the RDC commissioned a report by Ward, Ashcroft and Parkman of Liverpool, chartered civil engineers, for a scheme of sewerage and sewage disposal and estimates for its construction. It is unbelievable that this scheme was not commissioned until 1964. The treatment works which comprised of a primary sedimentation tank, a biological filter and a secondary sedimentation tank (capable of an initial capacity of 500 head at 30 gallons per day, space being provided for ultimate duplication in order to serve 1,000 head) cost approximately £15,000 (including £2,000 for rotary distributors, filter and sludge bed media). The contractors for the work were Clee Hill Ltd of Ludlow.

At the time of design, the population of Bangor village was 300, so that the initial design for a population of 500 provided for a 67% increase in the population. Since realisation of the scheme, extensive council and private development has caused the population to increase to 450, approaching the initial capacity of the works. Planning consent had been granted for a large development of a further eighty-two dwellings and consequently the council implemented the planned extension of the sewage treatment works to its ultimate capacity of 1,000 head in 1970. This extension involved the duplication of the primary sedimentation tank and percolating filter, together with a means of improving the efficiency of the existing sludge drying beds, which could not be extended owing to space restrictions. Provision was made for the ultimate replacement of the existing sewage ejector, which would become inadequate as the load upon the works approached capacity. Minor modifications were also carried out in order to increase the operating efficiency and standards of safety.

Refuse collection

For centuries the villagers had regarded the river as their own personal sewer and refuse disposal site. Any unwanted item was thrown into the water. Near the bridge was a communal ash pit where people could deposit the ash from their fires, but some people were throwing any waste into the pit. By the last quarter of the nineteenth century there were demands for everyone to stop fly-tipping and in April 1901 the parish council erected a notice banning the practice. The occupants of Kiln Cottages were suspected of fly-tipping in February 1903 when their houses were declared insanitary and the sanitary inspector had permission to install a tank for the collection of surface water and to supply earth closets.

Erection of a notice did not stop the problem and in 1923 these cottages were again requested to stop tipping down the bank and a letter was sent to Bent's Brewery asking for the provision of a suitable place for their tenants to dump refuse and night soil as the tip by the bridge was a nuisance. The reply came back that they already supplied a tip for the use of their tenants. In 1931, a nuisance was complained of along Graig Lane and a warning notice banning the practice was erected.

After continual complaints of tipping near the bridge and elsewhere the RDC and the parish council approached Major Peel to see if they could use the tip in Overton. Their request was granted and they then looked into the feasibility of buying an incinerator to reduce the quantity of rubbish that was carted to the tip but decided against buying one when the RDC agreed that the collection of refuse in the parish was their responsibility and a house to house survey was made to ascertain the amount of house refuse that need to be removed to the tip. They then advertised for a person to set up the service.

The tender of William Jones of School House, Bangor, for the collection and removal of home rubbish from Bangor to the Overton tip at 3s per motor load was accepted and notices were put up in Bangor to inform the residents that their rubbish would be collected every Friday. In August 1932 the refuse collection commenced but two years later Jones gave notice that he wished to terminate the contract. When no satisfactory tender had been obtained, he agreed to a new contract at the increased price of 5s per load. Bangor was gradually cleaning up its act and being dragged into the modern age.

Electricity

Bangor used to have six street lights which, according to the *Wrexham Advertiser*, were situated outside the Royal Oak, the Buck, the Red Lion, the Ship, the New Inn and the Star. But, when all but three of these inns had closed, the lamps vanished. It was not until 1896 that a parish meeting,

One of the 1902 lamps scan be seen on the corner of Winifred Cottage.

chaired by John Mort, was called to discuss a scheme for street lighting. The suggestion had been to illuminate the streets between Bangor and the station by means of oil lamps and a rough estimate of the cost was given of 20s to 28s for each lamp and the running cost would be 1½d for each lamp per night. The first meeting voted against the installation of street lighting.

A public subscription to raise money for such a scheme was initiated with the enthusiastic support of Mr Sutton of Althrey, Mr Parry and the rector. By 1900, the lamps had been ordered from the Orion Gas & Oil Lamp Company and by 1902 they had been erected just in time for the celebrations for the coronation of King Edward VII. To celebrate this dual occasion it was proposed that the young and old of the parish be given a tea with the balance of the money collected. It is not recorded how many lamps were bought, but it is not thought they extended as far as the station and may only have been erected in the High Street. The *Wrexham Advertiser* reported: 'The risks which are forever associated with the road turns in Bangor village will now be considerably minimised by the handsome coronation lamps which have been erected'. The turns which the reporter was referring to were probably those on the High Street/Whitchurch Road and the High Street/Overton Road junctions. One of these lamps on the corner of High Street and Whitchurch Road attached to the corner of Winifred Cottage, can be seen in an old photograph.

In 1902, the parish council complained that the lamps were put up without their authority and declined to have anything to do with them. In December 1904, a newspaper sarcastically reported 'Things are evidently looking up in Bangor: one of the street lamps was alight.' Things had not improved by 1907 when it was reported that:

> There is no sign of anything being done to light the public lights in Bangor. It seems quite a farce to vote a sum of money towards the purchase of lamps for the lighting of the village when, for three years, they should not be used. Why not raise a few shillings like they have done in Overton and light them during the winter months.

One or two houses had their own electricity generator (Deeside possibly being one) and there were private firms such as Gamble of Overton that erected power lines to supply electricity to the public but they were expensive and often unreliable. Municipal power stations were gradually being built and with the development of the National Grid in 1925/6, electricity became much cheaper and it was not long before the residents of Bangor began clamouring for a supply to be brought to the village.

In 1925, an approach was made by the North Wales & South Cheshire Electricity Board with regard to the development of electricity supplies in the district. General J.H. Lloyd attended a conference at Llandudno in 1930 on behalf of the RDC with instructions to call attention to the isolated position of the Maelor with respect to the supply of electricity and to enquire whether it was proposed to supply the area. A plan was submitted showing the position of above ground power lines in the area and asking if there were any local objections. There were none and work supposed to have commenced in early 1932. By 1937 however, for whatever reason, the company had still not covered the Maelor and the RDC's patience was at an end and they requested details of the cost of receiving a supply from North Wales Power Company in Rhostyllen. Once again, war intervened and plans were shelved.

Talks were restarted after the war but it was not until 1962 that Bangor finally received an electricity supply. After Councillor Tom Parry had attended a talk by a member of the Civic Trust on how villages could be improved, he had suggested that the electricity cables should be placed underground so that no 'concrete monstrosities' and overhead wires would spoil the appearance of Bangor. He was also responsible for the design of the street lamps in wrought iron with a blue mercury vapour that were at one time a feature of the village. The lamps in High Street were fixed to the walls of certain properties with wrought iron brackets, two of which can still be seen on the corner of the Buck Hotel and on the corner of The Croft (at the junction of High Street and Whitchurch Road). There is a third lamp at the rear of Althrey Lodge Cottage which the owners were able to purchase when it was offered for sale. There were several of the tall street lamps in the village until a few years ago, the last one being on the corner of Laurels Avenue. This has now been replaced with a modern, orange, neon light.

Alderman Tom Parry.

The coming of the electricity supply was marked by a small ceremony in a room in the Buck Hotel overlooking the High Street when Councillor W.A. Peters, vice chairman of Overton Rural District Council, in the presence of R.N. Pegg (sub-area manager, Manweb), symbolically switched on the supply. Everyone who had agreed to be connected could finally put away all the oil lamps, gas cylinders and gas mantles and look forward to a clean source of heat and light at the press of a switch.

One of Tom Parry's lamps attached to the Buck Hotel.

Many people had expressed dissatisfaction with the electricity supply provided by Mr Gamble and the dangerous state of the overhead wires. It was commonplace for there to be sudden breaks in supply, usually only lasting a few seconds. This still happens today and it has been suggested that when Manweb took over the supply they must have used some of the old power lines.

R.N. Pegg, sub-area manager Manweb, and others at the Buck Hotel when electricity was connected to Bangor.

19. Clubs, Societies and Events

Many clubs were started at various times in Bangor. The earliest known ones were the friendly societies that acted as benefit clubs in times of hardship. Members paid a small weekly sum to the club which enabled them to receive monetary assistance in times of ill health or death. They were first established in Britain during the eighteenth century, but their heyday was in the nineteenth and early twentieth centuries, before the establishment of the old age pension in 1909 and the National Health Service in 1948. The clubs usually held an annual club dinner that was the highlight of their year and was the scene of much singing, eating and drinking. Bangor's first such society was founded in 1762 and, under an Act of 1793, friendly societies had to be registered with the Quarter Sessions. On 20 December 1794 the local Quarter Sessions ordered

> ... that the Articles of Bangor Club be received and deposited among the records of this Court in pursuance of an Act of Parliament passed in the 23rd year of the reign of his present Majesty entitled 'An Act of Encouragement and Relief of Friendly Societies.

Similarly, on 18 July 1811, the Quarter Sessions ordered; 'that the Bangor Club Articles be filed amongst the records of this court pursuant to the statute in this case made.'

Any money that had accumulated in the club to the credit of an individual could be bequeathed in a will to a beneficiary. In the will of 1787, a gentleman named William Leicester stated,

> And whereas I am a member of a certain society established in Bangor and as such entitled both to the sum of 40 shillings towards the expenses of my funeral and to the sum of £7 to be paid to my executor.

The 1804 will of William Edwards, a yeoman, recorded:

> The money that may become due upon and after my decease as being a member of a society club held at Bangor I leave to Mrs Amy Downward.

For some reason this club lapsed and in 1857 an article in the *Wrexham Advertiser* stated that:

> ... this club was established 95 years ago and is being reinstated. There are 170 members with a total in property and funds of over £1000. A Committee met at the New Inn in Bangor on 31st December last when it was unanimously resolved to augment the payments to sick members and pensioners. The former from 6s per week to 8s per week and the latter will be raised from 1s 6d per week to 4s per week. Contributors pay 4d per week.

Many friendly societies were started by or in public houses and were affiliated to national organisations such as the Loyal Order of Buffaloes, the Ancient Order of Foresters and the Independent Order of Oddfellows, all of which rendered the same basic assistance to members in times of need. Some held public functions to raise money for good causes. In 1881, the Victoria Lodge of the Order of Oddfellows held their anniversary celebrations when shooting galleries were erected in the village and they did a roaring trade. At intervals during the day, the church bells were rung. At 11 a.m., the Whitchurch Rifle Volunteers Band arrived and headed a procession of the members which paraded around the village and visited the houses of several of the neighbouring gentry. They afterwards marched to church and an anniversary dinner was served at the Red Lion which was followed by the giving of loyal and patriotic toasts and the singing of numerous songs. At six o'clock in the evening, there was dancing on the green at the back of the inn.

Sometimes a sports day was held as in July 1899 when the Turn O'Dee Lodge of the Loyal Order of Ancient Shepherds marked their anniversary with a march to the church headed by the Farndon and Holt Brass Band. Sports competitions on the Groes field followed the church service, comprising foot and bicycle races, pony, Galloway and trotting handicaps. There was also dancing in the evening to the music of the Pen-y-Cae Brass Band.

Bangor Academicals

This group was first formed in 1975 as a five-a-side football team by some of the young male newcomers to the village who played in a league at the Plâs Madoc Leisure Centre. A name was needed for the team and Bangor Academicals was suggested which has stuck ever since. They also entered a team in the Wrexham Quiz League (playing at the Royal Oak) and played skittles at the Bickerton Poacher. Later, whilst maintaining an active interest in various sports, they enhanced their social experiences and, together with their wives, were involved in a diverse range of activities including wine safaris, theatre visits, a pantomime, an overseas visit and the celebration of an important date in history. In recent years, fundraising for charity has become an important annual feature of the Academicals' activities. The group currently has thirty-nine members, of whom twenty-four joined in the early years.

Athletics

There was no athletic club in the village but there was a family who had a formidable reputation as runners. The Jarvis family, particularly Jack Jarvis and his son Tom, had won so many races that the prizes were taking over the house. Tom and his trainer, Jim Tudor

Tom Jarvis with his trainer, Jim Tudor, and some of the prizes he won at sports events. [Sybil Hughes]

of Vernon Street, Wrexham, had their photograph taken with many of the prizes that he had won – cups, trays, teapots, coffee pots, clocks, vases, tankards, epergnes, cutlery and even an oil painting.

Bangor Bowling Club

Quite when the first bowling club was formed in Bangor is not known but it had been in existence for a number of years by the time of the 1935 annual general meeting. At that date the treasurer, Arthur Done of Royton, had been connected with the club for many years. It had its bowling green on the Groes field by kind permission of Mr Fearnall. The club was in a healthy position financially and membership stood at ninety-two, including ten boys aged between ten and fourteen in the juvenile section. During the previous twelve months the member-ship had increased by thirty-nine which no doubt reflected the input by various people in the improved facilities of the club, namely former police inspector Mercer who provided a pavilion, J. Suckley of Halghton who gave fencing material and William Austin Peters who provided floodlighting for the green.

Jack Jarvis, father of Tom. [Sybil Hughes]

In 1935, J. Taylor won the senior handicap competition beating H. Antley 21-6. E. Hoadley Smith of the Buck Inn gave the first prize, a set of woods, and the second prize, also a set of woods, was donated by R. Burney of Wigan, both prizes being presented by Arthur Done. The junior section handicap was won by Sidney Bennett who beat Ronny Stevenson by 21-20. Mrs William Griffiths of the post office and the Revd Baldock donating the prizes. The runners-up, J. Pritchard and N. Dunbabin, received prizes donated by George Dunbabin, a ship's officer, which were presented by the Revd Baldock. Mr Suckley won the Bowling Badge competition and the runner-up was Reg Betteley (both were from Halghton). The season ended with a hot-pot supper.

The following officers were elected for the 1936 season: Revd Baldock (chairman), Arthur Done (treasurer), Inspector Mercer (secretary), E.L. Mytton (assistant secretary). The captain was W. Jones and vice captain E. Price. The committee members were: William Griffiths, J. Suckley, J. Bartlem, W.A. Peters and Edward Jones. The following year William Griffiths (Post Office) was appointed secretary and the chairman was the new rector, the Revd R.H. Owen. This club seems to have been a casualty of the war.

A bowling club was again formed in 1989/90 on part of the sports field with the enthusiastic support of a dedicated number of residents. The first officers were Roy Binner (chairman), Alex Barkley (treasurer) and Ted Brett (secretary). A hedge has been planted around the green, seats placed and a shed erected. Now the club is planning to have its own toilet after years of sharing the gentlemens toilet in the sports pavilion.

Bangor Royal British Legion

In December 1932, at a well-attended meeting of ex-servicemen held in the institute it was unanimously decided to form a branch of the British Legion for Bangor and district. The following

Left: Eddie Robinson and his sister Hazel standard bearers for the Bangor branch of the Royal British Legion. Right: Women's branch of the Royal British Legion parading to a service in the church.

officers were appointed: Colonel Fenwick Palmer, Cefn Park (president); Revd F.R. Baldock (chairman); P. Humphreys (treasurer); T.B. Woodcock, Worthenbury (secretary). Over fifty members were enrolled and the branch served the districts of Bangor, Worthenbury, Isycoed, Overton, Penley, Pickhill and Cross Lanes.

Eddie Robinson became the standard bearer for the Bangor branch in 1953. He won many standard-bearing competitions, including the county championships for ten consecutive years, and the Wales area competition twice, but his proudest moment came in 1971 when he became the first ex-RAF serviceman, and the first Welshman, to win the Legion's national standard bearing competition. He was the production manager at Fullwood & Bland in Ellesmere. He died in 1975. His sister Hazel, representing the Bangor Women's section, became the first woman national standard bearer for Wales in 1968–9. The Bangor Branch folded in 2010, following the deaths of Ron Evanson and Harry Clegg and George Humphreys leaving the village.

Bangor Carnivals
Bangor has held carnivals at various times, the first to be mentioned in the *Wrexham Advertiser* being in 1930 when a rose queen was chosen by the children.

1930	Daisy Jarvis, crowned by Miss Pitcairn Campbell.
1931	Edna Berry, crowned by Mrs Ormrod.
1932	Lavinia Marian (Wendy) Mallalieu, aged nine, crowned Carnival Queen.
1933	Olive Humphreys, aged nine, sister of George (Dode) was not formally crowned as Mrs Mallalieu of the Buck Hotel, who was to have performed the ceremony, was indisposed.

In 1938, Olive Humphreys was chosen as Miss Bangor at a dance held in Overton Village Hall and then competed in the Miss Maelor competition. The following year, Violet Spoor was chosen as Miss Bangor but could not go on to compete for the 'Miss Maelor' title as she was away on holiday.

The Bangor carnival was revived in 1976 following a suggestion by the Cub Scouts' chairman, Dave White. This was held on the racecourse with a tug-of-war competition and an inter-pub river crossing contest 'Walk on Water' at Turn o'Dee. This latter contest involved teams attempting to walk on duck-boards or pallets strung in a line across the river. The boards sank beneath a person's weight when they stepped onto them,

Daisy Jarvis the first Rose Queen in 1930 with her attendants, Edna Berry (the second Rose Queen) on the right and Wendy Mallalieu (the third Rose Queen) in the centre.

throwing them off balance. The secret to success was to run across. There were also an up-river canoe race, a canoe polo match and raft races.

The following year, the committee became more ambitious and planned a Jubilee Festival Week to celebrate the Queen's Silver Jubilee with an event organised for each evening of the week leading up to the Saturday Carnival.

Saturday, 18 June	Festival Barn Dance
Sunday, 19 June	Raft Race, etc on the river
	Model Railway Exhibition

Mrs Ormrod having crowned Edna Berry as the second Rose Queen (on the left) and the retiring Rose Queen – Daisy Jarvis (with 'Rusty' Spoor in between them). The boy on the right (holding the crown on a cushion) is Leslie Griffiths.

Olive Humphreys, 'Miss Bangor' 1938.

Monday, 20 June	Model Railway Exhibition
Wednesday, 22 June	Crafts Exhibition
Thursday, 23 June	Jubilee Roadshow (Chester Theatrical group)
Friday, 24 June	Festival Prize Bingo
Saturday, 25 June	Carnival Day

The carnival day itself started early with Morris dancing competitions followed after a break by the street procession with a silver band, a fife and drum band, a fancy dress parade, dance troupes, vintage cars, floats and the Carnival Queen herself. Events on the field included: Morris dancing, rally cars (which were available to drive) an army display by the Army Cadets, model steam train rides, clay pigeon shooting and vintage engines and machinery. Roy Jones had the crown specially made at the British Aerospace factory in Broughton and Viv Lavis-Jones lined it with red velvet with a band of white faux fur. She also made a red velvet cloak and several of the sashes. A total of £685 was made from all the carnival week's events. To raise more money for the sports field the committee commissioned a ten-inch Royal Silver Jubilee plate in a limited edition of 480, made by Enoch Wedgwood and selling at £2.50. The sale of the plate raised £695 which boosted the carnival's proceeds to the magnificent sum of £1,380.

In the following years the events were extended over two weeks, with the last carnival in 1982 lasting for three weeks. In 1979, the carnival took place on the sports field for the first time. In 1983, when the chairman wished to step down from organising the events, no one was willing to take over although several people had said they would help on the day. The event was a victim of its own success and after seven very successful years the carnivals came to an end again. The Carnival Queens were:

1976 Karen Roberts, daughter of Joe and Freda Roberts of Abbot's Way

1977 Karen Bryan, daughter of Peter and Margaret Bryan of Sandown Road.

1978 Becky Walker, daughter of Dave and Sue Walker of Willow Court, crowned by Mike Smith, Wales Football Manager

1979 Sheila Done, daughter of Marian and Les Done of Bank Farm, crowned by Tony Brookshaw, driven by Les Newland in a red Ford Grenada, loaned by Kirby's of Wrexham, standing with her head through the sunroof waving

1980 Sian Hughes, daughter of Audrey and Phil Hughes of Chester Way, crowned by Eric Woodward

1981 Mary Jones, daughter of Dennis and Pam Jones of Abbot's Way, crowned by the mayor of Wrexham, Councillor John R. Thomas

1982 Carol Johnson, daughter of Cyril and Jane Johnson of Station Road, crowned by the mayor of Wrexham, Mrs Rose Nicholson

*Carnival Queens
(clockwise from top left):
1977 Karen Bryan.
1981 Mary Jones.
1980 Sian Hughes.
1979 Sheila Done.
1978 Becky Walker.
1982 Carol Johnson.*

Bangor Christy Minstrels

The first mention of the minstrels was in 1903 when they gave an entertainment at Overton in aid of local charities. In March 1908, they gave a performance in the Bangor schoolroom to a crowded audience. The curate, the Revd G.E. Browne, introduced the various items in the programme, with special praise and an encore given to a duet *You shan't come and play in our backyard* rendered by Bertie Young and Nelson Love. The programme included a comic song by Tom Antley, a song *If those lips could only speak* by David Poynton, banjo rhymes with William Griffiths and a comic duet by David Poynton and Dick Shone. One of their next performances was given at the church fete in June 1908 where in a field in front of the rectory, they gave an entertainment to a large audience. Many members of the church choir sang with the Christy Minstrels which was a very popular form of entertainment.

Bangor Cricket Club

The first mention of cricket in Bangor is in June 1882 when Archibald Peel of the Gerwyn, presented the scholars of Bangor Boy's School with new cricket bats, wickets and a ball. The Revd Frank Okell, an enthusiastic cricketer, helped to form a cricket club in May 1924 and was appointed captain with Walter Crosse as vice captain. Captain Barker was the honorary treasurer and Barry Nuttall the honorary secretary. Their opening match of the season was against Overton.

The following year the rector was again elected captain with Walter Crosse and P. Hodginson vice captains, Mr Pady of Pickhill was the secretary and William Griffiths of the post office was the treasurer. The club lost one of its keenest members when the rector left the village to become the vicar of Eccleston later in the year.

At the AGM in January 1926 the following officers were elected: president – Oliver Ormrod, secretary – H. Pady, captain W. Griffiths and Mr Stevenson; vice-captains H. Nuttall and Mr Hodgkinson. The committee was composed of the officers and the Revd Baldock and playing members of the team (George Jarvis and Archie Morris). The subscription was fixed at 2s 6d. Mr Stevenson offered a bat for the best batting average, which was accepted. Mr Hodgkinson was appointed groundsman and Mr Buck volunteered to assist him. It was decided to enlarge the playing pitch and Tuesdays and Thursdays were agreed upon as practice nights. The boys would practise on Wednesdays.

Bangor Cricket XI – Revd Okell in striped blazer c.1924. [Lady Bibby]

In March 1927, a dance was held in aid of the cricket club at the Assembly Rooms at which J. Lewis and Philip Humphreys were the MCs, assisted by W. Griffiths (treasurer), H. Pady (secretary), A. Morris, Mr Stevenson (captain) and Oliver Ormrod (president). Herbert Pady's band played for the dancing.

The last mention of the club was in June 1928 when it was reported in a Wrexham newspaper that:

> The vitality which until late years was connected with the Cricket Club has died out and this despite the efforts of Mr Pady, the energetic secretary, who has done all he could to keep the club active but received no backing. There is the chance of the boys taking the game up but something should be done, considering the expense and trouble taken in providing an excellent pitch. Bangor is one of the best sporting parishes in the district but it has never taken kindly to cricket.

The club must have been reformed post the Second World War as Jeremy Stratton remembers watching his father playing cricket with Tom Parry as wicket keeper. There was a wooden hut that served as a pavilion and a Mr Dutton owned a Dennis petrol-driven, water-cooled lawn mower and kept the pitch mown.

When the new sports field was opened, there was talk about having a cricket pitch on part of the site but the surface was never smooth enough for a serious game to be played.

Bangor Boy Scouts, Girl Guides, Wolf Cubs and Brownies

In February 1930, at a meeting convened by Mrs Barker, daughter of Oliver Ormrod of Pickhill Hall, it was decided to form a company of Girl Guides for Bangor and Pickhill but it is not known how long this remained active. In the 1970s the 1st Worthenbury Guides was formed under their captain, Mrs V. Underwood, with assistant guiders Mrs Hughes and Miss Knight and they met in the Old School, Worthenbury.

Bangor Cub Scouts who took part in a Wrexham Gang Show in 1984. [Photo by Geoff Wilding] Front row (R–L): Daniel Hunter, Richard John. Back row: Graham Pierce, Simon Gresty, Michael Nicholls, Daniel MacKreth.

In 1975, the Bangor-on-Dee Brownies were formed under guiders Val Stevenson and Denise Manchester and met in St Dunawd's School for many years where they planted two commemorative trees in the grounds. They won the Gwydir Jones Trophy on several occasions and took part in pack holidays. The Bangor Brownie pack joined 800 members from all over Clwyd in celebrating seventy years of the formation of Brownies in 1984 at a camp held in Prestatyn. Many members of the Bangor Brownies went on to join the Worthenbury Girl Guides.

Bangor had a Wolf Cub Pack in the 1950s and when Peter Furber moved to the village he became involved with them and they had the use of a Scout hut in Graig Lane. The Scout hut fell into disrepair when the Cubs disbanded and was taken down as it was deemed unsuitable for use due to its lack of sanitation.

In September 1975, the Cubs reformed with Dave White as chairman, John Griffiths as treasurer and Ken Manchester as the Group Scout Leader, helped by his wife Denise as Cub Scout Leader and assisted by Carolyn Chance as Assistant Cub Scout Leader.

The site of the old Scout hut was used for the occasional campfire cooking competition and games until eventually, when Mountfields estate was built in the 1990s, the site was sold to Gordon Mytton for a pumping station.

The Cubs competed very successfully in the Wrexham and District Swimming Gala, winning the annual Wrexham and District Cub Scout Swimming Gala Cup on several occasions and also took part in the Cub Scouts Football League with great enthusiasm.

Some members of the pack took part in the bi-annual Wrexham Scout Gang Show at the William Aston Hall in Wrexham and went on camping holidays to Cwm Penmachno. They also entered and won decorated float competitions in the Bangor carnivals, using Peter Furber's wagons – one year, using the Knights of the Round Table as the theme (set against a backdrop of a castle) or another year Space Travel, with the Cubs wearing silver space suits attached via umbilical cords to a silver rocket.

In 1998, Ken left the Cub Scout pack to become Clwyd County Area Commissioner for Scouting and successfully held the Scouting 2007 Centenary Camp on the Bangor Race Course that was attended by about 1100 Cub Scouts, Scouts and Leaders. Tony Grice took over as Cub Scout leader for Bangor and later went on to become Scout leader in Overton. Eventually, due to a lack of trained leaders, the Bangor Cubs Scout pack was disbanded.

Many of the older Cubs went on to join the Overton Scout troop and attended World Jamborees in countries as far away as Canada and Australia and still maintain the friendships which they made. In 2002, two ex-Bangor-on-Dee Cub Scouts, who became Queen's Scouts, were chosen to proudly carry the Welsh flag for the Colour Party at the Annual St George's Day parade in front of the Queen at Windsor Castle.

Bangor Football Club

The first mention of a Bangor football team and a football pitch is in an issue of the *Wrexham Advertizer* of March 1881 when Archibald Peel of the Gerwyn presented the scholars of Bangor Boys' School with a football, and Mr Fearnall of Royton kindly allowed a piece of land called the Groes to be used as a football pitch. Over the years, the youth of the village were allowed to use the field as a sports field with varying degrees of success. They played in competitions against other village teams and were ably supported by their friends who raised money on their behalf by organising various functions such as a dance held in the Assembly Rooms in April 1929 in aid of the football club run by the secretary, Fred Tibbott.

The Friendship Club

The Friendship Club was formed in April 1988 from the remaining members of the Senior Citizens Club that used to meet each month in the Community Centre until the centre was closed in 1981. Mrs Daphne Long was the chairman, Mrs Joan West took on the post of secretary and Mr Carr agreed to be treasurer for the first year, followed thereafter by Frank Davis. Daphne Long gave up the post of chairman after a couple of years and they did not appoint anyone else to that post. Joan West was secretary for eleven years, with Frank Davis as treasurer for eleven years. They ran the club with an average yearly membership of fifty-five, most of whom regularly attended the monthly meetings in the village hall. They had talks and demonstrations and held social events and the club was a great success. When Mrs West reached the age of eighty, she felt that it was time for someone else to take over the running of the club. At almost the same time Frank Davis suffered a stroke and unfortunately no one else was prepared to take on the organisation and the club folded in 1999. The money was divided between the members with each person receiving £20, and the balance in the account and the crockery was given to the village hall.

Bangor Gymnastic Club

In 1933, the Girls' Gymnasium Club was formed and a successful whist drive and dance was held in the Assembly Rooms to raise funds for equipment. The whist drive prizes were presented by Mrs Price (police station). The instructor was Ted Roberts of Bangor who had over twenty years experience in the army. By August, they were proficient enough to give their first display of gymnastics at the annual Harvest Festival. The club folded after war was declared.

Overton & Bangor Horticultural Society

This society was formed in 1865 and usually met in the grounds of Bryn-y-Pys. By 1874, Erbistock had joined and it became the Overton, Bangor and Erbistock Horticultural Society. Hugh Peel donated many of the cups and prizes for the various classes of fruit and vegetables for which there was keen competition amongst the residents of the villages. In the early years, the society held an annual hedge cutting competition which usually took place at Eyton House, the farm of Frank

Lloyd and in 1906 there were thirteen entrants. William Chesters and Joseph Matthews, both from Bangor, were placed third and fourth respectively and in the absence of Hugh Peel, the prizes were distributed by A.G.P. Child, the Bryn-y-Pys estate manager. The following year, the competition was won by William Chesters of Bangor and two other Bangor men took two out of the first four prizes. As several of the previous years' winners were deemed to be 'old hands' it had been decided to ban them from entering and the winner was the youngest of the entrants. The society ceased to function due to lack of support in 1931.

Bangor Isycoed & District Horticultural Society

This society had its origins in the Food Production Society formed by Edward Griffiths (gardener to Pitcairn Campbell at Deeside), Samuel Dunbabin and Joseph Spoor, with the aim of encouraging the growth of as much produce as possible for the needs of the parish during the First World War. After the war, in 1921, it became the Bangor & District Horticultural Society with Edward Griffiths as its secretary. Most of the shows were held on the Groes field by kind permission of Robert Fearnall. In 1931, when the Overton Flower Show had been abandoned through lack of support, Major Peel offered the cups to the Bangor Society as awards at their shows. In 1937, Mr Barlow resigned as secretary after twelve years in office and Harold Bellis was appointed in his place. The society was very successful with the various classes being keenly contested and the list of winners published in the Wrexham papers each year. In 1938, it was described as the Bangor Flower & Cheese show. The eighteenth and final show was held on 8 September 1939 after which the society became yet another casualty of the war.

Bangor Library

The library was established for the use of the inhabitants of the village and surrounding district in October 1879 by C.E. Thorneycroft of Bangor and Harold Lees of Pickhill Hall. To celebrate its inauguration they held a tea party at the Buck Inn. The library consisted of over 250 volumes of history, theology, biography and fiction. There were also a number of children's books. This library may have been originally accommodated in one of the schoolrooms but a year later a club and reading room was formally opened in 'a very suitable house in a central spot.' After an ample supper given by Mrs Lees to the members to inaugurate the opening of the club, Mr Lees was elected president for the ensuing year and a committee of management, consisting of five honorary members and five ordinary members, was appointed. James Hunt (junior) was elected secretary and Mr Webster, treasurer. The clubroom was well equipped with daily and weekly papers and monthly magazines. In December 1920, a new library was opened with a splendid selection of books thanks to Captain H. Harrison. Arrangements had been made for the selection of books for lending to be changed twice a year. Mrs Oliver Evans agreed to act as librarian. Some years later, after Johnnie Spoor had put up shelves, the library was moved into the village institute.

The Rifle Club

This was formed in August 1902 by a group of enthusiasts led by Mrs Ormrod of Pickhill Hall who produced the Rules of the British Rifle League, along with some ideas on the formation of rifle clubs. General Savage Mostyn read them over and discussed them with those present. Each member would pay 1s to be affiliated to the league and 6d to the Bangor club for working expenses, out of which a certain amount of ammunition would be allowed for competitions and practice. A number of members were enrolled and a committee formed consisting of Messrs Ratcliffe, Davies, Fitzjohn (all of Bangor), George Goderich and Richards (of Overton), A.A. Walker and T. Powell (of Marchwiel), W.T. Cheetham and K. Mackenzie (of Cross Lanes), Thomas Nunnerley and P. Jones (of Pickhill) and Peate of Eyton. Mrs Ormrod was appointed secretary and treasurer and Mr Lloyd Jones as assistant. Sergeant Major Edwards was appointed superintendent of shooting.

The question of a suitable 500-yard firing range was next on the agenda and possible sites were discussed. In the meantime Oliver Ormrod offered to make inquiries as to whether the old Endowed School could be had free or rented for a small sum, so that the club could practice indoors. The Morris tube, a kind of miniature rifle, was used in the army for indoor use and what was deemed to be good for the regular soldiers was thought to be good enough for Bangor. The making of proper targets would prevent any damage to the walls and the committee would look out for a suitable open-air range for the next season. This request to use the hall was turned down, but a temporary 100-yard site at the Graig was offered and accepted until a more suitable one could be found. To raise money for the newly-formed club it was decided to hire the Wrexham Pierrots Troupe to put on an entertainment in November.

The rifle club did not get off to a good start in their second match competition against the Overton club, losing by 431 points to 393. The teams were Overton: F. Barrett, E. Studley, J. Ralphs, John Jenkins, C. Vaughan, George Goderfen, Martindale and A. Stockton. Bangor: Sergeant Major Edwards, T. Owen, J. Boffey, E. Fitzjohn, C. Ratcliffe, Large, Young and S. Spoor. Unfortunately, Mrs Ormrod, who was one of the most enthusiastic member of the Bangor Club, had died twelve months after its formation. Miss Ormrod of Pickhill Hall volunteered to act as secretary of the club in place of her mother and began her duties by opening the club's new open-air range at Isycoed. The 1904 AGM was held at Pickhill Hall in April at which Oliver Ormrod presided and one of his first duties was to present Lord Kenyon's prizes for their prowess in shooting to Mr Barrett (junior) of Overton, Sergeant Major Edwards and Master Large of Bangor, Martindale of Penley and Mr Lloyd Jones of Marchwiel.

One of the first matches of the 1904 season was against Wrexham Rifle Club at which they scored 504 against their opponents 470. However, Wrexham had their revenge in an October return match when Bangor lost by fifteen points. In order to practise over the winter months the club was offered, and accepted, the use of a large room at the Kiln Inn, Cross Lanes, where they could practise using the Morris tube. They had a good attendance of members and they were anxious to keep practising as they had had an excellent second year, losing only two away matches by a very small margin.

To keep up the interest of members over the winter a series of inter-club matches were arranged with teams made up of seven men, each of whom was allowed seven shots. The first match took place in January 1905 when a team led by S. Clutton beat one led by H. Fowles by 198 to 174. They also had a match against a team representing the Wrexham Cycle Club which they won comfortably. In April, the club had a match against the 1st Vol. Battalion, Royal Welsh Fusiliers at which the shooting was really good from both teams with W. Thompson of Bangor achieving the highest possible score (every shot being a bull's eye) that helped Bangor to win by five points.

In March 1907, they had a match against Holt that was a cliff-hanger to the end with first one side holding the lead and then the other and by the time the last two men went down to fire, the score was a tie. The last Bangor man, the captain, then edged the club ahead by just two points. There was very good shooting from both sides as can be seen from the individual scores: Bangor – E. Lloyd Jones, 49; T. Ankers, 46; H. Fowles, 50; T.S. Clutton, 50; T. Jones, 47; E. Edwards, 49; H. Griffiths, 43; J. Lloyd Jones, 48; E. Brookfield, 48 – total 430. Holt – W. Lewis, 50; H. Pridding, 48; T. Love, 49; W. Capper, 48; R. Mullock, 48; J.C. Redrope, 48; E. Bellis, 47; H. Jones, 45; J. Green, 45 – total 428. No doubt emboldened by their first-class performance the club entered a competition held in Liverpool where they found that they were outclassed.

In February 1908, Bangor was at the top of the newly formed Wrexham & District Rifle League having defeated the Wrexham and Rhos teams. Later that month, they held what they hoped would be the first of an annual event, a dance, to the music of John Morris's Band. Sergeant Major Edwards and Reginald Parry shared the role of Master of Ceremonies. In 1909/10, they had a poor shooting season, losing the first three matches which culminated in a nail-biting match in December with a team from the Wynnstay & Ruabon Club when the lead varied by no more than three points throughout, ending with Bangor losing by just one point.

The Bangor Rifle Club continued until the outbreak of war. On the restoration of peace, Bangor did not reform and a letter, printed in the *Wrexham Gazette* from T. Roberts, of the Brymbo Institute Miniature Rifle Club asked whether the various flourishing clubs before the war: Wrexham Conservative Club, Wrexham Church House, Wynnstay & Ruabon, Brynteg, Brynmally and Broughton, could be revived as Brymbo was the only one still active.

Bangor Quoiting Club

This club was also formed in 1903 and presumably operated from one of the three public houses, the Royal Oak, the Buck or the Red Lion. The club started off well with their first match when they defeated a team from Overton by twenty points. In 1911, they played a visiting team from Ruabon against whom they were very evenly matched and towards the end there were only a couple of points separating them. When the last man came to throw the Ruabon team won by just three points. The Bangor team consisted of: P. Bartlem, 3; W. Dunbabin, 7; J. Poynton, 9; T. Brooks, 8; D. Bartlem, 9; H. Dunbabin, 5; E. Brooks, 8; J. Spoor, 9; I. Hughes, 9 – total 67. This club was also a casualty of the First World War and does not appear to have been reformed.

Bangor Sports Field

After the public meeting in May 1977 it was decided to set up the Sports Field Management Committee with its own trustees and bank account. The first management committee was appointed and comprised: H. Laughland (chairman); R. Neville (vice chairman); R. Jones (treasurer); P. Bryan (secretary). The Development Sub-Committee chairman was Gordon Mytton, the Fund-Raising Subcommittee chairman was Roy Jones and the Negotiation Sub-Committee chairman was H. Laughland. They were given £1,000 from the Village Hall and half the income from the lottery each year until such time as they were financially secure.

In 1979, the Sports Field Project was entered in the Clwyd Voluntary Services Council's Local Endeavour Competition and was awarded first place and it was also announced that it had been

Part of the playing field.

given a loan of £4,000 from the National Playing Fields Association to enable them to complete the next phase of the project. The carnival was able to use the field for the first time in June 1979 when £425 was raised for the Sports field fund.

Over the years the sports field has gone from strength to strength, with an enthusiastic committee which purchased an additional acre of land and undertook the draining of the field, the laying of an all-purpose playing surface, the making of the tennis courts, the erection of a pavilion with changing facilities, the provision of toilets and a kitchen, the laying out of a car-park and the construction of a bowling green.

Bangor Tennis Club

The first mention of a tennis club is in Wrexham newspaper of January 1930 when a whist drive and dance was held in Twiss's Assembly Rooms in aid of the club funds. The MC for the whist was Harry Nuttall and for the dancing P. Humphreys and J. Doran. In October 1934, a successful dance was held in the Assembly Rooms in aid of the tennis club of which Miss Gladys Twiss was secretary and Mrs Parry of Wrexham was treasurer. Tennis may have been played on the Groes up to the outbreak of war but nothing more is known of the club, although tennis may have continued on the rectory or Deeside tennis courts.

Bangor Women's Institute

The Bangor-on-Dee branch of the Federation of Women's Institutes was formed in 1929 with Mrs Gossage of Gerwyn Hall as the first president, followed in 1930 by Mrs Pitcairn Campbell of Deeside with George Humphreys' mother, Ethel Humphreys, as the treasurer and Mrs Violet Williams as secretary. The meetings were held each month in the schoolroom at the rear of the Presbyterian Chapel, with larger meetings in the Assembly Rooms until the village hall was available for hire in 1966. In those days, the rules were very strict and members had to attend several meetings before they were allowed to stand for election to the committee. A record was kept of the names of all those attending at each meeting and the proceedings of a meeting were recorded in a minute book that had to be sent to headquarters when full. The committee meetings

Members of Bangor Women's Institute on the group's 50th anniversary in 1979.

were held in the homes of the various committee members. Only the minute book of 1987–97 and an attendance register for 1974–91 now survive.

Monthly meetings took the form of debates, demonstrations, talks and lectures. A competition for a flower arrangement or a cake would also be held each month and recipes would be exchanged. Despite the WI's reputation for jam and cake making, many of the meetings took a more serious form with current topics being discussed and debates held. On the outbreak of war in 1939, a series of first aid classes were held in Bangor by the medical officer, Dr Caspar of Overton, and keep fit classes were organised with the sanction of the local education authority.

By 1976, Mrs Tingay was the president and in 1979, on a suggestion of Mrs Joan West, the committee had china trinket boxes made to commemorate the 50th Anniversary of the founding of the Bangor Branch. These were made by the Royal China Company in Stoke-on-Trent and were given in their presentation boxes to the members. Mrs Marjorie Bayliss of Graig Cottage took over from Mrs Joan West as treasurer in 1981. Mrs Iris Caughey of Laurels Avenue became the president in 1985.

The 60th anniversary was commemorated with a miniature dish decorated with a black and white drawing of Bangor Bridge and church tower and inscribed 'Bangor-on-Dee W.I. 1929–1989'. Many years before, a lady from Gronant had made a tapestry wall hanging, measuring about 20 feet x 30 feet, featuring some of the resolutions that had been passed by the National Women's Institute over the years, and which is, or was, on display in St Fagan's near Cardiff. With the success of this in mind, it was decided to contribute towards a wall hanging to commemorate the date of the founding of each branch of the Clwyd Flint Federation. Some of the members of the Bangor branch

Bangor Women's Institute's 60th anniversary.
L–R: Mrs Betteley, Mrs Baker and Mrs Huxley.

embroidered a section depicting the Bangor Bridge, church and racecourse.

When the affiliation fees to the Federation were increased to an unsustainable amount in 1997, the decision was made by the Bangor branch to resign from the parent body. The group was renamed the Bangor Ladies, since when the membership has increased slightly. Mrs Iris Caughey was still the president with Mrs Marjorie Bayliss serving as treasurer and Mrs Dot Mytton as secretary. Mrs Barbara Kneale of Raggs Hill became the secretary in 2000 and resigned in 2012 and in 2006 Mrs Caughey handed over the presidency to Mrs Sonia Capstick.

Officers of the WI presenting Sister Heather of the Renal Unit with a cheque for £100 collected at a coffee morning in 1991. L–R: Marian Done, secretary, Sister Heather Jones, Dorrie Cooke (President) and Marjorie Bayliss (Treasurer).

Young Wives

Formed on 20 January 1972, the first officers were: Mrs Julie Hutchings (chairman), Mrs Diane Rowles (secretary) and Mrs Catherine Firth (treasurer). They initially agreed to meet twice a month. By the second anniversary they had seventy-five paid up members and the group has proved to be very successful and is still functioning today.

Youth Club

In 1974, after pressure from families with young children, it was decided to set up a youth club in Bangor and arrangements were made to call a special public meeting with John James, Deputy Youth and Community Officer. This resulted in the formation of the Youth Club management committee and the appointment of a paid Youth Club leader and the first meeting was held in September 1974. The club was very successful for the first few years, but interest fluctuated and when financial support from Wrexham Council was withdrawn the club folded. It has restarted and folded two or three times since with varying degrees of success.

20. Employment

Most job opportunities in Bangor parish were related to farming and many men were farm labourers and the women were employed in dairy work. Still more were employed in domestic and private service at the many large residences such as Emral Hall, Althrey Hall, Pickhill Hall and Plâs Fron, employing men as coachmen –such as in 1891, Alfred Checkett of the Lodge, Bangor or Henry Bursey of Cross Lanes in 1900. By 1913, when Henry's twins were baptised he was described as a motor driver. Men like Edward Griffiths of Deeside Cottage, Bangor were employed as gardeners. There were also service workers in each community, such as blacksmiths, wheelwrights, basket makers, saddlers and other mainly rural crafts. Then there were those employers that provided less traditional work such as the Great Western Railway on the Wrexham to Ellesmere railway line, and the General Post Office in the form of mail collection and deliveries, construction and maintenance linesmen of the embryonic communications network. The local highways authority employed roadmen to keep the verges and metal roads clean and tidy, and a roving gang filled and repaired potholes and occasionally resurfaced a section.

Cadbury's Factory

In the 1937–8, a very significant event took place in the area which was to affect employment prospects and local prosperity. The industrial age finally reached the south-eastern rural area of Denbighshire and the Maelor area of Flintshire when Cadbury Brothers of Bournville, Birmingham decided to build their third 'milk factory' (or creamery) in the parish of Bangor to supplement the output of two previously established units operating at Frampton and Knighton. The new factory was to change job prospects at a stroke. Cadbury's had a good reputation as a caring and forward-looking employer and it is not surprising that employment at 'the factory' became a prime ambition for many.

The company had gained a global reputation for the excellence of their chocolate, in particular Cadbury's Dairy Milk chocolate. The purpose of a milk factory was to utilise local milk supplies in an area of twenty miles radius of the factory and prepare the basic ingredients, mix them together before the final stages of blending, moulding and packaging which took place at other sites. The company purchased a property, Twll Farm in Pickhill Lane, Cross Lanes and began building a factory on one of the fields, adjacent to the railway, in August 1937 with a planned start date for production 1 May 1938.

A well-known local company, John Hughes, was awarded the contract to build the factory and, as they employed local men, were a popular choice. The principal of the company at that time was George Lockhart Wood of Maes-y-Nant, Cross Lanes (now the Cross Lanes Hotel). George Wood suffered from deafness but was a very competent woodworker and who personally carried out a tremendous amount of work for the church in Bangor, the mission in Cross Lanes as well as the building and fitting out of the church in Eyton. Whitalls of Birmingham worked on the boiler house necessary to contain four Lancashire boilers to generate steam used in the processing as well as drive two Bellis and Moreom generators which provided 200v DC electricity supply to the works. P.C. Richardson provided the steeplejacks to build

The Cadbury's creamery at Pickhill.

the 150 feet-high brick chimney, which was a very prominent landmark for many miles around until it became superfluous to requirements in the 1970s. The plant was fully tested on 28 April 1938, using water as a substitute for milk, and, well ahead of schedule, the plant was fully commissioned on 1 May 1938, processing a batch of 3,000 gallons of local milk. In the 'high tech' society we are now accustomed to in the twenty-first century, it might be considered reckless to utilise a green field site for a very efficient production unit in such a short gestation period, especially as there was no electricity supply in the area and lifting aids available would have been rather archaic. However, the fact that it was accomplished must be viewed as a testimony to the honourable business ethics of the time and the workers pride in their skills.

It was necessary for Cadbury's to engage some key workers who had gained experience in their other factories in order to ensure a smooth start, and these immigrant families were welcomed and quickly settled into the local schools and communities. Most of them must have liked the district as their descendants are still in the area, the family names Goulding, Kent and Harper coming immediately to mind.

The outbreak of the Second World War led to an unexpected expansion of the Cadbury factory as some of their buildings at Bournville were requisitioned by the Ministry of Works to be used for war production and, in view of the effect of air raids in the Midlands, it was sensible to disperse plant to less vulnerable sites. During 1942, work began on the construction of a new building and the conversion of one bay of the sugar and cocoa bean warehouse to house moulding and packaging machinery for the No Mould Department.

The majority of the new labour force was female, much to the delight of the young country lads who, with restricted travel facilities in wartime, had little opportunity to meet the opposite sex. They had not expected to work with such a bevy of beauties as had landed in their laps. Young ladies were recruited from the local villages and those from Overton, Eyton, Worthenbury and further afield cycled to work, used the railway to the newly-built Pickhill Halt or used a special bus service from Wrexham. The mixed workforce proved to be very popular and many long-lasting friendships and marriages resulted which have endured to the third generation. Whoever the recruitment teams were, they showed good taste.

The finished products from the No Mould Department were wrapped bars of ration chocolate, which was very dark chocolate with some of the sugar content reduced and replaced by salt. The company was no longer allowed to use milk in its chocolate but continued to receive milk that was then redistributed for human consumption throughout the north-west region.

Cadbury continued to operate the factory until 1971 when, as Cadbury Schweppes, they stopped production. After remaining empty for two years, it was taken over by the Milk Marketing Board for the production of dairy products. Dairy Crest then operated the site and the buildings were significantly changed. One block, which is still recognisable, is the original office block, which now carries a memorial tablet to honour those former employees who gave their lives in the armed forces between 1939 and 1945 in defence of the freedom we have today. In 2011, Dairy Crest announced that it was closing the factory and everyone waited to see who would take over the site. Cassidy & Ashton of Station Road in Chester gave a presentation in the village hall later in the year where they outlined their plans to adapt the buildings as a cheese-packaging factory operated by First Milk and everyone breathed a sigh of relief.

Blacksmiths

There were four blacksmiths' premises in Bangor at various times – the one with big arched doors, next to the hairdressers in Whitchurch Road, is the one that most people know and recognise.

For over two hundred years, members of the Clay family were the blacksmiths and their name probably derives from Cloy, Clay, Cley, Claie or Clais as it has been variously spelt. They were members of a wide-spread family of blacksmiths operating in the Maelor and surrounding areas. In 1731, the death of blacksmith Richard Clay was recorded in the Bangor burial register in February. Luke Clay was recorded in the parish registers as being the blacksmith at Halghton smithy in 1711 and his father was probably the Luke Clay of 'Eaton Isafe' [sic] who had his children baptised between 1675 and 1686. John Clay was the local blacksmith when he and his wife, Mary, had a son, also named John, in 1785. John (junior) had succeeded his father by 1820 when he gave evidence for Benjamin Harris the schoolmaster when he appeared at the Quarter Sessions. In 1851, the blacksmith was still John Clay and his wife Elizabeth (born in Worthenbury), both aged sixty-five. Living with them were four sons, a daughter and a thirteen-year-old grandson. By 1871, William Clay (aged forty-three) had taken over the smithy with his wife Harriet, brother Thomas, and his sons, John, William and daughter Elizabeth. In 1881, the blacksmith was still William Clay and he and his wife were living at the smithy with their daughter, Elizabeth, a letter carrier, and granddaughter, Hester. On the death of William in about 1886, Lizzie Clay moved with her mother to live nearby in what has since become known as Clay's Cottage. She died in 1932.

Joseph Spoor took over the business and eventually bought it in 1901. He had been born at Nº 8 Court, off Kitchen Street, Liverpool, in August 1861, the son of Joseph and Ann (née Brawn) Spoor. His father was employed as a 'labourer in a foundry' but by 1884 when his son married, he was described as a blacksmith. In 1881, Joseph Spoor (junior) was aged nineteen and employed by Joseph Kilvert at Coed-yr-Allt in Ellesmere as one of two blacksmith's assistants. Joseph would

Right: The Spoor family outside the smithy in Whitchurch Road.

Below: Joseph Spoor (right) and his son, John (left), with a group of stable hands.

have just completed his seven-year apprenticeship, probably with the same blacksmith. He must have moved to Bangor in the early 1880s as he met and married his wife Hannah, daughter of Edward Jones, cattle dealer, in Bangor in June 1884. On the marriage certificate the witness was a Richard Kilvertson who is thought to be the son of the blacksmith in Ellesmere. Joseph and Hannah's daughter, Christiana, was born in Liverpool the following year but by the time their son Joseph was born three years later the family were back in Bangor. They had another two children, John and Aaron. Joseph Spoor bought the smithy, the shop and the adjoining cottage from William Davies in 1901 for £500 when it was described as 'a dwelling house, shop, warehouse, malt kiln and garden.' In June 1918, Spoor hit the local headlines when he had a miraculous escape during a storm when lightening entered the home and tore the paper from the bedroom walls, descended to the rooms below and smashed a grandfather clock before entering a cupboard, smashing some of the contents. The pattern of one of the plates in the cupboard was driven from the face to the back so that the face of the plate was plain and the back was decorated. Joseph, who had been sitting by a window reading, had just made a move in the direction of the fireplace to light his pipe when the bolt struck the house and was unharmed. Mrs Spoor was fortunately visiting her daughter-in-law at the time.

When Joseph Spoor died in 1929, his second son John, or Jack as he was known, took over as the village blacksmith. The smithy had a good reputation among the

The Smithy in Whitchurch Road, 2013. The right-hand part of the rendered cottage ('Maralomeda') was a carpenter's shop before becoming a private dwelling.

racing fraternity and many owners came from miles around to have their horses shod with special lightweight shoes before their races. The family also ran a café in a room at the rear of the smithy and catered for functions such as the wedding of their daughter, Ruby, in 1948. A fire caused £2,000 worth of damage to the café in the early hours of the next morning, Easter Sunday, but they managed to save all the furniture, although a large quantity of crockery, kitchen equipment and wedding gifts were destroyed. The fire was prevented from spreading to the attached cottage and to the terrace of three cottages next door by the prompt attention of the Wrexham Fire Brigade. Another wedding reception, that of Miss Fanny Leach of Bangor, was to have taken place on Easter Monday, but their wedding breakfast was destroyed in the fire and the reception had to be held in the village Institute with family and friends rallying around with last minute baking and collection of food.

Lilac Cottage, Station Road. The left-hand side of this building was for a short time the smithy before it became a wheelwright's shop.

There was a second smithy attached to a cottage at the beginning of Station Road which was pulled down in 1950 for the first of the Abbot's Way council houses, occupied by the Evanson and Taylor families. In 1851, the blacksmith was Thomas Griffiths (aged forty-five) who, with his wife Martha, had six children – four boys and two girls. Thomas was still there in 1891. There was a Richard Griffiths listed as a blacksmith in an 1881 trade directory who may have been his son.

When Joseph Spoor first came to Bangor, he probably worked for the Griffiths family and when they gave up the smithy, he took over the tenancy and continued to run it together with the one in Whitchurch Road for a few years. There is a sale brochure of 1908 listing a freehold cottage garden and outbuildings 'occupied by Mrs Ann Davies, together with the old smithy and piece of land occupied by Mr Spoor, blacksmith, and being the footage to land belonging to Bent's Brewery Co. Ltd.' There is a photograph, that is thought to have been taken outside the smithy, in which Vera Roberts (née Spoor) identified her grandfather shoeing a horse.

Joseph Spoor (on the right, shoeing a horse) with possibly two sons in the photograph. A local stableboy with a pony stands in the doorway. One of the posters advertises 'Rural Sports & Dancing' at Bangor.

The third blacksmith shop was at the end of a terrace in Whitchurch Road, now converted into one property called Maralomeda that had been a smithy when John Jones lived there some time prior to 1812, but had become a wheel-wright's shop when it was rented by John Munford and then sold to him in 1814.

The fourth blacksmith's shop was at the side of Lilac Cottage in Station Road and is marked as such on the 1870 OS map. It later became a wheelwright's shop when it was occupied by a Mr Hodnett.

The Plassey

The present house was built in the nineteenth century on a fifteenth- or sixteenth-century moated site which may have had its origins in mediaeval times. The farm was bought at the beginning of the twentieth century by Francis (Frank) Lloyd, an auctioneer, who lived and farmed at Eyton House at the Plassey end of the Two-Mile Straight. He had bought an established auctioneer's business in 1890 and built up his main business, monthly horse sales which were held at Eagles Meadow at the bottom of the Wynnstay Hotel yard in Wrexham, into a thriving concern. In 1891, he sold the livestock and stock of grain of the Plassey on behalf of David Jones who was selling up prior to a visit to South Africa, and not long after this bought the property. He had the house altered and extended and established a dairy herd and a model dairy. His wife, Frances (Fanny), was said to have refused to live in the Plassey and remained resident in Eyton House. Frank Lloyd once described the road outside Eyton House as 'Infirmary Corner' because of all the accidents that occurred there. He lived at the Plassey and at Eyton House until his death, aged seventy-four, in 1926. He and his wife had eleven children – seven sons and four daughters and all but one son, Captain Stewart Lloyd, Royal Welsh Fusiliers, survived him. The Lloyd family continued to farm at the Plassey until 1955 when they sold the estate.

In 1960 the Brookshaw family (of horse-racing fame) bought the Plassey and farmed it until 1968 when they sold the herd to a neighbouring farmer who had lost his cattle to foot and mouth disease. The decision was taken to turn the now redundant model dairy into a restaurant (with the stalls intact) and the stables into a coffee shop. The other buildings were converted into individual shops such as fashion boutiques, a picture farming business, a hair salon, craft shops and a smithy. Now, together with an 9-hole golf course, a lake, a garden centre as well as a caravan site, the business employs a number of local people and looks set to continue doing so for many years to come.

21. Skeletons and the Supernatural

A skull

In 1978, a skull was found in the garden of Millstone Cottage, Whitchurch Road by the author when she was digging a place for a coal bunker in the bank at the back of her property. Having removed an old, field hedge the skull was found about two feet below. It was very yellow in colour, well preserved with the upper teeth in place, but minus the lower jaw. Not quite knowing what to do with it, but absolutely sure that the bin was not the right place, the police were contacted. Two officers and a police photographer then appeared and asked whether anyone from the locality had been reported missing in the last fifty years. The skull was sent to the north Wales coroner for examination and was later declared to be 'ancient' and offered back to the finder. The offer was declined and the coroner said that he would like to retain it to do further tests. Nothing more was heard about the skull and its whereabouts are now unknown.

George Bursey, the chairman of the Wrexham Smallbore Rifle Club heard of the find and remarked that as a young lad he remembered playing football in Bangor with some pals using two skulls that they had found as balls. He could not remember where they were actually found nor by whom. He said he knew that one skull ended up in the river but did not know what happened to the other one. This would have been about 1910/12 as he was aged seventy-eight at the time of relating the tale. He was born at Cross Lanes in February 1900 to Henry Bursey, a coach driver, and Annie Uren Bursey, and died in October 1999, having just failed to reach his father's age of 100.

Two skeletons

When the village hall was extended for the second time in 1986 the contractors found two skeletons whilst digging a trench for the footings. The side of the trench fell in revealing the bones. The coroner was notified and visited the site. He estimated the bones to be lying at a depth of approximately five feet (judged by the fact that when standing in the trench, he could not see over the top and he was six feet tall) and to be in a very good state of preservation having been buried in the clay layer which runs under the whole of Bangor. He stated that the bones belonged to more than two skeletons and was of the opinion that the church graveyard must at one time have extended beyond the present site as the skeletons had the appearance of having been decently and properly buried. The coroner consulted with the then incumbent, the Revd Philip Owen, and although he suggested that the side of the trench be made good and the bones left where they were found, it was decided to apply for a faculty to re-inter them in the churchyard. No entry was made in the burial register and no stone or marker was placed over the grave. The skeletons were declared to be 'ancient' as they were deemed to be more than 200 years old.

Ghostly appearances

There have been four reports of ghostly apparitions in Bangor.

The Puritan: Mr and Mrs Gorman bought Tŷ Graig on Station Road from Bob and Margaret Evers and tell an intriguing story of a resident ghost. One day, Mrs Gorman had dozed off in a chair and awakened to see the figure of a man sitting in the corner. She described him as a puritan, but could not say why she thought that except that he was dressed in black. This happened again in similar circumstances. She did not mention it to her husband as she knew that he would only say that she was a crazy woman. However, one day her husband said in passing 'I wish that man in the chair would go away.' He had seen the same apparition, again just after he had awoken from a cat-nap. They did not mention it to anyone and were particularly careful not to discuss it in front of their grandchild when she was staying with them. One day the little girl remarked that the old man in the chair had said that she had a very pretty mother. They made enquiries with Bob and Margaret Evers to find out if they had ever seen a ghost or any other unexplained 'happenings' in the years they had lived at Tŷ Graig, but were told that they had not.

The Monk: Tracy Adams of the middle shop tells of another unexplained ghostly sighting. She and her husband, Dave, had ordered a curry from a takeaway and the man who delivered it to their house in Church Avenue asked where the monk was, as the previous times he had called he had seen him in the churchyard. On Dave remarking that there was no monk, but that there had once been a monastery in Bangor many years ago, the man turned quite white and said that he was not coming again and could not get away quickly enough. He never came delivering again, someone else was sent.

The Schoolmaster: Terry and Pam Davies have had experiences of strange happenings at the schoolhouse. They were aware of another person in the room, perhaps sitting on the bed; of a shadow reflected momentarily in a wardrobe door; of a circle of bright, blue light moving quickly from a corner around the room to the door; of a feeling that someone was wanting to pass on the stairs. When a son's school friend stayed the night he was unable to sleep in the bedroom and took his duvet and slept in the lounge. Sometimes, as well as the feeling of a presence in the room, they experienced the smell of cheap Woodbine cigarettes. They say that they never felt that it was a malevolent ghost and never felt threatened and have grown quite used to its occasional appearances.

The Gardener: When PC Gary Bentley was living in the police house, Westgate House, in Overton Road in the 1970s he told of having seen a ghost standing by the well in the garden.

22. Old Houses

Although Bangor would have appeared quite different one hundred and fifty years ago it would have been recognisable, as the main road layout has not changed. But, during the twentieth century many of the old houses and cottages have been either demolished or altered and many new properties have been built on what were once orchards and fields. The following is a short tour of the village, with details of the buildings that have been demolished or altered, commencing at the bottom of Bryn Hovah hill. The 1840 tithe map property reference number, where known, is shown in squared brackets.

Overton Road

On the left hand side is **Althrey Woodhouse [1097]** owned in 1840 by Croxon Jones & Company (John Croxon, Richard Jones Croxon, James Thomas Jones and Thomas Longuville Longuville, solicitors of Oswestry). Edward Pearson occupied it from about 1832 until at least 1855 when it was bought by the Peel estate and rented in 1868 to Captain Francis Mostyn Owen. In about 1887, the six-year-old Lord Berners came here from Arley Hall to stay with his mother for four years until he was sent away to school. In later life, he wrote a book about his early childhood in which he mentioned his stay at Bangor.

In the early twentieth century, Stanley Harrison a racehorse trainer occupied the house and made great use of its stabling. His headman was Michael Daly, father of Dympna Daly. In 1936, Colonel S.V. Misa and his wife rented Woodhouse after he had retired from the army. He rejoined the army in 1939 and served as adjutant of the 8th (Denbighshire) Bn, Royal Welch Fusiliers, before

Althrey Woodhouse before renovation.

Althrey Woodhouse after renovation.

The old barn at Althrey Woodhouse.

being given the command of 9th (Caernarvonshire & Anglesey) Battalion, Royal Welch Fusiliers in 1942. He took up farming in 1949 when he bought Trench Farm, increasing the size to 200 acres and served on a number of agricultural committees. In addition, he was active in local affairs serving as a member of Flintshire County Council and later Clwyd County Council. He acted as stable manager of the racecourse for fifty years retiring in 1976 to live at Trench Farm.

The racehorse trainer Frank Lloyd and his wife, Thelma, bought the property from the Peel estate and started a series of renovations to the house and in particular to the old half-timbered barn before retiring to Bryn Hovah. Their daughter and her husband have now taken over its care and have further renovated the property. The date of an earlier house built on the site is unknown but, judging by the half-timbered barn, it must have been one built at the very latest by the seventeenth century. The present house was built above the cellars of a previous building.

Althrey Hall [1066] at the bottom of the long driveway is a fifteenth- or early sixteenth-century half-timbered Grade I-listed building. In 1840, it was owned by the Hon. Robert Henry Clive and was tenanted by Ester Barker. In 1851 the tenants were James and Margaret Barker. The hall must have been subdivided into at least two buildings as the Sutton family were the occupants from at least 1853, when Ambrose Sutton died, until his grandson, John Remer Sutton, died in 1943 and Remer Sutton and his brother Ambrose took over. Captain the Hon. A. Tyrwhitt, RN (who commanded HMS *Nile*) and his wife lived in a wing of the hall until 1903, then Colonel (later Brigadier-General) R.H.W. Dunn resided there until his death in 1917.

In 1986, Tom Smith bought the hall and began a comprehensive programme of restoration. A Victorian wing was taken down revealing a classic 'H-framed' medieval hall, with the porch, gallery and chapel added at a slightly later date. During the process of restoration, six post-holes were discovered under the floor in the main hall and these and other evidence indicated that there

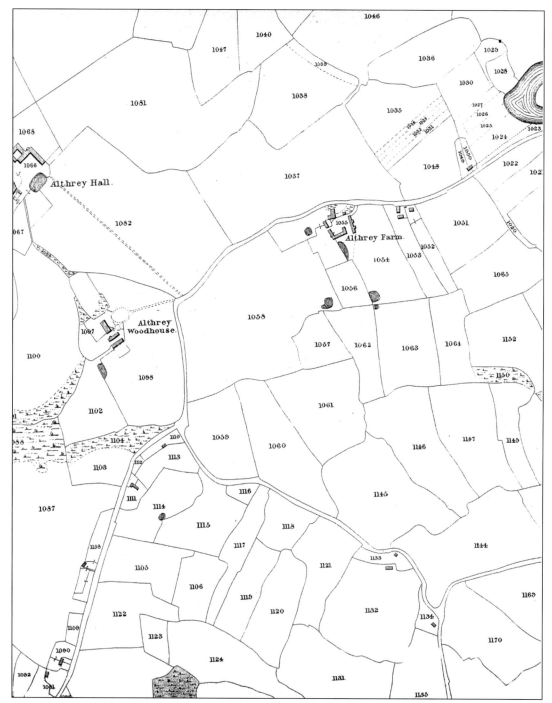

1840 Tithe Map of Bangor Isycoed (part 1).

had been at least two earlier buildings on the site. Archaeologists who swarmed all over the house and land said it was possible that it could have been the site of the monastery, particularly as the hall was built on slightly higher ground and never flooded. When a large Victorian chimney on the back of the hall was lit it smoked badly and on investigating the cause, it was found to be blocked and they discovered fifty-seven salmon fish-hooks inside. It had been used for the smoking of the Dee salmon. Smith demolished the chimney and replaced it with one more in keeping with the period of the hall. The kitchen was at the rear and to the left of the building, and when they dug down below the hearth they found the remains of earlier hearths. Each of the four main ground floor rooms had a staircase leading to a bedroom on the first floor with no connection to any other room. The maximum height of the doors was five feet four inches, giving an indication of the height of people in earlier times. When the renovations were underway and the seventeenth-century wood panelling was removed from a first floor room for conservation, paintings were discovered on two of the walls. One was of a couple in sixteenth-century attire thought to depict a descendant of Owen Glyndŵr's standard bearer. They have been identified by the Archaeological Conservation Unit of Cardiff University College as the son of the owner, Ellis ap Richard and his wife Jane Hanmer, a member of the Hanmer family, and may been painted about 1530. Some of their thirteen children appear to have scratched their names on the walls – sixteenth-century graffiti! The murals were in a very fragile state, being painted on a thin plaster lime-wash on top of wattle and daub, and the layers were beginning to separate. They required very careful restoration using modern solvents and acrylic resin before being recorded and then protected behind the panelling once again.

The house has a chapel that was a later addition at a time when Catholics were being persecuted. It leads off one of the bedrooms by means of a door fitted into the Tudor panelling. The chapel was said by Mrs Sunter Harrison to have had an escape route above the entrance door by which it was possible to cross from one end of the building to the other. This was blocked up by the electricians just prior to her visit in the early 1960s. The chapel has a painted ceiling that depicts a faded Celestial City with the letters 'I.H.S.' and 'N.R.I.' at each end of the painting. She thought that it could be the handiwork of Margaret Trevor who came to Althrey to reside with her cousins, the Ellises, in the seventeenth Century.

The hall now looks magnificent once again and, under the terms of the grant, Tom Smith allowed the public to view the house on completion of the work, but it was not long before he moved on to his next project. In 1998, he sold Althrey Hall to Mr and Mrs Clark and bought The Bryn farmhouse, part of the Gredington estate, which also required restoration. He has since moved on, via Adrefelin and Quinta Cottage in Overton, to his present project restoring a half-timbered property in Denbigh.

Althrey Farm [1055] was owned by the Hon. Robert Henry Clive (son of the first earl of Powis) in 1840 when Mr John Smith was the tenant. When Smith died in 1869, John Mort rented the farm until his death in 1909, aged eighty-four, when the tenancy was taken over by his cousin Joseph Cross Mort. The farm was later sold to the Bryn-y-Pys estate. It was latterly owned by Neville Jones who sold it to Gordon Mytton. Having developed the outbuildings for housing, Mytton sold the farmhouse and it is now undergoing restoration by a couple who are relocating there with their business from Holt.

Tom Smith in 2012.

Interior of Althrey Hall.

Althrey Cottage [1052] bought by Gordon Mytton and rebuilt in the 1980s. There is some confusion with Althrey Lodge that used to bear the same name. It is thought that this property was sold in 1900 when it was bought by John Mort of Althrey Farm.

Turn O'Dee Cottages were owned in 1840 by Mrs Anne Boodle. N$^{o.}$ 1 [1049] was rented to Edward Allman and N$^{o.}$ 2 (now called Afon Cottage) was rented to Edward Fennah. The cottages were bought by George Cambell some time prior to 1850 to add to his steadily growing portfolio of

George Cambell's boundary stone at N$^{o.}$ 1, Turn O'Dee Cottage.

property and the present owner of N⁰· 1 has dug up a boundary stone in the garden bearing date 1850 and the initials 'G.C.'

Turn O'Dee House, located next to Turn O'Dee Cottages at the end of the drive, has replaced a pair of cottages that were built after 1840, as they are not marked on the tithe map. Neville Jones owned one cottage and his wife the other

The pair of cottages that were replaced by Turn O'Dee House.

and when they left Althrey Farm at the end of the twentieth century, they had them demolished and a new house built on the site.

Althrey Lodge [1011] used to be known as Althrey Cottage when it as was owned and occupied by George Cambell (1802–76) and his wife Elizabeth in 1840. In 1842, he was a high constable for the Overton area. After his wife died, he married Charlotte in September 1858. As well as the cottage, stables and a coach house, he also owned the croft – a small piece of land **[1012]** – at the rear and a terrace of three cottages, all accessible from a cart track at the side, as well as a few of the fields around. He went on to acquire several farms, smallholdings, properties and land in Bangor and Cloy, and

Althrey Lodge.

Althrey Lodge became the hub of his empire. He had boundary stones erected on nearly all his properties and a plan of his estate was made showing the extent of his holdings in 1861 and again in 1873. This can be viewed in the Flintshire Record Office. After his death, his wife continued to live there until she died in 1886. The trustees of the estate sold Althrey Lodge in 1900 and George Goswell, a racehorse trainer, bought it and lived there with his family. Mr and Mrs Arthur Done lived here in 1929. In 1963, Mr and Mrs Coggins, who were said to be relocating to the Bahamas, offered it for sale. A. Kent Jones the local estate agency subsequently bought it privately on behalf of a client.

Althrey Lodge Cottage was converted from the coach house and stables belonging to Althrey Lodge with part of the croft (probably after the Goswells left) to make a separate holding with an entrance from the cart track at the side. The three cottages **[1013]** behind Althrey Lodge Cottage originally faced the river and were replaced by the present two north-west-facing two cottages, **Davro** and **Braemar**, during the twentieth century. Further up the cart track was where the

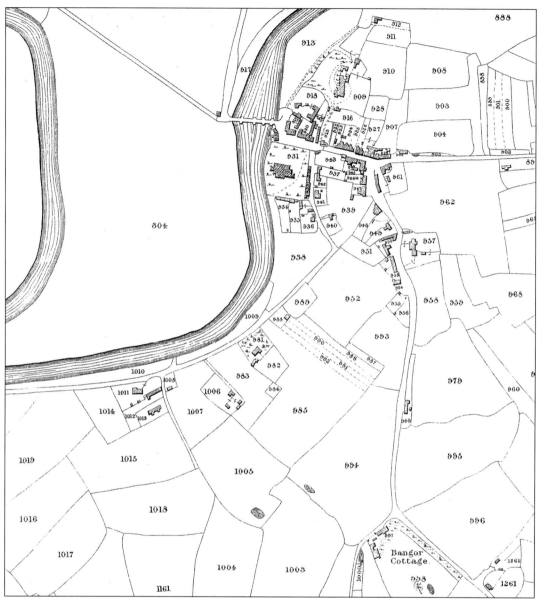

1840 Tithe Map of Bangor Isycoed (part 2).

Althrey Lodge Cottage converted from the stables of Althrey Lodge probably after Mr Goswell left.

piggeries once stood, now part of a modern bungalow named **Lyndale**.

Maes-y-Groes Cottage [1008] was located on the opposite corner to Althrey Lodge Cottage in 1840 and separated from it by the cart track. It was then owned by Mary and Jane Suckley and Margaret Swinley of Maes-y-Groes and was rented to Richard Davies. We have no idea of its age or style as it has long since been demolished. Opposite this cottage was an opening which led to the river to enable the people living in the vicinity to have access to obtain their water. When the river was in flood, the land in the Maes-y-Groes area was always inundated. For years they pressed for either a continuation of the bulwarks or for a wall to be built to protect their property and eventually the council agreed to raise the level of the road by about a foot.

Maes-y-Groes [1006] was owned in 1840 by Jane and Mary Suckley and Margaret Swinley. The site has been occupied from very early times and the earliest mention of it is in the bishop's transcripts when John Jones, servant to John Williams of Maes-y-Groes, was buried on 9 May 1673. The present house is only the latest of several dwellings on this site. It was bought in the 1960s by Margaret Hélaine and Marjorie Rees and sold by the former in the 2000s when she went to live in Overton. But, unable to settle, she returned to live in Post Office Cottage, previously the home of her sister Betty Starr. She died in 2012. The new owners of Maes-y-Groes have since demolished the old house and rebuilt it on the old footprint. In the field at the side of Maes-y-Groes stands an ancient oak tree, known as the Monk's Oak, that tradition says was the place where Augustine held his second meeting with the Celtic bishops. This would

Maes-y-Groes rebuilt in about 2010 on the same footprint and copying the same style as the old house.

The Monk's Oak at Maes-y-Groes in 2013.

make it over 1400 years old – it is old but not that old! The trunk is eight or nine feet in diameter and three quarters of the tree is now dead, but the rest sprouts new leaves every spring.

Deeside [981] was owned by Mrs Elizabeth Pool in 1840. The age of the house is unknown but set into a wall of an outhouse is a date stone of '176?' and part of the initials 'T.P.E.?'. In 1879, it was offered for sale at Queen's Hotel in Chester but was withdrawn from auction when the only offer of £1,600 failed to reach the reserve price. A magistrate, Henry J. Royds and his wife, Agnes, bought the property when it was offered for sale again in 1880 and lived there until they moved to Hatfield in Herefordshire where he died in 1910 aged sixty-six. The next tenant was the Hon. Alexander Parker (son of the sixth earl of Macclesfield and Lady Mary Grosvenor), brother of the first duke of Westminster's estate agent, who was resident from 1899 until the disastrous fire of 1904. In 1905, it was put up for sale, still fire-damaged, but the property did not reach its reserve and was withdrawn. It was afterwards bought by Mr and Mrs Pitcairn Campbell in 1911 but

Deeside as it is today.

The date stone in the wall of an outhouse at Deeside.

whether before or after it was repaired is not recorded.

Deeside Cottage [988], probably built in the eighteenth century, was situated next to Deeside, on the right as you approach the village, and separated from it by the footpath from Overton Road to Cloy Lane. Mrs Elizabeth Pool of Deeside owned it in 1840, along with two of the quillets of land behind the cottage. Her tenant was Charles Griffiths. Mr and Mrs Pitcairn Campbell became the owners in 1911 and the cottage was the residence of their head gardener, Edward Griffiths, for twenty-eight years until his death in May 1931. It was the scene of an inquest held in May 1930 when Edward's son, Bartlem Griffiths, aged nineteen, was drowned whilst swimming in the river. The cottage was sold in about 1969, on the death of the previous owners and was bought by John and Elizabeth Jones. It became an unfortunate casualty of the building of the new river bridge and the young couple had bought it not realising that it lay in the path of progress. They were very happy there and desperately fought the compulsory purchase order but had to eventually admit defeat and the house was demolished. They had taken photographs which remind us that progress comes at a cost.

The **pinfold or pound**, marked on the 1912 OS map, was located opposite Deeside Cottage and was used to accommodate stray animals that had been impounded by the parish constable. The owner had to pay a fine for their retrieval. The pinfold, of medieval origin, was usually a fenced enclosure, but this one had been re-sited and built in brick at a cost of £13 13s in 1856, much to the annoyance of a nearby resident, Mrs Bentley, who complained about the nuisance. In 1896, it was reported to be in a dilapidated condition and, after establishing that the Bangor ratepayers were the owners, the parish council agreed to its removal in 1900.

The Orchard [938]. Further along the road, opposite the entrance to Abbey Gardens (itself built

Deeside Cottage (exterior and interior) pulled down to make way for the new bridge.

on the site of the old quillets) and Abbeygate Walk, was an orchard owned by John Lewis in 1840. It was run latterly by Alfred (known as Griff), the father of Geoff Griffiths of Raggs Hill, as an orchard and nursery and is where the appropriately named houses, N°s. 1–4 The Nursery, were built in about 1970. Dode Humphreys said that when the builders were clearing the site they found a stone slab that they thought was the cover for a grave. However, knowing that if the find was reported the work would be held up whilst the area was investigated, it was hastily covered it up again. It is probable that this slab actually covered the well that once belonged to the nursery. On the other hand, it just might have been the evidence needed to support Derrick Pratt's theory that the churchyard at one time covered a much larger area. We may never know. There is a similar stone slab in the garden of the Old School-house, which is thought could be a grave cover or possibly the cover for the well that served both the house and the old Endowed School.

Orchard Villas, originally known as Orchard Cottages, located opposite the above nursery, were built in the twentieth century, sometime prior to 1912, on part of the land belonging to Orchard House. They belonged to Annie Elizabeth Evans until her death in 1927 and her tenants were Patrick Joseph McCarthy and Job Reeves. The headmaster, George Moss, lived there for a few years before moving to Wrexham.

Westgate House was built on Orchard House land after 1912 and its first occupant was John Mort. After he died in 1937 it became the police station until Bangor lost its resident policeman in the 1990s.

Orchard House [940], located opposite Millbrook House, is of unknown date as the deeds only go back to 1912, but was probably built in the eighteenth century. The owner, George Powell, sold it to Annie Elizabeth Evans and, on her death in 1927, it was conveyed to John Mort. Griffith Evan Jones rented it in 1924, followed by Lewis Ebenezer Mitton [Mytton], both former station-masters in Bangor. It was owned in 1840 by John Lewis and occupied by Elizabeth Danick. At one time, there was a track that ran through the grounds from the side of the smithy in Whitchurch Road to Overton Road.

Greylands [941]. Located at the side of Orchard House was a farmhouse now called Greylands that was owned by John Lewis in 1840

Orchard House thought to be eighteenth century.

and occupied by John Griffiths. Dode Humphreys had been told it was built on the site of Bangor's seventh public house, the Boar's Head. Thomas Antley occupied it from about 1913 until his death in 1939 when it was extended and divided into two properties, **Greylands** and **Greenacres**.

Greylands and Greenacres.

The **Schoolhouses and Endowed School [936]**. Where Millbrook House and the Old Schoolhouse now stand was the terrace of three, half-timbered, thatched cottages that burnt down in 1859. They were already old when the school was built in 1748. The detached thatched barn was not affected by the fire and was afterwards pulled down to enlarge the school playground.

Church Avenue. If you pass the old Endowed School (now the village hall which is described elsewhere) and turn left you come to the site of a row of five or six old cottages of which only two remain. The three cottages **[934]** nearest the river were owned by John Lewis in 1840 and tenanted by John Jones and others. The next cottage **[935]**, the largest, was behind the Endowed School and was bought by the trustees of the village hall in 1966 for a car park. The deeds go back to 1688 when it was owned by Roger Davies of Dongrey and his wife, Bridget, and their descendents retained ownership until 1794. This half-timbered house is shown in an artist's sketch of 1782, a copy of which is displayed in the church exhibition. Joseph Stokes the schoolmaster rented this cottage, as did a later schoolmaster, Benjamin Harris, and his wife, Anne. Anne Harris continued to rent it after her husband's death. It had been pulled down and rebuilt sometime between the date of the sketch and 1838 when Daniel Rowland Barker of Carden left it to trustees in his will. They sold it to George Harper of Moss Fields, Shropshire and it then passed through several owners until Mrs Rosina Fraser of Hanmer House, Salisbury Road, Wrexham sold it in May 1919 to Mrs Paterson Morgan, the wife of the rector of Bangor, for £200. It was used for church meetings for a short while and became known as the Church House, but it was never a rectory as such. In 1926, it was sold to Mr and Mrs Manning and then rented to various tenants.

Nine cottages [932 & 933]. Next to the village hall and separated from it by Church Avenue, was a terrace of cottages which was described by the rector as 'a grievous nuisance.' They were set partly in the churchyard and jutted out, narrowing the road. These cottages are shown on the 1840 tithe map, but it is not known how old they were or what they looked like. They were pulled down in 1864. In 1840, the first five **[933]** belonged to John Lewis and were rented by Charles Edwards and others. The next cottages **[932]** were owned by the Hon. Robert Henry Clive and were rented by Thomas Price and others.

Lock-up. Continuing up Overton Road, at the end of the terrace, was the old round house or lockup that was pulled down in 1885.

Pair of houses [937 & 942]. Located opposite the old lock-up was the site of the stocks and a property that in 1840 was a substantial pair of houses. These houses were pulled down about 1883 and were replaced by the cottage known as **Rosecroft** by the duchess of Westmoreland who had

it built for her head groom who was retiring. **Charcoal Cottage** may have been added later. Peter Furber told the author that when he was excavating the front of Rosecroft to put in gateposts, he uncovered substantial sandstone foundations of a previous building. He had the roof of the cottage raised and the cottage extended in the 1980s.

Rosecroft and Charcoal Cottage.

The Tollhouse [943]. On the right-hand corner of Overton Road was the cottage built *c*.1767 to take the tolls, with a gate across both roads. In 1840, it was on land owned by Sir Richard Puleston of Emral. We have no idea of the style of the building, except that it was likely to have been single storey. When the turnpike trust was wound up it was, quite rightly, thought more important to widen the road at the Overton Road/High street junction by demolishing the cottage than it was to preserve a little piece of history.

High Street

Bridge Cottages [930]. Turning left into High Street we come to the site of five cottages, now occupied by the War Memorial, that were demolished in 1914 to provide better access to the bridge. In 1840, the owner of three of them was Sir Richard Puleston and the occupants were Mary Fleet, Thomas Stotton and Edward Stoneby.

Dee Cottage [918]. Turning to the right, behind the present boathouse, was the dwelling that Mrs Sunter Harrison thought may have been known as the Malster's cottage. In 1840, it was

The old cottages by the bridge pulled down to improve visibility and access to the bridge in 1914. [Heritage Prints of Wrexham]

owned and occupied by John Lewis and included substantial buildings, a yard and gardens. It was known as Dee Cottage in 1860 when the contents were sold on his death. When a survey was conducted into the village water supply in the 1920s it was called **Dee View Cottage** and Ernie Young's grandfather, Walter, called it **Dee Villa** when he lived there during the twentieth century having moved from Graig Villa. The cottage was built of red brick with substantial attics with windows in the gable ends and slightly projecting end-chimneys. The windows to the front were three-light casements with stone lintels. The cottage had three points of interest – a date stone at first floor level with the initials 'I. L.' and the date '1796' within an oval border, and a Sun fire insurance mark. The initials were those of the original owner, perhaps John Lewis' father or

grandfather (the letter 'J' was often converted into an 'I' in inscriptions). The third thing of interest was a purse containing Georgian coins that was discovered hidden under the floorboards when the house was pulled down.

Dee Villa demolished in the 1950/60s.

Kiln Cottages [918] were converted into seven small properties from the outbuildings belonging to Dee Cottage by the new owner, probably after John Lewis's death in 1860. These cottages were called **The Square** in the 1901 census. They were pulled down in the 1950/60s.

The **Royal Oak Inn [919]** was owned by Sir Richard Puleston of Emral in 1840. There had been an inn on this site from a much earlier date. The present building is two-storey and was rebuilt in 1900 of half-timbered and rendered construction. The ground floor fronting High Street was split into two rooms with one room called the vaults that had a separate entrance from the High Street, identified by the curved canopy over the doorway. There used to be a building at the side of the pub, with a bay window that was used by the landlord as his office and a study for his daughters. One day, during the 1960s a lorry on its way to Brymbo stalled on the bridge. Its brakes failed and the lorry ran backwards into the building, causing so much damage that it was decided to demolish it. Sylvia Niven, the daughter of the licensee, had been working in the study at the time and had just left the room when the accident occurred. Not long afterwards, the decision was taken to pull down all the buildings at the rear of the hotel, which greatly improved access to the bridge and provided much needed space for a car park.

Bridge House [920] is a Grade II-listed building which stands next to the Royal Oak, and divided from it by an alleyway. It was split into three dwellings and was owned by Sir Richard Puleston in 1840. His tenants at that time were William Thomas, Edward Allman, Thomas Paddock and Martha Edwards. One of these tenants lived in an old cottage attached to the back of what is now **Old Bridge House**, which was, and still is, accessed from the alleyway. This cottage may have had a malt kiln at the rear and may well have been the property once known as the **Maltster's House**. We have no idea of the style or age of any of the original buildings that faced Overton Road. George Cambell bought them from the Emral estate and, employing the Overton builder John Edge, had them either rebuilt or remodelled, with a new frontage and higher roof line, to an almost symmetrical design with a central shop front in 1856. The houses contain cellars that used to (and probably still do) fill with water when the river was in spate. The present building is three-storey, of red brick in Flemish bond with sandstone bands between the storeys and with the upper windows alternating between flat-headed and round-headed openings. The middle section consists of shop premises with living accommodation over. The right-hand part, where E.L. Mytton's son lived with his family, has now been incorporated into the Buck Hotel.

The Royal Oak, Bridge House and the Buck Hotel.

The Buck Hotel [921]. This early eighteenth-century inn was part of the Emral estate. It is 2½ storeys high, of rendered brick with dormers windows. It still contains the first floor room that was once used as a courtroom by the local magistrates. It had a range of stables set against the wall dividing the inn from the rectory Lodge, that were destroyed in a fire in May 1937. The damage was estimated at over £200 and the cause of the blaze was believed to have been a lighted cigarette. The Buck was sold in 1905 to Bate's Brewery, Wrexham, for £1,225.

Rectory Lodge [915]. John Douglas designed the present building for the duke of Westminster in 1897. It replaced an older lodge, date and style unknown, that the duke's predecessor had bought with some land from the Revd Maurice Wynne in 1832. The rectory drive used to be to the left of the lodge and was moved to its present position when the duke gave a strip of land for a driveway to improve access to the school in 1902.

The **Old Rectory [909]**. Up the drive alongside the rectory Lodge is the Old rectory, now called **Bridgeman House**. It served as the rectory until 1985.

The old **Infants' School [919]**. In the far left hand corner of the rectory garden, next to what is now N⁰· 1 School Close, was the site of the leaking old cottage (accessed from the Rectory drive) that was used as an

Rectory Lodge rebuilt by John Douglas in 1897 for the Duke of Westminster.

infants' school, about which the government inspector was so scathing. It was in use until the National, or Free, School was built in the mid 1800s. In the 1980s Gordon Mytton converted the old school into part of School Mews and his mother lived in one of the cottages.

Chapel House [923] was built about 1839 on land owned by Isaac Pickering as an Independent or Congregational chapel. At some stage it ceased to be used as a chapel and was later converted into a dwelling.

A small two-storey cottage **[923]**, owned by Isaac Pickering, was attached to the Post Office and was lived in by Luther Williams, the village cobbler, in the 1920s before the Evanson family took over. On one night a week Ron Evanson's mother used to cook chips in her boiler to sell to customers. The cottage was pulled down after the Abbot's Way council houses were built *c.*1950 and Ron was given the tenancy of N⁰· 1. Cliff Knight bought the small cottage in 1950 soon after he became postmaster and demolished it to obtain access to his land at the rear of the post office in order to build a garage.

The **Post Office** and **Orme Lodge [923]**, both eighteenth century, were owned by Isaac Pickering in 1840 and were at various times all one property and at other times divided into the present two cottages, each with its own entrance door. There was a big room on the first floor that at one time spanned both cottages.

Post Office Cottage [924] is an eighteenth- or early nineteenth-century building that may have been owned by Isaac Pickering and rented by Edward Moses and Joseph Powell in 1840.

The High street as it looked prior to 1925. Note the cobbled pavement on the left, the brick fascia of the cottages and no War Memorial.

The Cottage [925] was originally two dwellings owned in 1840 by John Edge, Edward Hanmer and Elizabeth Bithill. Living there at that time were Timothy Roberts and Edward Pearson. The cottages were originally two-storey and Stan Adams had them converted by Tom Parry into one single-storey building in the 1950s.

Hendy [926] was owned in 1840 by the same three people as the previous cottage and was tenanted by Thomas Jones. Travers Twiss came to Bangor at some time prior to 1900 and purchased the attached cottage, part of **[927]**, and converted it into a café known as Twiss's Tearooms, and a grocer's shop (now called the Middle Shop) and run by his great-grandson Dave and Tracey

The High Street cottages as they look today.

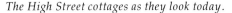

Adams. In 1922, Twiss applied to the RDC for a licence to store petrol and the remains of the old petrol pump can still be seen outside. At the far end of the shop was an archway with large wooden doors that joined the shop to the next property – The Croft. The remains of the arch can still be seen now forming the frontage to the pet shop.

The Croft, and **Deva House,** and what is now a hair salon **[927]**, form a group of taller houses that were owned in 1840 by the same three people as the previous properties. The tenants were Thomas Minshall, Roger Jones and Edward Hanmer. Edward Hanmer owned the garden **[928]** at the rear of the block. Deva House was the residence of the village

The archway now incorporated into the Middle Shop.

policemen for a few years. PC Parry's son, Tom, had a timber business up the alleyway at the rear of The Croft and when electricity came to Bangor he became an electrician and installed electricity in several properties, including the police house, before eventually becoming a builder. Tom Crawford and Mary Poynton later ran Deva House as a shoemakers and cobblers shop and then it became Miss Ainsworth's fishing tackle shop. The right-hand third of the block was owned by the Humphreys family and Mrs Humphreys (Dode's mother) ran a small general goods business from the front parlour. This became known to all as 'Olive's Shop' when it was taken over by her daughter. Olive sold the most wonderful Cheshire cheese which she would buy fresh each week from Nantwich. When she retired she let the shop to Les Newlands for a number of years who operated a small printing business there until he retired. This terrace of three properties all had tiny gardens to at front with railings around that were removed to widen the road.

The Stableyard [944]. Returning up the south side of the High Street we come to a Grade II-listed building, which was formerly known as the Ship Inn. A timber-framed property, it dates from the early seventeenth-century and the earliest date mentioned in the deeds is said to be 1670. It has been altered and extended over the years. In 1840 it was owned by John Edge, Edward Hanmer and Elizabeth Bithill and included with the inn was the cottage now known as **Fraser Cottage** and **Winifred Cottage** the property facing Whitchurch Road, both owned by the same trio and the

tenant was Joseph Sandland. In 1861, Jane Davies, the licensee, was summoned for permitting drunkenness on the premises. When two years later she was again found guilty of the same offence, the magistrates refused to

The butcher's shop in part of what is now the Stableyard premises c.1937. L–R: George (Dode) Humphreys, Mr Williams, –?–, Hilda Roberts, Mrs Williams.

The Ship Inn.

renew her licence and the Ship Inn was closed. Part of the premises was run as a butcher's shop by G.H. Williams and part as café up to 1965. Until recently it was a restaurant operated by the present owners, Dave and Cathy White, and is now a small hotel.

Fraser Cottage is of early nineteenth-century date but has been considerably altered and extended in recent years. It was the home of the village postman Jack Roberts. His wife was known as Mrs Postman Roberts – shortened to Mrs Possie Roberts – to distinguish her from the other Roberts' wives. In the twentieth century she let Dr Caspar use the front parlour as his surgery and used to sit in a chair by the surgery door making her privy to the conversation between the doctor and his patient. Consequently, she knew all the ailments and complaints of the villagers.

Station Road

A terrace of three cottages **[929]** with a yard was at one time attached to 'Olive's shop' on the left hand side, at the beginning of Station Road. This was owned by Edge, Hanmer and Bithell. The tenants at that time were Joseph Sandlands, Jane Hanmer and one cottage was empty. These cottages are referred to in the parish council minutes of November 1899 when 'the question of the dilapidated & insanitary condition of three old cottages near the blacksmith's shop abutting onto the highway to Worthenbury was raised'. The terrace was still there in December 1899 as the RDC had again received a letter from the local government board about the condition and recommending that council applied for urban powers to have them removed. They must have been knocked down soon afterwards.

Cottage and Smithy [906]. Next to the previously listed terrace was a cottage and smithy that were demolished in the 1950s to make way for the first of the village's council houses. The pair of houses Nos. 1 & 2 Abbot's Way, were occupied by Ron and Millie Evanson and Noel and Audrey Taylor. The smithy with the garden **[905]** was owned by Edge, Hanmer and Bithill and in 1840 was let to James Lee when it was described as a house, yard and garden. The right-hand part of this building became a blacksmith's shop which was run by the Griffiths family later in the nineteenth century.

Graig Lane

Brickyard [891]. At the beginning of Graig Lane was a cottage and a brickyard on the left-hand side, where the present house now stands. In 1840 it was owned by John Lewis. Walter Young lived there and called it Graig Villa before he moved his family to live in Dee Villa behind the Royal Oak. Ron Evanson, found an Elizabethan coin in the garden whilst digging a trench to install a telephone.

Graig Cottage [869]. At the bottom of Graig Lane is Graig Cottage, once owned by Peter Lloyd and bequeathed by him in 1781 for charitable purposes (the rent was to be used for the purchase

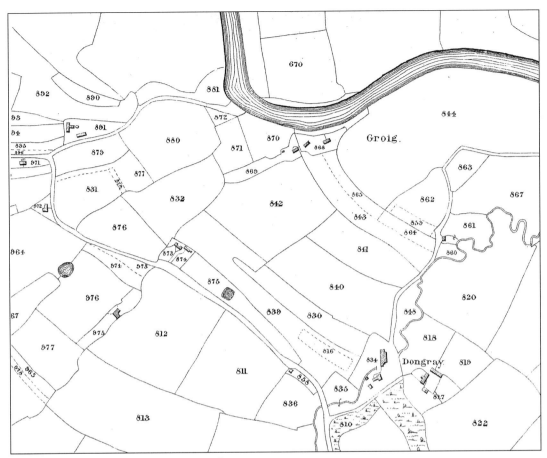

1840 Tithe Map of Bangor Isycoed (part 3).

of bread for distribution to the poor of Bangor). Thomas Edwards was the occupier in 1840. It served for a time as the police station and was sold by the charity in 1905. Marjorie Bayliss and her husband bought it *c*.1950.

River View [868], next to Graig Cottage, was once two sandstone cottages and another separate dwelling, all owned by William, John and Henry Churton and George and William Parker Churton and rented to William Williams, William Peers and George Jones in 1840. The separate cottage was later knocked down. The Robinson family owned the two cottages in the twentieth century and, after the death of Eddie Robinson and his sister Hazel, they were sold by auction for £72,000 in *c*.1988, and the new owners converted them into one property.

River View.

The Old Graig Cottage. Below: Wattle and daub panels inside the Old Graig Cottage.

Station Road (continued)

The **Old Graig Cottage [873]** is on the left-hand side of the hill set back from the road. It was owned by Richard Edwards in 1840 when the tenant was Thomas Edwards. In about 1970, Ron and Sybil (née Jarvis) Hughes bought the house from Mr and Mrs Joe Edwards. The history of the house is unknown, but from the tithe map the house appears to have once been twice its present size. The new owners were given planning permission to pull it down and to build a bungalow on the site. They had demolished a lean-to building at the side when news came through that it had been made a Grade II-listed building, which put a stop to any further development. The interior of the cottage contains wattle and daub and the windows are a rare surviving example of their type. The cottage is said to be at least early eighteenth or possibly seventeenth century. The owners have since re-roofed and re-pointed the property and repaired the windows to ensure it is watertight and have handed it over to their son. When Ron was digging the front garden, he found a silver coin dated 1653 which suggests that the site was occupied at the earlier date.

Fair Risings was built at the side of the plot where the original Tŷ Graig once stood, although nearer the road, in the early 1960s and was bought by Ron and Sybil Hughes in about 1968.

Tŷ Graig [974] was once owned by the 6th earl of Plymouth who inherited it in 1799 as part of the Althrey Hall estate when he was not quite ten years old. It is mentioned in his marriage settlement. On reaching his majority he began selling many or all of his holdings in Flintshire. He sold Tŷ Graig (or Graig House as it was known) to Richard Edmunds in 1818 and in 1840 it was rented by John Mottershall who also rented the croft alongside that extended nearly to the Millbrook. In the early part of the nineteenth century the original Tŷ Graig house was set back from the road, roughly on a line with the

Above: Old Tŷ Graig (date unknown).

Right: Tŷ Graig (built after 1840) in 1945 when it was sold. The shutters give the Georgian-style building quite a modern look. [M. & R. Evers]

Old Graig Cottage. There is an undated photo-graph that shows Tŷ Graig as a partially half-timbered building. I have not been able to find out when the present house was built nearer the road. Bob and Margaret Evers, the former owners, kindly allowed me to see the old deeds of the house.

A cottage **[858]** near the old railway entrance was pulled down when the railway was built in 1896. It was owned in 1840 by the Emral estate and rented by Roger Knowles.

The Mount. There has been a new front elevation attached to the old house.

The **Mount [975]** was owned and occupied in 1840 by Miss Elizabeth Davies. Unfortunately, the deeds do not go back very far so the age of the property is unknown. There are said to be inter-esting beams in the building that are thought to indicate a date of at least the eighteenth century and it may have been built on the site of earlier houses. The Mount may have been another of the properties belonging to the earl of Plymouth.

N$^{os.}$ **1 & 2, The Leeks [972]** were owned in 1840 by Samuel Chesters and his tenants were James Mottershead and Thomas Jones.

The Leeks Cottages.

Lilac Cottage(s) [971]. This property was a smithy on the OS map of 1879 and was later occupied by a wheelwright. Originally three cottages it was converted into one property by George and Helen Humphreys. In 1840, the owner was Peter Roberts and his tenants were Thomas Edwards and William Newns. Then it was just described as a house and garden. It was probably extended into three separate dwellings at a later date.

A terrace of three cottages **[897]** used to stand where the basket shop and house is now. In 1840, it was described as a house and garden, owned and occupied by Joseph Edwards. The house must have been extended and converted into three cottages after that date. Two of the cottages were demolished for the extension to the basket business and Cyril Johnson had the remaining cottage modernised and extended in 1980. An external brick wall was built around the building and the old cottage was then pulled down, all while continuing occupation. The basket shop has expanded con-siderably since the early days and is still run as a family business.

The terrace of three cottages where Johnson's Basket Shop is now located.

Whitchurch Road

The Star Inn [961]. Turning into Whitchurch Road is the old farmhouse, now known as **Dee House**. In 1840, the owner was Elizabeth Davies and her tenant was Samuel Chesters. It was run as a farm and inn until the magistrates refused to renew the licence in the nineteenth century. The Bennett family later ran part of the old buildings as a very successful small brewery. The farm buildings were converted into dwellings known as **Dee Court** *c*.1992. The brewery site is now occupied by a dental practice and builder's offices with frontages onto the Whitchurch Road.

Hill View and **Mount View** cottages were built in the latter half of the nineteenth century much as they appear today.

The Laurels farmhouse with Hill View and Mount View beyond.

The Laurels [957]. This is an eighteenth-century two-storey farmhouse with a large attic that was owned in 1840 by Mrs Elizabeth Edge and her tenant was Elizabeth Bithell. The farmhouse still retains its sliding sash windows to the front elevation, with wedge lintels and the living room has a substantial beam over a wide fireplace. When the house was re-plastered, vertical beams were discovered at intervals in many of the walls. The house appears to have been built on a sandstone foundation and may be on the site of a previous building. Between the Laurels and the entrance to the Laurels estate, was an orchard of 4½ acres belonging to the farmhouse that was sold in 1962 to a builder, H.V. Morris, for the erection of the first of the bungalows of the Laurels estate. At one time the village possessed several walnut trees, one of which used to stand by the entrance to the farmhouse. There was also one in the garden of **Millstone Cottage** and in **Walnut House** (the old New Inn). Carpenter Clement Robinson (1885–1954) and his wife came to live in Bangor in the early 1920s and they initially resided at The Laurels from where he ran his business. He later rented the end terrace cottage opposite and people still remember seeing coffins propped against the wall. Their three children, Joan, Clem and John were all born in Bangor.

Kiln Cottage [980]. In 1840, this was owned by William Lea and rented by Thomas Jones when it was described as a house and malt kiln with a narrow strip of garden to the front. The house, originally single storey, has been much altered over the years. Nᵒ· 2 Kiln Cottage was a later addition at the rear.

At the top of Bangor Bank, on the left-hand side is **Highgate House [1262]** that was owned in 1840 by Samuel Chesters and the occupier was Thomas Jones. It was built with a cellar that was almost constantly full of water having been erected near to, if not on top of, a spring. The house has since been 'gentrified' and wrought iron gates have been fitted.

Highgate Cottages [1261]. Next to the previous property are a pair of cottages owned by the executors of the late Daniel Barker – Daniel Boote, John Barker and John Pool in 1840. Their tenants were Daniel Jones and William Edwards. There was a boundary stone in one of the gardens that the author saw in the 1980s with initials and a date that can no longer be found and, unfortunately, the details cannot be recalled.

Bangor Cottage [997], also known as **Abbeygate Cottage**, across the road at the junction of Cloy Lane, was owned and occupied in 1832 by Joseph Warter, JP. He resided there until his death in 1874, aged sixty-eight. Mr and Mrs Webster then bought the cottage but he died in 1883. Lady Power and her son, Sir John Power, came to live in Bangor and rented Abbeygate from the owner, Mrs Meredith Jones, until Sir John's death in 1900. Captain and Mrs McNabb then lived there until 1906.

Bangor Cottage in the 1950s. [S. Harrison, FRO D/DM/1201]

The Cottage & Abbey View.

Returning to the village, on the left-hand side of Bangor Bank, opposite Kiln Cottages, is **The Bungalow** that was probably built at the end of the nineteenth century.

Abbey View and **The Cottage [954]**. Continuing past the bungalows that were the beginning of the Abbeygate Walk development in the 1960s, we come to a pair of semi-detached cottages of late eighteenth- or early nineteenth-century construction. In 1840 they were owned by Mrs Ann Boodle and her tenants were Jane Ralphs and John Montford. The earliest date mentioned in the deeds is 1848, when Ann Boodle sold Abbey View to George Cambell. Included with the properties were two gardens **[955 & 956]**. Garden N° 955 was later divided into two, half being given to each cottage, and N° 956, complete with pigsties, was sold for the building of the bungalows. The property was then sold to Richard Bostock and descended from him to Thomas Richard Bostock, his son, who also owned the attached dwelling. On his demise, both cottages were sold to Lieutenant-Colonel S.V. Misa.

A terrace of three cottages **[953]** lies behind the previous dwellings. The far end of the terrace, **Maralomeda**, was built in the eighteenth century as a blacksmith's shop with a cottage attached. Like Tŷ Graig, it was owned by the 6th Earl of Plymouth as part of the Althrey Hall estate. In 1812, he sold the blacksmith's shop that had been 'late in the holding of John Jones and now in the holding of John Munford' to maltster William Maddocks of Bangor who then conveyed it to the wheelwright John

The terrace of three cottages and smithy once belonging to the Earl of Plymouth.

Munford of Bangor for £52 10s. By the time of his death, John Munford also owned the two adjoining cottages and in his will (dated 1844) bequeathed the first two cottages (occupied by Thomas Ince, a tailor, and Thomas Sadler, a slater) to his unmarried daughter Mary Munford and the blacksmith's shop and tenement, in the occupancy of John Clay, to his married daughter, Elizabeth Hughes of Croxton, Eccleshall. In 1868, the terrace became the property of Elizabeth's granddaughter, Mary Ann, she having bought her siblings' share of the property for £350. On her death in 1943, the terrace was sold to the Bangor butcher, George Hubert Williams, for £365. He then sold the middle cottage (now called **Woodlyn**) in 1968 and in 1971 sold the end cottage and the smithy to Joan Duckett (née Robinson). In 1974, he sold the third cottage (**Millstone Cottage**) to Viv Lavis-Jones.

Plassey House and Court, formerly the **Red Lion Inn [950]**. Four flats were built by Gordon Mytton in the 1990s on the footprint of this former nineteenth-century inn. The stabling/barn was also converted into four dwellings. The inn had once had its own malt kiln and well. Legend has it that this well, known as Deiniol's, or the Monk's, Well once served the monastery. It was said to be one of the few deep wells in the village but was filled in when the property was converted.

The three or four thatched cottages in between the Plassey barn and Walnut House (New Inn) were probably demolished in the 1950s.

Three black and white, **thatched seventeenth-century cottages [949]** once stood on the land at the side of Walnut House. In 1840, they were owned by Thomas Bradshaw and occupied by John Roberts, Samuel Pickford and William Phillips. In the early part of the twentieth century they were occupied by the Jarvis, Mathews and Roberts families. One of the women was a laundress and some people still remember going to her with their washing. Mr and Mrs Jack Roberts lived in the one nearest to the old garage and Dr Morton used to hold his surgery in her back kitchen. When they moved to live in Fraser cottage opposite the post office, the surgery moved with them. They were probably demolished in the 1950/60s.

The **New Inn [948]** now **Walnut House**. This was an eighteenth-century inn first mentioned in the deeds in 1788. It was owned in 1840 by Thomas Bradshaw and his tenants were William Bebbington and James Clark. The building ceased to function as an inn *c.*1880 and was later bought by Austin Peters of Birkenhead. He made an application to the RDC for permission to erect a garage on land at the side of Walnut House in 1931. This garage closed for business in the 1990s when his son Stuart retired.

Rose Cottage, part of the old inn, is attached to the side of Walnut House and was the home of the Fowles family.

The **Boar's Head Inn** may have been one of the old buildings located behind the smithy. Sue (Vera) Roberts (née Spoor) found an old beam on the site on which the name was written.

The **Smithy [947]**. The Clay family were the blacksmiths at Halghton smithy from at least 1711 and members of the same family are recorded as blacksmiths in Bangor in 1782 when John and Mary Clay had their daughter christened in the church. In 1840, the smithy and attached cottage were owned by John Roberts and the tenant of the cottage was Mary Roberts. Joseph Spoor bought the business in 1901.

The terrace of three cottages [946], since converted into two (a third cottage had been added to the middle cottage, on the end nearest the smithy) as can be seen by the different heights of the windows. Its front door was subsequently bricked up and the two cottages were merged into one. It is now is called **Old Smithy Cottage**. Unfortunately the old deeds have been lost.

Rose Cottage at the side of Walnut House once the home to the Fowles family with their six children.

Clay's Cottage [946] is the last in the terrace. It took its name from its owner, Lizzie, Clay who, when her father the blacksmith died, bought the cottage and lived there with her mother. The property was one of several that was inherited in 1799 by the sixth earl of Plymouth and sold by him to Charles Bradley in 1812.

Old Smithy Cottage and Clay's Cottage.

The **Presbyterian Chapel [945]** was built on the site of an old cottage that was attached to **Winifred Cottage**. In 1840, the old cottage was owned by John Roberts and occupied by John Dunbabin. In 1869, the owner, William Thomas, gave the site for the building of a chapel which opened for worship in 1871.

Winifred Cottage is the last cottage in Whitchurch Road that was part of the Ship Inn in 1840. Dr Samuel Edwards Jones, used to hold a surgery here. Born in Cilcain and educated in Oswestry, he graduated in medicine in 1892 at the age of twenty-one. He commenced practice in Bangor in 1894 and, after eight years during which time he lived at Althrey Lodge, he entered into partnership with Dr Llewelyn Williams of Holt Street, Wrexham and moved to live in Wrexham. He had served on the parish council until his move to Wrexham and continued to hold office in many of the village societies and always retained an special fondness for the area. He

Winifred Cottage.

had a distinguished career both in medicine (being chairman of many committees) and in public life (he was mayor of Wrexham in 1901–11 and a county councillor). He died in 1935. Other doctors also used the cottage as a surgery including the Wrexham surgeon Mr Livingston Pow, who held a surgery on a Sunday morning in the right-hand cottage of a pair occupied by Mrs Johnson (these were later converted into one property). The present Overton doctors' practice has a surgery on the ground floor. The practice has just acquired the Chapel House for more up-to-date premises and it is planned to move the surgery there after conversion is completed in 2013.

Further afield in the parish of Bangor

Plâs Fron was built (or rebuilt) in 1657 for a Mr Holbrook who was most probably the William Holbrook who was Bangor churchwarden in 1668. The house was sold in 1694 to Weston Hassall. In September 1694, a Charles Hassall (possibly his son) was married in Bangor by licence to Christian Jones. They had three known children, Elizabeth (born December 1695), Jane (born August 1697) and Marion, a son (born in October 1700) all christened in Bangor. In 1711, his wife died and was buried in Bangor and eventually Charles married again and he and his second wife, Judith, had a daughter, Mary, who was baptised in January 1726. He was churchwarden for Sesswick and Pickhill in 1704 and again in 1716. In 1695, Charles gave 6d towards a brief from Neston Church rectory following a fire. Weston Hassall is recorded as having died in February 1726 and was buried in Bangor, but there is no entry in the parish registers for Charles Hassall and he may have rented out the house and left the area.

During the nineteenth century the house was occupied by Captain Paul Griffith Panton, JP, and his wife. Captain Panton was the last male representative of the Pantons of Anglesey. He had joined the Royal Navy in the Mediterranean in 1804, the year Napoleon was crowned emperor of France and the year before the battle of Trafalgar. For nearly twenty years he actively served his country. He became the chairman of the Wrexham Board of Guardians and always gave generously to the poor and needy. He and his wife were great supporters of the church and the local school

Aerial view of Plâs Fron prior to demolition.

and when he died in 1872 his family erected the screen around the organ to his memory.

Captain George C. Fenwick of Erbistock Hall, Royal Welsh Fusiliers married Mary Peel, the elder daughter of Archibald Peel of the Gerwyn, as his second wife in 1891. Her uncle, Sir Roger Palmer of Cefn Park, purchased the Plâs Fron estate from a J.R. Bennion and presented it to the couple as his wedding gift. Mary Fenwick's grandfather was a brother of Sir Robert Peel, prime minister in 1834 and 1841. Her mother was the sister of Sir Roger Palmer and her son, Lieutenant-Colonel Roderick George Fenwick, took the additional name of Palmer when he inherited Cefn Park from his uncle. After her husband died, she carried on his good work representing Sesswick and Pickhill on the RDC and was the first woman to be elected to the Denbighshire County Council. She represented Marchwiel on the Wrexham Town Council in 1921 and became a magistrate in 1924. She was keenly interested in the welfare of the poor and served on the Wrexham Board of Guardians. She was very active locally in church affairs, throwing open her garden for church fetes and events for various charities and took a great interest in the education and welfare of the young. Her younger son, Roger Mansell William Fenwick, was killed in the First World War and is remembered on a plaque in the church.

When woodworm was discovered throughout the building in the 1980s the decision was taken to demolish the house as the cost of treatment and general renovation was prohibitive.

23. Eyton Township

Eyton School

Eyton School was built as a combined church and school in 1869 (inscribed on a stone over the door) at a cost of £430. The architect was John Douglas and it was built on land given by Sir Watkin Williams Wynn, sixth baronet of Wynnstay. The building comprised a nave or schoolroom, originally entered by two porches and divided off by a large arch at the east end, and a chancel or classroom.

When the school opened in February 1870, there were about twenty-seven children of whom only five were able to read on entry. The school was inspected at frequent intervals and by May 1873, a newspaper reported that the inspector said 'the reading and writing are fairly taught'. The report on the school in 1877 was encouraging: 'this school has greatly improved since Miss Hall has had the charge of it'.

In April 1879, the *Wrexham Advertiser* reported the inspector had written:

> ... the work of the infants is good on the whole, they gave me some intelligent answers. The grammar of the II standard was very fair on the whole, the other standards very weak. The reading and arithmetic of III standard and the working out and arithmetic of the IV standard will need mush care. In other respects the school has passed a fair examination. The order was good and the children were very well mannered. The accounts were excellently kept.

Eyton School 2013.

EYTON NATIONAL SCHOOL, 1894.

RECEIPTS.	£	s.	d.	EXPENSES.	£	s.	d.
The Duke of Westminster, K G. (2nd Moiety)	10	10	0	Salary of Mistresses	82	1	10
Sir W. W. Wynn, Bart.	5	0	0	Lodgings of ,,	5	4	0
Edmund Peel, Esq.	10	0	0	To Monitors and Pupil Teachers ..	36	14	8
Sir Roger Palmer, Bart.	5	0	0	Books, Maps, Stationery, Drawing, &c.	11	13	6
General Hon. Savage Mostyn	2	0	0	Coals and Lighting ..	4	1	11
Oliver Ormrod, Esq...	2	2	0	Insurance	0	4	6
Lord Kenyon	2	2	0	Furniture and Repairs	4	8	0
E. Randles, Esq.	2	0	0	Cleaning	3	0	0
Mr. Parker, The Parkey	1	1	0	Sewing Materials	1	0	1
Miss Champion McGill	1	1	0	Balance in hand, Nov. 1st, 1894	5	7	0
Mrs. Yorke	1	0	0				
Capt. & Mrs. Fenwick	1	0	0				
Hon. Mrs. Tyrwhitt	1	0	0				
Capt & Mrs. Pocklington	1	0	0				
Mr. Ellis...	0	10	0				
Mr. C. K. Benson	0	10	0	Nov. 8th.—Paid for enlargement of School			
Miss Scott	0	5	0	Buildings, by voluntary Contributions,			
Rev. G. H. McGill	1	1	0	£230 : 0 : 0.			
Government Grant	65	1	0				
,, School Fees, 12 months	40	0	0				
Drawing Grant	1	17	6				
	£154	0	6		£154	0	6

Eyton School Accounts.

By 1880, HMI T. Morgan Owen reported:

The infants of the first class were good in spelling, about very good in colour, fair in intelligence, tables and writing, and pretty fair in form and arithmetic; those of the second class were pretty good in tables; imperfect in form and fair in all other respects. The geography of the second standard was pretty good as regards common definitions, but poor in others; of the third standard pretty fair in part. The needlework done in my presence was very fair; the specimen work was praiseworthy. The grammar of the second and third standards was pretty good; of the other standards moderately fair. The standard work was good in reading; the other is in process of improvement. Both tone and order were commendable. School accounts are remarkably well kept.

In February 1881, when the school was examined in religious knowledge by the HMI Revd E. Owen, he was impressed and reported:

The school is making good progress. The answering of the children was very creditable. Their repetition and writing from memory was praiseworthy, particularly so of the first two classes which was very good. Group 1: Mary bishop, Mary Griffiths and Margaret Roberts; Group 2:

Class of 1936/7. Front row: Doreen Brooks; Harlod Roscoe; –?–: George Roscoe; Joan Hughes; Margaret Steen; Les Baldwin; Glyn Hughes; Delia Corfield. Second row: Millie Ellis; Joyce Davies; Doreen Haycocks; Eric Roscoe; Roger Kyniston; Dennis Bryan; Eric Darlington; Sheila Hughes; Elsie Hughes; Mary Steen. Third row: Mary Jones; Brenda Hughes; Dorothy Darlington; Nora Davies; Peggy Hughes; Gwen Davies; Mabel Corfield; Moira Evans; Marg Corfield; Rhona Roberts; –?–; Mary Hughes, Betty Brooks. Fourth row: Mr Sellers (headmaster); Lionel Roberts; Herbert Ellis; Eric Hughes; –?–; Jack Hughes; Eric Parry; Frank Davies; Ron Cheetham; Joe Haycocks; Charlie Roscoe; Miss Samuels; Miss Ellis. Back row: Kathleen Carden; Marjorie Jones; Mona Johnson; Queenie Rogers; Ethel Richards; Hilda Duffy; Eddie Green; Dorothy Devonport; Jane Roscoe; Gladys Hughes.

Thomas bishop, Group 3: Catherine Williams, Sarah A. Haycocks and Alice Hughes; Group 4: Edith A. Barker, Mary Jones, Sarah A. Davies and James Griffiths.

In July 1884, the inspector was clearly pleased with his visit and reported:

Considering the great improvement that has taken place in this school and bearing in mind its tone and order, I feel justified in recommending it for the excellent merit grant. I hope to see the needlework and knitting at the next examination an improvement upon that of the past in quantity and quality. The infants were good in reading, alphabet, colour and objects generally, pretty good in repetition of tables (but good intelligently in this subject), spelling arithmetic, *viva voce* and writing letters, fair in writing their names and copying on blackboard and arithmetic on slates: imperfect in form they knew of natural phenomena. They should know a few exercise songs. They require some small books and some coloured pictures of an interesting as well as instructive character. Miss Cash will shortly receive her certificate.

Whenever any sizeable expenditure was needed to the fabric of the school, the managers and the people of Eyton held events to raise the necessary money. Such as when the inspector reported that new toilets or 'out offices' in 1902 were needed, a sale of work was held in the December, which raised the sum of £91 19s 0d. Two tenders had been received from Jenkins & Jones of Johnstown and from Dunbabbin of Bangor. It was decided to leave the rebuilding until the end of the school year, 31 March 1903. Six years later, the school was threatened with closure unless a list of repairs requested by the education authorities was undertaken. The managers of the school under the chairmanship of the Revd Elrington Bissett had rejected the scheme as they could not see their way to carry out the alterations and improvements requested. However, the money must have been found because the school has been functioning ever since.

Village Hall

Having seen the success of the First World War army hut purchased by the inhabitants of Bangor, it was decided to raise funds in order to purchase one and install it on brick foundations for use as a village hall. By the beginning of 1922 they had amassed the sum of nearly £100 from fetes and other entertainments and Mr Frank Lloyd the auctioneer offered a site on a twenty-year lease at an annual rent of 10s (50p) and by April of that year a hut had been purchased. On Good Friday, in torrential rain, a party descended on Park Hall Camp, Oswestry to carefully dismantle the chosen hut and later on that same evening the last plank was unloaded in Crabtree Green by a willing band of helpers. On 19 April, Mrs Ernest Lloyd cut the first sod and Mrs Bert Williams laid the first brick for the foundations. A handsome spade and trowel were presented to these ladies to commemorate the occasion.

After three months of untiring work by a team of volunteers led by Mr Pryce Davies, the hut had been erected and furnished. Five people were elected as trustees: the rector of Bangor (*ex officio*), Mrs Harry Roberts, Ernest Lloyd, Bert Williams and Joe Pryce Davies, and the new institute was used for the first time for a flower show as part of a fete on 2 August 1922. The hut was officially declared open on 21 August with a Grand Concert. Mr Pryce Davies was presented with an illuminated address for his untiring leadership and energy in driving forward the erection of the institute.

King George VI's coronation was celebrated in the institute with a tea for all the children. The older children (aged 7–16) were presented with books and the younger ones (aged 3–7) with medals. Afterwards everyone took part in sports on a field lent for the occasion by Mr Ernest Lloyd of Plâs Eyton who also distributed the money prizes. In the evening

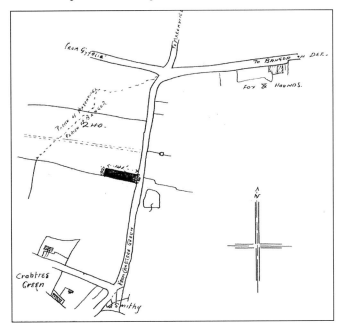

Site of the village hall on land leased from the auctioneer Frank Lloyd.

Eyton Church.

there was a firework display followed by a dance to music provided by a local band.

The Institute remained the centre of village life for many years until it became very dilapidated and failed to attract many bookings. In 1975, someone set the hut alight and within minutes it was blazing away. It has never been replaced.

Church

The church at Eyton was erected in 1869 as a building to serve the dual purpose of church and school. It opened for divine service on 8 February 1870. As already stated, the building comprised a nave or schoolroom, originally entered by two porches and divided off by a large arch at the east end, and a chancel or classroom as occasion demanded.

The rectors of Marchwiel and Bangor took it in turn to conduct divine service and it served the people of Eyton well until 1925 when divine services were transferred from the school to the institute. Throughout that time the hope was still maintained of building a church at Eyton and a building fund had been opened soon after the Great War and grew steadily. By 1938, it had reached £160, and the Revd F.R. Baldock, a former rector of Bangor, gave a site in a field next to the Institute. In the spring, a building committee was formed which comprised the Revd R.H. Owen (chairman); Mrs Guy Gossage, Mrs Victor Dennis, Mrs George Wood, Mr A. Done. Mr F.T. Cheetham, and Lt-Colonel R. Fenwick Palmer (churchwardens of Bangor); Mr G.L. Wood and Mr J.H. Sellars (honorary secretaries); Mr G.B. Williams (honorary treasurer) and Victor Denis, Herbert Morris, H. Roberts, Eric Jones, Pryce Davies, J.E. Parry, A. Brayne and J.F. Sellars. Thereafter, the fund began to mount rapidly as various people held functions such as Mrs Gossage's fete that realised £170, Mr Wood's fete £220 and Eyton's own fete brought in another £170. Subscriptions were also sought from both inside and outside the parish and at last the building commenced. The

Interior of Eyton Church.

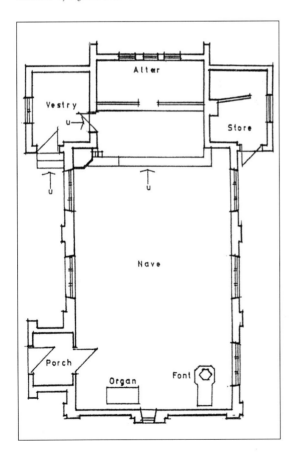

architect was a Mr Knott of London, the builder was Harry Jones of Holt and Victor Dennis was responsible for the drainage work and the levelling of the exterior ground. The church was planned on a rectangular design, with a seating capacity of eighty-five and was later fitted with oak pews. George Lockhart Wood of Maes-y-Nant (now Cross Lanes Hotel) gave invaluable service of both a financial and practicable nature. Most of the oak furnishings were made and given by him and he also supplied the lighting system. The organ was the gift of Mr Wood's mother, the font was given by Mrs Gossage and the pulpit by Mr G. Harrison. Local farmers volunteered to lay all the paths.

The church, alongside the institute in Crabtree Road, Eyton, was dedicated by the

Plan of the interior of Eyton Church.

Dedication of Eyton Church by the Bishop of St Asaph in 1939 with visiting clergy. The institute can be seen on the right. Below: Invitation to the dedication.

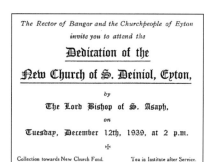

The Rector of Bangor and the Churchpeople of Eyton
invite you to attend the

Dedication of the

New Church of S. Deiniol, Eyton,

by

The Lord Bishop of S. Asaph,

on

Tuesday, December 12th, 1939, at 2 p.m.

✠

Collection towards New Church Fund.   Tea in Institute after Service.

Bishop of St Asaph on 12 December 1939 before a large congregation that included many former clergymen from Bangor; the vicar of Welshpool, the Revd F.R. Baldock; the vicar of Llanfynydd, the Revd Garmon Jones and the Revd Ellis Rowland, former curate of Bangor. On 6 October 1940, the archdeacon of Wrexham dedicated the pews made and fitted by Mr Wood.

The building is known as a mission church and is not licensed for weddings as it was dedicated and not consecrated. However, someone must have slipped up and forgot to inform the rector of Bangor, the Revd Richard Henry Owen, of this important fact as within twelve months of the dedication, the first wedding took place there, that of a Miss Nellie Cown (Cound in the Bangor register) and James Henry Gillam of Esclusham. Ten years later, Miss Brenda Mary Hughes and Graham Tyson Phillips of Ruabon were also married in the church by the Revd Garmon Jones, as were several of her friends. All the ceremonies were recorded in the Bangor parish register and no one questioned the validity of the services until the Revd Philip Owen arrived in the parish forty-six years later!

Appendix 1

Rectors

1300	William St John, son of Lord St John, Sequestration of profits of rectory to bring him up in study, 20 April.
1307	Re-appointment of him, at the request of Thomas Cardinal de St Sabina's to the rectories of Warnford, value 30 marks, and of Bangor, value 50 marks, in the dioceses of Winchester and Lichfield, which he obtained being under age, not in holy orders and not resident as well as the canonry and prebend of Rammesbyri in Salisbury, with dispensation to retain the same. [Papal Letters]
1325	John Chyney, 'The King presented, as true and undoubted Patron of the Church of Bangor, one John Chyney, upon the death of William St John'
1329	Wallis Dever, rector ecc. de Wythyndon, by exchange.
1333	William de Rossale, presented by Eubul Strange, Knt.
1334	Roger Dowlwas
1347	John de Wotynhall, rector of Stretton, diocese of Hereford, by exchange.
1349	Henry Blakebourn, on presentation of the Black Prince, in wardship of Roger le Strange, an infant.
1353	Robert de Trefford
1356	James Martin
1402	John Richard, outlawed in 1410 for adherence to Owen Glyndŵr.
1410	John L'Estrange, 'Dispensation to him, who is a Servitor of King Henry, and holds the above church, situate on the March and confines of Wales, where wars and burning have long gone on so that he cannot reside without great bodily peril, to hold another living with it.' [Papal Letters]
1418	John Leyott, '*Dec. Baccalaureus, Decanus Cestrie, rector ecclesiarum de Malpas et Bangor;*' prebendary of Lincoln, 1403; exchanged for prebendary in Gnosal College, Stafford, 1405; prebendary of Lichfield, 1406, obtained bull from Pope John to found a chantry at Hale; died 1428. Epitaph in Hale church according to Ormerod's *Cheshire*; in Alderbury according to Randle Holmes MSS [British Museum]. Gilbert Ireland in 1617 concerning his chapel in the chancel in Hale church and his seats within it quotes an inscription of Richard II '*Hic jacet* Mgr John Leyot rector of Malpas & Bangor who first acquired a free burial place by decree of Pope Urban VI.'
1428	Howell Kyffin, Ll.B., canon of St Asaph, 1406.
1448	William Wexton

1461	Thomas Wateford
1466	Rafe Heathcote
1511	James Stratebarrell
1523	Richard Pace, chief secretary to Henry VIII, divine and statesman, dean of Exeter, 1522; dean of St Paul's, 1519–32; rector of Llangurig, diocese of Bangor, 1520. He fell under the displeasure of Wolsey, and was deprived of all his preferments.
1527	William Knight, D.C.L., fellow of New College, Oxford; secretary to Henry VII and Henry VIII; sent on an embassy to the emperor Maximillian, 1514; dean of the collegiate church of St Mary in Pratis, Leicester, 1515; canon of Lincoln, 1516; of St Paul's, 1517; and of Bangor, 1520; Archdeacon of Chester, 1522; of Huntingdon, 1523; and of Richmond, 1529; canon 1537, and bishop, of Bath and Wells, 1541; died 1547. [*Alum. Oxon.*]
1542	Richard Gerrard, B.A., Oxford; rector of Grappenhall, 1522, and of Wigan, 1555; died 1558.
1582	William Charleton
1583	William Chaderton, D.D., fellow of Christ College, Cambridge, 1561; Margaret professor of divinity, 1567; president of Queen's College, 1568; Regius professor of divinity, 1569; prebendary of York, 1573; canon of Westminster, 1576; bishop of Chester, 1579; retaining in commendam this rectory and the wardenship of Manchester; bishop of Lincoln, 1595.
1595	George Bulley
1597	Richard Vaughan, D.D., bishop of Bangor, 1596.
1604	Sir Richard Murray, Bart., eldest son of Sir Charles of Cockpoole, came to England from Scotland with king James, and had a grant of this rectory with the chapels of Worthenbury and Overton Madock; warden of Manchester Collegiate Church, 1609. [State Papers, James I]
1604	Thomas Blaque, D.D., chaplain to the Queen; rector of St Vedast, 1571; rector of Great Brasted, 1570–1611; rector of Lambeth, 1577; rector of St Ewelme, 1580–96; dean of Rochester, 1592; died 1611.
1612	George Lloyd, D.D., fellow of Magdalen College, Cambridge; rector of Thornton, Cheshire; bishop of Man 1599–1604; bishop of Chester 1605–15.
1615	John Williams, D.D., Christ Church, Oxford; warden of Ruthin, 1606–21, where he died and was buried, '*qui qua decessit, natus in urbe fuit.*'
1621	George Trenwwy
1621	John Bridgeman, D.D., fellow of Magdalen College, Cambridge; chaplain to King James I, canon of Peterborough, 1605; of Exeter, 1613; of Lichfield, 1616; rector of Wigan, 1616; bishop of Chester, 1618; deprived by Parliamentary sequestrators; died at Morton Hall, 1652; buried at Kinnerley, Shropshire.
1640	Henry Bridgeman, M.A., fellow Brasenose College, Oxford, third son of former rector; rector Barrow, 1639; deprived by the sequestrators for his adherence to the Royalist cause.
1646	Robert Fogg. Intruder during the Commonwealth, previously Henry Bridgeman's curate. Said by Philip Henry, Presbyterian minister of Worthenbury, to have kept a coffin in his bedchamber. Ejected at the

restoration of the monarchy for refusing to use the Book of Common
Prayer. He died in 1776, aged 80, and was buried in Acton, Nantwich.

1660   Henry Bridgeman, M.A., restored, made dean Chester, 1660; bishop Sodor
and Man 1671–82. In conjunction with Bishop Isaac Barrow he founded a
school in the Isle of Man. Died 1682.

1682   John Lloyd, M.A., of Halghton, presented by Thomas Lloyd, who had
bought half the manor of Maelor Saesneg, with the advowson of Bangor,
from Charlotte, lady Derby. Buried 23 August 1687 in the chancel of
Bangor church.

1687   Hugh Morris, B.A., Jesus College, Oxford, son of Morris Griffiths of Guilsfield;
deprived as a non-juror 1690.

1690   William Lloyd, M.A., Brasenose College, Oxford, son of William Lloyd of
Halghton, gentleman. Resigned the living 1691.

1691   Rice [Rees or Rhys] Jones, M.A., of Cannock, Christ Church and Hart Hall,
Oxford, son of Thomas Jones of Criccieth, gentleman; died January 1736
after forty-five years, the longest serving rector of Bangor.

1736   John Fletcher, M.A., rector Hawarden, 1728–41. He was of Shuddebank,
Cumberland. Married Mary Lloyd of Halghton and Gwernhaelod daughter
and eventual heiress of Mary Phillips and Thomas Lloyd. Monument in
Overton Church. Ancestor of the Lloyd-Fletchers of Gwernhaelod and
Nerquis Hall. Died July 1741. Buried Bangor.

1741   William H. Phillips, M.A., nominated Frederick Lloyd, M.A., the next rector,
as his curate at £30 *per annum*, 1760. Buried in Bangor, 16 June 1762.

1762   Frederick Lloyd, M.A., Queen's College, Oxford, son of John Lloyd, of
Maesmynan, Caerwys, gentleman. Buried in Bangor, 30 April 1798, aged
sixty-eight.

1798   Maurice Wynne, D.C.L., Jesus College and All Souls' College, Oxford; vicar
Much Wenlock, 1793; son of Owen Wynne of Llwyn, Denbighshire, said to
be the last male descendant of the Wynnes of Gwydir, Llanrwst. Buried 3
June 1835 in Overton, aged seventy-five. Second longest serving rector –
thirty-seven years.

1835   George Augustus Elliot Marsh, M.A., minister St Mary's Chapel, Grosvenor
Square; evening lecturer St George's, Hanover Square; private chaplain to
the Earl of Huntington; married Julia, daughter of Thomas Murdock of
Portland Place. Buried 24 February 1867 in Bangor, aged seventy-seven.

1867   George Henry McGill, M.A., Brasenose College, Oxford; vicar of Stoke
Ferry, Norfolk, 1846–54; perpetual curate Christ Church, St George in the
East 1854–67; first rural dean revived deanery of Bangor; married Mary
Frances Champion, daughter of John Champion, Esq. Wrote pamphlets on
the London poor rates, occasional sermons and archaeological papers; died
1896 aged seventy-eight.

1896   Mordaunt Elrington-Bisset, (formerly Elrington), M.A., Pembroke College
Cambridge; curate of Cheltenham, 1884–6; of St Michael's Chester Square,
1887–96; rural dean,1903; married Florence Isabella Maude (died 1909),
daughter of Colonel and the Hon. Mrs Tottenham of Plâs Berwyn and of

Revd Elrington-Bisset.

Revd Okell.

Revd Owen.

Woodstock, County Wicklow, 1896; chaplain to the Guards, London, 1909; died 1927 aged sixty-seven, buried Bangor.

1910   Richard James Basil Patterson-Morgan, M.A.; curate of St John's, Northwich; renowned orator; married Miss Agnes Dronsfield, daughter of William Dronsfield, a Lancashire cotton millionaire, of Sandiway Lodge near Northwich (he later inherited the house and estate and resigned the living and acted as assistant curate of Sandiway church); died 1966, aged eighty-seven.

1920   Frank Jackson Okell, M.A., chaplain to the forces during the First World War; curate Sheffield 1919; vicar Eccleston 1925; rector Malpas 1936; rector Astbury, Congleton 1944; bishop suffragan Macclesfield; married Gertrude E.C. Houghton; died 1950, aged sixty-three.

1925   Frederick Ross Baldock, M.A.; curate Broughton, Hawarden; vicar Welshpool, 1937, canon St Asaph; Chancellor St Asaph 1947; married Leila Constance Woodhouse; died September 1950.

1937   Richard Henry Owen, M.A., Bangor, curate of Colwyn Bay 1924; vicar Llantysilio 1931–37; vicar Rhosymedre 1945–51; vicar Prestatyn 1951–67; vicar Brynymaen and Trofarth 1967–70; canon St Asaph; Archdeacon St Asaph 1964–70; married Dorothy Margaret Cooper; died 1977 aged seventy-seven.

Revd Garmon Jones.   *Revd Daniel.*

1945	Richard Garmon Jones, B.A., curate Conway 1928–29; curate Llanrhos 1930; rector Llanfynydd 1933–45; vicar Trofarth with Brynymaen 1954. Grandson of Rev. Elias Owen, antiquarian; married Norah Horrocks 1929; died Jan 1977, aged eighty.
1954	Leslie Mills Daniel, B.A., curate Holywell 1941–48; curate Llangollen 1948–54, married Anne Thomas; died Sept 1984 aged sixty-seven.
1985	Philip Roger Owens, Dip.Theol., curate Colwyn Bay 1971–74; curate Wrexham 1974–77; TV 1977–80; priest in charge Yoxford 1980–85; rector Flint 1998–2003; retired 2006.
1998	Iris McIntyre, M.A., chaplain Brockhill prison 2003–6; vicar Stourport & Wilden 2006.
2004	Adrian Walter Alexander Copping; curate Royston, St Albans 2004; rector combined parishes of Cilcain, Gwernaffield and Llanferres 2009.
2010	Susan Blagden, M.A., pastoral theology; curate Grantham 1999–2003; assistant chaplain Stoke Mandeville Hospital NHS Trust, 2003, ministry team leader, Bro Enlli, Aberdaron 2012.

Appendix 2
Churchwardens

The first column contains the names of the warden appointed by the rector, known as the vicar's warden. If the chosen person was from Bangor, then the townships of Eyton with Royton, and Pickhill with Sesswick appointed the other two. If the rector's choice came from one of the townships, then Bangor appointed their own representative. Prior to 1660, the names have been taken from visitation records (*) or the bishops transcripts (**). Afterwards, where there is a difference in names between the visitation records and the bishop's transcripts (such as in those in 1677), all names mentioned have been included.

1548	John Maddock	–?– ap Maddock	
1549–53	*Records missing*		
1554	John ap Griffith	Robert ap Edward	David ap Jenkyn
1555–1626	*Records missing*		
1627	John Puleston	Roger Griffiths	Edward Br–?–	Robert ap David
1628–34	*Records missing*		
1635	John Jeffreys	Thomas Ellis	
1636	John Wynn	Ellis Edwards	
1637–59	*Records missing*		
1660	Sidney Richard	William Overton	William Lloyd	John Jones Snr
1661	Francis Clarke	William Overton	John Decka	William Lloyd
1662	Ralph John Robert	John Hale	David Lloyd	
1663	John ap William	John James	Thomas Ellis	
1664	Edward Shone	Richard Basnett	Edward Taylor	
1665	Roger Dod	William Rowlands	Richard Rogers	
1666	Sidney John Richards	James Barton senior	Hugh Griffiths	
1667	Thomas Tonna	John Jones	Edward Price	
1668	William Holbrook	Sidney John Richards	John ap Shone	
1669	Edward Andrews	Humphrey ap Edward	Philip Oulton	
1670	George Bostocke*/ Burghall**	Edward Ellis	Richard Dod	
1671	John Edwards	John Randles,	James ap Edward	
1672	John ap William	Thomas Perkins	Edward Taylor (died)	John Wm Maddocks
1673	William Ravenscroft	William Edwards	Roger Davies	
1674	Richard Oulton	John Randles	Thomas ap Hugh	
1675	Hugh Taylor	Thomas Puleston	John ap Edward	
1676	John Edsbury	Randle Dartison	Edward ap Roger	
1677	Robert Davies	Roger Sidney	John Benjamin	Benjamin Maddocks*
1678	Hugh Lewis	Hugh Moore	John Jones	

1679	Roger Powell	Phillip Joy	David Eddowes	Thomas Rowland**
1680	Thomas Hanmer	John Rogers	Edward Davies	
1681	Francis Clarke, Snr	Richard Clarke junior	Thomas Davies	
1682	Andrew Meredith	Samuel Rogers	Ralph Roberts	
1683	Randle Pulford	Edward Hanmer	Thomas Povah	.
1684	John Puleston	Booth Basnett	John ap William	
1685	Roger Kendrick	Edward ap Shone	John Decka	
1686	Edward Wynne	Ellis Jones	Richard Clarke	
1687	Francis Griffiths	Thomas Decka	William Rowland	
1688	Thomas Tonna	John Price	Thomas Perkins	
1689	John Richards	Francis Clarke	John Rogers	
1690	William Lloyd	Robert Edwards	Thomas Harper	
1691	Thomas Clarke	Thomas Heskey/Hesketh*	Edward Swarton	
1692	Robert Baker	Philip Oulton	John Sidney	
1693	John Griffiths	John Evans	William Spencer	
1694	Ellis Edwards	Richard Jones	Thomas Evison	
1695	Roger Davies	Francis Clarke	James Humphreys	
1696	Robert Williams	Thomas Meredith	James Heskey/Hesketh	
1697	John Edwards	Edwards Griffiths	William Rowland	
1698	Edward Ellis	Robert Pennant	John ap Ellis	
1699	John James	John Carter	William Jones	
1700	John Jones	Simon Taylor	William Curry	
1701	Edward Wynne	Francis Clarke	Ralph Roberts	
1702	Thomas Rogers	Ellis Decker	Thomas Rogers	
1703	Richard Clarke	John Edwards	Edward Price	
1704	Edward Clarke	Roger Jones	Charles Hassall	
1705	John Puleston	William Edwards	Robert Baker	
1706	John Richards	Edward Hopley	Thomas Decka	
1707	John Smith	Owen Griffith	John Randles	
1708	Richard Jones	John Phillips	John Roberts	
1709	John Clarke	John Jones	Francis Abraham	
1710	Roger Jones	John Edwards	Robert Williams	
1711	John Evans	Robert Edwards	Thomas Bertley	
1712	Ralph Roberts	William Spencer	William Shone	
1713	Richard Clarke	Francis Clarke	James Humphreys	
1714	James Rogers	Thomas Evison	Edward Lloyd	
1715	John ap Edward	Roger Lewis	Edward Griffith	
1716	John Overton	Edward Wynne	Charles Hassall	
1717	Timothy Owen	Thomas Rogers	Robert Puleston	
1718	John Puleston	John Baker	William Edwards	John Richards
1719	Randle Randles	Owen Griffith	John Smith	
1720	Booth Basnett**/ John Basnett*	Richard Jones	John Ralphs	
1721	Robert Williams	John Phillips	John Griffith	
1722	John Evans	Thomas Price	John Clark	
1723	John Jones	William Spencer	Edward Lloyd	
1724	Booth Basnett	John Puleston	Edward Tunnah	
1725	Booth Basnett	Edward Tunna	James Royds/ James Rogers*	
1726	Edward Tunna	Edward Wynn	Richard Jones	

1727	Roger Davies	John Taylor	Thomas Evison	
1728	Francis Clarke	Thomas Evanson	Robert Puleston	
1729	John Baker	Richard Booth	Owen Griffith	
1730	Andrew Lloyd	Robert Evison	John Smith	
1731	George Broughall	George Rowland	Roger Jones	
1732	Thomas Pemberton	Daniel Tunnah	John Edwards	
1733	William Edwards	Edward Tunna	John Thomas	
1734	Roger Hughes	John Bradshaw	John Phillips	
1735	John Jones	Francis Evans	John Edsbury	
1736	John Jones	John Smith	John Thomas	
1737	Hugh Jones	Peter Lloyd	William Phillips	
1738	John Hankey	Jonathon Williams	John Jones	
1739	Trevor Davies	William Jones	Job Jones/John Jones*	
1740	William Overton	John Thomas	William Jones	
1741	Thomas Minshall	Richard Heskey/Hesketh	John Davies	
1742	Edward Hopley	Randle Randles	John Wynn	
1743	John Jones,	Edward Griffith	Thomas Evison	
1744	Roger Davies	Robert Puleston	John Edwards	
1745	Thomas Tunnah	John Puleston	Edward Wynne	
1746	Francis Clarke	John Jones	Kendrick Eyton	
1747	William Craven	Ralph Taylor	Roger Jones	
1748	John Jones	Hugh Jones	Edward Wynn	
1749	John Jones (died)	Edward Jones**	Randle Randles	Thomas Evison
1750	Randle Randles	John Hughes	Nathaniel Maurice	
1751	Jonathon Williams	Daniel Tunnah	John Phoenix	
1752	Humphrey Hughes	John Thomas	William Jones	
1753	Roger Griffiths	Daniel Taylor	Thomas Eyton	
1754	Thomas Probert	Ralph Wright	Randle Randles	
1755	Jonathon Williams	Richard Palin	Thomas Speed	
1756	Roger Davies	Francis Clarke	Thomas Davies	
1757	James Smith	Joseph Davies	John Rowland	
1758	Peter Lloyd	Edward Griffiths	Thomas Evison	
1759	George Taylor	William Harrison	Thomas Speed	
1760	Peter Downward	Thomas Jones	John Wynn	
1761	John Maddocks	Timothy Owen,	Robert Tamberlaine/	
			Jonathon Treen	
1762	Ambrose Nixon	Joshua Edwards	Robert Tamberlaine	James/John Poynton
1763	Edward Jones	Samuel James	William Jones	
1764	Humphrey Hughes	John Jones	James Davenport	
1765	Peter Lloyd	Edward Thomas	Thomas Evison	
1766	William Leicester	Hugh Jones	Thomas Eyton	
1767	Ambrose Nixon	Richard Palin	Edward Jones	
1768	Thomas Eyton	Thomas Randles	Thomas Speed	
1769	William Leicester	John Jones	John Rowland	
1770	John Hotchkins	John Pearson	Timothy Owens	
1771	Humphrey Hughes	John Taylor	James Davenport	
1772	George Taylor	John Davies	Randle Griffiths	
1773	Peter Downward	Thomas Jones	John Pointon	
1774	Peter Lloyd	Francis Clarke	Thomas Evison	
1775	Thomas Jones	Samuel James	John Ellis (Wynn?)	

1776	Ambrose Nixon	Thomas Evans	John Ellis
1777	John Davies	William Probert	John Evison
1778	Humphrey Hughes	Thomas Brereton	John Rowland
1779	James Smith	Hugh Jones	John Evison
1780	John Hotchkins	John Bradshaw	Thomas Davies
1781	George Taylor	Thomas Pearson	Randle Griffiths
1782	Thomas Jones	Randle Bennion	Thomas Speed
1783	Ambrose Nixon	Randle Randles	Thomas Evison
1784	James Smith	William James	John Wynne
1785	Samuel Jackson	John Davies	John Evison
1786	Peter Potter	Francis Clarke	Timothy Owens
1787	Humphrey Hughes	Daniel Evans	William Roberts
1788	James Lewis/	Charles Davenport	Edward Eyton, John Iveson**
			Samuel Lewis* & **
1789	John Davies	Edward Edwards	Edward Jones
1790	George Taylor	Tristram Davenport	John Wynne
1791	Henry Jones	Thomas Brereton	Thomas Poole
1792	Humphrey Edge	John Bradshaw	Thomas Davenport
1793	Robert Nickson	Hugh Jones	John Owens
1794	Joseph Stokes	Thomas Pearson	Owen Ellis/John Evison**
1795	James Smith	Thomas Randles	Thomas Poole
1796	Humphrey Hughes	Randle Bennion	William Roberts
1797	Thomas Hotchkins	William Jones	John Evison junior
1798	Peter Ellis	William Jones	John Evison senior
1799	Thomas Jones	John Davies	John Wynne
1800	Jeffrey Chester	Daniel Evans	Thomas Poole/
			Edward Eyton**
1801	Thomas Jones	Frederick Pearson	Edward Jones
1802	Peter Potter	Jonathon Phillips	John Dunbabin
1803	James Lewis	William Wynne	William Owens
1804	Thomas Dixon	Edward Edwards	Thomas Poole
1805	Charles Overton	Widow Davenport	John Bradshaw/
			Edward James**
1806	Humphrey Edge	Thomas Brereton	Owen Ellis
1807	Joseph Stokes	Thomas Bradshaw	Edward Davies
1808	James Smith	Hugh Jones	William Roberts
1809	William Boodle	Randle Bennion	Widow Davenport/
			George Davenport*
1810	Roger Hughes	John Randles	John Evison
1811	Thomas Baker	William James	John Wynne
1812	James Done	John Davies	Thomas Poole
1813	Joseph Edwards	John Wilson	William Rhoden
1814	William Salisbury	Joseph Evans	John Dunbabin
1815	Ann Francis	Charles Davenport	Edmund Jones
1816	John Stant	Thomas Edwards	Kendrick Edward Eyton
1817	William Maddocks	Samuel Newton	William Roberts
1818	Edward Hanmer	Charles Rowe	Edward Davies
1819	Thomas Jones	Hugh Dixon	Thomas Bird
1820	Benjamin Harris	Edward James	John Newnes
1821	William Dutton	David Matthews	John Evison

1822	Tristram Davenport	Thomas Wainwright	James Higginson
1823	William Taylor	John James	Ambrose Sutton
1824	Samuel Parker	John Pugh	Isaac Jones
1825	John Smith	Edward Edwards	Joseph Edwards
1826	William Orford	Thomas Bennion	William Tomlinson
1827	Joseph Sandland	John Roberts	Samuel Smith
1828	Joseph Warter	Thomas Bradshaw	George Dicker
1829	Edward Davies	John Edwards	Richard Edmunds
1830	James Done	Charles Rowe	Edward Pritchard
1831	Richard Broomhall	Richard Craven	John Ellis
1832	Edward Pearson	William James	William Bradshaw
1833	John Davenport	John James	William Roberts
1834	John Lewis	Joseph Sandland	Thomas Bird
1835	Charles Jones	John Pugh	Samuel Dunbabin
1836	Henry Edwards	John Edwards	James Higginson
1837	John Stontford	Hugh Dixon	Joseph Edwards
1838	Samuel Chester	John Griffiths	Richard Edmunds
1839	John Orford	Hamlet Wood	Richard Edmunds
1840	Robert Probert	Joseph Bradshaw	Charles Griffiths
1841	Randle Barker	William James	Benjamin Pointon
1842	Joseph Fowles	John James	Thomas Evison
1843	John Bevan	Thomas Shaw	Ambrose Sutton
1844	John Smith	Edward Lewis	Charles Higginson
1845	John Clay	John Lodge	Thomas Thomas
1846	John Edwards	John Ellis	John Lees
1847	Thomas Jones	James Price	John Davies
1848	Robert Bithell	John Pugh	Joseph Ellis
1849	George Cambell	Edward Dixon	William Bradshaw
1850	John Dicker	William Roberts	William Higginson
1851	Edward Davies	Colonel Keightly	Joseph Evans
1852	Samuel Acton	William Pearson	William Cheetham
1853	John Jones	William James	Benjamin Pointon
1854	John Jones	John James	Thomas Evison
1855	Thomas Thomas	Thomas Shaw	Job Mulliner
1856	Thomas Thomas	Edward Williams	William Roberts
1857	John Smith	Edward Lewis	William Roberts
1858	Thomas Thomas	Edward Dixon	H. Bayley
1859	Francis Jones	Edward Dixon	Thomas Evison
1860	John Clay	Edward Dixon	Thomas Evison
1861	John Clay	Edward Dixon	Thomas Evison
1862	John Clay	Edward Dixon	Thomas Evison
1863	John Smith	Edward Lewis	Job Mulliner
1864	John Smith	Edward Lewis	Job Mulliner
1865	John Suckley	John Jackson	William Roberts
1866	John Suckley	John Jackson	John Edwards
1867	Benjamin Bithell	William Cheetham	John Jackson
1868	Benjamin Bithell	Thomas Evison	George Marsh
1869	George Cambell	Thomas Evison	Anthony Marsh
1870	Ambrose Sutton	Samuel R. Peate	W. Tomlinson
1872	Edward Owen	Edward Lewis	Walter Richards

1873	J. Hewitt,	Thomas M. Shaw	Humphrey Morris
1874	R.E. Bickerton	Thomas M. Shaw	Humphrey Morris
1875	R.E. Bickerton	J. Roberts	Randle Richards
1876	Thomas Brassey	Edward Lewis	Samuel R. Peate
1877	Thomas Brassey	Harold Lees	Francis Lloyd
1878	Thomas Brassey	Harold Lees	Francis Lloyd
1879	Harold Lees	Thomas Fearnall	Thomas Blake
1880	Thomas Blake	Thomas Fearnall	William James Mackenzie
1881	Thomas Blake	Thomas Fearnall	William James Mackenzie
1882	Thomas Fearnall	William James Mackenzie	J. Bickerton
1883	Thomas Fearnall	William James Mackenzie	John Mort
1884	Thomas Fearnall	William James Mackenzie	John Mort
1885	H.J. Royds	Samuel R Peate	William James Mackenzie
1886	H.J. Royds	William James Mackenzie	Samuel R. Peate
1887	H.J. Royds	William James Mackenzie	Samuel R. Peate
1888	Ambrose Sutton	Francis Lloyd	William James Mackenzie
1889	George Griffiths	Francis Lloyd	William James Mackenzie
1890	George Griffiths	Francis Lloyd	William James Mackenzie
1891	John Edwards	Samuel R Peate	William James Mackenzie
1892	John Edwards	Walter Hughes	William James Mackenzie
1893	John Edwards	Walter Hughes	William James Mackenzie
1894	John Edwards	Walter Hughes	William James Mackenzie
1895	Gen. Savage Mostyn	Walter Hughes	William James Mackenzie
1896	George E. Fenwick	Oliver Ormrod	John Lewis
1897	George E. Fenwick	Oliver Ormrod	Thomas Fearnall
1898	George E. Fenwick	Oliver Ormrod	Thomas Fearnall
1899	George E. Fenwick	Oliver Ormrod	Thomas Fearnall
1900–03	Hon. A.E. Parker	Oliver Ormrod	Thomas Fearnall
1901	Hon. A.E. Parker	Oliver Ormrod	Thomas Fearnall
1902	Hon. A.E. Parker	Oliver Ormrod	Thomas Fearnall
1903	Hon. A.E. Parker	Oliver Ormrod	Thomas Fearnall
1904	George Fenwick	Oliver Ormrod	Thomas Fearnall
1905	George Fenwick	Oliver Ormrod	Price Williams
1906	George Fenwick	Oliver Ormrod	Price Williams
1907	William James Mackenzie	Oliver Ormrod	Price Williams
1914	William James Mackenzie	Oliver Ormrod	Arthur Done
1915	William James Mackenzie	Oliver Ormrod	Arthur Done
1916	William James Mackenzie	Oliver Ormrod	Arthur Done
1917	William James Mackenzie	Oliver Ormrod	Arthur Done
1918–27	Oliver Ormrod	Arthur Done	John Davies
1928–36	Oliver Ormrod	Colonel Fenwick Palmer	Arthur Done
1937–47	Arthur Done	Colonel Fenwick Palmer	Frank T. Cheetham
1948–59	Colonel Fenwick Palmer	George L Wood	Frank T. Cheetham
1960–6	Colonel Fenwick Palmer	Edward Huxley	Frank T. Cheetham
1967	Colonel Fenwick Palmer	Edward Huxley	John Done
1968	Colonel Fenwick Palmer	Edward Huxley	John Done
1969	Edward Huxley	Jack Richards	John Done
1970	Edward Huxley	Jack Richards	John Done
1971	Edward Huxley	Jack Richards	John Done
1972	Edward Huxley	Jack Richards	John Done

1973–81	John Done	Jack Richards	–?–
1981	Stanley Lloyd	John Lomax	Jack Richards
1982	Jack Richards	John Lomax	Stanley Lloyd
1983	Jack Richards	John Lomax	Stanley Lloyd
1984	Jack Richards	John Lomax	Stanley Lloyd
1986	Jack Richards	John Lomax	–?–
1987	John James	Robert Evers	Leslie Done
1992	Arfon Mytton	Leslie Done	Peter Roberts
1993	Arfon Mytton	Jean Christiansen	Peter Roberts
1994	Leslie Done	John Rixson	Alan Furber
1995	Leslie Done	Alan Furber	Jean Christiansen
1996	Leslie Done	Alan Furber	Hilda Turton
1997	Leslie Done	Alan Furber	Hilda Turton
1998	Leslie Done	Alan Furber	Hilda Turton
1999	Leslie Done	Alan Furber	Hilda Turton
2000	David Child	Hilda Turton	Rachel Wadon
2001	David Child	Hilda Turton	Rachel Wadon
2002	David Williams	Rachel Wadon	Jill Johnson
2003	David Williams	Brian Neale	Philip Morgan
2004	David Williams	Brian Neale	Philip Morgan
2005	Hilda Turton	Brian Neale	Philip Morgan
2006	David Williams	Brian Neale	
2007	David Williams	Brian Neale	
2008	David Williams	Brian Neale	
2009	David Williams	Brian Neale	
2010	David Williams	Brian Neale	
2011	David Williams	Brian Neale	
2012	David Williams	Brian Neale	
2013	David Williams	Brian Neale	David Roberts